# ARMADA

**Colin Martin** was Reader in Maritime Archaeology at St Andrews University and has directed excavations on three Armada shipwrecks. **Geoffrey Parker** teaches history at The Ohio State University and has published forty books. Both served as historical consultants on the BBC documentary *Armada*.

Further praise for *Armada*:

'Thoroughly explores both the English and Spanish sides of the "invincible" invasion, from the buildup, to the conflict, and the aftermath.' Jesse Russell, *New Criterion*

'Draws on the latest maritime and archival discoveries to tackle pressing questions about one of history's most famous naval clashes.' *History Revealed*

'Martin and Parker have produced an absorbing account of the Spanish Armada, synthesizing a vast amount of research into a highly readable narrative.' Catherine Scheybeler, *Mariner's Mirror*

'A magisterial study … It has no rivals as a comprehensive and authoritative account of the Spanish Armada.' David Childs, *Naval Review*

'A very vivid and uniquely detailed retelling of a familiar story – which Martin and Parker reconstruct with consummate skill – but also a passage to the sixteenth-century maritime world.' Elliot Jordan, *International Journal of Maritime History*

'Without question, it is the definitive first resort for any historian of the topic; it undoubtedly overshadows its rivals, countless as they are. It combines sure grasps of politics, strategy, naval and land warfare, and technology with a clear exposition and handsome production.' Neil Younger, *Journal of Modern History*

'Ironically, given that the Spanish Armada was one of the great disasters of its age, Martin and Parker's *Armada* is undoubtedly a triumph. Beautifully illustrated, delightfully readable, yet uncompromising in its scholarship, this will be the definitive work on the Armada for generations of historians to come. It is a must-have for all those who would seek to understand one of the defining moments of early modern history.' Jack Abernethy, *Journal of Military History*

'Those who claim you cannot improve on perfection need to explain this book. Martin and Parker's original account of the Armada campaign was the work from which all subsequent scholars took their lead; this one, with thirty years' worth of extra research and thought, sets a new benchmark. Magisterial.' Dan Snow, author of *On This Day in History*

'An elegant marriage between archival research and marine archaeology yields new light on the Armada and its benighted crews in a compelling account of the 1588 campaign. After reading this absorbing book, who can now still believe that history is static, carved in stone?' Robert Hutchinson, author of *The Spanish Armada*

# ARMADA

―⋄―

*The Spanish Enterprise
and England's Deliverance in 1588*

COLIN MARTIN
AND
GEOFFREY PARKER

YALE UNIVERSITY PRESS
NEW HAVEN AND LONDON

Published with assistance from the foundation established in memory of Oliver Baty Cunningham of the Class of 1917, Yale College.

Copyright © 2022 Colin Martin and Geoffrey Parker

First published in paperback in 2025

All rights reserved. This book may not be reproduced in whole or in part, in any form (beyond that copying permitted by Sections 107 and 108 of the U.S. Copyright Law and except by reviewers for the public press) without written permission from the publishers.

All reasonable efforts have been made to provide accurate sources for all images that appear in this book. Any discrepancies or omissions will be rectified in future editions.

For information about this and other Yale University Press publications, please contact:
U.S. Office: sales.press@yale.edu yalebooks.com
Europe Office: sales@yaleup.co.uk yalebooks.co.uk

Text designed and set in Adobe Caslon Pro and IM Fell by Tetragon, London
Printed in Czechia by Finidr

Library of Congress Control Number: 2022942455

Authorized Representative in the EU: Easy Access System Europe, Mustamäe tee 50, 10621 Tallinn, Estonia, gpsr.requests@easproject.com

ISBN 978-0-300-25986-5 (hbk)
ISBN 978-0-300-28524-6 (pbk)

A catalogue record for this book is available from the British Library.

10 9 8 7 6 5 4 3 2 1

*For*
*Paula Martin*

# Contents

*Conventions*     ix

INTRODUCTION     1

## Part I
### *The Fleets Assemble*

1. 'Arise O Lord and Avenge Thy Cause'     15
2. 'The great bog of Europe'     48
3. 'A fleet to impeach it'     67

## Part II
### *God's Obvious Design*

4. Armed Neutrality, 1558–80     101
5. Cold War, 1581–5     129
6. The Grand Design and its Architect     151
7. Phoney War     176
8. The Armada Takes Shape     194
9. Medina Sidonia Takes Charge     214
10. Advance to Contact     234

## Part III
### *'It came, it saw, it departed'*

| | | |
|---|---|---|
| 11 | Battle Stations | 255 |
| 12 | Stalemate in the Channel | 281 |
| 13 | The Test of Battle | 301 |
| 14 | 'God blew and they were scattered' | 321 |
| 15 | From Dispersal to Disaster | 343 |
| 16 | Analysis of Failure | 373 |

## Part IV
### *The Aftermath*

| | | |
|---|---|---|
| 17 | The Bitterness of Defeat | 411 |
| 18 | The Counter-Armada | 435 |
| 19 | If the Armada had Landed | 460 |
| 20 | The Armada in History and Legend | 482 |
| 21 | The Armada Shipwrecks | 512 |

| | |
|---|---|
| Epilogue | 539 |
| *Glossary* | *549* |
| *Chronology* | *553* |
| *Abbreviations* | *560* |
| *Notes* | *566* |
| *Bibliography* | *642* |
| *Acknowledgements* | *675* |
| *List of Illustrations* | *679* |
| *Index* | *689* |

Readers will find the following online at
https://yalebooks.co.uk/armada-appendices/

Appendix 1: The Spanish Fleet, Ships and Seamen
Appendix 2: The Spanish Fleet, Soldiers and Ordnance
Appendix 3: The English Fleet
Appendix 4: Guns and Gunnery
Appendix 5: Note on Sources

# *Conventions*

Dates: On 24 February 1582 Pope Gregory XIII ordered all Christians to advance their calendar by ten days, but different countries adopted the 'New Style' at different times: in Spain 15 October 1582 immediately followed 4 October; in most (but not all) of the provinces of the Netherlands in rebellion against Philip, 25 December immediately followed 14 December 1582; in the provinces 'loyal' to him, 22 February 1583 immediately followed 11 February; and so on. All dates in this book after 4 October 1582 appear in New Style unless otherwise stated, even for states (like England) which rejected the Gregorian Calendar; and throughout we have assumed that each calendar year began on 1 January (and not on 25 March, as in the Julian Calendar or 'Old Style' – OS in our notes). Thus Queen Elizabeth delivered her iconic speech to the army at Tilbury on 18 August 1588, just as the Armada rounded the north of Scotland.

Money: To avoid confusion and facilitate comparisons, all sums of money mentioned in this book have been given in Spanish ducats or pounds sterling. In the later sixteenth century, about four ducats made up one pound sterling. Each ducat was roughly equivalent to one escudo (or crown) and to 2½ florins; 10 florins were roughly equivalent to one pound sterling.

Proper names: Where an established English version of a foreign place name exists (Antwerp, Corunna, The Hague, Vienna) we have used it, otherwise we have preferred the style used in the place itself today (Mechelen, not Malines; Aachen, not Aix-la-Chapelle). Likewise, where a standard English version of the style and title of an individual exists (William of Orange, Philip II) we have used it, otherwise we have preferred the version used by the individual.

Transcriptions: Quotations from English sources have been modernized for ease of reading.

Translations:   Unless otherwise stated, translations from Dutch, German, Italian and Spanish sources to English are by Geoffrey Parker. Some technical terms, for example some ship-types, cannot be accurately translated into English, so the Spanish original has been retained. These are listed in the Glossary with explanations and approximate translations. The originals of all Spanish translations will be found in Colin Martin and Geoffrey Parker, *La Gran Armada. Una nueva historia* (Barcelona, 2023).

## *Introduction*

It was 10 August 1588 in the North Sea, and the summer weather was unseasonably bad. Before a brisk south-westerly gale, with her storm-canvas set, ran the English royal galleon *Victory*, scarred by recent battle. Her gaudily painted upperworks were stained by gun-smoke; the royal standard at the mainmast and the flags of St George which whipped from the fore- and mizzen-tops were in tatters. The rigging showed signs of makeshift repair, the bowsprit and mizzen mast had been splintered by shot, and the ship's longboat was missing. Although she was still seaworthy, *Victory* was in no condition to engage an enemy. Her shot-lockers, on which her whole fighting capacity depended, were empty.

Somewhere to leeward lay the huge Armada sent by King Philip II of Spain on 'the most important mission in the world, with the whole world watching': the conquest of England and its return to the Catholic Church.[1] Despite the longest and fiercest artillery battle which had ever taken place at sea, the Spanish fleet was still loose in the northern seas, its formidable order and discipline largely intact. Its ammunition stocks, though depleted, were not exhausted, while the massed companies of soldiers it carried still rendered the Armada invulnerable to boarding attack. Worst of all, the English no longer knew where it was, or what it might yet do.

In *Victory*'s great cabin her captain, Sir John Hawkins, Treasurer of the Navy, scrawled a postscript to the urgent report he had just completed, apologizing for his poor handwriting: it was done, he explained, 'in haste and bad weather'. His dispatch, addressed to Sir Francis Walsingham, Queen Elizabeth's secretary of state, showed Hawkins to have been an extremely worried man. The Spanish fleet, he warned, was still:

Here, and very forcible, and must be waited upon with all our force, which is little enough. There should be an infinite quantity of powder and shot provided, and continually sent abroad; without the which great hazard may grow to our country; for this is the greatest and strongest combination, to my understanding, that ever was gathered in Christendom. Therefore I wish it, of all hands, to be mightily and diligently looked unto and cared for.[2]

Eight days later England's Lord Admiral, Charles Howard of Effingham, 'in haste and much occupied' aboard his flagship *Ark Royal*, still felt anxious and uncertain about the Armada's movements and intentions, but like Hawkins he had no doubt about its formidable strength. 'Some made little account of the Spanish force by sea,' he confided to Walsingham, 'but I do warrant you, all the world never saw such a force as theirs was.' Even the redoubtable Sir Francis Drake was by no means confident that the threat had passed. Although the Armada might have been driven back towards Spain, a powerful invasion army headed by one of the most determined and capable military commanders of the age still lay on the Flemish coast, poised to embark for England. From his flagship *Revenge*, Drake warned on 20 August that the queen's ministers should not doubt that Alexander Farnese, duke of Parma, 'being so great a soldier as he is ... will presently, if he may, undertake some great matter ... My poor opinion is that we should have a great eye unto him.'[3]

England's best-informed contemporary opinion thus did not underestimate the enormity of the threat posed by Philip's fleet – and yet, as quickly as it had come, that threat evaporated. The Armada had no further tricks up its sleeve: it struggled on between Orkney and Shetland and into the Atlantic in an effort to gain sufficient sea-room for a safe run southwards to the ports of Galicia and Biscay. But fortune did not favour it. The autumn gales of that portentous year – the Winds of God, as their Protestant detractors would have it – blew early and with unusual violence, driving many of the returning ships towards the western seaboards of Scotland and Ireland. A large number were wrecked, often in cataclysmic circumstances, and the survivors were hounded down with little mercy (Figure 1).

For the Spaniards the Armada campaign proved an unmitigated disaster brought about as much by the forces of nature as by the hand of their adversaries. The English and Dutch, in contrast, saw it as both an overwhelming victory and a clear demonstration of where divine sympathy lay. The anxious realities expressed by the English commanders in the campaign's immediate aftermath were quickly swamped, in the euphoria of deliverance, by a tide of uncritical and patriotic fervour that saw the events as an affirmation of Protestant England's inevitable superiority over her Catholic foes.

1. The route the Armada took around Britain and Ireland, including the locations of some shipwrecks. The scale is in English leagues. The compass roses show the wind directions at various stages of the journey. A hand-coloured engraving by Augustine Ryther of a chart by Robert Adams, made in 1590.

That fervour, and the misconceptions it generated, have dominated English perceptions of the campaign ever since. The Armada story acquired a perennial appeal as the heroic and triumphant episode in a long maritime, military, economic and ideological struggle between England and her rivals. On any reckoning it is a good yarn, and it has provided generations of historians with an abundance of material from which to spin it.

Serious studies began in the late nineteenth century with the publication of selections of documents from both Spanish and English archives, albeit often accompanied by patriotic commentaries. For almost a century afterwards, those who studied the Armada tended to wallow in the rich but unreplenished pond provided by their late Victorian progenitors, even though the published sources represented (as their editors were at pains to point out) no more than personal selections of the documents they considered most relevant in the light of late nineteenth-century historical perceptions. It is time to examine the original sources anew.

2. Simancas Castle, Spain. The Spanish monarchy began to deposit its central administrative records here in 1540. The archive, originally housed under the dome of the tower on the far left, still contains the majority of the official papers concerning the Armada. Colin Martin took this photo in 1966 when Geoffrey Parker was working in the search room (the lower windows in the centre). They first met seven years later as colleagues at the University of St Andrews.

On the Spanish side much of the primary evidence survives in the archives of Simancas (AGS) (Figure 2). The king's councils and secretaries of state and war handled a mass of reports, memoranda and letters concerning the 'Enterprise of England' (as Philip called it), and they later formed part of the series *Estado* and *Guerra y Marina*. They are relatively well known, though still greatly under-exploited. Less familiar are the audited accounts concerning the men, munitions and provisions loaded aboard individual Armada ships, now in the series *Contaduría Mayor de Cuentas* and *Contaduría del Sueldo*. Some are extremely detailed, thanks to the obligation of each ship's clerk to 'record the powder, shot and match expended, noting down how much is used every day and for what reason, with what effect, and by whose order. Take particular note of the artillery pieces fired, and of their calibre and weight, and of the powder and shot consumed in firing them.'[4]

Beyond Simancas, the papers of the Armada's commander, the duke of Medina Sidonia, have survived almost intact, although now scattered between collections in England and the United States as well as in the ducal archive at Sanlúcar de

Barrameda. They shed light on important issues concerning the conduct of the Spanish campaign. The Armada's deputy commander, Juan Martínez de Recalde, kept a detailed journal of his voyage and also preserved some of the letters he exchanged with Medina Sidonia and others during and just after the battles in the English Channel, revealing major differences of opinion over both strategy and tactics within the fleet's High Command. Others aboard the Armada also left personal testimonies in the form of narratives, diaries, letters and (for those taken prisoner) interrogations.

The surviving records of the Armada's English opponents are similar but less plentiful. Elizabeth's Privy Council and her secretary of state handled a mass of reports, memoranda and letters concerning the defence of England and Ireland. Most are preserved among the Registers of the Privy Council (a daily compilation of decisions taken by the executive branch of government on matters great and small) and the State Papers series in The National Archives (TNA) at Kew, with more in the manuscript collections of the British Library and elsewhere. The National Archives also hold three series of annual accounts regarding the navy: those submitted each year by the Treasurer of the Navy, with detail on the equipment and movements of the queen's ships and the wages of all who served on them; and by the Victualler of the Navy, recording the quantity and cost of all provisions supplied to keep those aboard the ships at their posts. The Ordnance Office also submitted separate accounts for munitions supplied each year 'for the sea service', but those for 1588 have largely disappeared. Only those for Drake's western squadron survive in the Plymouth Archives. Lord Admiral Howard seems to have been the only senior English officer in 1588 to have kept a journal of the campaign, but neither he nor his commanders left a substantial personal archive.

The same imbalance affects diplomatic dispatches. Ambassadors from twelve foreign governments resided at the Court of Spain in the 1580s, and each wrote at least one lengthy dispatch per month to his home government, filled with details of the Enterprise. They also secured and forwarded copies of official documents, even top-secret ones like the Armada's order of battle. Philip II maintained ambassadors in the larger states, and his correspondence with them (preserved in AGS *Estado*) also sheds light on his plans. In contrast Elizabeth maintained permanent diplomatic relations with only three states in the 1580s: France, Scotland and the Dutch Republic. The dispatches of her envoys abroad are in TNA State Papers; those of the French and Scottish diplomats at her Court in 1588 have apparently disappeared.

The surviving administrative records for Elizabeth's only ally, the Dutch Republic, are even more scarce. The Algemene Rijksarchief in The Hague contains the correspondence of the central government with its English allies as well as with its own military and civilian personnel; the resolutions and correspondence of the States-General (the sovereign body); the minutes of the Council of State (charged with defence); and some records of the Admiralty of Holland. The Rijksarchief Zeeland in Middelburg contains both the correspondence of the provincial authorities with the States-General and the accounts of those who salvaged two large Armada wrecks in Dutch waters.

Over the past fifty years maritime archaeology has allowed us, quite literally, to go on board the ships themselves and examine them and their contents at first hand. In the terrible aftermath of the Armada more than thirty Spanish ships were lost off the western coasts of Scotland and Ireland; and the sites of eight have now been discovered and investigated. Between them they provide examples of several of the types of ship which sailed with the Armada: the Neapolitan galleass *Girona* off the coast of Antrim, Northern Ireland: the Basque-built *Santa María de la Rosa* in Blasket Sound off south-west Ireland; the Rostock-built *urca Gran Grifón* off Fair Isle, between Orkney and Shetland (Figure 3); the Venetian-built grain-carrier *Trinidad Valencera* in Kinnagoe Bay, County Donegal, Ireland. In 1985 the remains of three large Mediterranean cargo ships, *Santa María de Visón*, *Juliana* and *Lavia*, began to emerge in the surf off Streedagh Strand, County Sligo,

3. Archaeologist recording a gun on the site of the wreck of *Gran Grifón* off Fair Isle.

Ireland. Yet another ill-fated Mediterranean merchantman, *San Juan de Sicilia*, went down in Tobermory Bay, on the Isle of Mull in western Scotland, though her remains have been all but obliterated by more than three centuries of determined and destructive hunting for her elusive (because illusory) treasure.

Archaeological evidence from these Armada wrecks has revolutionized our understanding of the events this book seeks to chronicle and explain, particularly when viewed in concert with the wealth of documentary material available in archives and libraries around the world. To be sure, the broad outline of the Armada story remains the same: Philip II attempted to invade and conquer England but his plans miscarried, partly because of his own miscalculation and mismanagement, partly because of the superior defensive efforts of the English and their Dutch allies, and partly because of singularly adverse weather. But there is more to history than broad outlines. The evidence now available, both documentary and archaeological, allows us to follow each stage in the Armada story with greater certainty than before and, perhaps more importantly, to explain with greater confidence why events turned out as they did.

Instead of basing our narrative on the pseudo-patriotic jingoism and speculative theorizing which has characterized so many previous studies, we rely here on a wide corpus of information drawn from contemporary protagonists and from the physical remains of the wrecked ships. All the available evidence reinforces our belief that the Armada constituted a threat to England of overwhelming proportions, and confirms that the anxious concerns expressed by English naval commanders about the menace it posed were not misplaced. In perhaps only slightly different circumstances, the Enterprise of England might have become the crowning success of Philip's reign.

The conflict was the highlight, though not the last act, of a personal duel between two monarchs who knew and disliked each other (Figure 4). At the time no one could predict the outcome, and Spain should no more be denigrated for failing to achieve its objectives than England's deliverance should be ascribed to its innate superiority. All the protagonists demonstrated both formidable strengths and serious weaknesses in the conflict, and most emerged with honour. The story stands on its own terms and the only bygones to be forgotten are the myths.

The men who fought on both sides, in particular, deserve nothing less. As Sir John Keegan wrote in his classic study, *The Face of Battle*: 'What battles have in common is human: the behaviour of men struggling to reconcile their instinct for self-preservation, their sense of honour, and the achievement of some aim over which other men are ready to kill them. The study of battle is therefore always a study of fear and usually of courage.' This is especially true of naval warfare, which is conducted almost exclusively by machines – and by the late sixteenth century the sailing warship was the most complex machine to be found anywhere. Nevertheless, the story of the men who lived, fought and often died in the ships of the Armada campaign 'is still the fundamental story to be related'. We therefore follow the lead of Rear-Admiral José Ignacio González-Aller Hierro, the driving force behind the magnificent multi-volume publication of Armada documents, *La batalla del Mar Océano*, and dedicate our efforts to those on both sides who fought and died for their country in 1588, 'far from their homes, anonymous heroes known only to God'.[5]

4. Friends, 'frenemies', enemies. Left: Philip II of Spain, by an unknown artist, *c.* 1580, oil on canvas. Right: Elizabeth I of England, 'The Ermine Portrait', attributed to William Segar or George Gower, *c.* 1585, oil on panel.

## 5. The Theatre of Operations, 1588

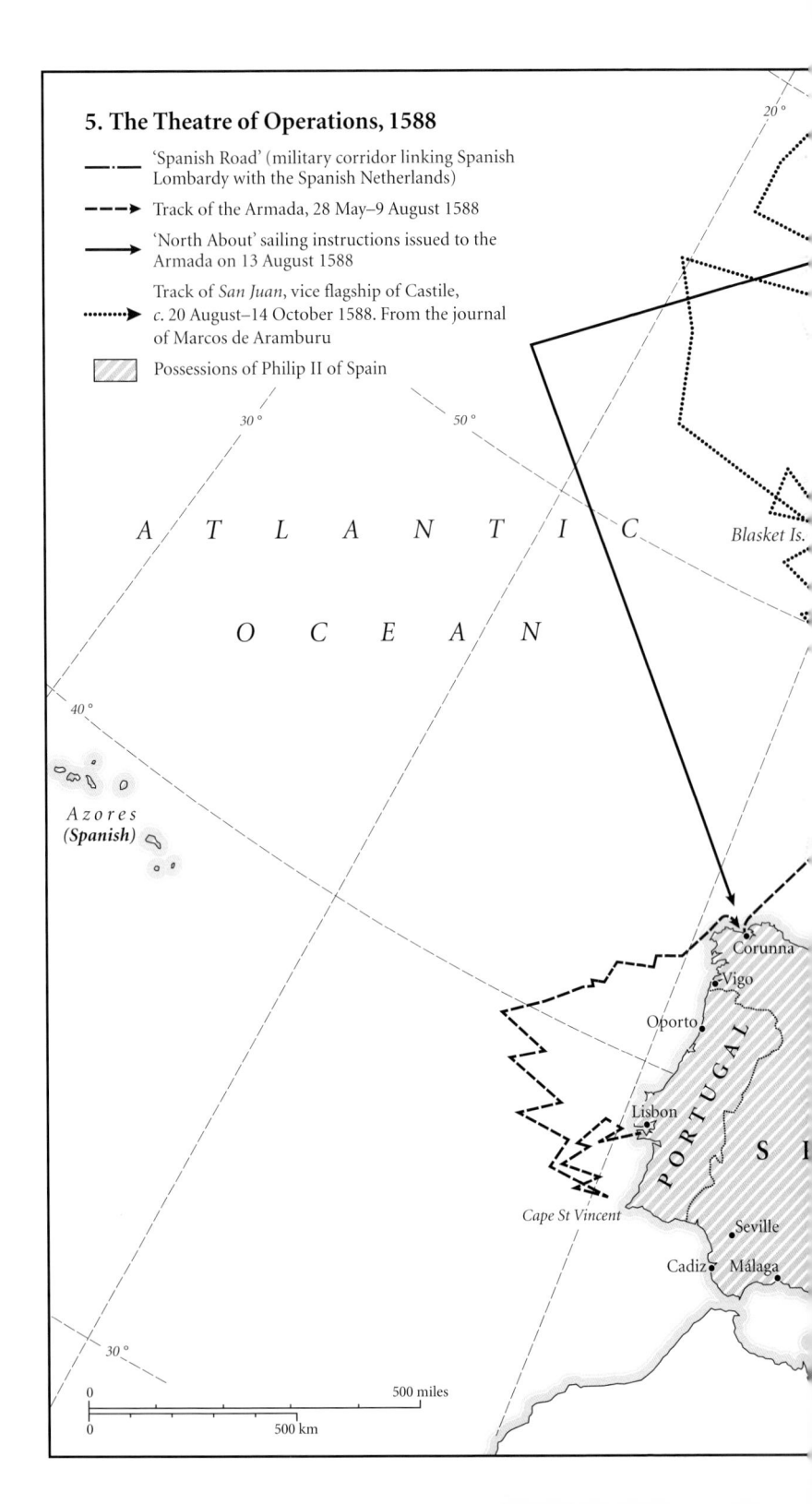

—·— 'Spanish Road' (military corridor linking Spanish Lombardy with the Spanish Netherlands)

– – ▶ Track of the Armada, 28 May–9 August 1588

⟶ 'North About' sailing instructions issued to the Armada on 13 August 1588

••••▶ Track of *San Juan*, vice flagship of Castile, c. 20 August–14 October 1588. From the journal of Marcos de Aramburu

▨ Possessions of Philip II of Spain

ATLANTIC OCEAN

Blasket Is.

Azores (Spanish)

Corunna
Vigo
Oporto
Lisbon
PORTUGAL
Cape St Vincent
Seville
Cadiz  Málaga

0 — 500 miles
0 — 500 km

10°
0°
10°
Faeroes
NORWAY
Shetland
Rockall
Orkney
St Kilda
SWEDEN
SCOTLAND
English fleet
breaks off
Edinburgh
North Sea
IRELAND
Dublin
DENMARK
Chester
Cork
ENGLAND
DUTCH
REPUBLIC
Hamburg
London
HOLY
Calais
Antwerp
SPANISH NETHERLANDS
Ushant
ROMAN
Rouen
Paris
Metz
EMPIRE
AUSTRIAN
HABSBURGS
F R A N C E
FRANCHE-
COMTÉ
Vienna
SWISS CON.
Geneva
Santander
SAVOY
Milan
VENICE
Bilbao
LOMBARDY
Venice
Avignon
Genoa
OTTOMAN
EMPIRE
Florence
TUSCANY
PAPAL
STATES
Barcelona
Ragusa
Rome
Naples
NAPLES
SARDINIA
Cartagena
Mediterranean Sea
Palermo
SICILY
N

## Part I
# The Fleets Assemble

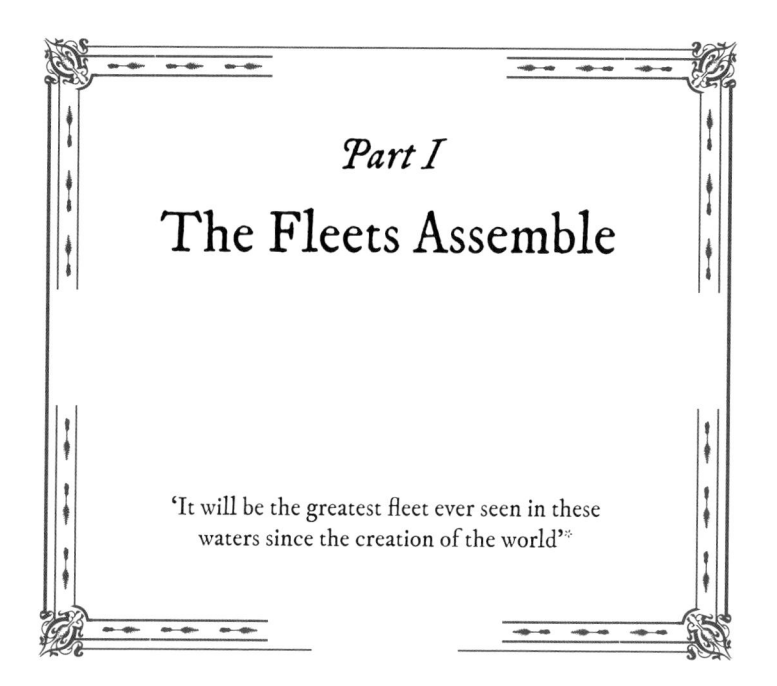

'It will be the greatest fleet ever seen in these waters since the creation of the world'*

**6.** Lisbon in 1662, with soldiers on parade in the square in front of the Ribeira Palace and a warship at anchor in the harbour.

# I

# 'Arise O Lord and Avenge Thy Cause'[1]

## On Parade

SHORTLY AFTER DAWN ON 25 April 1588, Don Agustín Mexía led seven companies of Spanish infantrymen, 1,250 soldiers, onto the broad plaza beside the River Tagus at Lisbon and lined them up as an honour-guard facing the Ribeira Palace, the seat of Portugal's kings (Figure 6).

Eight years before, Philip II of Spain had claimed the throne of Portugal on the death of the last ruler from the native Avis dynasty, unleashing an army led by his foremost general, the duke of Alba, and a fleet commanded by his foremost admiral, the marquis of Santa Cruz. Backed by skilful logistical planning, the invaders joined forces and advanced to the walls of Lisbon where they routed the troops mobilized by another claimant to the Portuguese throne, Dom Antonio. Forces led by Spanish grandees, including the duke of Medina Sidonia, soon overcame all opposition in the peninsula and in April 1581 Philip II of Spain was crowned Philip I of Portugal. Only the Azores archipelago in the mid-Atlantic, a thousand miles west of Lisbon, held out for Dom Antonio.

In 1582 Santa Cruz, who had extensive experience of amphibious warfare in the Mediterranean, organized a battle fleet ('armada' in Spanish) in Lisbon's Tagus estuary, and led it forth to impose Spanish control on the Azores. In an engagement in July off the largest island, São Miguel, Santa Cruz routed the fleet raised by Dom Antonio and executed all those captured. He returned in triumph to Lisbon, where the king received him in person. Only Terceira island continued to defy him, and the following summer Santa Cruz led an even larger armada including galleys and troop-transports from Lisbon and directed a successful amphibious landing.

After another round of executions, and the brutal sack of captured communities, all resistance collapsed and Santa Cruz again returned in triumph to Lisbon.

By then King Philip had returned to Spain where he turned his attention to creating an even larger armada, mobilizing ships, men, munitions and provisions from his dominions in Europe and America, and from his allies, until by 1587 he had assembled a task force of 30,000 men and 130 ships in the Tagus estuary. He instructed Santa Cruz to conquer England and restore its obedience to the pope: a venture known in Catholic circles as the 'Enterprise of England'.

To achieve these goals Philip had devised an ambitious strategy. The Armada would adopt a defensive formation as it advanced up the English Channel, relying on tight sailing discipline and the numerous soldiers aboard to fend off opposition until the fleet approached the ports of the Spanish Netherlands, where his nephew the duke of Parma had orders to assemble 27,000 troops and embark them on a flotilla of small ships. The two forces would then 'join hands' (the king's phrase) and cross the Narrow Seas together to establish a beachhead at Margate in north-east Kent. There the Armada would offload the siege-guns, draught animals, munitions and supporting services it had brought from Lisbon, and also 6,000 of its own troops to reinforce Parma's men. The invading army would then advance rapidly towards London, supported by the fleet in the Thames. With the support of its siege-train it would neutralize England's antiquated and weakly garrisoned defences, seize the capital, and either capture or kill Queen Elizabeth and her leading ministers.

Parma's soldiers were reckoned the best in the world and putting their boots on English soil offered Philip the most promising pathway to success – but boots on Spanish decks were needed to get them there. The seven companies of infantrymen drawn up outside Lisbon's Ribeira Palace were 'the best-looking and best-armed men that could be found' among the five Spanish *tercios* (regiments) embarked aboard the Armada (Figure 7). Appearances were deceptive, however. Officers and men were chosen because of their looks, not their unit cohesion, to serve as an honour-guard for the parade and the ensuing standard-blessing ceremony. They had come ashore the previous evening, while their comrades remained locked down on the ships. Guards posted ashore had orders to capture and execute any deserters (the fate of several previous fugitives).

On the stroke of 6 a.m. a procession emerged from the palace led by Philip's viceroy of Portugal, his nephew Cardinal Archduke Albert, who also served as the kingdom's papal legate and chief Inquisitor. Around his neck hung the emblem of the Golden Fleece, Spain's most prestigious order of chivalry, of which Philip was Grand Master and whose knights he addressed as *primo*: 'cousin'. At the viceroy's right hand rode a short, heavily built bearded man of thirty-nine, who also wore

7. Spanish infantry marching. Men with muskets and arquebuses lead with pikemen behind. Part of a frieze made of tiles commissioned in the 1580s to celebrate the victories of the marquis of Santa Cruz.

the distinctive Golden Fleece: Don Alonso Pérez de Guzmán el Bueno, twelfth lord of Sanlúcar de Barrameda, ninth count of Niebla and seventh duke of Medina Sidonia, who the previous evening had taken the oath to serve faithfully as Philip's Captain-General of the Ocean Sea, an office vacated by the death of Santa Cruz two months before. Medina Sidonia had sought to decline this honour, but Philip insisted. Now the reluctant duke was honour-bound to do his best in an enterprise he had come to believe was ill-judged and unlikely to succeed.

Next in the procession came Don Alonso Martínez de Leyva, aged thirty-seven, whom the king had appointed to lead the Armada's troops after they landed in England and also (though he probably did not know it) to take command of the Armada should Medina Sidonia fall. Don Alonso, resplendent in a suit of gilded armour presented by the king, had served with distinction in Italy, the Netherlands and both Azores campaigns; and early in 1588 Philip had briefed him in person on his operational duties.[2] At his side marched his brother-in-law, Don Francisco de Bobadilla: at fifty the Armada's most experienced military commander, with a distinguished record of active service in Italy, the Netherlands and Portugal, culminating in his appointment as overall infantry commander on the Terceira campaign five years before. Bobadilla also had good connections at Court, having grown up in the household of one of the king's principal advisers. Then came the *maestres de campo* (colonels) of the five Spanish infantry *tercios* embarked on the fleet, led by Don Alonso de Luzón of the *tercio* of Naples, who sported a moustache so luxurious that it attracted comment when the English captured him a few months later; and

Don Diego Pimentel of the *tercio* of Sicily. These two distinguished officers had led their troops from Spanish Italy to Lisbon the previous year. Nicolás de Isla was in command of the regiment which normally sailed on the guardships of the transatlantic convoys carrying the treasure that was the life-blood of the Spanish Empire. Don Francisco de Toledo and Mexía himself commanded the two *tercios* of volunteers raised in different parts of Spain specifically for service on the Armada. The reserve companies (*compañias sueltas*) had no colonel.

Each of the seven most senior infantry officers also commanded a fighting vessel in the Armada; six came from noble families, and five were knights in one of Spain's orders of chivalry. Some of the *aventureros* (gentlemen volunteers) and *entretenidos* (staff officers) who took part in the procession were also knights. Foremost among them marched Don Antonio Luis de Leyva (a distant cousin of Don Alonso), prince of Ascoli, whom many believed to be (in the words of Elizabeth's chief minister, Lord Burghley) 'the king of Spain's bastard': offspring of a supposed liaison between Philip and a lady of the Court.[3]

After the viceroy and the duke had completed their inspection, the parade marched off to the sound of fife and drum to Lisbon's great cathedral. Few townspeople lined the streets, and the Portuguese aristocracy were pointedly absent – Spain's recent conquest still rankled – but protocols had to be observed and the archbishop of Lisbon celebrated Mass and pronounced a general benediction on the Enterprise of England. Other native well-wishers included Sor María de la Visitación, a noblewoman sent to a nunnery as a child, who in 1584 had begun to display the stigmata of Christ's wounds. She also claimed to have experienced visions in which Christ and selected saints spoke to her. Many believed that her prayers had cured the sick and averted shipwrecks, and she received visitors and letters from far and wide seeking her intervention. Fray Luis de Granada, author of the best-selling *Book of Prayer and Meditation* and a celebrated preacher whose sermons had impressed the king during his stay in Lisbon ('even though he is very old and has no teeth'), became convinced that Sor María was a saint and composed a flattering biography that listed her 'miracles'. The viceroy asked her to bless the Armada and she graciously obliged.[4]

On 25 April the Armada's damask battle standard, so heavy that it took two men to lift, was laid on the cathedral altar and blessed. Its design affirmed the venture's strong religious overtones: images of a crucified Christ and the Virgin Mary flanked Philip's coat of arms, with the inscription *Exsurge Deus et vindica causam tuam*: 'Arise O Lord and Avenge Thy Cause'. The ships in the estuary and the soldiers drawn up outside fired three rounds in salute, and the garrison of Lisbon Castle replied.

After Mass the archbishop and clergy of the city processed through the streets towards the palace, followed by Albert and the senior officers. Medina

Sidonia's cousin Don Luis de Córdoba, mounted on a white charger, bore the now-consecrated banner aloft. They paused at a nearby Dominican convent where the duke (with some assistance) draped the unwieldy standard over the altar and held one of its tassels to mark the consecration of his own person to the cause it signified.

Finally the duke and viceroy stood on the steps of the palace while the honour-guard fired another volley, and those holding colours and pikes lowered them in salute. The senior officers then retired for a well-earned repast, while the soldiers were herded back to the ships. They would not leave Lisbon for more than a month, or disembark for more than two. The survivors would not return to Spain for five months or more. Almost half would not return at all.

## The Participants: Soldiers

A variety of sources, from documents in archives and libraries to artefacts recovered from Armada wrecks, provide details about the soldiers aboard the fleet. Only a few were born outside Spain. In February 1588 a Moroccan magistrate who had fled to Portugal and converted to Christianity offered to raise seventy 'men of his nation' to 'serve God and His Majesty' on the Armada, and asked permission to embark on smaller ships 'because they will be the first to land'. Medina Sidonia accepted, but with reservations: the new recruits, known as Moriscos (converts to Christianity from Islam) 'may not have colours or drums or other insignia', and they would receive a firearm but no salary.[5] In addition 'some Africans and people of mixed race [*negros y mulatos*]' sailed with the fleet – but according to one eyewitness 'very few of them survived because of the extreme cold' on the voyage. We know the fate of only two of the Africans: one was still alive when his ship ran aground on the Devon coast on the way back to Spain but died shortly after coming ashore; the other was thrown into the air when the ship on which he sailed exploded just after she returned to her home port. Miraculously he survived.[6]

Fearing that his ships had too few soldiers to achieve the king's goals, a month before the parade Medina Sidonia had issued a call for Portuguese volunteers, but only two gentlemen agreed to lead them (Albert 'spoke to others, but they refused'), and even they demanded higher wages and refused to serve on the same ship. Eventually, almost 2,000 local men embarked but Philip remained suspicious, insisting that 'the Portuguese troops should remain aboard the ships at all times, because I hear they serve better at sea than ashore. Those who land' in England 'must in all cases be the best and most experienced soldiers.'[7]

Who, then, were the 'most experienced soldiers'? They included 1,400 men drawn from the Spanish garrisons of Sicily, commanded by Pimentel (a veteran of the conquest of Portugal in 1580). They had sailed from Sicily to Cadiz and marched overland to Lisbon, arriving just in time to sail with Santa Cruz in July 1587 to the Azores to meet and escort home the annual treasure-fleet from the Americas. Four other contingents of infantry sailed with the marquis: 1,700 men drawn from the Spanish garrisons in Portugal; 1,500 who had served on the transatlantic guardships; 500 aboard a squadron from Vizcaya in northern Spain; and 2,500 raised by the cities and nobles of Andalucia. These men may have lacked combat experience but their voyage to the Azores and back, which lasted three months and covered 2,000 miles, had at least familiarized them with naval service in Atlantic waters. Six infantry companies that arrived at Lisbon in April 1588 also had naval experience. The company of Patricio Antolínez, raised in Burgos, had embarked on the transatlantic guardships at Sanlúcar in April 1586, spent the winter in Cartagena de Indias (now in Colombia), and returned in September 1587. It then sailed to Lisbon, where many were sent to reinforce other ships. Antolínez and his men boarded the *urca Gran Grifón*.[8]

The 'most experienced soldiers' aboard the Armada also included 1,600 men drawn from the Spanish garrisons in Naples commanded by Alonso de Luzón. Like the *tercio* created from the Spanish garrisons in northern Portugal and Galicia commanded by Toledo, they arrived in Lisbon too late to take part in the Azores operation, but all were familiar with military life, and some had been under fire. Thus Francisco Ruiz Matute had enlisted in a Spanish infantry company in 1567 and fought on Philip's Mediterranean galley-fleet, participating in the great naval victory of Lepanto in 1571 before returning to Naples. He became a company captain just before his *tercio* set sail for Lisbon, where he embarked on the ill-fated *Santa María de la Rosa*. Francisco Blanco, another veteran from the *tercio* of Naples, had served in the conquest of Portugal and the Azores, and then fought in the Netherlands until 1586 before fleeing to Naples, where he changed his name to Juan Ortega before enlisting in Luzón's *tercio*. Together they travelled to Lisbon, where they embarked on the equally ill-fated *Trinidad Valencera*.[9]

Perhaps 10,000 soldiers aboard the Armada could thus claim previous military or naval experience. The rest were raw recruits: the 2,000 Portuguese and Morisco volunteers; 2,500 more raised by the cities and nobles of Andalucia; 1,500 raised by the cities and nobles of Extremadura; and 1,500 from elsewhere in Castile. Instead of joining one of the *tercios*, these soldiers joined the reserves. The companies from Extremadura arrived so late that Medina Sidonia embarked them 'directly from the barges' that carried them across the Tagus, for fear they might desert if allowed to land. They received the weapons they would be expected to use in combat only after coming aboard, and powder and ball 'so that they could train, and have something in reserve for the expected combat', only after two weeks at sea.[10]

A disproportionate number of the other soldiers aboard the Armada came from Andalucia, both because the king had issued patents to raise a total of 5,000 men there for service on the fleet, and because almost all the troops already serving on the transatlantic guardships also came from the towns and villages of the Guadalquivir valley (Figure 8). Many came from the same place and continued to serve together, rather like the 'chums platoons' of the British Army in the First World War. Thus sixty-four Armada survivors ransomed in England in 1590 came from the small town of Écija, between Seville and Córdoba, because they had enlisted together when Captain Alonso de Zayas recruited a company there. Like him, they boarded *Nuestra Señora del Rosario*; and like him, they fell prisoner to the English when the ship surrendered after her first day in combat.

Each *tercio* usually comprised twelve companies. Within each company, soldiers belonged to a *camarada* – a group of six to eight men who shared a tent or billet, and cooked and ate together. This is an optimum bonding number: large enough for individuals to be mutually supportive, yet not numerous enough to encourage factions. An army's cohesion and strength depends on the interpersonal loyalty and support within these tight-knit groups.

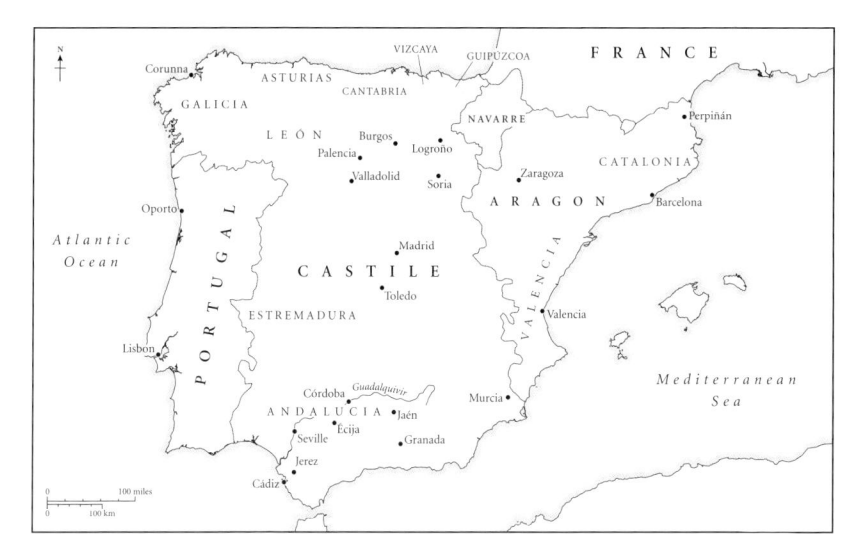

8. The provinces of Spain.

The fleet also included more than 500 *aventureros* and *entretenidos*, who brought with them not only some 600 'retainers able to fight' but also jewellery, including (in some cases) gold chains. These could be up to fifteen feet long, worn in loops. They were not merely decorative: links were pinched together rather than joined

**9.** Items of gold jewellery recovered from the wreck of *Girona*. Top left, a gold pendant in the form of a salamander, studded with rubies, while a ring (top right) bearing the same mythical emblem (supposedly an antidote to fire) perhaps belonged to the same individual. Bottom left, a lover's ring which even after four centuries beneath the sea brings a lump to the throat. It was given by his wife or sweetheart and depicts an unclasped girdle with a hand holding a heart with this timeless inscription: NO TENGO MAS QUE DARTE – 'I have nothing more to give you'. Centre right, Tomás Perrenot, the nephew and heir of Cardinal Granvelle (for many years Philip II's chief minister), wore a ring inscribed 'Madame de Champagney 1524' which had belonged to his grandmother Nicole Bonvalot. He perished with Leyva when *Girona* went down. Bottom right, Cameo with the head of one of the twelve Caesars (the other eleven were also found). Each was of lapis lazuli framed with gold embellished with pearls, and would have been linked as a necklace.

**10.** Other luxury items found on Armada wrecks include: a gold combination toothpick and ear-scoop (*Girona*); a silver scent bottle and glass dropper (*Girona*); and a nit comb (*Trinidad Valencera*). Top right, three silver forks of different designs, very early examples, from the wreck of *Girona*, which was crowded with survivors from earlier wrecks on the Irish coast. Centre, knife with a steel blade decorated with a fish symbol; the handle is of bone, the two sides held together with decorative copper-alloy rivets (*Trinidad Valencera*). Bottom right, Ming-dynasty export-quality porcelain bowl, also from *Trinidad Valencera*.

so that lengths could be detached to make payments – an early form of traveller's cheque. When *Trinidad Valencera* foundered off the Irish coast, a survivor estimated that 'the soldiers and wild people' relieved them of 'money, gold buttons, rapiers and apparel to the value of 7,300 ducats or there about' and 'money, plate and jewels' worth 1,200 ducats (Figure 9).[11] The senior commanders, like their retainers, also brought extra luxuries with them, including fine clothes and dinner services for use when they arrived in London (Figure 10).[12]

Many men aboard the Armada left wives and sweethearts behind. Only sixty-four women received permission to embark with their husbands on the *urcas Santiago* and *El Gato* (known in the fleet as 'the ships of the women'), presumably to carry out ancillary tasks as the army advanced into England. Many soldiers were probably unmarried because they were young – sometimes very young. Of 500 soldiers recruited for service on the Armada in summer 1587, ninety were teenagers and 320 were aged between twenty and twenty-five. Of almost 400 soldiers imprisoned in England and ransomed in 1590, forty-eight had enlisted before they turned eighteen and almost all the rest were under thirty. Of 133 other Armada survivors later integrated into the Spanish army fighting in the Netherlands, ten had enlisted as teenagers and most of the rest in their early twenties.[13]

The service records of the last group of survivors offer a unique insight into the experience of individual soldiers aboard the fleet, because the army's accountants listed everything supplied to each man so that it could be deducted later from his wages. The balance sheet is revealing. The soldiers who boarded the transatlantic guardships in March 1586 earned some 100 escudos over the next two years and had received almost all of it in money and goods (clothes, weapons, rations and so on) by the time they set sail for England. Likewise, Luzón's veterans received their wage arrears in full when they left Naples in May 1587 and earned a further 42 escudos by the time they sailed from Lisbon one year later, of which they had already received 41 escudos in money and goods.[14]

These figures reflect both the efficiency of Spain's military administration and Philip's ability to transfer large consignments of American treasure to Lisbon. Just before the parade 500,000 escudos in gold arrived from Seville, half of which Medina Sidonia used to issue two months' wages to each man. He divided the rest between the five most powerful ships in the fleet, ready for disbursement as soon as the Armada reached England: his flagship *San Martín* (Portugal), *Santa Ana* (Vizcaya), *Santa Ana* (Guipúzcoa), *San Salvador* (Guipúzcoa) and *Rosario* (Andalucia).

Perhaps this largesse raised collective morale, because as they boarded their ships some soldiers sang a popular ballad:

My brother Bart
For England departs
To kill Drake
And capture the queen.

When he returns from the wars
He must bring back in chains
A little Lutheran for me
And a Lutheran girl for my granny.[15]

## The Participants: Mariners

Most of the soldiers had spent the winter months billeted ashore, but most of the seamen had not, and (no doubt because of their close confinement) diseases raged through the ships. Typhus carried off the marquis of Santa Cruz in February 1588; and of 700 Basque seamen who joined the Armada and perished before it returned, almost half died before the fleet even departed. These seamen from Spain's north coast – one of the few contingents of the 7,000 aboard the Armada for whom we have details – differed from the soldiers in two respects. First, many were married: together, they left behind almost 350 widows and some 700 orphans. Second, they were almost all experienced. Many had sailed to the Azores and back the previous year, and before that had served an apprenticeship as *grumetes*, learning how to climb the rigging and work the sails, man the pumps, tie knots, crew the ship's boat, and follow orders. As in all sailing ships it was a hard life. In the chilling phrase of the *Naval Instructions* published by Judge Diego García de Palacio in 1587: 'The lash will soon teach those who do not already know their way round a ship.'[16]

Like the soldiers, many seamen aboard the Armada came from the same place – 150 of the Basque seamen lived in San Sebastián and the neighbouring port of Pasajes (Pasaia) – and some came from the same family. Martín de Villafranca from San Sebastián, owner and master of *Santa María de la Rosa*, was one of those who died in Lisbon; his son of the same name succeeded him and perished 'when the ship and everyone aboard foundered on the coast of Ireland'. Three Iriarte brothers from the small port of Zumaya all died on the campaign, albeit on different ships: Martín, a gunner; Lazaro, a carpenter; and Balthasar, a sailor. Although 'too young to marry', the three left their grieving parents 'in great poverty'.[17]

Personal details for one other group of Armada mariners survive: thirty captured seamen ransomed from English prisons in 1590. Many were in their thirties, and almost all were described as having a 'good physique' (*buen cuerpo*) – a phrase conspicuously absent from the list of soldiers ransomed at the same time. Again in contrast to the soldiers, these mariners and the eleven ransomed *grumetes* came from all over Europe: from the Baltic, France, Italy, the Netherlands, Portugal and the Adriatic, as well as from Spain's Atlantic ports. This variety is hardly surprising, because the Armada included ships from all those locations, embargoed on Philip's orders along with their crews. Perhaps half the 7,000 seamen aboard the Spanish Armada did not come from Spain.[18]

## Ten Generals for Ten Squadrons

The Armada left Lisbon organized in ten squadrons, each commanded by a Spanish 'general': nine from Castile and one from Catalonia.

Medina Sidonia, born at Sanlúcar de Barrameda and in command of the squadron of Portugal as well as of the whole Armada, was Spain's richest grandee. He governed more than 50,000 vassals, and a register of the estates and jurisdictions he inherited covered 400 folio pages. In 1579 the duke had organized the defence of Andalucia against a possible attack from Morocco, working closely with the galley squadron commanded by Santa Cruz, and the two also cooperated closely the following year in reducing the ports of southern Portugal to Philip's obedience. In 1581 the king ordered Medina Sidonia to lead an amphibious attack on Morocco, but he changed his mind and diverted the naval assets assembled in Andalucia to Lisbon for the Azores campaign. Unfortunately, two of the galleys prepared by the duke sank in Cadiz Bay in January 1582, and Santa Cruz sent a crushing reproach: 'I implore your lordship not to order galleys to sail at this time of year, because even if they are fully provisioned they may be lost.' Medina Sidonia objected to the rude tone and forwarded the letter to Philip, demanding a commission of inquiry to establish whether he had been at fault (if so, he offered to pay for the damage). This irritated the king. 'As if we did not have enough difficulties and problems, now I have this package from the duke of Medina Sidonia,' he scribbled angrily to his private secretary and chaplain, Mateo Vázquez. 'It's stupid to have the duke and the marquis at odds like this', especially since 'I don't think the marquis's letter is as bad as the duke claims'. Philip nevertheless instructed Vázquez to rebuke Santa Cruz, reminding him 'how much His Majesty esteems the duke, both for who he is and for all he does in the king's service'. So 'let there be no differences, but rather complete conformity between you'. The rebuke worked. In 1587 Medina Sidonia supervised the dispatch of a huge fleet of reinforcements from Andalucia to join Santa Cruz in Lisbon. Not one ship was lost.[19] Juan Gómez de Medina, from Cadiz, had accompanied Santa Cruz to the Azores in 1582 and served as vice-admiral of several transatlantic convoys. The central government rated him 'a soldier as well as a sailor' and in January 1588 appointed him general of the squadron of *urcas*: large merchantmen from northern Europe embargoed in the ports of Andalucia the previous year.[20]

Six other squadron commanders came from Spain's northern port cities. Juan Martínez de Recalde (Vizcaya), from Bilbao, was the son and grandson of seafarers who had served the Crown. Now in his mid-forties, he had commanded both transatlantic fleets and naval flotillas in the mid-Atlantic. In addition, as he reminded the king, 'I can truly say that Your Majesty has no subject of my rank with more experience, or who has sailed more often' in the seas around England, Ireland and the Netherlands. In 1572 Recalde had assembled and commanded a fleet sailing from Spain to the Netherlands, where he led his ships into battle against the Dutch rebels. Three years later he led a second fleet on the same route, and when storms forced him into the Solent he landed briefly at Southampton. In 1580 he transported an expeditionary force from Spain to Smerwick in south-west Ireland, gaining local nautical knowledge which would later save several Armada ships, including his own. He possessed one more asset: he had married the sister of Don Juan de Idiáquez, Philip's principal secretary of state, which gave Recalde valuable contacts at Court and a direct channel to the king. In March 1588, at Medina Sidonia's request, Philip appointed Recalde *almirante general* (deputy commander) of the Armada, 'because besides being a fine mariner he is a very good soldier'.[21]

Martín de Bertendona, aged fifty-eight and also from Bilbao, had an equally distinguished record. In 1554 he had sailed with the fleet which took Philip from Spain to Southampton for his marriage to Queen Mary Tudor, and in 1570 he commanded the fleet which brought Philip's fourth wife, Anna of Austria, from the Netherlands to Spain. For part of that voyage English warships commanded by Charles Howard and William Winter escorted his fleet: he would meet both officers and their ships again in the Armada battles. Bertendona had also fought the Dutch rebels alongside Recalde in the 1570s and commanded a squadron during the Azores campaigns of 1582 and 1583. In January 1588 Philip appointed him general of the Levant squadron, composed of large Mediterranean merchantmen.

Miguel de Oquendo from San Sebastián, in his mid-sixties, matched Recalde and Bertendona in naval experience. He too had played a prominent role in both Azores campaigns under Santa Cruz, and during the Armada battles some said he handled his flagship 'like a lancer' – an extravagant simile, perhaps, for his lumbering 1,200-ton *Santa Ana*, though not for his personal panache. Like Recalde, Oquendo enjoyed good connections at Court: when in May 1586 Philip decided to create a fleet from Guipúzcoa under Oquendo's command, he granted a personal audience to brief him – the only senior commander apart from Leyva to be so honoured. Oquendo was also wealthy despite his humble origins. He owned two large ships (both sailed with the Armada), considerable cash reserves and two slaves.[22]

Agustín de Ojeda, born in adjacent Fuenterrabía, had twenty-five years of naval expertise, including service on the transatlantic convoys, and on both Azores campaigns, when in 1587 Santa Cruz awarded him a handsome salary as a staff officer 'to serve near our person'. Medina Sidonia kept Ojeda on the flagship, giving him joint command over all the seamen aboard until in June 1588 he appointed him to replace the deceased general of the squadron of *pataches* and *zabras* (small, fast sailing ships embargoed in the Basque ports).

Don Pedro de Valdés, in his mid-fifties, came from the port of Gijón in Asturias and in 1565 had commanded the troops aboard a task force sent to destroy all French settlements in Florida. A decade later he joined Recalde's fleet sailing to the Netherlands, taking refuge from storms in Dartmouth on the way. In 1580 he commanded the squadron which captured Oporto for King Philip, but the next year catastrophe struck: sent to clear the seas around the Azores of opponents, Don Pedro made a rash attempt to capture Terceira and had to withdraw after suffering heavy casualties. He was court-martialled on his return and sent to prison, but in 1587 he sailed to the Azores as an *entretenido* on Santa Cruz's flagship. On his return Philip appointed him general of the Andalusian squadron, made up of large merchantmen embargoed by the Crown. Like Oquendo, he was wealthy: witness the handsome Renaissance-style Valdés Palace which stills stands in Gijón.[23]

Don Pedro's cousin Diego Flores de Valdés, also from Gijón and (like Oquendo) over sixty, had a similarly mixed record of command. His career began auspiciously: he had accompanied Philip on his journey from Spain to Southampton in 1554 and commanded the ship which brought him back from the Netherlands to Spain five years later. He was second-in-command of the expeditionary force sent to Florida in 1565, and subsequently led at least eight convoys safely to and from North America. This record led to his appointment in 1581 to command a fleet sent to clear English interlopers from the South Atlantic, but in this he failed spectacularly: he lost all but eight of his twenty-three ships and the English escaped. Nevertheless, when in February 1588 Philip decided to divert to Lisbon another flotilla of guardships assembled for a transatlantic crossing, he appointed Flores as its general. It reached Lisbon on 28 April and became the squadron of Castile.[24]

Of the other two squadron generals, Diego de Medrano, born in Soria around 1545, had fought in the Mediterranean for twenty years before Santa Cruz appointed him to command the galleys which played a crucial role at Terceira in 1583. Medrano and his galleys also accompanied the marquis on the Azores expedition four years later. Don Hugo de Moncada, born in Barcelona in 1557, was the youngest of the generals. He began his military service at age fourteen, rising to command a galleass in 1585 in which he sailed from Naples to Lisbon two years later. In February 1588 Philip appointed him general of the galleass squadron.

It is worth pausing to admire the collective experience of these senior naval officers. Oquendo, Recalde, Don Pedro de Valdés, Bertendona, Medrano and Ojeda – like three senior army officers (Bobadilla, Leyva and Pimentel) – had all sailed with Santa Cruz to conquer the Azores and come under fire. The first four were also familiar with northern European waters; Recalde, Bertendona and Diego Flores had even sailed up the Solent and landed at Southampton. Oquendo, Recalde and Don Pedro, like Diego Flores and Gómez de Medina, had commanded fleets.

Although Medina Sidonia had done none of these things, he regularly summoned the generals to his flagship and took advantage of their wisdom. Perhaps his willingness to learn reflected his education. Pedro de Medina, a noted humanist and author of books on navigation and history, had taught him to converse in Latin as well as Spanish, and imparted a knowledge of history along with an interest in current affairs. Leyva, too, had received a fine education. In his last known letter, as he faced the bitterness of defeat in August 1588, he invited his colleague Recalde to recite 'A poem written by Fray Luis de León, the great scholar, when his jealous rivals had him imprisoned by the Inquisition. When he regained his freedom, he wrote down this poem that I am sending to you now, because we need the temperament of a poet.' Little is known of the education of the other generals, but at his death Oquendo owned a small library; and Recalde knew enough history to compare Leyva's bravery under fire with that of El Cid Campeador, Spain's national hero.[25]

## Men Behaving Badly

Nevertheless, like all human beings, the Armada's senior officers had their flaws. In February 1588 the king's special representative in Lisbon exploded with indignation that other members of the High Command treated Recalde with disdain, despite the fact that 'he is without doubt the most competent and experienced man here; and as God is my witness, he suffers a great wrong in not having a seat on the Council of War. Is it his fault that his colleagues resent him [because of his low birth]'? Shortly afterwards, when Don Pedro de Valdés disagreed with his colleagues on tactics, Medina Sidonia duly relayed his dissent to the king but spitefully added: 'Perhaps he does not remember what happened to him in Terceira, at great cost to Your Majesty.'[26] Don Pedro's cousin Diego Flores de Valdés also attracted a fair degree of spite. On hearing of his selection as commander of the South Atlantic fleet in 1581, a rival observed that 'although it is certain that His Majesty likes the general [Flores], those who know him definitely do not'. Seven years later, on learning that Flores would command the squadron of Castile, a survivor of the South Atlantic expedition urged the king to 'appoint someone with more courage, one not so timid and risk-averse to fighting even when he holds the advantage, as we saw most recently in the fleet sent by Your Majesty to the Strait of Magellan'.[27]

Some of the fleet's commanders fell short of the standards expected of a Spanish gentleman: a pedigree untainted by illegitimacy, Jewish blood, heresy, or having worked for a living. Even Medina Sidonia did not meet all these criteria, because he was descended from the illegitimate daughter of an archbishop who was himself illegitimate. Gómez de Medina was 'descended from Jewish converts, and the Inquisition of Seville had burned or condemned one of his grandfathers': his promotion to squadron commander only went through because the king's naval advisers 'did not have time to ask the Inquisitors of Seville to provide details'. Both Oquendo and Don Juan de Acuña Vela, Spain's Captain-General of Artillery, had been summoned to appear before their local Inquisition on suspicion of abetting heresy.[28]

The murky past of several other Armada commanders came to light through the complex process required to obtain a knighthood in one of Spain's Orders of Chivalry (Figure 11). As Grand Master of each Order, Philip alone could make a nomination; but before it could take effect, his Council of the Orders sent investigators to the residence of each nominee to interview people – often dozens of people – with knowledge of their religious and personal background. The investigators, one a friar and the other a knight of the Order, asked a set of questions designed to determine whether the nominee was of 'pure blood [*limpieza de sangre*]'. Those who failed this test only received a knighthood if the king secured a papal dispensation to disregard the 'stains [*tachas*]' on their record.

The Armada's senior officers had accumulated a surprising number of 'stains'. Don Pedro de Valdés's knighthood went on hold after investigators found that two of his grandparents were the offspring of fornicating priests, and 'the whole world knows it [*todo el mundo lo sabe*]'. In addition, some said his father had sold vegetables ('albeit home-grown, not the produce of others'). Although the investigators

11. The insignia of Spanish knightly orders. Left: the Golden Fleece, on a golden chain (reconstruction drawing). Members of this Order associated with the Armada included Parma and Medina Sidonia. Top right: Cross of a Knight of Santiago (Don Pedro de Valdés, Diego Flores, Oquendo and a score of others aboard the Armada held this honour). Middle right: Cross of a Knight of St John of Malta. Below right: Cross of a knight of Alcántara (front and back) perhaps belonging to Don Alonso de Leyva, a Knight Commander of the Order (all from the wreck of *Girona*).

suspected this was just a slur spread by Don Pedro's 'enemies in the town and on the town council', 'the whole world' also knew that no sooner had Valdés got his knighthood than his father Don Juan had Don Pedro's wife murdered on suspicion of adultery, and that royal officials then arrested, tried and executed Don Juan.[29]

Miguel de Oquendo, too, faced determined local enemies. In 1562 the king had granted his petition to carry 'offensive and defensive weapons' at all times, because 'some people wish you harm, and you fear that they might injure or kill you'. Twenty years later, now a magistrate in San Sebastián, Oquendo browbeat his colleagues into approving funds for the squadron the king had asked him to raise and lead to the Azores, which meant that 'many people in this town hate him'. His enemies had a field day when the Council's investigators arrived later that year to collect testimony for Oquendo's knighthood. Witnesses asserted that his father had 'made ropes with his own hands', and that Miguel not only bought and sold goods but also maintained a factor in Cadiz to handle his merchandise.

In October 1583, after returning victorious from Terceira, Oquendo had stormed back to Court and complained that 'my enemies have waged war on me while I have been away, making accusations that are wholly untrue' explicitly to derail his knighthood. He also asserted that although he had indeed worked for a living, in Bilbao 'all the citizens, however noble, work for a living without compromising their noble status'. The Council of the Orders nevertheless 'resolved that he should not be given a knighthood for now', and the king had to obtain a papal dispensation to overrule them.[30]

Several of the Armada's military commanders also required similar royal intervention. Luzón did not receive a knighthood until 1598 because rumours that the Inquisition had burned one of his forebears at the stake for crypto-Judaism derailed previous nominations (although, as with Don Pedro de Valdés and Oquendo, some witnesses suggested that the rumours merely reflected efforts by local elite families to prevent him from getting a knighthood).[31] The Council's investigators discovered that the grandmother of Don Balthasar de Zúñiga, a staff officer aboard the flagship, was 'the granddaughter of the archbishop of Santiago, a priest'; and that the prince of Ascoli's mother was descended from a bishop who had converted from Judaism. In each case the king had to secure a papal dispensation before his nominee could receive a knighthood. Moreover, since 'the whole world' knew about such 'stains', they no doubt became the subject of gossip and jests aboard the fleet.[32]

The same was true of embarrassing misdeeds by other leading protagonists. During Holy Week 1581 a group of young courtiers in Madrid took advantage of the moment when all the candles in church are extinguished and the congregation makes a great noise during a 'Tenebrae' service, to kiss and grope any young women within range. Among those arrested, fined 2,000 ducats apiece and banished from Court were the count of Paredes, two sons of Don Diego de Córdoba (the king's chamberlain) and Ascoli. Not long after Ascoli's return to Court, he and another young aristocrat led their servants into the streets one night and began a serenade beneath a lady's balcony. High words attracted the attention of Don Diego de Córdoba's unruly sons and the rival groups soon 'drew their swords and slashed at each other' until relatives calmed them down. Once again the king exiled them all from Court.[33]

These miscreants were still in disgrace in March 1588 when Philip called on all noblemen to repair to Lisbon and join the Armada, and they seized the opportunity of redemption. Ascoli brought with him thirty-nine combat-ready servants, more than anyone else, so that he could (in Philip's words) 'follow in the footsteps of your ancestors by joining the Armada to serve me'. The king ordered Medina Sidonia 'to summon the prince to all meetings of the Council of War', and to 'listen to his voice and opinion in the matters discussed there'. The duke complied, granting him a place of honour by his side on the flagship's quarterdeck despite the fact the prince was only twenty-four and lacked any military and naval experience.[34] Other senior officers with chequered pasts included Juan Téllez Guzmán, marquis of Peñafiel and Medina Sidonia's cousin, sent to prison in 1587 after disgracing himself at Court. A year later he appeared in Lisbon as an *entretenido*, presumably after volunteering for the Armada in return for his freedom. Aged thirty-four, and accompanied by twenty-one retainers, the marquis embarked on the Portuguese warship *San Marcos*, commanded by Bobadilla; and when Bobadilla moved to the flagship to advise the duke on military matters, Peñafiel, despite his lack of naval experience, took command of the ship.[35]

Leyva, too, had once displeased the king. In 1581 Don Alonso threatened to kill a royal secretary suspected of adultery with the duke of Medina Sidonia's mother-in-law. Despite the duke's plea for clemency, Leyva was exiled from Court, but redeemed himself by serving on the Azores expedition the following year. In 1587 Philip sent him to Cadiz to help Medina Sidonia oversee the ships preparing to sail to Lisbon to join the Armada, 'on account of his experience and expertise in these matters'. Once in Lisbon, accompanied by thirty-six retainers, Don Alonso embarked on the great Genoese merchantman *Rata Encoronada* (Figure 12).[36]

Another former miscreant aboard the fleet was Captain Francisco de Cuéllar, who had enlisted while still a teenager as a soldier on the transatlantic guardships, and in 1580 took part in the conquest of Portugal. Cuéllar evidently served with distinction because the following year Philip appointed him 'captain on sea and land' of one of the warships led by Diego Flores into the South Atlantic; but he was accused of cowardice during the battle with the English and imprisoned aboard his own ship. He managed to clear his name soon after his return to Spain but did not receive his salary arrears until June 1587, when Philip sent Cuéllar and six other South Atlantic veteran officers to Lisbon to serve Santa Cruz on the Armada. Given their combat experience the seven expected to take command of one of the fighting ships, but by the time they arrived the marquis had already appointed 'gentlemen' (*hidalgos*) to every vacant post and so the newcomers sailed reluctantly to the Azores as staff officers. When they returned they refused to command lesser ships. Therefore, 'to avoid supporting vagabonds and men who shun the service of Your Majesty', the marquis 'dismissed them and terminated their salaries' and begged the king to 'make an example of them, as a warning to others' if they came to Court to complain. Instead, the captains swallowed their pride and agreed to serve as *entretenidos*. Cuéllar eventually sailed on *San Pedro*, one of the transatlantic guardships in

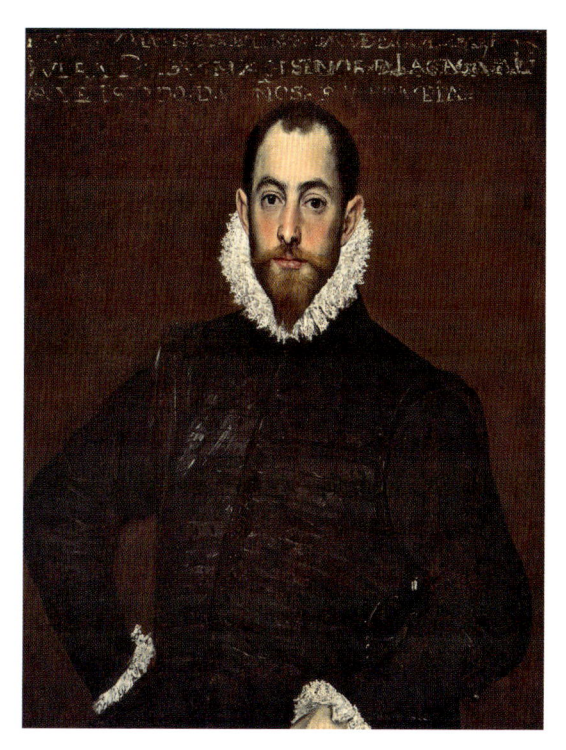

**12.** Portrait of Don Alonso de Leyva by El Greco, *c.* 1580. Don Alonso became a celebrity in 1578 when he raised a company of gentlemen volunteers in Italy and led them to fight for Don John of Austria, the king's brother, in the Netherlands. In 1586 some thought that he (rather than Santa Cruz) should command the royal fleet, because 'besides being a soldier as well as a sailor, he is affable and well-liked'; and a senior naval officer in Lisbon welcomed the chance 'to serve with such a famous soldier, and have him teach me the discipline of war' – unusually warm praise in a profession where criticisms far outnumbered compliments.[37]

the squadron of Castile, and just before she left Corunna his dream came true and he took over as her captain.[38]

Probably the best-known miscreant aboard the Armada was Lope de Vega, aged twenty-six. Royal magistrates had arrested him in a Madrid theatre the previous year on suspicion of circulating satires and, after a prison term, banished him not only from the Court but also from Castile. He reached Lisbon just in time to join Recalde aboard *San Juan de Portugal* and survived the journey to become Spain's most famous and prolific playwright. His participation in the Enterprise of England has been disputed, but his name appears clearly in a list of *aventureros* embarked on the fleet: 'Lope de Vega, from Madrid'.[39]

## The Ships

The Armada's command structure thus had serious weaknesses. So did its ships. As soon as Medina Sidonia arrived in Lisbon to take up his command in March 1588, he travelled around the fleet in a felucca (*falúa*) – one of ten small, sleek ships propelled by oars and sails, specially constructed in Lisbon the previous winter – and went aboard every ship anchored in the Tagus, even ordering the sails to be spread out on the decks for his inspection.[40] He asked each commander to submit a list of everything his ship lacked – cables, anchors, artillery, seamen, pilots and so on – and promised to supply them 'as fast as possible'. He shifted stores and munitions from ships he considered overloaded and paid special attention to the quantity of drinking water embarked. He then convened a committee of experienced subordinates to discuss how best to address the shortfalls. His hands-on approach and his efficiency, on which all his subordinates commented favourably, reflected his long experience of overseeing the dispatch of transatlantic convoys.

Governments in wartime often embargoed all large merchant ships found in local ports and afterwards selected those deemed suitable for amphibious operations which required the transfer of troops and munitions, paying the owner a fixed monthly rate for the ship and her crew until the end of the campaign. The Armada was no exception: embargoed merchantmen made up about two-thirds of the total (Figure 13 and Appendices 1–2). Some were constructed in Mediterranean ports, like *San Juan de Sicilia* from Ragusa, *Juliana* from Mataró in Catalonia and *Trinidad Valencera* from Venice (all in the Levant squadron). Others came from

13. Piece of carved decoration reused as part of a door but believed to have come from a wrecked Armada ship, now in the Clare Museum, Ennis, County Clare, Ireland. The curved plank clearly comes from a ship's hull, and the carving symbolizes a mercantile origin, with cornucopia, cloth-bale, barrels and books.

shipyards around the Atlantic, the Baltic and the North Sea, including *Gran Grifón* from Rostock (*urca*), *Santa María de la Rosa* from San Sebastián (Guipúzcoa), and *Nuestra Señora del Rosario* from Ribadeo (Andalucia). Most of the ships in the squadrons of Vizcaya and Andalucia, as well as the *pataches*, *zabras* and caravels used for communications, were also constructed in the shipyards of northern Spain.

Merchant ships need to transport large cargoes as economically as possible, which means capacious stowage and minimum operating costs; speed and manoeuvrability are less important. The hulls of European merchantmen – whether operating in the Mediterranean or the Atlantic – were therefore deep, tubby and box-like, with simple sailing rigs which required relatively few hands. The requirements for warships were the reverse: they needed to be fast and manageable, which meant the sacrifice of carrying capacity to create sufficient space for big guns that could engage an enemy at effective ranges, and embarking larger crews to serve them.

14. *San Martín*, right foreground, depicted in a fresco painted in the Hall of Battles at the Escorial to commemorate the naval victory of Santa Cruz off São Miguel in the Azores in 1582. Note the big guns on the two lower decks, the main deck and forecastle crowded with soldiers, and the holes in the sails caused by enemy fire. The boat towed behind her contains prisoners tied back-to-back. A friar hears their confessions before they are thrown into the sea to drown.

The Armada's vessels built specifically for combat fell into four categories. The squadron of Portugal included some of the largest sailing warships in the world. Medina Sidonia, like Santa Cruz before him, sailed in the flagship *San Martín*, built at Lisbon in the 1570s and carrying around fifty guns (different sources record slightly different totals) (Figure 14). She and *San Mateo* had played a prominent part in the battle off São Miguel, sustaining serious damage in the fight. The other seven galleons of the squadron were built in Portuguese shipyards after the Spanish conquest (Philip himself attended the launch of one of them, named *San Felipe* in his honour). Together with the galleass *Florencia* and two extra-large *zabras*, all had sailed to and from the Azores in 1587. Between them they carried around 400 guns, half of them large.

The squadron of Castile comprised smaller and faster fighting ships, built to escort the annual merchant convoys safely between Andalucia and Central America. The flagship, *San Cristóbal*, carried thirty-two guns; seven more warships had been built in shipyards near Santander to a standard design. The entire squadron carried almost 350 guns, a third of them large.

Galleys carried lateen sails which were used whenever conditions allowed, but for independent manoeuvre especially during battle their principal means of propulsion came from oarsmen, most but not all being prisoners or slaves (Figure 15). Designed explicitly for war, each galley carried a formidable array of artillery at the prow, which meant that (like a modern fighter aircraft) the whole platform had to manoeuvre to aim its ordnance. They could also perform vital work towing big sailing ships in confined waters and (thanks to their shallow draughts) the equally vital work of transferring men and munitions from ship to shore. Had they been available off Flanders in 1588 they could have protected Parma's landing-barges as they crossed the shallows where the deep-draught Armada ships could not operate. Some historians have seen the desire to include galleys in the Armada as a misplaced nostalgic reluctance to abandon a proven fighting machine, even though it was fundamentally unsuited to artillery-dominated naval warfare outside the Mediterranean. But both Medina Sidonia and Recalde wanted more of them.

Galleasses combined the capacious hull of a sailing ship with the ability to manoeuvre under oars. With a displacement roughly four times that of a galley, galleasses moved slowly when rowed, but in most conditions they could direct devastating firepower from the big guns on their fore- and aftercastles – some of them 50-pounders – at less adaptable sailing vessels. At Lepanto in 1571 six Venetian galleasses, operating in support of a conventional galley fleet, played a decisive role. But despite their impressive appearance, the galleasses' performance in the Armada campaign was to fall short of expectations (Figures 15, 16).

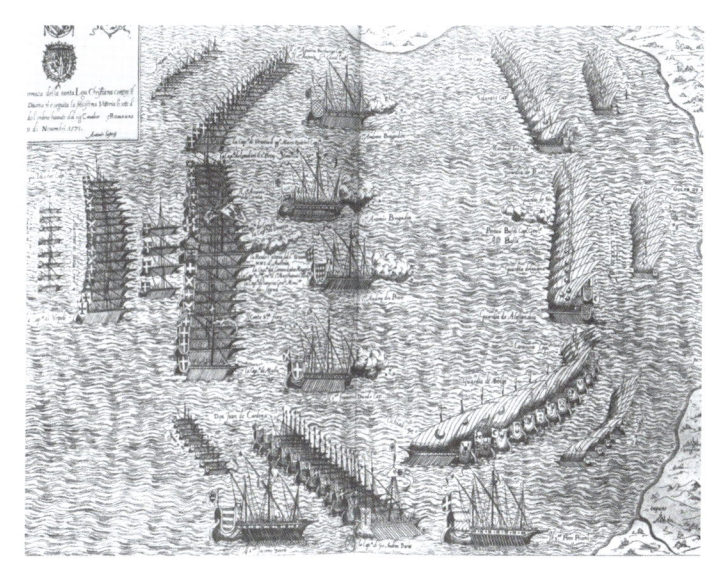

**15.** The battle of Lepanto, 1571. The Turks (right) rely on galleys, while the opposing Christian forces are led by larger galleasses carrying heavier artillery at their bows. Both sides are deployed in a half-moon formation, as the Armada would be.

**16.** A galleass, with her heavy guns mounted at bow and stern, and light swivel-pieces above the rowing bank. Valentine Dale, an English observer, commented on the vivid colours when he inspected the galleass *San Lorenzo* wrecked off Calais: 'The oars are all red, the sails had upon them the bloody sword [the red cross of holy war]; the upper part of the galleass was also red, signs and manifest tokens' – he continued self-righteously – 'of the bloody mind' that had sent them. The colour scheme is confirmed by this image (detail from the 'Greenwich Cartoon', Figure 35).

On 9 May Medina Sidonia's printer issued a pamphlet of forty-four pages, often known as the 'Lisbon muster', entitled *The Most Happy Armada that our Lord King Philip has ordered to assemble in Lisbon harbour*, filled with details on every ship, arranged by squadron, including the guns, munitions, soldiers and seamen aboard, as well as the names of all the officers, *entretenidos* and *aventureros*, and a note of the religious orders to which the 180 clerics aboard the fleet belonged (Figure 17).

It may seem curious that this compendium of information, which would today be classified as Top Secret, was published and disseminated by Medina Sidonia. The idea evidently originated with the duke because when one of the printed copies reached the Royal Palace on 3 June, Philip's private secretary forwarded it with the wry comment 'It's very detailed'. The king was furious: 'Yes indeed,' he scribbled. 'Printing these things could prove very dangerous, especially so early, because it will make our enemies aware of them.' Later, however, he accepted that the document might intimidate his enemies and impress his allies, letting all Europe know that the conquest had been achieved by Spanish arms and treasure (perhaps rendering more acceptable the king's claim to choose England's next monarch). Further editions soon appeared in Naples, Rome, Milan, Cologne and Paris.[41]

17. A page from the pamphlet *La felicíssima Armada*, printed at Lisbon on 9 May 1588, summarising the totals of the ships, soldiers, seamen, artillery pieces, powder, shot and so on. The only omission was the names of the 200 embittered English and Irish exiles aboard. This copy came into the hands of Lord Burghley, Elizabeth's chief minister, who translated the totals into English (bottom right).

**Table 1.1.** *The squadrons making up the Spanish fleet, as they left Corunna*[42]

| Squadron | Fighting ships | Support vessels | Total ships | Total sailors | Total rowers | Total soldiers | Total guns |
|---|---|---|---|---|---|---|---|
| Portugal | 9 | 2 | 11 | 1,058 | – | 2,647 | 266 |
| Castile | 14 | 2 | 16 | 1,078 | – | 2,579 | 326 |
| Galleys | 4 | 0 | 4 | 74 | 910 | 148 | 20 |
| Galleasses | 4 | 0 | 4 | 446 | 1,200 | 890 | 200 |
| Vizcaya | 10 | 4 | 14 | 800 | – | 1,986 | 234 |
| Andalucia | 10 | 1 | 11 | 720 | – | 2,089 | 251 |
| Guipúzcoa | 10 | 4 | 14 | 715 | – | 1,821 | 256 |
| Levant | 11/12 | 0 | 11/12 | 810 | – | 2,865 | 324 |
| *Urcas* | 22 | 0 | 22 | 646 | – | 2,375 | 387 |
| *Pataches* & *zabras* | 3 | 20/23 | 23/26 | 564 | – | 195 | 114 |
| Total | 97/98 | 33/36 | 130/134 | 6,911 | 2,110 | 17,595 | 2,378 |
| Caravels & feluccas | – | 16/17 | 16/17 | ? | 42 | – | – |
| TOTAL | 97/98 | 49/53 | 146/151 | 6,911 | 2,152 | 17,595 | 2,378 |

## Master of the Armada

Why did Medina Sidonia's pamphlet, printed at Lisbon on 9 May 1588, take more than three weeks to reach the king's desk? In part, the explanation lies in Philip's decision in 1583 to leave Portugal and return to Castile. Almost all letters and papers addressed to him were reviewed by one of the advisory Councils which met in the royal palace in Madrid: the Council of State for foreign policy, the Council of War for defence, the Council of the Inquisition for the affairs of the Holy Office; and so on. The Councils would forward each incoming paper to the king with a summary and suggest an appropriate response in a document known as a *consulta*. Philip read each *consulta* and either wrote or dictated his response. In winter he, too, resided in Madrid but in other seasons he divided his time between nearby secluded retreats, above all San Lorenzo El Real de El Escorial 50 miles north-west of Madrid in the Guadarrama mountains. There, from a small study overlooking the High Altar, Philip sought to run a global empire upon which the sun never set (Figures 18, 19).

**18.** The Escorial. Constructed under Philip II's personal direction, started in 1563 and completed in 1584. He intended the complex to serve as a monastery, library, seminary and family mausoleum as well as a royal palace.

Herein lay the first reason for the late arrival of Medina Sidonia's pamphlet describing the Armada: even the fastest courier required four days to ride between Madrid and Lisbon, and another day between Madrid and the Escorial. Distance explains a delay of a week, however, not almost a month. That stemmed from Philip's style of government.

The king abhorred personal interviews, preferring to transact all business in writing. In 1576, when rejecting the request of a senior military adviser for an interview, he informed his secretary: 'I would be glad to see him, but in all honesty I have very little time. And anyway,' he added, 'I forget so much of what is said to me at audiences.' Two years later, when Medina Sidonia asked for an audience to discuss how best to execute Philip's policy towards Morocco, the king replied: 'If you happened to be close to court, it might be useful to hear the details from you in person; but since your letters will be delivered to me in complete secrecy, I think it would be best if you wrote.'[43]

This was Philip's standard response: he insisted on receiving all information in writing. During the invasion of Portugal in 1580 he instructed his principal field commander 'to let me know *every day* what is going on'; and eight years later, during the Armada campaign, the king instructed his ambassador in Paris 'to advise me of everything *minute by minute*'. His ministers complied, and the torrent of incoming information convinced the king that he – and only he – had the 'big picture' necessary to take the correct decisions.[44]

To keep up with this torrent Philip worked on his papers for eight or nine hours almost every day, reading incoming letters and *consultas* before taking the final decisions himself, which he communicated to one of his secretaries either in a separate *billete* (note) or scrawled in the left-hand margin of the incoming document (left wide for this purpose). The king also signed most outgoing documents in person, up to 400 letters in a single morning (or so he once claimed). In 1575 an English diplomat in Madrid reported that Philip 'writes and dispatches by *billetes* more (they say) than all his secretaries'. A decade later, according to the Venetian ambassador:

> Someone who frequents the king's private apartments informs me that he is never idle, for besides his desire to read himself all the incoming and

**19.** Hub of empire: Philip II's study in the Escorial Palace. Note the original clock on the king's desk, with a candle in front of the clock face. The brass surround contains a reservoir of oil to keep the candle burning, so that Philip could keep track of time as he worked night and day. The window at the back connects with the High Altar in the Basilica, so that the king could also keep track of liturgical time. A picture of St Lawrence's martyrdom hangs to the right of the desk.

outgoing correspondence from all areas, and from all the ambassadors and ministers of his vast dominions . . . he covers every day with his own hand more than a ream of paper.[45]

Long before the typewriter, the photocopier and the word processor, Philip was drowning in a sea of paper. And he knew it. 'I have 100,000 papers in front of me,' he began one frantic note to a secretary; and one night in 1578 he complained to Mateo Vázquez:

> I have just been given this other packet of papers from you, but I have neither the time nor the strength to look at it; and so I will not open it until tomorrow. It is already after ten o'clock and I have not yet had dinner. My table is full of papers for tomorrow because I cannot cope with any more today.

A few months later he lapsed into self-pity. So many 'matters have come up that cannot be neglected: I do not believe that any human resources would suffice to deal with them all – especially not mine, which are very weak and getting weaker every day with all the things that have to be done.' Occasionally the number of pending decisions caused the king to lose his temper. One day in 1581 he complained to Vázquez that:

> Some things are going to have to wait, because one cannot do everything at once. Try to do something to hold them up because I cannot take any more. Anyone who looks at how I spent today will see that just two men detained me for more than two hours and left me with more papers than I can manage in many more [hours]. So I am shattered. God give me strength and patience.[46]

The king expected God to provide not only strength and patience, but also miracles to bridge the gap between intention and achievement, between means and ends. As bad news poured in from his commanders in the Netherlands and the Mediterranean in 1574, Philip warned Vázquez that 'unless God performs a miracle, which our sins do not merit, it is no longer possible to maintain ourselves for [more than a few] months, let alone years'. The arrival of news of further reverses, instead of leading him to reconsider his unsuccessful policies, reinforced the king's expectation of divine intervention. 'May God help us with a miracle. I tell you that we need one so much that it seems to me that He *must* choose to give us a miracle,' he lamented, 'because without one I fear everything will descend into the worst situation imaginable.'[47]

Philip's conviction that his policies advanced God's cause often led to friction with those responsible for executing them. When his lieutenants challenged a royal order to invade England in winter 1587, he blandly replied: 'We are quite aware of the risk that is incurred by sending a major fleet in winter through the Channel without a safe harbour, but . . . since it is all for His cause, God will send good weather.' In March 1588 he saw the delays in getting the Armada to sea in terms of a divine test: 'We must believe that Our Lord has permitted these setbacks so that, when they have been overcome with His assistance, we will see more clearly how we owe our success to Him.' A few weeks later, with Easter approaching, the king insisted that everyone aboard the fleet 'must avoid oaths, blasphemy and other offences against Our Lord, because earning His favour in this way [*granjear con esto su favor*] is the best path to victory'.[48]

## The Armada and the Supernatural

A few Catholics dissented. The coincidence of a partial solar and a total lunar eclipse early in 1588, following a rare astronomical alignment of Saturn, Jupiter and Mars, led many to foretell an imminent catastrophe. In Carmagnola, a French enclave in the Alps, Giorgio Rizzacasa published a book of predictions in 1586 which claimed that if Philip 'lives for two more years – which according to the stars seems highly doubtful – he will experience ill luck [*infelice sorte*] in almost all his actions', especially those involving the sea. In Rome, Joseph Creswell, a Jesuit chosen by the pope to help re-catholicize his native England should the Armada succeed, went to consult 'a holy man who enjoyed such contact with Our Lord that he might well have known something of His plans'. The 'holy man' discouragingly but accurately predicted that the fleet would 'go up in smoke', and Creswell remained in Rome.[49]

Similar prophecies of doom circulated in Spain. Those of Lucrecia de León, a young woman who lived in Madrid, attracted widespread attention after she predicted the death of Santa Cruz three weeks before it happened. She had already foretold the victory of Francis Drake (Lucrecia was very specific) in a great naval battle against the marquis, and on 1 May 1588 she described a dream that showed St James – 'Santiago', Spain's patron saint – riding behind the Armada on a horse with no legs, holding a lance with no point, proclaiming 'I keep my strength for God's war' – implying that the Armada sailed only to satisfy Philip's pride. Lucrecia's dreams, and the predictions of other popular prophets like Miguel de Piedrola, achieved such fame that a 400-page *Treatise of true and false prophecy* denounced those who 'foretold that Spain would be lost in this year of 88' and reassured readers that 'the Devil may well want to prevent the Enterprise of England, which with God's help is under way, and to this end He may spread fear and misgivings; but this will avail him little because God has imbued those who will command it with great dedication' as well as great confidence.[50]

As the Armada prepared to set sail, conventional religious faith permeated Spain despite the prophets of doom. Pedro de Ribadeneira, a prominent Jesuit, composed an *Exhortation to the soldiers and captains who sail on this campaign to England* that confidently asserted: 'We are not going on a difficult enterprise, because God our Lord, whose cause and most holy faith we defend, will go before us; and with such a captain we have nothing to fear.' In Rome, the pope granted a Jubilee Indulgence not only to all who sailed on the Armada but also to those who prayed for its success. All over Spain religious processions to implore divine favour took place every Sunday and holiday, and in Madrid a printed pocket itinerary was published to guide the faithful from church to church on their quest for the Armada indulgence. In the Escorial the entire royal family spent three hours daily in relays at prayer before the Holy Sacrament.[51] All the Italian ambassadors at the Court of Spain shared Philip's confidence that the Armada would triumph since (in the words of one) 'we have God on our side, and it is to be believed that He will not abandon His cause, which in this case is the same as that of His Majesty'.[52]

The General Orders issued to the fleet by Medina Sidonia on 21 May 1588 exuded a similar confidence in divine favour. 'First and foremost,' they began, everyone:

> From the most senior to the most junior, must understand that His Majesty's principal motive in preparing and undertaking this venture has always been the service of God our Lord, and to bring back to the church many countries and souls oppressed by the heretics, enemies of our Holy Catholic Church, who have forced them to join their sects and errors. To ensure that everyone remains focused on this goal, as we are obliged to do, [all officers] must order everyone under their command to embark only after confessing and taking communion, with the great contrition for their sins that I hope they will show, so that God will guide and lead us.

The duke also decreed punishment 'at my discretion' for 'any soldier, sailor or other person in the Armada' who blasphemed or profaned 'the name of God, Our Lady, or the saints' during the voyage; and according to one report the duke ordered each captain to submit a list of all women (*Weibsbilder*) aboard their ship and 'they found somewhat more than 600. They were not only brought ashore but expelled from Lisbon ... This made the soldiers restless, but they were consoled by the thought that there were many pretty girls [*hübsche Weiber*] in England'. To cover all eventualities, the duke asked his confessor to secure absolution in advance for 'any excesses and sins' that his men might commit, either aboard the fleet or ashore in England.[53] He also ensured that religious calls, or summons, regulated all shipboard routines. At dawn each day the ships' boys chanted the *Salve* at the foot of the mainmast, and at sunset the *Ave María*. Time was marked by a thirty-minute sand glass, each turn being accompanied by a short prayer. Eight such half-hourly spells marked the passage of a four-hour watch, and on the seventh call the off-duty crew prepared to take over. On Saturdays they sang the *Salve* and the *Litany of Our Lady* (Figure 20).

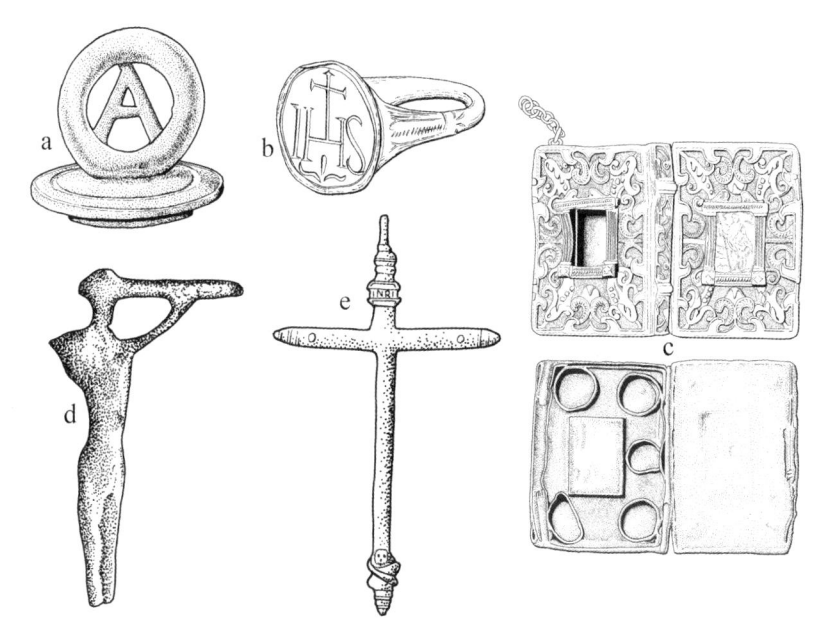

**20.** Religious finds from the *Girona* wreck-site include: a) a silver-gilt lid from a set of altar vessels (the 'A' denotes Aqua); b) a gold ring with circular bezel inscribed IHS, the sacred monogram; c) a gold box in the form of a book decorated with a representation of St John the Baptist; its interior is divided into five circular compartments within which were traces of wax, identifying them as having held Agnus Dei discs (these were made in vast numbers by melting the wax from the previous year's Easter candles from the churches in Rome, and were blessed by the pope); d) part of a silver crucifix, eroded by movement on the seabed; e) a copper-alloy pectoral crucifix, with INRI inscribed near the top (you can see the holes where the body was fitted).

The duke himself displayed great personal devotion. On hearing of his appointment, Ribadeneira speculated that 'God Himself chose him as commander of the Armada, and as His instrument to carry out such a holy and glorious enterprise' on account of Medina Sidonia's exemplary piety. While waiting for a favourable wind in May the duke consulted not only Sor María de la Visitación but also 'a saintly friar called Antonio de la Concepción, whenever I can, and he is very confident that Our Lord will grant Your Majesty a great victory'.[54]

His deputy, Juan Martínez de Recalde, showed equal devotion. In July 1588, when illness kept him confined to his bed, 'I placed certain holy relics on my liver and my arm' to help them recover; and when the fleet survived severe storms virtually intact, Recalde opined that 'God reunited the fleet almost as fast as He dispersed it to make us understand that without His favour we can achieve nothing. And since He has reunited it, He wants us to achieve our goal and His service.' Recalde also had a conscience. In 1577, just before leaving the Netherlands after five years of bitter fighting, he appeared before the magistrates of Antwerp and offered to satisfy anyone who could substantiate a claim against him. Six years later, after returning from the victorious Terceira campaign, he 'retired to a convent to do penance' for his part in the sack of the island. He would do the same after returning from the Armada campaign to expiate his part in its failure.[55]

Other senior officers shared these values. Diego Flores had placed one of his daughters in a nunnery, and he owned one silver and one gold cross, a religious medal and several relics. Oquendo owned a portable altar, two religious statues, and several paintings of the Virgin Mary and the Saints. In January 1588, with the Armada confined to the Tagus, Oquendo felt sure that all would be well, 'if we just fulfil our own obligations and leave the rest to Him who has the power'. Two months later he declared that 'even if we sail with few men and little artillery, I trust in God that we will do our duty' and therefore prevail over the heretical English.[56] Leyva felt the same. As he boarded a galleass for the journey from Cadiz to Lisbon in July 1587, Don Alonso looked forward to 'the victory that we hope God will give to this fleet'; and nine months later, windbound in the Tagus, he felt confident 'that God will soon send a favourable wind, and that this magnificent fleet [*tan suntuosa armada*] will make good use of it'. Even after he grasped the reality of the Armada's defeat, he wrote two letters which invoked 'God' eleven times in just over 1,000 words.[57]

A few days before the standard-blessing ceremony, a papal agent in Lisbon asked a senior Armada officer in confidence, 'If you meet the English fleet in the Channel, do you expect to win the battle?' 'Of course,' replied the officer. 'How can you be so sure?' asked the emissary. The officer responded:

It is well known that we fight in God's cause. So, when we meet the English, God will surely arrange matters so that we can grapple and board them, either by sending some strange freak of weather or, more likely, just by depriving the English of their wits. If we can come to close quarters, Spanish valour and Spanish steel (and the great masses of soldiers we shall have on board) will make our victory certain. But unless God helps us by a miracle the English, who have faster and handier ships than ours, and many more long-range guns, and who know their advantage just as well as we do, will never close with us at all, but stand aloof and knock us to pieces with their culverins, without our being able to do them any serious hurt. So we are sailing against England in the confident hope of a miracle.[58]

Many historians have taken this response as irony, but at least one senior officer believed that he had already been saved by a miracle. In December 1585 Don Francisco de Bobadilla and some 3,000 Spanish soldiers fighting in the Low Countries found themselves trapped by Dutch forces on a tiny island between the rivers Maas and Waal. Surrender seemed inevitable until, following the discovery and veneration of a buried image of the Virgin Mary, a sudden fall in temperature froze the rivers and allowed Bobadilla to lead his troops to safety across the ice. Every devout Catholic regarded this as a miracle.

A Portuguese Jesuit aboard the fleet summarized the spiritual exaltation of his comrades on the eve of departure: 'Such was their confidence in God that there was not a man who could be persuaded of anything that went against this conviction: that God would grant them victory against the heretics and enemies of the Holy Catholic Church.' Their faith was apparently rewarded on 11 May, when a light easterly breeze sprang up. The duke ordered some of the bigger vessels to proceed to the mouth of the Tagus and anchor there, and he 'got into a felucca and sailed among them to speed things up'. He also 'saw to it that the galleys helped the *urcas* whenever they needed it' as they manoeuvred. That same day a special envoy sent by the duke of Parma, together with five pilots familiar with the Flemish coast, arrived at Lisbon with news of Parma's preparations.[59]

On 28 May, when the wind again blew from the east, the duke 'fired a gun', the signal for all ships to raise anchors. Once again, he 'boarded a felucca to get the Armada to sea' and the following day galleys towed his flagship and some other big vessels to the mouth of the Tagus. Two days later 130 large ships, ten caravels and ten feluccas had cleared the bar without the loss of a single vessel. When Medina Sidonia gave the order for 'the largest fleet that has ever been seen in these seas since the creation of the world' to turn northwards towards Parma's army, the world held its breath.[60]

2

# 'The great bog of Europe'

———≪❊≫———

PHILIP II'S MASTERPLAN FOR THE conquest of England depended on the Armada 'joining hands' with an army of 27,000 soldiers, camped near the coast of Flanders and commanded by his nephew Alexander Farnese, duke of Parma. As soon as the fleet arrived, the king expected Parma and his men to embark on the 300 small invasion transports assembled in the harbours of Dunkirk and Nieuwpoort and cross the Channel to the designated landing-zone in Kent. But without the Armada's protection they would be helpless. In the shoal waters beyond the coastline they could glimpse the sails of shallow-draught Dutch gunboats, carrying 1,200 musketeers trained for naval combat and pledged to destroy any of Parma's forces that put to sea. Just over the horizon a squadron of larger Dutch warships, reinforced by Queen Elizabeth's Narrow Seas fleet, lay in wait to intercept and annihilate Parma's flotilla should it make a sudden dash for England.

Most accounts of the 1588 campaign concentrate on the naval battles of the main fleets as the Armada advanced up the Channel, and pay scant attention to the vigil maintained by the forces in the Dover Strait. But their role was just as important, because although the Armada sailed against England it also aimed to terminate a long-standing challenge to Spanish power in the Netherlands.

## The Dutch Revolt

The seventeen provinces of the Netherlands ruled by Emperor Charles V formed part of the world's first transatlantic empire, and when he abdicated in 1555 they all passed to his son Philip II. Some provinces, including the most prosperous – Brabant, Flanders, Hainaut, Holland and Zeeland – had been familiar with firm government from Brussels for more than a century; other provinces, including Friesland, Gelderland, Groningen and Utrecht, had been annexed by Charles himself. The seventeen provinces received a single federal structure in 1548, becoming the newest state in Europe, but each retained a lively spirit of independence, accentuated by their distinct histories and traditions, their unique institutions, and their different languages: French in the south; German and East Dutch in the east; West Dutch and Fries in the north and west (Figure 21).

The Protestant faith, also born in the first half of the sixteenth century, found it easy to penetrate this patchwork of jurisdictions, customs and languages. Before long Calvinism, Anabaptism and Lutheranism all had their devotees in different parts of the Low Countries. It was to counter the spread of these heresies that in

21. South-east England and the Netherlands, 1588.

1559 Philip decided to increase the number of Catholic bishops in the Netherlands, to sharpen the laws against Protestantism and to extend the scope of the Inquisition.

All these initiatives required money, and money remained in short supply. In 1564 lack of funds had forced Philip to freeze the creation of new bishoprics, and two years later to suspend the enforcement of heresy laws and the activities of the Inquisition. The Protestants soon took advantage of these concessions. In spring 1566 they began to organize open-air prayer meetings defended by armed guards. In the summer the lack of a firm response by the central government led to a campaign of iconoclasm, in which small groups of Protestants first smashed Catholic religious images and then demanded the right to worship in churches as well as in the fields. According to Margaret of Parma, the king's sister and his regent in the Netherlands, by August half the local population had converted to Protestantism and 200,000 people had taken up arms against the government.

The king and his Spanish advisers took Margaret's highly alarmist (and, as it turned out, grossly exaggerated) estimates of Protestant strength at face value and resolved to send Spain's most experienced general, the duke of Alba, to the Netherlands at the head of 10,000 Spanish veterans, with orders to restore order and extinguish heresy. Alba and his soldiers marched from Lombardy to the Netherlands, arriving in August 1567. They immediately began to arrest and imprison dissidents.

The presence in the Netherlands of a professional army, commanded by the most successful general of his day, immediately transformed the international situation in northern Europe. The duke and his troops constituted a permanent challenge to the security of neighbouring states: France, England, Scotland and the semi-autonomous principalities of Germany. Their rulers now felt sufficiently threatened by Philip to offer support to the Protestant exiles and rebels led by William of Nassau, prince of Orange, when he invaded the Netherlands in 1568 and again in 1572. Although Orange's first attempt proved a costly failure, the second achieved partial success: the invaders gained control over much of Holland and Zeeland.

For three years the outcome lay in the balance. Not only did the impressive fortifications of many Dutch towns complicate Spain's reconquest: so did geography. The provinces in revolt, surrounded by the sea, were a confusion of broad rivers, islands and peninsulas. Lakes, marshes and waterways further impeded communications. In the words of an English traveller, Holland and Zeeland constituted 'The great bog of Europe. There is not such another marsh in the world, that's flat. They are an universal quagmire . . . Indeed it is the buttock of the world: full of veins and blood, but no bones in't.'[1]

This 'buttock' was also defended by a fleet of ships able to operate close inshore and capable both of blockading all Netherlands ports loyal to the king and of preventing vessels sent from Spain from landing troops on Dutch territory. In 1572 several ships from Spain, in a fleet commanded by Juan Martínez de Recalde, ran aground on the Flemish coast. Three years later most ships in a second fleet, jointly commanded by Recalde and Don Pedro de Valdés, failed to reach the Netherlands at all. Philip made no further attempt to gain control of the North Sea until 1588.

But Spain did not give up the struggle. Alba assembled a massive force of 60,000 soldiers, known to its contemporaries and to posterity as the 'Army of Flanders', and hurled it against one rebellious town after another: Mechelen, Zutphen and Naarden fell in 1572, Haarlem in 1573. His men sacked each of these towns and massacred a large part of their populations, irrespective of sex or age, and sometimes despite previous promises of clemency. But to no avail: Alba's draconian policy only intensified the resistance of the towns still in rebellion, and Philip recalled the duke in semi-disgrace at the end of 1573. This, too, failed to end the revolt. 'There would not be time or money enough in the world to reduce by force the twenty-four towns which have rebelled in Holland' and Zeeland, wrote Don Luis de Requesens, Alba's dispirited successor, in October 1574, 'if we are to spend as long in reducing each one of them as we have taken over similar ones so far'. Philip agreed. The fate of the Netherlands, he lamented, 'is very much at risk, with so many troops and no money to pay them ... Unless God performs a miracle, our affairs there cannot be improved without money.' Indeed, he sighed some days later, 'I think the Netherlands will be lost for lack of money, as I have always feared.'[2]

His fears soon came true. In September 1575, crippled by the cost of fighting constantly for more than three years, the Spanish treasury declared bankruptcy and the flow of money to the Army of Flanders abruptly ceased. The rebellious towns lit bonfires of joy when they heard the news, and with good reason: before long Philip's unpaid troops in Holland and Zeeland either deserted or mutinied. In November 1576 the Spanish infantry launched a desperate assault on Antwerp, the largest city in northern Europe, captured it, and then for several days carried out a brutal rampage in which they killed perhaps 8,000 people and destroyed 1,000 houses. It became known as 'the Spanish Fury'. The leading Catholics of the provinces still under Spanish control now made common cause with the Protestant rebels, led by Orange, who soon presided over a new 'government of national unity' established in Brussels and responsible to a States-General (parliament) representing all the provinces, languages and religions of the Netherlands.

This marked the high point of the Dutch Revolt. The States-General demanded that Philip accept them as his lawful government and that he appoint only officials of whom they approved. Even more provocatively they insisted on freedom of worship for Protestants throughout the Low Countries. No early-modern ruler could accept such demands – not least because, as the king's advisers in Spain pointed out, concessions in the Netherlands would probably lead to similar demands from his other dominions. Instead, Philip decided to use force to regain his defiant provinces and began to rebuild the Army of Flanders. Troops and treasure assembled in Spanish Lombardy travelled to the Low Countries via the 700-mile military corridor established by the duke of Alba, known to contemporaries as 'the Spanish Road', to defeat the Dutch by attrition and weight of numbers. From the autumn of 1578 these formidable troops were moulded into a superb fighting force by the tough and energetic prince (and later duke) of Parma.

Parma was an ideal choice as commander-in-chief. In the first place, as Philip's nephew, his royal blood entitled him to deal directly with sovereign rulers and gave him an effortless social superiority over the prickly Netherlands aristocracy. Secondly, he had grown up at the Court of Spain, where he developed useful contacts among the king's ministers and at the same time learned the complex processes by which policies were made (and unmade) at the highest levels. Thirdly, his wide travels provided a valuable appreciation of Europe's geography. In 1557 he had accompanied Philip to England and thirty years later, on the eve of his planned invasion, he reminisced about the pleasures of Greenwich Palace because 'he knew the place well, for that he was there, being then young'. The prince also became fluent in French, German and Spanish as well as in his native Italian. He then served as a staff officer in the Spanish Mediterranean fleet and took part in the great naval battle of Lepanto in 1571 (Figure 22).[3]

22. Alexander Farnese, duke of Parma (1545–92), by his Court painter Otto van Veen, c. 1585. He wears his insignia of the Golden Fleece and an exquisite suit of armour, giving him a regal aura.

Although only thirty-two when he took command of the Army of Flanders in 1578, Parma could draw on extensive political and military experience. He also possessed impressive personal resources. In most years his Italian estates sent 50,000 ducats to support his household in Flanders, and he raised far more – by 1592 almost 1 million ducats – in loans secured on his personal credit. Parma used these funds to maintain his own diplomatic service and a glittering court, and to attract an entourage of noblemen who came to 'learn the art of war in his school'. When Amadeus, brother of the duke of Savoy, arrived in 1587 with strict orders to participate in 'all military endeavours', he joined relatives of the duke of Mantua and the grand duke of Tuscany, attached to Parma's headquarters. That same year Don Juan de Idiáquez, Philip's secretary of state, sent his son and heir Alonso to lead one of the cavalry companies earmarked for the invasion army from Flanders. Several senior officers who sailed on the Armada – including Bobadilla, Leyva and Mexía – had also served in Parma's 'school' and had come to admire and respect him.[4]

## The Spanish Reconquest

This formidable combination of power and influence enabled Parma to offer a wide range of rewards, bribes and promises at opportune moments to advance his cause. In 1578–9 his subtle diplomacy drew the Catholics of the southern Netherlands back into the royalist camp, and throughout the 1580s he secured the surrender of numerous strongholds without a siege. As an English officer fighting with the Dutch army bitterly remarked on hearing of the premature capitulation of yet another town: 'Everyone knows that the king of Spain's golden bullets made a bigger breach in the heart of the traitor in command than their battery' made in the walls.[5] Parma proved equally adept in the use of force. On the one hand he tried to murder those who refused his bribes. At Philip's instigation he placed a price on the head of William of Orange, and sponsored various would-be assassins until in 1584, in return for 25,000 ducats and a patent of nobility, one of them succeeded. On the other hand his 60,000 soldiers – Spaniards, Italians, Burgundians, Germans, and some English and Irish Catholics as well as native levies – compelled more than seventy rebellious towns to surrender.

In 1581 Parma devised a grand strategy which would double the size of the Spanish Netherlands. Observing that Flanders and Brabant, the richest provinces in revolt, depended for their prosperity on waterborne trade, the duke realized that if he could control the Flemish coast and block the Scheldt below Antwerp the entire inland network of rivers and canals would be paralysed. Without access to the sea all the major towns caught in his net would have to submit.

Parma's neighbours in north-west Europe viewed each success with grave dismay. The 'great bog' occupied a position of permanent strategic importance, since an army stationed there could intervene in France and the Rhineland or even, given a fleet, in England and Scotland. That is why the creation of the powerful Army of Flanders, first under Alba and again under Parma, caused a diplomatic revolution in northern Europe.

Looking back in 1589, Elizabeth I's principal adviser, William Cecil, Lord Burghley (born in 1520), mused that 'The state of the world is marvellously changed, when we true Englishmen have cause for our own quietness to wish good success to a French king and a king of Scots.' For the previous 500 years England had generally opposed – and often made war on – the rulers of France and Scotland, usually in alliance with the rulers of the Netherlands. Admittedly, Burghley continued, the two kings 'differ one from another in profession of religion, but seeing both are enemies to our enemies, we have cause to join with them in their actions'. He saw this change as 'the work of God for our good' and expressed gratitude for 'His miraculous goodness, for no wit of man could otherwise have wrought it'.[6]

The rulers of England, France and Scotland therefore welcomed the continuance of a rebellion in the Low Countries because it absorbed a large part of Philip's resources in fighting a war which he seemed unable to win. Thus in 1572 virtually all the Netherlands' neighbours sent support to William of Orange's invasion; in 1574, when the rebel cause seemed to be faltering, France began to send regular subsidies; and in 1578, as Spanish military success recommenced, France and England again took the overtly hostile step of sending troops to fight for the Dutch.

Nevertheless, when Parma launched his master strategy in 1581 the Dutch Revolt seemed doomed. The religious divide made the Catholic and Calvinist rebels uneasy bedfellows; petty provincialism made Holland and Zeeland reluctant to pay for the defence of Brabant; above all, the rebellion seemed likely to collapse (according to an English observer) 'for want of good government; for there is a number that commands in the country, and few will obey'. A few months later he repeated: 'Every man will command, and few . . . will be commanded, so there is no order nor good government among them.'[7]

For a while it seemed he spoke too soon, because the prince of Orange persuaded François de Valois, duke of Anjou and heir presumptive to the French throne, to become 'prince and lord of the Netherlands'. In 1581 the States-General declared Philip deposed from all his Netherlands titles, and Anjou arrived at the head of 10,000 troops to take over. Furthermore, he declared that he would persuade the queen of England to marry him and place her resources alongside his in the defence of Dutch liberty. 'Froggy' (as the contemporary English song had it) 'went a wooing' and in February 1582 returned to the Netherlands claiming that he was engaged to Elizabeth, and bringing with him as a token of this new attachment her favourite, Robert Dudley, earl of Leicester, and her secretary of state, Sir Francis Walsingham. They all attended a ceremony at which William of Orange, in the name of the States-General, invested Anjou with the regalia and dignities of the dukes of Brabant. Representatives of the other provinces soon followed suit and the duke, his new titles officially recognized by both France and England, became in effect sovereign ruler of the provinces in revolt against Philip.

It did not last. First, in March 1582 an assassination attempt plotted by Parma left William of Orange seriously injured. While he convalesced, Anjou and the States-General fell into disagreement. Early in 1583 the duke's French troops attempted to take control of the leading Low Countries towns, but they failed and Anjou left the Netherlands in disgrace. He died a year later.

Parma's accomplished veterans exploited the confusion to capture most of the ports along the Flemish coast and then struck inland, capturing Bruges and Ghent, the largest towns of Flanders. In September 1584 they began a huge engineering project to close the Scheldt some 30 miles below Antwerp and so cut off all access to the sea. It consisted of a great timber bridge 800 yards long, its central section floating on anchored pontoons, defended by a complex of emplacements containing almost 200 guns, with booms moored upstream and downstream. Some regarded the bridge, completed at the end of February 1585, as one of the wonders of the age and Parma staked everything upon its success: 'The siege will never be abandoned,' he boasted to a visitor, 'and this' – pointing to the bridge – 'will either be my tomb or my pathway into Antwerp'.[8]

Many contemporaries considered Antwerp, with a population of 80,000 and a five-mile circuit of powerful modern fortifications, to be impregnable. Certainly, the States-General did little to help the city until April 1585, when a fleet from Holland commanded by Justinus of Nassau, Orange's illegitimate son, moved to the mouth of the Scheldt while several ships filled with explosives floated down the river on the ebb tide from the beleaguered city towards Parma's bridge. An Italian, Federico Giambelli, had designed these floating bombs with considerable ingenuity. He had constructed some to explode on impact, and others with delayed fuses to detonate as the ship neared the bridge. Others still were simple fireships, filled with devices which exploded when the heat reached them (Figure 23).

Just as Giambelli had intended, the unpredictability of his 'infernal machines' caused confusion and indecision among the Spaniards. The whole idea of explosive ships was new, and few appreciated the cataclysmic danger they presented. When the largest 'hellburner', which had been set to blow up almost harmlessly in the middle of the river just short of its target, spewed out its colourful pyrotechnics, the defenders of the bridge gathered to watch the display. Even Parma came for a while, and he had only just started back for his headquarters when one of the other vessels, primed to explode on impact, hit the bridge. At least 800 Spaniards

23. The hellburners of Antwerp. Detail from one of five engravings of Parma's bridge over the Scheldt included in *The Low Countries Wars* by the Jesuit historian Famiano Strada, commissioned by Parma's son to write a history of his father's exploits. The artist captured the moment when one of the 'infernal machines' constructed by Federico Giambelli struck the boats in the centre of the bridge. The other incendiary devices burn harmlessly in the river. Over ninety editions of Strada's work had appeared in various languages by 1700.

were killed, many more were injured, and Parma himself was knocked down by the shockwave. The terrible experience of the exploding ships was not easily forgotten and the 'hellburners of Antwerp' entered the vocabulary, and the irrational fears, of every Spanish soldier and sailor. Nevertheless, Parma's seasoned troops soon recovered their discipline and their wits: they temporarily made good the damage, stood to their battle stations, and prevented Justinus and his fleet from exploiting their advantage. Antwerp surrendered in August 1585.

Parma had achieved a great deal against heavy odds. Within four years he had driven those in revolt against Philip back into an enclave scarcely larger than they had held in 1572, and the surrender of Antwerp allowed him to contemplate how best to complete the reconquest with the formidable cosmopolitan army he commanded. Its soldiers came from a wide range of social and geographical backgrounds. Some were outlaws who had enlisted to escape punishment at home, others were the younger sons of noblemen seeking glory; the troops from Spain, Italy and Burgundy had marched up the Spanish Road to join units raised in Germany and the Netherlands; some officers and men had thirty years of active service – in effect, Parma's army had become their home. Their integration is reflected in the friendly games they played on holidays, which pitted teams from north of the Alps (the *oltramontani*) against those from further south (the *citramontani*). In the words of Paolo Rinaldi, Parma's chamberlain and chronicler, the soldiers of the Army of Flanders 'were powerful men, well-armed and of martial aspect, highly trained and always ready to obey and to fight'.[9]

Englishmen who had seen the Army of Flanders in action shared Rinaldi's high opinion. George Gascoigne, an eyewitness, viewed the storm and capture of Antwerp in 1576 as a 'victory being miraculous and past man's capacity to comprehend how it should be possible' and attributed the outcome to the 'order and valour' of the Spanish infantry, adding: 'Caesar himself had never any such soldiers' because 'their continual training in service doth make them expert in all warlike stratagems'. Sir Roger Williams, who later advised Elizabeth on how to defend England against an invasion, agreed: 'To speak truth,' he wrote, 'no army that ever I saw, passes that of the duke of Parma for discipline and good order.' And Sir Roger had good reason to know, because he had fought with the Spaniards in the Netherlands from 1574 until 1578, and thereafter against them. The earl of Leicester, in command of England's land forces at Tilbury in the summer of 1588, had likewise seen the Army of Flanders in action, and deemed them 'the best soldiers at this day in Christendom'. Parma commanded the perfect instrument to achieve military success.[10]

The Dutch, in contrast, were losing the ability and will to resist. They had failed to save any of the towns of Flanders and Brabant from capture, and now they were bankrupt. In 1583 lack of funds forced them to suspend interest payments on state debts, and even the tomb of the prince of Orange was (according to an English visitor) 'the poorest that ever I saw for such a person, being only of rough stones and mortar, with posts of wood coloured over with black'.[11] The Dutch lacked not only money but also leaders. If their problem in 1581 had been too many commanders, by 1584–5 they had too few: following the assassination of Orange no one in the young Republic had adequate experience of war or diplomacy. Orange's son Maurice, although allowed to succeed his father as governor of Holland and Zeeland, was only seventeen, and many years would pass before he gained the skill and sagacity required to reconcile the differing interest groups within the Dutch state. Indeed, in the wake of Parma's victories, a vociferous peace party grew up within the rebels' ranks, anxious to make a deal with their former master while they still had something to bargain with. In July 1585, when the States of Holland proposed to levy another tax for the defence of Brabant, the town council of Gouda (in Holland) withheld its consent and argued instead for immediate negotiations with Spain for 'a good peace'. Only the dispatch of loyal troops brought Gouda to heel.

Perhaps, Parma mused, he should exploit these divisions by invading Holland and Zeeland as Alba and Requesens had done, and hope for the best; but the experience of 1572–5 had demonstrated the dangers and difficulties of that course. Moreover, it had proved so difficult to regain the major towns of Flanders and Brabant that ultimate success sometimes seemed miraculous – but one day, Parma reminded Philip, 'God will grow tired of working miracles for us.' He therefore concluded that negotiation was a better option for bringing the Dutch Revolt to an end, but the States-General refused to negotiate. Despite the loss of Antwerp, he complained, they 'show no sign of anything except renewed obstinacy'. Why?[12]

Parma harboured no doubts. In September 1585 he informed the king that 'English troops are arriving [in Flushing] every day, and already number four or five thousand men. It seems that the queen of England wishes openly to take up the [rebel] cause ... for one can clearly see from the letter she has written to them how much assistance and encouragement she is prepared to give'. It might therefore be easier and more effective, he reasoned, to divert his forces from fighting the Dutch – who were certainly in no position to mount a counter-attack – and instead eliminate their foreign supporters. With the outbreak of civil dissension in France following the death of Anjou, further assistance from that quarter seemed unlikely; and, for the same reason, no French reprisals would be possible should Spain decide to deal with the Dutch rebels' other persistent supporter across the English Channel. In December 1585 he urged Philip to mobilize his forces to destroy Elizabeth.[13]

## Preparing for the Invasion

The king had reached the same conclusion and ordered the raising of troops in Spain to reinforce the Army of Flanders for an assault on England, but the hostility of France as well as England meant that recruits had to be transported to Genoa, and then march along the Spanish Road across the Alps. It took at least three months, and the journey left many men exhausted.

The build-up began with 2,000 recruits raised in Castile in the spring of 1586 by Don Antonio Manrique specifically for the Enterprise of England. On reaching Luxembourg the following December the survivors unslung their guitars and began to dance and sing, to the disgust of the veteran troops who never 'danced and whirled, an indecent thing in war, except with Flemish ladies'. The recruits became known as the *tercio de la zarabanda* (regiment of the saraband), because they carried on 'as if they were in Spain. But they very soon forgot the tunes and dances because the trials and miseries that befell them in the Low Countries gave them no more time for such diversion.' They also soon lost their commander: Manrique insulted and threatened the Judge Advocate General, forcing Parma to degrade and exile him ('the mildest punishment I could impose, given the nature of his offence'). He therefore redistributed Manrique's recruits to reinforce the veteran *tercios*, and to learn from them.[14]

In February 1587 the king decided to recruit two more Spanish *tercios* to reinforce Parma's army in preparation for the invasion of England: one in Castile under Don Antonio de Zúñiga, the other in Catalonia under Don Luis Queralt (Figure 24). When Zúñiga arrived in Genoa in August he led 2,662 men, but only 2,000 remained by the time they reached the Netherlands three months later, and 200 needed hospital treatment. According to Parma:

> They came not only without arms but also without clothes and they were badly treated. It is a shame to see them. So bad are they that I do not believe such misery has ever been seen in the Spanish nation, which makes me ashamed, not just on compassionate grounds but that soldiers of Your Majesty and of the Spanish nation should have been seen by people along their route so broken and ill-treated.

By the spring of 1588 only 1,500 men remained and Parma redistributed them to reinforce the veteran units.[15]

Queralt's *tercio* of 1,900 Catalans, many of them former bandits who had received a pardon in return for enlistment, also arrived in poor shape after the long

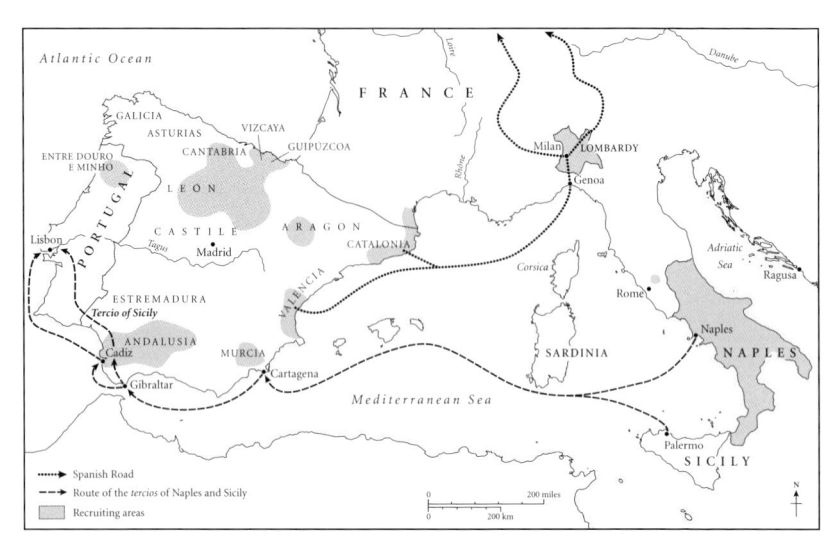

**24.** The areas of Spain and Italy where Philip recruited troops in 1587–8 intended for Flanders and Lisbon.

march along the Spanish Road, and by April 1588 their strength had fallen to 861. Parma only kept them as a separate *tercio* because of their distinctive language, which earned them the nickname 'the *tercio* of the parakeets [*tercio del papagayo*] because of how they sounded when they tried to speak Castilian with the rest of the troops'. Philip also authorized the levy of two *tercios* of Italians, one from the kingdom of Naples and the other from the states of his allies in central Italy, a total of 9,000 men. They, too, travelled up the Spanish Road in 1587 and suffered heavy losses along the way.

In February 1588 Parma estimated that the recruits newly arrived from Spain and Italy 'have diminished from their initial strength by at least one-third, with many more men sick'. This dramatic reduction reflected not only the recruits' lack of training in basic survival skills, but also the scarcity of food and shelter in the areas where Parma billeted them on arrival. '[It] may justly give cause of wonder how so many living in a wasted and greatly spoiled country should notwithstanding be victualled,' wrote an English observer. 'Viewing the country for the space of forty miles in length, and somewhat more,' he continued, 'the villages were desolated, and razed in a manner to the ground, no inhabitant to be found in them, scarcely any houses but here and there scattered.' Parma had achieved a major logistical triumph in maintaining so many men amid this unpromising environment.[16]

Early in July 1588 one of the Italian noblemen at Parma's headquarters reported that 'The soldiers are all standing by, close to Dunkirk and Nieuwpoort, and everything required for the Enterprise of England is ready.' Besides '4,000 gentlemen adventurers' like himself, he estimated the invasion army at 27,000 men, with 12,000 infantry and 2,000 cavalry remaining to defend the Netherlands (Table 2.1).[17]

Table 2.1. *Parma's invasion army*[18]

| Units | Soldiers |
| --- | --- |
| 4 Spanish *tercios* | 6,000 |
| 3 Italian *tercios* | 7,000 |
| 8 German regiments | 12,000 |
| 11 Walloon regiments | 16,000 |
| 1 Burgundian regiment | 1,000 |
| 1 Irish regiment | 1,000 |
| 15 cavalry companies | 1,500 |

Cavalry made up only a small part of the invasion force: most of the animals carried by the Armada and accompanying Parma's troops were intended to draw the heavy artillery-train once it landed in England. Everything depended on the infantry recruited from all over the Habsburg lands in Europe. The Irish *tercio* formed an exception: most were Catholic infantry recruited to serve in the Dutch army who had changed sides the previous year, reinforced by some English Catholic exiles.

Of course, defects remained. In July 1588, only two weeks before the Armada arrived, Queralt begged Parma to 'order that we should be given weapons because (as your highness well knows) we lack them'. As soon as they had them, Queralt promised, 'I shall get the troops out once or twice a week, as I have already begun to do, and place them in formation and drill them as much as I can'; but without weapons, his men could not complete even basic training. Notwithstanding such shortcomings among some of the new recruits, however, both friends and foes agreed that Parma's invasion force was in superb shape to undertake the Enterprise of England.[19]

Evidence concerning the vessels assembled to carry the troops is more equivocal. As Sir William Winter, with a lifetime of naval experience behind him, observed in June 1588:

Whereas it is said that the prince [of Parma]'s strength is 30,000 soldiers, then I assure your honour it is no mean quantity of shipping which must serve for the transporting of that number and that which do appertain to them, without the which I do not think they will put forth; 300 sail must be the least; and, one with another, to be counted 60 tons.[20]

By then, although Winter did not know it, Parma had almost met this target. According to the records of his fleet, Dunkirk harbour sheltered almost 100 vessels – twenty-six warships (several displacing over 150 tons), twenty-one barges, together with perhaps fifty merchant ships – with almost 200 more boats, most of them barges, in and around Nieuwpoort (Figure 25). Their total displacement exceeded 30,000 tons.

25. Great uncertainty surrounds the adequacy of the ships and supplies assembled by the duke of Parma to transport his troops to England in the summer of 1588. Some soldiers complained that they were crushed into the appointed boats without food. Parma, however, anticipated that the Channel crossing would only take between eight and twelve hours, so that on the one hand few provisions would be needed for the actual journey (and in any case he had embarked them on other vessels) and, on the other hand, the troops could be packed fairly tightly into the boats. This sketch of how the Spanish army crossed the Rhine in 1605 demonstrates the possibilities.

As soon as he heard that the Armada had left Lisbon, Parma ordered all seamen to report to their ships upon pain of death, and had his men practise embarkation and disembarkation repeatedly. In June (according to an English source) the duke 'came to Dunkirk and viewed the fleet and rowed out of the mouth of the haven to view it'. From that point on, he ordered anyone who needed to visit his soldiers or his ships to be blindfolded.[21] Parma's flagship flew a 'royal standard' of red damask bearing on one side the Spanish coat of arms and on the other a depiction of Christ crucified, flanked by the Virgin Mary and St John the Baptist. Other ships flew ensigns that displayed the cross of Burgundy, the arms of the seventeen provinces of the Netherlands, and of Spain. All flags were 'scattered with flames of fire', as a sign that they would be unfurled in war; furthermore, according to an English source, the Spanish companies at Dunkirk 'set up their ensigns in the ships wherein they were to embark' in readiness. Specially constructed magazines at both Nieuwpoort and Dunkirk overflowed with munitions and provisions, with more stored in nearby houses and monasteries: the Greyfriars convent in Dunkirk alone housed 1,000 tons of gunpowder. Parma also stockpiled 7,000 pairs of wading boots; ovens to bake bread aboard the ships; 'scaling-ladders, mattocks, spades, shovels and hatchets'; and 'flat-bottomed boats . . . prepared on purpose to carry horse[s], for they have within them both rack and manger and other necessaries' to keep the animals stable and safe in transit. Based on detailed reports from their spies, on 13 July the States of Zeeland concluded that Parma's troops were fully prepared to embark for any destination he chose 'with his ships in such readiness that they could set sail in 10 to 12 days'.[22]

## Parma the Conqueror?

This immense mobilization plunged Parma into debt. His household accounts and correspondence reveal loans taken out in 1587–8 from a remarkable variety of sources, including the nuns of St Catherine of Siena and the Jesuit College in Rome (both charged him 7 per cent interest). These unlikely creditors reflected the duke's deep personal piety. The chronicle of his life and deeds compiled posthumously by Rinaldi recorded in minute detail the duke's exemplary devotions: where and how often he confessed and took communion; how he left time every Saturday for special prayers to the Virgin Mary; how he made sure his soldiers had access to the Holy Sacrament if they fell mortally ill. He ended his chronicle of Parma's career with a selection of 'Sayings of Alexander Farnese', which included numerous pious utterings like 'Nothing requires correction more urgently than taking religion as a joke.'[23]

Rinaldi did not exaggerate. In 1587 Parma created a special chaplaincy for the spiritual welfare of his troops (the *missio castrensis*) and asked the General of the Jesuit Order to send twenty-four fathers 'from various nations' to preach to his troops 'during the Enterprise we are now preparing'. Shortly afterwards he secured a papal bull creating the 'Confraternity of the Holy Sacrament among the soldiers in the Netherlands'. When news of the Armada's approach arrived, according to one (admittedly hostile) source, instead of travelling directly to Dunkirk, Parma made a diversion to pray before the Black Madonna at Halle in Hainaut 'for his blind devotion's sake'.[24]

Parma's personal faith manifested itself in other ways. At an audience on 18 July 1588 with Dr Valentine Dale, one of Elizabeth's peace commissioners, the duke stressed England's vulnerability because if war came, and 'if the battle be lost of your side, it may be to lose the kingdom and all'. Dale boldly replied that one battle rarely sufficed 'to conquer a kingdom in another country', as Parma should know himself 'by the difficulties of the recovery of that which is the king's own by succession and patrimony. "Well," said [Parma] "that is in God's hand."' The duke did not change his mind on this point when it became clear that the Enterprise had failed. According to Dale, 'The duke of Parma, sore offended with God, hath said he verily thinketh that God is sworn English.' More modestly, he assured Pope Sixtus V that 'since this has pleased our Lord God, we must believe that it was for the best, and for His greater glory'. He also urged the pope to send funds 'both to pay the great debts that we have accumulated for this venture, and also to encourage His Majesty to persevere with it'.[25]

What would Parma have done in England after the conquest? Philip II's orders were clear. 'The minute you set foot in England,' he instructed his nephew, 'you must proclaim that you come to reform religion' and 'restore the true and traditional Catholic faith'. This, the king believed, 'will calmly win over the Catholics' of England. Parma must inform 'the heretics that they will be allowed to reconcile and be pardoned and will not forfeit their property if they agree to convert. The legate who is on his way [Cardinal Allen] will bring with him the power to give absolution.'[26] Nevertheless, Parma had disobeyed equally clear royal orders during his campaigns in Flanders and Brabant. In 1584, when he forced Ghent to surrender, he at first insisted that the magistrates should 'humiliate themselves, showing complete submission and obedience, and declare themselves ready to accept and welcome whatever terms His Majesty might offer'; but under pressure from his Netherlands advisers he abandoned this demand for unconditional surrender.

Instead, he allowed Protestant citizens to remain in the city and even practise their faith in private for two years while they sold their property. To induce other rebellious towns to surrender, although he insisted on the immediate departure of the rebel leaders, he promised amnesty (*'oublie du passé'*) to everyone else. He also agreed not to prosecute anyone for past crimes and granted a period of transition before the Protestants must either convert to Catholicism or depart: two years at Brussels, four years at Antwerp. When Bruges surrendered, he allowed Protestants to remain permanently, provided they caused no 'scandal'. In the felicitous phrase of Violet Soen, 'Clemency was the carrot, warfare the stick'; and although Philip protested vigorously when he learned of these concessions, he allowed them to stand.[27]

Would Parma have implemented a similar combination of carrot and stick in England? Probably not. The king expected Sixtus to nominate the uncompromising founder of the English College in Douai, William Allen, as archbishop of Canterbury with full legatine powers; and he intended Allen to head an interim government in England until the pope could invest the person he chose as Elizabeth's successor. Furthermore, Philip's instructions to his nephew warned that many of the vanquished English would falsely claim to be Catholics, and so he must trust 'only the Catholics who will accompany you, men whose faith you have tested, so that no one can fool you'. Some of these men were political exiles, like Charles Neville, earl of Westmoreland, who had fled after the failure of the Northern Rebellion two decades before; others were religious exiles, like Archbishop Émonn MacShamhradháin of Armagh, primate of all Ireland. The Armada likewise carried many exiles as well as 180 members of religious orders, some of whom had authority to recover for the Catholic Church all the lands and rights confiscated at the Reformation. It seems unlikely that they would allow Parma to offer clemency to the Protestants of England and Ireland as he had done to those of Bruges, Ghent, Brussels and Antwerp.[28]

## A Diplomatic End to the Conflict?

The scale of the religious and military preparations in Spain and Flanders alarmed Elizabeth, and she indicated to Parma her willingness to discuss terms for the withdrawal of her forces from the Netherlands, provided the initiative could seem to come from Spain (to save face with her Dutch allies). At the same time, and apparently independently, King Frederick II of Denmark offered his services as a mediator in the Low Countries Wars. Philip authorized Parma to explore both these peace initiatives, since they might reduce (even temporarily) English aid to the Dutch and perhaps secure some restitution for goods seized by English privateers on the high seas and in the Americas – but without reducing the military pressure on the Dutch or scaling back preparations for the invasion of England. Early in 1587 Dutch troops captured an envoy sent by Parma to Denmark, bearing full details of his talks with Elizabeth's ministers, which forced the queen to show her hand. She now announced her intention of beginning formal talks with Spain and invited the Dutch to join in.[29]

Her appeal divided the Republic. The inland provinces which bore the brunt of the war against Spain favoured discussions, but the States-General held firm and refused to send delegates to the peace talks. The queen persevered, however, and in February 1588 her commissioners arrived in Flanders with authority to negotiate a peace with Spain on two conditions: toleration for Protestants in the Netherlands and withdrawal of all foreign troops. Needless to say, Philip had no intention of making these concessions, but he instructed Parma to pretend that they might form a basis for discussion, both to divide the Dutch further and to confuse Elizabeth. Formal talks began in May at Bourbourg, near Dunkirk.

Perhaps the talks also confused Parma. According to an Italian envoy at the duke's court at Bruges on 29 July 1588: 'We spend our time here in banquets, fetes and games', and at one of them 'His Highness said that this year the war is turning into banquets, and the bullets are turning into tennis balls.' He erred: 300 miles to the east, at 7 p.m., the lookouts aboard the Armada sighted the coast of Cornwall. The following evening the English warships at Plymouth emerged to meet them.[30]

3

# 'A fleet to impeach it'

All that stood between England and defeat in July 1588 were the warships assembled at Plymouth to intercept the Armada as it approached from Spain, and the smaller flotilla in the Narrow Seas tasked with preventing a surprise attack by Parma's troops from Flanders. To be sure, a few hundred regular soldiers served in scattered garrisons along the kingdom's coasts and the Scottish border, and militia forces were on stand-by, but they were far from ready. Many were not even familiar with the terrain on which they might have to fight. Although the government commissioned surveys of the defensive arrangements in most coastal regions, many remained inaccurate and incomplete.

Last-minute haste and confusion also dogged the mobilization of troops. Even in London the government had only issued orders to arm 10,000 citizens in mid-March, and then could not find enough modern or serviceable equipment. Many received bows and arrows, but no training in their use. Not until 6 July, long after the Armada left Lisbon, did Elizabeth's Privy Council authorize the creation of a reserve army near London; and since this could only be achieved by depleting forces elsewhere, local officials received instructions to divide the militia of each southern county into three parts:

> Some to repair to the sea coast, as occasion may serve, to impeach the landing or withstand the enemy upon his first descent; some other part of the said forces to join with such numbers as shall be convenient to make head to the enemy after he shall be landed (if it shall so fall out); and another principal part of the said trained numbers to repair hither to join with the Army that shall be appointed for the defence of Her Majesty's person.[1]

Even then, the troops designated to protect the queen were instructed simply to be ready to go wherever directed 'upon an hour's warning'. Only on 2 August did the government decree full mobilization: 'Her Majesty's pleasure is that you should forthwith send [them] into Essex, unto the town of Brentwood.' From there the men must repair to Tilbury, where construction had started on a small fortress to protect the headquarters of the 'General of Her Majesty's forces in the South', Robert Dudley, earl of Leicester.[2]

It was all in vain because the Spaniards had no intention of landing in Essex. Their objective was eastern Kent, where in the past Romans, Saxons and Danes had all successfully stormed ashore. Philip had chosen well, for despite some last-minute and often ingenious improvisations by Elizabeth's hard-pressed commanders, England lacked an integrated defence system capable of withstanding a sustained assault by a professional army equipped with heavy artillery.

Some, indeed, regarded preparations by land as a wasteful farce. As Sir Walter Raleigh put it some years later, if an army 'be transported over sea' and the landing 'place left to the choice of the invader . . . such an army cannot be resisted on the coast of England without a fleet to impeach it', unless 'every creek, port, and sandy bay had a powerful army in each of them to make opposition'. Since this was obviously impossible, Raleigh believed that England's only sure defence lay in her 'many movable forts': the warships of the 'navy royal'. Her rulers must therefore 'employ good ships on the sea, and not trust to any entrenchment upon the shore'.[3]

## 'The flower of England's garland'

In 1588 Elizabeth possessed thirty-four 'movable forts', and according to Charles Howard of Effingham, her Lord Admiral (Figure 27), 'I think there were never in any place in the world worthier ships than these are'. He deemed them 'the strongest ships that any prince of Christendom has'. But, as Nicholas Rodger reminds us: 'Sea power cannot be improvised. In every age and every circumstance, the successful navies have been those which rested on long years of steady investment in the infrastructure essential to keep running the complex and delicate machinery of a seagoing fleet.' Such was the case with the fleet that met the Armada.[4]

The origins of Elizabeth's navy lay in the reign of her father, Henry VIII, who created a permanent defence establishment against the threat of Catholic attack following his excommunication by the pope. In 1546 he established a full-time Navy Board to oversee, among other things, the building, arming, victualling and upkeep of his warships. The illustrated inventory completed that year by Anthony Anthony, an official of the Ordnance Office, allows us to see Henry's 'navy royal' in frozen review, with special attention to the artillery aboard each vessel. The remains of one of the warships shown, the 600-ton *Mary Rose*, now on display and under study at Portsmouth, throw sharp light on the weapons technologies and tactical thinking of Henry and his naval experts (Figure 26).

Launched in 1509, by 1514 the *Mary Rose* carried fifteen bronze and sixty-three iron guns, all breech-loaders. A major refit – effectively a rebuild – took place in 1536. Details have escaped the documentary record, but the recovery of a major part of the ship's hull together with many guns and associated artefacts make it clear that her decks were reinforced to bear a much heavier armament, especially in the bronze muzzle-loading category. The ten such guns recovered between 1836 and 1981 include a 68-pounder cannon royal, a cannon, three demi-cannons, three culverins, and two demi-culverins. Despite some reduction in the weight and number of wrought-iron guns, Anthony's depiction of the ship shows her positively bristling with heavy ordnance on the broadside and stern, the lower tiers protected by lidded gun ports. The ship was still equipped for close-and-board tactics (note the shear-hooks on her spars), but she also had a ship-smashing capability to precede it.[5]

26. *Mary Rose*, from the Anthony Anthony Roll (1546).

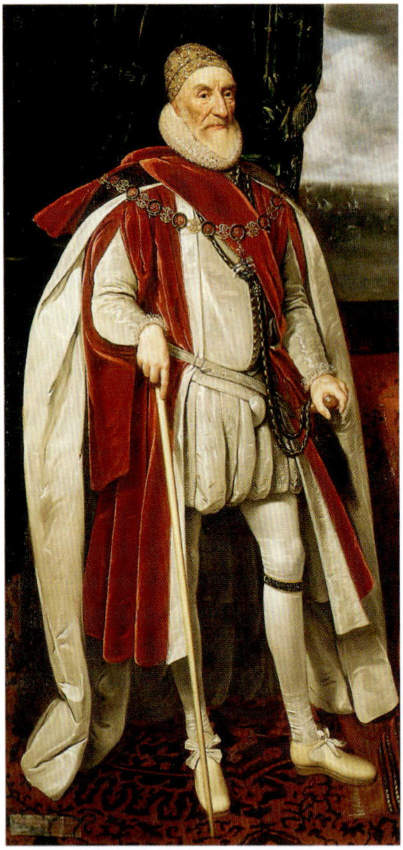

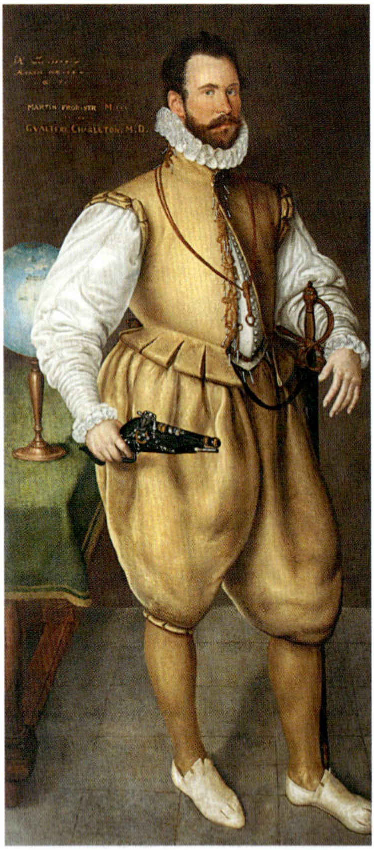
GVALTERI CHARLETON M.D.

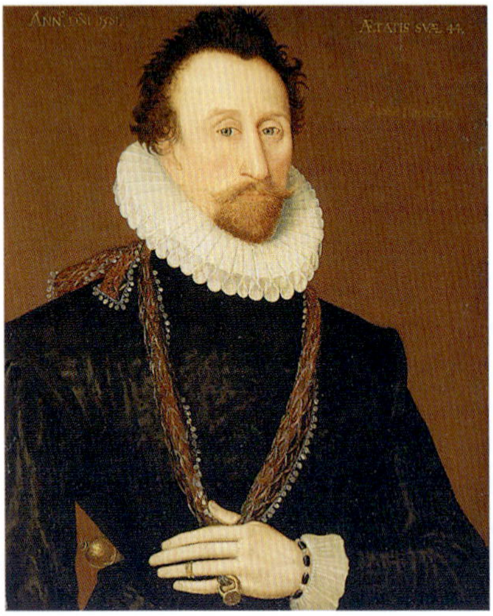
ÆTATIS SVÆ 44.

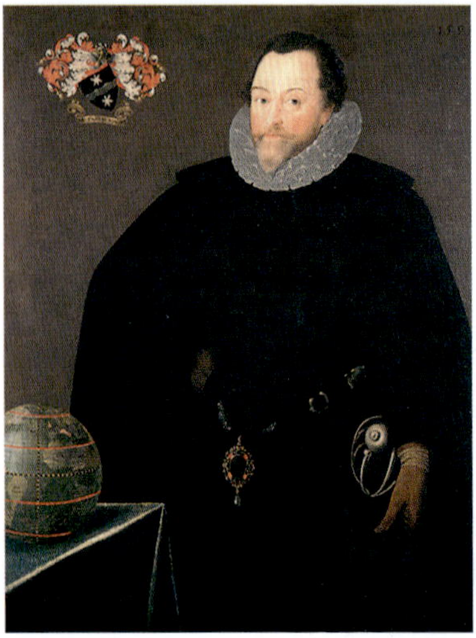

For most of the time such ships were laid up on a care-and-maintenance basis to minimize cost to the Crown, but in an emergency they could rapidly be mobilized for service in home waters. Since they were not designed to endure long periods at sea, all they needed to make them operational was food and munitions for a full complement of seamen and soldiers which, in the case of *Mary Rose*, amounted to some 100 and 600 men respectively. Virtually the full capacity of the ship was given over to the accommodation of weapons and men, who remained on board only long enough for a foray across the Channel, to land an expeditionary force in Scotland, or to repulse an enemy invasion attempt in home waters. Both for the preparatory bombardment intended to immobilize an enemy, and for the short-range salvoes designed to create confusion and alarm in the vital seconds preceding a boarding assault, she relied almost entirely on her artillery.

*Mary Rose* and her sister ships thus closely resembled those of the Spanish Armada a generation later, in that soldiers formed their primary weapon. Most of *Mary Rose*'s 600 soldiers were archers, trained from boyhood in the use of the yew longbow, who could release a barrage of armour-piercing missiles from ranges of more than 200 yards, at a rate of up to six per minute. For the final stage of a successful engagement – the physical boarding and capture of an adversary – 300 pikes and bills were provided. But the Anthony Roll included some ships of a different type. The 450-ton *Graunde Masterys* (Grand Mistress) had a long hull, low castle-works, heavy broadside armament and stern guns, all under a four-masted rig with lateen mizzens (Figure 28). Unlike *Mary Rose*, she and several sister ships carried no shear-hooks: a clear indication that closing and boarding did not form

**27.** Elizabeth's leading admirals. Top left: Lord Admiral Charles Howard, 2nd Baron Howard of Effingham (1536–1624), by Daniel Mytens. A formal full-length portrait done shortly after Howard retired from active service in 1618, it shows the fleet he commanded in action against the Spanish Armada thirty years before: still his main claim to fame. Top right: Sir Martin Frobisher (*c.* 1535–94) by Cornelis Ketel, 1577. Bottom left: Sir John Hawkins (1532–95) in 1581. A Plymouth merchant who made a fortune as England's first slave-trader, Hawkins introduced a series of crucial innovations while he served as Treasurer of the Navy from 1577 until his death. This portrait hung in the almshouse he set up in 1592 at Chatham to care for sick seamen. Bottom right: Sir Francis Drake (*c.* 1540–96) in 1591, by Marcus Gheeraerts. Painted when Drake was out of favour with the queen, the portrait stresses his achievements in her service: the jewel presented to him by Elizabeth, after he had 'singed the king of Spain's beard', hangs at waist level from a ribbon round his neck; the globe refers to his circumnavigation of the world; his sword hilt reminds viewers that he had fought for his country.

part of their intended repertoire. They were the precursors of the 'race-built' galleons which would give England a tactical edge in 1588.

Throughout his reign Henry took a close personal interest in the skilled and almost mystical art of gunnery, and with the help of foreign experts the gunfounders of England became renowned throughout Europe. Even at the beginning of his reign, as a contemporary put it, the king possessed 'cannon that would suffice to conquer hell', and by its close Henry's store of ordnance was truly formidable: almost 200 guns of 9-pounder calibre and above. Many of these pieces, including the biggest, were to be found on the decks of his warships. The navy that Henry bequeathed to his successors, while still mostly composed of troop-filled battleships designed for use in the Narrow Seas, thus carried the seeds of a revolutionary concept which would flower under Elizabeth: a sailing warship whose offensive capacity lay not in her soldiers but in her guns.[6]

By 1547, the year of Henry's death, the navy royal consisted of fifty-three well-gunned warships totalling some 10,000 tons. But it was a navy that England could not afford. In a cost-cutting exercise of a kind all too familiar in modern peacetime navies, ships were sold off or scrapped until in 1554 only thirty remained, mostly in poor condition. But then came one of history's great ironies. Philip of Spain, king consort of England by virtue of his marriage that year to Henry's daughter Mary, took a keen interest in English affairs, even when he was absent. The Privy

28. *Graunde Masterys*, from the Anthony Anthony Roll (1546).

Council sent him Latin summaries of their deliberations, which he returned with comments and suggestions, and in September 1555 the Council reported that most of the queen's ships were unseaworthy and should be brought to the Thames dockyards for repair. Philip welcomed the initiative because 'His Royal Majesty understands that the chief defence of the realm of England consists in this: that her ships are always ready and in good order. So that they can defend the realm from all invasion it will be fitting that they are always prepared and in readiness.'[7]

The Council hastened to act. Work began on three 'high charged ships' of 500 tons or more (a new *Mary Rose*, *Lion* and *Philip and Mary*, later renamed *Nonpareil*), followed in January 1557 by a decree which placed the Navy Board under the direct control of the Lord Treasurer, who 'with the advice of the Lord Admiral' would allocate the funds required to maintain a fleet capable of defending England. A few days later Queen Mary signed a warrant authorizing an annual payment of £14,000 to the Treasurer of the Navy, including £5,000 for 'building and repairing of ships' and another £1,000 for maintaining their rigging and 'other tackle and apparel'. Most of the rest of the money was earmarked for the sustenance of naval personnel, supervised by the 'Surveyor-General of Victuals for the Sea'. Payments (known as the 'ordinary') would be made in bi-annual instalments in advance, 'the same to continue during our pleasure': something known as a 'warrant dormant', because it was renewed automatically during the life of the monarch.[8] Shortly afterwards, again persuaded by Philip, England declared war on both Scotland and France. Over the next two years the Lord Treasurer spent more than £150,000 on the navy, including work on *Elizabeth Jonas*, another 'great ship' begun shortly before Mary died and Philip ceased to be king of England. All four galleons would distinguish themselves in 1588, fighting against his Armada.

Thanks to the efforts of Henry VIII, Philip and Mary, when Elizabeth Tudor came to the throne on her sister's death in November 1558 she acquired thirty-four warships; but would she continue her predecessors' high expenditure on the navy? Mary's 'warrant dormant' lapsed with her death, and in February 1559 the Navy Board tactfully enquired whether their new sovereign intended to issue a fresh one: 'Towards the maintenance of all the said ships, the queen's highness's pleasure is to be known for the continuance of the ordinary of £14,000 by the year from Christmas last, as well for the building and repairing of the same ships and provisions for the same.' To help her decide, the Board submitted a list of twenty-two royal ships with a total displacement of some 5,000 tons 'to be kept and preserved for the service of her Majesty'. They deemed the rest to 'be very much worn and of no consequence without great repairs to be done upon them' and 'not worth the new making'.[9]

Elizabeth, who inherited her sister's wars with both France and Scotland, decided to retain all the vessels recommended by her naval experts, as well as one of those they rejected (*Jesus of Lübeck*), and she renewed the 'warrant dormant'. In July 1559 she went to Woolwich to view the launch of the last great ship commissioned by her sister, naming her *Elizabeth Jonas* 'in memory of her own deliverance from the fury of her enemies, from which in one respect she was no less miraculously preserved than was the prophet Jonas from the belly of the whale'. Afterwards, 'Her Grace had a goodly banquet and there was great shooting of guns'.[10]

Some of Elizabeth's advisers still feared for her security. Sir Nicholas Throckmorton – the queen's relative as well as her ambassador in France – reminded her in April 1560 that with 'the French king Your Majesty's assured enemy, and the king of Spain your doubtful friend', she must take urgent steps to defend her realm against a surprise attack. Moreover, since 'the greatest defence you have is the sea, which being the wall of your realm is chiefly to be guarded':

> Nothing can so well serve as to continue your navy strong, and by the advice of the wise and experienced men of your realm to devise means how the same may be maintained and increased; and that also seeing that your greatest force and strength must be by sea, that good means may be found to encourage your nobility, gentlemen, and all others to apply themselves to that service.

In case the queen missed the point, Throckmorton exhorted her chief minister, Sir William Cecil, to 'Bend your force, credit, and device to maintain and increase your navy by all the means you can ... for in this time, considering all circumstances, it is the flower of England's garland ... It is your best and best cheap defence and most redoubted of your enemies and friends.'[11]

Throckmorton's message evidently got through because almost immediately work began in the royal dockyards on three more great ships: *Triumph*, *Victory* and *Aid*. In addition, the queen issued instructions praising the wisdom of 'our late dearest father King Henry VIII' for promoting naval readiness, and declared that 'our navy is one of the chiefest defences for the preservation of us and our realm against the malice of any foreign potentate'. Henceforth she required the principal officers of her navy 'once in the week (or more as the case shall require) to assemble themselves together' with the Lord Treasurer to discuss everything 'as shall be meetest for the good order of our navy'. In addition, every officer must become familiar with the duties of his colleagues 'to the intent that when God shall dispose His will upon any of them, those living may be able (if we shall prefer any of them)' to replace them. The 'flower of England's garland' was free to blossom.[12]

## The Dreadnought Revolution of Tudor England

By 1588 the queen's ships numbered thirty-four – the same number she had inherited – but both their combat effectiveness and their tactics were now very different. The 'Fighting Instructions' drawn up in March 1558 by William Winter, 'Master of the Ordnance of the Navy', contained an admonition that 'no ordnance to be shot but by the captain's licence and that not in vain', followed by two articles about procedures 'for the boarding of the enemy' – clearly envisaged as the primary means of combat. A year later, Winter submitted a declaration of all ordnance aboard the queen's ships, which provides an interesting comparison with the guns carried by the same number of ships in 1588 (Figure 29).

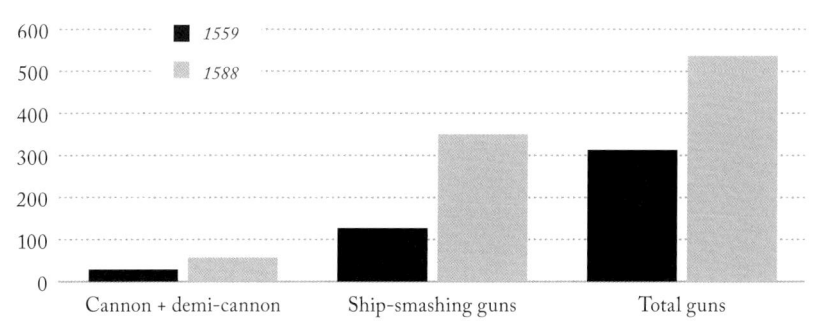

29. The firepower of the Elizabethan navy.

The queen's ships in 1588 thus deployed almost three times as many guns able to fire 'ship-smashing' rounds (9-pound balls and above) as their predecessors, and almost twice as many full cannon (firing a 50-pound ball) and demi-cannon (firing a 32-pound ball) – a clear indication that the Navy Board came to see bombardment rather than boarding as the primary means of combat.[13]

There was also a significant difference in the size of the crews aboard the queen's ships. In 1574 rumours of a Spanish invasion led Elizabeth to mobilize her navy, and the list of 'the number of men and furniture requisite for the setting forth of the same' included sixteen of the ships that would later face the Armada. Once again a comparison with 1588 is instructive. The tonnage of all sixteen warships remained much the same but they carried far fewer men (Figure 30).

30. Manning the Elizabethan navy.

The reduction in the number of soldiers by one-third is another clear indication that the Navy Board came to see its warships primarily as gun-platforms, not troop-transports.[14]

This critical change occurred in the 1570s, when the queen's shipwrights introduced a design known as 'race-built'. This involved a reduction in the castles fore and aft and a longer gun-deck, thanks to sleeker lines and a hydrodynamically efficient hull which combined (according to the master-shipwright Matthew Baker) 'the head of a cod and the tail of a mackerel'. At the same time rigging and sail-plans became more complex and efficient. These developments brought three important advantages. First, they made possible a revolution in armament: instead of castles carrying anti-personnel weapons, longer and stronger gun-decks permitted a significant increase in the weight of ordnance carried. Second, the sleeker lines allowed English warships to sail faster than their adversaries and to manoeuvre – and bring their guns to bear – with (for that age) remarkable agility. Finally, an increase in 'tumblehome' – the narrowing of the hull above the waterline – not only increased a ship's stability but made it much harder to board.

Moreover, English shipwrights began to commit their warship designs to paper, which had two further advantages (Figures 31, 32). First, shipwrights could share designs and construct 'classes' of warships to the same plans. Formulae based on proportions and arcs established a 'master frame' (some way forward of midships), creating a template from which the shapes of other frames could be resolved ('moulded') as full-scale patterns, allowing the preparation of frames before assembly. Previously, hull shape had been determined largely by eye with components 'faired' individually to fit as construction progressed: an inefficient and time-consuming process. Now successful designs could be replicated. *Galleon Leicester*, for example, constructed in a private shipyard in 1578 for privateering, was almost identical to the royal warship *Revenge*, launched the previous year, thanks to plans supplied by Matthew Baker. A decade later both ships would fight the Armada. Second, paper designs made it possible for shipwrights to learn from their contemporaries and predecessors, and thus improve their product.

The first of the faster 'all-big-gun battleships' of the Tudor navy was called *Dreadnought*, just like the similarly innovative capital ship of the Royal Navy in

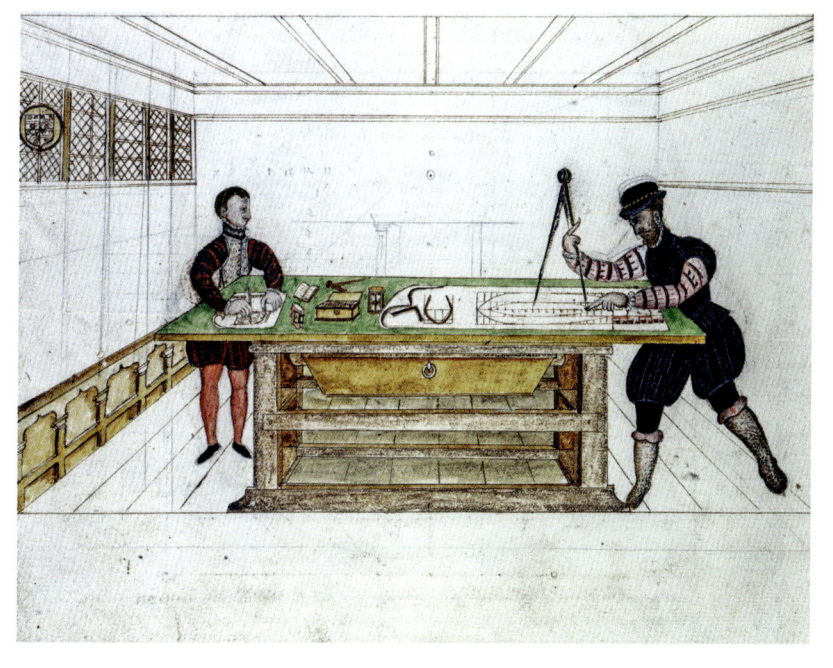

31. A shipwright and his apprentice at work, from *Fragments of Ancient Shipwrightry*, a volume of drawings, mathematical calculations and notes compiled by Matthew Baker, master-shipwright (*c.* 1530–1613). Although undated, it refers to ships built by Baker between 1570 and 1590 and may have been intended to teach his numerous apprentices in the royal dockyards.

the early twentieth century. Launched in 1573, she displaced 700 tons and carried 31 tons of ordnance. The ability to carry artillery weighing almost 5 per cent of total displacement was unprecedented, and the distinctive design and armament of the ship demonstrated that England's naval experts had anticipated the doctrine adumbrated three centuries on by the instigator of the later *Dreadnought*, Admiral Sir John Fisher: 'Strategy should govern the types of ships to be designed. Ship design, as dictated by strategy, should govern tactics. Tactics should govern details of armament.'[15] Fisher's Tudor predecessors had evidently worked out that the only effective strategy to defend England from invasion was to build warships capable of using artillery powerful and efficient enough to disable and disperse an enemy fleet from a distance.

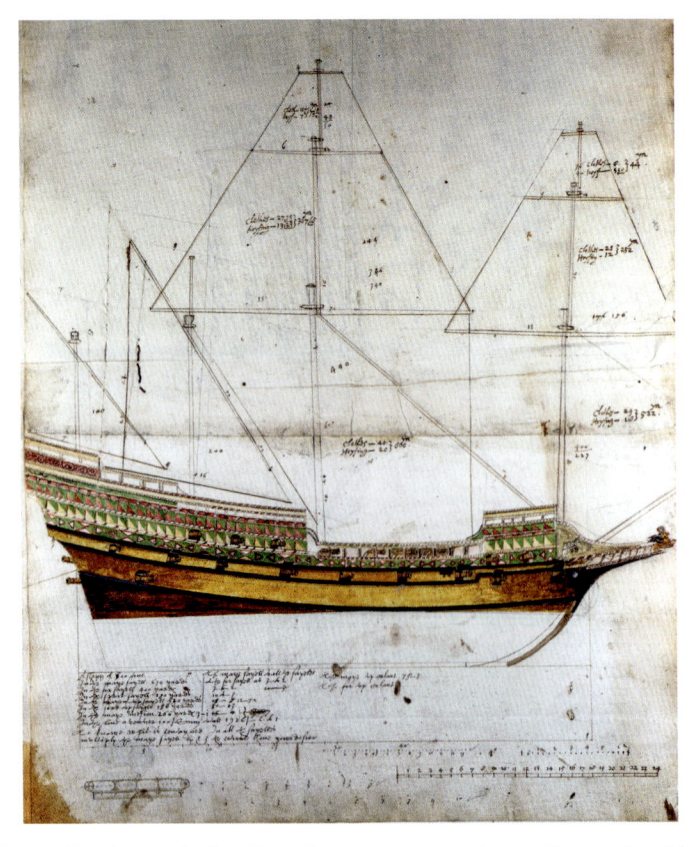

32. The profile of a race-built galleon from *Fragments of Ancient Shipwrightry*. Note the striking topmasts on the main- and foremasts.

## The 'reformation' of John Hawkins

Those Tudor predecessors nevertheless faced another major problem: how to produce enough ships like *Dreadnought* to safeguard the state, given that constructing a new galleon took at least two years. John Hawkins (see Figure 27) became Treasurer of the Navy in 1577, which gave him not only responsibility for managing the fleet's finances but also a direct say in policy and ship design. His profound knowledge of ships and seamanship, coupled with his personal experience of naval warfare, resulted in a multitude of improvements which in combination were revolutionary. The 'Bargain' he offered to Elizabeth promised that each year he would 'do such reparations as shall be needful, either in the making of a new ship, repairing in dry dock or any otherwise that shall be needful, so that the full number be kept as they are now at present'. Hawkins's naval 'reformation' (as he called it) involved an ambitious programme of rotation: he would construct eleven new galleons and 'reform' twelve older vessels to the new race-built design, and he provided a schedule of exactly 'how they are to be new built, one after another', down to 1599.[16]

    Other innovations devised by Hawkins, when added to the race-built concept, created truly revolutionary fighting machines. Hulls were strengthened to bear the weight and recoil stresses of heavy guns. This process had begun earlier, and can be seen in modifications made to the structure of *Mary Rose* shortly before she sank in 1545, including diagonal bracing between her frames and main gun-deck beams, and four decades later technical drawings by Matthew Baker show similar bracing (Figure 33).[17] Sails were redesigned and flattened so a ship could sail closer to the wind. Masts were heightened to carry more sail in good weather without endangering the ship in storms by making it possible to 'strike', or lower, the topmasts when necessary (see Figure 32). This not only improved a ship's sailing abilities but disadvantaged an adversary not so equipped. Writing a few years later, Sir Walter Raleigh enthused that 'It is not long since the striking of the topmast (a wonderful ease to great ships, both at sea and in harbour) hath been devised.' Raleigh also applauded the regular use of rotating capstans to raise anchors and perform other lifting tasks, instead of the traditional windlass. It was safer – the bars of an out-of-control windlass could be lethal – and more men could apply their combined strength, allowing heavier anchors and longer cables to be set out. 'By it, we resist the malice of the greatest winds that can blow,' Sir Walter enthused, 'for true it is that the length of the cable is the life of the ship in all extremities.'[18]

    Hawkins also oversaw the replacement of suction pumps with the more efficient chain pumps. This reduced the exhausting tedium of pumping water out of a ship,

**33a.** Top left: A shipworm (*Teredo navalis*). Top right: *Teredo* tunnels in wood from a shipwreck. Bottom: Example of hair-lined sheathing from a seventeenth-century wreck.

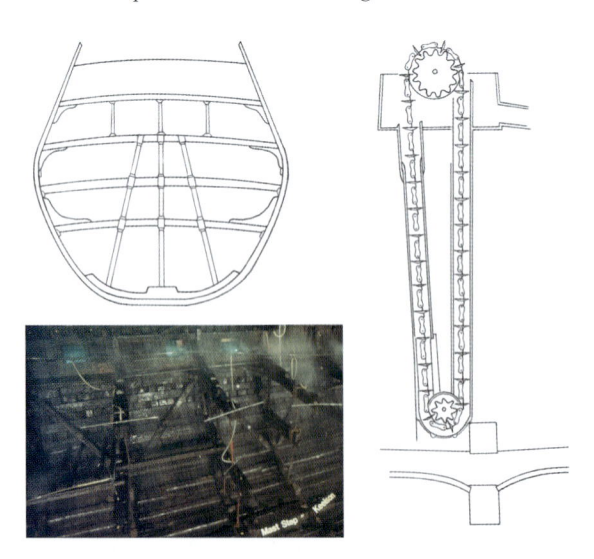

**33b.** Top left: Cross-section of a race-built galleon (adapted from Baker, *Fragments of Ancient Shipwrightry*) showing the reinforcing of deck-beams. In the words of Sir Walter Raleigh, 'we have added cross pillars to our royal ships to strengthen them, which being fastened from the keelson to the beams of the second deck, keeps them from settling'. Bottom left: Diagonal bracing on *Mary Rose*. Right: Diagram of a chain-pump.

which could quite literally mean the difference between life and death. He also found a way to thwart the humble shipworm (*Teredo navalis*; see Figure 33a), a seawater mollusc whose vestigial shells form a beak with which it eats into immersed wood, ultimately honeycombing it to destruction. From ancient times lead sheathing was used to protect the submerged parts of hulls, but this was heavy, expensive and prone to peel off with the working of a ship. Hawkins's solution was to cover the lower hull timbers with half-inch elm planking, sandwiching a layer of horsehair impregnated with tar. 'The thinner the better,' wrote a contemporary, 'for then the worm will presently [immediately] be at the tar (which he cannot abide); and so hath not the means nor room to work in and out of the plank'.[19]

Although in retrospect all these changes appear logical if not essential, at the time they seemed controversial and costly. Therefore, in order to persuade William Cecil, now Lord Burghley and Lord Treasurer, to accept his 'Bargain', Hawkins accused William Winter and others who had handled the repair of royal warships in the past of using poor materials and charging excessive prices. They did not accept defeat gracefully. Winter denounced Hawkins's offer as mere 'cunning and craft to maintain his pride and ambition, and for the better filling of his purse, and to keep back from discovering the faults that are left in Her Majesty's ships at this day'. One of Winter's associates submitted 'Articles of discovery of the unjust mind and deceitful dealing of John Hawkins', denouncing the 'baseness of the said Mr Hawkins in birth, mind and manners'. Two master-shipwrights submitted a detailed list of the defects they claimed to have found in individual ships: *Elizabeth Jonas* 'is very old' and 'we find her greatly decayed in her timbers'; *Triumph* 'we find much decayed in the timbers' and 'cannot be of any long continuance except these imperfections be remedied'; *Mary Rose* 'being very old, we find the great part of the timbers decayed' and so 'she is not to be built upon, but rather discontinued'; and so on.[20]

In February 1588 this barrage of criticisms forced Hawkins to present himself at Court 'to answer in his own defence'. Admiral Howard provided strong support, informing Burghley that 'I have been aboard of every ship that goes out with me, and in every place where any [man] may creep, and I do thank God that they be in the estate they be in, and there is never a one of them that knows what a leak means'. He predicted that Hawkins 'shall prove them arrant liars that have reported the contrary'. Nevertheless, in June, with the Armada at sea, Howard found it necessary to repeat his assurance that 'Her Majesty may be sure, what false and villainous reports soever have been made of them, she has the strongest ships that any prince in Christendom has.'[21]

Why did Elizabeth's senior naval officers try to discredit if not destroy each other at a moment of national crisis? Nicholas Rodger offers the most plausible explanation: 'corruption' was 'the all-purpose explanation for anything which did not work satisfactorily', and so 'accusations of corruption were usually just a bid to take over a contract from a rival . . . Contemporaries took it for granted that officials would make money from their positions; what they wanted to know was whether the crown was getting value for that money.'[22] The Armada campaign soon revealed the truth, because despite several months at sea and a major fleet action every one of the queen's ships returned to port in good condition, just as Hawkins had predicted. Nevertheless, it is worth noting that both he and Winter died rich. Although the official salary of each man never exceeded £250, their wills revealed that they owned landed properties, city mansions and lavish possessions. Each made bequests totalling at least £10,000 – almost enough to construct four race-built galleons.

## Band of Brothers?

In August 1588 Lord Henry Seymour, who commanded the English flotilla protecting the Narrow Seas, fretted about the serious divisions he perceived among his colleagues. 'I find my Lord [Admiral Howard] and his company divided in a manner to factions,' he lamented; and in a dockside altercation Sir Martin Frobisher threatened to eviscerate Sir Francis Drake – both, together with Hawkins, Howard's principal lieutenants (see Figure 27). It is nevertheless possible to read too much into this evidence of discord, coming at the end of several weeks at sea and several days under fire. The last will of Hawkins revealed the close bonds that united the queen's senior officers. He left 'my best diamond worth £100, or so much money in gold' to Howard; 'my best jewel, which is a cross of emeralds' to Drake; 'a diamond worth £20' to Sir Henry Palmer; £20 to William Borough; and forgiveness of a debt of £50 to Edward Fenton.[23] This amity was founded in part on blood – Drake was Hawkins's cousin, Fenton his brother-in-law – and in part on shared experiences. Drake had sailed with Hawkins on three trading voyages in the 1560s; Winter had helped to fund Drake's first solo raid in the Caribbean; Frobisher had served as his vice-admiral on the West Indies expedition. Throughout the 1588 campaign the Lord Admiral regularly consulted a Council of War that included Drake, Frobisher and Hawkins.

This 'band of brothers' spirit evidently developed after Elizabeth came to the throne. In Henry VIII's navy, as in the Spanish Armada, soldiers formed the majority of each warship's complement and it was therefore usual to appoint a soldier rather than a seaman as the vessel's captain, meaning that many captains lacked seagoing competence. The results could prove fatal. In 1545 Sir George Carew only came aboard *Mary Rose* when a hostile French fleet appeared. He immediately 'commanded every man to take his place and the sails to be hoisted; but the same was no sooner done, but that *Mary Rose* began to heel'. Sir George's uncle, Sir Gawen Carew, in command of a sister warship, 'seeing the same, called for the master of his ship and told him thereof, and asked him what it meant, who answered that if she did heel she was liked to be cast away'. Sir Gawen then came close and asked his nephew 'how he did, who answered that he had a sort of knaves whom he could not rule'. A historian of the family explained this remark:

> He had in his ship a hundred mariners, the worst of them being able to be a master in the best ship within the realm; and these so maligned and disdained one another, that refusing to do that which they should do, were careless to do that which was most needful and necessary, and so contending in envy, perished in forwardness.[24]

Many people (including Henry VIII) watched *Mary Rose* founder, and the ignorance displayed by her captain of what it meant when a ship heeled over in the wind apparently led to changes in the structure of command. In 1578 the dedication to a book on navigation praised young Howard of Effingham for learning 'things, although not usual to noblemen', which were 'yet most necessary unto all manner persons that haunt the seas', ranging from 'the meanest matters, as all manner of cordage and tackle within board, namely sheet, halliard, bowline, tackle, and helm', up to 'the use and practise of the astrolabe'. That same year, as he began his circumnavigation of the world, Drake warned his crew:

> Here is such a controversy between the sailors and the gentlemen, and such stomaching between the gentlemen and the sailors, that it doth even make me mad to hear it. But, my masters, I must have it left. For I must have the gentleman to haul and draw with the mariner, and the mariner with the gentleman . . . As gentlemen are very necessary for government's sake in the voyage, so have I shipped them for that purpose, and to some further intent; and yet though I know sailors to be the most envious people of the world and so unruly without government, yet may I not be without them.[25]

Drake's doctrine soon became standard on English warships. A list of potential naval captains drawn up for Burghley in 1586 contained seventy-six names, including five noblemen, eight knights and eighteen esquires, the majority of whom had previously commanded warships at sea, as well as eighteen gentlemen, all with considerable naval experience. The rest were evidently professional seamen.[26] Both groups knew how to 'haul and draw'. When Howard led a squadron of warships to Flushing to stiffen Dutch resistance to Spain, the ship commanded by Seymour (whose aunt, Jane, had married Henry VIII) ran aground just outside the harbour. Howard praised Seymour because 'although many of the ship went out to save themselves for fear, he would by no means stir out of her, but said he would abide her fortune and so encouraged them all. I and Sir William Winter came presently aboard of her, where we found my Lord Harry sparing no labour for her help'. A few months later, on blockade duty off Dunkirk, Seymour apologized for dictating a letter instead of composing it himself because 'I have strained my hand with hauling of a rope, whereby I cannot write'.[27]

Elizabeth's senior officers looked after their crews as well as their ships. In 1596, when he led a large fleet to capture Cadiz, Howard manifested great solicitude 'for all his followers of all sorts and degrees, but especially for the poor toiling and continual labouring mariner, himself daily making enquiry how they did, and *calling to them by name* to know in what case they stood, and what they did lack, bidding them boldly to utter their wants'. Howard also recognized the limits of his authority. During the naval action in Cadiz harbour he 'called to the master of his ship and bid him with all speed put nearer' to the fighting so he could take part; but 'the master craved pardon of his lordship and told him it was a thing impossible to be done in that place' without the ship running aground. 'His lordship being wonderfully discontented with this answer, and chafing inwardly as it appeared manifestly in his countenance', nevertheless gave way and called for his pinnace, in which he went to another ship of shallower draught, where in 'the very hottest of the battle' he 'in person discharged four great pieces' at the enemy.[28]

England's defences by sea in 1588 did not depend solely upon the warships of the navy royal. The queen could also draw upon a powerful 'Volunteer Naval Reserve'. Thirty of the privately owned ships that fought with Howard displaced between 200 and 400 tons and carried up to forty-two guns: they were warships in all but name, and several had considerably more combat experience than the carefully husbanded royal fleet. Only two of the queen's ships had sailed under Drake to the Caribbean in 1585, but all twelve armed merchantmen that accompanied them later served against the Armada. The raid on Cadiz two years later, again commanded by Drake, comprised six royal ships and seventeen armed merchantmen, almost all of which also fought in 1588. This should not surprise us, for many of these private ships belonged to prominent figures in the queen's navy, and distinctions often became blurred. Howard himself owned seven warships, which he normally used for privateering but in 1588 they all fought the Armada. Hawkins owned three, and Drake two. All were commanded by their owners' relatives or commercial partners, thus creating remarkable unity within the English fleet.[29] Howard's relatives commanded several ships. Lords Seymour and Sheffield (*White Bear*) were his nephews; Lord Thomas Howard (*Golden Lion*) and Nicholas Gorges (commander of the supply squadron) were his cousins; Sir Robert Southwell (*Elizabeth Jonas*) and Sir Richard Leveson (aboard *Ark Royal*) were his sons-in-law. All provided the Lord Admiral with unwavering support.

## The Queen and her Navy

Howard could also usually count on support from his most illustrious relative: his cousin the queen. Elizabeth never boarded her fleet in action, as her father had done: during the invasion scare of 1545 Henry was dining with his captains aboard the flagship, anchored in the Solent, when a lookout spotted the French war-fleet approaching. 'He had a secret talk with the Lord Admiral' before going ashore to watch the action. The queen nevertheless took a keen interest in naval affairs. After dining aboard *Elizabeth Jonas* at Deptford in 1560, she and 'above 4,000 people on the water and the land' watched a simulated naval battle in which four pinnaces 'assaulted' a sailing ship and 'shot great ordnance' and 'all manner of artillery'. Just after the Armada campaign, the Navy Board ordered their master-shipwrights to make 'fair plats' (scale drawings) of some new ships and bring them 'to my Lord Admiral that her Majesty may see them'.[30]

Elizabeth made at least seven visits to view her ships at Deptford, including the memorable occasion in 1581 when she came aboard Drake's *Golden Hind*, newly returned from her circumnavigation, knighted him on her deck and dined with him in the main cabin. The following year (a few months after Philip II watched the launch of *San Felipe* in Lisbon), the Treasurer of the Navy purchased two loads of birch 'to make a bower for her Majesty to rest in, being at the launching of the galleon' *Golden Lion*. Elizabeth also 'took a survey of the dockyard at Chatham' in 1573, and returned there nine years later with Francis, duke of Anjou, heir to the French throne. On that occasion:

> Her Majesty showed him all her great ships which were in that place, into most whereof her Highness and the prince and lords of his train entered. And not

without great admiration of the French lords and gentlemen, who confessed that of good right the queen of England was reported to be Lady of the Seas. Also, he beheld how all those ships were ready furnished and well appointed.[31]

Maintaining a large fleet in constant readiness is never cheap. In 1581 one of Elizabeth's ministers appealed to the House of Commons for new taxes in the following terms: 'One of our greatest defences therefore standing by sea, the number of good ships is of the most importance for us. What the Queen's navy is, how many notable ships, and how far beyond the navy of any other prince, is known to all men. And therewith also it may easily be considered how great charges be incident to the same.'[32] The Members of Parliament obliged, even though they could not know – as we do today – just how much the queen spent on her fleet.

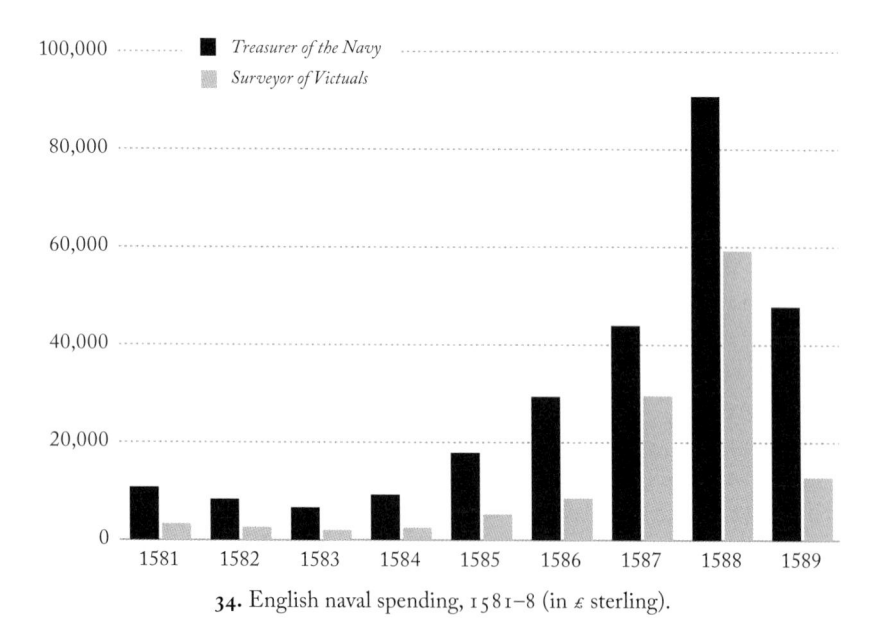

34. English naval spending, 1581–8 (in £ sterling).

In addition, the royal treasury spent about £5,000 annually on ordnance and munitions 'for the sea service' (Figure 34).

The Tudor state's willingness to spend so much on the navy is easily explained. No one could forget the trauma in 1545, when a French fleet landed troops on the Isle of Wight and 'came unto the haven of Portsmouth and there rowed up and down, there being never a ship at that instant in readiness, nor any such wind to serve if they had been in readiness to impeach them'. The queen, born in 1533, may not have remembered this disgrace clearly, but many could remind her: Winter had been with the fleet's commander, John Dudley, Viscount Lisle, and became close to Lisle's son Robert, earl of Leicester. The widow of Sir George Carew, Lisle's vice-admiral and commander of *Mary Rose*, became one of the queen's ladies-in-waiting; another of her ladies-in-waiting married Carew's brother (and fellow commander); Howard of Effingham's father had commanded another warship.[33]

Close ties bound Elizabeth to her entourage thanks in part to her traumatic upbringing. Her father had executed her mother (Anne Boleyn) and one of her stepmothers (Katherine Howard). Two of her other stepmothers had died in childbirth (Jane Seymour and Katherine Parr, who had helped to raise her). Her half-brother Edward approved the execution of one of her suitors, Thomas Seymour (also her stepfather, since he had married Katherine Parr). Her half-sister Mary imprisoned her twice, once in the Tower of London, on suspicion of treason. As queen she therefore placed her trust primarily in three groups of her subjects: those related to her mother (Walsingham's stepfather was Anne's brother-in-law; Howard was Anne's cousin); those who had shared her trauma (Leicester had been imprisoned in the Tower with her); and those who had supported her in adversity (Burghley had served as her confidential adviser during Mary's reign; Sir John Norris's parents had cared for her when under house arrest).

Whereas Philip II surrounded himself with knights of the Golden Fleece whom he addressed as 'my cousin' as a courtesy title, Elizabeth surrounded herself with men and women who really were her cousins – and she gave some of them nicknames, as a family member might do. She called Leicester her 'eyes' (and he played along, signing his letters to her 'your ŌŌ' rather than with his name); she referred to Norris's mother, an intimate companion, as her 'crow' because of her dark complexion; she christened Walsingham, who also had a dark complexion, her 'moor'; and called Burghley's son Robert Cecil, who had a slight spinal deformity, 'pygmy'.

Such familiarity did not spare members of the queen's inner circle from punishment when they displeased her. Elizabeth imprisoned or banished courtiers when she discovered they had conducted illicit sexual relations without her knowledge or married without her consent. She also engaged in what today would be called 'bitch-slapping': she hit with a candlestick a lady-in-waiting who had married without permission, breaking one of her fingers; and when the earl of Essex turned his back on her at a council meeting she boxed his ears.[34] Members of Elizabeth's Court had little choice but to put up with such humiliation because they felt certain that Philip would eliminate them, and perhaps their families too, if he ever gained the upper hand in England.

An analysis of Elizabeth's travels reveals the tight composition of her inner circle. Although in the course of her reign she stayed in the homes of more than 400 subjects, most belonged to the three groups of ultra-loyalists. She stayed with Leicester twenty-three times, with Burghley twenty times, with Norris (or his parents) ten times, and with Howard four times. Moreover, although the queen spent much of her reign on the move, she rarely strayed far from London, never travelling further west than Salisbury and Bristol, nor further north than Stafford and Norwich.

Elizabeth liked to travel for two reasons. First – and in this she resembled Philip – absence from the centre of government helped her (as historian Mary Hill Cole has noted) 'maintain an independent course of action and justify her cautious indecision'. Travel offered the queen 'an opportunity to keep her officials off-balance and to defer decisions'. Second, according to Ambassador Guzmán de Silva, one of the most perceptive foreign observers at her Court, the queen adored the attention. 'She travels through the field in a carriage open on all sides, so that the people can see her,' Guzmán wrote, and 'she sometimes orders the carriage to take the route where there seems to be the largest concourse of people. Then she stands up' so that everyone could see her better and applaud. Occasionally she miscalculated. One evening in 1581 Elizabeth rode out to Islington 'to take the air; where, near the town, she was environed with a number of begging rogues (as beggars usually haunt such places) which gave the queen much disturbance'. Thereafter Elizabeth travelled less often.[35]

Again like her former brother-in-law, the queen normally formulated her foreign and defence policy in one of her palaces – but there the parallel ends. Philip took most decisions alone, with limited input from a handful of secular and clerical advisers, and he rarely briefed his commanders in person. Instead, he entrusted the plans and policies he had devised to couriers who lacked the authority to offer details or explain his rationale; and he forbade subsequent discussion. By contrast, when faced by the existential threat of foreign invasion, and with virtually no experience to guide her, Elizabeth recognized the need for both consultation and delegation. In December 1587 her detailed Instructions for Howard on how best to use the navy to defend her realms not only left him room to use his 'own discretion and judgement' in interpreting her commands, but also added a striking conclusion:

> Forasmuch as there may fall out many accidents that may move you to take another course than by these our instructions you are directed, we therefore think it most expedient to refer you therein to your own judgement and

discretion, to do that thing you may think may best tend to the advancement of our service.

Eight months later the queen 'entered this morning into consultation' with her Privy Councillors about the partial demobilization of her forces, 'seeing (God be thanked) there is no apparent danger from the enemy'. Together they ordered Leicester to stand down most of the troops at Tilbury but only 'if [you] shall see no sufficient cause to the contrary'.[36]

The queen consulted her experts in person before taking other important decisions. In spring 1588 she summoned Drake, Howard, Hawkins and Winter to Court to discuss naval strategy, and on 23 April Howard notified Burghley – who as Lord Treasurer held ultimate responsibility for the navy – that she had made up her mind without him: 'I would have been very glad to have seen your Lordship myself, *but I could not obtain leave of Her Majesty*; and yet it were fit that I should make Your Lordship acquainted with Her Majesty's resolution touching the service on the seas, which God willing I will do before I depart.' Apparently this meeting did not happen, because four days later Howard coolly informed Burghley that 'It is now determined that I shall go westward with the greatest part of Her Majesty's ships, *whereof I have thought good to advertise Your Lordship*. The purpose and conclusion of her Majesty's intent, Sir William Winter or Mr Hawkins will advertise your Lordship at large' – that is, at least three naval officers had learned 'Her Majesty's intent' in person long before the Lord Treasurer, not only their superior but also her principal political adviser.[37]

Once again the queen allowed Howard remarkable flexibility. His new Instructions ordered him to 'repair to the west parts' of England and place his fleet:

> Between the coast of Spain and the said west parts as may best serve to impeach the great navy now prepared in Spain [from] attempting anything as well against our dominions of England and Ireland as also the realm of Scotland. [But] for that it is hard for us to give unto you any particular direction in this service, we hold it best for us to refer the matter to your own good consideration, to take that course for the furtherance of our said service, as to you in your own discretion shall be thought meet.

As Nicholas Rodger observed, 'Few commanders-in-chief in so critical a situation have ever been trusted with such complete discretion.'[38]

## Micromanagement

The queen was not perfect, however. Like Philip she could and did change her mind. Consider the letters exchanged on 27 March 1596 between two of her ministers charged with preparing royal commissions for Lords Howard and Essex to lead a massive naval assault on Spain. In the morning her secretary offered to read the commissions out to her but Elizabeth said 'she knew them already', so she signed them unseen. Then she had second thoughts and 'in the midst of the sermon' sent her secretary a message 'that I should stay those things which Her Majesty had signed'. After dinner she sent for him again 'and made me read the commission, and coming to the point of "invading the realms & dominions, &c.", Her Majesty would have it reformed thus, viz. "to invade such parts of the realms & dominions of, &c"'. Although the queen signed the revised commission the following day, she ordered that it be kept secret 'for some time'.[39]

Also like Philip, Elizabeth sometimes tried to micromanage operations. On 19 June 1588 she rebuked Howard for his decision to intercept the Spanish fleet off Corunna, because 'she thinketh it not convenient that your lordship should go so far south'. Instead, she ordered him to 'ply up and down in some indifferent place between the coast of Spain and this realm'. As it happens, the rebuke arrived after contrary winds forced Howard back into Plymouth, and it provoked perhaps the most outspoken reproach the queen would ever see. Her 'letter I do not a little marvel at', he began, because the decision to go to Corunna 'was deeply debated by those which I think the world doth judge to be men of greatest experience that this realm has', namely Drake, Frobisher and Hawkins. 'But,' Howard continued, '[I] am glad there be such there as are able to judge what is fitter for us to do, than we here' – even after four centuries, the sarcasm is deafening – and he 'most humbly pray[ed] Her Majesty to think that that which we meant to do was not rashly determined'. His sarcasm evidently found its mark, because – fortunately for the future of the Tudor state – the queen backed down. Howard soon received another letter:

> Whereby I do perceive Her Majesty's gracious goodness that she thinketh us to be so careful of her service as that she hath referred it unto me and such other my assistants here to do that which they and I think fittest and most convenient to be done for the more surety and service of Her Majesty and the state.[40]

## Hearts of Oak?

By then, Howard commanded 105 ships at Plymouth, including nineteen of the queen's galleons and forty-six large auxiliary vessels, manned by almost 10,000 officers, gunners, mariners and soldiers. Although no musters seem to have survived, we may surmise from the records of other expeditions that most of the men aboard the fleet were young. Only one of those who sailed with Drake to the Caribbean, and only ten who sailed with Fenton to the South Atlantic, were over thirty. Many who took part in these ventures died at sea, and the same was true in 1588. Before making his last attempt to intercept the Armada before it reached the Channel, Howard warned that 'We must now man ourselves again, for we have cast many overboard, and a number in great extremity which we discharged.'[41]

Some attrition was inevitable, because as Richard Hakluyt observed a few years later: 'No kind of men of any profession in the commonwealth pass their years in so great and continual hazard of life' as a mariner. This explained why 'of so many, so few grow to grey hairs'. Some losses were self-inflicted, however. For example, in February 1588 a rumour reached Howard that a few men aboard his flagship were 'something inclined to papistry' and he determined to purge them before the campaign began. His lieutenant proclaimed that 'he that was in his ship that would not be sworn against the pope, he would take him for a traitor and so use him'. Howard examined one suspect in person and only kept him aboard when he joined the rest of the crew with 'the book of Psalms, which he daily sang with the [ship's] company'. No doubt, as he would do on the Cadiz raid eight years later, Howard required the captain of each ship to 'take a special care to serve God, by using [the Book] of Common Prayer twice every day, except urgent cause enforce the contrary'; and at the setting of the watch 'every night by 8 of the clock' to arrange 'singing of the Lord's Prayer [and] some of the Psalms of David'. He certainly made sure that his ships carried thirteen preachers paid by the queen – an unprecedented number in the English navy (albeit only a fraction of the 180 clerics aboard the Armada).[42]

Howard also did his best to train the men aboard the fleet to use their weapons. Early in July he boasted that 6,000 of them would be able 'to land upon any great occasion', because 'they have been trained here under captains and men of experience, and each man knowing his charge, and they their captains. I had rather have them to do any exploit than any 16,000 out of any part of the realm.' Strangely, Howard opposed similar training for his gunners. In February 1588 he heard that by 'a mischance' in one of Drake's ships 'a piece broke and killed a man, with some other hurt', and he informed Walsingham that 'if you would write a word or two unto [Drake] to spare his powder, it would do well'. Apparently the only practice the gunners aboard the fleet received in firing and reloading their pieces was in the salvoes and salutes that were almost as frequent in the English as in the Spanish fleet.[43]

The opportunity for practice ended abruptly on 29 July. After his failed attempts to catch the Spanish fleet as it sheltered in Corunna, Howard was back at Plymouth in the process of loading stores and munitions in the inner harbour when Captain Thomas Fleming of the pinnace *Golden Hind*, one of the screen of pickets stationed in the Channel Approaches, arrived with momentous news: he had sighted the Spanish Armada, in formidable strength and good order. Immediately the leading English ships prepared for the tricky and laborious business of warping out of harbour with the ebb tide; but once the vital order had been given Howard could do nothing until his ships had cleared port and formed up in Plymouth Sound, ready to sail. Although the story may be apocryphal, these few hours would have given him ample opportunity to complete his game of bowls against Drake on Plymouth Hoe.

We must not mistake such confidence for complacency. In April 1588 Drake expressed doubts about 'the resolution of our own people, which I shall better understand when I have them at sea'. Three months later, Hawkins observed that although the warships were 'in most royal and perfect state', their crews were not: 'There be some in them that have no goodwill to see the coast of Spain with them, but cast many doubts how they will do in those seas.' Most looked to the supernatural for reassurance. Before embarking, William Monson (then a volunteer aboard one of the queen's ships) consulted the London astrologer Simon Forman about his chances of survival. Most of his shipmates hoped for divine protection. Those who in the course of 1588 wrote the letters that John Knox Laughton later printed in *State Papers relating to the defeat of the Spanish Armada* invoked 'God' more than 400 times. Drake's letters, in particular, were full of divine invocations. 'Your Highness's enemies are many,' he reminded Elizabeth on one occasion, 'yet God hath and will hear Your Majesty's prayers, putting your hand to the plough for the defence of His truth, as Your Majesty has begun. God, for His Christ's sake, bless Your Sacred Majesty, now and ever.'[44]

Others felt less confident. The previous year, the magistrates of Plymouth threatened that any resident who 'upon any attempt offered by the enemy absent himself' from the town, would suffer immediate confiscation of all property and perpetual exile ('never afterward to be admitted there nor allowed as a town dweller'). Shortly afterwards the royal commander in Portsmouth, another town of great strategic importance, complained to the Privy Council that 'Your Honours would think these speeches to be strange, if you should hear them – the meaner and poorer sort – to say that he would not sell horse and cart to defend his prince, country, family and children.'[45]

Perhaps these faint-hearts believed the doom-laden prophecies that circulated in England (as they did in Spain), triggered by the coincidence of a solar and lunar eclipse and the astronomical alignment of Saturn, Jupiter and Mars. A popular treatise noted the 'old, and common prophecy, touching the year *1588,* which is now so rife in every man's mouth', that 'very extraordinary accidents, as, extreme hunger and pestilence, desperate treasons and commotions, shall then fall out, to the miserable affliction and oppression of huge multitudes: or else, that an utter and final overthrow, and destruction of the whole world shall ensue'. Specific baleful prophecies also circulated. In 1584 a yeoman in Canterbury was tried for saying he hoped to see a change of religion within three years and predicting that 'the pope of Rome should have as great authority' in England 'as ever he did in Rome'. Two years later an Essex shoemaker was arrested for predicting that 'our queen shall live but a little while; she will be gone ere summer come'. In June 1587 a clergyman in Cambridge claimed that 'February come twelvemonths England shall have a new prince, and the prince shall reign but five months, and he shall be a papist.'[46]

The government took such prophecies very seriously – the archives contain copious details on these and other prophets of doom – and they found little comfort in the answers of leading English Catholics to the question, '[If] the pope or any other by his appointment and authority do invade this realm, which part do you take?' Almost half of those interrogated declared that they would either join or at least not oppose the invaders, and several others refused to answer a hypothetical question ('It is a future contingent and he knows not what he should do'). Very few declared unqualified support for the Tudor state.[47]

These sentiments have been termed 'pre-Armada millenarian pessimism', and the queen and her ministers deployed several strategies to counter it. They subsidized publications highlighting the 'barbarous cruelty and tyranny of the Spaniard' manifested in events like the sack of Antwerp, and claimed that Spanish troops were boasting that after their invasion 'we shall have the spoil of rich England' and 'embrace their fair wives, and make havoc of their long gathered riches'.[48] On 20 July John Whitgift, archbishop of Canterbury and primate of England, sent out an injunction for public prayers for deliverance to be said in all churches; and two weeks later, 'upon new advertisement of the discovery again of the Spanish Fleet', the Privy Council ordered all clerics to persuade their 'parishioners to join in public prayer to Almighty God the giver of victories to assist us against the malice of our enemies'.[49]

None of the protagonists could know what the imminent trial of arms would bring. None could be sure whose prayers would be answered or whose prophecies would come true. The two sides had very different aims, equipment and tactical doctrines, and neither knew the intentions, strengths and weaknesses of their opponents, let alone how best to respond. No one doubted the stakes, however. In his celebrated history of World War I, *The World Crisis*, Winston Churchill wrote that in 1916 Admiral Jellicoe, commander of Britain's Grand Fleet, 'was the only man on either side who could lose the war in an afternoon'. Admiral Howard held an even greater responsibility in 1588: he was the only man who could lose the war against Spain in an afternoon, and in doing so jeopardize the entire Tudor regime and England's Protestant faith.[50]

**(Overleaf) 35.** The 'Greenwich Cartoon' – so-called because it might have been a design for a tapestry. The English and Spanish fleets engaged, English school, 16th century. The ships are shown with accurate detail. As with other near-contemporary images, a galleass appears in the foreground. These vessels evidently made a great impression on contemporaries.

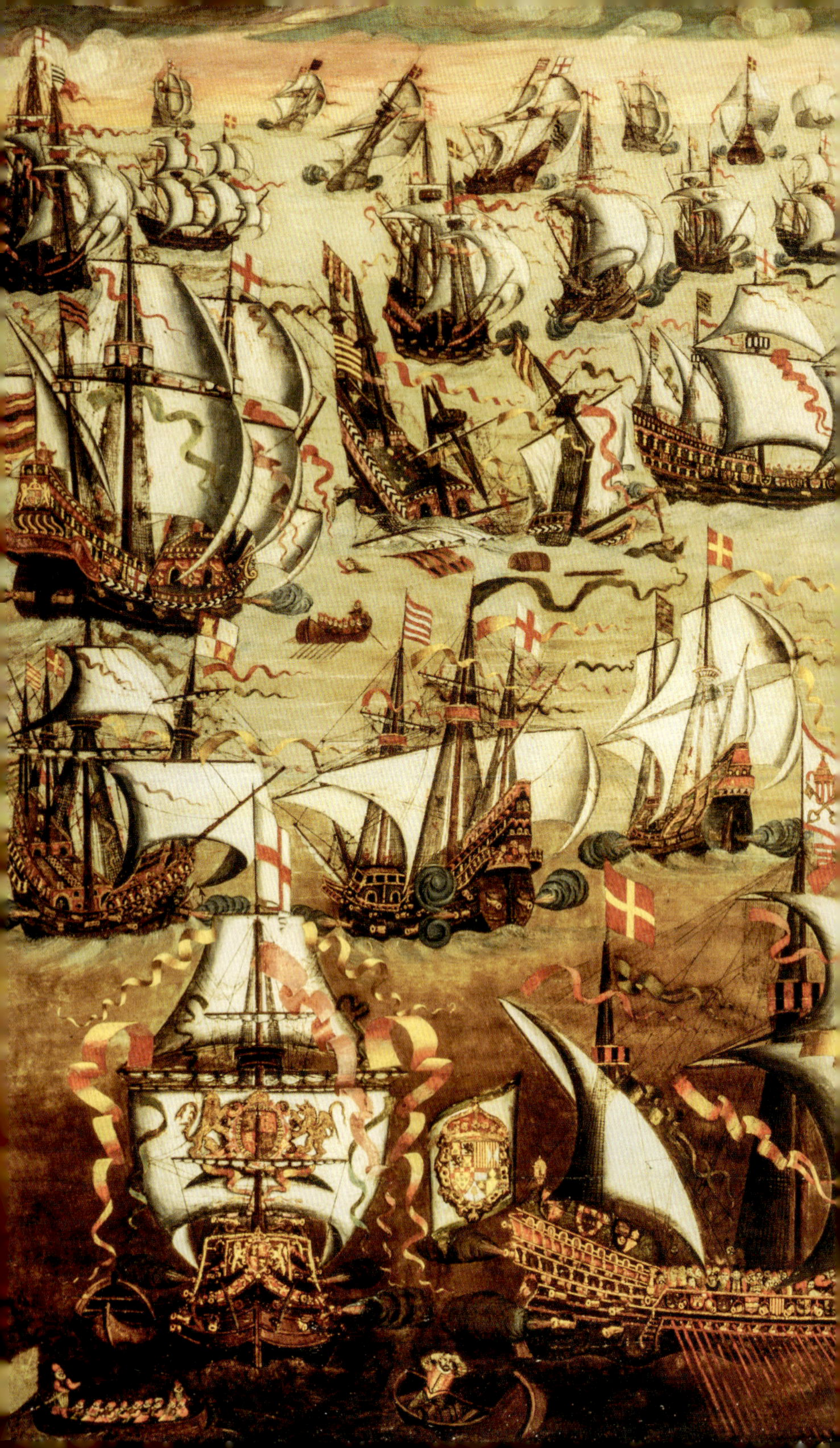

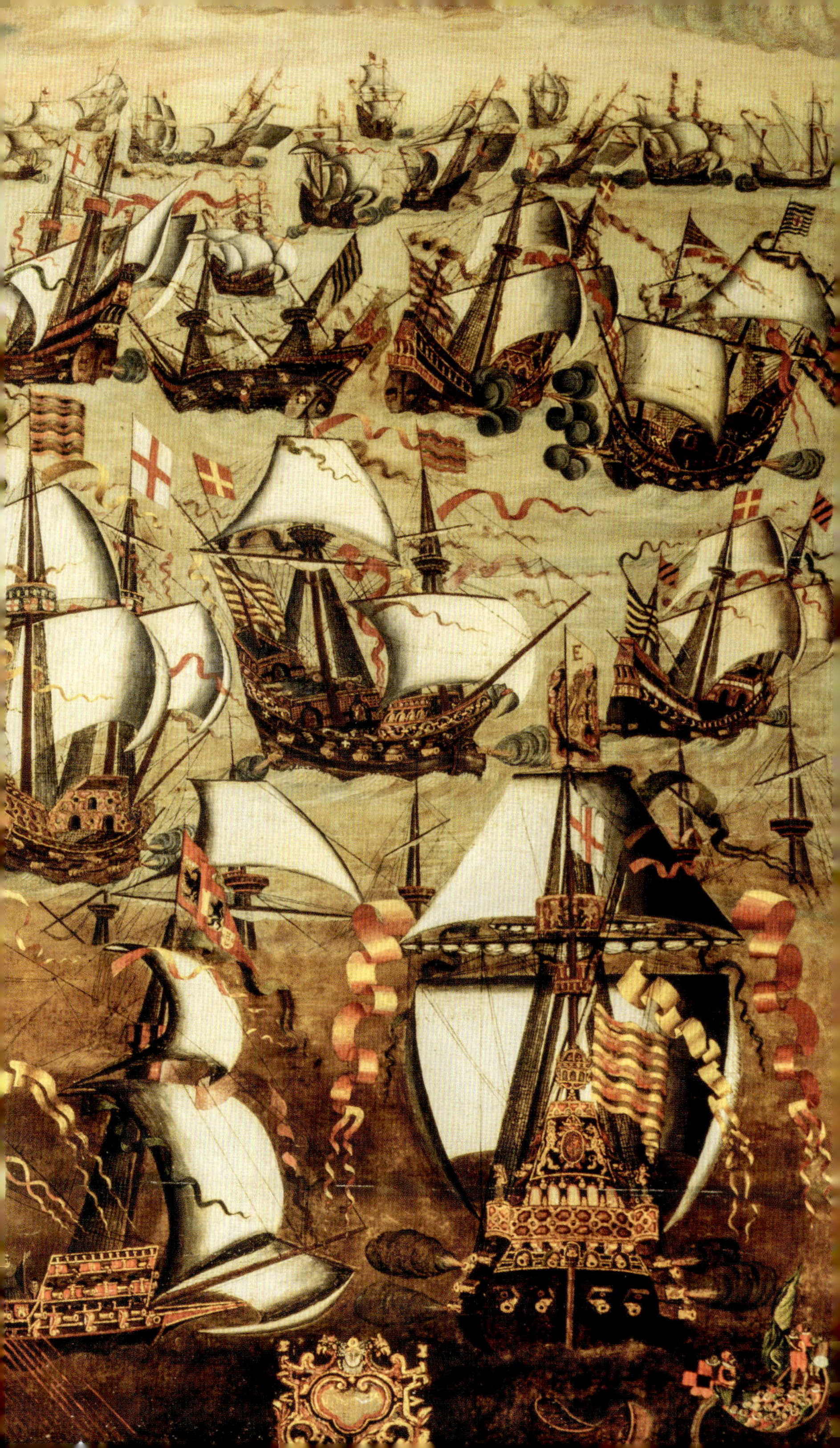

# Part II
# God's Obvious Design

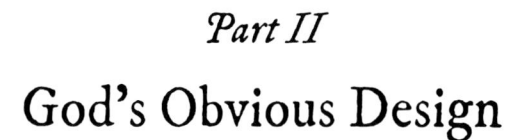

'I pray Your Majesty will hasten the Enterprise of England to the earliest possible date, for it would seem to be God's obvious design to bestow upon you the crowns of England and Scotland'

DON BERNARDINO DE MENDOZA TO PHILIP II,
28 FEBRUARY 1587[*]

# 4

# Armed Neutrality, 1558–80

## Philip, Elizabeth and Two Marys

For the first decade of her reign, which began in 1558, Queen Elizabeth made no change in traditional Tudor foreign policy. She remained a loyal friend of Spain and, like her predecessors, strove to destabilize the governments of France and Scotland. Initially, she had little choice because as Spain's ally she inherited a war with both France and Scotland: her elder half-sister Mary had married Philip of Spain, and at his request she declared war on France and its Scottish ally in 1557. Her decision soon yielded bitter fruits. In January 1558 the French captured Calais, England's only continental possession; and three months later the Dauphin Francis, heir to the French throne, married Mary Stuart, Queen of Scots. When Mary Tudor died the following November the young couple refused to recognize Elizabeth's title, and the ushers who preceded Mary Stuart on her way to the chapel royal shouted 'Make way for the queen of England'. After Francis became king in July 1559 he and his wife styled themselves in official documents 'Francis and Mary, by the grace of God rulers of France, Scotland, England and Ireland'; and, according to Elizabeth's appalled ambassador in France, the couple had the heraldic arms of England, Scotland and Ireland emblazoned on their great seal, furniture and dinner service (Figure 36).

36. The seal of Francis and Mary Stuart, claiming to be sovereigns of France, Scotland, England and Ireland.

As John Guy observed, 'This was highly provocative, tantamount to establishing a rival monarchy in exile. It was to taint the relationship of Mary and Elizabeth for the rest of their lives.' When in December 1559 Elizabeth sent Sir William Winter with a fleet to prevent French assistance from reaching Scotland, she instructed him to avoid 'any open declaration of war', with one exception. If he encountered French ships 'carrying the arms of England, to the dishonour of his sovereign and his country', then Winter might 'do that enterprise he shall see most hurtful to the French'. Otherwise he must preserve the fiction that he was acting 'upon his own head, and of himself as though he had no commission therefore of the Queen's Majesty' (a fiction the queen would use repeatedly when sending her warships to attack Spanish assets).[1] The following year Elizabeth's principal minister, William Cecil, submitted a memorandum warning her that the queen of Scots and her husband Francis 'be in their hearts mortal enemies to your Majesty's person'; that their 'malice is bent against Your Majesty's person; and that they will never cease'. He predicted that 'as long as Your Majesty and the Scottish queen live', she 'would not permit Your Majesty to live in an assured peace'. Some years later a colleague reminded Cecil of something 'your lordship did will me to hold [as] a principle: that popery and treason went always together. I trust also your Lordship will have it in mind.' He need not have worried: that 'principle' would underlie all Cecil's policies, domestic and foreign, until he died in 1598.[2]

Initially, Elizabeth adopted a slightly less draconian position, but she still refused Mary's request for recognition as her lawful successor. 'I know the inconstancy of the people of England, how they ever mislike the present government, and have their eyes fixed upon that person that is next to succeed,' she told a Scottish diplomat; adding that 'if it were certainly known in the world who would succeed me, I would never think myself in sufficient surety'.[3]

To understand such passionate views it is necessary to consider earlier developments. The story – and indeed the story of the Armada – began in the 1530s with the decision of Henry VIII of England to divorce his wife Catherine of Aragon in order to marry one of his Court ladies, Anne Boleyn. It was easier said than done: the divorce led to a breach with the papacy culminating in the separation of the Church in England from the Church of Rome, with Henry proclaiming himself England's 'Supreme Head'. These events had international significance, both because Catherine was the aunt of Charles V, ruler of Spain and the Netherlands and Holy Roman Emperor, and because the breach with Rome opened England to the influence of the continental Reformers who had already repudiated papal authority.

Foreign Catholic rulers soon struck back. They refused to acknowledge the validity of Henry's marriage to Anne Boleyn, and regarded the couple's only surviving child, Elizabeth, as a bastard. They also rejected the king's claim to be Supreme Head of the Church of England, and planned his deposition. In 1542 James V of Scotland launched an invasion of northern England, and three years later the French sent an expeditionary force which entered the Solent and landed on the Isle of Wight. Henry easily overcame both challenges. In the south Henry himself watched his fleet engage a French invasion force in the Solent. In the north his army routed the Scots invaders at Solway Moss and James V, already ill, died on hearing the news. His week-old daughter, Mary Stuart, succeeded him.

Henry died in 1547 and the crowns of England and Ireland passed to his only legitimate son, the nine-year-old Edward VI, whose regents introduced a full Protestant Church Order at home and continued the war against France and Scotland abroad. But Edward, a sickly youth, died six years later, and in spite of attempts by his regents to secure a Protestant succession, his crowns passed in 1553 to Mary Tudor, daughter of Henry and Catherine of Aragon. Mary had always remained a devout Catholic, despite prolonged harassment, and as queen she resolved to enforce her faith upon her new subjects. Within a month of her accession she also opened negotiations with her cousin Charles V about marrying his son and heir, Philip (Figure 37). The wedding took place in July 1554, and a formal reconciliation of England with the Church of Rome followed in November. Three months later officials started to burn English Protestants at the stake. More than 450 men and women perished over the next four years, and hundreds more fled to Europe to avoid 'the most intense religious persecution of its kind anywhere in sixteenth-century Europe'.[4]

37. A silver coin of Philip and Mary, claiming to be sovereigns of England, Naples, Spain – and France.

In January 1554 rumours about Mary's Spanish Match provoked 'the most dangerous rebellion that any Tudor ever faced'. Although the government thwarted some of the uprisings planned by the rebels, most of them Protestants and military veterans (which helps to explain their early success), Sir Thomas Wyatt marched on London at the head of 3,000 men from Kent. They crossed the River Thames at Kingston, where Mary's supporters had failed to destroy the bridge completely, and advanced on the capital. Wyatt repulsed an attack by loyal troops near Charing Cross and advanced down Fleet Street until he reached 'Ludgate, without resistance, his men going not in any good order or array'. Only Wyatt's decision to abandon his siege-guns in the interests of speed saved London, which was defended by thin medieval walls that could not have withstood an artillery bombardment.[5]

Mary later approved the execution of scores of rebels, including Wyatt, and the imprisonment of hundreds more. These included her half-sister Elizabeth (mentioned in documents exchanged between the conspirators) and several men who would later serve her, including James Croft and William Winter.

Although still in Spain, Philip knew about the rebellion because his library contained a copy of 'The diary of Thomas Wyatt's rebellion'; but early in 1555, as a gesture of goodwill, he persuaded Mary to pardon almost all the prisoners, including Princess Elizabeth, Croft, Winter and Robert Dudley (imprisoned for opposing Mary's accession). Nevertheless, a few weeks later, another group of conspirators planned to 'slay the queen and after that the king' as they watched a tournament, but 'there was such fear in their stomachs when they should have done it that they made scruple who should begin'. Once again the king found out about it: a year later a participant in yet another conspiracy against Philip and Mary revealed details to government interrogators.[6]

Despite the lavish distribution of pensions paid from his Spanish revenues, Philip remained unpopular in England, in part because the trial and execution of so many Protestants caused widespread disquiet and unrest, in part because the alliance between Philip and Mary led directly to the loss of Calais and all the English property within the port city. In addition, despite some false hopes, the queen failed to conceive an heir and Philip abandoned England in August 1555, returning in March 1557 but leaving again the following July. Although Mary's supporters blamed his absences for her apparent infertility, the true culprit was probably the cancer that killed her in November 1558.

Once again religion complicated the succession. Although Princess Elizabeth had felt it politic to attend Mass after 1555, she clearly had Protestant sympathies. To Catholics she was also the daughter of the adulterous liaison between Henry VIII and Anne Boleyn, and therefore disqualified from the royal succession. Mary Tudor had always regarded her as illegitimate. So too did Mary Stuart, queen of France and Scotland, the legitimate Catholic granddaughter of Henry VIII's sister, who consequently considered herself the rightful queen of England. Many Catholics agreed with her, but Philip was not one of them.

On hearing of his wife's death he gave orders that henceforth 'England, France and Ireland must be omitted' from his seals and style; and although several Catholics sought his approval for plots to overthrow Elizabeth Tudor in favour of Mary Stuart, he rejected them all. Instead, he welcomed the letters written by Elizabeth a few days after her accession assuring him of 'our zeal and affection to continue the old and perfect amity that from time to time hath been so friendly maintained' between their predecessors. She signed herself 'your sister and perpetual ally'. Philip reciprocated with letters addressed 'To the most serene princess Elizabeth, queen of England, France and Ireland, Defender of the Faith, our very dear sister and cousin'.[7]

With great reluctance Philip even offered to marry her. In January 1559, 'feeling like a condemned man wondering what is to become of him', he wrote a secret holograph letter authorizing his ambassador in London, the count of Feria, to offer his hand to Elizabeth – but only 'to serve God and to see if this might prevent that lady from making the changes in religion that she has in mind' (and only if the terms were better than those imposed on him when he married Mary Tudor). 'If it were not to serve God, I would never do this,' he confided to Feria. 'Nothing could or would make me do this except the clear knowledge that it might gain the kingdom [of England] for His service and faith.' After a few weeks Elizabeth Tudor rejected her graceless suitor, and soon afterwards began to implement the 'changes in religion' that would make England Protestant again.[8]

Just as Philip failed to prevent his 'very dear sister and cousin' from re-introducing Protestantism to England and Ireland in 1559, the following year he also failed to prevent her from invading Scotland to help Mary Stuart's Protestant opponents to victory. In a sense he had no choice. Although he made an advantageous peace with the French in April 1559, he rashly rejected an agreement with the Ottoman Turks, and so their fleets continued to threaten Spain and Spanish Italy. Four months later the situation seemed so bad that, despite his growing anxiety about developments in England and Scotland, he left the Netherlands and returned to Spain to concentrate on the defence of the Mediterranean.

Philip thus relegated the affairs of north-west Europe to the back-burner, so to speak – but with serious misgivings. As he prepared to depart for Spain he gave vent to his frustration at leaving England in Protestant hands in another secret holograph dispatch to Feria, still in London:

> This is certainly the most difficult decision I have ever faced in my whole life ... and it grieves me to see what is happening over there [England] and to be unable to take the steps to stop it that I want, while the steps I can take seem far milder than such a great evil deserves ... Nevertheless, at the moment I lack the resources to do anything.

Later in his rambling letter Philip returned to the point in a more forceful and calculating way. 'The evil that is taking place in that kingdom has caused me the anger and confusion I have mentioned,' he stated, 'but I believe we must try to remedy it without involving me or any of my vassals in a declaration of war until we have enjoyed the benefits of peace [for a while].' He added, 'My only aim is to get it right [*acertar* – one of the king's favourite words]', before lapsing into self-pity: 'May God grant that things turn out the way I want, but I am so unlucky that when I want something this much, it often turns out badly.'[9]

Philip recognized that, for the time being, although overthrowing Elizabeth might produce a religious triumph by restoring Catholicism to England and Ireland, it was likely to prove a political disaster by delivering both kingdoms to the French. When, early in 1560, she sent an envoy to ask Philip for assistance should the French invade her realm in the name of Francis and Mary Stuart, Philip ordered his regent in the Netherlands to prepare troops to help Elizabeth in case of need, 'given her importance to us, and the danger that would follow to our dominions if she and her kingdom were lost'.[10]

Mary Stuart returned to Scotland in 1561, after the death of her husband King Francis, but this made her even less attractive as an ally of Spain. On the one hand she chose mostly Protestants as her ministers and granted official recognition to the Reformed religion. On the other hand Mary remained a French princess: she wrote almost all her letters in French and in her will of 1566 ten of the first twelve beneficiaries were her French relatives. Philip still saw no advantage in toppling the unreliable but isolated Tudor queen simply to turn England into a French satellite under Mary Stuart. Instead, he continued to dream of winning Elizabeth back to the Catholic faith by peaceful means. In February 1568 he asked his ambassador in London, Guzmán de Silva, if 'you think one might hope that one day the queen might come to her senses and recognize her error' (that is: renounce Catholicism). He also asked if 'there are any persons about her or in her council who could lead her to do this?' He continued: 'If I could do anything useful to this end, I would do so with all my heart.'[11]

## Philip versus Elizabeth

The following month it seemed as though Philip might have changed his mind, because he refused to grant further audiences to Elizabeth's resident ambassador in Madrid, Dr John Man, on the grounds that he was a married Protestant cleric who had insulted the pope in public (calling him 'a tiresome little monk'). The king virtuously informed the pope that Dr Man's continued presence on Spanish soil might cause offence to God, 'whose service, and the observation of whose holy faith, I place far ahead of my own affairs and actions and above everything in this life, even my own'. He asked Elizabeth to recall her ambassador but stressed that nothing should 'disturb the warm friendship I feel for her, and expect will last for ever'. As a token of goodwill Philip ordered his officials to seize all copies of *A Pontifical and Catholic History*, recently published in Castile by Gonzalo de Illescas, because Elizabeth objected to some unflattering comments about her and both her parents. The king then had a second edition printed, purged of all passages 'that impugned the titles and esteem of the queen's person'.[12]

In June 1568 Philip decided to replace his ambassador in London, the experienced and urbane Guzmán de Silva, with Don Guerau de Spes, a Catalan gentleman with little or no diplomatic background. The king's instructions stressed the need to 'negotiate with grace and cheerfulness' to preserve the 'amity and alliance' that had long bound England to 'both the kingdom of Spain and the House of Burgundy'. He revealed that Guzmán had conveyed his sympathy to Mary Stuart 'on her misfortune, because she is a Catholic and also my sister-in-law' (Philip's wife was the sister of Mary's first husband). Spes should discuss with Guzmán whether to maintain contact, and if he approved 'you may send her the letter from me that I will give you' – but 'without entering into any specifics that might oblige me to do anything'. The fiery and inexperienced Spes had no intention of heeding these directions. Instead, he worked indefatigably to win Mary's confidence and to put her in touch with dissident English Catholics, whose desire to overthrow Elizabeth he also encouraged. With equal energy he strove to exaggerate and exploit any English slight or action that seemed to prejudice Spanish interests. In retrospect, it seemed to at least one diplomat that amicable relations with Elizabeth could have continued if only Guzmán had remained at his post.[13]

Spes first turned Philip and Elizabeth into enemies because of Spain's claim to a monopoly of all trade with, and all colonization of, the American continent. The claim arose from a papal decree that divided between the crowns of Castile and Portugal all lands discovered (and yet to be discovered) beyond Europe. This monopoly, enshrined in the treaty of Tordesillas signed by representatives from both kingdoms in 1494, remained largely intact at the time of Philip's accession, but in 1562 John Hawkins, a Plymouth merchant and shipowner who had traded with the Canary Islands (a Spanish possession off the Atlantic coast of Africa, and the staging-post for all ships sailing from Spain to America), decided to undertake a venture to take cloth and African slaves to the Caribbean, whence he would return to England with a cargo of hides and sugar. Although he made no application to the Spanish Crown for a licence, Hawkins was careful to pay all the taxes due to Spain and to behave throughout (as he saw it) entirely within the law.

The voyage made a profit, and Hawkins repeated it on a larger scale in 1564. This time the queen invested in the venture, contributing the 600-ton *Jesus of Lübeck*, an old warship from Henry VIII's navy withdrawn as unfit for front-line service. The enterprise proved as profitable as its predecessor, but the Spanish colonists were now less welcoming because royal officials, anxious to exclude all interlopers, had expressly forbidden trade with foreigners. Hawkins therefore felt obliged to underpin his trade with the threat of force, though the threat was (he asserted) simply a charade which allowed the colonists to claim, if challenged, that they had dealt with him only under duress.

Soon afterwards a chilling example of Spain's resolve to keep all 'interlopers' out of the Americas occurred. When news reached Philip that a party of 1,000 French Protestants (commonly known as 'Huguenots') had established a colony in Florida, he licensed a consortium of seafarers from northern Spain to destroy them, led by Pedro Menéndez de Avilés and including his relatives Don Pedro de Valdés and Diego Flores de Valdés. The Spanish task force swiftly outmanoeuvred the French until in October 1565 they offered to surrender on terms; but Menéndez reminded them that 'I was their enemy and waged war against them with fire and blood, for that they were Lutherans'. He therefore demanded their unconditional surrender, and when they accepted, Menéndez spared just a few and 'all the others I caused to be put to the knife'. When Diego Flores brought the king news of these events, Philip enthusiastically endorsed the executions and condemned the survivors to a lifetime of servitude rowing his galleys. He also knighted Flores and granted him a handsome cash reward.[14]

News of these events spread swiftly throughout the Protestant world, yet Hawkins undertook a third transatlantic voyage in 1567 with eight vessels: two of them warships from the navy royal (*Jesus of Lübeck* and *Minion*) and the others English traders, including *Judith*, a small vessel captained by Hawkins's young kinsman Francis Drake. At first things went well, and Spanish colonists around the Caribbean purchased the slaves whom Hawkins brought from Africa. Then, as his fleet began its homeward passage in September 1568, a sudden storm off the Florida coast seriously damaged it. Seeking shelter, the battered ships limped into the small harbour of San Juan de Ulúa on an island just off the coast of Mexico.

This led to a seminal incident in the evolution of English naval artillery tactics. The seaward side of San Juan de Ulúa had an artillery emplacement at either end of a long sea wall with a series of mooring rings which allowed ships to secure their bows to the quay and run out an anchor astern. The sole function of this haven was to shelter fleets carrying merchandise between Europe and America. At other times it was virtually deserted, as on this occasion, and Hawkins encountered no resistance. After his customary courtesies to the small garrison he set about repairing his ships and refreshing his men. Trading deals were done, hostages were exchanged, guns were positioned on shore in case of attack, and everyone observed a mutually beneficial status quo.

But as fate would have it, a fleet of galleons arrived from Spain bearing Don Martín Enríquez, the newly appointed viceroy of Mexico. Hawkins protested his friendly mercantile intentions and, backed up by physical possession of the harbour and its defences, obtained the viceroy's grudging permission to complete his repairs and depart. The Spaniards moored along the harbour frontage, tied to the quayside rings, and separated from the English by a beached storage hulk. *Jesus* and *Minion* were moored on one side of her; the Spanish flagship *San Pedro* and vice-flagship *Santa Clara* on the other (Figure 38). Thus the two fleets remained in a state of formal coldness for two days, during which Don Martín clandestinely moved men to positions from which they could overrun the guns on shore, and silently filled the hulk with soldiers. It would be, he thought, a classic boarding action with the added element of surprise. He had no qualms about breaking his word: in his view an agreement made with a pirate and heretic in a Spanish harbour had no validity.

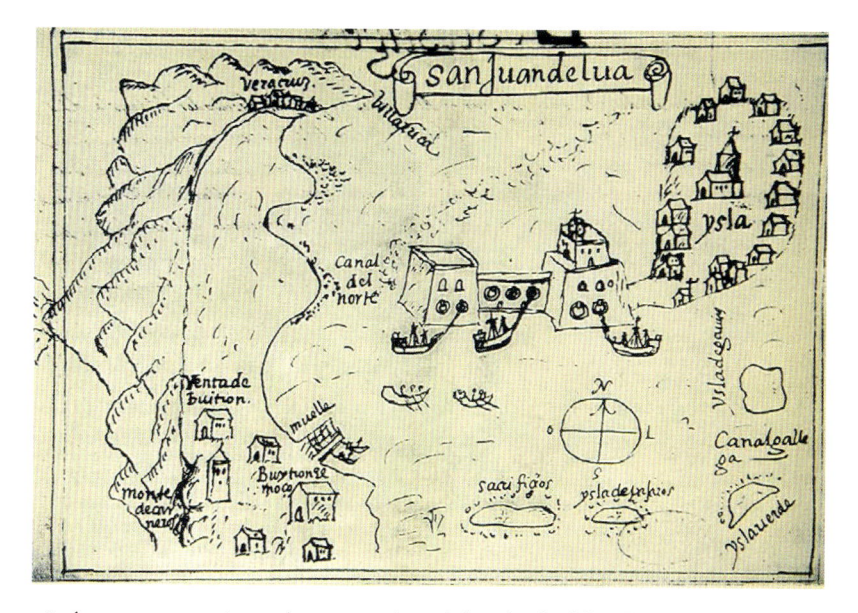

38. An anonymous sixteenth-century plan of the island of San Juan de Ulúa, just off Veracruz on the Caribbean coast of Mexico. The mooring wall used by Hawkins's ships and their Spanish adversaries in 1568 is at the centre.

When the viceroy judged the moment right he launched a surprise attack, but Hawkins had anticipated this eventuality. *Jesus* and *Minion* were moored fore and aft: both now cut their forward cables so they could haul themselves off by their seaward anchors, presenting their heavy bow artillery to the attacking Spaniards. The latter had planned a boarding assault, and when that proved impossible *San Pedro* and *Santa Clara* hauled themselves off by their own stern cables and the four warships slugged it out with their guns at 'about two ships' length' (in the confines of the harbour the other ships were powerless to act). Eventually, English guns manned by seamen prevailed over Spanish ones worked by soldiers. Within an hour Hawkins had blown up *Santa Clara*, shattered *San Pedro* and sunk another vessel. The enemy had been defeated at a distance, without boarding, by gunfire alone. This revolutionary tactic profoundly influenced Hawkins's views on warship design over the following two decades and determined how the Armada battles would be fought.

In the short term, however, it proved a pyrrhic victory. *Jesus of Lübeck* had to be abandoned along with three other ships and many men. Hawkins himself transferred to *Minion* and fought his way out of the harbour. Francis Drake's little *Judith* also escaped, though with an alacrity that later drew censure, and reached Plymouth in December. Hawkins arrived a month later, with only fifteen survivors. Scarcely a quarter of the 400 men who began the expedition ever returned to England. Elizabeth had thus lost to Spain one of her royal warships, with another damaged; many of her subjects had perished and others languished in captivity. The venture from which she had expected to receive a handsome profit yielded a serious loss.[15]

News of this signal defeat arrived at a delicate moment. The outbreak of a new civil war in France unleashed a wave of Protestant aggression against Catholic ships on the high seas. In November 1568 Huguenot privateers came upon five ships carrying over £80,000 in cash from Spain to the Netherlands. The French attacked and the treasure-ships ran for shelter in English ports. Don Guerau de Spes explained to Elizabeth that most of the money belonged to a consortium of Genoese bankers and formed part of a loan made to the duke of Alba: he asked her either to provide a naval escort direct to Antwerp or to transport it overland to Dover, ready to be shipped to the Netherlands. The queen agreed and, since the Huguenot pirates continued to threaten, most of the bullion came ashore; but at precisely this moment Elizabeth learned of the events at San Juan de Ulúa. She immediately ordered her officials to transfer the money to the Tower of London and placed the ships that brought it under temporary arrest.

The queen's intentions at this point remain unclear – she may have planned to use this windfall as a bargaining chip to secure compensation for Hawkins and freedom for his crew – but almost single-handedly Spes turned a diplomatic spat into a war. He asserted (wrongly) that Elizabeth had confiscated the treasure and urged Alba to embargo all English property in the Netherlands in retaliation, and asked the king to do the same in Spain. Both swiftly obliged, and naturally the queen reciprocated. She also placed Spes under house arrest and imprisoned some of the crews from the treasure-ships.

Direct intercourse between England and Spain now virtually ceased. Elizabeth had reluctantly recalled Dr Man but did not replace him, so she lacked a voice at Philip's Court to explain her intentions, and Spes remained in detention and almost incommunicado for six months – yet never had diplomacy been more necessary. In the Netherlands the defeat of an invasion led by the prince of Orange left Alba and his victorious troops free to meddle in the affairs of neighbouring states. In France religious wars prevented the beleaguered government from pursuing any coherent foreign policy. Above all, events in Scotland spiralled out of control. Encouraged by a letter of support from Pope Pius V, and confident that assistance from continental Catholic rulers would help enforce her claim to Elizabeth's throne, in February 1566 Mary Stuart declared publicly that 'there was no other queen of England but herself'. By then she had married Lord Henry Darnley, a relative whose claim to succeed Elizabeth on the English throne was second only to that of Mary, and in June she gave birth to a healthy son, the future James VI. This gave her a decided advantage over the unmarried and childless Elizabeth, but seven months later a group of nobles murdered Darnley and on 15 May 1567 she unwisely married one of the conspirators, the earl of Bothwell (and, equally unwisely, given her broader strategy, they married according to Protestant rites).

These dramatic events provoked a rebellion by her leading subjects, who imprisoned her, declared her deposed, and crowned her son James King of Scots in her place. Mary received little support from her subjects, whom she had failed to cultivate, and none from her French relatives, who were too absorbed in their religious wars to spare any help. When she escaped from her Scottish captors in May 1568, therefore, she rode into England and threw herself on the mercy of her only apparently friendly neighbour, Elizabeth. It proved to be a fatal error.

Because so many Catholics regarded Mary as the legitimate queen of England, Elizabeth could not afford to allow her cousin to take sanctuary with a sympathetic foreign ruler, nor yet to remain at large among the numerous and restless Catholic population of northern England. Irrespective of its morality or legality, Elizabeth (prodded by Cecil) concluded that her only option was to keep the queen of Scots closely confined – even though this left her cousin with only two choices: wait for Elizabeth to die or escape from prison with the help of sympathetic Catholics.

In November 1568 Mary wrote a letter reminding Philip II that he remained her brother-in-law, even though his wife Elizabeth de Valois, sister of Francis II, had died; and she stressed that 'I am an *obedient and devoted* daughter of the Holy Roman Catholic Church, in which I wish to live and die' (adding, untruthfully, 'I have never wavered in this'). Her appeal convinced Philip. He replied: 'I will treat her as a true sister, just as if we were children of the same mother, and as such I will help and assist her as much as lies in my power' (adding, significantly, 'provided she remains as devoted as she claims she wants to be to our Holy Roman Catholic Church').[16]

The king also informed his leading ministers that he would take advantage of 'the good opportunity which now presents itself to remedy religious affairs in that country [England] by deposing the present queen and giving the crown to the queen of Scotland, who would immediately be joined by all the Catholics'. He told Alba that 'it appears to me that, after my special obligation to maintain my own states in our holy faith, I am bound to make every effort in order to restore and preserve it in England as in former times'. The arrival of some news shortly afterwards, that Elizabeth had sent assistance to a new Huguenot rebellion, encouraged the king in such thoughts, 'because if she means to break simultaneously with me and with France ... clearly God must be allowing it on account of her sins and unfaithfulness, so that she will be lost'.[17]

Pope Pius V agreed and urged Philip to invade England and depose Elizabeth in Mary's favour. When the king ignored his overtures Pius, without Philip's knowledge, in 1569 presented Alba with a golden sword, the symbol of a warrior of the faith, and sent a letter exhorting him to invade England. Before the end of the year some Catholic nobles in the north of England led out their followers in an attempt to depose Elizabeth and restore the 'old religion' to the kingdom. One group of rebels captured the port of Hartlepool, 150 miles from Tutbury Castle where Mary languished, and started to fortify it, 'expecting aid from King Philip', while others marched south towards Tutbury, covering 80 miles in five days. Mary's custodian lamented that 'this castle is very weak and not able to resist' and 'we have a marvellous lack of armour, but especially of weapons'. Elizabeth was lucky that the rebel leaders lost their nerve and pulled their forces back to Scotland, allowing her to hunt down and execute those who remained in England.[18]

Then in February 1570 the pope issued a Bull which declared Elizabeth a heretic, absolved her subjects from their obedience, and excommunicated all who henceforth obeyed her. He sent copies to Alba (again without informing Philip) together with orders to ensure the Bull's diffusion in England and to take steps to depose her.

At first Philip was furious. Did Pius not appreciate that 'my knowledge of English affairs is such that I believe I could have given a better opinion upon them and the course that ought to have been adopted under the circumstances than anyone else'?[19] This was merely bluster. In fact, Philip did not know what to do next and he set out his dilemma in a tortuous twenty-two-page letter to Alba. Elizabeth had confiscated not only the treasure shipment from his bankers but also the goods of his subjects in England (worth almost £250,000). She had also welcomed his rebels (perhaps 30,000 Dutch exiles, mostly Protestants, resided in England); she had sponsored and strengthened Hawkins's trading voyage to the Caribbean; and she had licensed attacks on any ships sailing through the Channel under Spanish colours. 'In contrast,' Philip continued, 'the damage that she, her kingdom and her subjects have received from us is so little . . . that one could justly say that she has declared war on us, but we are at peace with her.' This unequal situation, the king insisted, could not continue: he must find a way of harming Elizabeth, and thereby bring her back to a state of peaceful co-existence.

His letter also contained a 'messianic' element. Philip reiterated his belief that God's service 'required' him to intervene in order to liberate the queen of Scots and restore Catholicism in England – especially since 'God has already granted that by my intervention and my hand the kingdom has previously been restored to the Catholic Church once.' Therefore, perhaps for the first but certainly not for the last time, he threw caution to the winds. He informed Alba that:

> Even though human prudence suggests many inconveniences and difficulties, and places before us worldly fears, the Christian certitude and the confidence that (with justice) we must have in God's cause will remove them, and inspire and strengthen us to overcome them. Certainly we could not avoid remaining with great guilt in our soul, and great regret, if because I failed that queen [Mary] and those Catholics – or, rather, the faith – they suffered and she was lost.

The king briefly reviewed possible strategies for achieving these ends: a surprise amphibious attack by his forces; a joint invasion with the French; or an assault on Ireland (representatives of the Irish Catholics had recently arrived in Spain to secure his support for their cause). He asked Alba to evaluate these plans, and meanwhile ordered him secretly to provide both the English Catholics and Mary Stuart with money, arms and munitions, and to send military advisers to help train her supporters. To facilitate all this, Philip enclosed a letter of credit for £75,000.[20]

Alba remained impervious to both the spiritual blackmail and the strategic musings of his master. He too had spent time in England and had noted the complexity of Tudor society and the strength of Protestant feeling, leading him to conclude that no firm alliance could be maintained with such an unstable country. The best policy was therefore to placate Elizabeth so that she would remain neutral. He now composed a detailed rebuttal of armed intervention.

'Even though the principal means must come from God, as Your Majesty very virtuously and piously suggests,' the duke began with heavy sarcasm (probably lost on his master), 'nevertheless since He normally works through the resources He gives to humans, it seems necessary to examine what human resources would be needed to carry out your wishes.' Alba ruled out an immediate invasion, with or without the French, because of the cost and Spain's strategic commitments elsewhere. He also pointed out that, although the English Catholics begged for assistance, they had made it very clear they did not want deliverance to come by means of a foreign army. The duke felt more positive about sending financial support to Elizabeth's disaffected subjects in Ireland, but since Ireland lay closer to Spain than to the Netherlands the operation was something 'that Your Majesty will be better able to arrange than me'.[21]

The northern rebellion and rumours of Spanish involvement led Elizabeth to make a major effort to mend her fences with Philip. On hearing that his new bride-to-be, Anna of Austria, would sail to Spain from the Netherlands, she appointed Howard of Effingham to command a fleet with orders to greet Anna in England's name and to offer her all support in her voyage. Howard must 'further say that although there hath, of late time, happened some show of unkindnesses' between her and Philip, 'which we impute to the mishap of evil-conditioned ministers, yet we cannot suffer any occasion to pass over wherein we may show any kindness' to Anna. Howard must also explain that by 'evil-conditioned ministers' she meant Spes, who had caused the rift through his 'words and unseemly speeches'.[22]

Philip chose to reject this olive branch. Instead, he took two important steps that perpetuated hostilities with Elizabeth. He welcomed to his Court Thomas Stukeley, an Irish adventurer who planned to lead an invasion to drive the English from his homeland. He also approved a suggestion from Spes (still in England, though closely watched by the queen's agents) that he should maintain contact both with discontented English Catholics and with Mary by means of a Florentine banker in London, Roberto Ridolfi, who enjoyed the pope's confidence and handled the funds secretly sent from Rome to England.

Philip's open support of Stukeley soon produced excellent results. Early in 1571 Elizabeth sent a special envoy to Spain, begging the king not to support her

Irish rebels, asking if she might send a new ambassador to negotiate a settlement of all outstanding issues; but instead of sacrificing Stukeley the king endorsed an ambitious plan devised by Don Guerau Spes and Roberto Ridolfi, entitled 'the Enterprise of England'.[23]

## The Ridolfi Plot

The full story of the Ridolfi Plot will probably never be known because too many important documents have been lost and much of the surviving information was extracted under torture (or the threat of it); but its broad lines are clear. It required a group of English Catholics to capture or kill Elizabeth, and free Mary Queen of Scots from her prison (not an impossible feat: she had escaped from custody before). They would then take her to the coast where a fleet manned by sympathetic Englishmen and commanded by John Hawkins (whom the Spaniards had attacked and almost killed at San Juan de Ulúa scarcely two years before) would 'convey' her to Spain. There she might marry Philip's half-brother, Don John of Austria, while her young son James would be betrothed to Philip's daughter Isabella. Elizabeth later claimed she could have tolerated all this ('Her Majesty thinks it no just cause to be offended with those devises tending to her [Mary's] liberty', according to Lord Burghley); what appalled her was clear evidence that Mary had connived in a plot to dethrone and perhaps murder her.[24]

Ridolfi left England in March 1571 armed with instructions, commissions and letters from his numerous contacts, all using the same unique cipher that he had supplied. With suspicious ease the queen's counter-espionage experts broke the cipher, allowing them to read all the correspondence concerning the Enterprise of England.[25]

After visiting Alba in Brussels and the pope in Rome, Ridolfi arrived in Madrid in June and met the king, Feria and various other senior ministers. Philip's reaction to this initial iteration of the Enterprise of England is worth detailed examination because the same cognitive dissonance would characterize his behaviour towards Elizabeth in 1587 and 1588. He also displayed the same desire to micromanage, refusing to recognize that the Ridolfi Plot was logistically impractical if not impossible. The activities of the French Protestants by land and sea compelled Don Francés de Álava (the Spanish ambassador in Paris) to entrust crucial dispatches about English and Scottish affairs – those from Alba and Spes as well as his own – to couriers in disguise who travelled on foot. Some letters took two months to arrive. Yet although the command system of the Spanish monarchy had slowed to a walk, it did not diminish the desire of the king and his ministers to control matters. 'For the love of God, send us hourly bulletins about what is happening,' the secretary of state berated Álava, because 'if you knew how much the king wants to know what is happening over there and in the Netherlands right now, you would write to him by airmail [*escriviría por el ayre*]'.[26]

The Ridolfi Plot also revealed how the prospect of restoring Catholicism to England led Philip to abandon his normal prudence. When the papal nuncio had an audience with the king soon after he had met Ridolfi, and urged him to support the Enterprise, 'His Majesty, contrary to his normal custom [at audiences], spoke at length and entered into great detail about the means, the place and the men' that he would devote to it. 'He ended by saying that he had wanted and waited for a long time for an occasion and opportunity to reduce, with God's help, England to the [Catholic] faith and the obedience of the Apostolic See a second time, and that he believed the time had now come.' The nuncio also reported that 'every day, at all hours, His Majesty asks Ridolfi for various pieces of information, to which he provides excellent answers. So that we have high hopes.'[27]

Philip's tenacity surprised even ministers who had worked with him for decades. 'I have never seen, nor would you believe, the zeal of His Majesty in this business,' one of them wrote to a colleague. 'It is extraordinary to see the ardour of His Majesty for the Enterprise of England,' he wrote to another – adding his surprise at 'how little it has been cooled by the news that the queen knows about Ridolfi's plans, and by the mistrust of the duke [of Alba]'.[28]

Philip's councillors interviewed Ridolfi on 7 July 1571 and afterwards cited God's will, the pope's blessing, the plight of England's Catholics and other 'inescapable' religious pressures to justify their unanimous endorsement of the plan either to capture or to kill Elizabeth in the autumn, while she was on her annual progress through the counties around London. This, they confidently predicted, would unleash a general rising of English Catholics led by the duke of Norfolk, which would in turn serve as a signal for Alba to send a fleet, reinforced by a flotilla already standing by at Santander in northern Spain, to escort 6,000 veterans from the Army of Flanders across to England to assist the rebels.[29]

One week later, after a further meeting with Ridolfi, Philip signed another letter to Alba affirming that Mary Stuart was 'the true and legitimate claimant' to the English throne, 'occupied by Elizabeth [*la Isabel*] through tyranny', and asserted that the duke of Norfolk:

> has the resolve, and so many and such prominent friends, that if I provide some help it would be easy for him to kill or capture Elizabeth [*le sería fácil*

*matar o prender a la Isabel*] and place the Scottish queen at liberty and in possession of the throne. Then, if she marries the duke of Norfolk, as they have arranged, they will without difficulty reduce [England] to the obedience of the Holy See, restore the Catholic faith, and renew to my entire satisfaction the ancient treaties of friendship that I and my predecessors have maintained with that Crown.

Philip promised to send Alba 'detailed instructions' soon – 'right now I only want to share my plan with you' – but he revealed that the conspirators had asked (via Ridolfi) for 6,000 infantry for England, 2,000 for Scotland and 2,000 more for Ireland, plus a reserve of 4,000 arquebuses, 2,000 suits of armour and twenty-five field guns. The duke must have these forces, and a fleet to transport them, ready within six weeks; and Philip promised to send £50,000 immediately for the venture ('I charge you expressly not to spend a single penny of this sum on anything else, however urgent it may be'). He concluded by assuring Alba that 'since the cause is so much His, God will enlighten, aid and assist us with His mighty hand and arm, so that we will get things right'.[30]

When Philip eventually sent Alba the 'detailed instructions' he had promised, he began by acknowledging that 'we must not undertake or start this venture, either by war or plot; rather it must be started' by Norfolk and his associates. He also expressed some doubts about Ridolfi's credibility but planned to operate on the assumption that the plot would unfold as planned: Alba must therefore be ready to intervene as soon as Norfolk had proclaimed Mary Stuart queen of England. Realizing that Alba would probably dismiss or disregard his orders as totally unrealistic, Philip administered another dose of messianic blackmail. 'No one can deny that this venture involves many and great difficulties, and that if it goes wrong we will incur considerable inconveniences (as you have prudently pointed out),' he conceded. Nevertheless:

> I desire to achieve this enterprise so much and I have such complete confidence that God our Lord, to whose service it is dedicated, will guide and direct it (because I have no personal ambition here), and I hold my charge from God to do this to be so explicit, that I am totally determined and resolved to proceed and participate, doing on my side everything possible in this world to promote and assist it.[31]

Before Alba's predictable protests reached him, the king made three important changes to the plan. First, he approved a bargain with an agent of John Hawkins, who was anxious to secure the liberty of the men captured in the Caribbean three years earlier. Instead of 'conveying' Mary Stuart to Spain, Hawkins now promised to lead a squadron of sixteen ships, then at Plymouth, to the Netherlands in September and help ferry Alba's troops to England. Afterwards, his ships would capture the Tower of London and then sail into the Medway and set fire to the royal warships anchored there. In anticipation, Philip released all of Hawkins's surviving crew captured in Mexico and imprisoned in Spain. Second, the king ordered Alba to increase the invasion force to 10,000 and designated Harwich in Essex as the landing-zone. Third, he authorized Alba to send money to Scotland to help Mary's supporters there to create a diversion – although he forbade the duke to send them any troops 'in order to avoid open war with the queen of England'.[32]

These changes made the plan dangerously complicated, yet the entire initiative remained in the hands of Norfolk and a bunch of unidentified henchmen. Until the latter captured or killed Elizabeth, and Norfolk brought his supporters out, the squadrons scattered between Plymouth, Santander and the Netherlands could not join forces, let alone start embarking Alba's troops. Furthermore, apart from the documents circulated by Ridolfi, no reliable evidence existed either that Norfolk (a Protestant) wished to lead a rising against Elizabeth or that any significant body of English Catholics would follow him if he did so.

Alba lost no time in drawing these fatal flaws to his master's attention:

> Your Majesty's letter has placed me in the greatest confusion, because at the beginning Your Majesty says that it is not your intention to take a course of action that would lead to the outbreak of war with our neighbours, yet you later tell me that you wish to help the duke of Norfolk ... Done in the way you describe, this would constitute a clear and direct declaration of war.

The duke then railed against the king's reliance on Spes, who 'lacks the experience of public affairs to deal with something as important as this', and on Ridolfi, 'who is not a soldier, and has not seen a military operation in his life':

> [They] think that one can conjure up armies out of thin air or pull them out of one's sleeve, and achieve with them whatever occurs in their imagination. To claim that at the same time one can create one army to capture the queen of England, and another to free the queen of Scotland, and that at the same time one can capture the Tower of London and set fire to the galleons in the river [Medway] – well, even if Your Majesty and the queen

of England agreed to cooperate to make it happen, it would not suffice to make it happen at the time they [Ridolfi and Spes] propose.

Therefore, the duke concluded bluntly, 'I have not even begun to make any preparations'.[33]

Philip's reaction to this devastating response was entirely predictable. On 14 September, dismissing all of Alba's practical objections, he repeated that:

> I am so keen to achieve the consummation of this enterprise, I am so attached to it in my heart, and I am so convinced that God our Saviour must embrace it as His own cause, that I cannot be dissuaded, nor can I accept or believe the contrary. This leads me to understand matters differently [from you] and makes me play down the difficulties and problems that spring up; so that all the things that could either divert or stop me from carrying through this business seem less threatening to me.

He reminded Alba that, if Spain did not act, Elizabeth would surely turn on her Catholic subjects and either kill or expel those who refused to convert, and then asked rhetorically: 'How many greater, more dangerous and more difficult obligations will that create for us? How shall we explain ourselves to God? What shame shall we feel if things come to that pass?'[34]

He need not have worried. Nine days earlier, on 5 September, acting on information about the plot supplied by Hawkins, Burghley sent a letter to Mary's custodian, 'haste, post haste – haste, haste – for life, life, life' (no other Elizabethan document would have such high priority). Mary must be informed immediately 'that it is now fully discovered to Her Majesty [Elizabeth] what practices that queen [Mary] has had in hand' with Norfolk, Spes, Ridolfi and others. Her gaoler must therefore 'tempt her patience in this sort to provoke her to answer' concerning 'her labours and devices to stir up a new rebellion in this realm [of England] and to have the king of Spain to assist it'. Mary must also be 'kept very strictly from all conference' (that is, deprived of all contact with the outside world).[35]

Mary vigorously maintained her innocence, but faced with the full apparatus of interrogation (both legal and physical) the conspirators in captivity soon provided most of the missing details. The bishop of Ross, Mary's senior diplomat, proved particularly eloquent. He asserted that the queen had first 'poisoned her husband, the French king'; then 'consented to the murder of her late husband, Lord Darnley'; and, the bishop predicted, Norfolk would have fared no better if they had married ('the duke should not have had the best days with her'). In short, she 'is not fit for any husband'. 'Lord!' exclaimed his interrogator, 'What a people are these, what a queen, and what an ambassador!' Elizabeth had Norfolk arrested, imprisoned in the Tower of London, tried and executed for treason; but she punished few others because (as Alba had always averred) there was virtually no evidence that the Catholics of southern England wished to change their allegiance.[36]

Why did Philip II, normally so rational and prudent, pursue for so long this over-ambitious, costly and misguided initiative in 1571, just as he would do again in 1587–8? To a degree the international situation justified his apparently irrational insistence on pressing ahead with the venture despite all obstacles. Alba had driven his opponents from the Netherlands, from which the invasion force would sail; France remained severely weakened by its religious wars; the Ottoman fleet had suffered a resounding defeat by the combined forces of Spain, Venice and the papacy at the battle of Lepanto in October. The king was right to fear that these advantages would not last. In 1572 the outbreak of a new Dutch Revolt and a powerful Turkish counter-offensive in the Mediterranean once more deprived Philip of the resources with which to topple Elizabeth – but he could not now restore harmonious relations with his 'very dear sister and cousin'. And he knew it. 'This is a bad business and, I fear, not only for the present but also for the future,' Philip scribbled on a letter from Alba revealing that the queen had ascertained Spain's involvement in the Ridolfi Plot. 'If this proves true, any number of victories over the Turks will not console me, because this is worse. I also fear that we ourselves bear the responsibility for the dreadful situation in which we find ourselves.'[37]

The Ridolfi conspiracy created a fatal rift between Elizabeth and her erstwhile suitor. The queen may not have been able to read (as we can today) the minutes of the Spanish Council of State and Philip's ciphered letters authorizing the invasion; but her intelligence reports left her in no doubt that he had lent support to a plan to depose and perhaps murder her. Elizabeth would never trust Philip again. In December 1571 she told the French ambassador at her Court that:

> The king of Spain had worked so hard to provoke and create havoc in [her kingdom] – of which she had proof in intercepted letters written with his own hand and by several of his ministers, and in the form of his tokens and rings intended for those who were to lead the said enterprise. She therefore no longer held herself restrained by the consideration she had always shown him until now.[38]

For a while Philip, too, showed little 'consideration' towards his former sister-in-law. In 1575 she sent an envoy to Madrid with instructions to reopen the English embassy, but only on condition that 'her subjects there and her ambassadors may have the freedom of their religion, without being molested by the Inquisition'. Inquisitor-General Gaspar de Quiroga urged the king to reject this, and instead to insist that all future English diplomats must be Catholics and revere the Holy Sacrament at all times, must not say or write anything against the Roman Church, and must refrain from discussing Catholic doctrine. Any deviation would incur the normal penalties imposed by the Inquisition. Not surprisingly, the English embassy in Madrid remained closed.[39]

Discovery of the Ridolfi Plot also encouraged Elizabeth to improve the defences of her realm, especially by sea. In 1572 her ministers compiled a dossier entitled 'Merchant ships in England', which listed 1,383 vessels between 6 and 240 tons, together with 'the masters' names, being in all the ports and creeks within the realm of England' – a unique resource in an emergency, regularly updated. The following year royal shipwrights launched the first 'race-built' galleon, *Dreadnought*, which carried heavy artillery equivalent to almost 5 per cent of her total displacement. Two more galleons followed almost every year.[40]

In addition, the queen now openly welcomed and protected refugees from Philip's 'tyranny' – especially if they came from the Netherlands – and from time to time she sent military and financial aid to keep the rebel cause there alive and ensure that the Spanish regime in Brussels would never again be strong enough to launch an invasion against her. She also tolerated – and sometimes directly supported – privateering expeditions against Spanish interests, starting in 1571 with a daring joint exploit by Francis Drake and his Devon men, some French Huguenots, and a group of former black slaves from Panama who had rebelled against their Spanish masters, raising the terrifying spectre for the Spaniards of white piracy allied with black insurrection. Despite the efforts of Diego Flores de Valdés, commander of the annual treasure-fleet, the allies destroyed Spanish property on the isthmus of Panama and gained plunder worth £100,000. Two years later the same allies seized a treasure-convoy worth around £50,000 in the same area. Drake's name now began to appear in Spanish sources as a man to be reckoned with.

In February 1574 Philip retaliated by ordering Pedro Menéndez de Avilés, the conqueror of Florida, to create a fleet both to clear the Channel of hostile shipping, whether English or Dutch, 'and to recapture some ports in the Netherlands occupied by the rebels'. To this end Menéndez must embargo 224 ships in the ports of Spain and choose the best to form a task force, and also recruit 11,000 soldiers. This was absurd: to locate and load the artillery and other equipment required to turn a merchantman into a fighting ship took months, and for such a huge undertaking (as Menéndez and several of Philip's councillors pointed out) 'it could take years'.

Moreover, once in northern waters, such a large fleet would need a safe harbour in which to shelter in case of need, and Spain no longer controlled one. After spending 500,000 ducats or more to no purpose, when plague carried off Menéndez and many of his men, Philip postponed the venture.

Some considered the mission impossible. 'I really do not know,' Don Luis de Requesens (Alba's successor) told the king philosophically, 'how it would have been possible to do everything in the time available, even if Menéndez had had the winds and the sea at his command.' Philip nevertheless persevered. Early in 1575 he decided to send a smaller fleet consisting of thirty warships, between twelve and twenty galleys, and thirty smaller vessels to regain control of the North Sea. The count of Olivares, a prominent minister in Madrid, prepared a plan that underlined two important weaknesses in this more modest project: the fleet needed far more heavy artillery and detailed charts of the waters it planned to dominate. Even then, absurdity crept in. Olivares asserted that Requesens 'must send duplicate copies of two charts'. One would provide details on the approaches to the Maas estuary; the other must cover 'the whole coast from Calais to the ports of Flanders, Zeeland and Holland, clearly showing all the sandbanks there, and the buoys and leading marks in use, and exact soundings with numbers'. This was a promising start, but Olivares then revealed his limited grasp of naval affairs: 'The council here will retain one copy of the two maps, and the commander of the fleet will take with him the other copy.' Eventually, fewer than fifty vessels (many of them small) set sail for Dunkirk in 1575, carrying reinforcements for the Army of Flanders. Storms drove several ships back to Spain and forced the rest (commanded jointly by Don Pedro de Valdés and Juan Martínez de Recalde) to take refuge in the ports of England's south coast where (despite some misgivings) the queen's officials assisted them.[41]

To express his gratitude for this generous treatment, Philip started to address Elizabeth again as 'Most puissant princess, our very dear and beloved sister and cousin', and sought to resurrect the 'diplomatic, family and geographical ties that link the two of us'. The queen took this as her cue to make another attempt to reopen an embassy in Madrid, choosing Sir John Smythe as her envoy, but once again Quiroga derailed the plan. At first, he refused to see the ambassador, and when in a moment of bravado Smythe eventually forced his way into the Inquisitor-General's chamber, they engaged in an unseemly shouting match. 'Let me tell you that if you were not an ambassador,' Quiroga yelled, 'I would punish you in such a way that it would serve as an example to you and those of your nation to pay attention to how you speak and who you are speaking to.' Smythe replied, 'I am not afraid of you or your threats', and then made a threat of his own: 'I will tell

His Majesty [Philip] so that he will see how little respect you show towards the queen, his sister.' To which Quiroga replied smugly: 'Tell him what you like. He will listen to me as much as to you – and perhaps more.' Quiroga was correct. 'I say that the queen must not succeed in placing an ambassador here with the freedom to practise his creed in private,' he told the king. Indeed, 'since the queen is who she is, we should not accept even a Catholic ambassador [from her]'. Smythe would be the last Tudor envoy received by Philip II.[42]

## Smerwick

In 1580 Philip decided to attack Elizabeth again, but clandestinely. A year earlier, with papal support, a party of Irish exiles had returned home to instigate a general rebellion. They landed at Smerwick, a wide and remote natural harbour close to the westernmost tip of Ireland, and spent the winter in a temporary fortification which they christened Castello del Oro (Golden Fort) (Figure 39). From there they launched an appeal to the Catholic powers of Europe for reinforcements.

A week after the duke of Alba captured Lisbon, in August, Philip sent him a detailed logistical plan for immediate intervention in Ireland, stressing that the pope offered strong support and inviting the duke's comments. Predictably, Alba strongly opposed the venture, still convinced that it was better to leave Elizabeth alone while she struggled to tame her dysfunctional kingdoms; equally predictably, the king overruled him. In September 1580 he authorized Juan Martínez de Recalde to convey to Smerwick some 800 volunteers raised in Italy and Spain under papal aegis, together with numerous pikes, powder and small arms to equip the Irish supporters they expected to join them.

After successfully completing his mission, Recalde left to survey the coasts of south-west Ireland before returning to Spain; meanwhile the reinforced garrison equipped Castello del Oro with modern bastions and awaited the general uprising. It never came. Instead, in an impressive combined operation, an English army under Arthur Grey, Lord Deputy of Ireland, arrived to blockade the Hispano-papal forces from the landward side shortly before a powerful naval squadron under Sir William Winter swept into the bay. At dawn on 8 November the warships began a steady bombardment. After disabling the garrison's guns, they levelled two of the bastions while the English troops advanced their siegeworks in preparation for an assault. The following night the defenders raised a 'white flag demanding a parley'.

**39.** Smerwick harbour in November 1580. A watercolour map created by or for Sir William Winter, Elizabeth's naval commander, which shows how his warships exchanged fire with the Castello del Oro defended by state-of-the-art fortifications and a Spanish and Italian garrison. Several ships, including *Revenge* at the centre, would serve against the Armada in 1588.

At first, they requested that they be allowed to leave with their lives, bags and baggage, but the English commander refused because their bastions 'were taken away [destroyed], their hearts I knew dismayed, their enterprise so vile and dishonourable towards our prince [Elizabeth]'. When Grey asked them why they had invaded Ireland, a Spanish captain asserted that 'the king had not sent them, but that one John Martines de Ricalde, governor for the king at Bilbao', had raised and transported them in his own name; an Italian 'affirmed that they were all sent by the pope for the defence of the Catholic Faith'. Grey pointed out that no declared state of war existed between Spain and England, and he denied that the pope 'could claim any princely power or empire'. Like Pedro Menéndez in Florida fifteen years before, Grey regarded his enemies as pirates and brigands, with no standing to negotiate a surrender: their only option was to 'render me the fort, and yield themselves to my will for life or death'. Again, like Menéndez in Florida, after his enemies made their unconditional surrender Grey had most of them slaughtered. The English soldiers and sailors entered the fortress, hanged twenty Irish men and women and hacked to death some 500 Italian and Spanish soldiers. Then 'the poor English soldiers that lacked hose and shoes, and were barely clothed', stripped the corpses and 'by means of this medley found to apparel themselves like Italians [*al modo italiano*]' – a particularly heartless image. Grey spared only twenty officers, whom he entrusted to his infantry captains, including Walter Raleigh (making his first appearance on the public stage) and Edward Denny, pending ransom.

Grey justified this savage treatment not only under the prevailing law of war – without a declaration of war, the defeated were not 'lawful combatants' – but also by citing the claim (made by one of those tortured) that Philip was preparing to send another fleet to bring 2,000 men as reinforcements, and that 'one Don Pedro de Valdesia should be general of this Armada'.[43]

Richard Bingham, deputy commander of the fleet, rejoiced that he and his colleagues had 'most worthily achieved this enterprise, and so nobly and liberally dealt with all sorts' of the queen's enemies. With government backing a London printer incorporated his account, and that of Grey, in a pamphlet celebrating *The prosperous success which God gave unto our English soldiers against the foreign bands of our Roman enemies . . . lately arrived in Ireland in the year 1580*, with a simultaneous Dutch translation. Eight years later, when a far larger number of Spaniards and Italians aboard a fleet led by Recalde and Valdés (among others) came ashore in western Ireland, both Bingham and Elizabeth would remember the savage precedent of Smerwick.

## Portugal and the South Atlantic

Philip scarcely noticed the massacre at Smerwick amid the general exultation after his forces conquered Portugal and gained its extensive overseas possessions, creating the first empire in history upon which the sun never set; and he quickly found alternative uses for both Don Pedro de Valdés and the reinforcements originally destined for Ireland.

In 1578 Philip's childless nephew King Sebastian of Portugal led an expeditionary force to Morocco. The poorly planned operation ended in August at the battle of Alcázarquivir, where Sebastian and many of his nobles perished. The last legitimate male in the direct line of the Portuguese royal house died in January 1580, leaving Philip, whose mother had been a Portuguese princess, as next of kin. There were other claimants, but none could match the king of Spain's power and proximity. The first phase of the conquest was the invasion of the Algarve in July by a small army from neighbouring Andalucia commanded by the duke of Medina Sidonia. He was supported by a large fleet of warships commanded by the marquis of Santa Cruz, which worked its way along the Atlantic coast from Cadiz to Setubal at the mouth of the Tagus. There the ships joined the duke of Alba, who had led 15,000 soldiers through the heart of Portugal. The army, together with a siege-train of twenty-two guns, now boarded the marquis's fleet and sailed across the mouth of the Tagus to Cascais – a journey of almost 70 miles – where the troops disembarked. In a brilliant combined operation, with the fleet providing close support, Alba entered Lisbon on 25 August and within two months the entire country was under Spanish control.

The following year Philip moved to the Portuguese capital, where he took the decision to send two amphibious expeditions to consolidate his new empire. The first, led by Don Pedro de Valdés, headed for the Azores archipelago, most of which refused to recognize Philip's title to the Portuguese throne. On 10 July 1581 the king himself 'got into the flag galley' and (according to his own report) spent the afternoon inspecting 'the fleet of fourteen or fifteen galleons, ships and supply vessels, carrying 1,000 Spanish and 1,000 German troops who are going to capture the island of Terceira'. It proved a miserable failure because of the impetuous carelessness of its commander: Valdés landed some 500 Spanish soldiers, cutting down all the defenders they encountered, but then the arrival of French and Portuguese reinforcements turned the tables and the Spaniards soon ran out of ammunition and almost all of them perished. Valdés was lucky to escape, but when he returned to Lisbon, Philip had him court-martialled and imprisoned.[44]

By then the king had entrusted the second task force to Don Pedro's cousin, Diego Flores de Valdés, whom he ordered to sail into the South Atlantic. According to available intelligence, the Strait of Magellan at its narrowest point was 'some 500 paces wide' and Alba commissioned Spain's leading military architects to design fortresses whose interlocking artillery fire would prevent hostile ships from entering the Pacific as Drake had done. In September 1581 Flores led twenty-three vessels and 3,500 men out of Cadiz with instructions to clear all intruders from the South Atlantic and to establish and garrison forts at the narrowest point of the Strait of Magellan. Neither he nor any of Philip's other advisers apparently knew that the Strait is in fact more than a mile wide at its narrowest point. The project was therefore doomed from the start.

The expedition to the Strait involved several of the same protagonists and revealed the same divergent naval tactics as the Armada campaign. Flores's Instructions required all artillery to be kept 'loaded and ready, even when it is inboard, so that if it were necessary to have use of it quickly, they have to do no more than aim it out of its gunports' – but said nothing about reloading. Flores also sent the majority of his ships, one commanded by Juan Gómez de Medina, to the Strait and ordered the rest to scour the South Atlantic for pirates. In January 1583 three Spanish ships, one commanded by Francisco de Cuéllar, discovered two English ships commanded by Edward Fenton (*Galleon Leicester* and *Edward Bonaventure*) refitting in a Brazilian port with their masts struck and their crews ashore. Cuéllar urged an immediate attack, while the Spaniards enjoyed the advantage of surprise, but his superiors decided to delay until the next day, by which time the English were ready to defend themselves. The Spaniards intended to board, but the heavy guns of their adversaries prevented this. While *Galleon Leicester* 'fired her broadside' into one of the Spanish warships, *Edward Bonaventure* 'sailed past her stern and fired all her artillery', killing the captain and thirty men, and wounding many more. According to one Spanish source, 'the two enemy ships fired so many artillery rounds into our vessel that she opened up in many places' and then sank. 'Numerous shot holes at the waterline' left another Spanish ship incapacitated. Both English ships therefore escaped. Both would fire their artillery again at Flores, Cuéllar and Gómez de Medina in 1588, with similarly devastating effects.[45]

Perhaps, as Carla Rahn Phillips has suggested, the expedition to the Strait of Magellan 'exceeded the physical capabilities of Spain's Atlantic fleet system': the Strait lay 8,000 miles from Cadiz, and detaching so many ships and stores for so long meant that there were not enough left to equip the regular fleet which should have sailed for Peru in 1581.[46] Human error exacerbated the scale of the disaster. Flores started with twenty-three ships but returned with only eight – a catastrophic loss – and the surviving principal officers accused each other of cowardice, leading to the trial and imprisonment of Cuéllar and others. Moreover, not only did the artillery on the two forts fail to close the Strait to enemy shipping because it was too wide: the sub-polar environment proved too harsh to support the garrisons. Of the 338 settlers who landed in February 1584 all but nineteen were dead three years later when an English flotilla commanded by Thomas Cavendish sailed through the Strait with impunity. He called the failing settlement 'Port Hunger'.

And while Flores and his fleet were away, Philip faced a far more serious naval challenge in the mid-Atlantic.

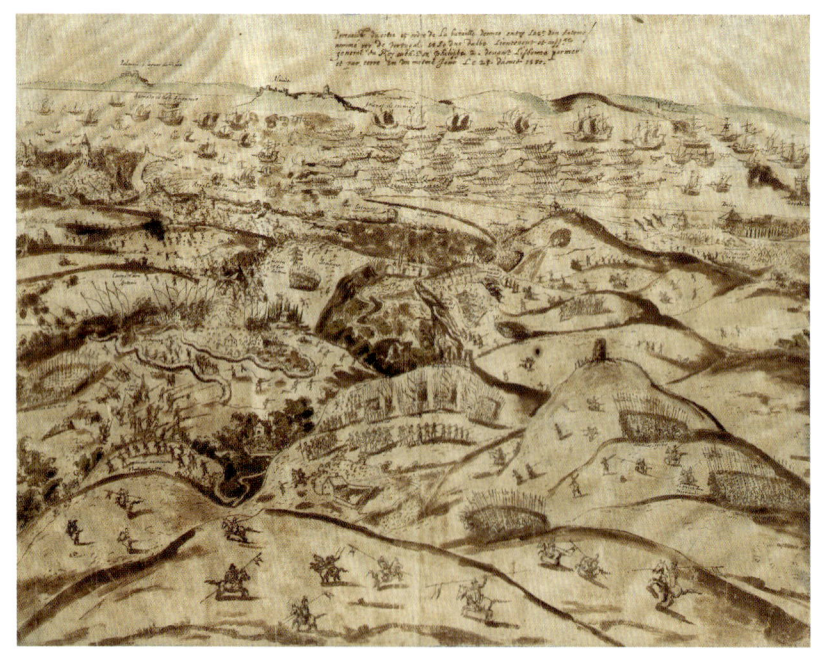

**40.** The Battle of Alcántara, 25 August 1580. The galleys and warships commanded by Santa Cruz advance up the Tagus (top). Meanwhile Spanish field artillery drives the Portuguese troops of Dom Antonio back from the Alcántara bridge (centre) and they flee towards Lisbon (left). The Spanish infantry prepares to advance. Although the caption is in French, the descriptions are in Spanish, probably by an eyewitness.

# 5

# Cold War, 1581–5

## The Struggle for the Azores

AMID THE EUPHORIA GENERATED BY the rapid conquest of Portugal, an important enemy of Philip II escaped: Dom Antonio, prior of Crato, an illegitimate scion of the ancient Portuguese royal family. One of the richest men in the kingdom before the Spanish invasion, and fluent in several languages, the fifty-year-old Dom Antonio was a charismatic figure who found many supporters for his claim to be the next lawful king of Portugal. In 1580 he raised an army to keep out the Spanish invaders, but they were routed at the battle of Alcántara bridge, just outside Lisbon (Figure 40). Dom Antonio then tried to make a stand at Oporto but failed again; and the following year a large manhunt coordinated by the duke of Medina Sidonia forced him to flee abroad.

But he still had friends and supporters. Above all, almost all the Azores archipelago, 1,000 miles west of Lisbon, recognized him, not Philip, as king of Portugal, and Dom Antonio sought foreign assistance for a full-scale invasion of São Miguel, the only island that had declared for Philip. In return for their support he offered the French king, Henry III, Madeira, Guinea and Brazil, and promised Elizabeth of England a fort in west Africa.

News of Philip's support of her Irish rebels in the Smerwick venture encouraged Elizabeth to show favour towards Dom Antonio and his cause, angering Philip's new ambassador at her Court, Don Bernardino de Mendoza. Like Don Guerau de Spes, Mendoza was a devout Catholic: he quoted the Bible frequently in his dispatches, read religious works in his spare time, and founded a chapel to the Virgin Mary in his home town. He also did all he could to advance the Catholic cause in

England, offering support to conspirators who sought to replace Elizabeth with Mary Queen of Scots. Having studied at the university of Alcalá, Mendoza was fluent in Latin, French and Italian – the language in which Elizabeth conducted her audiences with him.[1]

Mendoza also had more than a decade of military experience, first as a cavalry captain in Italy and the Netherlands and then as an adviser to both Alba and Requesens. He never allowed Elizabeth to forget this, sometimes prefacing his comments to her with phrases like 'Speaking as a soldier . . .'. In 1581, when he discovered that Dom Antonio had arrived in England and been received by the queen and her leading ministers, Mendoza scolded her at an audience, saying that since she 'did not seem to hear what he said to her, and act accordingly, it might be necessary to see if she would listen to artillery'. The queen snapped back that 'if I thought to threaten her or make her fear, she would put me in a place from which I could not speak at all'. Mendoza laughed this off: 'I told her that I knew monarchs did not fear individuals, especially not a woman like her who was so beautiful that she could vanquish lions; and she is so vain and superficial that her anger abated.' His misogyny blinded him. Elizabeth had already allowed Dom Antonio (whom she, like her Dutch allies, addressed as 'the king of Portugal') to issue letters of marque to several of her privateering merchants and she secretly loaned him £1,000 in gold to uphold his cause.[2]

Thus fortified, Dom Antonio travelled to France, where he assembled a fleet of fifty-eight vessels, including some Dutch and English privateers (two owned by Sir Francis Drake), which in summer 1582 sailed under the Portuguese flag to the Azores, commanded by a former colonel of the French guards, Filippo Strozzi.

In order to defeat this fleet, and complete the conquest of the Azores, Philip launched a major amphibious operation. There was nothing intrinsically novel about this: his armed forces had done the same against Tunis in 1573, to relieve Malta in 1565, and to capture Lisbon in 1580 – but such operations were extremely complex, requiring many warships and support-craft to work in close conjunction with substantial land forces. Efficient logistics, precision fleet drills and the fine balancing of copious resources, coordinated by expert commanders like Don Álvaro de Bazán, marquis of Santa Cruz, were essential ingredients for a successful outcome (Figure 41).

Galleys seldom ventured into the Atlantic in the mid-sixteenth century, however, where sailing warships carrying heavy artillery reigned virtually supreme. Yet until 1580 Spain's only sailing warships were the relatively lightly armed galleons that escorted the fleets of merchantmen sailing to and from America. Although extremely effective in their assigned role, they were no match for battleships of the

41. Portrait of the marquis of Santa Cruz by Juan Pantoja de la Cruz.

type now being developed in northern Europe. The squadron of Portuguese galleons, massively built and powerfully gunned, captured at the fall of Lisbon, changed all this: Philip now possessed some of the best sailing warships in the world.

Lisbon was also a superb naval base. The narrows at the mouth of the Tagus, defended by shore batteries with heavy artillery, made the wide roadstead beyond a safe haven for even the largest fleet. No other Iberian port could offer the same combination of almost unlimited capacity with almost total security both from enemies and the weather. Lisbon would provide an ideal springboard should Philip ever desire to mount a seaborne invasion of France, the Netherlands or England; and in 1582 it offered the perfect base from which to intercept Dom Antonio's fleet and conquer the Azores.

Philip's Instructions to Santa Cruz insisted on 'exemplary punishment' for all who opposed him: 'If anyone should now resist me, and take up arms against me, they cannot avoid judgement under the Laws of War' – that is, the marquis must summarily execute them. The king also included an unkind reference to the

Valdés fiasco: 'What matters now for your reputation and mine is that you get the job done this time.'[3] Suitably chastised, in July 1582 Santa Cruz led thirty ships and 8,000 men from Lisbon and encountered Strozzi's ships off the island of São Miguel. After several days of sparring for position the two fleets clashed in a close-range contest that lasted five hours. The senior Spanish infantry officer, although a veteran of Lepanto, considered that the battle had been fought 'with the greatest fury ever seen', and several participants commented on the large number of rounds exchanged. One of the principal galleons involved had only a single barrel of powder left at the end of the action. Spanish tactics were simple – individual captains singled out an enemy ship and fired their guns at short range before grappling and boarding – and by the end of the day Dom Antonio's fleet had lost ten ships sunk or captured. According to one account, the 'sides, masts and rigging' of the enemy flagship 'were so shattered by the battery we gave them that she sank'. Well over 2,000 men perished in the action, including Strozzi (who died of his wounds shortly after his ship surrendered), or in the summary execution of prisoners that followed, in accordance with the king's instructions (see Figure 14).[4]

Some naval experts thought that Strozzi had been unlucky to lose. His ships had proved nimbler than those of Santa Cruz and had used their artillery well, killing over 200 of Santa Cruz's men and wounding more than 500. In addition, they operated in mutually supporting groups of four 'to charge and assail each of them one of the great vessels of the enemy'. Thus when the galleon *San Mateo* dropped out of formation, Strozzi's ships surrounded her and fired 500 rounds, inflicting damage so extensive that it took over a year to repair. Most of the other victorious galleons also suffered damage and some got home only with difficulty – as depicted in the large commemorative fresco of the battle, commissioned by Philip for his apartments at the monastery of San Lorenzo de El Escorial.

All the same, Santa Cruz had won a great victory, and on his return he demanded immediate rewards from his master: 'The rank of grandee and the title of Captain-General of the Ocean Sea' plus the prestigious *encomienda mayor* of the Military Order of Santiago for himself and another *encomienda* for his son. This brazenness infuriated the king – 'What some people want is outrageous,' he exploded – but he eventually gave way, perhaps influenced by the general jubilation that greeted these new victories (Figure 42). According to a French diplomat at Philip's Court, some Spaniards boasted that 'even Christ was no longer safe in Paradise, for the marquis might go there to bring him back and crucify him all over again'. Others took to 'spitting in the faces of any Frenchmen they happened to meet in the street'.[5] Nevertheless, Terceira island continued to hold out for Dom Antonio and in spring 1583 he reinforced his garrisons there with 800 fresh French troops.

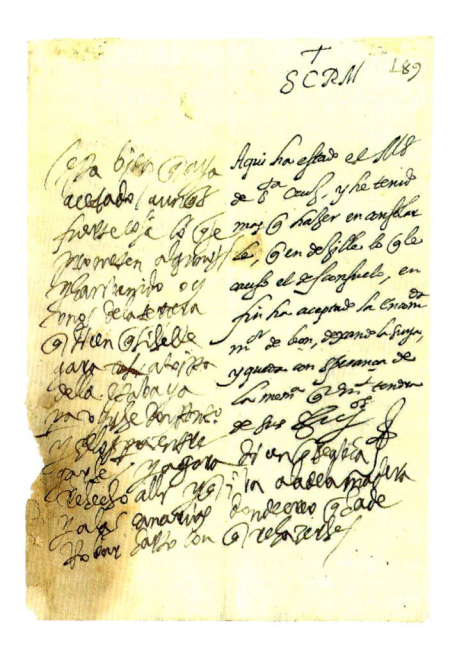

**42.** A *consulta*: the standard instrument of government in Habsburg Spain, with the recommendation by a minister (in this case Mateo Vázquez) on the right and Philip's reply scrawled in the wide left-hand margin. This exchange discusses the rewards demanded by Santa Cruz after his victory in the Azores in 1582, which the king considered (third line) *fuerte cosa* – literally 'strong stuff', meaning 'outrageous'.

Santa Cruz now prepared an overwhelming response. He assembled 15,372 men aboard ninety-eight ships, including twelve galleys, five galleons, two galleasses and thirty-one big merchantmen (to serve as troop-transports), as well as numerous smaller vessels and landing-craft. This time his aim was not to defeat a fleet – although his task force could certainly defend itself if necessary – but to land troops, together with their supporting equipment and supplies, on a suitable beachhead and then reinforce them until they could gain their objectives ashore.

Surprise formed an essential element of the plan. Dom Antonio expected a landing at the port of Angra and disposed his forces accordingly; but information from spies combined with personal reconnaissance persuaded Santa Cruz to deliver his main thrust at a beach ten miles from Angra, defended only by light earthworks and a few guns. He boarded one of the galleys himself, the better to direct operations, and his After-Action Report has a strikingly modern ring:

The flag galley began to batter and dismount the enemy artillery and the rest of the galleys did likewise ... The landing-craft ran aground and placed soldiers on the flanks of the fortifications, and along the trenches, although with much difficulty and working under the pressure of the furious artillery, arquebus, and musket fire of the enemy. The soldiers mounting the trenches in several places came under heavy small-arms fire, but finally won the forts and trenches.[6]

The entire Azores archipelago was now in Spanish hands (Figure 43).

43. The marquis of Santa Cruz directs an amphibious landing on Terceira island on 26 July 1583, by Niccolò Granello and Fabrizio Castello. The second fresco in the Hall of Battles at the Escorial honouring Santa Cruz shows the prominent role played by the galleys both in suppressing enemy fire on shore and in protecting the small boats carrying the landing parties.

## 'The World is Not Enough'

Philip's monarchy had suddenly become a truly oceanic power: his seaborne armies could apparently strike at any point on his enemies' coasts with surgical precision.

Such efforts could also count on a supportive ideology. When news of the conquest of Terceira arrived in Madrid, Cardinal Granvelle, the king's principal adviser on foreign policy, exclaimed:

> God's goodness is giving us so many advantages and favours that we must work hard to further His cause, and strive to liberate as many souls as possible from the chains of the Devil [that is, the Protestants], in the Netherlands as elsewhere – and all the more so, since in doing His work we are also doing our own.

The following day, when the good news reached the Escorial, the king's personal secretary and chaplain Mateo Vázquez assured him that:

> The care, zeal and resources with which Your Majesty attends to matters affecting the service of Our Lord ensures that He looks after those affecting Your Majesty. To have the sea under our control is most important . . . but more important still is the promise of more fortunate successes which we may expect from God's hand in return for the care with which Your Majesty has sought the honour of God and of His religion.[7]

His Majesty was not immune to such flattery. He commissioned another large fresco in the royal apartments at the Escorial to commemorate Santa Cruz's new victory; and 'a royal sculptor has received orders, it is said directly from His Majesty, to make some medals with designs that show his dominion over Portugal and the entire Atlantic Ocean'. Shortly afterwards, a courtier proposed a new royal motto, *Nihil nunquam occidit* ('Nothing is ever hidden'), 'so that all will know that the sun never sets on the kingdoms now unified' under Philip's rule, 'because as night falls in our hemisphere it is daytime in the other'. A gold medal struck in 1583 went even further: one side showed the king's head with the inscription 'Philip II, king of Spain and the New World', and the other bore the uncompromising legend NON SVFFICIT ORBIS ('The World is Not Enough') (Figure 44), a motto first applied to Alexander the Great. The king approved, and it soon became the logo of his global empire. When a party of Englishmen broke into the governor's residence in Santo Domingo in 1586 they saw the royal arms of Spain atop the globe, with a scroll 'wherein was written these words in Latin NON SVFFICIT ORBIS', which they condemned as a 'very notable mark and token of the insatiable ambition of the Spanish King and his nation'.[8]

Celebrations of Santa Cruz's naval victories took many forms. Recoveries from one Armada wreck included a bowl commemorating the Terceira campaign, which

**44.** 'The World is Not Enough'. This gold medal, probably struck in 1583, celebrated the successful annexation of Portugal with a phrase used by a Roman author about Alexander the Great – NON SVFFICIT ORBIS ('The World is Not Enough') – and placed Bucephalus, the horse that only Alexander could ride, atop the globe. The 'cloud' separating the word SVFFICIT represents God and reminds viewers that even world conquerors have limitations.

**45.** Pewter bowl found on the wreck of *Trinidad Valencera*. The Latin motto says 'For Fatherland and Friendship 1583'. St James, Spain's patron saint, rides triumphantly over the waves. The bowl presumably belonged to a veteran of the successful Terceira campaign who later sailed against England.

showed Spain's warrior patron saint with new attributes. St James still rides a charger, his cloak flowing in the wind and his sword-arm raised to strike down his foes; but those foes are no longer cowering infidels. They are the swirling waves of the Ocean Sea, waves that Spain would now subdue along with the human enemies who sought refuge among them, notably England (Figure 45).[9]

Elizabeth and her advisers viewed this spate of Spanish victories with trepidation. The likelihood of a full Spanish reconquest of the Netherlands, combined with command of the Atlantic, created an opportunity to repeat the Ridolfi Plot at a time when England possessed few allies. Dom Antonio was a spent force, his cause in Portugal discredited, and the leaderless Dutch Republic seemed likely to disintegrate.

Worse still, France clearly stood on the brink of civil wars even more terrible than those it had already endured. Until 1584 the conflict had pitted a minority of Huguenots, anxious to gain some official guarantees of toleration, against the Catholic government and its supporters. The death of Anjou in June of that year changed all that. Although incompetent and unprepossessing, the duke had fulfilled two important political functions: he was not only heir presumptive to the childless Henry III but also 'prince and lord of the Netherlands', a role that virtually guaranteed French support for the Dutch. His death jeopardized this special relationship, especially after the assassination of William of Orange the following month. Anjou's astute mother, Catherine de Medici, had no doubt that without those two leaders the king of Spain would quickly complete the reconquest of the Low Countries – and 'after that', she predicted, 'he will not fail to attack this kingdom [France] and England'.[10]

Henry III's closest male relative was now Henry of Navarre, leader of the Protestant party – and therefore totally unacceptable to Philip, who commissioned Don Juan de Zúñiga, a protégé of Granvelle with extensive experience of foreign affairs, to work out the best policy to prevent Navarre's succession. Several cogent analytical papers came back within the week, all starting with the premise that 'Your Majesty is obliged to make sure that no heretic succeeds [to the throne of France], both because you have a duty always to defend and protect the Catholics and because any heretic must necessarily be an enemy of Your Majesty.' Zúñiga therefore recommended an alliance with the French Catholics who had formed a paramilitary organization, known as 'the League' and dominated by Henry duke of Guise, Mary Stuart's cousin, expressly to prevent Navarre from becoming king.[11] In December 1584 Philip's agents signed a treaty at Joinville (Guise's headquarters), which recognized Cardinal Bourbon, an ally of Guise, as the heir to Henry III, and guaranteed an annual Spanish subsidy of 500,000 ducats to the League. In return the League leaders promised to do their best to further Spain's designs elsewhere in Europe, including the surrender to Spanish agents of Dom Antonio, who had taken refuge in Catholic Brittany.[12]

Philip reaped an immediate benefit from his new alliance: in March 1585 Henry III formally rejected an invitation to assume Anjou's mantle in the Netherlands. But this provoked an immediate backlash in London: two days after hearing of Henry's decision the Privy Council resolved to send assistance to the Dutch. They also assured them cryptically that 'Drake's voyage goes forward'.[13]

## The Virgin Queen Flexes her Muscles

Sir Francis Walsingham, Elizabeth's secretary of state, prepared the crucial policy documents. A staunch Protestant, Walsingham had spent most of Mary's reign in exile. Perhaps that is where he learned to fear Catholic conspiracies against Protestant England and in favour of Mary Stuart. In December 1568 he forwarded to his colleague William Cecil a warning from Paris 'that both France and Spain have here within this realm a practice in hand for the alteration of religion and the advancement of the Queen of Scots to the crown'. Even though the 'advertisement is so general and descends to no particularities', Walsingham argued that given 'the malice of this present time . . . there is less danger in fearing too much than too little, and that there is nothing more dangerous than *security*' (by which he meant complacency). The Ridolfi Plot fully vindicated his alarmist views and won over not only Cecil (Lord Burghley from 1572) but also the councillor whom the queen trusted most, Robert Dudley, earl of Leicester. Henceforth, as Patrick Collinson has observed, this triumvirate 'formed an unusually coherent conciliar regime, which was more often divided from Elizabeth than within itself' (Figure 46).[14]

In particular, the triumvirate shared the same foreign policy goals. They all identified Mary Stuart as Elizabeth's principal enemy and believed that only her elimination could ensure the safety of their own sovereign. They also favoured a dual strategy to sap the power of Philip II, and thus prevent a coordinated attack from Spain and the Netherlands: supporting the Dutch Revolt, and impeding Spain's overseas trade, especially with the Americas. No sooner had William of Orange and his followers raised the standard of rebellion in the Netherlands in 1572 than Walsingham predicted that 'upon the good success or evil success' of their venture depends the 'common cause of religion'. Should Orange fail, 'Her Majesty cannot promise to herself any great safety, having so dangerous a neighbour, whose greatness shall receive no small increase, if he overcome this brunt. I pray God

**46.** The queen's advisers. Top: Robert Dudley (1532/3–1588), 1st earl of Leicester, unknown English workshop, *c.* 1575. Leicester's influence with Elizabeth was so great that more than sixty portraits of him survive, many produced for courtiers anxious to show their loyalty and thus, perhaps, induce him to speak to her in favour of their interests. Bottom left: William Cecil, 1st Baron Burghley (1520/1–1598), Lord High Treasurer, unknown artist, after 1587. Bottom right: Sir Francis Walsingham (*c.* 1532–1590), attributed to John de Critz elder, *c.* 1589.

therefore that Her Majesty may incline to do that which may be for her safety.' On this occasion Walsingham failed – after some vacillation, Elizabeth refused to provide open support for Orange – but in 1577 the triumvirate persuaded her to dispatch a fleet commanded by Francis Drake through the Strait of Magellan and into the Pacific Ocean, where it would surprise and plunder Spanish shipping. 'Drake,' the queen told him bluntly, 'I would gladly be revenged on the king of Spain for divers injuries that I have received' – but then she 'swore by her crown that if any within her realm', including Drake himself, made Philip aware of the plan 'they should lose their heads'.[15]

Drake complied: when he left Plymouth in December 1577 with a small fleet of heavily armed ships (funded by Elizabeth, Leicester and Walsingham among others), no one else had divined his true destination. His appearance off the Pacific coast of South America less than a year later, having traversed the Strait of Magellan, came as a complete surprise to the unarmed Spanish merchantmen sailing there, and he returned to Plymouth in September 1580 with 23,000 pounds of silver, 100 pounds of gold and much high-value merchandise. One source estimated the total value of Drake's cargo at £2 million – five times England's annual revenue – all of it seized from subjects of the king of Spain. The queen put Drake's ship on display at Deptford as a national monument to England's achievements, knighted him at a public banquet on the main deck, and granted him £10,000 from the profits of the voyage – although she ordered that this transaction be kept 'most secret to himself alone'. She also forbade publication of any account of what later became known as Drake's 'Famous Voyage'.

Such inconsistency reflected Elizabeth's quixotic personality: vain, secretive and shrewd, over the years the queen had learned how to play off the men who surrounded her in order to leave herself the greatest freedom of manoeuvre. Although intermarriage and family connections united her councillors, several of whom were also related to Elizabeth through her mother, they seldom managed to impose their policies on an unwilling queen. She rarely attended meetings of her Privy Council, instead seeking the opinion of each member individually and then 'leaking' it to the rest. If the council persisted in urging a policy of which she disapproved, Elizabeth would stage a series of temper tantrums until they dropped the issue.

Only two matters led the queen to act irrationally. The first was Robert Dudley. Mystery shrouds the exact nature of their relationship. In an unguarded moment in 1566 Leicester told a foreign diplomat that 'I think I know Her Majesty as well if not better than anyone else who had become close to her, because I began to know her intimately [*familièrement*] before she turned eight.' Moreover, if she should decide to marry (which he considered unlikely), Leicester declared: 'I am pretty sure she will not choose anyone but me', because 'Her Majesty has told me that openly more than once'. Perhaps the earl exaggerated – there is evidence only of 'heavy petting' (as it might be called today) during his visits to the queen's bedchamber in the two years after her accession – but although she never married, Elizabeth seems to have treated Leicester as her surrogate husband. In another unguarded moment, in September 1585, while on his way to the Netherlands to command the troops she had sent to support the Dutch Revolt, Leicester spent a night in the queen's company. The morning after, he confided to Walsingham that 'I find Her Majesty very desirous to stay me' – that is, to prevent him from leaving England – 'and this last night worst of all. She used very pitiful words to me of her fear she shall not live and would not have me from her.' She did not let him leave England until December, seriously undermining the Dutch cause.[16]

The second matter that led Elizabeth to behave irrationally was the threat of assassination – and not without cause. While she was incarcerated by her half-sister Mary in the Tower of London in 1554, the government apparently tortured other prisoners 'to find out a knife that should cut her throat'; and the Ridolfi Plot was the first of many that aimed to murder her as the prelude to re-catholicizing her kingdoms. Lest any doubted how easy it was to assassinate rulers during the Renaissance, the murder of her cousins Henry Darnley and James Stuart in Scotland, of her ally William of Orange, and of Henry III of France served as brutal reminders.[17]

The impact of the queen's fears for her own safety on decision-making emerges clearly from a letter written by a frustrated Burghley after a meeting of the Privy Council in Windsor Castle 'at night' on 10 September 1586. 'Here we are still in long arguments but no conclusions do last, being as variable as the weather, such is Her Majesty's disposition to cast more perils than we can perfectly resolve to Her Majesty's contentation,' he complained. 'There have been arguments these three days, but yet no conclusion.' The date and place of Burghley's irritated letter explain both the delay and the lack of 'conclusion'. The queen had retreated with her Privy Council behind the walls of Windsor, then her strongest fortress, because irrefutable evidence had just arrived of another plot to assassinate her and replace her with Mary Queen of Scots, assisted by a foreign invasion.[18]

The irrefutable evidence came from Walsingham. In the spring of 1583 he had managed to suborn a clerk in the French embassy in London who provided access to the ambassador's correspondence, including the papers he handled for Mary Stuart. Almost immediately these revealed a plot involving Francis Throckmorton, a young Catholic gentleman, and Walsingham had him arrested for treason. A search of Throckmorton's house revealed 'two papers containing the names of certain Catholic noblemen and gentlemen' prepared to assist him in eliminating Elizabeth, and a list of suitable 'havens for the landing of foreign forces'. Under torture, Throckmorton incriminated both Mary and Mendoza. In January 1584 the Privy Council summoned Mendoza and told him that the queen had ordered him to leave the country within fifteen days, to which the ambassador coolly replied that 'since I had not given her satisfaction as a minister of peace I would henceforth do my best to satisfy her in war'. He was more outspoken still in a letter to his government: 'The shamelessness of these people has brought me to a state where I desire to live only to avenge myself upon them, and I hope that God will let this happen soon and will give me the grace to be His instrument of vengeance.'[19]

## 'Annoying the king of Spain'

The Privy Council did not intend to wait for Mendoza to strike. A few days later Burghley drew up 'A memorial of divers things necessary to be thought of and to be put in execution for this summer, for the strength of the realm to prepare for martial defence against either rebellion or invasion'. Commissioners must visit the south and west coasts and survey possible landing-zones, where 'some sconces and trenches [should] be made to cover the arquebusiers to impeach landings'. The queen's ships, reinforced by larger private vessels, would deploy in three squadrons, 'whereof the one would lie about the Isles of Scilly, the second about the Isle of Wight, the third near Harwich'. The greatest problem, Burghley realized, was whether to prepare for an attack in the west from Spain, or in the east from the Spanish Netherlands. He therefore negotiated a naval alliance with the prince of Orange, who promised to send a fleet of twenty warships to support Elizabeth in case of invasion.[20]

In July 1584 one of Philip II's subjects managed to murder Orange; and Throckmorton, tried and convicted of treason, went to the block. The combination of these events, both involving Philip, prompted the Privy Council in October to devise and circulate a 'Bond of Association', pledging 'the utter extermination' of anyone who 'shall attempt any act, or counsel or consent to anything that shall tend to the harm of Her Majesty's royal person'. Although the Bond did not mention Mary Stuart by name, it stipulated that any 'pretended successor by whom *or for whom* any such detestable act should be attempted' must perish. The council circulated copies to each county, collecting hundreds of signatures. As John Guy observed, as far as Mary was concerned 'it was a licence to kill'.[21]

That same month the Privy Council also conducted a major foreign policy review. They concluded that, in the wake of the death of Anjou and Orange, the Dutch Republic seemed doomed without foreign aid and they urged the queen to intervene. In addition, they accepted that eventually Spain would make another attempt to topple the Tudor regime; but there unanimity ended. One group of councillors argued that the best response to the Spanish threat was to concentrate on domestic defence – strengthening the fleet, fortifying the coasts, organizing supporters of the regime to fight more effectively in their own defence – but offering no provocation to Spain abroad. 'So would England become impregnable,' they concluded, 'and she on every side be secure at home and a terror to her enemies.' Other councillors (led by Burghley, Leicester and Walsingham) argued that this was not enough. If Philip ever reconquered the whole Netherlands, they stressed, his power would be 'so formidable to all the rest of Christendom as that Her Majesty shall no wise be able with her own power nor with the aid of any other, neither by sea nor land, to withstand his attempts'. In such an eventuality Elizabeth would become prey to Philip's 'insatiable malice, which is most terrible to be thought of, but most miserable to suffer'. For Tudor England to survive it must halt Spain's progress in the Netherlands while at least one committed continental ally (the Dutch Republic) remained, rather than waiting until Elizabeth would have to stand and fight alone. As Burghley put it: if Philip 'once reduce the Low Countries to absolute subjection, I know not what limits any man of judgement can set unto his greatness'.[22]

For a few more months, fearful that open support for Philip's Dutch rebels would provoke all-out war with Spain, the queen hesitated; but she showed no such restraint concerning attacks against his possessions overseas. In July 1584, just after learning of Orange's assassination, John Hawkins sent Burghley a paper entitled 'The best means how to annoy the king of Spain', whom he deemed 'the mortal enemy of our religion and the present government of the realm of England'. He suggested three strategies: an attack on the Iberian long-distance fishing fleets; an assault on the Caribbean where 'the islands will be sacked, their forts defaced, and their brass ordnance brought away'; and recognition that 'the king of Portugal may in his [own] right make war with the king of Spain'. Dom Antonio would then authorize anyone who 'upon their own charge would serve and annoy the king of Spain as they might, both by sea and land', and Elizabeth would permit those who collected the loot 'to retire, victual and sell in some port of the West Country'. He concluded cryptically: 'The voyage offered by Sir Francis Drake might best be made lawful to go under this licence also, which would be secret till the time draw near of their readiness.'[23]

Shortly afterwards Elizabeth created a special fund of £10,000 'to be issued from time to time' on the orders of a commission consisting of Burghley, Walsingham and the Lord Admiral, Howard of Effingham. They immediately gave Drake enough money to assemble a fleet of fifteen ships and twenty pinnaces, with 1,600 men (500 of them soldiers) for an expedition to the Moluccas, claimed by Dom Antonio as king of Portugal. The total cost was estimated at £40,000, of which the queen promised to contribute half. Drake would raise the rest himself.[24] Although in December 1584 she changed her mind and suspended the project, she made sure that Drake received enough money to keep his fleet in being. She also allowed a small colonizing expedition to sail to America and establish a precarious settlement at Roanoke in what is now North Carolina.[25] Then in March 1585, as soon as she learned that Henry III had rejected the Dutch offer of sovereignty, the queen authorized negotiations with envoys sent by the Dutch Republic to conclude a formal alliance against Spain. The following month, as a gesture of support, she suspended all English trade with those parts of the Netherlands loyal to Philip.

This news arrived in Madrid as ministers discussed how best to support the efforts of the duke of Parma and his troops to recapture Antwerp. Cardinal Granvelle argued that the sudden seizure of all Dutch shipping in Spain and Portugal, followed by a prohibition of the rebels' lucrative trade with the Iberian Peninsula, might bring the revolt to a swift end. 'In my opinion,' he wrote, 'Holland and Zeeland could easily be reduced if we deprive them of the trade with Spain and Portugal.' The ideal time, he suggested, was either the autumn, when the Iberian ports would be full of Dutch vessels loading wine, olive oil and other newly harvested crops, or the spring, when they brought Baltic grain. He also recommended the blanket seizure of all foreign vessels, except for those of Catholic states: 'We should arrest all of them, and afterwards discuss which should be released and which should not.'[26]

## The Lurch into War

Elizabeth's suspension of trade with the Spanish Netherlands in April 1585 played right into the hands of such 'hawks', and the following month Philip ordered the embargo of all foreign ships in Iberian ports, save only the French (on account, he claimed, of their small size). Characteristically, he carried it out in a complex and clandestine manner. 'Do it,' he instructed his agents in the ports:

> in such a way that, for the present, it will be understood that ships belonging to the rebels of all my states, and those from Hanseatic [ports] and Germany,

and from England, will be embargoed on the grounds and with the pretence of wanting to create a great fleet. Having done this, once they have been embargoed and detained, we will know what we have in all areas [of the peninsula] and can better ordain what should be done.[27]

Accordingly in July, again as Granvelle had suggested, the king ordered the release of all German and Hanseatic vessels (with compensation for the period of detention), and later of the English. This left only the Dutch, whose embargoed ships he eventually either incorporated into royal service or sold by auction to help fund his fleet.[28]

In one respect the gambit worked extremely well. Dutch trade with the Iberian Peninsula collapsed as scores of vessels from Holland and Zeeland suffered arrest and the Republic immediately halted further sailings to Spain and Portugal. The total of Dutch ships leaving the Danish Sound – most bound for Iberian destinations – fell by one-third and stayed low for three years. By contrast the decision to embargo non-Dutch ships proved a disaster. The king's officials seized almost 100 English ships and their cargoes, throwing their crews into prison and handing some over to the Inquisition; but there was one exception. A party of Spanish officials from Bilbao came aboard the large and well-manned *Primrose*, partly owned by John Hawkins (Figure 47). At first Francisco de Guevara, the senior Spanish magistrate who was fluent in English, distracted the master and crew by 'making merry' while pinnaces filled with soldiers took up pre-assigned positions. Suddenly, Guevara announced that he had a warrant to arrest the ship and ordered his men to board *Primrose*; but the ship's master, furious at the deception, ordered his crew to resist. After killing seven or eight of the boarders, and wounding many more, the ship gained the open sea, taking with her not only Guevara and several members of his entourage but also a copy of the embargo decree.[29]

The Spanish government never seems to have considered how the embargo of English vessels might appear to Elizabeth and her advisers. Granvelle, the architect of the scheme, did not care – on one occasion he dismissed the English as 'ordinarily of an unpleasant nature who hate foreigners ... I dislike them intensely and the best of them is not worth a fig' – but even he realized that it would be foolish to halt trade with England at the same time as with the Netherlands. It would be far better, he argued, to release the English ships after verifying their identity because later, in the absence of the Dutch, 'we shall soon have our ports full of them' – and that would be the optimum time to impose a separate embargo targeting English vessels.[30]

## The Primrose of London,

with her valiant aduenture on the
**Spanish coast, bearing of the burthen**
of 150. Tunne.

Declaring the maner how 97. Spanyards came aboord the same ship, the course of the skarmish, and how by their valiantnes they discomfited them. Whereunto is added the copie of the Kinges commission for the imbarment of all English Ships. Truely published by Humphrey M...ee.

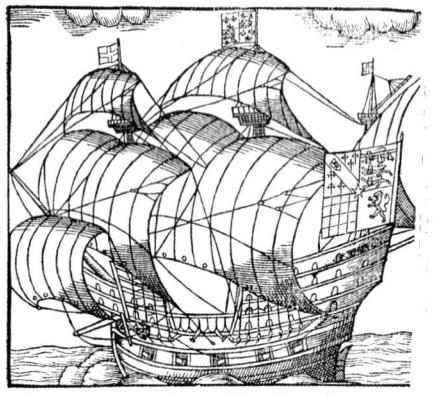

¶ Imprinted at London for Thomas Nelson. 1585.

**47.** The title page of *The Primrose of London*. Two printed pamphlets telling the story of the ship's 'valiant adventure' and escape from her Spanish captors appeared in 1585, indicating her importance to English readers. This one contained a copy of Philip II's embargo of all foreign vessels found in Iberian ports.

Elizabeth and her ministers of course knew none of this. Instead, they studied the exact wording of the embargo decree brought by *Primrose* and immediately noted that, because it exempted the French, it affected only ships from Protestant lands. To Walsingham, always prone to detect Catholic conspiracies, this seemed deeply sinister:

> The late arrest made in Spain of our ships and the ships of others well affected in religion, with a special exception ... of the French cannot but be interpreted as a manifest argument of secret intelligence and mutual concurrency likely to be between the French and the Spaniard for the ruin and overthrow of the professors of the Gospel.[31]

Interrogation of the Spaniards captured aboard *Primrose* offered little reassurance: one informed his captors that 'hearing that the Hollanders seek aid in England and fearing lest they shall be aided', the king of Spain 'means by this arrest to fear [deter] the English from aiding them'. Moreover, an intercepted letter from a Spanish merchant in Andalucia to his partner in Rouen spoke unequivocally of 'the state of war that now exists with England'.[32]

Military and naval preparations therefore went ahead apace. Walsingham had already prepared a 'plot for the annoying of the king of Spain', even though he recognized that such 'inconveniences' might provoke a Spanish counter-attack; but Philip's embargo played right into his hands and the queen now threw caution to the winds. Walsingham advised William Harborne, his secret agent in Istanbul, to persuade the Ottoman sultan 'if it were possible, to convert some part of his forces' from attacking the Shah of Iran and deploy them instead 'against Spain, thereby to divert the dangerous attempt and designs of the said King from these parts of Christendom'. In June 1585 Leicester invited Dom Antonio to return to England, and the next month Elizabeth signed a treaty that bound Scotland, through its pliable yet ambitious young king, James VI (Mary Stuart's only child), more tightly to her side. She also commissioned a naval squadron to sail to Newfoundland with orders to attack the Iberian fishing fleet there (it later returned to England with many prizes and about 600 captive mariners).[33] Shortly afterwards the Privy Council drew up regulations for the issue of licences for subjects affected by the embargo, allowing them to make good their losses by plundering any ship sailing under Philip's colours 'in as ample and full a manner as if it were in the time of open war between Her Majesty and the said king of Spain'. The queen also ordered Drake to prepare 'some special service to be by him executed, tending greatly to the benefit of us and our realm', to purchase stores, and to impress 'mariners, shipwrights, smiths, carpenters, and divers other needful artificers, workmen and labourers' for 'the voyage he intends, with the favour of Almighty God, to make to foreign parts'.[34]

A few days after signing these warrants, but before making a public commitment to the Dutch, Elizabeth sought clerical reassurance, asking her prelates to declare 'Whether a prince may defend the subjects of another prince from being forced to commit idolatry?' John Whitgift, archbishop of Canterbury, declined to answer, not only because 'it is a matter of council and of state, wherewith it becomes none to intermeddle but such as are called thereunto' but also because 'I know not Her Majesty's ability to maintain and defend that which they [the Dutch] require of her'. Unsatisfied with this vague answer, the queen asked him explicitly: 'Whether Her Majesty be bound by the word of God to assist the Dutch Republic against the king of Spain?' This time, after pointing out that Philip might employ a parallel rationale for assisting the Catholics of Ireland, Whitgift replied that 'Considering the manifest peril if overthrown' which both England and the Dutch would face, and considering 'their just cause, I think Her Highness is to depend upon the providence of God and bound to assist them'.[35]

This evidently convinced Elizabeth, because on 20 August, at her palace of Nonsuch, she signed a formal treaty that (together with a supplementary treaty three weeks later) obliged her to provide the Dutch with over 6,000 soldiers for their army, to pay one-quarter of their defence budget (a share estimated at £125,000 each year), and to supply an experienced councillor to coordinate government in the rebel provinces and lead their army. In return the Republic promised to surrender the strategic ports of Flushing, Brill and Ostend to England, as sureties until it could repay the queen's expenses. The treaty of Nonsuch came too late to save Antwerp, which fell on 17 August, but within a month more than 4,000 English troops had arrived at Flushing, one of the Dutch ports ceded to Elizabeth by treaty.

The queen also tried to align her policy with that of the Turks. Walsingham informed Harborne in Istanbul that, 'given the success of the said King of Spain's affairs in the Low Countries', Elizabeth was 'now fully resolved to oppose herself against his proceedings'. Harborne must therefore 'use all your endeavour and industry in that behalf, the rather for that it is most evident that if the said king might be kept thoroughly occupied, either by some incursion from the coast of Africa in itself or by the galleys' from Istanbul against Italy. Measures 'to annoy [Philip] from this side of Europe,' Walsingham continued, would leave Spanish power 'so weakened and divided as it would be no small advantage to Her Majesty'. But:

> If you shall see that the Sultan cannot be brought altogether to give ear to this advice you shall, after you have done your best to gain this first point, procure at least that by making show of arming to the sea for the king of Spain's dominions, [he can] hold the king of Spain in suspense, by means whereof he shall be the less bold to send forth his best forces into these parts, which may serve to good purpose if you fail of the first.[36]

Meanwhile, on 24 September, Drake's squadron of twenty-five ships with eight pinnaces, carrying 1,900 men (1,200 of them soldiers), sailed from Plymouth. The commanders included veterans of Drake's circumnavigation and of the Azores battles, as well as several men prominent at Court – Francis Knollys (Leicester's brother-in-law), Christopher Carleill (Walsingham's stepson) and, for a time, Sir Philip Sidney (Walsingham's son-in-law and Leicester's nephew). Another connection between the fleet and the Court lay in the ships: the queen supplied two warships, John Hawkins owned at least four vessels (one of them *Primrose*), Leicester owned two, and Admiral Howard and Sir William Winter each owned one.

On 7 October 1585 the task force arrived off Galicia in north-west Spain. At first Drake tried to negotiate with the local magistrates, claiming that it was all about the embargo: the queen had sent him 'to demand the cause of imprisoning her subjects and taking their goods from them as if it were open war', and to ascertain if 'it were the intention of the king of Spain to hold them thus by force and thereby to give cause of war'. When the negotiations faltered Drake's men came ashore and conducted raids on local villages, desecrating churches, collecting booty and taking hostages.[37]

Why exactly Drake chose to raid Galicia remains unclear, for neither his commission nor his instructions seems to have survived. One of his senior officers later gave four reasons: to find shelter from an approaching storm; to take on water and redistribute stores; to draw up 'Articles of Order' for the fleet; and 'lastly, which was not the least, to make our proceeding known to the king of Spain'. He need not have worried: no sovereign could overlook such an act of naked aggression. As Don Diego Pimentel, a senior Armada commander captured in 1588, told his interrogators: 'The reason why the king undertook this war [against England] was that he could not tolerate the fact that Drake, with two or three rotten ships, should come to infest the harbours of Spain whenever it pleased him, to capture its best towns and plunder them, and to interdict our trade with America.' Balthasar López del Árbol, another officer aboard the Armada, told his captors the same: 'The cause why the voyage was taken in hand, as he hath heard, was to be revenged of the injuries done by Francis Drake and the English ships against the king.'[38]

Elizabeth's numerous aggressive acts in response to Philip's embargo decree – not just the raid on Galicia but also kidnapping the fishing fleet, welcoming Dom Antonio, issuing letters of marque, sending soldiers and subsidies to assist rebellious subjects, and trying to mobilize the forces of the sultan – led her to print a justification for her actions in several languages. She rehearsed her efforts to 'continue very good friendship with the king, as his good sister' until two of his ambassadors, Spes and Mendoza, supported an invasion 'with a power of men, partly to come out of Spain, partly out of the Low Countries'. It was to forestall another attempt that she had sent assistance to her Dutch neighbours, at their request, and had garrisoned 'some few towns upon the seaside next opposite to our realm, which otherwise might be in danger to be taken by the strangers, enemies of the country'.[39]

She thus presented her actions in the Netherlands as self-defence, not a declaration of war, but she could not do the same with the raid on Galicia. The diplomatic corps in Madrid agreed with the Imperial ambassador, Count Khevenhüller, who reported that 'people here don't need to hear the drums beat again' to know that hostilities had begun. 'In my opinion, with this act the English have removed their disguise and mask towards Spain.' Burghley agreed: England, he wrote, was now about 'to sustain a greater war than ever in any memory of man it hath done'.[40]

---

Philip's foreign policy towards England had thus backfired again. As with the treasure-ships fifteen years earlier, the king and his ministers underestimated both the resources and the resolve of Elizabeth. For the first time since signing peace with France in 1559 a major European ruler had (in effect) declared war on Spain, and for this Philip had mainly himself to blame. He had repeatedly broken one of the cardinal rules of Grand Strategy: that, usually, 'less is more'. Although major states must maintain a substantial military force to protect their strategic interests in key areas, peripheral challenges are best met through non-military means – indeed the trick is to do as little as necessary to counter each challenge. Alba had been right: Elizabethan England was inherently unstable and so should be left alone. Given the existence of an influential 'peace party' among Elizabeth's councillors until at least 1584, and given the permanent uncertainty surrounding the succession should the childless queen die, there was no reason to doubt that the skilful deployment of non-military instruments would minimize English interference abroad while enhancing Philip's reputation for resolve and strength. Now, having repeatedly failed – and been seen to fail – to bring England back into the Habsburg orbit by diplomacy and plots, and having provoked an open attack on Spanish soil, the question was no longer whether Philip would counter-attack, but when and how he would deliver that counter-attack.

# 6

# The Grand Design and its Architect

## 'The most potent monarch of Christendom'

THE UNION OF SPAIN AND Portugal made Philip II the ruler of an 'innumerable, not to say infinite, multitude of kingdoms, lordships, provinces and various dominions in all four quarters of the world'. He now governed, according to one of his subjects, 'the greatest empire that has been seen since the creation of the world'. Even his enemies agreed. One fearful Englishman deemed the king of Spain 'the most potent monarch of Christendom', who 'hath now got a command so wide, that out of his dominions the sun can neither rise nor set'. According to another, Philip had become 'A prince whose empire extended so far and wide, above all emperors before him, that he might truly say, *Sol mihi semper lucet*: the sun always shines upon me.'[1]

Who was the 'me' upon whom the sun always shone? In 1582 an envoy from the Netherlands provided a vivid description of his sovereign. 'He is of less than average height with broad shoulders and chest, and a large pale face' with prominent lips, 'especially the lower one, a sign of his Habsburg ancestry. His eyes are somewhat red, like those of a man who reads and works a lot, even at night, because he insists on seeing practically everything.' In 1588 a French diplomat noted few changes. 'He is getting thinner, as people do as they get older', but otherwise:

> He is assiduous in attending to business, with everything passing through his hands. He trusts no one and delegates to no one, as if he were still only 40. He continues to spend many hours in devotions, and also many in recreation: when the weather allows, he goes out with his children in a coach,

shooting deer (or watching others shoot them) and sometimes fishing. They come back late.

Philip spent the summers 'outside Madrid, because he likes the buildings, the gardens and the country air which is much purer than that in the cities. He finds more time there to attend to business, and fewer people to distract him.' One of Philip's senior ministers confirmed this: 'Our Master loves peace and quiet and likes to govern and control the world in silence, relying on people who do the same.' Indeed, 'we have ample proof that the people he likes best are those who make the least noise'.[2]

The king also dressed with quiet understatement. Although he had a new suit of clothes made every month, the design and the colour – black – remained the same. Sometimes he 'dressed down' even further. An ambassador reported that Philip received him attired 'very plainly', just 'clad in a plain black cloak with cloth cap'; and one of the monks at the Escorial later noted that the king attended services 'looking just like a physician', adding 'He did not even wear a sword.' When Philip met his future son-in-law, the duke of Savoy, for the first time in 1585 he arrived 'dressed in black without any pomp, except for his insignia of the Golden Fleece', and that is how he appears in a formal portrait done two years later, when he was sixty (Figure 48).[3]

Even when attired 'very plainly', Philip could still intimidate his subjects. As a noblewoman irreverently observed when the king nominated a man of obscure origins to be primate of all Spain: 'His actions now resemble the miracles performed by Christ, who made men out of clay.' The future saint Teresa of Ávila reported that in his presence 'I felt completely confused when I started to speak to him, because he fixed his penetrating gaze on me and seemed to see deep into my soul ... I lowered my eyes and told him what I wanted as quickly as possible.' In his funeral sermon for Philip in 1598, a Court preacher claimed that 'with a sideways glance he sent some men to their graves' and asked rhetorically: 'How many great scholars, how many valiant captains, were unsettled, trembling, and mute in the presence of His Majesty?'[4]

In part, this was a facade. The king also exhibited a strong measure of self-doubt, perhaps fostered by a sense of inferiority when he compared himself with his remarkable father, Charles V, the victor of numerous battles, an instinctive leader, a cosmopolitan traveller fluent in five languages. Yet this heroic ruler had produced only one legitimate heir to succeed to and govern the vast empire he had created, and the careful education in the art of government that Charles provided for him only served to heighten Philip's awareness of the need for success in order to prove himself worthy of his father and his mission, and of the disgrace of failure.

The anxiety to live up to the only standards that he knew and revered led Philip to obsess about 'getting things right' (*acertar*: one of the commonest terms in his vocabulary). Thus in 1576 he assured the Inquisitor-General of Spain that 'I want to get everything right, especially in matters where religion is concerned'; 'I want so much to get right the appointment of a president [of the Council of Castile]'; and 'I shall not cease to think about everything, to make sure we get it right'– three examples taken from his correspondence with a single minister in a single year.[5]

The desire to *acertar* provides the key to Philip's distinctive style of government: an insistence on taking all important decisions himself, ensuring that he knew more about public affairs than anyone else. To be sure, this offered him advantages – above all, it allowed Philip to take decisions at his own pace – but it also

**48.** Philip II, by Alonso Sánchez Coello, 1587. Formal portraits of the king in later years normally portrayed him dressed simply in black, conveying his majesty not through the outward symbols of kingship but through dignity and 'serenity'. His only ornament here is the insignia of the Order of the Golden Fleece. Sánchez Coello intended this understated portrait of his master, then aged sixty, to go to Pope Sixtus V, but Grand Duke Ferdinand of Tuscany opened the package and refused to part with its contents.

brought disadvantages. Most significantly, it gave him the freedom to change his mind, sometimes repeatedly, and to put off or overlook difficult choices until it was too late. In 1584 Cardinal Granvelle, who had served the king since his accession, complained bitterly about Philip's tendency to procrastinate:

> I see in all matters these delays, so pernicious and in so many ways prejudicial to our own affairs, including the most important ones, which become lost to view with so much delay. And the reason is that His Majesty wants to do and see everything, without trusting anyone else, busying himself with so many petty details that he has no time left to resolve what matters most.

Three years later the papal nuncio in Spain made a similar complaint: 'His Majesty wants to see and do every single thing himself, yet that would not be possible even if he had ten hands and as many heads.'[6]

The most comprehensive indictment of Philip's desire to micromanage came from Don Juan de Silva, who had served the king for half a century as page, soldier, ambassador and councillor. 'The detailed attention that His Majesty devotes to the most trifling things is a subject for regret,' Silva confided to a colleague, 'because when a man finds things to do in order to avoid working, it is what we call a pastime; but when he works in order to find things to do it cannot be given the name it deserves.' He continued:

> Although His Majesty's brain must be the largest in the world, like any other human being he is not capable of organizing the multitude of his affairs without making some division between those that he should deal with himself and those that he cannot avoid delegating to others. It is equally true that His Majesty does not make this distinction ... Instead he leaves nothing entirely alone and takes from everyone the material that should be delegated (concerning individuals and details), and so does not concentrate on the general and the important because he finds them too tiring.[7]

## The King and God

The desire to *acertar* also reinforced the king's deep religious faith. He attended Mass daily; heard a sermon at least once a week; confessed and received Communion at least four times a year; and went on 'retreat' during Holy Week, as well as at times of severe emotional strain. He also spent much time in private devotions. According to one of his valets, 'not a single day passed in which the king did not spend a long period' in 'contemplation or mental prayer'. Another valet claimed that the king always travelled with 'his books of devotions, and kept open in front of him the small portable oratory that he always took with him' with 'images of the Crucifixion and of Our Lady in silver bas-relief, which had plenary indulgences attached to them. His Majesty spent several hours a day thinking about and pondering divine and spiritual matters.'[8]

The monks at the Escorial noticed that sometimes when he was at prayer or in contemplation, tears would roll down the king's cheeks; and deeply religious people, including the future saint Ignatius Loyola, detected in the king a piety of profound and unusual intensity. Philip showed a special interest in relics, above all those recovered from Protestant countries and sent to the Escorial. At his death, the king's collection contained 7,422 relics, including twelve entire bodies, 144 heads and 306 complete limbs, some accompanied by a label written in his own hand (Figure 49).[9]

49. Reliquaries at the Escorial, containing some of Philip II's relics. The 'keeper of relics' at the Escorial claimed that the royal collection included at least a fragment of the bones of every known saint except three. Although only a fraction of the original collection has survived, each golden casket contains a certified body part of a saint.

Philip often equated his own political interests with those of God. In 1573, with breathtaking presumption, he reassured an ailing minister: 'I hope that God will give you good health and a long life, since you are engaged in God's service and in mine, *which is the same thing*.' Two decades later he called on the Council of the Inquisition to continue doing 'what is best for the service of God and myself, and the authority of the Holy Office, *because one cannot be separated from the others*'.¹⁰

These uncompromising assertions that religious principle should always prevail over political calculation amounted to messianic imperialism. Philip convinced himself that he possessed a direct mandate to uphold the Catholic faith at almost all times and in almost all places. Many of his subjects agreed. Luis Cabrera de Córdoba's *History of Philip II, king of Spain*, the best account of the king's life written by someone who knew him personally, opens with a striking frontispiece. The king, in armour and with his sword drawn, stands as the sole barrier preventing heavily armed men from attacking the Virgin Mary, who has placed the king's cloak over her arm while she holds the cross against her shoulder with one hand, and raises a chalice in her other hand (Figure 50).

50. Frontispiece of Luis Cabrera de Córdoba, *History of Philip II, king of Spain*, engraved by Pierre Perret. The first part of Cabrera's study appeared in 1619, providing the best account of Philip's life and reign written by a contemporary. The author portrayed him throughout as defender of the faith – starting with the image on the first page. Here Philip in armour (and garters) uses his sword to protect the Virgin Mary from the enemies of the Catholic Church, with the Escorial in the background. A motto stating that 'The first priority is religion' separates the protagonists.

With such godliness in his heart and mind, it is not surprising to find that Philip and his advisers attributed every success to divine intervention and favour, and rationalized each defeat or failure either as a punishment for their sins and shortcomings or as a test of their steadfastness and piety. When in 1586 the American treasure-fleets arrived safely in Seville with a bumper consignment of gold and silver, the king assured his ministers that 'God has done this'. Conversely, when news of a spate of military reverses arrived at Court, a minister tried to console his master with the thought that:

> God, who can do anything, is our greatest strength in these troubles, since we have seen that He always looks out for Your Majesty, and in your greatest necessities gives the greatest signs of favour ... These indications arouse great expectations that, since Your Majesty fights for the cause of God, He will fight – as He has always done – for the interests of Your Majesty.[11]

## Governing the First Empire on which the Sun never Set

Philip's style of decision-making, with its combination of micromanagement and messianic zeal, had dire political consequences. The primary task of rulers, like the leaders of any corporate organization, is to define clear objectives for their enterprise, develop a plan for achieving those objectives, and then systematically monitor progress by adjusting the plan to circumstances whenever necessary. Their task is to ask the 'open questions' – what, when and why – and visualize how the enterprise should evolve over the next few years; they must also choose and coach subordinates to realize these goals, and delegate execution to them. Policy should never be confused with execution. Leaders set goals and give directions; managers implement them.

According to modern organizational theory, the least efficient and least successful corporate system is the 'crisis management' model, in which the leader attempts to do everything in a dictatorial and secretive manner, reduces employees at all levels to simple functionaries and then, overwhelmed by the burden of responsibility, restricts the goals of the organization to coping with each successive challenge and trying to avoid mistakes. This style of leadership, sometimes termed a 'zero defects mentality', was the one adopted by Philip. Thus, before giving his final approval for any major action, he waited until he believed everything was perfect. In 1571, as the Venetian ambassador in Madrid waited anxiously for Spain's galleys to put to sea and join the fleet of his allies, he noted with irritated fascination the king's insistence that 'Where naval warfare is concerned, every tiny detail takes up the longest time and prevents voyages, because not having oars or sails ready, or having insufficient quantities of ovens to bake biscuits, or the lack of just ten trees or masts, on many occasions holds up for months on end the progress of the fleet.' Moreover, once the last oar, sail, oven and mast had been acquired, the king expected everything else to happen like clockwork.[12]

This assumption was of course wholly unrealistic, given the limitations imposed by sixteenth-century technology and communications, but two assets blinded Philip to this critical defect. First, he maintained the largest and best intelligence service in Europe. In 1574 an ambassador at the Court of Spain complained enviously that the king disposed of so much information 'that there is nothing he does not know'.[13] Philip maintained permanent embassies in Rome, Venice, France, Genoa, Vienna, the Swiss Cantons and Savoy (also in Lisbon until 1580 and in London until 1584), as well as temporary missions elsewhere when occasion required; and he provided each of his ambassadors with funds to purchase top-grade information. In the 1580s the chief papal cipher-clerk, the English ambassador in Paris and the comptroller of Queen Elizabeth's household (to name just the most prominent) all accepted Spanish bribes in return for intelligence. Moreover, whereas the ambassadors and ministers of other European states normally sent one dispatch each month to their principals, Philip expected at least one dispatch each week and in times of crisis he demanded one each day.

The superb courier service at his disposal reinforced Philip's dangerous belief in his omniscience. The contract made by his father with the Taxis (or Tassis) family created chains of postal stations linking Spain with Germany, Italy and the Netherlands, and every week scores of official messages passed safely along those post routes. The network could be expanded whenever need arose. Thus in 1567 the duke of Alba established a chain of postal stations, each with two horses, along the Spanish Road that connected Milan with Brussels, providing an alternative link with Spain whenever war rendered other routes unsafe. Couriers managed to convey messages from Brussels to the king in eleven, ten and, in at least one case, only nine days: an average speed of almost 100 miles on horseback each day. In 1571 news of the victory of Lepanto covered over 2,000 miles in three weeks: again an average of almost 100 miles a day. The following year a galley carrying messages from Philip's fleet in Messina reached Barcelona – almost 1,000 miles away – in only eight days. As the historian Giovanni Ugolini observed, letters travelled faster than anything else in early modern Europe.[14]

Nevertheless, like all rulers, Philip resembled the captain of a riverboat: he could maintain steerage way only as long as his ship moved faster than the current.

Paradoxically, his insistence on acquiring ever more data, feeding his illusion that this empowered – entitled – him to micromanage both policy and operations, slowed down his ship of state and thus diminished his control.

Earlier in the reign the king seemed aware of this problem. He usually briefed his principal lieutenants in person, or at least entrusted his instructions to a minister capable of explaining his intentions in detail, and he sometimes delegated the final decision on critical operational issues to those whom he tasked with implementing them. Thus in 1567 he spent four days closeted with the duke of Alba to discuss the policies to follow in the Netherlands, and afterwards provided extremely detailed instructions, but he still made a vital concession: 'I delegate all these matters to you, as the person who will be handling the enterprise and will have a better understanding of the obstacles or advantages that may prevail.' In 1574 he granted Alba's successor, Don Luis de Requesens, similar latitude: 'This is what seems best to me but you, holding responsibility for these things, will do what you see to be most fitting for my service, and for the advancement of what lies in your hands.'[15]

Philip seems to have abandoned this prudent practice after the conquest of Portugal. In 1585 one of the king's secretaries advised a colleague that in decision-making one should do 'what His Majesty used to say to ambassadors', namely (and here he shamelessly imitated the king's style, using the '*vos*' form): 'You who are on the spot and hold the matter in your hands, will see and do what you understand to be most appropriate.' The key phrase was '*used* to say': by then, Philip drafted crucial policy documents and sent them by courier to those tasked with their execution. 'Waste no time in complaints and questions,' he instructed his subordinates, and instead 'Believe me, *as one who has complete information on the present state of affairs in all areas.*' This was ridiculous. Even if the king had possessed 'complete information on the present state of affairs in all areas', it would have been of little use by the time his instructions reached their destination because 'the present state of affairs' would have changed.[16]

Philip never seems to have recognized these constraints as he planned and prepared the Armada; and yet, in the words of an eminent modern strategic analyst: 'There is only so much that any human can absorb, digest and act upon in a given period of time. The greater the stress, the more individuals will ignore or misrepresent data, mistake and misconstrue information, and the greater will be the prospects for confusion, disorientation and surprise.' In short, 'More information from more sources, made available more quickly than ever before, equals system overload.' In the sixteenth as in the twenty-first century, 'Processing and transmission technologies far outstrip our ability to assimilate, sort and distribute information.' Even if, as Don Juan de Silva speculated irreverently, 'His Majesty's brain must be the biggest in the world', events would show that it was still too small to micromanage the conquest of England.[17]

## The 'Enterprise of England'

Philip's insistence on taking all major decisions himself attracted to his Court many English and Irish exiles who yearned to topple the Tudor state and restore Catholicism to their homeland by force. Some, claiming to be God's mouthpiece, accused the king of defaulting on his special relationship with Heaven. 'I do not know how Your Majesty will be able to excuse yourself before Our Lord if you fail to assist and support the people and the groups who with such zeal and such religious conviction ask you for help,' Thomas Stukeley, a prominent exile, chided Philip. Except for Ridolfi, however, until 1583 no conspirators against Elizabeth received the king's open support. Admittedly the troops who left for Smerwick in 1579 and 1580 departed from a Spanish port in Spanish ships, but Philip disavowed them as soon as things went wrong.[18]

The conquest of the Azores rekindled the king's interest in the 'Enterprise of England'. After their victory at Terceira 'the captains who accompanied the marquis of Santa Cruz said openly that now we have Portugal, England is ours; and little by little we shall also gain France'. Santa Cruz shared their euphoria, urging Philip to 'look to God, since the cause is so just and so much His', and to remember that:

> Victories as complete as the one God has been pleased to grant Your Majesty in these islands normally spur princes on to other enterprises; and since Our Lord has made Your Majesty such a great king, it is just that you should follow up this victory by making arrangements for the invasion of England next year.[19]

For the benefit of his master the marquis reviewed past amphibious operations, from the successful landings of the Romans and Saxons, through those of the Yorkists and Lancastrians in the fifteenth century, down to the Ridolfi Plot. He concluded that any future Spanish invasion should aim for London, since it was the seat of government and was easily accessible from the sea. Moreover, as Sir Thomas Wyatt's rebel army had proved, it lacked modern defences; and once the expeditionary force from Spain landed in the Thames estuary, reinforcements would readily be available from the Army of Flanders.

Philip thanked the marquis 'for all you wrote in your holograph letter, offering yourself to lead a new campaign, which you suggest for next year'; but, he continued, 'these are matters that cannot be discussed with certainty now, because they depend on the timing and the events that will take place between then and now'.[20] Although he asked Santa Cruz to prepare feasibility studies for the overthrow of Elizabeth Tudor he also planned to use the troops aboard the fleet, once they returned, to expel the Morisco population of Castile 'as the Catholic Kings [Ferdinand and Isabella] had done with the Jews' ninety years before. Don Alonso de Leyva would command the operation, assisted by Don Francisco de Bobadilla. In the event Philip abandoned this project after the fleet returned from Terceira 'because the veterans were needed in the Netherlands', so Bobadilla led them to Italy and up the Spanish Road to the Netherlands, where they helped force Antwerp to surrender.[21]

However, Philip did not entirely abandon the Enterprise of England. He had seen for himself in the 1550s that the Tudor regime did not fully appreciate the need to maintain a powerful navy (see chapter 3) and could not unify its Catholic and Protestant subjects. He also knew some members of that regime personally (including Howard, Leicester and Burghley); and several other councillors accepted his pensions, notably James Croft, one of the commissioners sent to Flanders to negotiate peace in 1588. Finally, Philip had also seen for himself Elizabeth's pliability when faced with threats from her older sister, and her willingness to attend Catholic worship for five months after her accession to gain his favour. He may have thought he could still intimidate her.[22]

While waiting for Santa Cruz to send his invasion plan, in September 1583 the king asked the duke of Parma for his thoughts on a cross-Channel surprise attack. Success in the Low Countries, he reminded his nephew, depended on 'finding a way to prevent England from fuelling this war', and he asked Parma whether, given sufficient resources, he could prepare and launch an invasion that would eliminate Elizabeth and replace her with Mary Stuart. The duke did not rule out the possibility, and he forwarded a detailed 'Description of the ports of England', compiled by a Catholic exile. He expressed a preference for a surprise attack across the Channel by the Army of Flanders, rather than a direct invasion from Spain; but given the precarious military situation, he suggested that it might be better to complete the conquest of the Netherlands before turning upon England.[23]

Philip appears to have accepted his nephew's advice. In November 1583 Don Juan de Zúñiga received a diffident letter from the count of Olivares, his successor as Spanish ambassador in Rome, announcing that Pope Gregory XIII 'has proposed that His Majesty should marry [Mary] Queen of Scots, saying that in this way he can once more become king of England'. He added, no doubt for Zúñiga's eyes alone: 'The pope expressly told me to write this to His Majesty, but through embarrassment I have chosen to write to you instead.' Inevitably the king saw the letter and scribbled: 'I do not feel any embarrassment at being told what should be done; but I do feel it with something so inappropriate as this – the more so because I know that I could not fulfil the obligation of either governing that kingdom [of England] or of going there, having so many other duties that it is impossible to fulfil even those as I would wish.' The king felt no more eager to marry Mary Stuart than he had been to marry Elizabeth Tudor twenty-five years before.[24]

The death of Pope Gregory and the election of Sixtus V in May 1585 changed everything. Sixtus immediately told Olivares about his zeal to commission 'some outstanding enterprise' for the Catholic faith, specifying either the conquest of the Muslim stronghold of Algiers or the invasion of England. The ambassador dutifully passed these details back to his master, but the king angrily endorsed the letter: 'Doesn't [the reconquest of] the Low Countries seem "outstanding" to them? Do they never think of how much it costs? The English idea lacks substance.'[25]

For a while Sixtus obligingly shifted his attention to the possibility of recapturing Geneva, formerly possessed by the dukes of Savoy and now the citadel of Calvinism, but in August he again proposed the invasion of England as a prelude to the final reduction of Holland and Zeeland. Once more Philip rejected the idea, albeit slightly less firmly. After emphasizing the cost and the long duration of the war in the Netherlands – 'entirely to avoid concessions over religion' and 'to maintain obedience there to God and the Holy See' – the king urged Olivares to impress upon the pope the strategic dilemma facing him:

> Let His Holiness judge whether I can undertake new enterprises, with this one [the Dutch war] in its current state ... because one cannot deal effectively with more than one thing at a time. And let him consider whether reducing the pressure [in the Netherlands] for anything else would be right, or a service to Our Lord ... because the war there is fought against heretics, which is what the pope wants. He should not think me idle as long as it continues.

Philip therefore invited the pope to contribute to the costs of maintaining the Army of Flanders and so facilitate a speedier victory in the Netherlands. Perhaps to distract Sixtus, he also urged his son-in-law, the duke of Savoy, to recapture Geneva.[26]

Sixtus refused to be distracted. Besides browbeating Olivares in Rome, he tried to change the king's mind through Luigi Dovara, a Tuscan diplomat sent to Spain some months earlier to promise financial aid from both the pope and the grand duke if Philip attacked England. Discussions with Philip's advisers in July and August proved inconclusive and Dovara had practically abandoned hope when on 11 October news reached the king that English troops had landed in Galicia four days before and opened hostilities against the local population.[27] Drake's audacity proved the last straw for Philip. Although taken completely by surprise – 'you must realize that the event was so unexpected that we cannot provide you with any help from here', he apologized to his beleaguered officials in Galicia – he ordered Don Juan de Zúñiga to prepare a thorough review of Spain's international situation in the light of this unwelcome development.[28]

## The Zúñiga Plan

Like his earlier analyses of the impact of the duke of Anjou's death (see chapter 5), Zúñiga's response represented Spanish strategic planning at its best. He first identified four major enemies – the Turks, the French, the Dutch and the English – and then evaluated the current threat level posed by each. He reasoned that the Ottoman sultan, previously Spain's foremost antagonist, had committed so many resources to the struggle with Iran that Philip need only maintain a defensive posture in the Mediterranean. The French, also once a major threat, now seemed so thoroughly mired in their own civil disputes that although it might be necessary to intervene at some stage to prolong them, the cost to Spain would probably not be high. This left the Dutch and the English. The former had been a thorn in Philip's side since the outbreak of rebellion in 1572; but although costly and humiliating, at least the problem remained confined to the Low Countries. The English menace seemed quite different. It had arisen recently and it threatened the entire Hispanic world, because Elizabeth supported the Dutch and Dom Antonio as well as Drake.

Zúñiga argued that since the queen had now openly broken with Spain, 'to fight a purely defensive war is to incur a huge and permanent expense, because we need to defend the Indies, Spain and the convoys travelling between them'. Therefore, he reasoned, an amphibious attack in overwhelming strength on Elizabeth's realms represented not only the most effective response but also the cheapest. Admittedly, the diversion of resources to the Enterprise of England might temporarily halt the reconquest of the Netherlands and compromise the security of Spanish America, but Zúñiga argued that Philip must take these risks because English aggression threatened his entire monarchy.[29]

Events soon vindicated Zúñiga's analysis. Parma reported a massive build-up of English forces in Holland, paid for by English subsidies, culminating in December

1585 with the arrival of Leicester to serve as governor-general of the rebellious provinces; while Drake continued his destructive progress from Galicia, through the Canaries and the Cape Verde Islands to the Caribbean. In Madrid, Granvelle fretted that 'the queen of England makes war on us so boldly and dishonestly, and yet we cannot get our own back'. In Lisbon, Santa Cruz composed a 'Discourse' that reviewed essential defensive measures to guard against the possibility (soon to become reality) of further attacks by Drake in America.[30]

These pusillanimous responses infuriated Don Rodrigo de Castro, archbishop of Seville, who had worked with the king to re-catholicize England in the 1550s. 'I wish we would cease to place our trust and base our policies on always having good luck,' he railed to a prominent minister in Madrid, 'because a single misfortune (which normally follows) leads to the loss of the reputation that underpins the authority of kings and princes . . . Let me tell Your Lordship how embarrassed I feel that there is now someone who can wrest mastery of the seas from a powerful king like ours.' Castro then directed his fire against Santa Cruz's 'Discourse'. What was the point (he enquired witheringly) of chasing after Drake, 'who is a fine sailor and leads a fleet that is well-equipped with everything he needs?' Surely the best way to end the English menace would be to attack Elizabeth while her leading admiral was absent from home waters. 'If we are going to undertake this operation,' Castro argued, 'there will never be a better time than now.' The king, who read this letter, endorsed it: 'The necessary orders have already been given.'[31]

They had indeed. On 24 October 1585, less than two weeks after hearing that Drake's forces had landed in Galicia, Philip entrusted Luigi Dovara with letters informing both Sixtus and the grand duke of Tuscany that he now accepted their invitation to undertake the conquest of England. He sounded only two notes of caution. First, 'Although His Holiness and His Majesty agree and are of the same mind about this enterprise, the lack of time (since putting the venture into effect requires extensive preparations) excludes the possibility of doing it in 1586, and so it will have to be delayed until 1587.' Second, because the total cost of the enterprise seemed likely to exceed three million ducats, and with Spain's finances already stretched to the limit by the war in the Netherlands, the king declared himself 'happy to contribute what he can, but states that it cannot be more than one third – or at the most one half – of the cost. The rest will have to come' from his Italian allies. In all other respects, however, Philip's response seemed positive, even enthusiastic.[32]

As soon as letters of commitment arrived from Rome and Florence, Philip signed further letters concerning the conquest of England which (just as Ridolfi had proposed) would involve the Army of Flanders. On 29 December 1585 he invited Parma, fresh from his triumphant reconquest of most of Flanders and Brabant, to propose a suitable strategy for invasion. Four days later he authorized Olivares to discuss with the pope three important questions concerning the operation: How would the invasion be justified to the world? What role would His Holiness and the grand duke play? And who would rule England after the death of Mary Stuart (still the obvious successor to Elizabeth and explicitly recognized as 'my sovereign' by many Catholics)? The ambassador must also insist that Parma would command the expeditionary force.[33]

It was one thing to decide that England must be invaded, however, and quite another to make it happen. Seaborne invasions had either overthrown or seriously undermined nine English governments since the Norman Conquest of 1066, with at least seven other successful landings by major forces and many other lesser raids. Philip and his ministers studied these various operations carefully and concluded that three strategies offered a reasonable prospect of success. The first consisted of a combined operation by a fleet strong enough both to defeat the opposing English navy and to shepherd across the Channel an army large enough to accomplish the conquest, just as William I had done in 1066. The second possible strategy involved a surprise assault, as Elizabeth's grandfather Henry Tudor had done in 1485. Finally, Philip could assemble an army in secret near the Channel while launching a diversionary assault on Ireland, which would draw off most of England's defenders and leave the mainland open to invasion by the main force (the Smerwick operation of 1579–80 seemed to show the way). That all three possible strategies received consideration in the wake of Drake's raid reflects great credit on the vision and competence of Philip and his 'national security advisors'; that they decided to undertake all three of them at once does not.[34]

## The Santa Cruz Plan

Confusion commenced in February 1586 when Santa Cruz responded to Archbishop Castro's rebuke by submitting an eloquent paper arguing that the best way to defend the Iberian world against 'pirates' like Drake would be an amphibious attack on England, which – predictably – he offered to command. Equally predictably, Philip demanded more details, instructing the marquis to prepare 'a paper showing the way in which you believe this could be effected, should circumstances permit'.[35]

This marked a radical departure in Philip's strategic thinking towards England, because previous plans had involved an invasion launched from the Netherlands, not from the Iberian Peninsula. Nevertheless, Santa Cruz seized the opportunity and in March 1586 sent the king a detailed proposal grandiloquently entitled 'The fleet and army that it seems would be necessary to assemble for the conquest of England'. The marquis prudently omitted both the precise strategy and the exact target envisaged, because 'the business is such that it is absolutely impossible to deal with or discuss it in writing', but we may speculate that the ultimate target was Kent, as it would be in 1588, with a preliminary descent on the south coast of Ireland (perhaps Waterford or Wexford, since many subsequent strategic papers designated these areas for attack). In any case the immense quantity and nature of the munitions specified, from capital ships down to the last pair of shoes, made clear that Santa Cruz aimed to emulate William the Conqueror, leading an invasion in overwhelming strength. As with his successful Terceira operation, the task force would assemble at Lisbon and strike from there as a single amphibious operation, landing an army in irresistible strength with all the necessary supporting services at a place that would take the enemy by surprise.[36]

Santa Cruz's proposal contained four elements, starting with transport. He estimated that he would need 150 ships totalling 77,250 tons to bring the projected 55,000 invasion troops to their destination. They would comprise forty-five fighting ships, including the galleons of the Portuguese Crown; forty large merchant vessels from Ragusa, Venice, Naples, Sicily and the Mediterranean coast of Spain; thirty-five Basque merchantmen from Biscay and Guipúzcoa; and thirty German *urcas* already in Iberian ports after having transported naval stores from the Baltic. An additional 400 support vessels of various sizes and types would assist with the mustering and preparation of the great fleet.

The second element in Santa Cruz's proposal concerned getting this massive force to the landing-zone. He argued that the role of this Armada, while at sea, must be wholly defensive. The engagement off São Miguel had demonstrated the futility, from the Spanish point of view, of a duel of heavy artillery which achieved victory at the expense of the capacity to exploit that victory ashore. The fleet would therefore sail – as it would in 1588 – in such a way that rigid formation discipline coupled with vigorous self-defence would bring it to Elizabeth's shores, if not unscathed, then at least sufficiently intact to put the third phase of the operation into effect: to land and secure a beachhead for the army. To this end 200 specially designed landing-craft would be built. This would doubtless prove the most difficult and crucial part of the whole enterprise; but it was one where Santa Cruz and many of his subordinates had recent and successful experience. It would be little different from the Terceira landing, except for the larger scale, and Santa Cruz took care to specify those ingredients that had brought him victory before. The forty galleys and six galleasses he demanded would now come into their own. Though unsuited for open-water combat with armed sailing ships, and vulnerable in heavy seas, oared warships would prove deadly in sheltered waters close to land and screened from seaward by the main fleet. They could operate right up to the beaches and neutralize shore positions; they could transfer heavy loads, including field- and siege-artillery, from the fleet to the beachhead; and once the initial landing-zone had been consolidated they could support the army's flank as it advanced on London, securing the rivers and harbours as required, just as they had done in Santa Cruz's advance up the Tagus to Lisbon a few years before.

Once the troops and their equipment had disembarked on the beaches, the operation would move into its fourth and final phase: the conquest of a considerable part of Elizabeth's kingdom (Santa Cruz did not specify its limits). For this the army would require everything necessary to ensure quick success, since speed would be of the essence. A swift blow at some vulnerable yet important part of the Tudor state would provide the most certain solution to the English problem, and perhaps the cheapest one too. To put the issue beyond doubt, Santa Cruz calculated that he would need 55,000 soldiers, including many veterans, supported by a siege-train organized into four batteries each of twelve 40-pounder *cañones de batir* and four 25-pounder heavy *culebrinas*, plus sixteen heavy field guns, twenty-four lighter guns and twenty swivel-pieces. An appropriate number of draught and pack animals, wheeled transport, and specialist artisans would accompany the artillery-train, together with 3,000 pioneers to construct field fortifications and siegeworks and to clear obstacles (see Appendix 4).

Santa Cruz's general staff would include administrative officers, a medical service, and a contingent of military police. Although the planning document made no mention of it (perhaps the marquis felt that this was something Philip would like to attend to himself), there would certainly be a strong chaplaincy department to maintain the crusading zeal of the troops and add spiritual conversion to the temporal subjugation of the English heretics. The prodigious undertaking would cost, according to Santa Cruz's meticulous reckoning (calculated down to the last earthenware platter), 1,526,425,798 *maravedís*, or about 4 million ducats: roughly £1 million.[37]

No doubt, like most commanders when asked by their political masters to draw up a plan of action, Santa Cruz deliberately overestimated his requirements to allow for the probability that they would later be scaled down. He probably also worked on the assumption that a smaller force might be able to do the job (albeit with less certainty of outright success). Be that as it may, mobilization of the task force he had proposed began almost immediately. On 2 April 1586, after a high-level policy meeting at the Escorial, the king authorized naval preparations in three places. Santa Cruz (who attended the meeting) would create a fighting fleet at Lisbon, to be called 'The navy for the defence of my realm, and for the destruction and punishment of the pirates who threaten its coasts'. Medina Sidonia would raise troops and concentrate supply-vessels in the ports of Andalucia. Juan Martínez de Recalde, Spain's most experienced Atlantic seaman, would embargo eight large merchantmen and four *pataches* in the Cantabrian ports to form a new squadron. He would then lead them to Lisbon, and from there the combined fleet would 'sail to Ireland and form a bridgehead' before either invading England or creating a diversion which would allow 'Your Majesty to carry out the conquest of Holland and Zeeland, or at least exchange your gains for the places that the queen holds in the Netherlands, and thus destroy that voracious monster which gobbles up the troops and treasure of Spain', namely the Dutch Republic.[38]

At precisely this moment news arrived at Court that Drake had captured and sacked Santo Domingo, capital of the Spanish Caribbean. An English officer gloated that Philip had 'never had the like piece of service performed since first the Indies were found' and 'neither has he nor any other prince had so great things done by so few hands'. Worst of all, from the king's point of view, 'We do not know what our enemies plan to do next.' He fretted that Drake and his men 'might have caused the Blacks on Hispaniola to rebel', and therefore ordered Santa Cruz to forget about 'the other project under discussion' (the invasion of England) and instead lead the fleet he had assembled to the Caribbean and destroy Drake. Perhaps realizing that the marquis would not welcome this drastic change of plan, Don Juan de Idiáquez added a holograph message of his own to the royal order, ending with a veiled threat: 'Your Lordship owes a lot to His Majesty.'[39]

The marquis's reply accepted the need to react decisively to the emergency in America, 'both to serve God, by preventing the heretics from gaining a base in the Americas, and to preserve our reputation'; but he claimed he did not yet command sufficient forces to achieve these goals. In addition, his spies in England warned that reinforcements for Drake were about to leave. Perhaps, Santa Cruz speculated, the 'pirates' intended to seize and fortify an American base (as indeed they did, at Roanoke) and he therefore insisted that a successful expedition to dislodge the English would require, in addition to his existing forces, 10,000 new troops, twelve galleys (essential for an amphibious landing), twelve siege-guns and 230 extra artillery pieces, plus sufficient powder and shot. Santa Cruz's arguments left the king unmoved. He refused to sanction the removal of any galleys from Iberian waters, or to await reinforcements, and he asserted that the English were far weaker than the marquis claimed. He therefore ordered Santa Cruz to leave Lisbon for the Caribbean at once. 'Everything depends on your rapid departure,' Philip insisted in his reply dated 20 April 1586.[40]

## The Parma Plan

That same day, in Brussels, the duke of Parma completed and dispatched his own detailed plan for invading England, as requested by the king. His twenty-eight-page letter began by regretting the lack of secrecy surrounding the king's intentions: even ordinary soldiers and civilians in the Netherlands, he asserted, now openly discussed the best way to invade England. Nevertheless, he believed that three basic precautions might still save the Enterprise. First, the king of Spain must have sole charge 'without placing any reliance on either the English [Catholics] themselves, or the assistance of other allies'. Second, the French must be prevented both from sending assistance to Elizabeth and from intervening in the Netherlands. Third, sufficient troops and resources must remain behind to defend the reconquered Netherlands against the Dutch after the invasion force had left.

After meeting these conditions, Parma suggested detaching a force of 30,000 foot and 500 horse from the Army of Flanders and ferrying them across the Channel aboard a flotilla of seagoing barges to launch a surprise attack on England. Provided his destination remained a secret, the duke felt he could undertake the invasion with a fair chance of success:

> given the number of troops we have to hand here, and the ease with which we can concentrate and embark them in the barges, and considering that we can ascertain, at any moment, the forces that Elizabeth has and can be expected to have, and that the crossing only takes 10 to 12 hours without a following wind (and 8 hours with one).

'The most suitable, close and accessible point of disembarkation,' he concluded, 'is the coast between Dover and Margate, which is at the mouth of the river Thames... This would allow us to march on London so fast that we could take it by surprise.' In essence, this represented the second invasion strategy: a surprise assault.

Only two paragraphs of Parma's long letter addressed the possibility of naval support from Spain, and even then only in the context of the worst-case scenario: if Elizabeth somehow discovered details of his plan, depriving him of the element of surprise. In that case, he suggested, since Drake's exploits had forced the king to mobilize a fleet to protect the Atlantic, the new navy might 'either sail suddenly up here to assist and reinforce the troops who have already landed [in Kent] and keep open the seaway between the coasts of Flanders and England. Otherwise – if your fleet is large, well-provided, well-armed and well-manned – it could create a diversion that will draw the English fleet away' from the straits of Dover. This corresponded to the third possible strategy for invading England, the one later favoured by Napoleon Bonaparte: a powerful naval decoy to facilitate an attack by a relatively unprotected invasion army.[41]

To some extent the long delay before Parma's proposal arrived at Court reduced its appeal. The king had asked for it in December 1585, yet Parma only complied four months later. Moreover, he entrusted it to a special messenger, the engineer Giovanni Battista Piatti, and sent him to Court by the longest route: along the Spanish Road to Italy, and then across the Mediterranean. Piatti did not deliver Parma's proposal to the royal cipher-clerks until 20 June, and the king's advisers spent four more days debriefing him about the exact amount of shipping available in the ports of Flanders to ferry a major army across the open sea, and about the possible advantage of a landing-place closer to London.

By then news of Drake's further depredations in the Caribbean had caused turmoil in the Spanish capital. The Imperial ambassador in Madrid marvelled at Philip's apparent lack of urgency in exacting revenge:

> I cannot work out the king's plan, because the Armada [in Lisbon] is taking shape so slowly . . . In the streets [*auf den Gassen*], people say that it cannot set sail this year. This makes no sense to me, unless the king has some secret intelligence or ruse: if so, it's no wonder that we are being deceived in our discussions. God forbid that it's the king who is being deceived.[42]

The gossip 'in the streets' of Spain continued, and in July Mateo Vázquez complained to the president of the Council of Castile, responsible for maintaining law and order in the capital, that:

> The people of Madrid are talking very freely about the damage done by the Englishman Francis Drake, using brazen and careless words, implying that we failed to take appropriate steps to stop him. This raises the suspicion that someone is trying to unsettle people, instead of stressing the great prudence and wisdom with which His Majesty has acted and is acting to do everything possible.

The president replied suavely (and revealingly) that 'although there are always some wicked people and unquiet spirits everywhere, in this case I do not believe that those who talk about this do so because they are wicked'. Rather 'everyone can see how much England and the Englishman Francis Drake affect public affairs here': it was only natural for people to talk about it. He therefore suggested that Philip should create a special committee to discuss (and be seen to discuss) 'all matters of state and war that involve the English'.[43]

## The Grand Design

Since 'open government' had never been Philip's style, instead of creating a special committee he turned Parma's assessment over to Don Juan de Zúñiga, already charged with implementing the preparations advocated by Santa Cruz, and Zúñiga in turn sought the advice of Bernardino de Escalante.

The archives of Philip's government are full of letters and memorials written by men like Escalante, often (like him) priests who lived and worked far from government circles. Born in Laredo, the son of a prominent naval captain, Escalante had sailed to England with the king in 1554 and spent fourteen months there before enlisting as a soldier in the Spanish army in the Netherlands. He later returned to Spain, went to university, and evidently studied geography as well as theology, for he later wrote an excellent treatise on navigation before becoming a priest. After his ordination he served as an Inquisitor until in 1581 he entered the service of the fire-eating archbishop of Seville, Don Rodrigo de Castro. Escalante sent more than twenty papers of advice to the king, most of them concerned with the war with England and some clearly influenced by Castro's aggressive attitude. Moreover, he periodically met senior ministers to discuss his suggestions.

In June 1586 Zúñiga invited Escalante to the Escorial, where he reviewed in detail the competing invasion strategies proposed by Santa Cruz and Parma. He even drew a campaign map to illustrate the alternatives – the only cartographic effort concerning the Enterprise of England to survive (Figure 51). Escalante suggested a combined operation. A fleet of 120 galleons, galleasses, galleys, merchantmen and *pataches*, together with an army of 30,000 infantry and 2,000 cavalry, should be concentrated in Lisbon and launched against either Waterford in Ireland or Milford Haven in Wales. At the same time the Army of Flanders should be reinforced, first to tie down the English expeditionary force in Holland, and then to cross the Channel in small ships in preparation for a surprise march on London while Elizabeth's forces dealt with the distant bridgehead established by the Armada.

This ingenious scheme, backed up by a wealth of detail on the political and physical geography of the British Isles, evidently convinced Zúñiga, because his own letter of advice to the king largely reiterated the plan proposed by Escalante. Zúñiga added only a few refinements. He argued that once Santa Cruz had established a beachhead and made the seas secure, supply-ships assembled by Medina

Sidonia in Andalucia should bring reinforcements and replenishments. He also made some suggestions about Parma's options after the invasion. If London fell, the duke should create an interim administration pending the investiture of a new ruler. Since Spain would gain no advantage from the direct annexation of England 'because of the cost of defending it', the newly conquered realm should be bestowed on a friendly Catholic ruler. Zúñiga regarded Mary Stuart as the obvious candidate but recommended that she should marry a dependable Catholic prince, such as Parma himself. If English resistance proved stronger than anticipated, however,

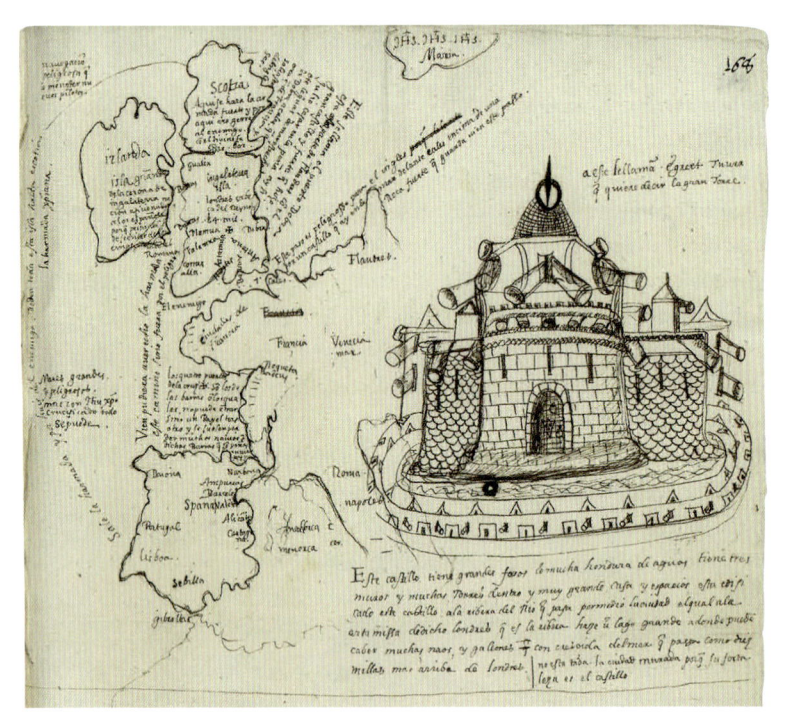

51. Campaign map for the conquest of England sent to Philip by Bernardino de Escalante, 1586. First (on the left) Escalante noted that a fleet from Lisbon might undertake a daring voyage through the North Atlantic directly to Scotland, where it would regroup before launching its main attack. 'The seas are high and dangerous,' Escalante warned, 'but through Jesus Christ crucified everything is possible.' An attack into the Irish Sea offered a second potential strategy, although Elizabeth's warships (labelled 'the enemy', at the entrance to the English Channel) made this a high-risk operation too. No less dangerous would be a surprise attack from Flanders to Dover and on to London, defended by 'E Greet Tura' (The Great Tower). Escalante's memory of England had evidently faded, because he placed 'Dobra' (Dover) in East Anglia and 'Antona' (Southampton) in Kent.

the duke should use his presence on English soil to secure three key concessions. First, there must be complete toleration and freedom of worship for Catholics throughout the kingdom. Second, Elizabeth must withdraw all her troops from the Netherlands, and surrender the places they garrisoned directly to Spain. Finally, England must pay a war-indemnity, and the invasion force should remain in Kent until it was received. With such high stakes, and with such a complex operation, Zúñiga concluded (as Philip had already done) that it would be futile to attempt anything during the present campaigning season; so he suggested that the Enterprise of England should be launched in August or September 1587.[44]

The king apparently made only one significant change to these suggestions before 26 July 1586, when he sent to both Parma in Brussels and Santa Cruz in Lisbon his Grand Design, henceforth referred to (for security reasons) as 'the agreed strategy' (*la traza acordada*), to overthrow Elizabeth Tudor and return England to the Catholic Church. The marquis would lead an Armada of irresistible force from Lisbon in summer 1587 – one year later – carrying all available troops together with most of the equipment (above all a powerful siege-train) needed for the land campaign, directly to Ireland's south coast. There it would land assault troops and secure a beachhead, thus drawing Elizabeth's naval forces away from the Narrow Seas. After two months – and here lay the critical new dimension – the Armada would suddenly leave Ireland and make for the Channel. At that point, and not before, the main invasion force of 30,000 veterans from the Army of Flanders would embark on a flotilla of small ships, secretly assembled, and under Parma's personal direction they would sail to a landing-zone on the Kent coast, henceforth referred to (for security reasons) as 'the agreed place': *la plaza acordada*, while the Grand Fleet secured local command of the sea. Parma's troops, together with reinforcements and the siege-train from the fleet, would land near Margate, make a dash for London and seize the city – preferably with Elizabeth and her leading ministers still in it.

One wonders whether Philip realized the enormous dangers posed by his hybrid Masterplan. Santa Cruz's original proposal contained much merit. The events of 1588 proved that once the Armada got to sea it experienced little difficulty in moving 60,000 tons of shipping to the Narrow Seas, despite repeated assaults upon it. The operation at Kinsale in 1601 (see chapter 18) showed that an amphibious force from Spain could easily seize and fortify a beachhead in southern Ireland. Parma's concept of a surprise landing in Kent also had much to recommend it: his troops had repeatedly shown their mettle under his leadership, and the untested and largely untrained English forces, taken by surprise, would have found it hard to withstand the Army of Flanders once it got ashore. The Armada's undoing ultimately arose from the decision to unite the fleet from Spain with the army from the Netherlands as an essential prelude to launching the invasion; and that decision came directly from Philip II.

Why did he do it? The king had seen active service in two victorious campaigns against France, in 1557 and 1558. In 1580 he had approved a strategy for the conquest of Portugal, which involved the daring transfer of a large army and its equipment from Setubal to Cascais, a sea journey that lasted three days and covered some 70 miles (considerably more than the distance from Dunkirk to Dover). The following year, at Lisbon, Philip inspected in person the fleet assembled to recover Terceira; and although it failed, in 1582 he oversaw the assembly of a far larger amphibious force there which executed a major operation in the Azores, 1,000 miles away, and he welcomed its triumphant return. The king also possessed direct experience of the route that both components of his Grand Design would follow. In 1554 he had sailed with a fleet from Corunna to Southampton, a journey completed in just one week, and five years later he had sailed back relatively easily from Flushing to Santander. In between, he crossed the Channel between England and the Netherlands three times.

For all that, the king remained an armchair strategist: technical, tactical and operational issues all remained closed books to him. Furthermore, he refused to move closer to the action, ignoring all suggestions that he should return to Lisbon to oversee the assembly of the fleet in person. It therefore took at least a week before Santa Cruz received a solution to each problem referred to the king, and Parma had to wait between four and six weeks. More seriously, Philip refused to brief either of his commanders in person: instead, both received a copy of 'the agreed strategy' of 26 July 1586 by courier (albeit Parma's copy went with the same messenger, Piatti, who had brought the prince's own suggested strategy to Court).

The deleterious consequences of Philip's style of leadership for the Armada campaign cannot be overstated. Looking back on how the Western Allies had won World War II, the Chairman of Britain's Joint Chiefs of Staff stressed the critical importance of periodic meetings between all the principal protagonists to hammer out a common strategy:

> We were working strategy three to six months ahead the whole time. *It was essential for us to meet round a table. We found you could not do it by an interchange of papers* and as we drew near the time to gather and make a conference, it became clearer and clearer that, *until we got around a table, we could never really solve those intricate problems of strategy that confronted us.*[45]

The 'intricate problems of strategy' that confronted Philip in the 1580s remained unsolved largely because he refused to meet his principal commanders 'around a table'. They therefore could not make him explain precisely how two large and totally independent forces, with operational bases separated by 700 miles of ocean, could attain the accuracy of time and place necessary to accomplish their junction, or how the vulnerable troop-transports to be collected in Flanders would be able to evade the Dutch and English warships stationed offshore to intercept and destroy them.

Unfortunately for the venture, the only ministers in Madrid with the authority and the knowledge to raise objections, Granvelle and Zúñiga, both died in the autumn of 1586, so no one could insist that Philip devise a fall-back strategy, a 'Plan B'. To some diplomats in Madrid the king now seemed 'imprudent and thoughtless, fit only to live among monks', because 'unchecked by rivalry with France' and without anyone to restrain him, he had become a prisoner of 'his own nature, which appreciates devotion more than love'.[46]

This was not how the Spanish elite at the time saw the international situation, however. The prominent merchant banker Simón Ruiz and his international correspondents welcomed the news that the king planned to send a major fleet against England, for they saw it as the only way to restore security to Spain's trade with the rest of Europe. The president of the Council of the Indies, responsible for New World affairs, likewise argued that only a direct strike on England could safeguard the Americas. Even the normally prudent duke of Medina Sidonia submitted a ten-folio handwritten memorandum which presented the creation of a powerful Spanish navy as indispensable for the nation's prosperity and security. He urged 'that this should be set in hand at once, and in earnest, and let it be understood that it will not suffice simply to oppose what the English send: [the fleet] will need to go into the Channel'. The duke (who little thought that he would eventually lead the Armada himself) also recommended that 'in all parts – in Italy, as in Vizcaya, Guipúzcoa, Portugal and Andalucia – preparations and activity should be undertaken, because it will become known in England and will make them draw in their horns'.[47]

The king agreed. A stream of commands now flowed from his desk which set the Enterprise of England in motion. He ordered the new squadron raised by Recalde to defend northern Spain to sail to Lisbon. He issued commissions to levy troops all over Spain to man the Armada. His viceroys in Naples and Sicily must send troops, victuals and munitions to join Santa Cruz, and to transport these assets they must embargo suitable merchant ships, guarded by four of the heavily gunned galleasses stationed in Naples. Philip then turned his attention to a diplomatic offensive designed to ensure that, at the critical moment, no foreign power would raise a finger to save Elizabeth Tudor from her fate.[48]

# 7

# Phoney War

## Regicide

In the event, Elizabeth herself provided Philip's greatest diplomatic success when on 18 February 1587 her officials executed Mary Queen of Scots. Perhaps they saw no alternative. The Ridolfi Plot was the first of many conspiracies that aimed to kill Elizabeth and replace her with Mary Stuart, creating a vicious circle. With so many plots afoot, Mary had become too dangerous for Elizabeth to set at liberty; and yet, detained in a succession of draughty castles with little opportunity for exercise, entertainment or outside recreation, a successful conspiracy offered Mary her only chance of freedom. Intrigue therefore became her principal pastime.

In summer 1586 Anthony Babington, a young English Catholic who had once served in Mary's household, devised a new plot to assassinate Elizabeth and some of her leading ministers. The queen of Scots rashly expressed her support for Babington in writing, and since Walsingham managed to intercept, decipher and copy the conspirators' entire correspondence, he arrested Babington and thirteen other conspirators. They were tortured, tried, convicted, hanged, castrated and disembowelled. Shortly afterwards Mary was moved to Fotheringhay Castle, near Peterborough, where Walsingham revealed her treasonable correspondence with Babington to a special commission comprising Elizabeth's leading councillors and nobles. The verdict was inevitable: execution for treason.

In assessing the severity of these punishments it is important to remember the underlying insecurity of the Elizabethan regime. The childless queen, now fifty-three, could not live for ever, and Mary was her closest relative. Although parliamentary statutes barred a Stuart succession, parliament had enacted similar statutes barring the succession of both Elizabeth and Mary Tudor, and in each case a later parliament had revoked them. Many prominent Elizabethans in 1586 remembered these earlier events. Some (including Elizabeth and Leicester) had languished in prison during Mary's reign; at least a thousand others (including Walsingham and his brother-in-law Robert Beale, clerk of the Privy Council) had fled the country to avoid the risk of being burned at the stake for their Protestant faith. They could hardly expect better treatment from a new Catholic regime.

They were right. The king liberally annotated the deciphered text of a letter from Don Bernardino de Mendoza, now Philip's ambassador in Paris, which included Babington's suggestion that the plotters should 'capture or kill' four of Elizabeth's ministers: Burghley, Walsingham, Hunsdon and 'Conoslybel'. Interestingly, Philip insisted that Burghley be spared, writing: 'He does not matter so much, because although he is a heretic he is very old, and he is the one who favours peace talks; but it would be advisable to do as he [Babington] says with the other three.' In fact, Mendoza (and Babington) had proposed *four* other names, but the royal cipher-clerks, unfamiliar with Elizabeth's ministers, had written 'Conoslybel' instead of 'Knollys y Beale' in the decrypt read by Philip. The king thus sanctioned the murder of someone he could not even identify.[1]

Although Burghley, Walsingham, Beale and their colleagues never knew about this letter, they certainly believed that an international Catholic conspiracy lay behind the plots to replace Elizabeth with Mary. Every new setback suffered by the Protestant cause abroad, and every new plot detected at home, increased their fear of an imminent Catholic assault on the Tudor state. In summer 1586 no one knew how much foreign support Babington had secured, and as a precaution John Hawkins took eighteen warships to reconnoitre the coasts of Spain and Portugal and look for evidence of naval preparations. During his three-month cruise Hawkins took prisoners who confirmed the worst: Spain was indeed preparing a huge invasion of England.

Playing on these fears, and on rumours (possibly invented) of yet another plot to replace Elizabeth with her cousin, this time involving French Catholics, in December the queen raged at an audience with a French ambassador, with 'some passion, which appeared in her countenance', that 'the Queen of Scotland had always pursued her, and that it was the third time that she had sought to make an attempt upon her life by an infinity of means'. She also claimed that 'nothing had ever touched her heart so keenly'.[2] Walsingham and Burghley exploited her anger to draft a warrant condemning Mary Stuart to death and they ordered William Davison, joint secretary of state with Walsingham, to make a fair copy ready for the queen's signature. On 11 February 1587, in a tense interview, Howard of Effingham convinced his cousin Elizabeth that she must sign the warrant. Having done so, she entrusted it to Davison. At the same time she ordered the two secretaries to compose a letter to Mary's custodian, Sir Amias Paulet, reproaching him for not finding 'some way to shorten the life of that queen [Mary], considering the great peril she [Elizabeth] is subject to hourly, so long as the said queen shall live' – in other words: why had he not murdered her in secret? The secretaries reminded Paulet that he had subscribed to the Bond of Association, which allowed him (in view of the Babington plot) to put Mary to death legally, and that his failure to do so 'cast the burden upon' Elizabeth, despite 'knowing as you do her indisposition to shed blood, especially of one of that sex and quality, and so near to her in blood'. Paulet received the letter at Fotheringhay the following day, and immediately replied with outrage that he had 'lived to see this unhappy day, in which I am required by direction from my most gracious sovereign to do an act which God and the law forbids'. He concluded: 'God forbid that I should make so foul a shipwreck of my conscience, or leave so great a blot to my poor posterity, to shed blood without law or warrant.'[3]

Paulet's refusal to murder Mary arrived in London on 13 February, and Burghley immediately summoned to his apartments nine other members of the Privy Council (including Leicester, Walsingham and Howard) and showed them the warrant signed by the queen. They all signed a document authorizing the regicide and gave it to Beale, who carried it post-haste to Fotheringhay, accompanied by an executioner whom Walsingham had thoughtfully kept in readiness. Mary died with dignity on the scaffold on 18 February 1587 (Figure 52).

These men played for high stakes because they had high hopes. A few months earlier, after reading the compromising correspondence between Mary and Babington, Walsingham predicted that 'if the matter be well handled it will break the neck of all dangerous practices during Her Majesty's reign'; and an eyewitness of the regicide opined that the 'fatal stroke this day [will] excuse her from being accessory to any like matters that may happen henceforth'. And so it proved: the plots against Elizabeth died with the queen of Scots. Some therefore considered that Davison and Beale had done a good day's work for the Protestant cause. The queen was not among them.[4]

News of the execution arrived in London later that same day while Elizabeth was out riding, and afterwards she 'talked for a long time with the king of Portugal [Dom Antonio]'. Fearing her wrath, her councillors maintained a discreet silence for as long as possible, but at '3 p.m. every bell in the town began to ring and there were bonfires in every street, with feasting and banqueting, as a sign of great rejoicing'. The queen 'taking notice thereof and asking the reason, thereby she

**52.** The execution of Mary Queen of Scots, February 1587. The earls of Kent and Shrewsbury sit in judgement on the queen, with Elizabeth's other commissioners standing behind them. Her servants kneel in prayer to her left. Afterwards the queen's clothes are burned (far left).

came first to know' that Mary was dead.[5] Her thoughts turned immediately to the probable international repercussions of the regicide of a former queen of Scotland and France who was not her subject but an anointed ruler, the mother of James VI of Scotland, and close relative of both Henry III and Philip II.

The initial French reaction to news of Mary's execution was alarming. In Rouen angry mobs seized English ships and destroyed English goods. In Paris outraged clerics delivered inflammatory sermons calling for revenge, and exhibited pictures outside their churches luridly portraying the atrocities committed against English Catholics by the Elizabethan regime. In Scotland King James (now aged twenty) expressed outrage that his mother had been killed without prior consultation, and many of his subjects felt the same. He sent envoys to France and Denmark to discuss mounting a joint assault on Elizabeth, who was widely compared with the evil Queen Jezebel of the Old Testament.

Elizabeth desperately searched for scapegoats. First she blamed the commissioners who had carried out her instructions, but they pointed out that the warrant bore her signature and must be obeyed. Then she accused the Privy Councillors who had approved the deed without her knowledge, but they too pleaded that the warrant had full legal force. Finally she turned on Burghley, who had coordinated the whole affair, and on Davison, who had released the signed warrant without (she alleged) her express command to do so. She therefore had Davison tried, imprisoned in the Tower, fined heavily and threatened with execution (although she freed him after just eighteen months, waived his fine and continued to pay his salary as secretary of state until he died). She also ostentatiously humiliated Burghley, forbidding him to come to Court for four weeks. Even in June the queen still 'entered into marvellous evil speeches' when she caught sight of him, 'calling him traitor, false dissembler and wicked wretch, commanding him to avoid her presence, and all about the death of the Scottish queen'.[6]

This was not an atmosphere conducive to the rational formulation of foreign policy. In April, almost two months after the execution, Walsingham complained that 'The present discord between her Majesty and her council hinders the necessary consultations that were to be desired for the preventing of the manifest perils that hang over this realm.' A few days later he apologized to a colleague in the Netherlands for failing to advise him on the correct policy to follow there, but 'we could not draw Her Majesty to any resolution. The late severe dealing used by her Majesty towards Mr Secretary Davison and others of her council makes us very circumspect and careful not to proceed in anything but wherein we receive direction from herself.'[7]

Yet seldom had the need for 'direction from herself' been greater. Philip's agents were everywhere, capitalizing to the utmost on the regicide and using it to justify their master's maturing plans to extirpate the tyrannous 'English Jezebel'. In the same month as Mary's execution the Venetian ambassador in Madrid noted in wonderment that 'the Spaniards are moving towards their great object in various ways and from many sides, no less by diplomacy than by preparations for war, and even by a union of the two'.[8]

At first not everything went Philip's way. In the Mediterranean a risk existed that the forces of Islam might launch a new attack on his possessions, or those of his allies, while the better part of Spain's army and fleet was committed in the Atlantic. So Spanish envoys travelled to Istanbul with orders to negotiate an extension of the armistice signed three years earlier with the Ottoman sultan. Elizabeth's diplomats swiftly rose to the occasion. Her unofficial ambassador in

Istanbul, William Harborne, persuaded the sultan that he would gain nothing from a deal with Spain and Philip's agents went away empty-handed. Therefore, although the Turks did not launch another attack in 1587 or 1588, the government in Madrid remained fearful that they might.⁹

Elizabeth's diplomats also succeeded in Scotland. Matters there were severely complicated by the phantom will of Mary Queen of Scots. In May 1586 she had informed the Spanish ambassador in Paris that she intended to 'cede and grant by will my right to the succession of this crown to the king, your master'. In all probability she never made the will (although Philip II ransacked the archives of Rome, Paris and Simancas to find some trace of it), but Elizabeth's agents intercepted Mary's letter describing it and sent a copy to James VI. Realizing that his mother's action threatened to disinherit him both from his Scottish kingdom and from his expectation of succeeding eventually to the English Crown, the young king made clear his support for Elizabeth. He continued to pocket his annual English subsidy of £4,000, and he later imprisoned a Spanish envoy sent to woo him.

The loyalty of some of James's subjects seemed less sure. Rumours of pro-Spanish sentiment in Scotland alarmed Elizabeth so much that in September 1587 she created an army of 6,000 foot and 400 horse on her northern border and kept it there for almost a year. In spring 1588 the Catholic Lord Maxwell began a rebellion in south-west Scotland with the declared intention of providing the Spaniards with a base (although King James rode out to suppress it in person); and in August, with the Armada off the Firth of Forth, alarming reports reached the queen that some Scottish border lords 'have said openly [that] so soon as they shall hear that the Spaniards be landed in any part of Scotland, they will ride straight into England, though the king say no'.¹⁰

English and Spanish agents also clashed in France. Following the 1584 treaty of Joinville, the Catholic League took possession of several strategic towns with Henry III's permission; their leader, the duke of Guise, already held numerous strongholds in the provinces of Champagne and Burgundy. All these places lay in the east of France, but in April 1587 Guise's troops seized three towns in Picardy, near the frontier with the Netherlands, and replaced the royal garrisons with League troops. They failed to capture their principal objective, however, because a royalist spy in Guise's household overheard a conversation about the need 'for some way to take the town of Boulogne, which was said to be necessary for them to receive and shelter the reinforcements they were expecting from Spain'. He alerted the city's garrison, which refused to admit Guise's men. To encourage this welcome spirit of independence, Admiral Howard led part of the English navy to Boulogne and offered any necessary assistance.¹¹

Elizabeth also provided the Huguenots with funds to raise troops in Germany to fight for the leader of the French Protestants, Henry of Navarre. Throughout spring 1587 rumours of their approach circulated, detaining both the duke of Guise and a detachment of the Army of Flanders in the east to resist them. When 11,000 German mercenaries, partially funded by Elizabeth, finally crossed the Rhine in August, the Catholic army easily outmanoeuvred them and inflicted a sharp defeat before they could join forces with Navarre; but their distracting presence detained Guise in eastern France. So in spite of spending over 400,000 ducats in subsidies to the League, and sending a small army in its support, Philip failed to gain a safe Channel port as a potential refuge for his fleet. It proved to be another crucial defect: with the port of Boulogne in friendly hands, the outcome of the Armada might have been very different.

## Seeking Funds and Intelligence

The Enterprise of England now received the king's undivided attention. On the one hand he strengthened economic sanctions against his remaining European enemies. In May 1586 he prohibited all trade from England to Spain: henceforth English goods arriving on neutral shipping would be confiscated as contraband. In January 1587 he ordered a new embargo of all ships from the Netherlands, followed by a detailed search to ascertain if any came from the rebellious provinces. Eight months later he forbade the import of Dutch goods aboard neutral ships.[12] On the other hand the king cancelled or postponed other ventures that might absorb available resources. In 1586, despite the devastation caused by Drake's raid, he rejected a plan by the Council of the Indies to improve the defences of the Caribbean. 'No one regrets the damage and no one desires a remedy more than I do, if only we had a way to execute it as we wish,' he informed the council, 'but your plans create a lot of problems, and the biggest one is the lack of money with which to pay for it all.' Philip likewise turned down the request from his viceroy of India for the dispatch of 'more troops, ships and munitions than normally leave each year' to attack the sultan of Acheh (Sumatra), because 'the large number of ships of all sorts, troops, munitions and military equipment' assembled for the Armada 'cost so much'. He also vetoed a proposal to construct a fortress at Mombasa in east Africa and rejected a request from the Spanish colonists of the Philippines to launch an invasion of China – both to avoid diverting resources required for the Enterprise of England.[13]

Concern about the need to economize was well founded. In 1585 the grand duke of Tuscany estimated that the conquest of England would cost just over 3 million ducats (£750,000). A year later Santa Cruz put the total cost of his proposal for the Enterprise at 4 million ducats (£1 million); but early in 1587 a group of the king's senior advisers estimated that 'seven million ducats will be needed to implement the plans made, and to be made, for this year'.[14]

The rising cost of the enterprise increased the king's anxiety to secure the financial contribution promised by Sixtus V. In spring 1586, regretting his earlier offer to pay one-third of the total, the pontiff informed the Spanish ambassador in Rome that a papal subsidy was superfluous since the king would have to invade England anyway 'in order to avenge the insults done him; on account of the advantage this would provide in dealing with Holland; and because he cannot by any other means safeguard his trade with the Indies'. (Ambassador Olivares speculated that the pope's Italian upbringing made him see 'avenging insults' as the mainspring of all public affairs.) Eventually, Sixtus agreed to contribute one million ducats, but only on proof that the invasion had taken place: he required confirmation, certified by a notary, *either* that the Armada had left Lisbon *or* that the army had landed in England, and he allowed Philip to choose the 'trigger' for payment. The king eventually opted for the latter – evidently considering it more likely that Parma would somehow find a way to get his army ashore than that Santa Cruz would ever get his fleet to sea. His error would cost him a million ducats.[15]

The pope's distrust seems to have aroused the king's own suspicions: on the back of a letter from Rome, Philip ruminated on the risk that should Sixtus die unexpectedly his successor might refuse to honour the commitment. In November 1586 these doubts became demands: all the cardinals must swear that, in the event of Sixtus's death, if elected pope they would honour his promise to pay. The king acknowledged the risk that this involved: 'Even though my desire to arrange this may lead to a breach of secrecy, because it may require a meeting of the College of Cardinals, nonetheless it is a point of such importance that it should not be forgotten. Because if we are not protected, we may find ourselves deceived.' Eventually the parties resolved their difficulties and on 29 July 1587 two Roman bankers received a special deposit of one million ducats in gold from the papal treasury, payable as soon as a public notary verified that Parma had landed in England. On the same day Sixtus agreed that Philip should nominate a new ruler of England willing and able to restore and uphold the Catholic faith. Until the investiture of that nominee, the task of re-catholicizing England would be entrusted to Cardinal William Allen, the senior English Catholic priest in exile, assisted by members of the various religious orders travelling with the Armada and with Parma's army. These clerics would also superintend the restoration to the Church of all lands and rights lost at the Reformation.[16]

The pope showed little enthusiasm for these terms, but he now had no choice. With Mary Stuart dead and France paralysed by civil war, the restoration of Catholic worship in England depended utterly on the efforts of Philip II. For the king, too, the battle of wills with Sixtus involved losses as well as gains. He had devoted countless hours to these tortuous negotiations – letters from Olivares bear far more of his holograph annotations than letters from Parma – yet, even so, the deposited money would remain available for only four months: unless the bankers received the agreed certification of Parma's landing by November 1587, the million ducats in gold would return to the papal vaults.

Worse, the king's foolish insistence on securing compliance from every cardinal meant that they, as well as many others, learned important details concerning the Enterprise of England. The Dutch found this out in December 1587 when they captured and interrogated Oda Colonna, an Italian officer serving in the Army of Flanders whose uncle was a cardinal. Colonna tried to secure his freedom by revealing everything he knew about the Armada: its funding, organization and destination. Amazingly, although the Dutch immediately sent a transcript of Colonna's interrogation to England, no one at Elizabeth's Court seems to have believed it. Not until May 1588 – five months later – did Walsingham order further questioning of 'Colonna the prisoner', as a matter of urgency.[17]

In part this strange oversight reflected the dilemma experienced by governments in all ages: how to distinguish true from false intelligence. In the case of Colonna, the dilemma became more intense because his information directly contradicted the data on Spain's intentions transmitted by Elizabeth's ambassador in Paris, Sir Edward Stafford.

On the surface Stafford boasted superb qualifications, both social and professional, for England's foremost diplomatic posting. His stepmother, Mary Boleyn, was Elizabeth's aunt; his mother served as lady-in-waiting to the queen and often slept in her bedchamber; his wife, Lady Douglas Sheffield, was the sister of Lord Admiral Howard. Stafford had undertaken continental missions for Burghley to Germany and France, and served repeatedly as Elizabeth's confidential envoy to her sometime suitor, the duke of Anjou. When Anjou first arrived in London he stayed in Stafford's house. His appointment as ambassador to the French Court in 1583 therefore came as no surprise, but Stafford nevertheless possessed two disadvantages. First, his wife had been Leicester's lover and bore him at least two children before he jilted her: the Staffords therefore detested the earl and tried to undermine his influence, and that of his ally Walsingham, with the queen. Second, Stafford was very short of cash. He complained several times that he lacked the funds to discharge his responsibilities properly and asked the queen to lend him money even if she could not afford to pay his salary. Since she gave him no satisfaction he ran up huge debts and squandered not only his own money but also the substantial sums sent to him by the queen to distribute among her French supporters. In February 1587, desperate for money and outraged by the execution of Mary Queen of Scots, Stafford approached Ambassador Mendoza and declared himself ready to serve Philip in any way possible, short of encompassing Elizabeth's death, in return for cash.

For the next eighteen months the ambassador proved as good as his word, repeatedly revealing to Mendoza confidential information received from England and sending a stream of false information on Spain's pacific intentions back to London. In May 1588, as the Armada prepared to leave Lisbon, he suggested that its true target was Algiers; in June he assured Walsingham that it would soon sail for America. On 31 July, the very day the two fleets had their first encounter off Plymouth, Stafford insisted that the Armada remained at Corunna, too damaged ever to leave.

Elizabeth thus had to balance the reassuring news sent by her own ambassador and kinsman against the alarmist revelations of Oda Colonna, as well as the detailed reports from her spies in Portugal, Spain and Italy concerning the scale and purpose of Philip's military, naval and diplomatic preparations. Fearing the worst she authorized a number of costly defensive measures. Between 1585 and 1588 the Navy Board built or purchased sixteen new vessels and repaired the rest. She also ordered the embargo of all ships in English ports, and from these special commissioners chose sixty-four armed merchantmen, thirty-three supply-vessels and forty-three pinnaces to serve if needed with her own warships. At the same time repairs to the fortifications along the south coast resumed; and orders went out to disarm known Catholics. To hedge her bets, however, Elizabeth also opened negotiations with the duke of Parma. No sooner had the queen signed the Anglo-Dutch treaty of Nonsuch in August 1585 than she sent him an envoy explaining her action and exploring the possibility of reaching an accommodation.

## 'Singeing the King of Spain's Beard'

In spring 1587 Elizabeth suddenly changed her mind and authorized a far more aggressive measure. She may not have seen Philip's promises to send assistance from both Spain and the Netherlands to Anthony Babington and his associates, 'with the greatest possible speed as soon as he knew that the venture had succeeded', confident that 'God would be pleased to permit what they plan, since the time has perhaps arrived for Him to advance His cause'. But she had plenty of circumstantial evidence that the king once more sought to depose and destroy her. She therefore turned again to Sir Francis Drake, who for some months had been seeking backers in England and the Netherlands for a new naval expedition 'to assist the king of Portugal, Dom Antonio, or on some other service'. Now, the queen ordered him to take his ships to sea 'for the honour and safety of our realms'.[18]

What exactly did this mean? If the queen ever issued written instructions for Drake's voyage, they are apparently lost, but his subsequent actions suggest that she ordered him to attack the ports where Philip was assembling ships, men and munitions, and to do as much damage as he could to keep the various parts of the Armada from joining together. To this end Elizabeth provided six of her own warships – almost a fifth of the navy – to reinforce the vessels already assembled by Drake, his friends (including Hawkins, Winter and Howard) and a consortium of London merchants.

As soon as he received the queen's commission Drake galloped straight to Dover, where he found the queen's ships, and immediately sailed with them to Plymouth, followed by the London contingent. On 12 April, less than three weeks later, he led a fleet of sixteen ships and seven pinnaces out of Plymouth Sound. Drake's parting message to Walsingham maintained the ambiguity of his purpose: 'The wind commands me away. Our ship is under sail. God grant we may so live in His fear as the enemy may have cause to say that God doth fight for her Majesty as well abroad as at home.'[19]

He left just in time. One week later the queen changed her mind again, in response to the simultaneous arrival in London of another soothing message from Stafford about Philip's pacific intentions, and of an envoy sent by Parma to promote peace talks. She now expressly forbade Drake 'to enter forcibly into any of the king's ports or havens, or to offer violence to any of his towns or shipping within harbour, or to do any act of hostility upon the land', and she sent a pinnace bearing her new orders speeding after the fleet. Moreover, in spite of every attempt to prevent the news leaving England, Ambassador Stafford in Paris learned that Drake intended to attack Cadiz and immediately leaked the information to Mendoza, who sent a warning to Spain by express courier.[20]

Neither message arrived in time. The queen's pinnace never caught up with Drake, who sighted Cape Finisterre on 15 April; and although Mendoza's courier completed the journey from Paris to Madrid in eleven days, he only delivered his urgent message to the king's cipher-clerks on 30 April. The previous evening, as the population of Cadiz watched the spellbinding feats of an acrobat in the main square, Drake and his powerful fleet had glided into the harbour.

Preparations for the Armada had by then reached a critical stage. Long-term stockpiling of provisions was in a particularly delicate state, because sixteenth-century Europe enjoyed few food surpluses. Supplies of the magnitude required might be difficult to obtain at any price should the notice given be too short; and, without tin cans and freezers, all types of food enjoyed a short shelf-life. Orders for biscuit and salt meat had been placed with contractors at Alicante, Cartagena and Málaga: to meet them, forty new biscuit ovens had to be built at Málaga alone. Government agents signed a contract in Milan for a large consignment of rice; nearly 200 tons of cheese came from the Baltic, transported in twenty Hamburg hulks. Other vessels from northern Europe brought essential naval supplies – pitch, cordage, timber and sailcloth – via the 'north-about' route around the British Isles, to catch the most reliable winds and avoid interception by the queen's ships in the English Channel.

Meanwhile Philip's agents negotiated bulk contracts for the supply of military equipment. In Seville the duke of Medina Sidonia ordered a large number of campaign tents, shoes, leather canteens and knapsacks for the invasion troops. The same city later supplied picks, shovels and gabions for the pioneers (see Appendix 4). According to the secretary of war, equipping so many new recruits meant that 'after providing them with weapons not a single arquebus, pike or musket will be left in the whole of Spain'.[21]

Securing enough suitable ships also required extraordinary measures. To reinforce the flotillas already assembled at Cadiz, the Basque ports and Lisbon, the king's officers embargoed private merchantmen throughout the Iberian world. In December 1586 the viceroy of Sicily seized five great ships constructed to carry bulk cargoes: *Trinidad Valencera* from Venice, *Rata Santa María Encoronada* from Genoa, *Anunciada* and *San Juan de Sicilia* from Ragusa, and *Juliana* from Barcelona. Three months later Medina Sidonia embargoed thirty Dutch and German merchantmen in the ports of Andalucia, including *Gran Grifón*, which became the flagship of the squadron of *urcas*, *San Pedro Mayor*, which became one of the fleet's hospital ships, and *Santiago*, which became known as 'the ship of the women'. Other royal officials seized *St Andrew*, a Scottish trader suspected of carrying contraband, at Málaga, and the English *Charity* at Gibraltar.[22]

Since the Armada had not yet become a coherent force, most of its scattered components remained vulnerable to attack. Moreover, the need to keep the main fleet in Lisbon ready for action seriously compromised the ability of other coastal regions to defend themselves. No one knew this better than Drake. He also knew that, although the Armada would eventually sail from Lisbon, the main activity currently centred on Spain's great southern port, which possessed extensive facilities for equipping and victualling the Indies fleets. With its wide entrance Cadiz may have been less secure than Lisbon, but it possessed forts, artillery and a powerful galley squadron. Trusting in their protection, by April 1587 nearly sixty vessels lay crowded at anchor in the harbour: *urcas* and coasters loading for Lisbon, the tuna-fishing fleet, and merchantmen of all types from small caravels to a 700-ton Genoese carrack. This motley and disorganized collection of ships and stores became the target of Drake's pre-emptive strike.

Flying no colours until the last moment to avoid identification, the English fleet entered the outer haven on 29 April. Drake immediately detached two warships to seize the bridge at Zuazo, the only route by which a relief army could reach Cadiz (the bridge, here '*Puente*', clearly shown at the bottom of the campaign map drawn by William Borough) (Figure 53); but they saw two galleys apparently guarding the spot. Not realizing that the galleys were there to be careened, and lacked crews and artillery, the English withdrew – thus forfeiting their best chance to capture and sack the town. Instead, they bombarded the largest ship in the outer harbour,

53. A map of the Cadiz raid of 1587, drawn by William Borough, Drake's second-in-command. Borough had studied cartography at the House of Trade in Seville and was fluent in Spanish. This explains the accurate representation of the shore batteries and the shoals that guarded the entrance to Cadiz harbour. It also shows the movements of Drake's fleet, starting with 'M' (upper left: 'our fleet at anchor upon a bravado'), with particular attention to the perilous position of Borough's own vessel, the vice-flagship *Lion*.

the great Genoese carrack, and before night fell they had not only sunk her but also burned five more cargo ships. The following day the English burned, sank and captured many other ships, including a large galleon belonging to Santa Cruz, as well as considerable quantities of food, munitions and stores destined for the Armada. However, that afternoon Medina Sidonia arrived with militia companies which he deployed to defend the town. He also set up new shore batteries which began to engage the raiders.

Meanwhile a flotilla of Spanish galleys made two attempts to repel the intruders, but on both occasions 'the superior range and power of the artillery' of the English ships forced them to withdraw; and in a show of bravado Drake fired a heavy-calibre shot right over the town, hitting houses on the far side. Having liberally resupplied his fleet with provisions seized from the enemy, on 1 May Drake prepared to lead his fleet to sea again, but when the wind fell he engaged in a bizarre display to emphasize his success: he decked his ships with all their flags and banners, and arranged a concert 'by the many musical instruments aboard his ships' as he exchanged gifts with the commander of the galleys, Don Pedro de Acuña. When Don Pedro's men returned, they reported in amazement that 'everyone they saw aboard his ship, from the humblest cabin boys to the most exalted soldiers, was dressed exactly alike: that is, [in] coarse cloth of the same colour. Only Drake wore velvet.' Sir Francis also began to negotiate an exchange of prisoners with Medina Sidonia, offering to free twenty-five sailors from Vizcaya in return for five Englishmen (the prize crew of a caravel separated from the English fleet and captured by Spanish galleys), but early on 2 May the wind picked up and he led his fleet away. Despite the '200 culverin and cannon shot at us' by Spain's galleys and shore batteries, only Borough's vice-flagship, *Lion*, suffered any damage.[23]

For some time Drake's destination after 'singeing the king of Spain's beard' (as he called his exploit) remained a mystery. Medina Sidonia sent off warnings of the possible danger: to the Canaries, to Lisbon and to the Court. He even sent one of his own ships to the Caribbean with orders for the annual treasure-fleet to remain in Havana until further notice. Drake had other plans. After an unsuccessful attempt to catch Recalde's Vizcayan squadron on the high seas, and an abortive landing at Lagos on the Algarve coast, on 5 May his men captured the castle and harbour of Sagres, near Cape St Vincent, desecrating churches and again replenishing supplies.

Drake had now seen for himself that 'there was never heard of so great a preparation as the king of Spain hath and daily does make ready for England', and he realized that 'if those forces join, it will be very perilous. Wherefore our intent is (God willing) to use all possible means to hinder the same.' He therefore interdicted the Armada's supply route between Andalucia and Lisbon, capturing or sinking virtually any vessel that tried to run the gauntlet of the English blockade. 'It hath pleased God,' he reported on 27 May, 'that we should take ships, barks, carvels and divers other vessels more than a hundred, most laden, some with oars for galleys, planks and timber for ships and pinnaces.' Above all he had taken 'sixteen or seventeen hundred tons of hoops and pipe-staves which would have made 25 or 30 thousand tons of casks, with many other provisions for this great army which the king of Spain is making ready'. All of this 'I commanded to be consumed into smoke and ashes by fire, which will be unto the king no small waste of his provisions, besides the want of his barks'. In mid-May one diplomat in Madrid estimated that the English had already caused damage equivalent to £175,000.[24]

At this point Drake apparently intended to lurk off Cape St Vincent until ordered to do otherwise, and he begged the queen to send reinforcements; but a few days later he headed for the Azores instead. Many of the London merchant ships, their crews decimated by disease, decided to return home, accompanied (much to Drake's fury) by Borough in the damaged *Lion*; but on 19 June, off the island of São Miguel, the rest of the English fleet (once again flying no colours until the last moment) captured the Portuguese carrack *São Phelipe*, which had wintered in Mozambique and was travelling home unescorted. Drake brought the huge vessel and a cargo later valued at £140,000 into Plymouth harbour on 7 July 1587. The queen presented him with a magnificent recompense for his exploits: the 'Drake jewel' (Figure 54).[25]

54. The 'Drake Jewel', presented to Sir Francis Drake by Queen Elizabeth to thank him for 'singeing the king of Spain's beard' in 1587. One side contains a locket with a portrait of the queen by Nicholas Hilliard, the most famous English miniaturist of his day, covered by a phoenix, one of the queen's emblems. The side shown here is a cameo of sardonyx which shows the profile of an African superimposed over a European, probably inspired by Drake's alliance with the 'Cimaroons' of America in 1576. In the 1591 portrait of Drake (see Figure 27) the jewel hangs conspicuously from his belt.

## To the Azores (again)

Philip and his ministers worked hard to make good the damage. Certainly the loss of so many ships was a serious blow – many of the vessels that eventually sailed with the Armada were inferior in quality to those lost at Cadiz – and the destruction of stores (especially, as Drake had noted, the barrel-hoops and barrel-staves) also proved tiresome. Nevertheless, more than enough of everything remained to supply a formidable navy, and the build-up of ships, men and munitions in Lisbon continued apace. Recalde's Vizcayan squadron evaded Drake and entered the Tagus safely in May, and the veteran *tercio* of Sicily commanded by Don Diego Pimentel, stranded at Gibraltar by Drake's presence off Cape St Vincent, marched overland and reached Lisbon in July.

The principal concern of Philip and his advisers was that Drake's raid might form part of some larger enterprise. Specifically, once they heard of his departure for the Azores, their concerns turned to the security of the fleets scheduled to arrive from America and Asia. Medina Sidonia had warned the former to stay put, but the king desperately needed the treasure it carried to pay for his military and naval preparations; moreover, other ships sailing home from India still knew nothing of Drake's presence.

The king could not decide what to do next, and he issued a stream of orders and counter-orders in a vain attempt to control the constantly changing naval situation. In June he directed the merchantmen bringing munitions from Italy, sheltering from Drake in the ports of Andalucia, to sail to Lisbon escorted by the galleys defending Cadiz and the Indies Guard galleons assembled there. As soon as they reached the Tagus, Santa Cruz must lead these warships, together with those he already commanded, to the Azores in pursuit of Drake. When contrary winds kept the Andalusian fleet in Cadiz, on 5 July Santa Cruz asked permission to sail with only the ships already in Lisbon. The king agreed, and thereupon sent orders to Andalucia that although the merchantmen and the galleys should leave for Lisbon as soon as possible, the Indies Guard galleons should head straight for the Azores. On 15 July Santa Cruz and Recalde led thirty-eight warships carrying 6,000 soldiers down the Tagus and on to the Azores, there to await the treasure-fleets. By then, however, the commander of the Andalusian squadron, Don Martín de Padilla, was halfway to Lisbon and the courier carrying the king's new command did not reach him until 20 July. He at once ordered the escort galleons to set course for the Azores. But then the king learned that more English raiders lurked off the Iberian coast and became fearful that the escort galleons, if they travelled alone, might be intercepted and overwhelmed; he ordered them to remain with

Padilla. Don Martín received this order later on 20 July and recalled the galleons just dispatched. Then news reached the Escorial that Barbary corsairs had been sighted passing through the Strait of Gibraltar, and the king feared they might attack Cadiz in the absence of the galleys; so on 20 July he ordered Padilla to return to Cadiz as soon as he had escorted the transports to Lisbon. Finally on 30 July, after receiving further alarming reports about the strength and intentions of the English fleet, the king commanded the galleys to return to Cadiz immediately from wherever they might be. As it happened, Padilla made good time and reached Lisbon on 4 August. He received the new royal directive there four days later and left for Cadiz that same night.[26]

This amazing chapter of contradictions shows Philip's strategic style at its worst. Convinced that he alone had 'complete information on the present state of affairs in all areas' (see chapter 6), the king could not resist micromanaging operations; and the more reality diverged from his plan the more he saw things he wanted to change. For a time Providence seemed to smile on him. A convoy of 106 vessels from America, carrying treasure and trade goods worth 16 million ducats, reached the Azores and the safety of Santa Cruz's ships on 26 August. The marquis promptly escorted them back to Cadiz, leaving Recalde with his squadron to protect any carracks from India still en route. In the event, Santa Cruz did not return to Lisbon until 28 September; Recalde, escorting one more carrack to safety, did not arrive until 10 October.

The rejoicing occasioned by these impressive feats of coordination ended the panic that Drake had caused throughout the Iberian Peninsula. During the summer Lisbon had witnessed anti-Spanish sentiments, with many Portuguese muttering that no carracks had been lost to enemies under Philip's predecessors, and complaining that their new masters 'wanted to take away the cream of all that was good in Portugal'. They also noted that the Spaniards in Lisbon seemed completely unaffected, 'going to their bull-fights and playing their games as if nothing had happened'. Meanwhile, in Madrid, foreign diplomats filled their dispatches with news of the latest exploits (both real and rumoured) of 'el Draque', with speculation about his next move, and with criticisms of the government's apparently ineffective response. According to one ambassador the king went so far as to 'swear by the life of the prince his son that he would be avenged. Then, having heard how people talked in Madrid about his delay in getting his fleet to sea, he exclaimed "So now they have lost respect for me even in Madrid, and say that all the harm that Drake has done and is still doing arises from my slothfulness!"'[27]

Whether or not this anecdote was true, Drake's raid forced the king to rethink the entire Enterprise of England. On a tactical level, since a state of war now clearly existed with Elizabeth, Philip decreed that English seamen captured by his ships should be treated as prisoners of war, not as pirates (until this point captains, masters and pilots had been beheaded, and the rest sent to the galleys).[28] On a strategic level the need for a direct assault on England seemed more pressing than ever. In the words of Don Juan de Idiáquez, a Basque whose family had long been prominent in central government and who was now Philip's secretary of state: 'With the English established in Holland and Zeeland, together with their infestation of the Americas and the high seas, it seems that defensive measures cannot deal with everything. Rather, it obliges us to put their house to the torch' in order to force them to withdraw from the Netherlands. Slightly later another royal minister delivered a similarly belligerent message in the wake of the Cadiz raid. The 'Enterprise of England', he asserted to the papal nuncio in Madrid, was now even more essential both to assure the safety of the fleets sailing between Spain and the Americas and to maintain the king's 'reputation, to avoid being subjected every day to similar mishaps like this one'. The crucial question facing Philip now was how best to achieve these ambitious goals.[29]

# 8

# The Armada Takes Shape

## The Masterplan Revised

Drake's exploits compelled Philip II to revise his overall strategy for the Enterprise of England. It had never been popular with Parma: as early as April 1586, even before the king first sent him the Masterplan, the duke complained that everybody knew about Spain's intentions, so the Enterprise would lack the vital element of surprise. The delivery to him of the papal sword, the same symbol of crusading virtue accorded to the duke of Alba in connection with the Ridolfi Plot, also symbolized the unwelcome publicity and lack of security that now surrounded the entire operation.

For several months – a measure, it would seem, of his disapproval – Parma held back his comments on the Masterplan; then, on 31 October, he enunciated all his doubts in a long letter. First, he asked the king bluntly whether Spain could afford the operation, since the cost of building up sufficient forces in Flanders to defend recent conquests, as well as to conquer Ireland and England, would be crippling. 'And I shall be bold to say,' wrote the duke, 'with the freedom that your Majesty allows me, that if you find yourself without adequate resources to undertake such a great enterprise as this . . . I incline to the view that it would be better to defer or drop it.' If the king wished to persist with his plan, Parma continued, he should consider a second point. 'It seems to me that it would be most useful if the Armada from Spain were ready for action at the same moment [as his own invasion from Flanders], because I am afraid that the Irish dimension may do us some mischief.' On the one hand, argued the duke, Elizabeth might deduce that there would be a second attack and raise troops abroad for her defence; on the other hand the Armada might well be unable, through adverse winds or other unforeseen circumstances, to move as precisely as the king's plan demanded.[1]

Philip's reply oscillated between uncertainty and irritation. He pointed out that he had scheduled the invasion of Ireland to take place only two months before Parma's assault, so that Elizabeth would scarcely have time to recruit foreign mercenaries. Instead, he predicted, she would withdraw troops from south-east England for service in Ireland, thus reducing opposition to Parma's cross-Channel attack. Nevertheless, the reservations of his outspoken subordinate shook the king's confidence. At one point in his letter he asked Parma to consider whether it might be better for the Armada to land on the Isle of Wight instead of in Ireland. In a holograph addition he explained rather forlornly: 'We cannot avoid building up the Armada we have here, because of the need to defend Portugal and for other things; and having created it, at so much cost, it would be best not to lose the chance of doing something with it.'[2]

This display of vacillation encouraged Parma to compose an even stronger critique of the royal plan. In January 1587 he unequivocally condemned both the seizure of an Irish springboard and the idea of a prior landing on the Isle of Wight. The king (his nephew boldly suggested) should concentrate on one thing at a time: if there must be an Armada, then let it sail straight for the Flemish coast and make the Narrow Seas safe for the Army of Flanders to effect its crossing.

Once again the king wavered. As he reviewed his nephew's many criticisms and complaints, he stumbled upon a devastating objection – one which, in the event, he later forgot. In a remarkably convoluted sentence, Philip expressed anxiety about:

> The need to make the Channel safe, because of the risk of sending a fleet like ours to sail between France and England at the appointed time (which often sees very bad weather in the Channel) without having a safe port in either, or in Flanders (except for Dunkirk, which apart from being the only one available is not suitable for ships of large draught), which would force the Armada to face bad weather; leaving aside the general advantages, and the more detailed knowledge of those coasts, which the enemy fleet will have. All these are points of substance, and I am looking into them.[3]

The king did not look very far, perhaps because of a counterblast from his principal policy adviser. 'The immense cost of the preparations, both in the Netherlands and here, made me hesitate before sending Your Majesty this paper,' Don Juan de Idiáquez apologized, 'because this enterprise is voluntary and there is an ancient maxim that one should avoid voluntary enterprises in which the costs will exceed the gains. In this case, even if we acquire the whole kingdom [of England], we cannot expect the benefits to equal the cost of conquest and occupation.' Nevertheless, Don Juan continued: 'This venture seems to me essential for our defence', because 'dominions as extensive as those of Your Majesty cannot be protected and safeguarded except by punishing those who challenge you so hard that it deprives them of their strength, and leaves others trembling about their fate'. Therefore, Philip must destroy the Tudor state. Lest the king remain unconvinced by strategic logic, Idiáquez deployed a further argument that he knew would prevail:

> This service would be so acceptable to Our Lord that it is impossible that His hand will not appear openly, both in the execution of this venture and in what follows, as a reward for someone who thus serves Him. I think that everyone has an obligation to serve Him according to their resources . . . and God has granted Your Majesty so much power and favour that it can be taken as a certain token of the favourable outcome of everything you undertake for His service.[4]

Confident that his arguments would convince the king, on 28 February 1587 Idiáquez reminded the duke of Medina Sidonia (tasked with collecting the ships which would sail from Andalucia to Lisbon as a second supporting wave) that the Armada's true purpose was to get the English to withdraw from both the Netherlands and the Americas; and 'since this cannot be achieved on the [English] mainland at the first stroke, we might start with Ireland, which we could use either as a pledge to exchange for the places they hold in the Low Countries, or as a springboard for a second strike against England'. This apparently convinced the king because preparations continued apace for both the diversionary landing of the Armada in Ireland and the invasion of Kent from Flanders.[5]

As time passed, however, Philip began to tinker with his Masterplan. He asked Medina Sidonia whether the escort galleons of the Indian Guard, now gathered beneath the duke's imposing castle at Sanlúcar de Barrameda, should instead reinforce the Armada. Initially the suggestion appalled the duke, who pointed out that 'the link between the two continents is the foundation of the wealth and power we have here', because the treasure from Philip's transatlantic possessions formed the life-blood of the entire empire; but Drake's raid on Cadiz changed his mind. Now he favoured adding to the Armada not only the escort galleons but also the larger merchant ships assembled for the next transatlantic fleet, as well as the galleasses from Naples and the ships embargoed to carry troops and munitions from Sicily to Spain. He further recommended forming these separate units into a single fleet that would sail to Lisbon together. The king agreed and issued the necessary orders.[6]

Then in June 1587 Philip decided that Ireland was indeed a bridgehead too far. Now, he informed Parma:

> Because the Armada here must first deal with meeting and protecting the fleets coming from America, I do not think it will be possible for it to reach the Channel before your own crossing. This should not matter, but rather confirms what is already arranged, because neither the person you sent here [Giovanni Battista Piatti], nor you after his return, asked that the Armada should come before, but only afterwards.

Therefore, 'The best course seems to me that, almost at the same time or as close to it as possible, we attack in three directions': an invasion by Parma from the Netherlands; an attack by the Armada from Spain on the Isle of Wight or Southampton; and an uprising by a group of Scottish Catholics to whom Philip sent both subsidies and encouragement.[7]

After this dramatic announcement, the king fell relatively silent for almost a month. Historians have found it hard to explain the hiatus, but the reason is simple: Philip's health had collapsed. Long before Drake's raid a note of deep weariness had crept into his directives. 'You can send me a memo about these matters,' he wrote to a secretary on 6 February 1587, 'so that I can look at it along with the rest; although, the way things are these days, I don't know when that will be.' The next day, he complained that 'I cannot handle any further business, because I have a terrible cold, and now I cannot read or write . . . So you can see from this how impossible life is just now.' Still the king soldiered on. On 9 February he complained that papers were still being brought for him to read and sign at 10 p.m. ('Look what I get to cure my cold!'); and on 14 February he lamented that 'I have been here, working on my papers for a long time, but while I've been at it, ten or twelve more dossiers have arrived. Everything else will have to wait until tomorrow.' With increasing frequency the king left papers unread because he 'had no time', or 'could not face them'.[8]

Just after learning about Drake's raid on Cadiz, Philip became seriously ill. By late May he could cope only with the most urgent papers. In mid-June his valet regretted that the king was so restless 'that I can no longer take advantage of that hour after he wakes up, which is the best time to read him state papers, because then he is alone and has the leisure [to listen]'. Ten days later the same valet lamented that 'the king's eyes are running all the time, his legs are very weak and his hand still painful; and the world is waiting.'[9]

Part of the problem lay in Philip's insistence on micromanaging everything. Admittedly he had come to trust Don Juan de Zúñiga, who drafted the Armada Masterplan; but Zúñiga died in November 1586. This left a gap at the centre of power. In May 1587, at the beginning of the king's illness, his secretary of state for war vented to a colleague his frustration at 'the considerable time wasted in consultation, for His Majesty is slow in replying and time is lost that cannot be regained'.[10]

Medina Sidonia now came to the rescue. Deploying to optimal effect his experience in getting fleets to sea, he assembled eighty-six ships off Sanlúcar and on 11 July 1587 watched Don Alonso de Leyva lead them all off towards Lisbon, 370 miles away. The fleet included the great ships of the future Levant and Andalusian squadrons, the four Neapolitan galleasses, and twenty-eight *urcas*. Three weeks later they all entered the Tagus safely, firing salvoes with such exuberance that one eyewitness claimed he could no longer see the sea for smoke. Leyva took command of all the ships now in the Tagus until Santa Cruz returned, and on 5 September informed the king that 'his' fleet was ready to leave Lisbon just as soon as Santa Cruz and his warships returned from the Azores.

## A Dialogue of the Deaf

What should the Armada, united at last, do now? To sail against England so late in the year involved grave risks. Some recalled the fate of Charles V's expedition against Algiers in 1541, when the emperor disregarded all professional advice and began his campaign in September. One month later storms destroyed half his fleet (over 100 ships) and much of its equipment (including 200 artillery pieces and 2,000 horses). Even before Santa Cruz returned to Lisbon, Philip's Council of War expressed their fear of a similar outcome. 'In view of the uncertainty concerning the time at which the marquis and his fleet may return', they reasoned, and 'without knowing the strength in which they will return (whether because they have encountered and fought the enemy, which would cause some damage, or because of storm damage or sickness among their crews) . . . we cannot predict or plan what may happen after the ships get back.' One councillor went even further: 'It is already clear,' he told the king, 'that we cannot undertake any other major enterprise this year beyond escorting home the treasure-fleets.'[11]

Philip, his health now restored, vigorously rejected such caution. Instead, on 4 September 1587 he issued yet another set of detailed Instructions for the

Enterprise of England to both Santa Cruz and Parma. The purpose of the venture, the king reiterated, remained unchanged: to restore England to the Catholic Church and to end English attacks on Spain's interests. Two paragraphs then explained that the unfortunate delays caused by Drake's raid, the need to escort home the treasure-fleets, and Elizabeth's efforts to gain foreign support, left no time to secure a base in Ireland before going on to invade England. Therefore, Santa Cruz must lead all the ships assembled in the Tagus 'in God's name to the English Channel, proceeding along it until he should anchor off Margate Cape, having first sent word to the duke of Parma of his approach'. The king asserted that 'the roadstead of Margate is excellent, but without defences'; that the port of Margate 'could ill withstand the assault' by the troops aboard the Armada; and that, from Margate, Santa Cruz's ships would be 'able to prevent the union of the [enemy] vessels in the river of London and on the east coast of the island, with those of the south and west coasts'. Therefore, 'the enemy will hardly be able to collect a fleet with which he would dare to seek out ours'. Philip also asserted that he had instructed Parma, 'as soon as he should see his crossing made secure by the presence of the Armada at Margate', to 'pass across his whole camp in small vessels of which there will be more than enough in those ports [of Flanders – albeit] for the crossing only'.

The king forbade objections to the new plan with his usual providential rhetoric. 'It is clear that great risks are involved in moving a mighty Armada in winter, particularly in [the English] Channel with no port secured,' he conceded; but 'God, whose cause this is, will give of His bounty suitable weather'.[12]

The Instructions left some vital questions unanswered. First, before securing Margate and its anchorage, should the Armada go to the ports of Flanders where it would find Parma's army fully embarked and ready to cross; or must the invasion barges make their way to the Kent coast alone and meet the fleet there? And in the former scenario, how would the deep-draught ships of the Armada negotiate the shallows and sandbanks that fringed the Flemish coast? Or, if it took the latter course, how could a fleet anchored at Margate protect the troop-transports from attack by the Dutch and English blockading squadrons on their journey?

The parallel Instructions sent to Parma shed no light on these vital matters. 'I have decided,' the king told his nephew:

> That as soon as the marquis of Santa Cruz gets the treasure-fleet safely to Cape St Vincent (which we hope to hear about from one hour to the next), and surrenders them there to the care of the galleys of Spain, he will sail straight to Lisbon. There he will pick up the rest of the fleet that awaits him

and they will all sail directly, in the name of God, to the English Channel, proceeding along it until they drop anchor off Margate Cape.

The king promised Parma that the fleet would send advance warning of its approach, and continued: 'You will therefore be so well prepared that when you see the Narrow Seas thus secured, with the Armada riding off Margate Cape or else cruising off the mouth of the Thames . . . you will immediately send the whole army over in the boats you have prepared.' The king repeated his assurance that, until the army was safely across, the Armada would concentrate on keeping enemy ships at bay; and he commanded Parma, for his part, not to stir from the Flemish coast until the fleet arrived. But on precisely how Parma would cross the 50 miles separating Dunkirk from Margate, the king wrote not a word. It was, to say the least, an unfortunate oversight.[13]

As usual, the king communicated his Instructions to both Lisbon and the Netherlands by courier, rather than by sending a special messenger primed to answer questions about the plan. He also ordered Parma to stop complaining. 'I cannot refrain from reminding you,' he scolded his nephew:

> That, apart from the initial idea of this enterprise and the selection of yourself to command it (which were my decisions), everything else connected with your end of the venture, including the resources and plan prepared, were according to your own directions of which you alone were the author. Moreover, for its preparation and execution, I have given you in great abundance everything that you asked of me.

All further criticisms of the plan must now cease.[14]

A similar bombardment greeted Santa Cruz after he returned to Lisbon on 28 September. A royal missive on 10 October ended: 'There is no more time to waste in requests and replies; just get on with the job.' Two weeks later the king reminded the marquis spitefully that 'it is now almost a month since you arrived [in Lisbon] yet you have not got everything ready, as you promised me'. He continued: 'So much time has been lost already that every further hour of delay causes me more grief than you can imagine. And so I charge and command you most strictly to leave before the end of the month.' Further letters, wheedling and hectoring by turn, left the king's desk in the Escorial for Lisbon almost daily, but the marquis answered each with excuses ranging from the perennial problems of logistics to the damage wreaked by a cyclone that struck the Tagus on 16 November. When the king belittled his objections, Santa Cruz finally lost his temper: 'If His Majesty continues to insist, I will sail with the Armada as a gentleman volunteer but not as its commander.'[15]

This dialogue of the deaf astonished the diplomats in Madrid, who closely monitored the progress of the Enterprise of England. In mid-November the Venetian ambassador, Hieronimo Lippomano, obtained a copy of Santa Cruz's measured refutation of one of the king's unrealistic tirades and wondered why Philip would refuse to believe his most experienced admiral. Lippomano discerned three possible reasons. First, Philip always found it 'difficult to change plans, once he has decided on something'. Second, his supreme confidence 'in the course of his good fortune' led him to assume that God would reward his efforts provided he performed his own part to the full. Finally, thanks to the mass of intelligence at his disposal, Philip always saw operations in each theatre in an international context, which made him anxious to act before the favourable situation changed. Two weeks later Lippomano's colleague Khevenhüller made a similar point: 'If the Turks were to undertake something, even with only 150 galleys, it would cause [the king] great difficulty and effort, because the [Atlantic] ocean is now full of English ships and pirates who are doing great damage.' Nevertheless, Khevenhüller continued: 'The longer the Armada preparations last, the less prepared it is to sail. There are now only 5,000 soldiers ready: the rest are dead or fled . . . It has cost the king so much money, certainly more than two million ducats thus far, and yet it has done nothing.'[16]

Although Philip never saw either of these pessimistic analyses, he would surely have agreed with them. He frequently impressed upon his subordinates that although they understood the needs of their own theatre of operations, he always focused on the 'big picture'. In September 1587 he warned Parma: 'Next year we might find ourselves with a Turkish fleet attacking Italy, should the Sultan make peace with the Persians'; and, in addition, the French might reconcile their differences, make peace and prevent him from annexing England. A month later Philip reminded Santa Cruz that 'the difference between success and failure is measured in days if not in hours'.[17] He also obsessed about how every delay to implementing the Masterplan increased the strain on the royal treasury. Each day the Armada cost him 30,000 ducats, and Parma's army cost him a further 15,000 ducats. Therefore, Philip told his ministers in Madrid, 'finding money is so important that all of us must concentrate only on that and on nothing else. I do not know what will come of whatever victories we may win without money, unless God performs a miracle.' The king did his best: in March 1588 he even sold the jewels of his late wife Anna of Austria to raise funds for the Enterprise and every Saturday he demanded a statement of the amount of money in the treasury and personally determined which obligations could be met and which must wait.[18]

The king soon had another reason to worry. On 30 September 1587, having learned that Santa Cruz had at last returned from the Azores, he informed Parma that the entire Armada was now ready to sail against England. Therefore, if Elizabeth should move her fleet down to Plymouth in response to this threat, leaving the Thames estuary unguarded, he urged his nephew to slip across the Channel alone and launch a surprise attack. Just possibly exploiting reports from his agents in Lisbon that the Armada was in fact far from 'ready to sail against England', Parma expressed enthusiasm for the dramatic change of plan and boasted to the king on 14 November that:

> I am entirely resolved, in the name of God and with His holy assistance, to put to sea myself on the 25th ... And unless we hear that there is an [enemy] fleet in the Channel which might prevent us from crossing, and if God is pleased to bring us safely to land and favour us ... I hope we shall be able to give a good account of ourselves to Your Majesty.[19]

Now the king panicked, fearing that if Parma had indeed undertaken his solo venture he might become stranded without the fleet from Spain. He therefore fired off another barrage of letters urging Santa Cruz to head for the Channel even if he could lead only forty-eight ships (10 December), and finally even if he could lead only thirty-five (21 December). Parma, for his part, received a barrage of royal letters enquiring whether he was already in England – and, if not, why not?[20]

On 31 January 1588, apparently forgetting his earlier expression of enthusiasm, the duke wrote back furiously to Philip, 'Your letters seem to infer that I may have done what Your Majesty emphatically ordered me not to do' – to cross the Channel before he knew that Santa Cruz and his fleet were ready to protect the operation:

> Your Majesty is perfectly well aware that, without the support of the Armada, I cannot cross over to England with the boats I have here, and you very prudently ordered me in your letter of 4 September not to attempt to do so until the marquis arrived ... Your Majesty has the right to give absolute orders, which I receive as special favours and execute; but for you to write to me now with a proposal which runs so contrary to the previous express orders and command of Your Majesty, causes me great anguish. I beg you most humbly to do me the very great favour of telling me what to do next.

The letter – perhaps the most disrespectful and critical that Philip ever received from a subordinate – remained uncharacteristically free of annotations from the royal pen.[21]

## Elizabeth Prepares

Paradoxically, this deluge of orders and counter-orders – many of them intercepted by English spies – brought Philip an unexpected benefit: it confused and exhausted Queen Elizabeth and her ministers. In June 1587 Burghley complained to a confidant that the avalanche of business left him with 'scant leisure to breathe'; and five months later he was 'so oppressed' by 'the heaps of affairs that this busy time breeds' that 'I assure your lordship I am weary to live'. The results of the confusion and fatigue appeared in the queen's Instructions to Admiral Howard dated 30 December 1587. They began confidently enough – 'Being sundry ways most credibly given to understand of the great and extraordinary preparations made by sea, as well in Spain by the king there as in the Low Countries by the duke of Parma' – but then uncertainty set in. 'It is also meant that the said forces shall be employed in some enterprise to be attempted either in our dominions of England and Ireland or in the realm of Scotland.'

Unable to assess these multiple threats, the queen attempted to parry them all. She ordered 'our servant Drake' to take part of the fleet to the West Country where he would 'ply up and down between the realm of Ireland and the west part of this our Realm', in case a fleet from Spain made a surprise attack. Meanwhile Howard should 'ply up and down, sometimes toward the ~~North South~~ North and sometimes towards the South' – the double strikethrough is eloquent! – 'as to you in your own discretion and judgement shall be thought may tend best to the impeaching of the attempts and designs' of Parma. If the troops assembled in Flanders attempted to cross the Channel or attack one of the Dutch ports garrisoned by Elizabeth's troops, Howard must summon Drake to join him; conversely, if the Armada appeared in the Channel approaches, Howard should send reinforcements to Drake. The result was chaos. According to a well-informed observer in London: 'Our preparations by land go as fast forward as our sea matters, for we have mustering everywhere and lieutenants and colonels appointed to every shire to be ready upon any sudden invasion' – whether from Spain, Flanders, Ireland or Scotland.[22]

Howard deemed a surprise attack by Parma the greatest threat. In February 1588 he sailed to Harwich and warned Burghley that it 'is a place to be made much of, for the haven has not his fellow in all respects not in this realm, and specially as long as we have such enemies so near us as they be in the Low Countries' – a warning that would later lead the queen to locate most of her land assets to repel an invasion in Essex. A month later, back at Dover, Howard begged for clearer orders because 'This is the year that makes or mars. And it were a great deal better that some did weep than all England should cry.' Perhaps stung by this rebuke, a few days later the queen 'ordered Sir Francis Drake to repair with his fleet to the coast of Spain to withstand that nothing be attempted either against Ireland or Scotland, and in case they have a meaning to come into the Narrow Seas, that there my Lord Admiral shall encounter them with his strength'.[23]

Then, in 'expectation of some good conclusion' of her negotiations with Parma, the queen dragged her feet again. Drake despaired, reminding the queen that if 'The king of Spain means any invasion in England, then doubtless his force is and will be great in Spain; and thereon he will make his groundwork or foundation, whereby the prince of Parma may have the better entrance, which in mine own judgement is most to be feared.' Therefore, Drake continued, 'to prevent this, I think it good that these forces here [in Plymouth] should be made as strong as [possible] . . . for that they are like to strike the first blow . . . and the sooner we are gone, the better we shall be able to impeach them'. He begged the queen to relocate her entire fleet to Plymouth and authorize an immediate attack in full strength on Lisbon. The queen was not convinced, and sent Drake 'some particular notes, and withal a commandment to answer them' concerning 'how the forces now in Lisbon might best be distressed'. Drake confessed that he was working on intuition – 'Truly this point is hardly to be answered as yet' – but reminded his sovereign that 'The advantage of time and place in all martial actions is half a victory, which being lost is irrecoverable.' He reiterated his plea that she relocate the bulk of her fleet to Plymouth and then send it to blockade Lisbon. The queen evidently discussed Drake's proposal with Howard, Hawkins and Winter in person until they reached a consensus, because on 27 April 1588 Howard informed Burghley that 'It is now determined that I shall go westward with the greatest part of her Majesty's ships.'[24]

Howard nevertheless remained at Court for another month. Perhaps Burghley persuaded Elizabeth that it was dangerous to send so many of her naval assets so far away, but then Drake rode up from Plymouth. On 17 May a member of the queen's entourage reported that 'My Lord Admiral remains at the court, having Her Majesty's Navy in readiness. Sir Francis Drake is also there, having his fleet ready also in the West' – although no one knew whether 'both of them are to go to sea' or await the outcome of the peace talks in Flanders.[25] The crucial decisions came soon afterwards. On 20 May the Privy Council authorized the issue of £2,000 to

Drake, 'to be now carried down with him to be employed' in preparing his ships at Plymouth; and on 23 May, 'for divers considerations', Elizabeth ordered Howard to join Drake in Plymouth. The two commanders must then deploy their joint assets 'as may best serve to impeach the great navy now prepared in Spain [from] attempting anything as well against our dominions of England and Ireland as also the realm of Scotland'.[26]

Howard acted swiftly. He led most of his fleet from the anchorage of the Downs on 21 May, leaving only a small squadron under Seymour and Winter to guard the Narrow Seas. 'The wind serving exceeding well', they arrived off Plymouth within forty-eight hours and Drake 'came forth with his 60 sail very well appointed to meet' them. Together they entered Plymouth harbour and dropped anchor. Howard intended only 'to stay these two days to water our fleet' and then 'take the opportunity of the first wind serving for the coast of Spain' where he hoped to intercept the Armada (which, unknown to him, had left Lisbon one week earlier).[27]

In the event, eighty-seven English ships put to sea on 8 June, but contrary winds kept them 'beating up and down with much foul weather' and after a week they re-entered Plymouth Sound to take on more provisions – but in this they encountered a major obstacle. The fleet carried almost 10,000 men, more than twice the population of Plymouth, and its needs could not be supplied from local resources: they must come from London, which meant reliance on favourable winds. Howard and Drake did their best. In July the Surveyor-General of Victuals praised them 'for the placing of six men to a mess at sea' (much like the *camaradas* aboard the Spanish ships), because 'thereby their victuals [are] much lengthened'; but he still estimated that it would take a month to collect another month's supply of food for all aboard. Throughout the campaign Elizabeth's commanders complained that they had enough food to sustain the fleet only for a few weeks and sometimes only a few days.[28]

## A New Commander for the Armada

Philip II faced problems of a different sort. He spent Christmas 1587 confined to his bed and was unable to get up even to eat until 17 January 1588. Not until the 20th did his valet pronounce him capable of governing his empire – and his Armada – once again.[29] During this power vacuum a furious and frustrated Don Alonso de Leyva arrived in Madrid. A week after surrendering his command to Santa Cruz, Leyva had begged the king to grant him some official position with the fleet, 'even if you only appoint me to serve as a cabin-boy'; but no appointment arrived and instead the marquis either ignored or humiliated him. In January 1588 Don Alonso left Lisbon and denounced Santa Cruz's shortcomings to the Council of War. Specifically, he insisted that the Armada 'needed a council where people of quality and distinction meet and discuss its affairs', including all the squadron and infantry commanders. He also suggested that three or four 'gentlemen of distinction' (including himself, naturally) should transfer to the flagship to provide constant advice to the marquis. The council endorsed his recommendations. On 28 January Philip signed patents nominating all those suggested by Leyva and instructed the marquis to start consulting 'all the nobles and notable gentlemen who have gone to serve me' on the fleet.[30]

These humiliating restrictions were in fact a smokescreen. Although Santa Cruz continued to assert that the Grand Fleet would leave shortly, the king no longer believed him. He therefore dispatched to Lisbon the count of Fuentes, the tough and resourceful nephew of the late duke of Alba, with orders to 'light a fire under the marquis' and to compel him to 'state clearly whether he wants to go as instructed or stay behind, because in the latter case we will issue the appropriate orders' and name another commander.[31]

Philip also asked the marquis to 'tell me, before you leave, the order you intend your ships to follow as they sail', and where they would regroup 'in case a storm or misfortune' should scatter the fleet. These were eminently sensible measures (although Philip had never before interfered with his commanders' operational discretion in this way) but later in the same document the king undermined them both. After restating that the Armada must attempt nothing against England until it had 'joined forces' with Parma, he added in his own hand an assurance that if Parma learned that the entire enemy fleet lay off 'Margate Cape, he would find a way to send to the said Cape the largest force of ships and men that he can' (a totally unrealistic assurance which would later create a fatal misunderstanding). Philip even saw fit to give the marquis a lesson in tactics. After claiming that 'it is not necessary to advise such an expert on the way to draw up your fleet on the day of battle', he proceeded to inform Santa Cruz that 'the aim of our enemies will be to fight using their superiority in artillery' whereas 'we must concentrate on getting to grips and grappling'.[32]

The lesson proved redundant. Fuentes arrived in Lisbon on 30 January to find Santa Cruz seriously ill and in deep despair, feebly trying to direct the fleet's preparations from his sickbed. The marquis claimed that he awaited only reinforcements from Seville before setting forth, to which Fuentes rudely replied: 'Why don't you look at my Instructions? You will see there that you should leave behind even the unserviceable hulks, to avoid losing time in getting the rest ready.' Thereupon the marquis 'read the text of my orders three times'. Fuentes added testily: 'I can't imagine why.'[33]

Even at the height of his powers Santa Cruz had been a fighting admiral rather than a staff officer; he had got things done by a combination of bombast, ruthless energy and a lifetime's experience of war. The Armada was now beyond such simple cures, and in any case Santa Cruz had lost the physical stamina and the will to apply them. According to a Scots merchant in Lisbon, once he learned that 'there was another governor come to govern Portugal, and he appointed to go with the Armada, the sorrow and grief [the marquis] took, being unwilling to go, was the occasion of his death' on 9 February. The Enterprise of England was now on the verge of collapse.[34]

Months of bad management compounded by bad luck had inflated even simple problems into crises. The preparation and embarkation of the task force's siege-train offers a case in point. The field carriages of the eight *cañones de batir* to be shipped aboard the Levant squadron turned out to be rotten and of an outdated pattern, so it was decided in October 1587 to replace them before embarkation; but since seasoned timber could not be obtained at such short notice, green wood was used in its place. Then the ship carrying the specially made iron fittings for the carriages was wrecked. The work was not completed until January. Further difficulties arose when the time finally came to embark the siege-train. On 2 January 1588 the Captain-General of Artillery in Lisbon, Don Juan de Acuña Vela, informed Philip that the guns must be embarked immediately, despite Santa Cruz's assurances that the matter could wait. On 30 January Acuña Vela reported that he had managed to stow only five of the *cañones de batir* aboard the Levantine ships: he had hoped to get the remaining three aboard that day but the galleys, which alone could handle such heavy loads, were otherwise employed. The Levanters' big tenders, also required for the operation, were not available either: they were working flat out distributing biscuit among the fleet. Four days later Acuña Vela reported that two more siege-guns were now aboard but one remained ashore. Similar difficulties beset other aspects of the fleet's preparations. A month after Santa Cruz's death Acuña Vela complained about 'how much money I have to spend every day, because there are a million things to spend it on, and everything is so expensive – both the initial purchases and transporting them here'.[35]

Despite the prodigious expenditure, by this stage the Armada had been reduced to a shambles of 104 unseaworthy ships and rotting supplies and – more critical because less easily cured – of dispirited, disillusioned and sick men. The strength of the *tercios* assembled in Lisbon fell by 500 men each month. More than 200 seamen from the province of Guipúzcoa died in Lisbon before they set sail. A 'Summary of soldiers and seamen on the fleet who have died' ended with the chilling entry: 'and 122 died in the hospitals, whose names we do not give or know, because they arrived so sick that they died almost immediately'.[36]

Santa Cruz himself soon joined them, carried off by typhus like so many of his men. Few mourned his death. According to a Lisbon chronicler the marquis had been proud, avaricious and cruel, so that although he was worth over half a million ducats only four people accompanied his coffin to the tomb, 'and his death was regretted by no one'. On hearing of his death Ambassador Khevenhüller reflected: 'In 1587 I was right to predict that the Armada would not leave that year; now in 1588 I do not trust myself to make a prediction. Like everyone else, I think that all these preparations are intended to facilitate and secure a good peace.'[37]

For once the ambassador's pessimism proved misplaced. The death of the marquis allowed Philip to appoint Don Alonso Pérez de Guzmán el Bueno, seventh duke of Medina Sidonia, as his new Captain-General of the Ocean Sea. He would succeed where Santa Cruz had failed: in two months he got the Armada to sea (Figure 55).

55. Don Alonso Pérez de Guzmán el Bueno, 7th duke of Medina Sidonia. An undated portrait by an unknown hand shows the commander of the Armada in later life but still supervising the shipping in the anchorage outside his palace at Sanlúcar de Barrameda, where this painting now hangs. He holds a small paper, testimony to his career as an administrator.

In 1582 Juan de Escalante Mendoza, who had almost thirty years' experience commanding transatlantic fleets, completed a manuscript treatise that described the qualities of the ideal commander of a large fleet. He must be, 'from Seville, well-born and of good lineage; a good Christian and experienced in naval matters, having made other voyages on the same route to the same destination'. He must also be discreet, just, learned and vigilant, 'as well as being brave, bold and skilful with weapons. He must be physically fit, able to jump with agility into any ship's boat whenever he needs to visit another ship in the fleet, no matter how rough the sea or how strong the wind . . . He must also be perceptive, decisive and diligent in any battle he has to fight.' Escalante presented his treatise to the king, who deemed it too valuable to print: instead, he had the original manuscript deposited in the House of Trade at Seville 'so that it can be used there when necessary'. He also arranged for a personal copy to be sent to him.[38]

How did the duke measure up to Escalante's criteria? Although born and bred in the ducal castle at Sanlúcar de Barrameda, 50 miles from Seville, Medina Sidonia was head of one of Spain's richest aristocratic families and second cousin to the king himself. The Jesuit Pedro de Ribadeneira testified to the duke's piety. He hailed his appointment 'because of who he is and the favours he has always done' for the Jesuit Order, and claimed that 'God himself chose [the duke] as Captain-General of the Armada, and entrusted this holy and glorious venture to him.'[39] Although Medina Sidonia lacked combat experience, he was a superb horseman and an expert jouster; and he experienced no problem in 'jumping with agility' into a ship's boat. He was no stranger to military command. In 1580 he had led an army during the Portuguese campaign and seven years later he saved Cadiz from being sacked during Drake's 'beard-singeing' exploit. His effective response on this occasion earned the praise and gratitude of Spanish policy-makers: one veteran minister in Madrid recommended appointing the duke to run the whole central government.

The duke exuded energy and at one point Philip reproached him 'for the excessive work you do yourself, and the amount you write with your own hand' and begged him to remember that 'late nights are bad for you'. Much of the excessive work concerned the timely dispatch of the annual convoys that sailed from Andalucia to America. One observer testified that 'since he came of age, the duke has done nothing in Sanlúcar except prepare fleets, navies and dispatch boats' for America. He had also assembled the fleets led by Diego Flores and Gómez de Medina to the South Atlantic, and the reinforcements sent to Lisbon in summer 1587. In short, 'Nobody knows more about these matters than the duke.' And that was exactly what the Armada now needed if it were ever to sail at all: not another fighting admiral but a determined and practical man with the personal qualities and administrative skills needed to turn the muddle at Lisbon into a coherent fighting force.[40]

Although the duke had also participated in planning the Armada, taking part in ministerial discussions on the impending war with England in 1586 and again in 1587, he neither desired nor expected high military command. In 1580 he had solicited appointment as governor of Lombardy, one of the most important posts in the monarchy, but soon decided that he did not want to go. His repeated excuses and procrastination eventually secured his release. Perhaps the duke recalled this success as he read Philip's letter dated 11 February 1588 announcing that, since Santa Cruz was clearly too ill to lead the Armada, the duke must go to Lisbon and replace him; but this time he could not avoid the poisoned chalice.[41]

Medina Sidonia's pleas to be excused have been used to discredit him. 'The limited experience I have of going to sea shows that it will be the death of me,' he complained to Don Juan de Idiáquez (whom he suspected, correctly, of having proposed his appointment to the king). He also claimed that (despite being the richest nobleman in Spain) his recent visits to Madrid 'have created serious debts, so that I now owe 900,000 ducats, and have not a penny to spend on this new venture'. More convincingly, he asserted that:

> Neither my conscience nor my sense of duty will allow me to accept this commission. The forces collected are so great and the enterprise is so important that it would not be right for a person like me, lacking all experience of seafaring or war, to take charge of it ... Even if I possessed these qualities, appointing me without warning like this means that I would be going in blind, since I know nothing about the state of the Armada, or the officers aboard it, or the strategy it must follow, or the information available on England and its ports, or the correspondence which the marquis carried on with people there.

'For all these reasons,' he concluded defiantly, 'I will not discuss any further accepting a task which, without doubt, I will perform badly since I shall be travelling blind, forced to follow the advice and views of others without knowing which is good and which is bad, or who might wish to deceive or discredit me.' He made only one concession. If his role would 'be to go to Lisbon simply to get the fleet out of there – which is something I do know how to do – then I will go'; but once he had prepared the Grand Fleet for departure, the king must appoint someone else to lead it into action.[42]

Medina Sidonia's refusal to 'discuss any further' commanding the Armada arose from more than the personal rationale given in his uncharacteristically disorganized and rambling letter. In a second letter dated 18 February 1588, written after he had recovered from the shock of his nomination and collected his thoughts, Medina Sidonia submitted a damning assessment of the whole Enterprise of England, which he believed to be ill conceived and (consequently) almost inevitably doomed to failure.

Remarkably, the king never saw this letter. His health remained poor for most of February, and he complained of pains in his stomach, of tiredness, of over-work. Urgent correspondence accumulated on his desk – some unopened, some unread, most unanswered; but Medina Sidonia's letter of 18 February was not among them. It had been intercepted and retained by the two councillors of state who had inherited the mantle of Don Juan de Zúñiga: Idiáquez and Don Cristóbal de Moura, a Portuguese whose diplomacy and duplicity had played a key role in the annexation of his native land in 1580. They now attended continuously upon the king and handled the day-to-day receipt, filing and dispatch of the immense quantity of paperwork generated by the Enterprise of England. Nothing of consequence escaped them.

When, in the course of these duties, they opened Medina Sidonia's frank letter of 18 February, they were appalled. '*We did not dare to show his Majesty what you have just written,*' they chided the duke, adding 'Do not depress us with fears for the fate of the Armada, because in such a cause God will make sure it succeeds.' They also warned him of the consequences of refusing such a signal honour. Everyone knew that the offer had been made; to refuse it now would lead to accusations of ingratitude, selfishness, even cowardice. 'Remember that you would entirely forfeit the reputation and esteem you currently enjoy for courage and wisdom if what you wrote to us became generally known (although we shall keep it secret).'[43]

Dismayed by this unexpected development, Medina Sidonia asked for an audience with the king, but (as usual) Philip refused. The duke thereupon wrote a holograph letter to Philip's secretary, Mateo Vázquez (whom he knew would show it to the king). He began by repeating that he had 'cleared his conscience by telling His Majesty what he should do in this matter' and confirmed that 'nevertheless I have bowed my head and will obey'. But he wanted something in return. The wealthiest aristocrat in Spain asserted that accepting his new post 'will leave my family deeply in debt. I have a young wife and four children, the oldest only nine years old, and sacrificing myself like this' for the king's service 'causes me acute pain'. To ease that pain he asked for the grant of large estates (*encomiendas*) to two of his sons 'before I embark'. The duke even specified that one of these estates should be the *encomienda mayor* of the Order of Santiago just vacated by Santa Cruz, and concluded with a reminder that 'I am giving up a lot, and I am about to do something I neither know nor understand, with great inconvenience and anxiety.'[44]

This brazen attempt at extortion infuriated Philip, but he instructed Vázquez to draft a soothing letter assuring the duke 'that whatever may happen to him – and I hope that God will show him favour – I will look after his children as they deserve even if he should die on this campaign (which I hope will not happen, but that instead he will return fortunate and victorious). I always take care of those who serve me. Therefore, he should depart carefree and happy.'

Philip then added 'for your [Vazquez's] eyes alone: I plan to bestow *encomiendas* on two of his sons when he returns, or if he falls (which God grant does not happen) – but do not tell him or anyone else about this until then'. The king then added, with uncharacteristic enthusiasm: 'If my presence were not so essential here [in Madrid], to provide what is necessary for the Armada and for many other things, I would not hesitate to join the Armada, and with great confidence that it would go very well for me. That's for sure, right?'

He instructed Vázquez to 'take what you like from what I have written, to animate and encourage' the duke, 'because he certainly has no reason to feel [demoralized] as he does. Rather he should feel very happy and inspired that he is going on this mission'[45] (Figure 56).

The duke was not the only Armada commander who felt demoralized. Just before his death, Santa Cruz had a conversation with Martín de Bertendona, recently elevated to command the Levant squadron, in which they agreed that the key problem with the Masterplan was the lack of a deep-water port in friendly hands between the Isle of Wight and Flushing, and they reviewed with alarm the sorts of difficulties that could arise in the Channel when storms blew and they had nowhere to shelter. After summarizing this conversation in a letter to the king, Bertendona added: 'I really wish that Your Majesty could be present' at debates in Lisbon on how best to prepare for the Enterprise. 'It would be very different to discuss them in the presence of Your Majesty, where you could not fail to hear the truth, rather than discussing them there [at Court] *where those who do not understand can give their opinions just like those who do.*' 'But,' he concluded serenely, 'since it is Your Majesty who has decided everything, we must believe that it is God's will.'[46]

Such rhetoric helped to disguise the fact that human affairs have a tendency to become disorderly and that deviations from the predicted pattern require constant correction. As the eminent mathematician John von Neumann pointed out: 'Failure must not be thought of as an aberration, but as an essential, independent part of the logic of complex systems. The more complex the system, the more likely it is that one of its parts will malfunction.' Von Neumann therefore insisted on the need for 'redundancy'. Complex systems, such as modern aircraft, require duplicates of all essential parts, so that if one fails another can take over. The system may not function as efficiently with the duplicate, but it will not fail. Because Philip's complex Masterplan did not include any 'redundancy', it required every component to function perfectly at all times. In that sense he and Bertendona were absolutely correct: without divine intervention, the Enterprise of England was probably doomed.[47]

56. In a *billete*, Philip informs his secretary, Mateo Vázquez, that he has read 'the letter and memorials' in which the duke of Medina Sidonia begs not to be appointed to lead the Armada. Philip tells Vázquez how to draft an answer in his name, including the assertion that he would like to lead the fleet in person. The passage '*Y esto es cierto. Verdad*' – a most unusual construction – forms a self-contained sentence, almost as if Philip tried to convince himself as he wrote that all would be well.

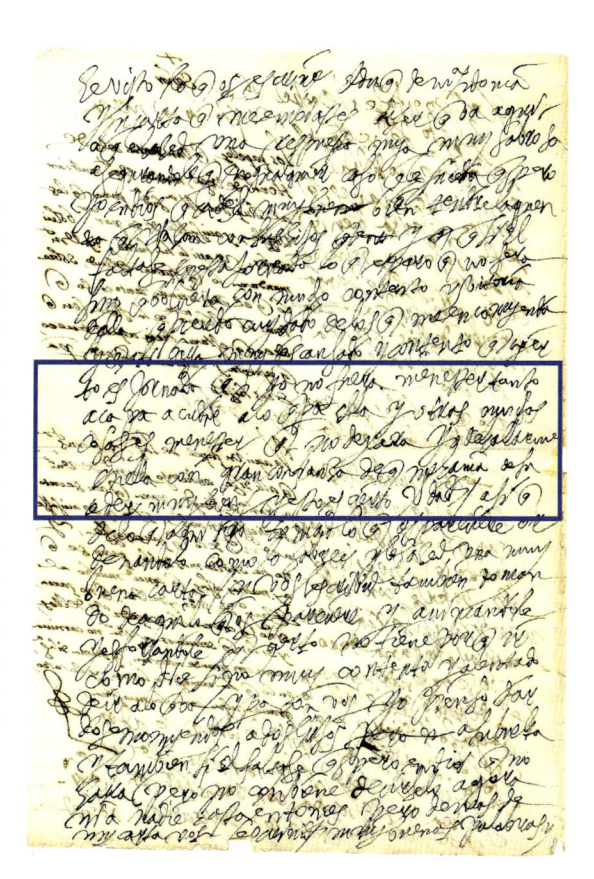

# 9

# Medina Sidonia Takes Charge

―――⋘❋⋙―――

### Minor Miracles in Lisbon

MEDINA SIDONIA TOOK HIS TIME. He did not leave Sanlúcar for Lisbon until 5 March, but he travelled in style: a train of twenty-six horses and twenty-nine mules carried his baggage. His entourage of almost sixty included four guitar players, 'a Moor to take care of the horses', and an eminent Dominican, Friar Diego Calahorrano, who received almost 40 ducats to purchase devotional works for the voyage, including a copy of *A Pontifical and Catholic History* by Gonzalo de Illescas, the book which had incensed Queen Elizabeth twenty years before (see p. 107).

While he waited impatiently for the duke's arrival in Lisbon, Fuentes did his best to maintain morale. He improved care for the sick, assisted by Leyva, Luzón and some other senior officers 'who each spend their days helping in the hospital'. He arrested some soldiers who had deserted from the fleet, including three who had arranged a mass defection; and with the king's enthusiastic backing, he had them hanged 'by way of example'. He protested that although Recalde 'is without doubt the most competent and experienced man here, as God is my witness he suffers a great wrong in not having a seat on the Council of War'. Above all, Fuentes struggled to secure more munitions for both men and ships. Lisbon had five gun-foundries when it surrendered to Spain and its new masters created another on a wharf by the river. It came into production late in 1587 and Fuentes reported to the king in February 1588 that 'by sheer willpower' he had secured fourteen artillery pieces from the new foundry, with seven more guns in production.[1]

The condition of the Armada was thus already improving by the time Medina Sidonia and his entourage rode into Lisbon on 14 March, but the duke took immediate steps to improve it further. The following day he demanded that the king appoint Recalde *almirante general*, or second-in-command of the fleet; and he began a detailed inspection of the fleet in person. His subsequent report to the king highlighted some critical deficiencies, including water ('As I went from ship to ship, I asked specifically how much water each one carried' and found the fleet was at least 1,000 barrels short); powder ('less than half of what we need'); artillery ('we need to redistribute all the big guns because it would be impossible to use them in their current positions'); and muskets (the three newly raised *tercios* had none, and Acuña Vela did not have enough weapons to arm even half of them). The duke and his expert advisers also discussed munitions. Some veterans told him that 'the day the marquis of Santa Cruz landed on Terceira [in 1583], even though some of the guns on the fleet did not fire, they consumed 1,800 quintals of powder'; and, they continued, the Armada carried only 3,000 quintals, 'which is less than half of what we need'. The duke ordered the immediate acquisition of munitions to fill these shortfalls. He also ordered an increase in the rounds for each gun from thirty to fifty, but this provoked a bitter argument among his advisers. Don Francisco de Bobadilla, the Armada's senior military commander, later recalled asking Acuña Vela: 'If the enemy did not allow us to board them, and we were skirmishing with artillery for four days, I would like him to tell me what we might do on the fifth if we carried so few rounds.'

Summarizing all this information, on 26 March Medina Sidonia informed the king: 'Although some people here may have told you that this Armada is so well-prepared and organized that it can set sail in a few days, I can tell you now that I have found everything in such a different state that this would be impossible.' He then repeated the fundamental misgiving he had expressed a month before: 'I tell you all this so that I can beg Your Majesty more effectively, as I do now, to reconsider whether the Armada should sail or not?'[2]

Philip's response was predictable. 'We must believe that Our Lord has permitted these difficulties,' he asserted, 'so that when we have overcome them with His aid, everyone will recognize more clearly that we owed every success to Him.' In other words, God was simply testing His faithful servant. The king repeated his injunction that everyone on the Armada must 'avoid oaths, blasphemy and other offences against Our Lord, because *earning* His favour with these measures is the best path to victory'.[3]

## Minor Miracles Abroad

Confident that God and the duke would resolve all remaining problems in Lisbon, the king turned his attention to the diplomatic isolation of England. The keystone of this policy remained the paralysis of France. In April 1588, in return for the payment of 100,000 ducats (£25,000) in gold, the duke of Guise promised to engineer a general rebellion by the Catholic League the moment he heard of the Armada's departure. But he could not control the enthusiasm of his subordinates. The following month Catholic mobs took over the streets of Paris; and when Henry III deployed his Swiss Guards to preserve order the entire capital erupted into violence, erecting barricades against the Guards and forcing the king to flee. The 'Day of the Barricades' made Guise the master of Paris and shortly afterwards he became 'lieutenant-general of the kingdom'. The senior French diplomat in Madrid warned his master that 'Spanish money will make a mark on the subjects of Your Majesty that will not easily be effaced and inflict a wound on your kingdom that will not heal'.[4]

Philip had hoped that Guise would force Henry to make further concessions, above all free access to the ports of Boulogne and Calais; but even without those crowning achievements, as the Armada got under way the French economy ground to a halt. According to the English ambassador: 'I never did see, nor no man has seen it, since France was France, that ever money was [as] impossible to be gotten as it is here now among all sorts, for all traffic ceases and for money there is none to be seen.' Neither Henry III nor the French Protestants could now save Elizabeth.[5]

Philip's diplomacy also ensured that the Dutch rendered little aid to England. In part it was an English 'own goal'. Leicester's government of the Netherlands had proved a disaster. The earl took the oath as governor-general of the Netherlands in January 1586 and immediately tried to create a strong central executive, to levy higher taxes for defence, and to purge the provincial governments of those who opposed his policies; but all these initiatives failed because he could not placate the prickly Dutch leaders as William of Orange had done. Leicester also failed to prevent Parma from capturing several frontier towns; worse, early in 1587 two of his English subordinates betrayed to Spain the strategic town of Deventer and a fort that dominated Zutphen. These defections totally discredited the earl and 'there grew a wonderful alteration in the hearts and affections of the people against the English. They uttered lewd and irreverent speeches of his Excellency and the whole nation.'[6] Then, in June 1587, Parma laid siege to the deep-water port of Sluis on the Flemish side of the Scheldt, and managed to throw a bridge of boats across the estuary below the town (as he had done at Antwerp), which cut it off from the sea. Elizabeth hurriedly sent reinforcements and money to Sluis not just because it was defended by English troops but also because it was a port from which England could be invaded. But on 4 August, its walls breached by some 14,000 rounds from Parma's guns, the English garrison ran out of powder and surrendered. Somewhat shaken, Elizabeth now begged her Dutch allies to join her in negotiating with Parma. When they refused, Leicester attempted to seize several strategic towns in the Republic, as the duke of Anjou had done three years before. Like Anjou he failed; and in December 1587, again like the duke, he abandoned the Netherlands and went home.

The Dutch now seemed incapable of defending themselves. They maintained 20,000 troops in garrisons, with only 11,000 as a field army, plus 6,000 English veterans: without the latter, the Republic's landward defences would collapse. The situation by sea was no better. In 1584, a few months before his assassination, Orange had stated the urgent need for ten 'good ships' to patrol the coasts in case of Spanish attack, but the States-General refused to comply. Instead of building warships of 300 and 400 tons, as the prince had suggested, they hired a few converted merchantmen of 200 tons. When in May 1588 some Dutch vessels arrived at Dover to assist the English fleet, they were deemed too small to be of service and sent home. If the Armada's target had been a port in Holland or Zeeland, the Dutch could have done virtually nothing to resist. The reconquest of the Low Countries, and therefore the Dutch Revolt, might have been over in a matter of weeks.[7]

Nevertheless, as Parma well knew, the Armada's objective was to conquer England, not the Dutch Republic. Continuing the talks with Elizabeth therefore served his purpose well because they not only caused confusion about his intentions but also called into question England's commitment to defending the Dutch. On Philip's orders Parma hinted at concessions and each time Elizabeth accepted the bait, even allowing her commissioners to negotiate in Spanish territory at Bourbourg, a town near Dunkirk. Philip reasoned that the talks 'will increase their sense of desperation later when, God willing', the invasion began. If the English asked why he mobilized, Parma must reassure them 'that it was normal to have weapons in one's hands to secure a good peace'.[8] The duke also exploited divisions among the English commissioners. He encouraged one – James Croft, who had long pocketed a Spanish pension – to break ranks and discuss terms for a complete English withdrawal from the Netherlands, and then made political capital by leaking the news to the suspicious Dutch. To be sure, Elizabeth gained something from the talks, above all an observation post in Flanders from which to monitor Parma's mobilization; but by forfeiting the trust of the Dutch she lost far more.

After the capture of Sluis, Parma concentrated on assembling sufficient troops for a successful invasion of England, and sufficient vessels to transport them. He had greater success with the first. Thanks to the passage of troops raised in Spain and

Italy along the Spanish Road, and widespread recruiting in Germany, by spring 1588 Parma commanded a force of 27,000 men ready to launch against England, while still leaving behind enough soldiers to defend the Spanish Netherlands (see chapter 2). He proved less successful in finding sufficient vessels to transport his invasion army.

In November 1587, when Parma assured the king that his forces were ready to launch a surprise attack (see chapter 8), his own records reveal that only sixty-seven vessels lay in Dunkirk harbour, and that even they lacked 370 guns and 1,630 seamen. Nieuwpoort harbour contained many barges and other small craft, with more in Sluis; but his biggest vessels – including a 400-ton flagship – lay at Antwerp, hemmed in by Dutch blockaders. Admittedly Parma made plans to strengthen his naval forces by hijacking thirty Scottish merchantmen with their six escort vessels as they sailed from Danzig to Aberdeen, and he sent 10,000 ducats in gold to Catholic leaders in north-east Scotland to arrange it; but neither the gold nor the ships were ever seen again.[9]

Parma now became profoundly uneasy about his ability to get the army across. 'My vessels here,' he reminded Philip in December, 'are no good for anything except transport, because for the most part they are barges and cobs, which in a fight would be so small and frail that four warships would be able to sink every boat they met.' Moreover, far more than four warships now awaited him. In the same letter, apparently for the first time, Parma mentioned the presence of a powerful Dutch blockading squadron, commanded by Justinus of Nassau, and warned Philip that the Armada would need to clear the sea of all enemy warships before his forces could reach 'the appointed place'. Subsequent letters to the king stressed this problem with increasing stridency. In March 1588, for example, Parma lamented that the English were:

> Forewarned and acquainted with our plans and have made all preparations for their defence; so that it is manifest that the Enterprise, which at one time was so easy and safe, can now only be carried out with infinitely greater difficulty, and at much larger expenditure of blood and effort. I am anxiously awaiting news of the departure of the duke of Medina Sidonia with his fleet ... [to protect] my passage across, so that not the smallest hitch should occur in a matter of such vital importance. Failing this, and the cooperation of the duke with me both before and during the landing as well as afterwards, I can hardly succeed as I desire in Your Majesty's service.[10]

It seems curious that none of these communications bears holograph comments from the royal pen, because Philip normally festooned incoming mail that interested him with notes and observations. For example, when in March 1588 he read a letter from a magistrate lamenting that he had just bought a ton of cheese for the Armada at one *real* per pound, the king found time to write in the margin: 'This is very little for a very high price: he should replace it, if he can find cheese at a better price.' The absence of comments on Parma's warnings about the defects of his troop-transports does not mean that the king did not read these letters, but it does suggest that he did not fully grasp their significance.[11]

## Medina Sidonia's Triumph

Medina Sidonia, on the other hand, fully grasped the naval threat posed by England. In a letter to the king in March 1587 about how best to protect the next transatlantic convoy, he stressed the scale of the crisis caused the previous year 'when John Hawkins, with six galleons of 400 tons' and some smaller ships had paralysed Iberian commerce in the Atlantic, 'because his ships sailed so well, carried little freight, and were careened and well-equipped'. He feared the consequences if 'Francis Drake or some other pirate' now appeared, because 'if they gain the weather gage, given the heavy artillery which they carry they can do us all the harm they want, sinking our warships and disabling the rest. Then they can capture them without risking any damage because our galleons cannot come to grips if the enemy does not wish it.' The only way to defend the convoys, Medina Sidonia opined, was to add more fighting ships 'armed with the heaviest guns which can be found', accompanied by twelve galleys.[12]

Once he got to Lisbon, the duke did his best to implement his own advice. He added some powerful armed merchantmen, including the huge *Lavia* and *Regazona*, as well as the galleons originally assembled to guard the 1588 transatlantic convoy, now named the 'squadron of Castile'. The duke also commissioned additional carpentry work to several galleons intended to create or extend the 'castles' at the bow and stern, 'because they are very open, and the soldiers would not be able to fight or take shelter'.[13] These structural changes were important, because ship design always requires a balance of advantages and penalties. Compromises must be struck between maximizing the positive attributes desired for a particular function and the price to be paid in negative ones.

The duke also did his best to add galleys. Santa Cruz had insisted that the Armada would need twelve galleys, but Philip refused to release more than four of those which protected the Tagus. The day after his arrival at Lisbon, Medina Sidonia informed the king that three of the four seemed too decrepit to cross the Bay of Biscay, and sent a list of eighteen galleys currently in Spain's southern ports, together with the age and condition of each (data he had at his fingertips, thanks to his work coordinating Spain's southern defences), plus a reminder that 'galleys are the sinews of this fleet'. He wrote in vain. Only the four ancient galleys from Lisbon would sail with the Armada, and (as Medina Sidonia had feared) not one reached the English Channel.[14]

The duke had more success in adding heavy artillery to the fleet, even embarking trophies from former victories (see Appendix 4). A bronze gun bearing the royal arms of Francis I of France, perhaps captured at the battle of Pavia in 1525 (when Francis himself was taken prisoner), was loaded aboard *San Juan de Sicilia*, while *Trinidad Valencera* received a huge Turkish *cañon de batir*, possibly a prize taken at Lepanto seventeen years earlier. More importantly, Medina Sidonia took steps to speed up production in the Lisbon foundries. Royal guns normally bore the king's arms and name, but such embellishment took time, so the duke secured a special dispensation to omit the royal insignia on all guns produced from the 'new foundry'. This step was entirely sensible, but production pressures also took their toll on quality. Horrifying accidents occurred when inadequately baked moulds burst, or when guns failed their proofing tests. In one such incident a weak gun exploded, killing two gunners and taking off the arm of a third. Perhaps as a result, many pieces were not properly proofed, and some substandard guns were evidently passed fit for service.[15]

The duke also 'devoted three entire days, without attempting anything else', to reorganizing the companies of Spanish infantry in Lisbon into five *tercios*; but 'that leaves me with a thousand other things to do. Although none of them is major,' he complained, they all took time. He managed to cut some corners by taking over a print shop in Lisbon whose presses ran off multiple copies of his various orders, with blank spaces for non-standard items (a technique he had used when preparing the transatlantic fleets) (Figure 57).[16]

## Life On Board

Everybody complained about life aboard the ships of early modern Europe. A letter written by Eugenio de Salazar, a judge from Madrid, about his Atlantic crossing in 1573 no doubt reflected a typical experience. He started with a detailed description of the sounds and smells of everyone aboard being seasick when the voyage began, before turning to the rituals under sail: the shanties sung by sailors to coordinate common tasks like raising and lowering the sails and the anchors; and the performance of dances, plays and songs in the evenings, sometimes accompanied by musical instruments. The same happened on at least some Armada ships because the artefacts recovered from the wreck of *Trinidad Valencera* included a

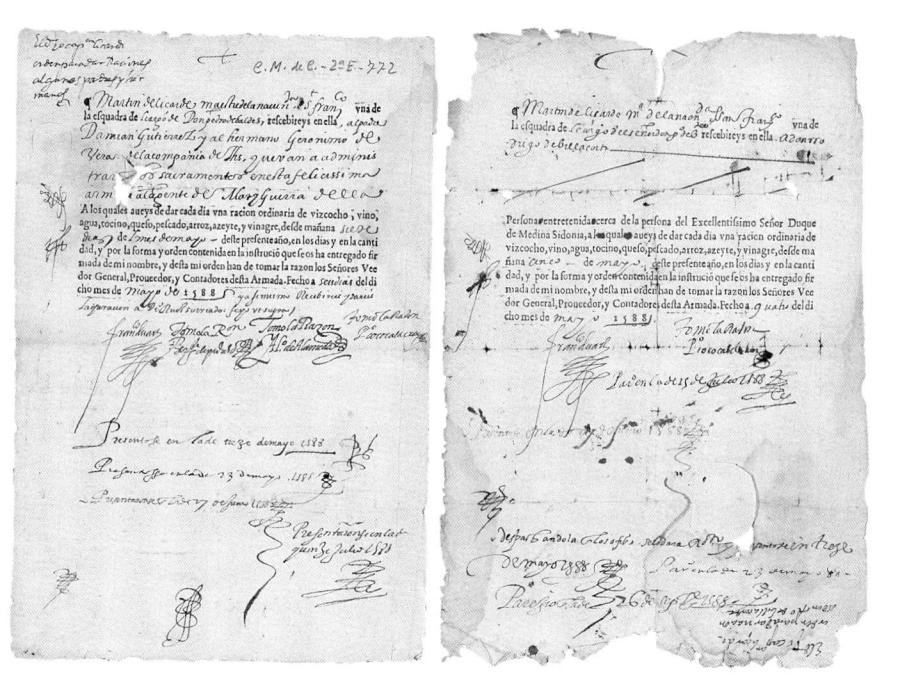

57. Two examples of the pre-printed forms introduced by Medina Sidonia after he took command of the Armada. Both forms ordered the master of *San Francisco*, vice-flagship of the squadron of Andalucia, to issue daily rations: one to two Jesuit priests and the servant who accompanied them; the other to an *entretenido*. Pedro Coco Calderón, one of the two chief accountants with the fleet and author of one of the most detailed accounts of its voyage, signed both forms. The masters of other Armada ships would receive the same forms with different details.

cittern and a tambourine (Figure 58). Nevertheless, Salazar noted, 'Travel on land is pleasant' because:

> If today you pass the night in the house of a hostess who is old, dirty, quarrelsome, wretched and greedy, tomorrow you will find one who is young, clean, modest, generous, pretty and pious ... whereas at sea there is no hope that the journey, the lodgings, or the host will improve. Instead, each day everything gets worse and more tiresome with the increasing tasks of the voyage and the lack of ship's stores as they become scarce and worse.

Salazar's ordeal lasted four weeks; the odyssey of most of those who survived the Armada campaign lasted four months.[17]

222   ARMADA

**58**. A tambourine (top) and the fingerboard of a cittern (below), both from the wreck of *Trinidad Valencera*.

**Table 9.1.** *Spanish and English weekly rations*

| Spanish |
|---|
| *Daily* |
| 1½ lb biscuit or 2 lb fresh bread, 1⅓ pints wine or 1 pint Candia wine (stronger), 3 pints water (for all purposes) |

| Monday | Tuesday | Wednesday | Thursday | Friday | Saturday | Sunday |
|---|---|---|---|---|---|---|
| 6 oz cheese | 6 oz fish (tuna/cod) or squid or 5 sardines | 6 oz cheese | 6 oz bacon | 6 oz fish (tuna/cod) or squid or 5 sardines | 6 oz fish (tuna/cod) or squid or 5 sardines | 6 oz bacon |
| 3 oz beans or chickpeas |  | 3 oz beans or chickpeas | 2 oz rice |  |  | 2 oz rice |
|  | 3 oz beans or chickpeas |  |  | 3 oz beans or chickpeas | 3 oz beans/ chickpeas |  |
|  | 1½ oz oil |  |  | 1½ oz oil | 1½ oz oil |  |
|  | ¼ pint vinegar |  |  | ¼ pint vinegar | ¼ pint vinegar |  |

| English |
|---|
| *Daily* |
| 1 lb bread or biscuit, 1 gallon beer |

| Monday | Tuesday | Wednesday | Thursday | Friday | Saturday | Sunday |
|---|---|---|---|---|---|---|
| 1 lb bacon | 2 lb fresh or salt beef | ¼ stockfish or ⅛ ling | 2 lb fresh or salt beef | ¼ stockfish or ⅛ ling | ¼ stockfish or ⅛ ling | 2 lb fresh or salt beef |
| 1 pint peas |  | 4 oz cheese |  | 4 oz cheese | 4 oz cheese |  |
|  |  | 2 oz butter |  | 2 oz butter | 2 oz butter |  |

## Figure 59. Medical Services on the Armada

A medical contingent of eighty-five was listed at Lisbon, its personnel and equipment to be transported in two hulks, *San Pedro Mayor* and *Casa de Paz Grande*. The latter was abandoned at Laredo and her people reallocated to *San Pedro* and other ships. Religious and medical services were closely linked – their joint purpose was to look after the health and well-being of the men during the voyage and provide a field hospital for the land campaign. An inventory of hospital equipment to be brought ashore begins with a full set of vestments and liturgical equipment.

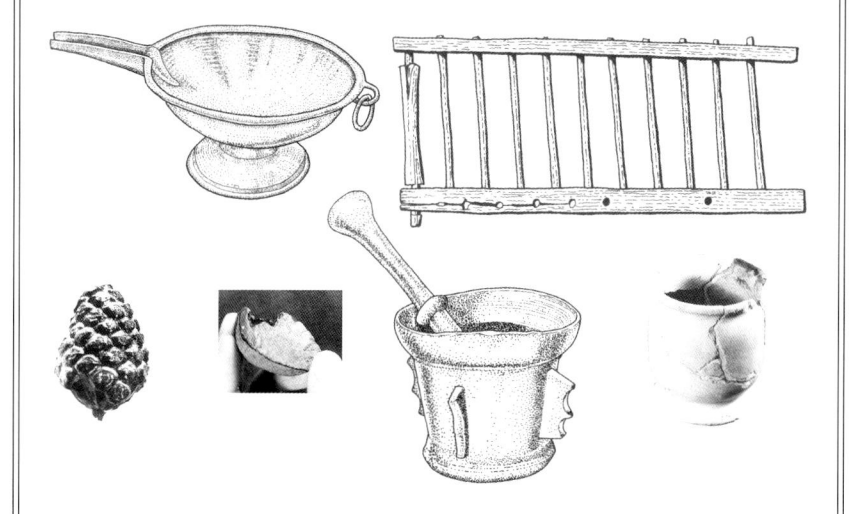

Top left: a pewter pap-dish for feeding patients. Top right: part of a cage for keeping live poultry. Bottom left: pine cone and brazil nut, both high-protein treats for invalids. Bottom right: mortar and pestle for crushing and mixing ingredients for medicines and small pot for storing ointment (all from *Trinidad Valencera* except for brazil nut from *Santa María de la Rosa*).

Glimpses of the Armada's medical services have emerged from the wrecks. In the absence of effective modern remedies, treats such as nuts, raisins and sweetmeats were welcome morale boosters. Fresh meat was often available for invalids, live chickens being housed in cages on deck and sheep towed astern in the ships' boats. And from the documents come several examples of the Armada's commanders showing concern for their men. Leyva and Luzón, for example, helped out as volunteers in Lisbon's hospital before the fleet sailed, and in the stormy Atlantic Recalde sent Leyva live lambs as comforts for the sick.

Although sickness and mortality were high while the fleet was mustering at Lisbon, once the men were embarked under Medina Sidonia's humane and efficient regime their health improved. When the Armada sailed in July only 250 remained unfit for service, though conditions again deteriorated when the fleet became storm-bound at Corunna. But the duke's organisational skill again alleviated the situation with medical interventions and fresh supplies. During the fighting casualties were relatively low. Poor weather, prolonged starvation, and disease on the dreadful voyage home would be the primary killers.

Medina Sidonia did his best to anticipate and alleviate these problems. As soon as he arrived in Lisbon he got rid of food that had become putrid, and loaded fresh provisions and more water (Table 9.1). He designated two of the *urcas* as hospital ships, and stocked them with medicines and herbal remedies, and made sure that other vessels carried rudimentary medical equipment (Figure 59).

The duke was powerless to mitigate three other miseries of shipboard life – lice, fleas and rats (Figure 60) – but he exacerbated a fourth: overcrowding. His flagship *San Martín*, for example, had about 20,000 square feet of sheltered deck space, much of it occupied by guns, munitions and stores. Working and moving about the ship required further space, and the elite demanded extra facilities and comfort for themselves and their retainers. So of perhaps 10,000 square feet available aboard for personal occupancy, Medina Sidonia and his staff occupied 3,000, leaving 7,000 for the 300 soldiers and 177 seamen aboard – rather less than 16 square feet for each man, his equipment and his personal effects for a long voyage.

Another of the duke's signal achievements was to provide each ship with navigational aids. In September 1587, Don Juan de Idiáquez had sent Santa Cruz a rutter (a mariner's handbook of sailing instructions) showing 'all the harbours and

**60.** The skull of a rat, from the wreck of *Trinidad Valencera*.

anchorages in enemy territory, which arrived here from the Netherlands three years ago', replete with annotations by both Parma (who had sent it) and Philip (pointing out numerous errors). Idiáquez also mentioned that 'in Lisbon, His Majesty's cosmographer Luis Teixeira is making a chart', and concluded: 'I hope to God that this description and the chart, the advice of experienced pilots, and the guidance of Our Lord who in such a cause will perform miracles for Your Lordship, will give you the victory we desire.'[18]

This was ridiculous and Medina Sidonia knew it. A week after his arrival in Lisbon he informed the king that given 'the lack of pilots in this fleet with knowledge of the English Channel', he had ordered the six most experienced mariners:

> To meet every morning and afternoon in the house of Juan Martínez de Recalde to correct the rutter and to advise me of the best course after we enter the Channel. They will also prepare sixty detailed charts, to issue to the larger ships, together with their itineraries and sailing orders. The smaller ships will receive the same itineraries and sailing orders so that all will be advised and informed of the navigation required of them.

'And thus,' the duke concluded, with an implied rebuke to both his predecessor and his master, 'I think we will have made a start on something that some here did not understand.' In case Philip missed the point, he added: 'Although these and other matters which we are handling may seem trifling, they are all necessary and essential to advance the service of Your Majesty.'[19]

Recalde and his mariners worked fast: a week later the duke signed a copy of the 'Rutter of the coasts of Brittany, Normandy and Picardy as far as Flanders and

England, with St George's Channel and Bristol and part of the Irish coast'. His Lisbon printer turned it into a twenty-page pamphlet and ran off multiple copies. Perhaps the committee worked too fast. The rutter included detailed information on the different depths and 'bottoms' to be found in various parts of the Channel, and how to recognize different landmarks ashore, so that pilots without direct experience of the area (and ships without pilots at all) might fix their position as the fleet advanced. But it only went as far as Calais and the Downs. Worse, it assured Armada captains that once they reached the anchorage bounded by the Goodwin Sands, 'You will wait there for a pilot to take you either to London or Dover.' If they wished to sail from there to the Low Countries, they should cross the Channel to the Flemish coast 'and when you are off Blankenberge you will fire a gun and a pilot will come out to take you to Flushing'. At a time when Spain was at war with both England and the Dutch Republic, it is hard to imagine more dangerous advice. Recalde and the pilots had evidently cannibalized commercial rutters composed in peaceful times.[20]

The duke's efforts to produce useful charts proved more successful. On 12 May 1588 Ciprián Sánchez, 'master chart-maker, living in Lisbon', delivered to the flagship '85 detailed charts of the coasts of Spain, England and Flanders, together with their soundings' – although his work rested on a fine irony. The only soundings available to a Lisbon cartographer at this time were those included in *The Mariner's Mirror*, a recent publication by Lucas Wagenaer, a Dutch Protestant, printed in Leiden, a rebellious Dutch city that had twice defied Spain's efforts to recapture it (Figures 61, 62).[21]

Medina Sidonia's early achievements as Captain-General of the Ocean Sea were quantitative as well as qualitative: he managed to increase the size of the fleet from 104 ships in February to 150 ships and ten feluccas in May, and the number of troops from scarcely 10,000 to 18,973: almost 3,000 musketeers, more than 10,000 arquebusiers, and 2,000 pikemen 'who have been equipped with arquebuses'. They were now supplied with swords, helmets and suitable clothes. Many men languishing in hospital were cured. Provisions and water were stowed according to a carefully planned turnover system (although the chief victualler still complained that much of the biscuit, bacon, cheese and fish had to be thrown overboard 'because it is two years old').[22]

Above all, the abysmal morale of the men gave way to pious fervour. Pedro de Ribadeneira, who had worked with Philip to convert England thirty years before, had been writing an *Ecclesiastical history of the schism of the kingdom of England*, but news of Drake's raid on Cadiz in May 1587 led him to complete it in haste. He called for 'the conversion or destruction of the heretics of

England' and the beheading of Elizabeth since she had 'ordered the beheading of a queen of France and Scotland for being a Catholic, her own niece and successor'. Ribadeneira also composed an *Exhortation to the soldiers and captains who sail on this campaign to England*, which confidently asserted that 'We are not going on a difficult enterprise, because God our Lord, whose cause and most holy faith we defend, will go before us; and with such a Captain we have nothing to fear.'[23]

## The Masterplan Laid Bare

By May 1588 Philip had thus managed to mobilize 140 ships and 18,000 troops for the Enterprise of England in Lisbon, with 300 small craft and 27,000 troops standing by in Flanders. The Dutch lacked the power by both land and sea to offer effective opposition, and Elizabeth's forces on land were stretched to the limit. Some 6,000 of her best troops remained in the Netherlands, and 6,000 more soldiers whom she could neither spare nor afford guarded the Scottish frontier in case of an invasion from the north. No one knew where the blow would fall. On 7 June, confined in Plymouth Sound, Admiral Howard complained that 'God knows which way the Spanish fleet will bend, either to England, Ireland, or Scotland', and warned that 'if the wind hold here but six days they will knock at our door'.[24]

A few days later the queen and her ministers had a stroke of luck: some ill-timed Catholic propaganda allowed them to eliminate the risk of an attack from Scotland or Ireland. In spring 1588 Cardinal William Allen, still in Rome, composed two tracts in support of the Enterprise and sent them to Antwerp to be printed in large numbers for distribution after the invasion took place. One was a sixty-page pamphlet entitled *Admonition to the nobility and people of England and Ireland, concerning the present wars made for the execution of his holiness' sentence, by the high and mighty King Catholic of Spain*. The other was a single-page broadsheet: *A declaration of the sentence and deposition of Elizabeth, the usurper and pretensed queen of England*. Both documents denounced Elizabeth as 'an incestuous bastard, begotten and born in sin of an infamous courtesan', and called on all English Catholics to 'forsake her therefore betimes, that you be not wrapped in her sins, punishment and damnation'. Instead, they must 'unite themselves to the Catholic army conducted by the most noble and victorious Prince, *Alexander Farnesius, Duke of Parma and Placentia*, in name of his Majesty'.

Elizabeth did not lack friends and agents in the Low Countries, and in June she received a copy of the 'vile, slanderous and blasphemous book entitled *An*

*Admonition etc*, by a low-born subject of ours now become an arrant traitor named Dr Allen'. Burghley received a copy of the *Declaration* – a 'roaring hellish Bull', as he called it – on 4 July. The reaction was curiously muted. A royal proclamation called for the summary imprisonment and trial of anyone caught circulating these documents but did not name them (no doubt to avoid giving them free publicity). A letter to the peace commissioners at Bourbourg noted that in them 'the duke of Parma is expressly named and chosen by the pope and the king of Spain to be a principal executioner of these intended enterprises', yet Elizabeth merely instructed one commissioner, Dr Valentine Dale, to show the offending tracts to Parma and demand a response.[25]

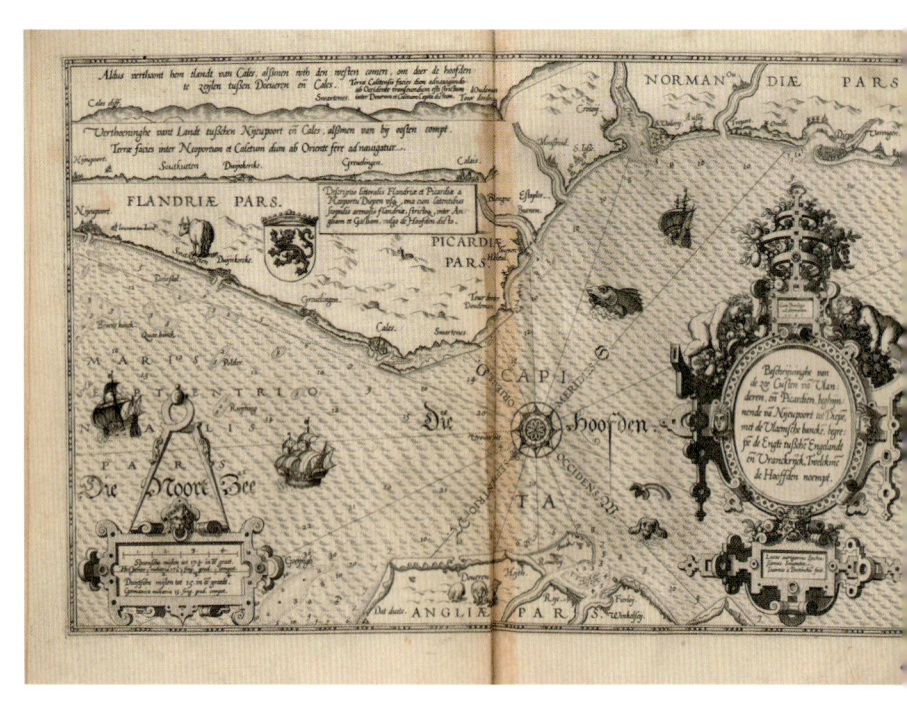

61. Lucas Wagenaer, *Speculum nauticum super navigatione maris occidentalis* (Leiden, 1586), included a detailed chart of the Narrow Seas from Dieppe (top right) to Nieuwpoort (top left) together with the north-east coast of Kent. Although created by a Dutch Protestant and printed in the Dutch Republic, such charts were relied upon by the Portuguese cartographers who created the maps (see Figure 62).

**62.** A Portuguese chart of the English Channel (oriented south-south-east). Although hand-drawn and coloured, with all details in Portuguese, in other respects the chart is identical to one of the same area printed in *The Mariner's Mirror* by the Dutch cartographer Lucas Wagenaer. The Portuguese cartographer carefully included Wagenaer's numerous soundings, an innovation in his charts. Dunkirk and Nieuwpoort, where Parma concentrated his forces, lie behind sandbanks upper left; the large anchor at lower left is labelled 'As Dunas' (the Downs anchorage) where Philip expected the Armada to wait for Parma. This chart may well have been captured when *Rosario* surrendered.

At an audience on 18 July Dale asked the duke if he intended to carry out the papal sentence of deposition against the queen. Parma replied that he knew nothing of Allen's *Admonition*, or of the 'Bull the pope had set forth, nor did undertake anything for him'. But, he warned Dale, given 'the *mal entendu* that hath been between his Master and Your Majesty' he would do whatever 'a soldier must do at the commandment of his Master' (emphasis in the original). The duke then added ominously, 'In my opinion you have more cause to desire [peace] than we, for that if the king my master do lose a battle he shall be able to recover it well enough without harm to himself, being far enough off in Spain; and if the battle be lost of your side, it may be to lose the kingdom and all.'[26]

The queen and her ministers correctly deduced from this exchange that 'Parma resolutely purposes to attempt London, however he may, whether by water or by land' – but did nothing more than discuss their options if London 'should be suddenly assailed'. Dale was appalled and wrote a furious letter which asked rhetorically:

> When Parma said he 'was a servant and a soldier and must do what his master commanded him', was not that enough for you to gather that 'Although of myself I look not to anything that the pope or his cardinals do, yet if my master and they have intelligence together, and my master command me to proceed to the execution of the pope's bull, I must do it'? And when he said, 'Her Majesty had more need to be desirous of peace than they, for if the king lost a battle he could recover it well because he was in Spain far enough off; [but] if the queen lost a battle it was the loss of her crown', was not that as much to say as 'We will give the queen a battle in England'?

Dale concluded: 'When all the forces were particularly described which are here in readiness expecting the navy of Spain, to be transported into England, is it not plain enough without a globe' that Parma and his soldiers would board Medina Sidonia's ships as soon as they arrived in the Narrow Seas and mount an invasion in overwhelming strength? On 5 August 1588 Dale signed a series of letters containing these crucial insights to his friends on the Privy Council and demanding action. He was just too late. The following evening, the Armada dropped anchor off Calais.[27]

## The Final Stages

By mid-May, thanks to heroic efforts by Acuña Vela and his team, the Armada carried a total of 123,790 artillery rounds – slightly more than 50 rounds per gun – as well as more than 5,000 quintals (250 tons) of gunpowder; a reserve of 1,000 muskets, 4,000 arquebuses and 5,000 pikes; a quantity of chain, bar and grape shot; and copious quantities of other munitions, including incendiary weapons. On 11 May some squadrons began to move down the Tagus, the larger vessels towed by galleys; but then the weather turned 'as boisterous and bad as if it were December' and a north-westerly gale howled up the Tagus estuary, forcing most ships to drop anchor again. Three days later the duke boarded a felucca and was rowed 'round the fleet, telling everyone to hurry up. I also made the galleys get close to the *urcas*' and 'if necessary tow them' down to the sea.[28]

On 21 May he distributed printed instructions to each captain, which established places for rendezvous in case of need. The first was off Cape Finisterre. In December 1587 Miguel de Oquendo had recommended 'sending some supplies to Corunna, in case the Armada encounters storms and has to enter a harbour in Galicia' and the king obliged, sending provisions to Corunna, and creating a chain of postal stations between the port and Madrid. Medina Sidonia nominated the Isles of Scilly as the next rendezvous, with the proviso that 'if by chance one or more ships become separated, they must not return to Spain on pain of death, loss of property, and condemnation as traitors. Instead they must proceed and wait for us on the south side of the island' (the duke seemed to think there was only one island in the archipelago). The third rendezvous was at Mount's Bay in Cornwall, at the entrance to the Channel.[29]

For another week these remained aspirational goals because adverse winds kept most ships anchored within sight of Lisbon. From his convent in the city Fray Luis de Granada speculated that 'God is punishing us', since 'the duke and the whole task force have been aboard their ships for three weeks, because they have lacked a wind to take them out, doing nothing except consume their rations'. They also consumed other vital provisions: Acuña Vela complained that the ships 'are using so much powder in firing salvos that I fear they will run short'. On 27 May Fray Luis lamented that despite all the prayers and processions 'the Armada is still here, because the weather has not allowed it to depart. It seems to me that Our Lord wants His Majesty to realize that even the greatest worldly power is worth nothing without His assistance.'[30]

The Almighty evidently relented the following day because the wind suddenly changed. The duke fired another salvo as a sign that all ships should weigh anchor, and once again he 'jumped into a felucca' to supervise operations. By sundown most of the Armada had cleared the Tagus and the galleys returned to tow two of the biggest Portuguese galleons, *San Juan* and *San Felipe*, out to join them. As he waited, the duke reassured his master that he understood his mission: to keep the fleet together, come what may, until he had 'joined hands' with Parma. Indeed, 'even if I learn that the enemy fleet is attacking Spain, I must not for that reason abandon the task that has been entrusted to me'.[31]

Two days later 140 ships and ten feluccas had cleared the bar with a single casualty: the *urca David Chico* sustained a broken mainmast as she left the Tagus, and the duke sent her ahead to Corunna for repair, escorted by the four galleys. Medina Sidonia was entirely justified in drawing the king's attention to 'everything I have done with this force [*máquina*], having found dangerously few men when I arrived, and everything so far behind schedule that I never thought I would see it in its present state in less than a year'. Others shared his immodest assessment. Bobadilla considered that getting the whole fleet safely to sea was a sign that 'God is with this Armada' and urged the king not to believe 'some who made haste to criticize this good duke'.[32]

---

Medina Sidonia's diligence raised Philip's spirits. On 12 May, at the Escorial, he took two of his children (Infanta Isabella and Prince Philip) with him on a fishing trip, 'and they visited the fish tanks and sent most of the catch' back to the monastery for the monks to eat. The following week the royal family set out again and spent a few days inspecting a new orchard. On 25 May Philip confided to Mateo Vázquez that 'If God is pleased to grant the Armada a favourable outcome, I have confidence that He will solve all our problems; but if not, it will be a disaster for everything – and I really dare not think about that. Instead I trust that He will have pity on His people.'[33]

For the next month, as they anxiously awaited further news, the king and his advisers tried to balance the spiritual and the material. On 17 June Don Cristóbal de Moura informed Parma:

> Here, we feel very downhearted about the slow progress of our Armada – albeit it is not the fault of His Majesty and those in his service – but there is nothing to be done in the things which God does except give thanks to Him. Let Him be blessed that everything has been made good and put in the state that Your Excellency can see from the enclosed letters. So here we have nothing else to say than to pray to God for success with the earnestness which the cause requires.[34]

The following day Philip informed Vázquez (with typical prolixity):

> I am resolved to neglect everything else and just concentrate on raising money, and I want you to help me with this because it is so important. Consider whether you should tell some of the ministers in Madrid to moderate the number of papers they send for a few days – although to avoid giving the reason, you can tell them that it is because I have been in pain recently.

He then apparently felt a twinge of guilt at telling a lie, because he continued, 'Or consider if it might be better to tell them nothing and let them send whatever they want. You will then put them on one side until we manage to get a grip on the other matters that are so important.'³⁵

Ten days later when the duke of Infantado, Spain's foremost aristocrat, complained that he had received no response to an earlier petition, Philip informed Vázquez (again with typical prolixity):

> You can tell the duke that you have reminded me [about this] several times, and that I very much wanted to see it; but that getting the Armada in Portugal to sea and related business have kept me, and still keep me, so busy that I have had no time for it. Also I have been indisposed with gout for some days – although that would not have held me back, unlike the Armada – and I needed and still need so much time and effort to find all the money which we have spent, and which we must still spend so that nothing on my part remains to be done in order to complete what has been started. Getting this done is so important that it leaves little time at present to do or think about anything else.

A few weeks later the king confided to Idiáquez: 'Things hang in the balance, and not just these affairs [of northern Europe] but of all areas. Please God, let the events advance His cause, and may He assist us as is so necessary.'³⁶

These documents capture the essence of the view from the Escorial. The king and his inner circle had done their best to mobilize every resource so that Philip could 'say that I have fulfilled my obligations'. Any setback, therefore, was 'not the fault of His Majesty and those in his service'. Everything now depended on the proper execution of the plan they had conceived and shaped with such care over the previous three years – assisted whenever necessary by the miracles to which, they felt, their prodigious efforts in God's cause entitled them.

# 10

# Advance to Contact

---

PHILIP AND HIS MINISTERS EXPECTED the Armada to solve all the strategic problems that faced them. In a holograph message to the Cortes of Castile in January 1588 the king reminded the deputies that 'You all know that the Enterprise that I have undertaken for the service of God and advancement of our Holy Catholic Faith is also for the benefit of these kingdoms, because it is the same cause.' A month later Idiáquez and Moura opined that 'The outcome of all our wars and ventures depends upon this Enterprise', namely the invasion and conquest of England.[1]

On 10 June Medina Sidonia sent a special messenger to Parma with the welcome news that the Armada was at last at sea and heading north. 'I hope that he will arrive in Flanders fifteen days before we do,' he explained to the king. 'This is very important, because it will allow the duke to prepare and get everything ready for when, God willing, I arrive.'[2] A second special messenger left the fleet that same day, begging the governor of Galicia to prepare ships carrying copious supplies of water and food ready for the Armada to pick up as it sailed by.

Medina Sidonia himself had helped to create an acute problem. His success in boosting the 12,000 fighting men on the books in February to almost 19,000 in May meant that they consumed provisions far faster than originally envisaged. The duke did what he could. His four galleys had towed the great ships of the Armada to sea and on 10 June he sent them directly to Galicia, 400 miles to the north, with orders to protect the ships carrying victuals for the fleet as it came abreast of Cape Finisterre. This moment arrived at dawn on 14 June – far later than the duke expected, because contrary winds had delayed his journey northwards – but the sight of the towering cliffs 'made everyone on the fleet rejoice'. Now, he informed Philip, 'if the weather permits me to press on, I intend to do so without a moment's delay'.

The arrival of this news at the Escorial prompted the king to make a rare joke. At the foot of a covering note to Idiáquez, Medina Sidonia wrote 'Please forgive me for not writing to you in my own hand', beside which Philip scribbled: 'It would be better to tell him that you won't forgive him if he *does* write in his own hand.'[3]

By then, the fleet's situation off Finisterre had deteriorated: no ships or galleys awaited it. After the Armada had cruised off Corunna for two days, the galleys escorted out some provisions. The duke sent them back for more, but the wind started to blow strongly from the south. Medina Sidonia now faced a critical choice.

63. The Armada's route, 30 May–21 June 1588.

Should he take advantage of the southerly wind and launch a surprise attack on England or should he wait for the supplies he desperately needed? He lingered in vain for another day and then gave the signal for the fleet to enter Corunna. By nightfall on 19 June his flagship *San Martín* and thirty-five other ships had anchored safely in the harbour (Figure 63).

## Disaster Strikes

The duke's decision fragmented the fleet. Nine vessels, including Gómez de Medina's *Gran Grifón* and Luzón's *Trinidad Valencera*, did not see the duke's signal and so continued northward. Mindful of the duke's threat to treat any captain who returned to Spain as a traitor, they sailed on to the designated rendezvous, the Isles of Scilly, to await the rest of the Armada. The main body also failed to enter Corunna that night, and so anchored beyond the headland, where a sudden and violent south-westerly gale scattered them. *Santa Ana* (Vizcaya), *Santa María de la Rosa* (Guipúzcoa), all four galleasses and several other vessels suffered serious damage.[4]

These mishaps broke the duke's spirits. On 24 June, when the scale of the disaster had become apparent, he composed two letters again urging the king to abandon the Enterprise of England. Medina Sidonia, it would seem, had got the measure of his master because he marshalled his arguments under two headings: first theology, then logistics. He began by noting the unusual severity of the recent storm. 'At any time it would be remarkable,' he observed, 'but since it is only the end of June and since this is the cause of Our Lord, to whose care the Armada has been – and is being – so much entrusted, it would appear that what has just happened must be His doing, for some hidden reason.' Perhaps, the duke suggested, the Almighty had issued a warning that Philip should abandon the Enterprise and instead use it 'to make some honourable arrangement with our enemy'. Next came logistics. The fleet's present situation was perilous: twenty-eight of its vessels, the entire artillery-train and some 6,000 soldiers were still missing.

The duke saw two alternatives – either press on regardless with the remaining ships or wait at Corunna for the missing vessels to return – and he perceived grave risks in both options. On the one hand, any attempt to carry out the Grand Design except in overwhelming strength would prove counterproductive, because the Armada would never be able to force its way up the Channel to reach Parma's army and shepherd it safely across the Channel. On the other hand, further delay would mean setting sail during the season when navigation in the North Atlantic was at its most hazardous.

The duke therefore boldly restated the fundamental objection he had voiced at the time of his appointment: 'The attack on such a large kingdom, with so many allies, requires far more forces than those that Your Majesty has assembled' – especially since, despite his best efforts, 'the strength of the Armada remains inferior to that of the enemy'. Moreover, once he got to sea, Medina Sidonia had found that 'the soldiers are not as well-trained as they should be', while 'I find that few officers, indeed hardly any, understand and know how to carry out their duties'. Yet the whole fate of the monarchy 'depends on the success or failure of this campaign, to which Your Majesty has committed all his resources – ships, artillery, munitions'. Losing these assets would 'put Portugal and America at risk and might even encourage another revolt in the Netherlands'. Therefore, the duke queried, might it not be better to cancel the whole operation? At the very least, these weighty considerations made it 'essential that the enterprise we are engaged in should be given the closest scrutiny'. 'I write this from personal experience,' he concluded (perhaps in a swipe at Idiáquez and Moura), 'so let no one deceive Your Majesty by saying something else.'

In another holograph letter that day the duke asked Idiáquez to make sure that this time the king saw his letter (no doubt a reference to the intercepted dispatch of 18 February) 'because my duty and conscience' obliged him to write, 'especially seeing that Our Lord has arranged matters, for His own hidden reasons, so differently from what we expected'. After stressing the unparalleled severity of the weather ('which would be unusual even in December'), he expressed his continuing sense of inadequacy. 'I greatly fear what is going to happen,' he wrote, 'because the fate of everything in this world has been entrusted to such a novice.'[5]

The courier departed; the duke waited. His letters placed his reputation, his high office and perhaps even his life at risk on two counts: first, suggesting that the king should make peace with his enemies came close to treason; second, and more serious, implying that Philip no longer had God on his side might, in the king's eyes, verge on heresy.

Nevertheless, Medina Sidonia was not alone in his misgivings. In Madrid, Ambassador Khevenhüller believed that the setback 'would greatly encourage our enemies and make the heretics think that God was on their side and not on that of His Majesty'; and according to the nuncio, 'the bad news about the Armada has upset not only His Majesty but this whole Court, because it seems that our Blessed Saviour does not approve of this enterprise'.[6] In Corunna the duke discussed the Armada's options with his Council of War. Don Jorge Manrique, inspector-general of the fleet, spoke first and claimed that it lacked sufficient bread and victuals to proceed – even though, according to Recalde, 'this was not true. Nevertheless, since [Manrique] claimed to have an exact record of everything, I had to keep silent.' The impetuous Don Pedro de Valdés did not keep silent. Instead, he argued vehemently for an immediate surprise attack. Things would never get better, Valdés claimed, and might well get worse: the Armada must strike now, while it still could. No doubt to the duke's profound relief, the rest of his senior officers agreed with Manrique that the Armada was too weak to proceed in its present condition, and the duke sent the king a summary of the debate. His covering letter on 28 June sought to discredit Valdés's dissenting opinion in a particularly mean-spirited way: 'Perhaps he does not remember what happened to him in Terceira, at great cost to Your Majesty' (a reference to Don Pedro's rash attempt to capture the island seven years before, ending in ignominious failure and a court martial).[7]

The duke's letter to Idiáquez that same day ('written on the flagship, with waves and storms as if it were Christmas') reprised the pessimistic tone of his earlier dispatches. He asserted that the performance of the fleet since leaving Lisbon had demonstrated it would be 'almost impossible' to keep it together in the Channel because neither the *urcas* nor the ships of the Levant squadron could keep up with the rest unless they had the wind directly in their sails. Moreover, 'since His Majesty has grouped all his naval resources' in the Armada, if it should meet with any misfortune 'it would imperil the grandeur of His Majesty, because his kingdoms do not have ten ships left, or artillery or other means for our defence'. And if the enemy should capture ports in America, or even interrupt the transatlantic trade, 'it would put an end to the strength of Spain'. As in his previous letters, the duke combined theology with logistics. Please understand, he told Idiáquez, 'that I am motivated only by my understanding of God's will, and by my belief that He does not want the Enterprise to proceed'. He continued morosely: 'Everything is lost; I can see that everyone's spirits are depressed, and those who know the most are the most discouraged. A month ago it was all so different. This astonishes me, and it could only happen if God willed it.' In conclusion Medina Sidonia could not resist repeating 'what I have told you so many times before, for the discharge of my conscience: someone must take charge of this force who understands what to do and has the experience that I lack'.[8]

As the duke awaited a response from the Court his fleet slowly reassembled. A *patache* sent to the Scillies found nine ships in good order, thanks to the efforts of Gómez de Medina (who as a squadron commander was the senior officer present). They had all returned safely to Corunna by 6 July ('having smelled England, because they were so close', as Recalde observed wistfully). Gradually other stragglers returned, and the great task of repairing and re-victualling the ships began. Medina Sidonia's wide administrative experience and tireless attention to detail once again paid rich dividends: 'The duke is working with great energy, as usual,' Recalde told the king. Like Admiral Howard, Medina Sidonia's style of command was neither remote nor aloof. Thus 10 July, a Sunday, found him in the bowels of the storm-damaged *Santa María de la Rosa*, supervising the stepping of a new mainmast. The task took six hours, but 'when it was finished,' he reported modestly to the king, 'I felt we had not done badly'.[9]

The atmosphere at the Escorial was very different. Medina Sidonia's pessimistic letter of 24 June 'came at a very bad time', the king complained, because 'I have to spend so much time on incoming papers that I believe it's making me walk badly'. He refused to read some of the documents that did reach his desk: 'Truly, I did not dare to read the letter about money' sent by Parma, 'because I already know how important it is, and reading more would do nothing except to give me more grief than I have already, which is more than enough about everything.' But he saw no alternative: 'The money must be spent, so that nothing on my part remains to be done to complete what we have begun. Taking it forward is so important that it leaves me little time just now to do or think about anything else.' He nevertheless gave the reports from Corunna his immediate and undivided consideration.[10]

The opening lines of the king's reply must have made Medina Sidonia blench. 'Duke and cousin', he began:

> I have received the letter written in your own hand dated 24 June, and from what I know of you, I feel sure that you brought all these matters to my attention because of your zeal to serve me, and a desire to succeed in your command. The certainty that this is so leads me to be franker with you than I should be with another.

After this terrifying start the rest of the missive, although firm, was considerate and mild in tone. The king restated each of the original reasons for the undertaking and used his perverse logic to demolish every one of the duke's objections. First the theology: 'If this were an unjust war, one could indeed take this storm as a sign from Our Lord to cease offending Him; but being as just as it is, one cannot believe that He will disband it, but will rather grant it more favour than we could hope.' Then came the logistics and strategy. The king reminded his doubting commander that the English had no allies, and that their forces remained inferior to those of Spain. With a following wind the fleet could be in the Channel within a week, whereas if it remained in Corunna it represented a sitting target, liable either to be destroyed at anchor or blockaded in port while the English ravaged the unprotected Iberian coasts and captured the next treasure-fleet. 'I have dedicated this enterprise to

God; and I chose you as the means to help me achieve it,' Philip thundered, 'and I am convinced that with God's help we shall overcome all obstacles.' He then issued a command that brooked no further dissent: 'Pull yourself together, then, and do your part!'[11]

The courier who delivered this document also brought rude letters from Idiáquez, who scolded the duke that he must trust in God, and 'man up [*haga pecho digno de su valor*]'; and from Moura, who urged him to 'put on some weight, get some sleep, and stop believing that you are responsible for Heaven's decrees. Instead you should accept them, because up there they know best what's best for us.' A few days later the king wrote again. 'You will have seen my decision clearly enough' in the previous letter, he told the duke – but as usual he repeated himself. 'You must not abandon the Enterprise because of what has happened but persevere at all costs with what we have begun, overcoming all difficulties that arise.' He continued: 'I hope to God that all these initial difficulties can be exchanged in the end for His greater glory' (another example of how the king saw divine favour as something that could be 'earned'). He concluded: 'Make sure to send me a courier every day with updates on the state of everything.'[12]

The point of this final injunction, of course, was to allow Philip a better opportunity to micromanage affairs, and he lost no time in doing so. Medina Sidonia had sent the king a copy of his recent letter to Parma, confirming that as soon as the Armada had 'reached the coast of England, I will let you know where I am so that Your Excellency can come and meet me. I hope very much,' he continued, 'that the coast has an anchorage large enough to shelter a fleet as large as this one, with a safe harbour nearby; but if not, we will have to make do with what we find.' He reiterated his need to know urgently 'the state of things over there, when you can set forth, and where we can meet'. He then reported that he had 'assembled the pilots and other experts aboard this fleet who are familiar with the whole coast of England and asked them to decide in which port this Armada might shelter, protected from the winds' while he waited for confirmation that Parma and his forces were ready. They named Beachy Head, Hastings and Romney.[13]

Events would reveal the wisdom of this Plan B, but once again Philip vetoed it. 'I am not surprised by the opinion of the pilots about suitable anchorages before you get to Dover,' he told Medina Sidonia, 'because they do not know that you have orders to press on to Margate Cape.' He now reiterated this goal. The central weakness of the king's operational strategy thus remained intact.[14]

Some thought that Medina Sidonia had made a serious error in taking shelter in Corunna. 'I cannot begin to tell you,' Recalde confided to Idiáquez:

The regret I feel that I lacked the health to go to the flagship and see the duke the day we saw the cape [Finisterre] and the galleys, because I know in my heart that we should have taken advantage of the good weather, which was exactly what we needed for our voyage. But instead we headed for this harbour because the courtiers [aboard the fleet], who always seek comfort and thought they would enjoy it here, got their way.

'But,' he conceded, 'since we have entrusted everything to God, He must have wanted it this way.'[15]

Recalde also blamed his commander for listening to those 'courtiers'. 'As a faithful servant of the duke, I do wish that he would be less credulous in some things and more resolute in others.' Apparently Medina Sidonia agreed, because he now summoned Diego Flores de Valdés, commander of the squadron of Castile, to serve on the flagship as his nautical adviser. The Council of War in Madrid reached the same conclusion and recommended the transfer of three other 'minders' to the flagship to compensate for the duke's inexperience: Don Francisco de Bobadilla, the most experienced military officer; Marolín de Juan, the senior pilot; and Miguel de Oquendo, commander of the squadron of Guipúzcoa, 'because of his familiarity with the North Sea'. 'We believe,' the councillors stated, 'that if the duke had consulted people of this calibre he would not have entered Corunna but instead would have undertaken the voyage.' Philip sent to Corunna Andrés de Alva, from the Council of War, to make sure that Medina Sidonia accepted 'those whom you, acting on my behalf, will direct to go over to his galleon, together with those whom he may deem most useful and who may be least missed from the vessels on which they now serve' – but he vetoed Oquendo ('to avoid leaving so many squadrons without a leader') while approving the transfer of Flores to the flagship. The choice of Flores, who knew more about convoys than battles, rather than Oquendo, would fatally affect the outcome of the Armada campaign.[16]

Nevertheless, the king's verbal spanking seems to have made Medina Sidonia almost a happy man. On 6 July, when the last of the scattered ships entered Corunna, he wrote jubilantly that 'the reunion of the fleet has been miraculous and makes us see that Our Lord has arranged the affairs of this Armada for His greater service'. A few days later he repeated: 'I hope that Our Lord will advance what remains to be done, to His great glory, giving us a very great victory. We are getting on top of everything; and although I struggle because I am alone here, I feel that Our Lord is giving me strength.' By 15 July his enthusiasm had increased even further. 'Since it is God's own cause, and since He has not forgotten the great service that His Majesty wishes to offer with this enterprise, He has been pleased to reunite the entire fleet without the loss of a single ship and with no loss for any of them. I hold this to be a great miracle.' He predicted that the Armada would set sail within the week.[17]

Recalde, as usual, harboured feelings that were both more pessimistic and more practical. 'According to the little that I have ascertained,' he informed Idiáquez (no doubt with heavy sarcasm, since he was second-in-command of the entire fleet and yet Medina Sidonia had only 'just done me the honour of seeing me'):

> The aim and destination of this Armada is to fight with the enemy as best we can and destroy him, as I hope God allows, provided the enemy wants to fight, as I expect he will. If not, we must sail to the Downs and there help and escort whatever ships are in Dunkirk and the army of the duke of Parma in safety to the location deemed most suitable, which should be the shortest crossing – say, six leagues – on one shore of the Thames or the other. That will take several days, because if we are to transport cavalry (as I hear) it cannot be done in a single transfer.

'When we have done that,' Recalde continued lugubriously, 'the first task for the Armada is to find a port capable of sheltering all of us' – but which one? 'I do not believe there is any harbour suitable for big ships between the Thames and Southampton; and that port, and those on the Isle of Wight, have numerous forts and castles.' Far better, Recalde thought, for the fleet to seize either Falmouth or Plymouth. Nevertheless, he concluded (just like Philip): 'We will sail with the strong and total desire to succeed, as the venture requires, and in the belief that God will guide us.'[18]

## Close Encounters

Neither Medina Sidonia nor Recalde mentioned (let alone challenged) the underlying strategic dilemma of whether to leave or stay in Corunna – no doubt because, given the situation in which the Armada now found itself, sailing to England as soon as possible had become the only sound option. Disbanding the fleet, which represented so much capital in both resources and prestige, before it had accomplished any of its objectives, would achieve nothing: as Philip observed, it would not even exert pressure on the English negotiators at Bourbourg. Worse, the English might descend on Corunna, just as they had done the previous year on Cadiz, wreaking havoc on the Armada as it lay helplessly at anchor.

That is exactly what the English planned to do. While the queen's commissioners continued to negotiate fitfully at Bourbourg, her admirals prepared to launch another pre-emptive strike against Spain. As soon as Admiral Howard arrived at Plymouth with his ships on 23 May he declared his intention to spend 'two days to water the fleet, and then God willing to take the opportunity of the first wind toward the coast of Spain'. A week later he led out 'eighty-seven sail of ships with me', intending 'to have borne over to the coast of Spain with all diligence; but we had not been fourteen hours at sea but the wind turned to the south-west and continued south and southerly for seven days, with very much wind as I think was ever seen at this time of the year'. Therefore, 'we had very much ado to recover Plymouth' on 16 June. While at sea they learned that the Armada, with '150 or 200 sail', had already left Lisbon but encountered headwinds, leading Drake to predict that 'either we shall hear of them very shortly, or else they will go to the Groyne [Corunna], and there assemble themselves, and make their full rendezvous'.[19]

Two weeks later Howard left Plymouth to attempt another surprise attack; but once again he was thwarted by storms off the Scillies, more storms off Ushant, and finally a flat calm when they were 70 miles off the Spanish coast. Eventually he gave up and on 22 July re-entered Plymouth, where the fleet started the laborious process of taking on provisions to replace those consumed on its fruitless voyage. It was just as well: the Armada was on the move again. As Howard later realized, 'the southerly wind which brought us back from Spain brought them out'.[20]

While he waited for that southerly wind, Medina Sidonia took several important steps. He re-emphasized the holy nature of the campaign and repeated the need to avoid swearing, gambling, sodomy and blasphemy, and ordered prayers to be said publicly aboard every ship twice daily. In an attempt to improve spiritual motivation, he sent all the clerics aboard the fleet to the island of San Antón in Corunna harbour where they set up tents and temporary altars. In batches of a thousand or more each man in the fleet confessed and received a blessing together with a metal medallion to wear around his neck showing the Virgin on one side and Christ on the other (Figure 64).

Understandably, morale aboard the fleet had waned, and the duke chose the island location partly through fear that his men might desert if allowed ashore. Some did indeed abscond: according to Dr Góngora, a medical officer aboard *Nuestra Señora del Rosario*, a number 'stayed in the Groyne [Corunna] and would not go forward'. These faint-hearts were probably no great loss. Recalde had already grumbled about the practice of entrusting companies 'to men who are very young simply because they are gentlemen'.[21]

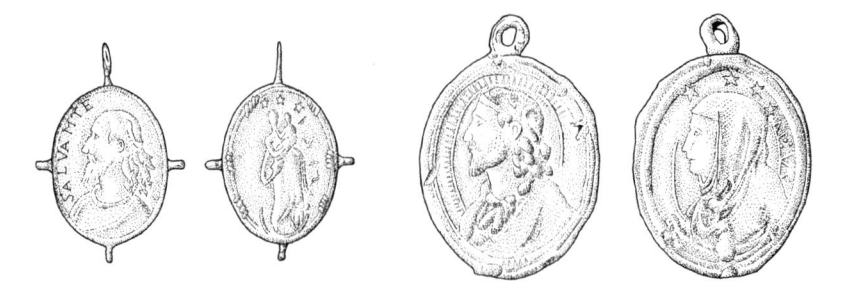

**64.** Two religious medallions, of copper (left) and pewter (right), examples of which have been found on several Armada wrecks.

Propaganda incentivized those who remained to stay the course. Some of those captured aboard *Rosario* reported hearing before they left Spain 'general speeches that they should all depart very rich from England'; others were assured that they would be allowed, 'in what place soever they should enter within [England], to sack the same, either city, town, village or whatsoever'; and that they would 'put all to the sword that should resist them'. As the English Catholic Tristram Winslade later told his captors: 'Their speech was to have landed as near London as they could, and to have rifled [sacked] it; and at their first coming not to have spared any man alive.' Other prisoners confirmed this: 'There was a plot laid to set fire in divers parts of the city of London, and to sack the same when it should be in an uproar, and so to follow on to the Court, where the queen should be, and make what means they could to kill her.'[22]

## Advance to the Channel

Whatever the truth of such stories, the morale of the fleet had rallied by the time it sailed from Corunna. On 19 July Andrés de Alva asserted that 'the storm that forced the fleet into this port was the work of God, because in Lisbon the captains did not realize the defects of their ships', but the 'bad weather they encountered revealed the faults in each vessel, and now that they have been remedied here they are in much better shape than when they left Lisbon'. Alva also stated that everyone now aboard 'serves with the greatest happiness imaginable and is eager to get to grips with the enemy'. In addition, reinforcements arrived, bringing the number of men aboard the fleet to almost 27,000, including more than 18,000 soldiers. Medina Sidonia even felt confident enough to reject some unsuitable newcomers.

When a contingent of 400 local levies arrived, he informed the king that they were old, infirm, undernourished and 'unfit to serve in any capacity' because 'not one of them can identify an arquebus, sword or any other weapon'. Rather than have them die aboard ship to no effect, and finding that the 'lamentations and misery of their wives troubled my conscience', he sent them all home.[23]

Medina Sidonia felt less confident about provisions. The chief victualler inspected all supplies, throwing many rotten items into the sea, and certified that the fleet still had enough cheese, fish, vegetables, wine and olive oil to last two months, and enough biscuit for 163 days; but the duke remained dubious. He reported to the king that 'since a good deal is damaged, or will become damaged', he had cut the daily ration for each man to one pound of biscuit and reduced the issue of meat.[24]

On 20 July Medina Sidonia convened two further meetings on the flagship – one of his Council of War, the other of his principal pilots – to debate what to do next. He insisted that each man deliver his opinion separately and the detailed record, sent to the king, revealed rare unanimity. Leyva (who spoke first) urged an immediate departure 'making all possible efforts, so that we can leave the path of despair and instead succeed in our voyage'. Diego Flores worried about the length of time required to get the entire fleet out of harbour and into the open sea, 'but because we are wasting time and provisions here, it seems less risky to go'. Recalde, who spoke last, adopted the grumpy tone that had become his hallmark: the weather was already as favourable as it was likely to get, 'and if the fleet had hoisted its sails at any time before 11 a.m. this morning, it would already have reached the open sea'. He therefore opined 'that if the weather tomorrow is like that today, we should set forth'. The duke then consulted his pilots, who unanimously endorsed Recalde's recommendation. They further suggested that, if the weather still seemed favourable at sunset, the flagship should fire a gun to authorize the fleet to start the final preparations, and another gun at midnight as a signal for each ship to start raising her anchors and make ready to unfurl her sails at dawn. Still the duke hesitated to take such a momentous decision alone, and at 7 a.m. on 21 July he ordered Recalde and a few other experienced senior officers and pilots to join him and Flores aboard the flagship to take the final decision. Since every ship had now weighed all but one anchor, they resolved that unless the weather changed the fleet should leave at midday. As at Lisbon, the entire Armada got to sea without a single loss – another remarkable feat of seamanship.[25]

Almost immediately a flat calm, and then a northerly wind, forced the fleet to drop anchor again and the duke feared that 'we may be forced to return to Corunna'; but then the wind shifted southerly. The flagship fired another gun at midnight as a signal for everyone to resume the voyage, but the rudder of the galleass *Zúñiga* broke and needed repair, and 'some ships took so long to make sail that the fleet had to wait until an hour after dawn to leave'. Nevertheless, by 25 July, having reached 'the latitude of 48 degrees' (level with the French port of Bordeaux), Medina Sidonia felt confident enough to send another *patache* to Parma, announcing his approach. A Cornish ship bound for Brittany for salt spotted them, and her captain noted with awe the great red crosses on the Armada's sails before fleeing homewards with his breathless story. The following day the weather changed again and brought three days of storms.[26]

The Armada now suffered some serious losses. Early on 26 July the galleon *Santiago* (Portugal) collided with *San Cristóbal* (Castile) and the ships were lucky to disengage with only minor damage. Dawn on 28 July revealed a far more serious calamity. The Vizcayan flagship *Santa Ana* – one of the most powerful vessels in the fleet, and therefore one of those chosen to carry 50,000 gold crowns from the royal treasury – was missing. While executing an order from Recalde to help repair the broken mast of a *patache*, she lost sight of the fleet and made for Mount's Bay, one of the designated rendezvous points. When she found no news of the Armada there, *Santa Ana* took shelter at La Hogue on the eastern side of the Cherbourg peninsula, and finally at Le Havre, where she would remain immobilized throughout the campaign.

All four galleys also dropped out. Their commander, fearing that his frail vessels could not withstand storms in the Bay of Biscay, asked the duke's permission to follow the coastline (as he had done between Lisbon and Corunna), but the duke refused. As a result, as almost everyone had predicted, all four proved unweatherly and made for French ports. One was wrecked as she tried to enter Bayonne; the convicts aboard another mutinied as she approached land; the other two limped back to Spain, leaking badly.

Worst of all, almost forty other ships were missing, including Valdés's *Rosario* and several other vessels from the Andalusian squadron. The duke ordered the Armada to shorten sail until the stragglers caught up, only resuming his voyage the following day when Valdés and his lost vessels, which had sheltered at the Scillies as instructed, rejoined the fleet.

Despite these setbacks, at 4 p.m. on 29 July – scarcely a week after leaving Corunna – lookouts on the flagship sighted the English coast. The duke immediately unfurled the royal standard, which displayed both the royal coat of arms and Christ crucified. He ordered everyone to say prayers of thanksgiving and authorized every ship to fire three artillery pieces (so much for a stealth attack!). 'The voyage has been so troublesome,' the duke reported to the king, 'that some people' – could he have meant Diego Flores? – 'voted that we should seek shelter; but I decided not to do that unless all the masts broke.' As Admiral González-Aller Hierro has observed: 'This was probably the happiest moment for Medina Sidonia on the entire campaign.' Even Recalde cheered up: everything had gone so well 'that it has made all of us happy, as you can imagine, and we have high hopes that each day will be better than the last'. According to Leyva, 'Tomorrow or the day after comes the wedding: that is, we will fight somewhere, with a near certainty of victory.' The duke expressed only two reservations at this stage. 'I cannot sail in this galleon any faster than the slowest ship in the Armada, because I need to protect them' (an attitude that would not survive contact with the enemy); and 'in all this time I have heard nothing from [Parma] or come across a single ship or person who can enlighten me, and so I am sailing blind'.[27]

Although he did not know it, the Armada now held a decisive advantage over its adversaries. Admiral Howard had returned to Plymouth Sound on 22 July after the abortive attempt to raid Corunna, his victuals all but consumed. It was not easy to replenish them in south-west England, a thinly populated area unaccustomed to providing the huge quantities of food required by the 9,500 men aboard the fleet. Yet haste was now essential because on 29 July 'an English pinnace came to reconnoitre the Armada' – no doubt Thomas Fleming's *Golden Hind* (see chapter 3) – and although some Spanish ships 'gave chase, she returned to the port [of Plymouth] at great speed'. Yet however fast Fleming travelled with his sensational news, he arrived too late for immediate action: the incoming tide meant that Howard could not get his fleet to sea before nightfall.[28]

The safety of England's principal defence, its battle-fleet, therefore depended on the efficacy of Plymouth's fortifications. A detailed map commissioned by Sir Richard Grenville the previous year shows artillery positions (Figure 65). The two batteries shown at Cawsand Bay to the west and Bovisand to the east, both of which Grenville considered 'a good landing' for seaborne invaders, required a 'new bulwark'. Without them, invaders could storm ashore and create fortifications that would paralyse the English fleet.

What of the other defences shown on Grenville's map? Although proving a negative is often hard, the municipal records of Plymouth for 1588 reveal that the town purchased some heavy ordnance, powder, cartridge bags and armour; but the Lord Lieutenant of Devon lamented the 'want of skilful people' with 'knowledge in making sconces and other fortifications', and made no mention of constructing any 'new bulwark'. Moreover, a petition to the Privy Council signed by both Sir Francis Drake and the mayor of Plymouth in 1590 leaves no doubt that the bulwarks shown on Grenville's map remained unbuilt in the Armada year. The petition began:

'The said town lies open to the enemy, not defended by any fort or rampart, [so] that he may, by the landing of a small force in the night, become master of their ordnance, and so possess himself of the town.' Tudor England was thus extremely fortunate that at 7 p.m. on 29 July 1588, 10 miles off the Lizard peninsula, 'Diego Flores argued that the flagship should take in sail and that we should wait in order to gain the weather gage, and the duke agreed.'[29]

65. The defences of Plymouth, spring 1587. Sir Richard Grenville's map, at a scale of almost two inches to one mile, shows twenty-nine artillery pieces sited according both to the lie of the land and the configuration of the deep-water channel. The red lines indicate ranges for each gun covering the channel that large warships would have to take to enter the bay, and also vulnerable landing-places. Nevertheless, twenty-nine guns seems a small number for the protection of so vital a haven; and other sources suggest that Sir Richard's proposals had still not been implemented when the Armada approached.

**(Overleaf) 66.** *The Seventh Day of the Battle of the Armada*, by Hendrik Cornelisz Vroom, *c.* 1600. The battle off Gravelines dominates the foreground. The fireships are in the middle distance, with the coast from Dunkirk to Ostend on the horizon.

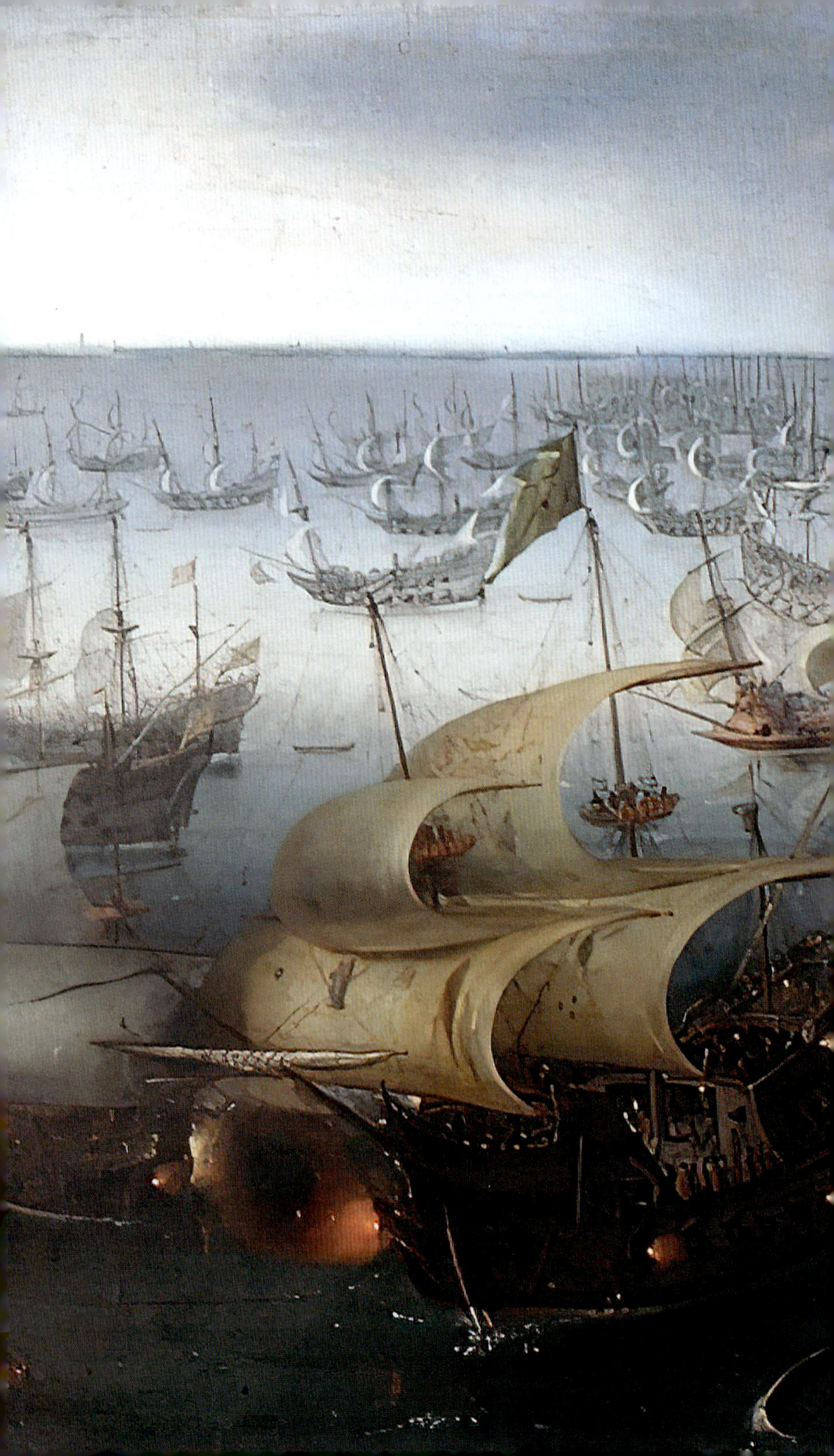

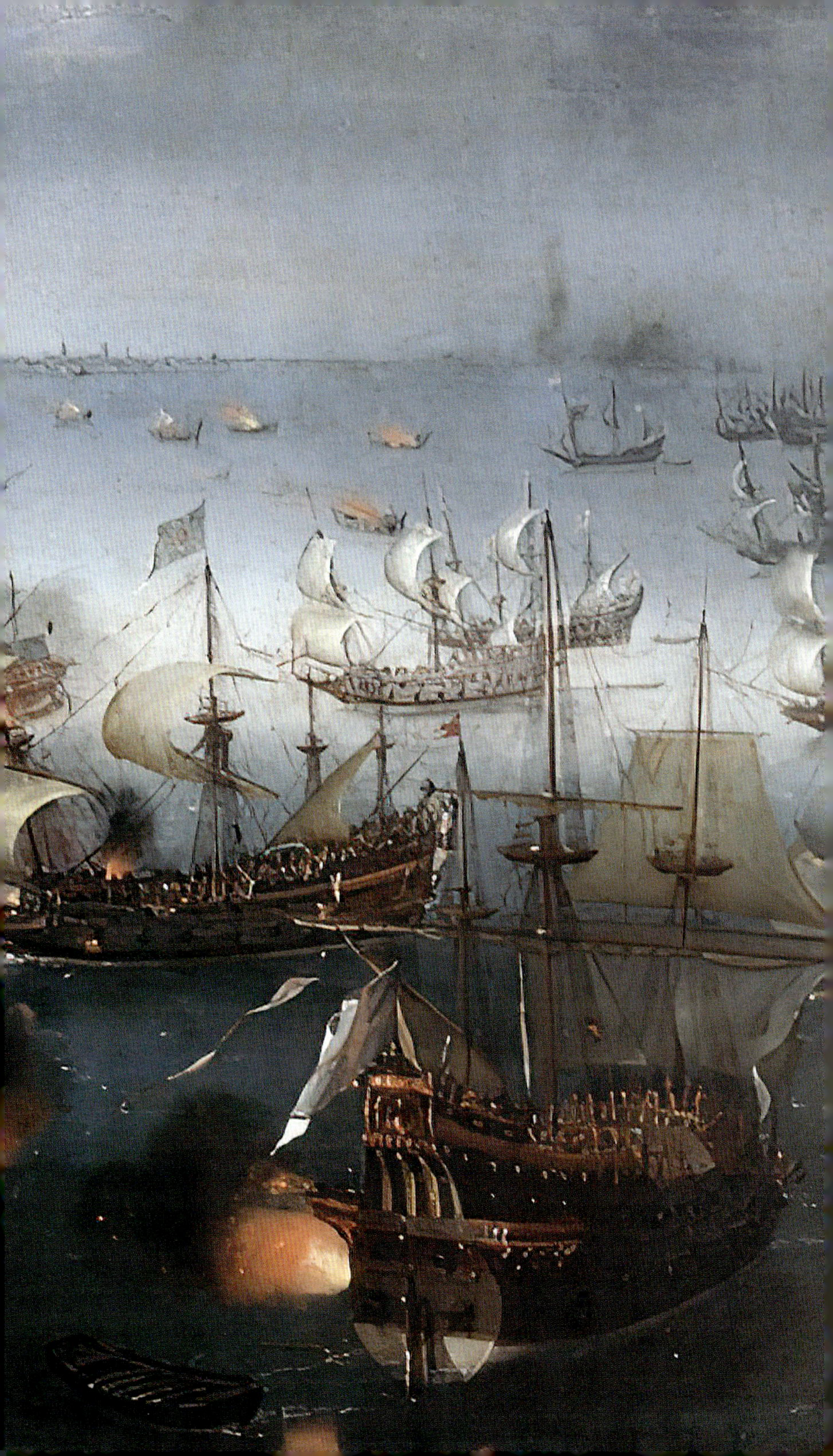

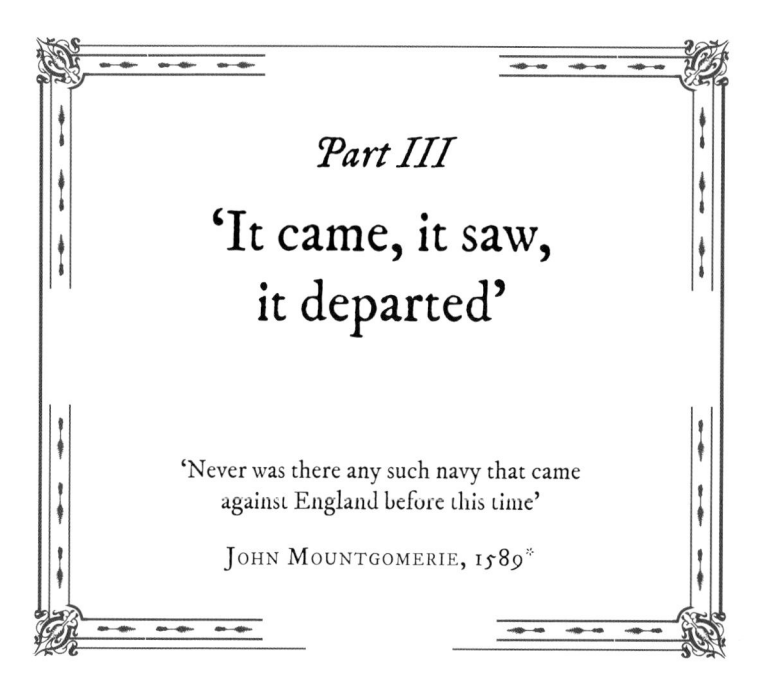

*Part III*

# 'It came, it saw, it departed'

'Never was there any such navy that came
against England before this time'

JOHN MOUNTGOMERIE, 1589*

## 11

# Battle Stations

─────⋘❋⋙─────

### The Enterprise of England: The Theory

P HILIP II SIGNED HIS INSTRUCTIONS for Medina Sidonia as Captain-General of the Ocean Sea on 1 April 1588 and sent them to Lisbon together with an updated version of a paper of advice prepared for Santa Cruz the previous September (see chapter 8). Between them they set out the royal vision of the Armada's strategic and tactical goals.

The duke must 'set sail in God's name for the English Channel, proceeding along it until he should anchor off Margate Cape' (the North Foreland), where Parma and his troops would join him 'as soon as he should see his crossing made secure by the presence of the Armada'. After this, the instructions juxtaposed details on the conduct of the fleet with measures to curb the immorality of its sinful human cargo on such a saintly enterprise. Theology and practical advice became inextricably muddled. There must be no blasphemy aboard the ships; the English fleet must be defeated if it tried to attack or halt the Armada. Drinking, gambling, feuding and (God forbid!) womanizing must be rigorously punished; the two dukes must cooperate fully on terms of equality and respect. Above all Medina Sidonia must keep in constant touch with Parma – a feat Philip apparently assumed would be easy, since the duke could 'either put a trusted messenger ashore on the coast of Normandy, who can then travel safely with a verbal message; or send a letter to a port in Flanders by sea, using the special cypher I am sending now.' The king's instructions closed with two injunctions that reaffirmed his intention to micromanage everything from the Escorial. 'I charge you to inform me in minute detail of everything you do and everything that happens.' Furthermore, 'You may not depart from these instructions, or from anything else I may add or order later according to news and developments.'[1]

Neither document explained exactly how the Armada would 'make secure' Parma's crossing to England – indeed Medina Sidonia would not even know where Parma intended to land until he reached his destination. According to the 'Secret Instructions' that Philip also signed on 1 April 1588: 'After you reach Cape Margate, which you must overcome all obstacles in your path to reach, *you will find out where the duke my nephew wants you to put ashore the soldiers on the fleet destined to support him.*' It specified only that Don Alonso de Leyva would lead those soldiers ashore at the appointed place and would thereafter take his orders from Parma.

At least the Secret Instructions laid out a 'Plan B'. If by some mischance the rendezvous with Parma proved impossible, then (and only 'after consulting my nephew') Medina Sidonia might sail back through the Channel and 'enter the eastern approach of the Solent, which is wider than the western approach and goes further inland'. He should aim to 'capture the Isle of Wight, which does not appear strong enough to resist. Once captured you will have a safe haven in which to gather the fleet. You must therefore fortify it strongly.' Although Philip delegated the immediate decision on what to do next to the two dukes, he insisted that afterwards 'It is really important that I know as soon as possible what has happened, so I can send advice and issue orders about what to do next. I therefore exhort you once again to keep me constantly informed of what you are doing.' The man in the Escorial would remain in charge.[2]

Philip also signed a third set of Instructions on 1 April, this time for Parma. In effect it set out a Plan C: what to do if the duke landed in Kent but did not 'succeed as we wish, so that you find that you cannot compel the English by force of arms to make peace'. In this case, Parma must use his presence on English soil to secure three concessions. First, the re-admission of all those banished for their religious beliefs, and the free exercise of the Catholic faith throughout the kingdom. Second, the surrender to Spanish forces of all Dutch towns held by English troops (especially the deep-water harbour of Flushing, which commanded the sea approaches to Antwerp). Finally, the payment of a war indemnity sufficient to cover the damage inflicted by England (though Parma might drop this demand in return for the other two concessions).

These were exactly the concessions suggested by Don Juan de Zúñiga in October 1586 (see chapter 6), but the king added two more. First, 'it would be a mistake to think' that English Protestants 'will keep any promises they make' and so Parma must not only take some prominent people as hostages but also garrison some

'English towns for a few years, to see how they carry out their promises' regarding toleration for Catholics. Philip added the second modification in his own hand. Even after Parma had landed in Kent:

> You must not end the peace talks with the English commissioners. Instead, you should instruct our delegates to persevere and tell their counterparts that the best thing they can do for their country is to offer terms so advantageous to me that they would justify you in withdrawing your forces. But if your campaign goes well, and has good prospects of success, you must not accept any terms they may offer you, however favourable. Instead, with God's help, you must complete the conquest.

Despite the obvious importance of this document, the king did not send it directly to Parma. Instead, he entrusted it to Medina Sidonia in a sealed package, to be opened only after the two dukes had 'joined hands'.[3]

It is hard to explain why Philip felt the need for such caution, beyond his normal disposition to act with 'secrecy and dissimulation', just as it is hard to explain why he continued to meddle from afar with the arrangements he had made. But meddle he did. Two days after signing these Instructions he responded to Medina Sidonia's request to delay the Armada's departure until Diego Flores de Valdés arrived with the transatlantic guardships gathered in Andalucia: 'As soon as I hear from Sanlúcar about the galleons, and how ready they are to leave, I will decide whether or not you should wait for them, and [if so] whether you should wait for them in the Tagus or out at sea.' The duke 'must therefore have everything ready to carry out instantly whatever I tell you to do'. This was totally unrealistic since 400 miles, or at least four days' travel, separated the Escorial both from Lisbon and from Sanlúcar.[4]

On 23 April Philip meddled again. He signed a commission for Leyva to take command of the Armada in case the duke died or became incapacitated, and sent it to Recalde with strict orders that 'if God grants the duke life, this package must be sent back to me unopened when you return. No one is to know about this, except in the circumstances described.' He then realized an obvious weakness: since Leyva remained ignorant of his future role, 'We should think about what to do if Juan Martínez [de Recalde] should die.' No evidence exists that he did so. The Armada therefore set sail with no contingent chain of command.

That same day, at the end of a long letter to Medina Sidonia addressing his complaints about the general shortage of munitions, the king added a holograph postscript:

When you meet with the enemy fleet, do not fire your guns from afar but wait until you can fire at close range, so that they hit the target. That way you will have more than enough powder and shot. Do this even if the enemy starts shooting early – in fact, let's hope they do so [*ojalá lo hiciesen*] because they will use up their ammunition, and then we can give them the thrashing that they deserve, as I hope to God will happen.

Characteristically, after Philip appended his signature he added a postscript to his postscript: 'Concerning all this, and the rest of what needs to be done in the battle, it would be good if you issued precise instructions and orders to all the senior officers, so that everything will be ready in time.'[5]

## The Enterprise of England: The Practice

Medina Sidonia obliged on 7 May, when he sent the king 'a sketch, poorly drawn in a hurry, that shows the order of battle I have devised'. Although the original 'sketch' has not survived, a heavily corrected document in the duke's archive, entitled 'The manner in which we must fight with the galleons', shows that he planned to deploy his fleet in three sections: a main 'battle' of thirty large ships flanked by two 'horns' or 'wings' of fifteen ships each.[6] Fortunately for historians, Vincenzo Alemanni, the Tuscan ambassador in Madrid, saw the sketch and commissioned two neat copies, which he sent to his master. Both are now in the State Archive of Florence (Figure 67).[7] They show that the duke had adopted the tactical doctrine advocated by the Iberian naval writers Fernando Oliveira of Portugal and Alonso de Chaves of Castile.

Alemanni apparently gained access to Medina Sidonia's original 'design' for the Armada's order of battle. He made two copies and sent them to the grand duke of Tuscany on 28 May 1588.

Bobadilla (#3) would lead the left wing supported by Bertendona (#15), and Recalde (#9) would lead the right wing. Each wing or 'horn' had twenty large ships (each one marked 'o'), followed by a screen of *pataches* (d). These would communicate with a reinforcement of six other large vessels commanded by Marcos de Aramburu (#10) on the left, and six more under Gómez de Medina (#11) on the right. The four galleys (e) and eight more ships under Don Pedro de Valdés (f) formed the rearguard. The 'battle' consisted of the four galleasses (b); the ships commanded by the duke, Oquendo, Flores and Isla (#5, #6, #7, #8); and four more vessels commanded by Leyva (a), followed by the rest of the Armada (c).

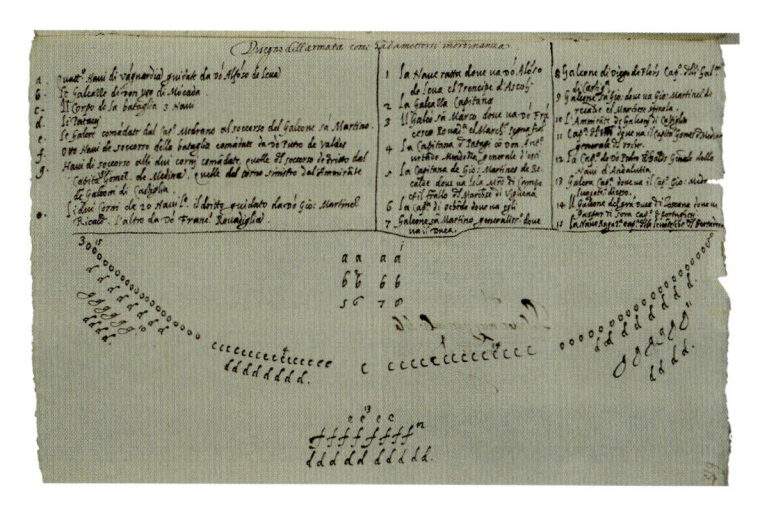

**67.** Medina Sidonia's battle plan for the Armada. The Tuscan ambassador to Spain, Vincenzo Alemanni, apparently gained access to Medina Sidonia's original 'design' for the Armada's order of battle. He made two copies and sent them to the grand duke of Tuscany. Below is a translation and diagrammatic representation.

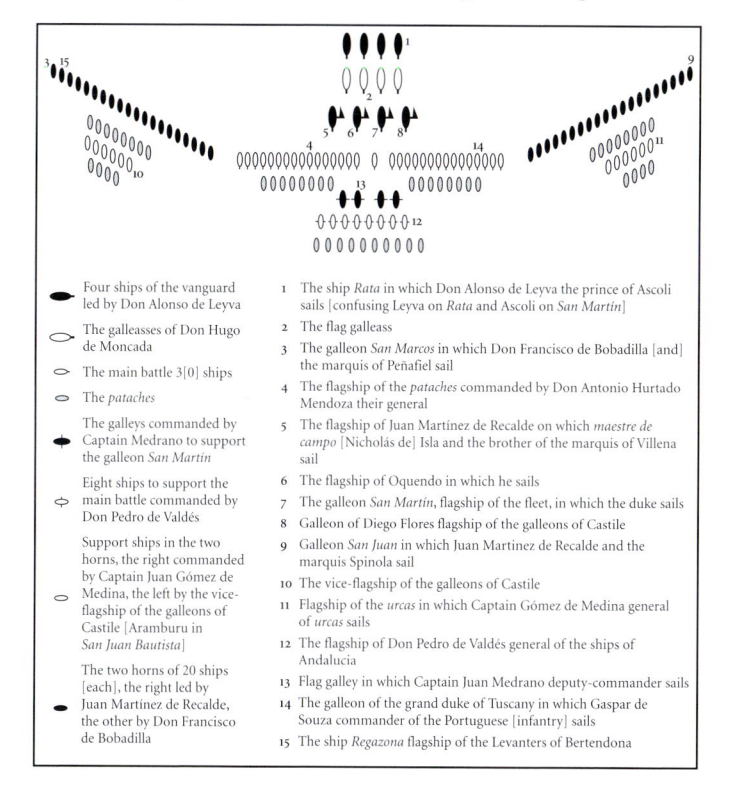

| | | | |
|---|---|---|---|
| ● | Four ships of the vanguard led by Don Alonso de Leyva | 1 | The ship *Rata* in which Don Alonso de Leyva the prince of Ascoli sails [confusing Leyva on *Rata* and Ascoli on *San Martín*] |
| ◁ | The galleasses of Don Hugo de Moncada | 2 | The flag galleass |
| ⊂ | The main battle 3[0] ships | 3 | The galleon *San Marcos* in which Don Francisco de Bobadilla [and] the marquis of Peñafiel sail |
| ○ | The *pataches* | 4 | The flagship of the *pataches* commanded by Don Antonio Hurtado Mendoza their general |
| ◀ | The galleys commanded by Captain Medrano to support the galleon *San Martín* | 5 | The flagship of Juan Martínez de Recalde on which *maestre de campo* [Nicholás de] Isla and the brother of the marquis of Villena sail |
| ⇦ | Eight ships to support the main battle commanded by Don Pedro de Valdés | 6 | The flagship of Oquendo in which he sails |
| | | 7 | The galleon *San Martín*, flagship of the fleet, in which the duke sails |
| | | 8 | Galleon of Diego Flores flagship of the galleons of Castile |
| ○ | Support ships in the two horns, the right commanded by Captain Juan Gómez de Medina, the left by the vice-flagship of the galleons of Castile [Aramburu in *San Juan Bautista*] | 9 | Galleon *San Juan* in which Juan Martínez de Recalde and the marquis Spinola sail |
| | | 10 | The vice-flagship of the galleons of Castile |
| | | 11 | Flagship of the *urcas* in which Captain Gómez de Medina general of *urcas* sails |
| | | 12 | The flagship of Don Pedro de Valdés general of the ships of Andalucia |
| ● | The two horns of 20 ships [each], the right led by Juan Martínez de Recalde, the other by Don Francisco de Bobadilla | 13 | Flag galley in which Captain Juan Medrano deputy-commander sails |
| | | 14 | The galleon of the grand duke of Tuscany in which Gaspar de Souza commander of the Portuguese [infantry] sails |
| | | 15 | The ship *Regazona* flagship of the Levanters of Bertendona |

In a manuscript treatise of *c.* 1540 Chaves advised battle-fleets 'to sail in wings [*en ala*] because all [the ships] can see their enemies and fire their artillery without impeding each other. They must not sail in line [*en hila*], with one behind the other, because that would cause serious harm, since only the ships in the van can fight.' In 1552 Oliveira's *The Art of War at Sea* (the first manual of naval warfare to appear in print) concurred: 'It is never safe at sea to allow opponents on your beam; rather you should always keep them ahead when you are fighting . . . Never expose your broadside to them.' Sailing warships should therefore place only lighter pieces, such as breech-loaders, on their broadside and mount all their big guns at the bow, just like a galley. This meant adopting a crescent formation in battle, again like galley fleets. Medina Sidonia had another reason to deploy his fleet in this way: that is how he organized the transatlantic convoys that left Sanlúcar.[8]

Nevertheless, two squadron commanders raised vehement protests. Bertendona complained to Philip that 'I could not have a worse position in the order of battle' (presumably because he would have to take orders from Bobadilla, who did not command a squadron), and Don Pedro de Valdés dismissed the entire crescent concept 'because the enemy's ships sail so well, they could be ahead of our vanguard at dusk and attack our rearguard the following dawn. Unless we take precautions they could do us great damage with little risk to themselves.' Valdés therefore made a counterproposal: the fleet should advance with the 'weak and slow vessels in the centre, and the fighting ships divided equally into a rearguard and vanguard around them, so that should the enemy attack from behind the whole fleet could turn about so that the vanguard became the rearguard and vice versa'. Don Pedro was undoubtedly right but the duke overruled him. Although he knew that Drake and part of the English fleet were at Plymouth and might wait until the Armada had passed and attack from behind, he assured Philip that:

> I am ready for him, as Your Majesty can see from our battle-plan, because I will be able to fight him with either of our two 'horns', reinforced by two of the galleasses which will accompany the four lead ships; and I will be able to deal with the rest of the enemy fleet, reinforced with the other two galleasses which will accompany my flagship.[9]

## The 'Troubleshooters'

Many interpretations of the Armada's formation have assumed that its various squadrons operated as discrete tactical units under their respective commanders, but this cannot be correct. Apart from the fact that two generals – Flores (Castile) and Recalde (Vizcaya) – did not sail with their squadrons, Medina Sidonia's sketch shows no squadron cohesion except for the four galleys ('e' in the sketch, lower centre) and the four galeasses ('b', upper centre). Apart from those oared vessels, responsibility for defending the fleet lay with the flagship *San Martín* and a contingent of large ships (including those commanded by Leyva and Oquendo) in the 'main battle', and a select group of powerful ships in key locations throughout the fleet.

The duke's sketch named fifteen ships: the flagships of all ten squadrons, plus one more from the squadrons of Castile (*San Juan Bautista*) and Levant (*Rata Encoronada*), and three from the squadron of Portugal (*San Marcos*, *San Juan* and *Florencia*). Each ship was commanded by a senior officer and each carried a strong contingent of veteran infantry. It seems likely that this elite group served as what we might term freelance 'troubleshooters'. While the duke insisted that the rest of his ships must hold their stations come what may, he expected each troubleshooter to act on his own initiative in response to any attack on the formation. He probably also tasked them with protecting each other, since there was little point in the fleet reaching its destination without its principal ships and top commanders. That would explain why Valdés in *Rosario* was sailing to assist Recalde in *San Juan* when he met with disaster.

Perhaps because *Santa Ana* (Vizcaya) and the galleys never reached the Channel, and *Rosario* and *San Salvador* were captured after the first day's fight, Medina Sidonia seems to have designated new troubleshooters to replace them. One was *San Juan* (Castile) commanded by Don Diego Enríquez, son of the viceroy of Mexico who had almost captured Hawkins at San Juan de Ulúa twenty years before (see chapter 4). Although the duke appointed Enríquez general of the Andalusian squadron to replace Valdés, 'having seen him serve with great diligence and skill in the naval encounters', he remained in command of *San Juan*.[10] The other new troubleshooters were presumably chosen from among those vessels mentioned by eyewitnesses as regularly engaging with the enemy: *San Felipe*, *San Mateo* and *San Luis* (Portugal); *Gran Grín* and *María Juan* (Vizcaya); *Nuestra Señora de Begoña* (Castile); *Santa María de la Rosa* (Guipúzcoa); *San Juan de Sicilia* and *Trinidad Valencera* (Levant); and *San Salvador* (*urcas*). Apart from the purpose-built Portuguese warships, these later choices were all big merchantmen that carried large contingents of veteran infantry under experienced officers. They would pay a heavy price for their prominence in the fighting: battle damage prevented all but four of them from returning to Spain.

## Battle Stations

Once he had got the Armada to sea, Medina Sidonia turned his attention to how best to deploy the hundreds of men crowded aboard each of the larger vessels. Philip's Secret Instructions of 1 April 1588 devoted a paragraph to 'the battle formation and the tactics to be adopted in the fight', should one occur. 'I can give you little advice, since those questions must be decided at the time according to circumstances,' the king began unhelpfully, but continued:

> You should take special note that the enemy's aim will be to fight from a distance, since he has the advantage of superior artillery ... while ours must be to attack, and to come to grips with the enemy at close quarters; and to succeed in doing this you will need to exert every effort. That you might be forewarned, you will receive a detailed report of the way in which the enemy arranges his artillery so as to be able to aim his broadsides low in the hull and so sink his opponents' ships.[11]

The 'detailed report' came from Francisco de Guevara, the unfortunate magistrate abducted on the English ship *Primrose* three years before (see chapter 5) and recently returned from captivity. Guevara had used his fluency in English and his powers of observation to good effect. 'The English warships,' he warned the king:

> Carry much excellent artillery. In order to sink the ships of their enemies, they have adapted their gunports for heavy artillery so that once they deploy each piece they can raise the breech and fire low at the side of an enemy ship. The bullet then passes through to the other side and exits so low that it can sink any ship. I understand that they have used this tactic several times.

'Since they are such good gunners,' Guevara continued presciently, 'if it comes to an artillery duel, Your Majesty's Armada will lose.' Therefore, 'it would be better to board the enemy ships first'.[12]

Medina Sidonia evidently bore this advice in mind when on 7 June he signed a document setting out what everyone aboard his flagship should do if they came under fire. Even its title was reactive: 'The order I give and issue *for the defence* of this flagship'.¹³

*San Martín* had a main gun-deck near the waterline, a second gun-deck above it, and above that a top deck open at the waist but covered fore and aft by elevated castle-works. Medina Sidonia and his entourage – the prince of Ascoli, Don Balthasar de Zúñiga and about a dozen noblemen – would stand on the open quarterdeck or poop, which curved upwards to provide a platform from which they could monitor the battle and direct operations. The ship's captain, Marolín de Juan (also the Armada's chief navigator), took responsibility for the day-to-day operation of the flagship under sail. Orders were issued by voice or whistle calls – the latter's high pitch was designed to cut through the noise of battle or foul weather (Figure 68). The duke also appointed four officers 'to direct the gunners and make sure the soldiers fighting on this deck fire properly' (curiously, he could name only two: the other two should be 'artillery officers with plenty of experience'); a fifth to take charge of the lower deck and 'the corridor around my cabin'; and a sixth to 'defend the forecastle, together with the soldiers stationed there, and the noblemen and their servants whom I shall name' (Figure 69). Small groups of marksmen would perch precariously in the fighting-tops (extended platforms on the crosstrees, protected by makeshift defences of coiled rope and mattresses) (Figure 70).

The duke only addressed how to carry out an attack when he described the *plaza de armas*: the open waist between the two castles, and the hub of the flagship's military capability. There, an officer on each side must 'make sure that everyone would fight, whether to defend or attack the enemy, with the valour and vigour that we expect from them'.

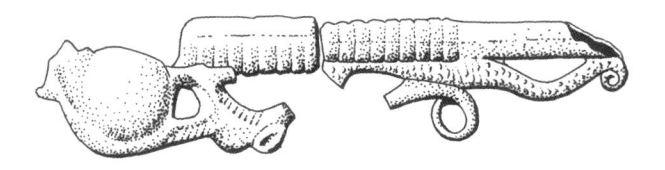

**68.** A silver bosun's whistle from *Girona*.

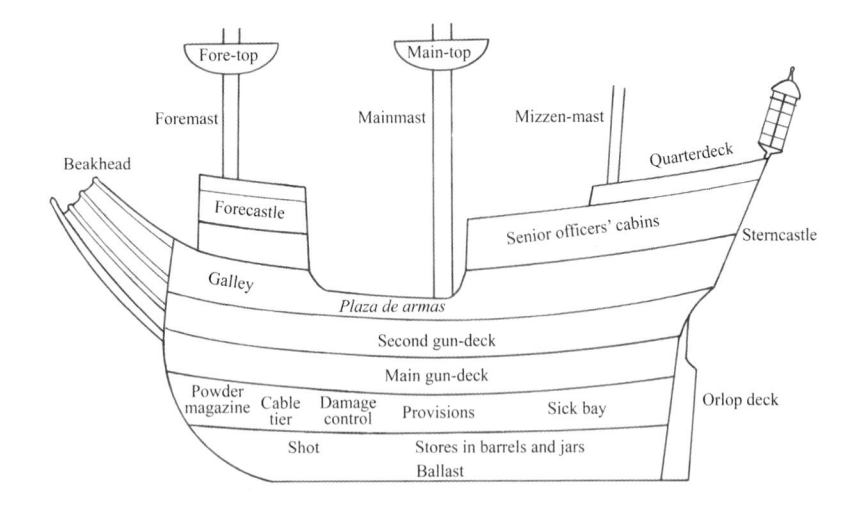

**69.** A diagrammatic representation of *San Martín*. The table below indicates the battle stations assigned to the troops on board *San Martín*, according to Medina Sidonia's battle order of 7 June 1588.

**Table 11.1.** *Locations of arquebusiers, musketeers and retainers on* San Martín

| Location | Arquebusiers | Retainers | Musketeers |
|---|---|---|---|
| The main deck where most of the big guns are | 36 (18 each side) | | |
| The same deck, on both sides | | 20 | |
| The second deck, my retainers and those of the gentlemen | 50 | 30 | |
| In the corridor leading to my cabin | 6 | | 5 |
| Below the quarterdeck, the mizzen mast and the foremast, on the right side | 26 | | 14 |
| On the left side of those two masts (13 to each mast) | 26 | | 14 |
| On the forecastle | 20 | | 12 |
| In the maintop | 4 | | 8 |
| In the foretop | 4 | | 4 |
| On the sterncastle | 30 | | 43 |
| **Total** | **202** | **50** | **100** |

70. A Spanish ship full of armed men, including in the fighting-tops. In close actions these positions high above an enemy's deck could bring down a deadly fire on an enemy, as Britain's Admiral Nelson would discover to his peril at the battle of Trafalgar in 1805 (detail from Figure 66).

## Incendiary Weapons

Medina Sidonia placed great store on incendiary weapons intended to deliver shock and awe at the climax of a boarding action at sea. Inexpertly handled, however, they could be as dangerous to friend as to foe. The duke therefore ordered that they should be 'entrusted only to the most experienced men' because in the hands of 'those who do not understand the management of them, great damage may result' (Figure 71).

The Armada's administrative records described three types of incendiary weapon, and examples have been found on some of the wrecks. The commonest were 'fire-pots' (*alcancías*): pinch-waisted earthenware bottles filled with a mixture of gunpowder, spirits and resin. They could be thrown by hand or swung from a lanyard, and would explode on impact and scatter their fiercely burning, napalm-like contents. They would be particularly effective when lobbed down from the fighting-tops.

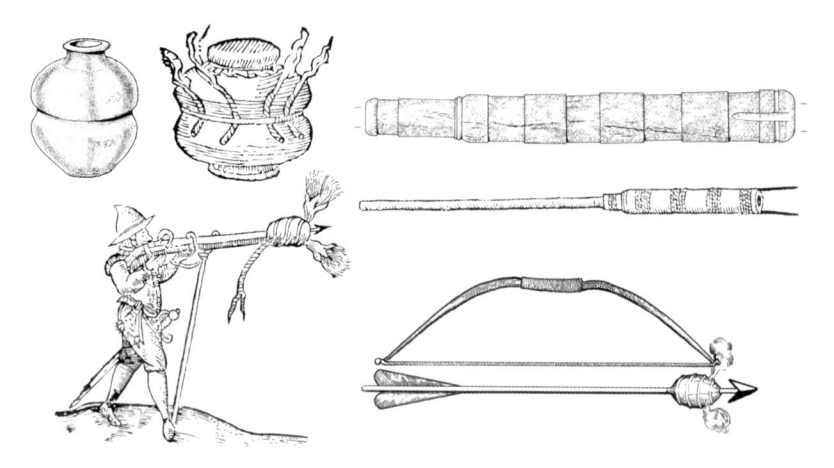

71. Incendiary weapons (not all to same scale).

Top left: *Alcancía* (fire-pot) (*Trinidad Valencera*) with a contemporary example with lighted fuses around its waist from *Tartaglia's Colloquies* (1588). Low-firing temperature ensured a brittle fabric that shattered on impact. Its short neck had a flared rim for securing a wax-impregnated cloth cover, like a traditional jam jar.

Top right: *Bomba* (fire-trunk) (*Trinidad Valencera*) with a contemporary illustration. Cord bindings reinforce it at intervals, and recesses were cut on either side of the mouth to fix a pair of iron points which enabled it to double as a short pike or, if thrown, embed itself in a target.

Bottom: Although the fleet's lading lists do not mention fire-arrows, a nocked wooden arrow shaft was found on *Trinidad Valencera*. Perhaps some Armada ships carried arrows or darts with pitch-impregnated cloth bags filled with a flammable mixture and a wooden fuse-plug, as were found on *Mary Rose*.

The *bomba*, or fire-trunk, consisted of a wooden tube, closed at one end and mounted on a shaft. It contained alternate 'slow' and 'furious' charges. The 'slow' phase spewed out a tongue of fire like a flamethrower which, as it burned out, ignited a 'furious' explosive charge laced with broken glass or metal filings that caused high-velocity scatter wounds. This was repeated over four or five cycles, each lasting several seconds – long enough to cover the vital final moments before boarding a ship, provided it did not explode prematurely (Figure 72). Santa Cruz's 1586 proposal for the Armada also mentioned incendiary darts (*dardos arrojadizos*).[14]

Curiously, the duke's battle orders said nothing about the possible use of fireships, but he devoted much attention to procedures akin to a modern warship's damage-control systems – how to 'put out fires' (*matar fuegos*) – and with good reason. The presence of gunpowder in an environment dominated by timber, tar, cordage and sailcloth, together with the smouldering slow matches with which weapons of all types were detonated, made fire an ever-present and deadly hazard, even without the stress and confusion of battle. A hundred half-butts filled with water were placed throughout the ship, especially on the gun-decks, together with wet blankets, buckets and scoops. Room was even found for two tubs on the main fighting-top and one on the foretop. Giant syringes operated by two men – one to hold and aim it, the other to depress the plunger – served as fire extinguishers. Sails were particularly vulnerable to conflagration and were doused prior to combat. As they became empty during the voyage, water and wine casks filled with seawater would become a fire-fighting reserve (Figure 73). Jars of vinegar were held ready to cool the guns, since overheating not only reduced their performance but weakened them and created a serious risk of fire or explosion. 'Friars, surgeons, pages and everyone

72. A replica fire-trunk (*bomba*) in action. Constructed for filming the BBC series *Armada* in 1988, the replica *bomba* demonstrated the weapon's propensity to 'cook off'; that is, to detonate as a single large explosion rather than a controlled sequence of bursts. This underlines Medina Sidonia's concern that such devices should only be handled by 'the most experienced men'. Happily, 400 years later, anachronistic health and safety protocols prevented serious injury.

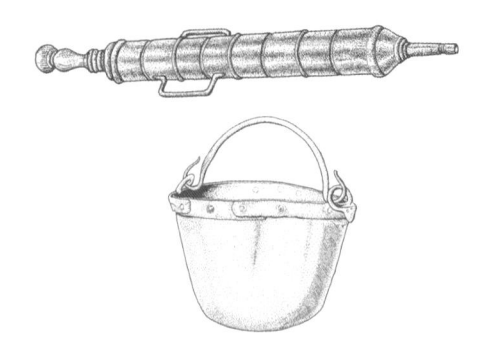

73. A fire-fighting syringe similar to those used on Armada ships (from the Museum of London, probably from the Great Fire of 1666); a copper bucket suitable for fire-fighting, from *Trinidad Valencera*.

else unable to fight' manned a first-aid station in the hold, immediately above the ballast, next to a detachment of carpenters who stood ready with lead sheets, nails, cowhides, planks and tools ready to deal with shot damage. The carpenters could be lowered over the side of the ship to repair holes near or below the waterline by nailing hides over them so that external water pressure would help to make a seal, and diving underwater if necessary.

The campaign journal compiled by Alonso Vanegas, the senior gunnery officer aboard *San Martín*, sheds further light on the dispositions on the flagship. In preparation for action the guns were loaded, manhandled into position, and lashed securely to the ship's side with their muzzles protruding through the ports. Each was under the charge of a specialist gunner, and an officer was allocated to each side of the two main gun-decks to control and direct their fire. A crew of up to six soldiers, withdrawn as required from their action-stations on the ship's decks, aimed each artillery piece under the gunner's direction. The soldiers then returned to their fighting stations. Once the initial artillery salvo had been fired, therefore, the guns could not be reloaded unless the soldiers returned to do so.[15]

What else did the duke expect his men to do if they came under fire? Most of the 300 infantrymen aboard the flagship were equipped with firearms, and 'the sailors and others who lack an arquebus but know how to use one will receive one from the ship's reserve. The rest will receive a pike.' To this end, two dozen short boarding pikes 'with the steel tips greased' were placed at strategic intervals around the ship. Other weapons included the officers' halberds and partizans, and shear-hooks for bringing down enemy rigging. Hooks were also mounted at the ends of yard-arms for the same purpose (see Figure 26).

On 13 June, as the fleet approached Cape Finisterre, each soldier armed with a musket or arquebus received powder, match and 'lead to make balls in preparation for when we fight [*para hazer balas para el tiempo de pelea*]'. The duke also expected these men to 'use some munitions so that they could drill [*para que se excitasen*] and keep the rest in reserve'. The ship's gunners received no such training, however, and although they did fire numerous salvoes of celebration or salutation they usually did so without using roundshot. They aimed and fired their big guns at a target for the first time when the English fleet attacked on 31 July.[16]

## Last-Minute Preparations

As the Armada approached Cape Finisterre, Medina Sidonia informed the king that 'every day when the sea allowed' he had 'summoned the squadron generals and some of the most experienced mariners to the flagship, to share with them my thoughts on how to make this operation succeed so that, having considered the pros and cons, we could take the decisions that seemed best'. Now, he continued, 'I have just ordered each general and each *maestre de campo* to inspect the ships and men for whom they are responsible, and to make sure they are ready to follow the orders I have issued concerning the way they should fight' (suggesting that each ship received battle orders similar to those for *San Martín*). In particular, these senior officers must verify that 'the soldiers have their weapons ready' and that 'when we sight the enemy fleet everyone knows what he has to do and will take up his position in an orderly fashion'. They must also 'notify me of any repairs needed for the artillery' and other weapons. At the end of his letter, Medina Sidonia assured Philip that:

> As soon as we have passed Cape Finisterre I will order all the ships to clear their decks, so that not a cabin, bed, box or trunk remains on them. All will be stowed below, and whatever cannot fit there will be thrown overboard. I will start with this galleon and inspect as many others as I can in person, sending trusted messengers to the rest, to ensure my order is executed throughout the fleet without exception, so that every ship will be as ready for action as if we faced the enemy.[17]

This order remained a dead letter, because of the duke's decision to head to Corunna instead of pressing on to England, but on 18 July he and his Council of War debated once more what tactics to adopt when they encountered the English fleet. By then some senior commanders appear to have developed doubts about the crescent formation. Leyva felt confident that 'such a sumptuous fleet [*tan suntuosa armada*] will produce excellent fruit', and he had 'little fear of our enemies because in my opinion they will want to test their fortune in small packets, and not in a single day'. Nevertheless, he continued, 'they are sure to be watching for any isolated ship which they can capture'.[18] Don Pedro de Valdés exploited such misgivings by advocating his alternative tactical disposition and eventually he prevailed. Medina Sidonia reported that at the council meeting on 18 July 'all of us here who serve Your Majesty, both soldiers and sailors, decided that we need to change the battle-plan', namely 'that there should be a single formation, with a vanguard, main battle and rearguard' – but, he added, 'we are still discussing which ships will go where', and he would notify each captain of his assigned position after he had worked this out. It was too late. The new list was evidently still not finalized when a change in the wind allowed the Armada to leave Corunna, because when the duke sighted the enemy fleet he ordered his ships to deploy in their original crescent formation. He only adopted the alternative proposed by Valdés after the disastrous first few days of combat.[19]

In contrast Medina Sidonia rejected some sensible advice sent by Idiáquez: 'You must place your trust in just two or three (or four) advisers, such as those just appointed by His Majesty' – namely Bobadilla and Flores. The duke must remember that 'although thousands of men are gathered aboard the fleet, Your Excellency is in sole charge, and you alone will be held responsible for the outcome.' So, Idiáquez continued, 'do not go back to consult your council afterwards when you should be executing decisions already taken'. Perhaps the duke ignored such tedious tactical advice because of his conviction that 'Our Lord will surely guide everything so that it serves Him best'.[20]

This was certainly the king's assumption. His last letter to Medina Sidonia before the Armada set sail, signed on 12 July, assured the duke that 'before you join hands with the duke of Parma, my nephew, the enemy fleet will already (with God's help) be destroyed, or else will have withdrawn because it did not dare to fight you'. He concluded: 'Go in the name of God who will surely advance His cause.' The enthusiasm of Tristram Winslade, an English Catholic exile aboard *Nuestra Señora del Rosario*, was probably typical; after his capture in the first day's fight he told his interrogators that 'They thought themselves to be able well enough to encounter the queen's navy, and supposed themselves to be the stronger for that their ships were greater in bulk and well furnished with men.'[21]

## The English Fleet

What, then, of the queen's navy, waiting 500 miles to the north? Its core consisted of sixteen of the queen's ships displacing between 400 and 1,100 tons (Appendix 3). We have found no sources on the proposed disposition, crews and armament of the English fleet comparable with those available for the Armada. However, one written account described their deployment as they left Plymouth (Figure 74). The ships at the heart of the formation were carefully arranged, with each of the queen's galleons matched with a merchantman (larger galleons with smaller merchantmen and vice versa) and a pinnace to communicate with other groups. The older, less manoeuvrable warships sailed at the centre of the formation, with the race-built galleons on the wings. Like Medina Sidonia, Admiral Howard deployed many smaller, lightly armed vessels because even if they could do little in action, at least from a distance a larger number of masts and sails might intimidate the enemy.

And what then? No participant on either side described Howard's initial tactics, perhaps because the confusion of war, exacerbated by the dense smoke from the guns, precluded objective analysis. Later historians have suggested that the first attack launched from windward was in line ahead, with the flagship leading and the rest following astern, but this does not agree with the only source to mention Howard's disposition before battle was joined. According to William Stukeley, sailing at this stage on *Rosario*, 'the enemy fleet appeared to windward, with perhaps 60 ships deployed in wings [*en ala*]', implying that Howard initially retained a 'three abreast' formation with two wings. He did not approach '*en hila*' (the term used to describe a line-ahead attack).[22] Michael Lewis was surely right to draw two conclusions: that on the basis of the campaign charts created by Robert Adams 'a *fleet* line-ahead' was 'neither attained nor attempted'; and that according to the surviving written sources 'the whole fleet never even tried to act as one corporate body. Again and again we glimpse groups of ships led by the Lord Admiral or Drake or Frobisher, operating quite independently from the rest' but 'not, apparently, coordinated by any one mind'.[23] Instead, the main fleet held its position to windward of the Armada, at a safe distance, and from time to time small groups of ships would attack the Spanish trailing horns, firing as they advanced and bringing their other guns to bear as they came about before returning to the main body.

These tactics were no secret. When Philip was preparing to send Pedro Menéndez up the Channel with a large fleet in 1574 (see chapter 4), Antonio Fogaza, a spy in London, warned him that Elizabeth commanded several 'great and powerful ships carrying heavy artillery close to the waterline ... which they fire into the side of the enemy ship, sinking it, and also causing confusion with the smoke'. Fogaza

'A description in what order our fleet shall keep together in fight; and it is to be understood that the first in every front are Her Majesty's ships'

|  | | | |
|---|---|---|---|
| Twenty more 'good ships' in 'wings to deal with stragglers' | ***Revenge*** (vice-admiral)<br>*Minion* of Plymouth<br>***Charles*** | ***Ark Royal*** (admiral)<br>*Galleon Leicester*<br>***Disdain*** | ***Elizabeth Bonaventure***<br>*Bark Talbot*<br>*Bark Young* | Twenty more 'good ships' in 'wings to deal with stragglers' |
| | ***Golden Lion***<br>*Margaret & John*<br>***Advice*** | ***White Bear***<br>*Minion* of Bristol<br>*Larke* | ***Nonpareil***<br>*Thomas* of Plymouth<br>*Elizabeth Drake* | |
| | ***Hope***<br>*Brave* of London<br>*Hind* of Exeter | ***Elizabeth Jonas***<br>*Hopewell* of London<br>*Hart* of Dartmouth | ***Dreadnought***<br>*Golden Noble*<br>*Golden Hind* | |
| | ***Swiftsure***<br>*Bark Burr*<br>*Diamond* | ***Triumph***<br>*Galleon Dudley*<br>*Chance* | ***Foresight***<br>*Mayflower* of London<br>*Passport* | |
| | ***Mary Rose***<br>*Spark* of Plymouth<br>*Delight* | ***Victory*** (rear-admiral)<br>*Tiger* of Plymouth<br>***Moon*** | ***Swallow***<br>*Tiger* of London<br>*Unity* | |

'Now follow five in sequel, although three abreast as before, and of the best merchant ships'

| | | |
|---|---|---|
| *Bark St Leger*<br>*Bartholomew*<br>*Red Lion* of London<br>*Ascension* of London<br>*Minion* of London | ***Aid***<br>*Merchant Royal*<br>*Hercules* of London<br>*Edward Bonaventure*<br>*Toby* of London | *Hope* of Plymouth<br>*Royal Defence*<br>*Golden Ryall*<br>*Centurion* of London<br>*Frances* of London |

74. The English order of battle, July 1588. The arrangement of the English fleet in three squadrons is not surprising: in 1545 both Winter and Howard's father had served in a fleet drawn up in a similar fashion. In his engravings of the campaign (see chapter 12), Augustine Ryther depicted each of the queen's ships (here indicated in bold type) with more and larger sails, leading two or three smaller vessels.

added: 'I myself saw them do this against the French thirty years ago' (no doubt a reference to the battle in the Solent in 1545).[24] John Hawkins did much the same at San Juan de Ulúa in 1568, as did Sir William Winter at Smerwick in 1580 and Edward Fenton in Brazil in 1582 (see chapter 4). All four, as well as some of their officers and men, participated in the Armada campaign.

A watercolour representation of the naval operation at Smerwick, prepared either by or for Sir William Winter, showed the tactic described by Fogaza in action (albeit deployed against a fortress projecting into the sea, rather than a moving ship: Figure 39). The bigger vessels, *Revenge* (then a brand-new ship, commanded by Winter) and *Swiftsure*, stand off in deep water, unanchored but with sails furled, bombarding the fort with their bow-chasers. The smaller vessels (*Aid*, *Tiger*, *Marlyon* and *Achates*) take advantage of their shallow draught to run under full sail towards the enemy, firing as they go, and then coming about to present broadsides and finally their stern guns at close range. All six ships would later employ the same tactic against the Armada.[25]

Winter's watercolour also reveals the simple device that made these quick-firing tactics possible. He ferried ashore some heavy guns to bombard the fort, together with their carriages: tiny but unmistakable, they are all of the efficient four-truck shipboard design. These had been in service at least since 1515, when a survey recorded that the big guns aboard Henry VIII's warships were mounted on four-wheel 'trotills'. Several examples were recovered from the wreck of *Mary Rose*, which sank in 1545; and they are clearly visible in a collection of technical drawings prepared in the 1570s by the queen's master-shipwright, Matthew Baker (Figures 75, 76).

By 1588 the guns on most English ships – and certainly on all the race-built galleons – were mounted on such compact carriages with a flat bed, stepped cheeks, and four small solid wheels or trucks. When run-out, the guns protruded well beyond the gunports while the inboard ends of the carriages barely extended beyond the breeches. This gave the crews space to reload, adjust and fire the guns.

75. Detail from Figure 39, showing English guns on truck carriages brought ashore to the 'mariners' trench' to bombard the Castello del Oro at Smerwick in November 1580.

76. Detail of a truck carriage on an English galleon, from *Fragments of Ancient Shipwrightry*, a collection of illustrations by Matthew Baker, one of the queen's master-shipwrights, between 1570 and 1590. Note the hinged gunports on the lower deck, and the way all guns are aligned to fire forwards.

In his textbook *The Art of Shooting in Great Ordnance* the master-gunner and mathematician William Bourne stressed the vital importance of using small trucks for big guns at sea, both because if the wheels 'be too high, then it will keep the carriage that it will not go close unto the ship's side', and because the guns on the lower gun-deck might need to be hauled inboard rapidly if rough seas made it necessary to close the gunports. Sir Henry Mainwaring's *Seaman's Dictionary*, composed in the early seventeenth century, made a telling comparison. Having explained that '*Trucks* are those little wooden wheels (being made without any spokes) that the carriage of the ordnance do run on' aboard ships, and that '*Tackles*' include 'the gunner's tackles [ropes and pulley blocks], with which they haul in and out the ordnance', he bluntly stated that 'The fashion of those carriages we use at sea are much better than those of the land, yet the Venetians and Spaniards (and diverse others) use the others in their shipping.'[26]

His view was echoed by Sir William Monson (who, in his youth, had taken part in the Armada battles), when he wrote that the Spaniards used two-wheeled carriages, 'which makes them dangerous and unserviceable, for their pieces so lying cannot be traversed from side to side but must be shot off directly forwards as they lie'. Carriages such as these can be seen in the 'Greenwich cartoon' (Figure 35). Although the artist was presumably English, the accuracy evident in this contemporary depiction supports its general veracity.

Archival and archaeological evidence confirms Mainwaring's judgement: many of the Armada's guns were indeed mounted on carriages with two large wheels and long trails. Thus in April 1588 Don Pedro de Valdés noted that 'The *urca* named

*Santa Ana* has a culverin of 31 quintals and 93 pounds of Naples which, because it is very long and is mounted on a land carriage [*cureña para de campaña*], cannot be used on the said hulk because there is not sufficient space for it.' Valdés therefore ordered the gun to be brought aboard his larger ship, *Nuestra Señora del Rosario*, where he apparently felt it might come in useful.

Some Armada documents mention 'sea carriages' (*encabalgamientos de mar*). The account of munitions salvaged from the flag galleass *San Lorenzo* noted twenty-nine *encabalgamientos de mar* specifically for the twenty-nine big guns aboard; and the same was presumably true for the other galleasses. The wreck of *Trinidad Valencera* revealed a long two-wheeled carriage of the type described by Mainwaring: with its gun mounted it would have constituted an assembly 19 feet long on a deck barely 36 feet wide. Similar carriages have been found among the remains of *Lavia*, off Streedagh Strand.[27] Solid tripartite wheels have been noted on both the *Lavia* and *Valencera* sites. Figure 77 shows the almost complete *Valencera* carriage. It lacks only

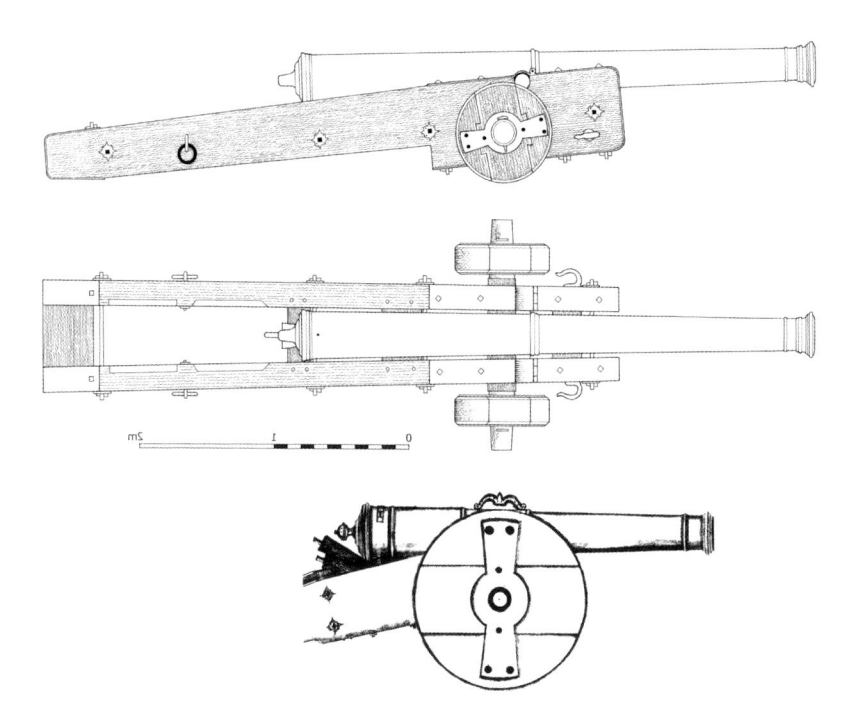

**77.** Top: Venetian sea-carriage from *Trinidad Valencera*, reconstructed from its substantial remains with a hypothetical gun fitted to its proportions (a calibre of about 14 lb). Bottom: drawing of a Spanish *encabalgamiento de mar*, with large tripartite wheels, 1594.

wheels, but spoked and solid examples of appropriate dimensions have been found elsewhere on the site. The solid version has been chosen for the reconstruction, while a hypothetical gun has been scaled to fit the carriage. It would have been a 13-pounder *media culebrina* with a bore of around 4¾ inches. None of the archaeologically investigated sea-carriages is Spanish, but the Simancas drawings suggest that such two-wheeled carriages with trails were the norm on Spanish ships at this time.

In 1587 a list of munitions supplied by Medina Sidonia to eleven ships that would join the squadron of Andalucia included some 'new gun carriages made of pine with wheels of pine', and specified that 'the new wheels of pine for the carriages must be three and a half palms high', namely 29 inches. Diego García de Palacio's textbook *Naval Instructions*, published in Mexico City that same year, described how to build and arm Indies guardships similar to the ones which would form the squadron of Castile, and included a statement that shipborne gun carriages must have 'solid wheels three palms' – about two feet – 'in diameter'. Neither Medina Sidonia nor García de Palacio seems to have realized that guns mounted on *encabalgamientos de mar* with solid wheels two feet and more in diameter could not come close enough to the ship's side to allow them to be elevated or traversed. Moreover, because pine is prone to break or shatter, wheels made of that wood might not survive the stress of combat. Perhaps some of the Armada's guns were mounted on compact four-truck carriages like the English ones, because a Portuguese drawing of about 1590 shows one, but if so they were not numerous (Figure 78).[28]

**78.** A four-wheeled truck carriage drawn by an unknown Portuguese engineer between 1582 and 1596. This image, one of several types of compact gun carriage in an anonymous volume of watercolours, suggests that Portuguese galleons in 1588 may have carried at least some guns mounted on truck carriages.

## The Naval Balance

England's naval guns were not only mounted on compact truck carriages: they were also shorter. This made them easier to work on shipboard because shorter barrels left more space for the crews to haul the guns back with tackles for reloading.

Of course, it was still not easy. William Bourne filled several pages of his textbook with advice on how to achieve the coordination required between gunner and steersman, so that shots could be fired on the downward swing of a roll to hit an enemy's hull below the waterline. However, for most of the 1588 campaign Howard managed to stay to windward of the Armada (having the 'weather gage') thanks to the superior speed and handling qualities of at least the race-built galleons. This meant that the Spanish ships often heeled away from their adversaries, presenting the normally submerged parts of their hulls (what contemporaries called the area 'between the wind and the water') at which the English could fire without the risk of being grappled and boarded.

The English enjoyed further advantages over the Spaniards. On average their ships carried one seaman for every two tons of shipping, whereas each Armada sailor had to work seven tons of shipping. To some extent the Spaniards made good this deficiency by employing soldiers to carry out general duties on the ships and provide gun crews in action – but they remained for the most part regular infantrymen, who seldom got on well with their nautical counterparts. Few had served at sea before and virtually none, except perhaps those attached to the squadrons of Portugal and Castile, had previously fought aboard the ships on which they now sailed. The same was true of their officers. Nicolás de Isla was the only *maestre de campo* with experience of transatlantic navigation, having commanded the infantry companies aboard the Indies guardships; but the king placed him in command of *Santa Ana* (Vizcaya). Leyva, Bertendona, Recalde and Don Pedro de Valdés as well as Medina Sidonia were all new to the ships they commanded.

Moreover, the Armada was 'Spanish' in name only: the mariners aboard came from a wide range of ports in the Baltic, Atlantic and Mediterranean, speaking many languages. All the officers and men aboard the English fleet, by contrast, were familiar with the armament of their particular vessels and with how to handle them on shipboard. They all spoke one language and used a common standard of weights and measures; they were all mariners (although those detailed to man the guns were still officially described as 'soldiers', they were specialist naval ratings); and they had learned to work as a team under a commander who was first and foremost a seaman. In addition, most were familiar with the theatre of operations. On 16 August, when the queen ordered Lord Seymour and Sir William Winter to leave their station in the Narrow Seas and 'repair to the north parts, for the better strengthening of the Lord Admiral', they summoned 'the wisest, most skilful masters and pilots of our company' to a 'conference', which 'conclude[d] that it is better for us to keep our strength here, than otherwise to put it to hazard'.[29]

Finally, many English masters and pilots possessed reasonably accurate charts of the seas on which they sailed. In 1585 Howard himself had shown to the Privy Council a copy of Wagenaer's *Mariner's Mirror*, just published in Dutch. Deeming it 'worthy to be translated and printed into a language familiar to all nations', their lordships encouraged Wagenaer to produce a two-volume Latin edition. In 1587 the clerk of the Privy Council began to translate the Dutch original into English, while a team of engravers produced superior versions of the original charts with all the information in English, the meridian based on London (not Enkhuizen), some corrections and a few additions (see Figure 94).[30]

The English edition of *The Mariner's Mirror* even showed some of the 'beacons', a network of mutually visible fire signals that could rapidly transmit news of an invasion around most of the country, and also serve as mustering-points when invasion threatened. In 1585 the Privy Council ordered the lord lieutenant of each shire to inspect both beacons and militia, and at least in Kent this prompted a local antiquarian, William Lambarde, to prepare multiple copies of a map that showed not only the location of the fifty beacons in the shire but also the sight lines between them (Figure 79). As the Armada sailed along the coast of Cornwall on 30 July 1588, William Stukeley noticed that 'they lit many bonfires ashore' – but even he did not realize that those bonfires transmitted to the queen and her Privy Council the vital intelligence that the Armada had finally arrived. Two days later, 'having very lately discovered the arrival of the Spanish fleet and army near the coast of this realm', at Elizabeth's palace of Richmond the Privy Council initiated a stream of defensive measures: troops to defend the queen must assemble in Essex; Catholics must be arrested and imprisoned; the clergy must arrange public prayers for victory.[31]

Nevertheless, these and other prudent defensive measures would have been too late if the Armada had attempted to enter Plymouth Sound or land on the Isle of Wight, because dangerous delays hampered their implementation. Thus on 5 August, when the Privy Council informed its officials that 'the Spanish navy is passed by the Isle of Wight and [is] very shortly likely to be upon the coast of Sussex', the Armada was in fact approaching Boulogne. Luckily for England communications by sea sometimes achieved better results. Late in the evening of 31 July, off Start Point in Devon, Drake sent Seymour a letter marked 'haste post haste' and entrusted it to a pinnace. She arrived at Dover two days later at 11 p.m.: a transit of forty-eight hours, notably faster than the equally important messages

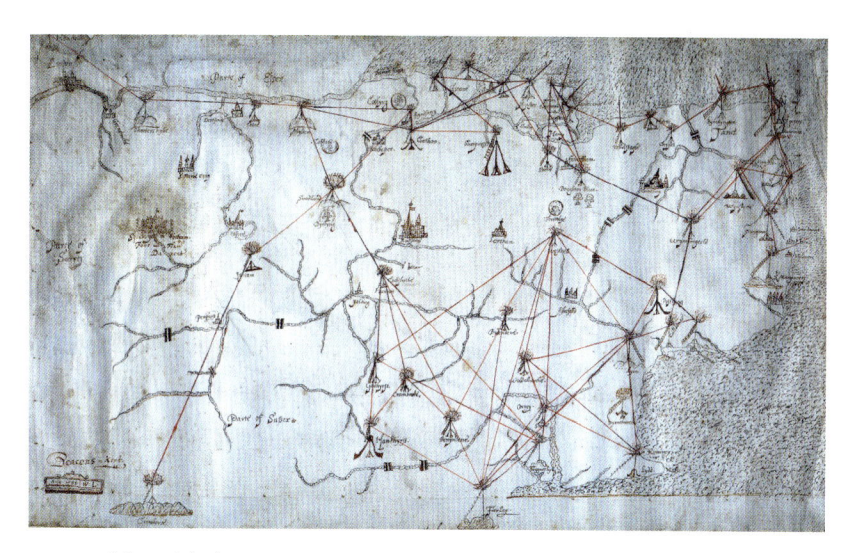

**79.** Map of the beacon system in Kent in 1585, by William Lambarde. One of many copies commissioned by the Lord Lieutenant, all at a scale of 1:230,000. The red lines show how news of a Spanish landing would travel from the five beacons on the Isle of Thanet, linked to the mainland by a single bridge, to those on Shooter's Hill and Highgate, both visible from London.

sent by Medina Sidonia to Parma (see chapter 13), and it contained vital information on the Armada's strength and fighting potential.[32]

No less important was England's ability to supply its fleet's needs. Ships sailed out of almost every port to join Howard as he passed by; and on 7 August Seymour and Howard 'joined hands' off Calais, increasing their total strength to 130 vessels. Admittedly, the following day Howard sacrificed eight small vessels as fireships, but this was far less debilitating than Medina Sidonia's loss of three major warships and all four galleys. The English fleet also received munitions. Most came from the Ordnance Office in the Tower of London: on 2 August four lasts (about 4½ tons) of gunpowder to Seymour, and two lasts and some roundshot to Howard; on 3 August five lasts of powder to Portsmouth; on 4 August ten lasts to the Downs, half by land and half by sea 'with all expedition'; and on 5 August 'seven lasts of powder and some quantity of bullets'. The Privy Council also empowered the surveyor-general of victuals to requisition food and beer for the fleet, which he sent to Dover. More provisions came from individual towns. For example, the small port of Topsham in Devon supplied £240 of victuals and munitions to Howard as he passed by; and on 12 August the magistrates of Newcastle sent him five lasts of powder and 'a good quantity of shot . . . from the demi-cannon downward'. The Armada, by contrast, received no replacements for the tons of powder and thousands of artillery rounds fired in the Channel battles, and only a little food and drink from the governor of Calais.[33]

Nevertheless, as the Armada deployed in battle-order at dawn on 31 July, few Englishmen underestimated the threat it posed to the survival of Tudor England. In his After-Action Report prepared for Admiral Howard concerning the 'marvellous plot to have taken us' hatched by Philip II and Parma, John Mountgomerie paid tribute to:

> [The] huge and mighty navy of ships which they brought, which so far surmounted our expectation that we never supposed that they could ever have found, gathered and joined so great a force of puissant ships together, and so well appointed with their cannon, culverin, and other great pieces of brass ordnance, with so many men, so many muskets, and all other furniture, according both for sea and land; that it appeared they spared not for any cost to bring their wicked purpose to pass. For never was there any such navy that came against England before this time.

Only the test of battle would determine if it would prevail.[34]

## 12

# Stalemate in the Channel

---

### First Blood

**B**Y DAWN ON 30 JULY the Armada was level with Falmouth: 20 miles east of the Lizard but still 60 miles west of Plymouth. Knowing that he was at last beyond the reach of the king's meddling pen, Medina Sidonia decided 'to let Your Majesty know that I plan to travel very slowly with this Armada, in battle formation'. Furthermore, since he now realized that anchoring off Margate Cape (as Philip had instructed) made no sense, the duke announced his intention 'to lead this fleet to the Flemish coast' instead. He was well aware that 'the Flemish coast has no port or shelter for these ships, so that the first storm that they encounter will drive them onto the sandbanks, where they will be lost', and so 'to avoid that obvious risk' – might that phrase contain a hint of criticism? – 'I have decided to travel no further than the Isle of Wight until I learn what Parma is doing'. He closed his letter by lamenting that during the whole voyage he had encountered no other ship able to provide information about either Parma or the English fleet.[1]

The Armada now resumed its advance and 'we steered towards Plymouth until about five in the afternoon'; but at that point once again the flagship *San Martín* 'struck sail, whereupon they all struck sail all night'. Recalde was furious. The previous day, in a letter to his brother-in-law Martín de Idiáquez, he had stressed the need 'to ensure that the enemy comes out to fight, and to provoke him to do so. Although I am no friend of making threats [*bravatas*], we should do so as we pass before the port of Plymouth, even if we waste a day doing so.' He now wrote in his journal: 'I opposed taking in sail until [we reached] the very mouth of Plymouth harbour', but the duke ignored him. Instead, a fast *patache* commanded by Lieutenant

Juan Gil, who 'had lived in England for some years, knew the country, and could speak its language', set out to gather intelligence. At midnight Gil returned with four English fishermen 'who each independently affirmed' that the enemy fleet was at Plymouth and 'numbered sixty vessels, twenty large. They are very long, with few upperworks, and they carry a lot of artillery capable of firing at long range'.[2]

Medina Sidonia again summoned his Council of War to the flagship, shared the new intelligence with them, and asked their opinion on what to do next. Leyva urged an immediate attack on Plymouth because once the two fleets became entangled at the harbour mouth, the Spaniards could board their adversaries and the shore batteries would not be able to fire for fear of hitting their own ships. Recalde supported his colleague, and the council 'resolved we should make for the mouth of the haven and set upon the enemy, if it might be done with any advantage; but otherwise keep our course to Dunkirk without losing any time.' The duke sent senior officers around the fleet in feluccas to inform every captain that they would assume battle-order at dawn the following day. He also decreed that all sails must remain furled until then.[3]

The duke had made a catastrophic mistake. The information brought by the four English fishermen was true when they left port, but seriously out of date by the time dawn broke on 31 July. Under cover of darkness Admiral Howard had undertaken a bold manoeuvre to exploit Medina Sidonia's unexpected but welcome decision to mark time. First, as soon as the tide turned, Howard warped all his ships out of harbour into Plymouth Sound (Figure 80). Then, after the moon rose around 2 a.m. he sent a small squadron under Drake to tack westward between the Spanish fleet and the coast. He also 'left five ships in sight' of the Spaniards so they would 'think that the rest of their fleet was also there', and thus distract them while he led the rest of his vessels across the front of the Armada and around its seaward flank, thus gaining the weather gage. It was a brilliant feat of seamanship that gave the English fleet a tactical edge it never lost.[4]

At dawn Medina Sidonia responded by running up his battle-flag, the prearranged signal for the Armada to take up its fighting formation, with a score of capital ships in each trailing 'horn' and the rest in the centre. The fleet spanned at least two miles. It was an awe-inspiring sight, and only trained and disciplined officers and seamen could have executed such a large and complex manoeuvre involving over 130 ships, especially ones with such varied sailing qualities. Whatever its weaknesses might be – and at this stage Howard and his officers had no means of gauging them – the Armada would clearly not be a soft touch.

Since there had been no formal declaration of war between England and Spain, Howard deemed it proper to follow tradition before battle commenced by issuing a formal 'defiance', or challenge. William Stukeley described how 'a small ship of about 80 tons' detached itself from the English fleet 'and, travelling at amazing speed, fired six or seven guns from one side, and the same again from the other, and four guns from her bow and stern. Having done this, she returned to the enemy fleet' as swiftly as she had come. The ship bore an appropriate name: *Disdain*.[5]

Formalities complete, at 9 a.m. on Sunday 31 July Howard launched his attack. He first engaged the wing commanded by Leyva, nearest the coast, and afterwards

80. The English fleet leaves Plymouth Sound on the night of 30/31 July. Drake leads one squadron in a series of long tacks westwards between the Armada and the coast, while Howard leads the rest of the fleet in front of the Armada. The two commanders then reunite behind their adversaries, having gained the weather gage, and Howard sends *Disdain* to issue a formal challenge. Hand-coloured engraving by Augustine Ryther of a chart by Robert Adams, made in 1590.

the one commanded by Recalde. Some Armada vessels broke station in the face of this assault, and sought shelter among the main body, but Recalde in *San Juan de Portugal* stood firm and for some time attracted most of the English fire. Recalde himself recorded that the English 'fired more than 300 rounds' at his ship, killing fifteen men and damaging 'with their shot the most important parts of the rigging, namely the mainmast stay and the foremast, with a shot that went right through it' before help arrived from the other troubleshooters. Around 1 p.m. Howard withdrew to a safe distance, some four miles astern.[6]

English reactions to this first engagement varied. Howard felt that 'we did some good, and I dare say [did] them some harm'; but, he admitted, 'we durst not adventure to put in amongst them, their fleet being so strong'. Drake commented that 'we had them in chase, and so coming up unto them there passed some cannon shot between some of our fleet and some of them', while Hawkins described the same incident as 'some small fight'.[7] Clearly the disciplined formation of the Armada and its evident strength produced the effect for which it had been designed: the English dared not come close, even though their guns could only inflict serious damage at close range. According to Henry White, captain of a 200-ton auxiliary, *Bark Talbot* (later to be one of the fireships): 'The majesty of the enemy's fleet, the good order they held, and the private consideration of our own wants did cause, in mine opinion, our first onset to be more coldly done than became the value of our nation and the credit of the English navy.'[8]

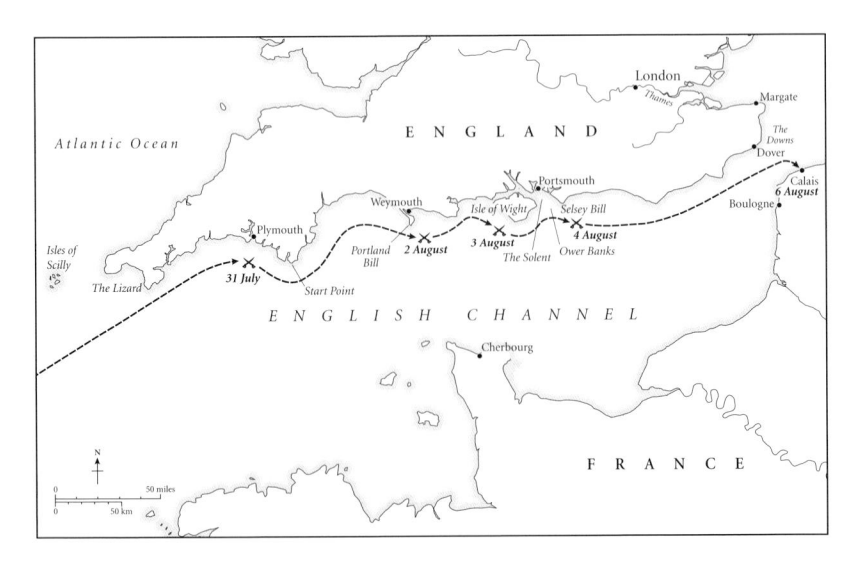

81. The Armada's advance to Calais.

Some Spaniards also felt dissatisfied with their initial behaviour under fire. Alonso Vanegas, the senior gunnery officer aboard *San Martín*, estimated that the Armada ships had fired 750 rounds on 31 July whereas the English had fired at least 2,000. The damage inflicted on *San Juan* forced Recalde to abandon his station while his crew carried out emergency repairs. Moreover, in his report to the flagship, Recalde predicted that since the 'Levant ships do not carry as much heavy artillery as the enemy, the latter will get closer and cause them damage'. If even the lion-hearted Leyva, in command of *Rata Encoronada*, 'gets the same bombardment that I received he will not be able to resist, because he carries no heavy artillery to keep them at bay'.

Recalde attributed all these problems to the decision not to attack Plymouth: 'I do not know why we failed to execute what we decided about going to the entrance to Plymouth harbour, and thus allowed the [English] to gain the weather gage from us – because otherwise they could not have managed it. There are some very experienced people out there and we were like novices and made the wrong call.' He concluded bitterly: 'What's done is done, and there is no reason to keep on discussing it. But it is very necessary to make sure in future that our enemies do not consume us little by little, and without any risk to themselves. We should rather put all our eggs in one basket, and the sooner the better for this fleet.'[9]

As Recalde vented his frustrations and struggled to repair his ship, two major disasters struck the Armada. First, around 3 p.m., a tremendous explosion rent the Guipúzcoan vice-flagship *San Salvador*, one of the ships chosen to carry some 50,000 gold crowns from the royal treasury (Figure 82). Mystery surrounds the cause of the blast. One explanation blamed sabotage by a German gunner, who was allegedly being cuckolded by a Spanish officer (what the lady was doing aboard in the first place remains unclear). Another more plausible version had 'the captain falling into a rage with the gunner and threatening to kill him if he shot no better'. In a fit of professional pique, the story continued, 'the gunner cast fire into the powder barrels and threw himself overboard'. Perhaps, however, it was simply an accident: according to the captain of a *patache* sent to rescue the ship, 'so much powder was on deck to serve the artillery that firing all the guns at the same time' generated the fatal spark. With so much gunpowder about, and so many lighted matches and fuses on the decks, it is remarkable that such catastrophes did not occur more often.[10]

Whatever the cause, *San Salvador* sustained extensive damage. The blast blew out the aftercastle and the two decks beneath and disabled her steering-gear. Half the 400 men on board were either killed or badly burned by the explosion or drowned as they tried to escape. Stukeley reported that since the stricken ship

**82.** *San Salvador* abandoned and on fire, 31 July. The Armada continues up the Channel in its half-moon formation, with two galleasses protecting each 'horn'. The English fleet follows to windward.

'was drifting towards the enemy fleet, the duke ordered a gun to be fired and came about to offer help and throw her a cable. He then went to the prow, so he could supervise this himself.' Thanks to Medina Sidonia's vigilance some of the fires aboard *San Salvador* were extinguished before they could reach the main magazine, which contained more than seven tons of gunpowder. The duke also oversaw the evacuation of some of the wounded, dreadfully burned, to the hospital ship *San Pedro*; and his *pataches* towed the damaged vessel into the middle of the fleet so she could be repaired.[11]

The other casualty on 31 July was even more significant. Don Pedro de Valdés in the flagship of the Andalusian squadron, *Nuestra Señora del Rosario*, one of the heavily armed 'troubleshooters' charged with the formation's defence and (like *San Salvador*) carrying more than 50,000 gold crowns from the royal treasury, decided to sail to Recalde's rescue – but she collided with a Vizcayan ship on the way.

*Rosario*'s bowsprit broke off, ripping the sail on the foremast. Seeing the danger, Don Pedro turned his vessel about, put her into the middle of the fleet, shortened sail so he could carry out repairs, and informed the duke that he would stay to windward while the work took place. At this point the sea began to get rough, and the foremast itself broke and fell onto the mainmast. *Rosario* was now without sails, except the mizzens, which did not suffice to steer her. Don Pedro fired more than eight guns as signals to request help, and when none came he sent Stukeley in a small boat to report his situation to the duke in person (Figure 83).

Stukeley persuaded Medina Sidonia to order 'a galleass that was close to Don Pedro to help him, and the duke himself came close to the galleass, shouting orders, but the galleass did not go to the rescue'. The captain of the *patache* which managed to come alongside *Rosario* speculated that the other ships hesitated 'because of fear, given the proximity of the enemy'. The captain offered to save Valdés and the treasure, but Don Pedro 'refused, saying that he would not leave unless all his men could leave too, and that he preferred to die in the company of his soldiers'. The *patache* returned and 'the entire Armada sailed past Don Pedro's ship, leaving her behind in clear sight of the enemy'.[12]

Friar Bernardo de Góngora, who escaped with Stukeley from *Rosario* to the flagship, knew who to blame for this heartless decision: 'The duke was willing to help and assist him, but Diego Flores de Valdés forbade him to do so, since it would put the entire fleet in jeopardy.' In view of this, the friar observed disapprovingly, 'the duke continued on his

**83.** *Nuestra Señora del Rosario* disabled, abandoned and surrounded by debris, 1 August 1588. *Revenge* and two smaller English vessels tentatively approach, leaving the rest of the English fleet in disarray. The Lord Admiral and three other vessels, without Drake's stern lantern, have come perilously close to the Armada's rear.

way and left the good Don Pedro and his company ... in the power of the enemy, who were never more than a league behind us'. The conclusion was unmistakable: 'Immediately, the word went round the fleet that no ship should take any risks, because if a flagship had not received any relief, who would rescue the rest from any danger in which they might place themselves?' Those later appointed by Philip to examine and explain the Armada's failure would conclude that 'the loss of Don Pedro's ship was the origin and cause of all later disasters'.[13]

Don Pedro was furious, believing that his commander had dishonourably abandoned him in the face of the enemy. Recalde thought the same and pleaded with the duke to wait while both *Rosario* and his own *San Juan* could complete their necessary repairs. Medina Sidonia agonized – 'If I could have remedied the situation with my blood,' he assured Recalde, 'I would have gladly done so' – but he accepted the advice of Diego Flores (who detested his cousin Pedro) that his paramount duty was to maintain the fleet's progress towards Flanders as swiftly as possible (Figure 84).[14]

The first English vessel to probe the abandoned Andalusian flagship's apparently formidable defences was the 200-ton *Margaret and John*, a merchant ship from the squadron provided by the City of London, which at about 9 p.m. came up and

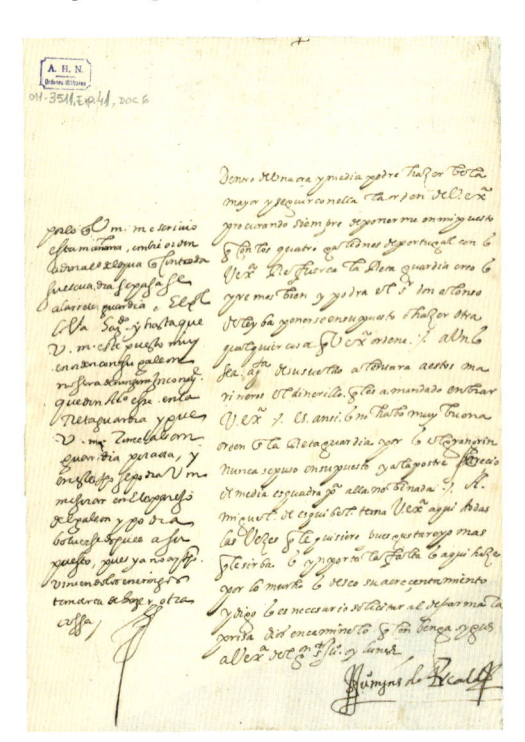

**84.** A *billete* sent by Juan Martínez de Recalde on Monday 1 August 1588 to the duke of Medina Sidonia, reporting on his efforts to repair the damage to his ship inflicted by English gunfire the previous day. The duke's secretary wrote a short reply in the left-hand margin, initialled by Medina Sidonia, which ended 'our enemies are closing in' (*viniendo los enemigos tan cerca*).

discharged her muskets into *Rosario*'s towering bulk. Don Pedro responded with two cannon shots, and after further desultory skirmishing *Margaret and John*, which was clearly incapable of taking *Rosario* by force, left to rejoin the fleet.

At dawn the following morning Don Pedro found himself in the presence of a far more formidable foe: the sleek and gaudily painted galleon *Revenge*, carrying the flag of Sir Francis Drake. How precisely the vice-admiral of the queen's navy came to be there, all alone and far from his allotted station, has been a subject of dispute ever since. The night before, Drake received orders to set watch for the fleet by displaying a lantern on his stern for everyone else to follow, so that the English ships could remain in contact with the Armada's ponderous advance, albeit at a safe distance. According to an irate Martin Frobisher, however, 'Sir Francis was appointed to bear a light all that night, which light we looked for, but there was no light to be seen.' Frobisher offered a simple explanation: after Drake observed that *Rosario* 'had spent her masts, then like a coward he kept by her all night because he would have the spoil. He thinks to cozen us of our shares of 15,000 ducats, but we will have our shares, or I will make him spend the best blood in his belly.' Sir Francis scarcely bothered to argue (perhaps to avoid drawing to Frobisher's attention the fact that *Rosario* had carried more than 50,000 ducats, not 15,000). Instead, he claimed half-heartedly that he had glimpsed strange sails in the darkness and, apparently forgetting about the lantern, had gone to investigate, 'not knowing what they were'. When dawn broke he found, to his professed surprise, that 'we were within two or three cables of *Rosario*'. 'Ay marry,' retorted Frobisher, 'you were within two or three cables length, [because] you were no further off all night.'[15]

Whatever the truth of the matter, the morning of 1 August found Sir Francis and Don Pedro at the start of what would become an extraordinary relationship. At first the Spaniard refused to surrender; then he refused to discuss surrender with anyone except Sir Francis in person; but when at last Valdés came aboard *Revenge* under a flag of truce, and Drake pointed out to him the hopelessness of his position, his defiance crumbled. He asked to be left alone for a few moments to make up his mind and then he emerged, his face all flushed, to announce his surrender.[16]

Pandemonium broke out on *Rosario*. Although Stukeley and three other English Catholics aboard had managed to escape, Tristram Winslade and a few others remained, fully aware that they could expect no mercy from their countrymen. Many Spaniards may have feared a similar fate; certainly, most seem to have forgotten that 'this ship carried 52,000 ducats belonging to the king and twelve trunks of the duke's fine clothes'. Much of this loot now disappeared. Some may have vanished during its transfer to *Revenge* in thin canvas bags – 'there is great likelihood,' a contemporary opined, 'that some of the treasure was purloined away' – but it seems unlikely that Drake would have been so naïve or unobservant as to let any such irregularity take place, at least on the part of others. Don Francisco de Zárate, whose ship Sir Francis had plundered in 1579 off Acapulco, had noted with grudging admiration that 'when our ship was sacked, no man dared take anything without his orders. He shows them great favour, but punishes the least fault.'[17]

In the end scarcely half of *Rosario*'s riches reached the queen's treasury, probably because Valdés and Drake struck a deal. At his interrogation by the English Privy Council, Valdés stated that his ship carried 'near 20,000 ducats, as also vessels of silver worth another thousand'; a month later Drake certified to Howard that he had received from *Rosario* 25,300 ducats. Both men were lying, and both must have known it.[18]

All this lay in the future. Following the capture of *Rosario* on 1 August no one was available to argue with Drake because the previous night, without his lantern for guidance, the English fleet had lagged behind. According to Howard, when dawn broke even the nearest of his ships 'might scarce be seen . . . and very many out of sight, which with a good sail recovered not his Lordship the next day before it was very late in the evening'. The chart by Augustine Ryther shows Howard and three supporters perilously close to the Armada's rear, while the remainder of his fleet lags far behind. Drake's dereliction of duty not only placed the flagship in grave danger but also gave the Spaniards a full twenty-four hours' respite: as Stukeley noted in his journal, 'Today our fleet did not exchange fire with the enemy.' Medina Sidonia had hoped to use the respite to patch up *San Salvador*, as Recalde managed to do with *San Juan*, but in the late morning her captain reported that the ship was taking on too much water and could not be saved. The duke therefore sent two *pataches* to bring off the wounded, the artillery and the treasure, and then scuttle the ship, but 'they could not get to the treasure because it was in the ballast, with the collapsed decks on top of it'. They also failed to recover the artillery or to sink the ship 'because they could not find a drill, hammer or axe or any other tool'. The duke therefore sent a felucca to rescue the wounded, 'but before she had covered a third of the distance, she had to turn back because enemy ships approached'. Once again, according to Stukeley, 'the duke followed the advice of Diego Flores de Valdés because he was a person of such experience; and Flores said that remaining would place the whole Armada at risk, given its state at that time.'[19]

About fifty of the most seriously wounded Spaniards were still on board when Hawkins and a prize crew arrived later that day, but finding 'the stink in the ship so unsavoury and the sight within board so ugly' they left abruptly and ordered her to be towed to Weymouth. The rest of the Armada continued its slow progress up the Channel.

## Round Two

The English had still not divined the Spanish Masterplan. Thanks to the beacon system, the queen and her ministers knew within a day that the Spanish fleet had been sighted, but they had no idea 'what course they may take, and in what place of the realm they may attempt to land'. They therefore guessed (wrongly) 'that the enemy will attempt to land in some place in Essex' and sent orders to the various counties to assemble and send troops there. Howard had no better intelligence. 'We mean so to course the enemy as that they shall have no leisure to land,' he informed the governor of Portsmouth on 1 August, and begged him to send 'all such ships as you have ready furnished'. Although his strategy was sound, at this stage his tactics were not, because he also begged the governor to send 'as many tall men as you can get in so short a time'. It is hard to imagine what role 'tall men' would have played except in the case of hand-to-hand fighting, in which the Armada would almost certainly prevail.[20]

The next encounter occurred early on 2 August when the wind fell, becalming both fleets just west of Portland Bill (Figure 85). At about 1 a.m. Recalde, Leyva and Oquendo came aboard the flagship *San Martín* and argued that ideal conditions now existed for the galleasses to close with some isolated English warships. Medina Sidonia promised Don Hugo de Moncada, commander of the four galleasses, one of the estates that (he thought) Philip had promised to give to his son 'if he performed his task well';

85. The battle off Portland Bill, 2 August. Frobisher and other English ships have become detached close to Portland Bill and are being attacked by galleasses. Meanwhile English warships, firing forwards, attack the Armada's protective line of troubleshooters. A small group of English ships attacks the Armada's seaward wing.

but 'the galleasses did not do what they could and should have done. At dawn, they were still half a league from the enemy fleet.'[21]

Then a fresh breeze sprang up from the east to give the Spaniards, for the first time, the weather gage. Responding to the danger, Howard led his galleons, close-hauled, towards the north-north-east, hoping to place himself between the Armada and the shore. But Medina Sidonia used his advantage of wind to counter this attempt, forcing the English ships to come about in a reach towards the south-south-west.

These moves gave the Armada's troubleshooters a chance to show their prowess. For the first time since the fighting began some of the larger ships now came to close quarters. Bertendona's *Regazona* led the charge, followed by Leyva's *Rata Encoronada* and Oquendo's *Santa Ana*; but although 'they came very near to boarding, and they say that Bertendona could have done so if he had been willing to engage any vessel except the enemy flagship', his adversaries prudently turned seaward and opened the range. An artillery duel continued for more than two hours, without discernible tactics on either side beyond a strong Spanish desire to grapple and board, and an equally strong English determination to stay clear and rely on their big guns.[22]

While this skirmish was taking place well to seaward off Portland Bill, a separate action developed just to the west of it. Five English ships lay close inshore in a flat calm: four merchantmen from the London squadron and Martin Frobisher's *Triumph*, the largest ship in the English fleet. The Spaniards saw a golden opportunity to close and board and Medina Sidonia dispatched Moncada with his four galleasses to deal with Frobisher's isolated force. The oarsmen propelled the galleasses towards their prey, and although *Triumph* used her 'excellent artillery which fired with extraordinary speed, killing several soldiers', the great guns of the galleasses pounded one of the smaller English vessels until some of its soldiers seemed ready to abandon ship. Next, the galleasses managed to damage *Triumph*'s rudder and the captain of the musketeers on *San Lorenzo* called on Don Hugo to increase speed so that they could reach the ship and take her. However, 'he replied that he was doing all he could, but that he had no orders from the duke to board'. At this point, the wind suddenly rose, and *Triumph*'s boats hauled her to safety.[23]

This failure infuriated Medina Sidonia, who dispatched a staff officer to 'say aloud to Don Hugo . . . certain words which were not to his honour'. Later that day the duke also sent a message to Moncada which began: 'A fine day this has been! And if the galleasses had done their bit, as I expected, it would have gone badly for the enemy.'[24]

Medina Sidonia now faced other perils. Howard had taken advantage of a change of wind to lead a number of his more powerful galleons in a thrust at the heart of the Armada. The Lord Admiral 'called unto certain of Her Majesty's ships then near at hand and charged them straitly to follow him, and to set freshly upon the Spaniards, and to go within musket-shot of the enemy before they should discharge any one piece of ordnance'. Once again they attacked in groups, firing their guns only at close range. After the action Drake gave £107 'in reward to the company of the *Revenge*', an additional £10 'to the master gunner and his company', and £2 'to the musicians' (Drake's accounts do not specify what the ship's musicians did to merit their reward). Howard claimed that the bombardment that day, 'all the fight long within half-musket-shot of the enemy', had forced the Spaniards 'to give way and flock together like sheep'. Recalde agreed. His own ship, he recorded in his journal, 'had fought without any succour from any other ship in the Armada, because they all seemed to want to take refuge one behind the others. So they all fled from the action and collided together: it is a disgrace to mention it.'[25]

The account of Stukeley, aboard the Spanish flagship, suggests that perhaps Howard and Recalde exaggerated:

> Diego Flores warned the duke that some ships were in danger of getting in the middle of the enemy fleet and said that the flagship should turn back. The duke did so, and soon found himself facing the whole enemy fleet, without being assisted for a long time. The enemy bombarded the flagship hard, although she responded in such a way that the last enemy ships kept their distance.[26]

Vanegas, also aboard *San Martín*, agreed with Stukeley. 'The English flagship, followed by their whole fleet, passed by us, each ship firing at our flagship in turn', but 'we faced them and used our artillery, so that the last of the enemy's ships fired from further away'. Nevertheless, Vanegas admitted, in return for some eighty outgoing rounds the flagship received 500 hits, some of which struck the hull and rigging and carried away the flagstaff and one of the mainmast stays. Another Spanish observer claimed that for 'more than an hour we could not see the flagship because of the gun smoke'.

So ended another depressing day for the Armada, and Stukeley (whose views surely reflected those of the senior officers aboard *San Martín*) at last grasped the fleet's inherent tactical disadvantage: 'Today [2 August] we finally realized that we could not board the enemy if he did not wish it, because he had enjoyed such a good opportunity of boarding our isolated flagship. We also saw today the advantage that the enemy holds over us: they can keep their distance thanks to the speed of their ships, and they carry better artillery than we do.'

After the English disengaged, Medina Sidonia took some key decisions. First, since he still had no word from Parma to confirm that his invasion force was ready, he dispatched another *patache* to Flanders, seeking an urgent update on the state of the preparations there. Next he reorganized the Armada's tactical formation. Accepting the battle-plan which the unfortunate Don Pedro de Valdés had proposed at Corunna, the duke ordered that:

> The Armada should travel in two squadrons, vanguard and rearguard. The rearguard will be reinforced by the best ships in the fleet, half under the command of Juan Martínez [de Recalde] and the other half under Don Alonso de Leyva. [Moncada] and the flag galleass, together with two other galleasses, will go in the rearguard with Juan Martínez, and the fourth galleass will go in the vanguard with me.

English sources subsequently referred to the Armada's new formation as a 'plump' or 'roundel'.

The duke sent out six *pataches*, each with a sergeant-major and a hangman, 'to make sure that ships in the fleet would keep in place according to the new order', and to issue a warning that he would hang any captain who failed to do so. He also ordered Moncada to make sure that the three galleasses in the rearguard 'should conceal themselves, and then rally immediately to all opportunities that arise without the need for further orders' (no doubt another allusion to Don Hugo's apparent reluctance to attack *Triumph*).[27]

It was not that the extended formation with 'horns' had proved defective. On the contrary, in spite of several serious losses, and in the face of a strong English fleet to windward, the Armada had demonstrated both its tactical and strategic strengths; and Medina Sidonia had shown great skill in commanding it. In the words of an officer aboard *Revenge*, the Spanish ships 'do keep such excellent good order in their fight, that if God do not miraculously work, we shall have wherein to employ ourselves for some days'. Moreover, although Vanegas reckoned that the two fleets had expended 5,000 rounds on 2 August, some of it at close range, neither side had inflicted much damage upon the other. Both commanders must have felt surprised and disappointed at the mismatch between the high expenditure of precious munitions and the lack of damage caused.[28]

Paradoxically, this worried the English more than the Spaniards. As Hawkins reported to Walsingham, the artillery duel had been 'sharp and long' and had cost 'a good part of our powder and shot': he therefore opined that it would not be wise to continue the fight until they had replenished their stocks of ammunition. The English had reached a moment of crisis. It was one thing to have nimble ships that could take advantage of wind and tide, and thus keep the Spaniards at arm's length, but to defeat the Armada it was necessary to destroy its ships, not just run rings around them. On the one hand, Howard and his subordinates could see that their vaunted heavy artillery, despite the expenditure of so much shot at moderately close range, had not inflicted serious damage on the Spanish ships. On the other hand, if the English brought their ships much closer they ran the risk of being boarded and overwhelmed by the numerous soldiers on almost every Armada vessel.

In strategic if not in tactical terms the Spaniards had proved themselves to be the superior force. As soon as the gunfire stopped, with the English fleet temporarily neutralized by its ammunition crisis, the Armada simply shook itself back into formation and continued its advance towards Dunkirk. Yet Spanish victory did not depend solely on maintaining the Armada's progress: to succeed, the fleet must rendezvous with Parma's army.

The Council of War aboard *San Martín* on 29 July had recommended that until the arrangements were clear, and Parma's readiness was assured, they should proceed no further than the Isle of Wight; otherwise the fleet would need to ply up and down the Narrow Seas while it waited for Parma. There can be little doubt that by the evening of 2 August, with the Isle of Wight looming on his port quarter, Medina Sidonia gave some thought to seizing the Spithead anchorage shown on his charts, off Portsmouth. There, at least, he might find a safe and defensible haven until Parma made contact, and he might even be able to establish a beachhead on the Isle of Wight.

## The Isle of Wight Alternative

The English were equally aware of this possibility – but how could they prevent it? Their strategy (insofar as they had one) had been to cut out and overwhelm individual members of the Spanish fleet: to 'pluck their feathers by little and little', as Howard put it. On 3 August, having obtained some meagre replenishment to its ammunition stocks, the English fleet was presented with another excellent featherplucking opportunity. As dawn broke a large ship trailed behind the landward flank of the Armada, close to the western entrance to the Solent. The straggler was Gómez de Medina's wide-bellied flagship *Gran Grifón*. Although the *urcas* were generally regarded as non-combatants, *Grifón* was a gallant if clumsy member of the Armada's troubleshooting elite, and she might have been left behind as a decoy, to tempt English ships to close and precipitate a general boarding engagement. Instead, as the nearest English ships crowded on sail to catch the light morning airs a powerful galleon, almost certainly Drake's *Revenge*, glided abeam the wallowing *Grifón* and gave her a salvo at close range. *Revenge* came swiftly about to give her another, then crossed her stern to rake *Grifón* with gunfire. It was a devastating example of the mobile artillery tactics that individual English captains were beginning to adopt: *Grifón* was hit by at least forty roundshot, half of them below the waterline. And yet she hung grimly on, with 200 or more angry soldiers resolutely at their posts despite serious casualties, eager to board and capture any English ship rash enough to clap sides. The incident once again demonstrated the Armada's underlying strength. It might be battered, but it could not be destroyed; yet unless it was destroyed, its military potential remained overwhelming.

As the fight around *Grifón* developed, more ships became involved. Recalde's *San Juan* received another 200 incoming rounds and *San Martín* received 130. Now Medina Sidonia sent the galleasses to extricate the damaged *Grifón* and gave the signal for a general engagement. According to Vanegas the two fleets expended another 5,000 rounds. One of the galleasses scored a direct hit on one of *Revenge*'s masts but otherwise, once more, neither side reported serious damage. The English then drew off, preferring to delay the Spaniards rather than precipitate an all-out battle. The duke turned his ships about, and the Armada continued relentlessly on its way.[29]

The next few hours of the campaign were crucial because the Armada had at last reached a commanding position close to the Solent's eastern entrance, presenting Medina Sidonia with a serious dilemma. The king had repeatedly insisted that the fleet could only attack the Isle of Wight if the rendezvous with Parma should fail. Yet until Medina Sidonia knew what practical arrangements Parma had made for their rendezvous, his only sensible course was to find a secure anchorage in which to shelter and if necessary defend the Armada. No such anchorage existed between the Isle of Wight and the Downs, which might allow him to convince the king subsequently that entering the Solent had been a wise response to changing circumstances. But events soon removed this option.

The previous evening, in response to his sustained lack of success, Howard had ordered a major reorganization of his forces. A Council of War aboard *Ark Royal* decided to arrange the fleet into four quasi-independent squadrons under the commands of Howard, Drake, Hawkins and Frobisher. Instead of a loose agglomeration of captains who, apart from a general obligation to support the flagship, acted as individual circumstances dictated, each squadron now received tasks which, if performed in unison, should force the Armada clear of the Solent (Figure 86).

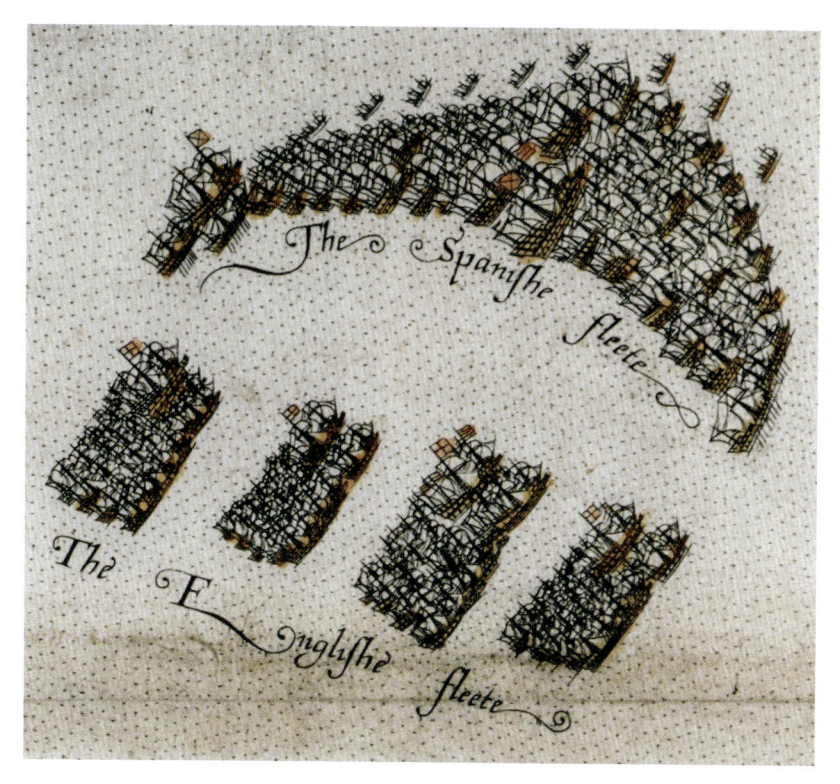

**86.** The two fleets continue up the Channel. The English fleet now sails in four squadrons, conserving its ammunition but ready for a more coordinated attack. The Armada is still shown in its crescent formation, with two galleasses protecting each wing. The large ship with a flag on the left is Recalde's *San Juan*.

4 August was the feast of St Dominic, whom Medina Sidonia held in special veneration and from whom he claimed descent. He felt confident that the saint would now bring him good fortune. Daybreak revealed that the Portuguese galleon *San Luís* and the *urca Duquesa Santa Ana* had fallen astern the main body. Like *Gran Grifón* the previous day, they presented the English – probably deliberately – with obvious targets. But this time there was no wind. Hawkins, whose squadron lay closest to the Spanish stragglers, lowered his ships' boats to tow his warships to the attack. Medina Sidonia responded by advancing the three galleasses attached to the rearguard, one towing Leyva's *Rata Encoronada*. As the ranges closed the English opened the gunports on their lower decks and the galleasses became the

main targets of the English bombardment. One began to list, another lost her lantern and a third received some damage to her prow. *San Juan de Sicilia* and *Anunciada* offered support, but the English countered with a heavy bombardment. Eventually the galleasses took *San Luís* and *Duquesa* in tow and brought them into the safety of the fleet.

At this point a south-westerly wind sprang up, enabling the immobilized sailing ships on both sides to manoeuvre again. On the left wing, Frobisher had taken his squadron into the difficult tidal seaway to the east of the Isle of Wight. Perhaps in an attempt to force a passage into the Solent, Medina Sidonia led a group of powerful galleons towards it. As they approached, Frobisher in his vast *Triumph* seemed to be in difficulties (quite possibly feigned) and lowered his boats to tow the ship clear. Then a breath of wind filled *Triumph*'s sails and she took on way. Medina Sidonia fired a gun to call off the chase.

Recalde, who had been closing in on Frobisher, and who had acquired first-hand experience of leading a fleet into the Solent in 1575, was furious:

> We were gaining the weather gage, and some of our ships were gaining ground on many of the enemy's, so we gave them chase. As we were thus harassing the enemy and pressing home our victory, however, our flagship fired a gun to call us back . . . In my opinion we should not have desisted as our flagship did until we had either made them run aground or else followed them into a port. Nor was it wise to sail with our fleet beyond the anchorage [Spithead] near to the Isle of Wight until we had heard from the prince of Parma, because it was the best anchorage in the whole Channel for every eventuality.[30]

Perhaps Recalde was right, but his account omitted an important obstacle: while the principal Spanish ships were engaged at the entrance to the Solent, a furious and unexpected English attack suddenly developed nearby. This assault was delivered 'in such a way', according to a Spanish eyewitness, 'that we who were there were cornered, so that, if the duke had not gone about with his flagship, we who were victorious until that point would have come out vanquished that day'. The surprise attack fatally unbalanced Medina Sidonia's dispositions, and he abandoned his last chance of forcing the Solent.[31]

This outcome brought gains to both sides. They had fired another 4,000 rounds on St Dominic's day and, according to Howard's journal, 'Forasmuch as our powder and shot was well wasted, the Lord Admiral thought it was not good policy to assail them any more until their coming near unto Dover.' Instead, he used his privilege as commander-in-chief to confer well-deserved knighthoods on Hawkins and Frobisher.

Medina Sidonia, too, welcomed the respite. He wrote again to Parma, bringing him up to date with his increasingly serious tactical situation:

> The enemy's fleet has come to bombard me so that we have had to turn and face them, and most days they have bombarded us from morning until night, without ever letting themselves go alongside our armada, even though for my part I have done everything possible and given them every occasion. Sometimes our ships have been in the middle of their fleet, all to the end that one of their ships should board and so bring on the battle.

He begged Parma to send him powder, and roundshot of the same calibres his ships had almost expended: 4-, 6- and 10-pounds. It is notable that he did not request heavier shot.[32]

On 5 August the fleets lay becalmed, giving time to carry out repairs. That night Recalde and his crew managed to repair the mainmast damaged by shot in the first encounter: 'We worked all through the night without the enemy noticing it, so that they would not realize the damage the mast had suffered. Before dawn we had made seven "fishes" [tapered splints, hollowed to fit round the mast] with seven bindings to fasten them, and we blackened them with pitch so that the repairs would not be visible'. Recalde's ingenuity and expertise saved his ship.[33]

The next day the westerly wind resumed, and the fleets again got under way. On the morning of 6 August, Boulogne on the French coast came in sight. What should the Armada do now? Philip's Instructions had specified 'Margate Cape' (the North Foreland) as the place where the fleet would 'join hands' with Parma, but with the English in battle-array three miles astern this made no sense. Yet with no word from Flanders, should the fleet go directly to Dunkirk to pick up the invasion force, trusting that it would be ready? Or should it hold back?

The official campaign journal of *San Martín* set out the dilemma now facing Medina Sidonia:

> There were different opinions on whether to anchor in that roadstead, and most favoured going on; but the duke, understanding from the pilots he had brought with him that if he proceeded further the currents would force him out of the Channel and into the North Sea, determined to anchor before Calais, seven leagues from Dunkirk, where Parma could come and join him. And so at 5 p.m. he ordered the whole fleet to drop anchor.

The account of a Portuguese Jesuit on the flagship adds details. 'Most of the senior officers argued that we should proceed, especially a man with great experience in naval and land warfare [presumably Recalde] who argued vehemently that we should not anchor off Calais but rather keep sailing until we had cleared the Narrow Seas.' But, the Jesuit continued, 'the pilots warned that if we continued, the currents would force it beyond the Channel and into the North Sea'. And that is why the fleet dropped anchor at 5 p.m. The duke now urged Parma to send him 'forty or fifty flyboats' so that 'we can hold off the fleet of the enemy until Your Excellency can come with all the rest [of your forces] and we can capture some roadstead [presumably Margate] where this Armada can anchor in complete safety'.[34]

We must once more salute Medina Sidonia's achievement. He had twice got the Grand Fleet to sea without losing a single vessel; and he had led it to Calais, only 30 miles from the Army of Flanders, almost intact. His success made some of his adversaries panic because, as the Elizabethan satirist and pamphleteer Thomas Nash reminded his readers a few years later: 'A man standing upon the Calais sands may see men walking on Dover cliffs' – and vice versa. On 7 August messengers from Dover arrived at the English Court saying that the previous day 'they discerned the Spanish fleet lying over against Calais and our fleet [while] sending out boats to land to refresh their men with victual and other necessaries'. Some courtiers expressed 'much grief' that Howard 'had suffered them to pass on so far without fight, and that he [had] prevented not the opportunity they have now gotten of refreshing their men'. Medina Sidonia must now have felt – and with some justification – that he had fulfilled his master's command, and despite overwhelming odds had 'done his part'.[35]

## 13

# The Test of Battle

---※---

### The Fatal Flaw

There can be few sets of military or naval correspondence so unidirectional as the letters exchanged between the dukes of Medina Sidonia and Parma as the Armada made its way from Lisbon to Calais. On 10 June, as he approached Cape Finisterre and confidently anticipated that he would reach the rendezvous within two weeks, Medina Sidonia sent 'a well-armed *patache* with oars' to inform Parma of his progress, pointing out that because of the coastal sandbanks and the lack of a deep-water port in Flanders, there could be no link-up close to shore. His next letter, dated 25 July, simply confirmed that, after the delay at Corunna, he was again on his way. No acknowledgement arrived to either dispatch, but Medina Sidonia persevered. On 31 July, as the Armada approached Plymouth, he asked Parma to send him pilots who knew the coast of Flanders 'because without them I would not know where to shelter vessels as large as the ones I bring with me if I should encounter the least storm'. He also asked 'Your Excellency what I should do, and where I should wait, in order for us to join forces'. Don Francisco de Bobadilla sent a letter with the same courier urging Parma 'to come out in person as soon as you see this fleet in the anchorage that it should reach, even if it cannot be with all the ships and men that you have assembled, because that will determine nothing less than the success of this fleet'.[1]

Off the Isle of Wight on 4 August, still without word from Flanders, Medina Sidonia wrote once more to remind Parma that 'Your Excellency should be ready to put to sea and find me' at a moment's notice. The following day, off Beachy Head, it occurred to Medina Sidonia that perhaps the small warships assembled in Dunkirk might be able to close with the English and engage them until his bigger vessels could get alongside and board. He therefore dispatched another messenger to beg Parma to send him '40 or 50 flyboats or other small and light warships' immediately. He also sent a pilot to explain to Parma why the Armada was making such slow progress, and how much it needed the reinforcements already requested.[2]

In spite of all these communications, when the fleet reached Calais the following day no word had arrived from the shore. Medina Sidonia came close to despair. 'I have written to your Excellency every day, telling you my location and that of the fleet,' he began another reproachful letter to Parma, 'and not only have I received no reply to any of them, but no acknowledgement of their receipt.' He repeated that 'if you cannot set forth at once with all your ships, you should send me the 40 or 50 flyboats which I asked for yesterday'. On 7 August he sent two more messages repeating 'our urgent need to find a port, without which this fleet will be lost because our ships are so big'. He continued plaintively (and pointlessly), 'this fleet cannot just sail up and down' while it waited for Parma, 'because our big ships are always to leeward of the enemy, unable to do anything to them however hard we try'.[3]

Here was an extraordinary situation: the joint commanders of the greatest amphibious operation in the Atlantic to that date had no effective contact with each other. Much has been made in the past of Parma's silence, some (including many Spaniards at the time) going so far as to accuse the duke of deliberately trying to sabotage the enterprise; but this is either malice or fantasy. It assumes that travel by land or sea in early modern Europe was easy, rapid and regular. Of course it was not. In the sixteenth century a journey between two locations might take days, weeks or even months, depending on the vagaries of the weather, the state of roads and bridges, the availability and mode of transport, the political situation, and the presence or absence of pirates or bandits along the route. A letter sent from Brussels or Paris to Madrid, for example, might reach its destination in as few as ten days; but in the summer and autumn of 1588 a combination of atrocious weather at sea and sustained activity by Huguenot partisans on land meant that some important communications took three weeks or more. Others did not arrive at all.

Moreover, when one of the correspondents was on the move, like Medina Sidonia aboard the Armada, the situation became infinitely more difficult. Even a messenger from the fleet who eventually found his way ashore would encounter difficulties in finding his way back, because the ships by then would have moved on to a different, and unknown, location. To make matters worse English and Dutch warships patrolled the waters over which messengers from the Armada had to travel. Even the duke's last messenger dispatched from Calais to Dunkirk, a land journey of relative safety, took two days to cover the 30 miles that still separated the fleet from the army.

Medina Sidonia here betrayed a fatal lack of familiarity with the realities of naval warfare (one cannot imagine his predecessor, Santa Cruz, making the same elementary error). It never seems to have occurred to him that all his messengers had either to run the gauntlet of hostile ships lurking in the Channel, or else make for the French coast and hope to find relays of horses ready to convey them overland all the way to Flanders. It was foolish to assume that they would arrive – let alone return with an answer – much before the Armada reached 'the appointed place'. The duke made few serious errors during the campaign. But this one was crucial.

In the event not one of the couriers sent from the Armada to Flanders did much good. Francesco Moresin, sent from Finisterre on 10 June, reached Flanders in eleven days; but the storms that dispersed the Armada off Corunna soon made nonsense of his message. Don Rodrigo Tello de Guzmán, sent from the Bay of Biscay on 25 July, took seven days to reach Parma. Medina Sidonia entrusted to Lieutenant Juan Gil his letter of 31 July, written when the fleet approached Plymouth and announcing that he now planned to make straight for the Flemish coast; but Gil did not leave until the following morning, when the fleet was off Portland Bill, and did not reach Parma's headquarters until early on 6 August. Only then did the duke start to prepare for the embarkation process, ordering the troops stationed inland to head towards the coast. The messenger dispatched off the Isle of Wight arrived late on 6 August, just as the Armada dropped anchor off Calais, and only then did Parma order embarkation to begin. Medina Sidonia's last desperate letter from Calais 'arrived in Dunkirk on the 9th, at 10:30 a.m.' – by which time the English fleet had forced the Armada into the North Sea. So although Medina Sidonia repeatedly expressed regret at his slow progress, and sought by every means to increase his speed, as Philip had exhorted him to do, from Parma's perspective he arrived too soon.[4]

On the evening of Saturday 6 August a reply from Parma finally reached the Armada as it huddled before Calais. At first the *patache* bearing it was mistaken for an enemy vessel and fired on, but its message must have made Medina Sidonia's heart miss a beat, for it was dated 3 August and replied to his letter of 25 July, revealing Parma's total ignorance of the fleet's proximity. In addition, Parma declared that since he 'had not embarked a barrel of beer, still less a soldier', he would not be able to join forces until the following Friday.

On Friday? Another six days? Medina Sidonia was horrified, because the Armada now faced a situation he dreaded: it had reached the rendezvous without securing command of the sea. 'To encourage the soldiers' aboard his fleet, the duke 'spread the word that they would win a great victory two days from now'; but in a new letter to Parma he stressed his perilous position. Admiral Howard lay at anchor one mile to windward, now reinforced by Lord Henry Seymour and Sir William Winter with the warships stationed in the Downs; to leeward lay the dangerous shallows known to mariners as 'the Banks of Flanders' – made even more dangerous because the Dutch had removed all the navigation and leading marks before the Armada arrived (Figure 87).

Medina Sidonia's cumbersome task force could not get any closer to Parma's embarkation ports: it could only wait at anchor in its exposed position off Calais and hope for the best. Perhaps in other circumstances the duke could have detached the galleasses and a few of the smaller galleons and sent them to drive off the Dutch blockaders (it was for such a task that a strong contingent of galleys had originally been planned). But given the proximity of the English fleet he dared not divide his forces. Yet no one – least of all the duke – supposed that the English would allow the Armada to remain unmolested for a further six days.[5]

87. The situation on 6 August. The Armada is anchored off Calais, with the English fleet poised to windward. Seymour's Narrow Seas squadron is leaving its anchorage in the Downs to join in the final assault which will be precipitated by a fireship attack.

The testimony of Don Diego Pimentel, one of Spain's senior infantry commanders taken prisoner two days later, revealed the fleet high command's total ignorance about the state of affairs in Flanders. Pimentel assured his Dutch captors that he had expected Parma to make a dash for the Armada with whatever forces he had ready. When asked if he did not realize that a powerful Dutch squadron lay outside Dunkirk, ready to oppose any attempt by Parma and his men to come out, Pimentel reiterated that:

> They had never once thought that the duke, with 100 ships, a multitude of coasters and barges, and an army of around 40,000 men, would not be able to sally forth as planned. It seemed strange to him that the duke, having such strength, should not have come out, or at least sent out enough barges with musketeers to drive back the warships of Holland and Zeeland.

Even if this entire advance guard perished in the attempt, Pimentel reasoned, it would have allowed the rest of Parma's invasion fleet to slip out and join the Armada.[6]

Pimentel's testimony probably reflected the thinking of Medina Sidonia at this point because, as his interrogators smugly noted, Don Diego was 'related to the principal families of all Spain' and had no obvious reason to lie. If so, three distinct misconceptions become clear, and they explain the failure to make the vital rendezvous required by Philip's Grand Design. First, Medina Sidonia assumed that news of the Armada's approach would have preceded it. This, of course, had not been so. The first news of the Channel battles to reach the Netherlands came (ironically) from the English diplomats at Bourbourg: at 3 p.m. on 6 August they received a letter from London announcing that the queen's ships had encountered and engaged the Armada off Plymouth. The delegation at once began to pack its bags, to the open amazement of the Spanish negotiators who (unaware of the Armada's progress) suspected that their departure might be 'some subterfuge or cover' intended to secure diplomatic concessions from Spain. The truth only emerged a few hours later.[7]

Medina Sidonia's second misconception stemmed from the first. He convinced himself that (having been forewarned) Parma would have embarked all his troops before the Armada reached the Narrow Seas, and would therefore be able to send out some warships to drive away or at least divert the Dutch blockaders as soon as the Grand Fleet approached Dunkirk. If it proved impossible to storm ashore in Kent, he invited Parma to lead out the troops embarked in their barges and 'help him capture the Isle of Wight'. As Parma pointed out to the king, these suggestions 'show clearly how ignorant the duke is about the qualities of the ships here'. Nevertheless, perhaps as a safeguard against subsequent blame, Parma convened a committee of local pilots and naval commanders and asked them to evaluate the feasibility of Medina Sidonia's suggestions. The council unanimously condemned the idea of sending a few warships against the Dutch blockaders as 'ill-conceived and unreasonable, against all the laws of land and sea warfare because of the risk that they would be lost, along with all the men on board, before they reached the Spanish fleet'. They likewise deemed 'utterly impossible' a voyage to the Isle of Wight because it 'would last seven or eight days', far beyond the endurance of the duke's barges, or of the men and animals embarked on them. Parma therefore remained adamant that Medina Sidonia must stick to the king's Grand Design: to defeat or drive off the enemy fleet 'to secure the passage from Dunkirk to Margate for all the soldiers assembled in Flanders'.[8]

There was more to Medina Sidonia's ignorance than poor communications, however: it stemmed from a fundamental failure of comprehension. Here the duke must bear some of the blame because the necessary information had long been available to him. In mid-May Francesco Moresin had arrived at Lisbon with a status report on Parma's preparations. His news was not encouraging: losses among the troops in winter quarters had dangerously reduced the number available for embarkation; and the Flanders flotilla contained few escorts for the unarmed low-freeboard landing-craft and barges designated to transport the troops. Perplexed, Medina Sidonia turned to the king for guidance, but received little help. Philip replied that the 10,000 soldiers aboard the fleet which he had earmarked to reinforce Parma's forces once they landed in England would more than offset the reduced number of troops in Flanders; and he simply ignored the lack of escort vessels, passing the responsibility for clearing the seas squarely back to Medina Sidonia. Parma's vessels, Philip repeated, were not of a kind 'that can put out and seek you at a distance, unless you have cleared away all enemy ships from the straits first, because they are transports and not fighting ships'.[9]

Medina Sidonia seems to have forgotten, or failed to grasp, this vital fact. On 10 June, off Finisterre, he revealed his misconception in a letter to Parma confirming that he 'was coming towards Your Excellency' and promising to 'write again to you when I enter the Channel so Your Excellency will know where this fleet is, so that you can lead your [ships] out'. Medina Sidonia even sent an extra *patache* 'so that Your Excellency can use it to tell me the state in which you find yourself, when you can come out, and where we can meet'. On reading a copy of this letter, the king immediately spotted the error, and scribbled in the margin 'This cannot be unless he [Medina Sidonia] makes it safe first.' He lost no time in firing off an anguished protest to the duke:

> I will not repeat here what I have told you so often, except to say that ... the main point [of the plan] was to go on until you could join hands with the duke my nephew ... I am sure you will have done this and proceeded to that location and made safe the duke's transit, because his ships are not able to come out and meet you further off until you have cleared the crossing of enemies: they are merely transport vessels, not fighting ships.[10]

At last the king seems to have recognized the principal defect in the plan he had imposed, but Medina Sidonia still did not. As the English coast came into view he again erroneously informed the king that 'the intention is that the duke of Parma should come out with his ships to the place where I arrive [that is, to the coast of Kent] without making me wait for him for a moment. On this depends the whole success of the campaign.'[11]

As soon as Parma received Medina Sidonia's letter of 10 June he penned yet another protest to the king. 'Medina seems to believe that I should set out to meet him with my small ships, which is simply impossible. These vessels cannot run the gauntlet of warships; they cannot even withstand large waves.' Perceptively but vainly, Philip annotated the margin of this letter, received on 7 August, the day before disaster struck his fleet: 'Please God, let there not be some slip-up [*embarazo*] here.'[12]

## Parma Prepares

The duke of Parma did not learn of the Armada's delay at Corunna until 21 July – ironically, the day it set forth again. A week earlier he had sent Moresin on a second mission to Medina Sidonia, repeating his warning about the need for the Armada to gain command of the waters off the Flemish coast before he could safely bring out his forces; but a bizarre combination of shipwreck, storms and an encounter with the English fleet delayed Moresin and he did not reach Spain until 2 August. Medina Sidonia's misconception therefore persisted, and he continued to send Parma futile letters asking where and when the rendezvous would take place right up to the moment he anchored off Calais.[13]

A third serious misconception compounded the other two. The Armada's commanders clearly believed that only a handful of enemy ships blockaded the

Flemish coast. They apparently did not realize, as Parma did, that the Dutch could deploy not only a small navy but also a sizeable reserve of large, shallow-draught merchantmen capable of carrying both soldiers and artillery. Parma's main concern, therefore, was to keep the Dutch fleet divided, because once it assembled off Dunkirk or Nieuwpoort it could confine his own ships to their harbours.

To avoid this situation Parma had adopted three stratagems. First, he kept most of his troops well away from the Flanders coastline, deployed to give the impression that they might be preparing to invade Holland or Zeeland. Second, the duke deliberately sowed confusion by moving his assets around unpredictably. On the day the Armada reached Calais, a senior English army officer in the Netherlands testified to Parma's success in this, complaining that the duke had:

> within these sixteen days often embarked [his troops and] descended again, speedily marched toward Brabant and as hastily retired again, sometimes dispersing his regiments into several garrisons and suddenly uniting his force again ... holding all in fear ... For though the smoke trouble and blind all, yet no spark of fire is kindled, and [we remain] uncertain where the flame will first burst forth.[14]

Parma completed the deception by dividing his invasion fleet among several harbours. About seventy vessels, including his 400-ton flagship and a large galley specially built by a team of ship's carpenters brought from Italy, were at Antwerp. Another flotilla lay at Sluis, captured by Parma the previous year. The duke expected the big ships to sail down the Scheldt from Antwerp, 'liberate' the flotilla confined in Sluis, and then proceed to Nieuwpoort and Dunkirk to embark the invasion army; but when he carried out a personal reconnaissance of the estuaries and channels along the north coast of Flanders he observed that over 100 Dutch ships lay in wait in the Scheldt to forestall precisely this manoeuvre. He reluctantly concluded that none of the Antwerp ships could reach Sluis safely by that route.

Ever resourceful, the duke therefore decided to leave the larger warships where they lay, in order to pin down the Dutch blockaders, and moved the rest towards the coast along inland waterways. Pioneers deepened the canals and broke some dikes to increase the level and flow of water until in March 1588 all the smaller craft from Antwerp and other ports along the Scheldt moved to Ghent. At the same time some 200 seamen recruited in Hamburg and Lübeck arrived overland to reinforce the crews aboard the flotilla.

Inevitably, the Dutch noticed these developments and tried to disrupt them. On 6 March a small vessel from Zeeland sailed into Dunkirk harbour, allegedly carrying butter and cheese for the troops gathered there. The harbour was 'full of vessels from the front to the back', forcing the new arrival to anchor some way off, so that when the bombs concealed in her hold exploded that night they only destroyed two of Parma's ships and severely damaged five more. But they also shattered all the glass windows in the town and reinforced Spanish fears that their enemies would resort to 'hellburners'.[15]

When the Dutch placed another blockading squadron before Sluis, ruling out any thought of a sortie from there too, Parma set his pioneers to work again. This time they deepened the rivers and dug new canals to link Sluis with Nieuwpoort, culminating in a 'cutt' ten yards wide and almost two yards deep opened on 5 April. Now, although the larger and better-armed vessels were once again left behind, a host of barges and other flat-bottomed craft could reach Nieuwpoort (Figure 88).

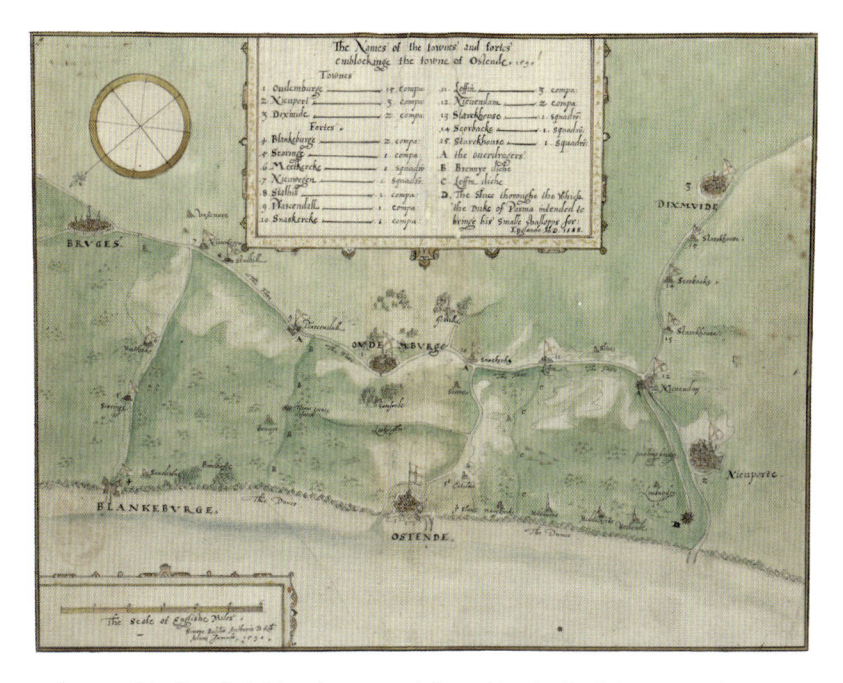

88. A map of the Dutch-held enclave around Ostend by the English cartographer Robert Adams in 1590 reveals the topography of one of the embarkation areas for the invasion army two years earlier. Near Nieuwpoort ('D': bottom right) Adams marked 'the sluice through which the Duke of Parma intended to bring his small shallops for England'. The duke's headquarters at Bruges appears at upper left; the other port of embarkation, Dunkirk, is off the map to the right – 'a long way off', as one of Philip's advisers observed acidly to Parma after the failure of the Armada.

By June 1588, against heavy odds, seven merchantmen and 173 flat-bottomed craft rode in Nieuwpoort harbour, ready to coordinate their activities with the warships and transports at Dunkirk. An English spy reported that although most of the vessels were 'open and have no defence when they be boarded', and lacked heavy artillery, he deemed them 'ready, and most of them ready laden with victual'. As soon as he received news of the Armada's arrival off Calais, Parma not only started to embark his troops in both Flemish ports, but also ordered the ships in the Scheldt to move downstream to draw off more Dutch blockade ships. He also 'suffered no stranger . . . to come to him, or to see his army and ships, but he blindfolded them'.[16]

The duke's complex web of deception worked. Contemporary Dutch records reveal a complete failure to discern Spanish intentions. Some of the Republic's leaders, dismayed by the continuation of the talks at Bourbourg and the absence of a decisive battle in the Channel, feared that the Armada would attack either Flushing or Amsterdam. Others fretted that even if the Armada landed troops in England, the Army of Flanders might still take advantage of the distraction to launch a surprise assault on a Dutch town. On 12 July 1588, with Parma's entire army ready to sail out from Dunkirk and Nieuwpoort at any moment, Justinus of Nassau, the Dutch admiral in charge of blockading the Flemish coast, commanded only twenty-four ships. By contrast thirty-two ships cruised off Sluis, 135 blockaded the Scheldt and another 100 stood guard further north around the entrance to the Zuider Zee and the Eems. All suggestions by the Dutch federal government that more vessels should be concentrated off Flanders ran into bitter opposition from the political leaders of Holland and Zeeland who, as late as 10 August – two days after the battle off Gravelines – still feared that Philip really intended to attack them. 'I think,' Lord Henry Seymour remarked, that the Dutch 'desire more to regard their own coast than ours'. Admiral Howard was more blunt: as he closed with the Spanish fleet, he observed bitterly that 'There is not one Flushinger nor Hollander at the seas.'[17]

Thus, in spite of subsequent accusations that he had been unprepared, Parma largely achieved his vital objective: surprise. The Dutch failed to divine what he intended to do, and their forces remained widely dispersed. Even their blockade of Dunkirk remained incomplete. The duke managed to send out four ships on 1 March 1588, one on 1 May, three on 7 June, one each on 30 and 31 July and 1 and 2 August, and three on 5 August, while two Armada vessels managed to enter Dunkirk, take on stores and leave again shortly afterwards. On reading a report about this, Lord Burghley scribbled angrily in the margin 'Wherefore serves Justinus and his ships of Zeeland?'[18]

Nevertheless, to concentrate an army of 27,000 men at the two designated embarkation ports, to embark them (along with horses, provisions, weapons and equipment) on the 270 vessels concentrated there, to get both flotillas to sea and then to join them into a single force, presented major logistical challenges. Parma estimated that the complete operation would require six days. Therefore, since he only received confirmation of the fleet's proximity on 6 August, his forces could not be fully ready until 12 August – but if on that day the Armada might escort him across the Channel in safety, he could soon be marching on London.

At first it seemed that this might be possible. On the one hand, the English fleet was lucky to recover from two serious missteps. First, Medina Sidonia's decision 'upon a sudden to anchor' on 6 August took Howard by surprise. At first he thought it a ruse to the effect 'that our ships with the flood [tide] should be driven to leeward of them' (a ruse which no doubt Howard himself would have attempted), but 'it was soon espied and prevented by bringing our fleet to an anchor also in the wind of them'. The next day the strong tide caused *White Bear* and three other ships to collide with *Ark Royal* and they became 'all tangled together, so as there was some hurt done by breaking of yards and spoil of tackle'; but 'by a great favour of God' no ship suffered 'destruction'.[19] On the other hand M. de Gourdan, the French Catholic governor of Calais, welcomed the Armada. He allowed a number of senior officers from the fleet (including Inspector-General Don Jorge Manrique, Victualler-General Bernabé de Pedroso and Paymaster-General Juan de Huerta) to go ashore and purchase water, fresh vegetables and other food. A stream of victuallers now plied between the anchored Armada and the shore.

It may have been the warmth of Gourdan's welcome that convinced the English commanders they had to act without delay. Thanks to Seymour's squadron Howard now commanded around 140 sail, but he still worried that it might not be enough to prevail. For all he knew, Parma might already be embarking his forces at Dunkirk. The survival of the Tudor state thus depended on preventing the Armada from reaching them.

## Send in the Fireships!

A Council of War aboard *Ark Royal* on the morning of 7 August resolved to launch a fireship attack against the Armada that night. Conditions were perfect. The Spanish fleet was crowded together at anchor, and its commander seemed uncertain of his next move. To leeward lay the Flemish shoals, on which the Spanish ships might be driven. Best of all, from the English point of view, the conjunction of spring

**89.** Eight fireships attack the Armada off Calais. Note the small oared vessels close inshore waiting to intercept them.

tides and a freshening westerly breeze could bring the fireships swiftly into the Armada's heart (Figure 89).

Eight fireships were prepared at a cost (subsequently minutely calculated by the owners to claim compensation) of £5,111 10s 0d. It was, as an eminent naval historian observed, 'perhaps the cheapest national investment that this country has ever made'. Meanwhile one of Seymour's ships sailed defiantly towards the anchored Armada and delivered a broadside. The guns on the galleass *San Lorenzo* 'returned the favour' and the intruder fled; but the escapade made a deep impression on the men aboard the Armada. 'We all admired her daring,' wrote an officer on *Gran Grifón*, 'but above all we marvelled that they had such fine, agile ships which could come and go as they pleased, unlike ours.'[20] More important, the spectacle distracted the Spaniards while Howard's men packed the eight fireships with combustibles, and loaded their guns with double shot to discharge spontaneously as the fire took hold, adding a psychological dimension to the stratagem. No Spaniard could forget Federico Giambelli's terrible 'hellburners of Antwerp' (see Figure 23), and everyone knew that the great pyrotechnician now resided in England. Howard deliberately played on these fears, and aimed not so much to destroy ships as to create confusion and panic throughout the Armada. Thereafter, he reasoned, the forces of nature, aided by the English fleet, would accomplish the rest.

So it transpired. Medina Sidonia had anticipated such an attack and prepared accordingly. Before night fell he set a screen of *pataches* to windward of the Armada, with orders to grapple and tow clear any fireships that might approach. When at midnight the attack came, two fireships were intercepted and dragged into the shallows – an act of great heroism on the part of the nameless *patache* crews – but the remaining six fireships careered towards the midst of the Grand Fleet. Medina Sidonia had anticipated this eventuality too. He ordered each ship in the rearguard to prepare rowing boats with soldiers aboard and sent out staff officers in feluccas with orders that any vessel in the path of a fireship should slip her cables and stand clear until the danger had passed, after which she should re-anchor.

These were sensible precautions, and in other circumstances they might have worked. The English boats towing the fireships turned back as soon as they came within range of *San Lorenzo*, but Howard had chosen a perfect time to launch his attack. With the tide running north at two knots or more, and a following wind, the fireships took only fifteen minutes to reach the Armada's rearguard, their pre-loaded guns discharging as the heat reached them. According to a Jesuit with the fleet, Recalde urged the ships 'not to raise the anchors, but instead to send out more rowing boats and use long poles and rods to divert the fireships; but this had no effect because God had decided on a different course of action'. Most captains simply cut or buoyed their anchor cables and fled – one eyewitness estimated that the Armada 'left behind something like 300 anchors' – and the strong currents combined with the rising wind made it almost impossible for them to regain their positions and re-anchor while they waited for Parma. Although no Armada ship caught fire, the fleet degenerated overnight from a disciplined and still formidable fighting force into a scattering gaggle of panic-stricken ships. The Armada had lost its cohesion, on which its effectiveness and future security depended.[21]

The command structure, too, temporarily lost its cohesion. When the prince of Ascoli in a felucca reached the side of Recalde's ship, which was already making sail, and shouted up a summons for the admiral to attend a council meeting on the flagship, *San Martín*, Recalde growled back that 'this was no time for me to leave my ship, and that my advice counted for nothing'. The prince replied that 'his vote too did not count' because of 'the confusion reigning in the flagship'. Captain Vanegas confirmed this impression, stating that 'someone [perhaps Diego Flores?] suggested that the duke should leave the flagship, because the fireships were getting close and their artillery could inflict serious damage, whereas the flagship could not turn about because other ships were manoeuvring in her path. But the duke considered this advice dishonourable.' Medina Sidonia therefore stayed where he was.[22]

## The Day of Decisions

Medina Sidonia now knew exactly what to do: he declared that 'if he had many lives he would lose them all to uphold his honour'. He apparently experienced only one moment of doubt. According to a subsequent account, when the duke found himself next to the flagship of the Guipúzcoan squadron he called out to her commander: 'Señor Oquendo, what should we do? We are lost.' 'I don't know,' came the sarcastic reply. 'Why don't you ask Diego Flores?' – adding 'I intend to fight and die well. Please send me more ammunition.' This stiffened Medina Sidonia's resolution. Several other accounts of the battle by Spanish survivors commented that the arrival of *San Martín* had saved them, 'because the English feared our flagship'.[23]

When dawn broke, Medina Sidonia fired three guns to summon the rest of the fleet to rejoin him, but according to Stukeley 'only a few vessels close to the flagship did so: the rest of the Armada kept going.' Nevertheless those 'few vessels' gradually formed a ragged but determined protective shield for the more vulnerable ships behind them. Sir William Winter, boasting thirty years' experience of naval command, observed this tactical manoeuvre for the first time with detached professional interest. 'They went into a proportion of a half-moon,' Winter wrote, and 'their admiral and vice-admiral, they went in the midst ... There went on each side, in the wings, their galleasses, armados of Portugal, and other good ships, in the whole to the number of sixteen in a wing, which did seem to be of their principal shipping.' It was the old trailing-horns defensive posture, this time composed almost exclusively of the troubleshooters, and they now became the target of an unprecedented naval bombardment that would destroy three and cripple many of the rest.[24]

The English fleet had wisely remained at anchor throughout the night, but between 7 and 8 a.m. on 8 August the squadrons led by Drake and Hawkins targeted the left of the Spanish rearguard. One squadron headed for Recalde in *San Juan*, supported by Pimentel in *San Mateo*, Don Francisco de Toledo in *San Felipe*, and the Vizcayan *María Juan*; the other squadron made for the flagship, supported by the marquis of Peñafiel in *San Marcos* and Oquendo in *Santa Ana*. Then, between 9 and 10 a.m. a third English squadron under Seymour and Winter attacked the right of the rearguard: Don Diego Enriquez in *San Juan Menor*, Leyva in *Rata Encoronada*, Bertendona in *Regazona*, Don Diego Téllez Enríquez in *San Juan de Sicilia* and perhaps also Don Alonso de Luzón in *Trinidad Valencera* (the surviving sources are ambiguous). Only Lord Admiral Howard was missing from the general attack, because his attention had shifted elsewhere.

In the confusion that followed the fireship attack Moncada's flag galleass, *San Lorenzo*, had been slow to cut her anchor cables and had collided with Leyva's enormous *Rata Encoronada*, severely damaging *San Lorenzo*'s stern and breaking her rudder so she could not steer. Seeing the fireships approach, many of her soldiers escaped up ropes cast down from *Rata*, while the 'poor convicts at the oars began to cry out pitifully and to hammer at their chains and fetters in the hope of escape by jumping in the sea, preferring to die by water than by fire'. All this seems to have disoriented Moncada. With the English bearing down on him and the Armada in full retreat, he tried to steer the galleass using only her oars, hoping the tide would carry her to Dunkirk. He rejected the offer of two French boats to tow him (for a price!) into neutral Calais, but *San Lorenzo* ran aground on a sandbank just off the port and heeled over as the tide ebbed so she could no longer deploy her big guns (Figure 90).[25]

Howard could not afford to leave such a powerful vessel in his wake but since the deep draught of *Ark Royal* prevented him from closing in, he sent an assault party in ships' boats to capture *San Lorenzo*. After a ferocious hand-to-hand struggle, during which Moncada died with a bullet in his brain, about a hundred Englishmen boarded and sacked *San Lorenzo*. They singled out a Jesuit priest who had remained aboard 'and beat him up, delivering several blows to his head, calling him "papist" and ripping off his clothes'. He managed to escape only after the English turned their attention to ransacking their prize. The rampage ended when they roughed up a French boarding party and Governor Gourdan threatened to use the guns of Calais to blow the galleass and everyone in her to pieces unless the English immediately

**90.** The galleass *San Lorenzo*, having lost her rudder in a collision, ran aground on a sandbank at the entrance to Calais harbour. While the other English squadrons engaged the scattering Armada, Howard sent small craft to attack *San Lorenzo*. Although she was captured and her Spanish crew fled, the guns of Calais eventually drove the English off (detail from Figure 91).

withdrew. By then Howard was certain that the galleass would never reach Parma and led his squadron into the fierce battle which had already raged for three hours along the fringes of the shoals off the coast between Gravelines and Ostend.[26]

It is difficult to determine what happened next, and in what order. As one eyewitness put it, he knew what had happened to his own ship but 'because of the great smoke could not discern' what happened to other ships; so although many first-hand accounts survive, they sometimes contradict each other. Nevertheless, we can identify three features which marked this battle as radically different from anything that had gone before. First, the superior sailing qualities of the English galleons impressed everyone. According to a staff officer on *San Martín*: 'Their ships were undoubtedly better than anything we have in Spain' – above all 'they could turn around faster than the best-trained horse'. The captain of a vessel in the squadron of Castile concurred: the English galleons 'were the best I have seen in my life, in both artillery and sailing qualities. Even without their topsail and mainsail, the slowest of them travelled much faster than our fastest ship.' This provided a critical advantage in a firefight.[27]

91. At dawn on 8 August, Medina Sidonia found himself exposed with only four ships nearby as the English decided to attack in strength. At lower right three grounded Spanish ships are shown in flames – presumably *San Mateo*, *San Felipe* and *María Juan* – although in fact none were burned.

Second, much of the firefight took place at very close range (Figure 91). Pedro Coco Calderón aboard *San Salvador*, one of the troubleshooters, reported that when Don Francisco de Toledo, in command of the Portuguese galleon *San Felipe*, saw that the English bombardment had destroyed his upper deck, broken both his pumps and left his rigging in shreds, he brought out the grappling hooks and ordered his men to board any ship they could, shouting to the enemy to come to close quarters. In reply, they summoned him to surrender with honour; and one Englishman, standing in the maintop with sword and buckler, called out 'Hey, good soldiers: surrender on the honourable terms we offer you.' By way of answer, a musketeer fired a shot that brought him down in sight of everyone. Encouraged by this success, Don Francisco 'ordered his men to fire their muskets and arquebuses, which caused the enemy to withdraw, whilst our men called them cowards and used opprobrious words about their pusillanimous behaviour, calling them chicken and Lutherans, and daring them to return to the fight'. *San Mateo*, a Portuguese galleon that had played a heroic role in the battle for the Azores in 1582, experienced an even closer encounter with an English galleon. As the two vessels passed one another, their sides scraped together and a single foolhardy Englishman, 'short and swarthy, leapt aboard' *San Mateo*, 'but our men instantly cut him to pieces'.[28]

The third novelty of the action on 8 August was the ability of the English warships to use their heavy guns to inflict crippling damage. They seem to have adopted the tactics used against *Gran Grifón* five days earlier: a group of ships targeted an isolated vessel and then manoeuvred in sequence, discharging their great guns forward, broadside and astern – and they did so rapidly at close quarters: 'The enemies fired their artillery just like we fired our muskets,' Vanegas observed bitterly. Winter agreed: on 8 August 'out of my ship there was shot 500 shot of demi-cannon, culverin, and demi-culverin; and when I was furthest off in discharging any of the pieces, I was not out of the shot of their harquebus, and most times within speech one of another' (which amid the clamour of battle must have been very close indeed). Many Spaniards testified to the devastating results. Father La Torre, aboard *San Martín*, reported that 'cannon balls rained down on us. One passed right through the mizzen mast, another took away a capstan, and a third went through the ship from the stern to the prow.' Vanegas recorded '107 direct hits on the hull, masts and sails by cannon shot, which would suffice to destroy a rock'. According to a Portuguese Jesuit on *San Martín*, 'We later weighed some of the incoming cast-iron rounds aboard the ship, and they were 50 pounds; and although parts of the galleon had seven layers of planking, the cannon balls went through them as if they were just one layer.' Only the heroic efforts of two naked divers with oakum and lead patches halted the water pouring into the hull from the rounds that hit below the waterline. The flagship only got back to Spain thanks to three great hawsers frapped around her hull.[29]

Pimentel's *San Mateo* was less fortunate. Bombarded for four hours by thirteen English warships, 'she became a thing of pity to see, riddled with shot like a sieve'. Moreover, the recoil of her own guns, fastened directly to the hull frames, 'pulled her internal structure apart'. When she began to gape open, 'Pimentel asked the duke to send a diver to see if the inflow of water could be halted', and to send a pilot. Medina Sidonia obliged, and also ordered some ships to bring off the men aboard *San Mateo*, but 'with night falling and the seas rising, they could not get there'. Pimentel refused to abandon his ship, and the wind and tide carried her towards the coast of Flanders.[30]

Meanwhile twelve English warships pounded *San Felipe*. They destroyed her rigging and rudder, brought down her foremast, and (according to Coco Calderón) 'knocked out five guns on the starboard side', while 'an Italian gunner (later killed by a cannon ball) managed to spike one of the big guns on the stern' (if true, an egregious example of sabotage). At 7 p.m. 'Don Francisco de Toledo, seeing that his ship was doomed', fired two guns to request assistance, 'and the *urca Doncella* came alongside. Toledo and 300 of his men transferred to her', but then 'Don Francisco said that if he was going to drown, he preferred to do so aboard his own galleon' and returned to *San Felipe*.[31]

Recalde blamed Medina Sidonia for what happened next. He complained in his journal that everyone had watched the enemy fleet pummel the two galleons:

> until the numerous incoming rounds they received left them unrigged so that they could not sail. Seeing them in this state, neither the flagship nor any of the other ships would help; and when I wanted to do so, the duke sent to tell me that I should stay on course and not hazard my ship for anyone. This brought shame to me and to everyone else.[32]

At dawn on 9 August *San Felipe* lay grounded in the shallow waters between Nieuwpoort and Ostend and, although Toledo and his men got safely ashore, the Dutch sent ships to take possession of what remained of the vessel. Meanwhile three warships from Flushing, filled with English troops, closed in on *San Mateo*. As she had lost her mainmast and had other sails damaged, the men aboard had no chance of escape, yet they fought for two hours, killing several of their assailants. Eventually Pimentel and his men surrendered, 'reserving their lives'; nevertheless, no doubt enraged at the death of their comrades, 'at their first coming aboard' everyone whom the English 'could lay hands upon was either thrown overboard, slain, or wounded'. In the end, 'of 457 which were in the ship at her first coming out of Spain there was but 127 brought ashore; which were such poor souls and so mangled that presently the Governor [of Flushing] sent 60 of them over into Flanders to carry news to the prince of Parma what was become of the rest'.[33]

The English inflicted serious structural damage on several other ships. According to a gunner aboard *San Juan de Sicilia*:

> An enemy squadron surrounded her and subjected her to a bombardment so heavy that she was completely shattered ... Many rounds struck the ship from the top to the bottom, and from the bow to the stern, some below the waterline in places difficult to repair ... The ship was so damaged and battered by cannon balls that she could only move forward with great effort and difficulty.[34]

*Santa María de la Rosa* also suffered serious underwater damage; and *Rata Encoronada* and *Gran Grifón* sustained hull damage so severe that eventually their crews had to run them ashore. Oquendo's flagship, *Santa Ana*, 'lay open through incoming shot, so that the pump was working night and day'. *San Pedro* (Castile), Francisco de Cuéllar's ship, 'was badly holed by very large cannonballs which the enemy fired into her in several places'.[35]

Despite the intense bombardment, only one Spanish ship actually sank during the battle: the Vizcayan *María Juan*. Surrounded and battered by English ships, and as her captain was 'in speech of yielding' to her assailants, 'before they could agree on certain conditions, [she] sank presently before their eyes'. Of almost 300 men aboard only a single boatload survived.

Human casualties aboard many other ships were also high – Vanegas estimated the Armada's overall casualties at the battle off Gravelines at 600 killed and 800 wounded – but perhaps the most serious loss was strategic. As Sir Francis Drake gloated in a letter to Walsingham: 'God hath given us so good a day in forcing the enemy so far to leeward as I hope in God the prince of Parma and the duke of Sidonia shall not shake hands this few days; and whenever they shall meet, I believe neither of them will greatly rejoice of this day's service.'[36]

---

The action waned between four and five in the afternoon, apparently because English ammunition began to run low, but the Spaniards now faced another menace. To escape they must sail, without adequate pilots or charts, into the unknown shoal waters off the Flemish coast. Aboard the flagship:

> The pilots discovered that we were very close to the sandbanks, and the duke sent out *pataches* to warn the Armada that it should steer away from the coast of Flanders and follow him. Our enemies seemed ready to engage with our flagship, and the few ships with us, but we believe that they did not do so because they could see we were heading for the sandbanks. As the wind rose, the pilots told the duke that unless it soon abated it would be impossible to save a single one of our ships.

The pilots did not exaggerate: at this point *Trinidad Escala* 'found herself in water only six fathoms deep, and she needed five'. According to Father La Torre, 'There was scarcely a man aboard the fleet who could sleep that night; we were all wondering when we would run aground.' So the men prayed, or cried to the Virgin to save them, while the chaplains took their confessions, until dawn broke to reveal that their prayers had been answered: 'While we were thus facing disaster, God granted that the wind changed and the fleet managed to sail away north, away from the sandbanks.' Vanegas was surely not alone when he wrote that gaining the open sea again 'seemed like a miracle – and indeed it was'.[37]

Although the miracle allowed Medina Sidonia to rally his ships, the Armada no longer had an objective for which to fight. As Leyva wrote to Recalde shortly afterwards: 'Even before this misfortune we knew that entering the North Sea was a mistake.' Recalde agreed: 'Once we entered the North Sea, the enterprise was doomed.' So what should they do now?[38]

## 14

# 'God blew and they were scattered'

---

### The Armada (almost) Surrenders

AT DAWN ON 9 AUGUST 1588 William Stukeley reported that 'our flagship found itself with only six other ships, with the rest more than a league away. Since the English fleet had followed our great stern lantern, they were close to our flagship.' The apparently miraculous change in the wind to the south-west allowed the Armada to clear the Flemish shoals and enter the North Sea, but it had lost its cohesion (Figure 92).[1]

92. A medal celebrating the dispersal of the Armada, defeated by adverse winds. Obverse: The final battle. Legend: FLAVIT YHWH [in Hebrew] ET DISSIPATI SUNT 1588 ('God blew and they were scattered'). Reverse: Church on a rocky island amid violent waves with the shield of Count Maurice of Nassau below. Legend: ALLIDOR NON LAEDOR ('I am assailed not injured').

The duke and his officers made their confessions and prepared to continue fighting. The guns of *San Martín* fired three times as a signal for the rest of the fleet to rally. To Medina Sidonia's anger and embarrassment this evoked no response, and he sent a staff officer to round up some of the pusillanimous captains. Twenty were brought to the quarterdeck, and Father La Torre recorded the grim dialogue that followed:

'Did you hear the guns?' Medina Sidonia asked furiously.

'Yes,' they replied.

'Then why did you not rally?'

'We thought your flagship was sinking, and the guns were a warning for us to hasten away to safety.'

After a short pause the duke coldly delivered his verdict. 'Hang the traitors.'[2]

In the event Medina Sidonia relented and only one captain was 'hanged from the yardarm of a pinnace and paraded around the fleet to publicize his crime'. He was Don Cristóbal de Ávila, captain of the *urca Santa Bárbara* and Medina Sidonia's neighbour at Sanlúcar. Another defaulter, Captain Francisco de Cuéllar of *San Pedro* (Castile), was spared the death sentence but deprived of his command and placed in the custody of Don Martín de Aranda, the fleet's Judge Advocate General, aboard *Lavia*. The duke demoted several more captains for cowardice, and next day sent staff officers to visit all the ships to warn their captains 'that they would be hanged if they failed to keep their station'.[3]

Suitably chastened, by 11 a.m. the Armada had deployed once more in battle-order; but the English kept their distance, and later that day the duke took in sail and fired a signal gun to summon a Council of War. As they came aboard *San Martín* the senior officers would have noticed many differences since their visit on 29 July – sails riddled with shot, splintered timbers, spars and rigging still tangled on the deck, bloodstains everywhere. The composition of the council also differed. Of those who just eleven days before had endorsed the decision to advance up the Channel with all possible speed, only Bertendona, Gómez de Medina, Leyva, Ojeda and Oquendo sat down with Diego Flores, Bobadilla and the duke. The rest were absent. The English had killed Moncada and captured Don Pedro de Valdés; the prince of Ascoli, Marolín de Juan (chief pilot), Don Jorge Manrique (inspector-general), Bernabé de Pedroso (chief victualler) and Hierónimo de Arceo (the duke's secretary) were all stranded ashore. Recalde even refused to attend when the duke sent a felucca to collect him 'because he felt disheartened by the lack of courage they had all shown, and by the confusion aboard the flagship, and because in some other meetings his opinion had counted for nothing'. He obeyed the duke's second summons, but with great reluctance.

Once his principal officers had taken their seats in his great cabin, the duke summarized the serious problems they now faced: 'The Armada has run out of ammunition because of the large quantity expended in four days of fighting, something rarely seen. Many seamen and gunners (the most essential personnel) have been killed or wounded. Gunfire has badly damaged the galleons and the largest ships, and there is nowhere along the coasts here where we could put in for repair.' The duke asked his officers whether, bearing all this in mind, the Armada should turn back and make another attempt to rendezvous with Parma. Should it seek a friendly harbour in northern Germany or Norway in which to refit, and then return the following spring? Should it hasten back to Spain, now virtually without naval defences, via the north of Britain? Or should it surrender to the English?[4]

There can be no doubt that the council debated this shocking final option. A few days afterwards Leyva complained to Recalde that the duke and his advisers on the flagship 'did not tell us about anything until after it had been decided; neither did they call us to the council except when they discussed starting talks about surrendering to the enemy.' Other sources compiled later said the same. According to Captain Vanegas, aboard *San Martín* though perhaps not present at the council meeting, 'some told the duke that if he wished to save their lives, he should make peace with his enemies', but:

> The duke replied that he was confident that Our Lord and his Blessed Mother would lead him to a safe harbour. Nevertheless, if They willed another outcome, no one would say of him that he had behaved differently from his ancestors. Even though others [one wonders if 'others' referred to the pusillanimous Diego Flores] told him that he could not in conscience allow so many people to drown, he did not want to hear them and instead told them not to speak to him about it any more.

Bobadilla supported the duke's resolve with an impassioned speech. 'This is the day to die fighting in the service of the king, as every member of my dynasty and family has done in the past', adding that 'it is better to die fighting with honour than to fall into the hands of those perfidious and heretical enemies'.[5]

Leyva and Recalde agreed, arguing vigorously 'that we should return to the Channel and that we should complete and execute there what our king commanded', and they apparently convinced their colleagues. According to the duke's campaign diary, the council unanimously decided that if the wind permitted the Armada should turn about, attack the English fleet, and return to the Channel for a second attempt to pick up Parma and invade England. Only if the wind proved contrary would it attempt the long return to Spain via the north of Britain – 'this voyage of Magellan' as Leyva ironically termed it. The senior officers then returned to their ships to wait for a favourable wind.[6]

They did not wait long. The following day, perhaps pressured once again by Diego Flores, the duke ordered the Armada to cut and run. 'On Wednesday 10 August,' Recalde recorded, 'the decision to return to Spain was notified to the whole fleet.' In addition, 'the duke gave orders that all ships should reduce the rations to a half pound of biscuit, a half pint of wine and a pint of water to each person per day, so that supplies should not run out because of the long voyage'. This was a most serious step, because even if all the food aboard was edible – and much clearly was not – this represented a daily intake of fewer than 1,000 calories, scarcely enough to sustain life, let alone health, for an extended period.[7]

Recalde was furious, writing to the duke the following day, 'We have certainly made a dreadful decision, but I trust that God will let us return to Spain.' This proved too much for Medina Sidonia. Although almost invariably courteous, this time he returned Recalde's note with the tart comment, written in his own hand: 'We could not have done anything else, for the reasons discussed at the council that you yourself attended.'[8]

Perhaps fatigue explains the duke's irritation: he would later claim that 'I have not got a wink of sleep, day or night, for a month'. Many others aboard Armada ships complained of exhaustion. A group of prisoners captured on 8 August said that 'the English had bombarded them so much that they had got no rest for four or five days'; and when relieved of his command, Captain Cuéllar protested that he had not slept for ten days. The men were also hungry. Father La Torre reported that the fireship attack left the crew aboard the flagship 'exhausted from all the tasks they had performed the night before, and in preparing the guns – and none of them had eaten'. A Jesuit aboard the Portuguese galleon *Santiago* commented that 'on the day of the battle we did not have time to eat, such was the fury of the combat and difficulty of movement'.[9]

Spirits sagged further as the Armada headed north. One survivor aboard *Gran Grifón* reported that 'everyone was extremely sad, so that no one spoke; nor did the duke respond when we fired a salvo as we passed by his ship'. According to Cuéllar, 'At this time the duke was withdrawn and very sad, and no one could talk to him.' Recalde apparently retreated to his cabin and did not emerge for three weeks.[10]

## The Fleets Disengage

Not long after Medina Sidonia had convened his council to discuss what the fleet should do next, Howard did the same. About 3 p.m. on 9 August the Lord Admiral 'shot off a warning piece and put out a flag of council'. He and his commanders agreed that the Armada would probably not seek refuge in the ports of Germany or Norway, 'a very dangerous place for such huge ships and such a number'. They also considered that the Spaniards would keep sailing north and 'dare not anchor for fear of such a stratagem as lately hath been used' (that is, a second fireship attack – and Howard had indeed prepared ships for that purpose). In any case, without the anchors abandoned off Calais, the council felt sure that their adversaries would 'be utterly undone' if they tried to find shelter in a Scottish harbour. Rather, they predicted that the Armada would 'bear about the north part of Scotland, and so go about to recover their own country again that way'. They therefore resolved that Lord Henry Seymour's squadron should leave that evening 'in the twilight [so] as the enemy might not see' and then 'guard the Thames mouth from any attempt that might be made by the duke of Parma'.

The following day Howard got his principal captains to ratify this controversial decision. They signed an affidavit that they would pursue the Armada until it drew level with the Firth of Forth but no further, because of 'our want of victuals and munitions'. Otherwise, the affidavit boasted, 'we would pursue them to the furthest that they durst have gone'. They were bluffing. As Howard admitted privately: 'We set on a brag countenance and gave chase, as though we had wanted nothing.' In fact they wanted everything: their shot-lockers were empty and their men were starving. Many were mortally ill.[11]

Luckily for the English their opponents knew nothing of this, and for the next two days the two fleets performed a cautious dance (Figure 93). As Recalde noted with a combination of puzzlement and frustration: 'The enemy fleet stayed about one league from us very gallantly, as well they might, because those who had previously fled from us were now chasing us; and to prove the point, whenever four or six of our ships turned back towards them, they fled again.' By the time they reached the Firth of Forth the situation aboard the English fleet had become desperate. According to some reports, 'my Lord Admiral was driven to eat beans and some to drink their own water [i.e. urine]'. Around noon on 12 August Howard made a final bombastic flourish: he drew up his fleet in battle array, 'shooting off a great volley of ordnance for joy', and then led his ships back to the Channel.[12]

93. The two fleets in the North Sea, off Northumberland. Detail from a chart showing the route around Britain and Ireland taken by the Armada in 1588 (Figure 1).

One Armada ship after another now reported difficulties in keeping up with the main fleet. *Lavia* lacked her spritsail and foretopsail; *San Juan de Sicilia* and *Trinidad Valencera* had few sails left to set. On 10 August another vessel from the Levant squadron broke her spritsail mast in a collision with a Portuguese galleon, which also suffered damage. Recalde favoured halting the whole fleet to allow time to repair the damaged ships, because 'the enemy does not want our blood' but 'only wants to give us the freedom to depart'. The duke refused. Although he characteristically blamed himself for all the reverses – 'Our Lord be praised, because it seems He is punishing us just for my sins, to which I attribute everything' – he stuck to his decision to return to Spain as quickly as possible, before supplies of food and water ran out.[13]

Recalde and Leyva continued to fear the worst. The former worried that 'our enemies might return and refresh themselves and wait for this fleet at Cape Finisterre in order to finish it off, instead of following us'. Leyva disagreed. 'I don't think that they will go to Finisterre,' he replied to his colleague. 'Rather we should expect to see them off Ireland. Wherever it is, from what we now know, I shall be sorry to see them: that is something I never expected.' A few days later Leyva became even more pessimistic. 'If it should thunder one night,' he told Recalde glumly, 'our fleet will run away thinking that the enemy has come upon us. God help us and free us from these Columbuses and Magellans.'[14]

The 'Columbuses and Magellans' – namely Medina Sidonia and his staff, led by Diego Flores de Valdés – nevertheless remained resolute. On 13 August they ordered that the mules and horses be thrown overboard to save water (they would drink more water than they were worth as meat). They also issued sailing instructions for the homeward voyage. 'The course that is first to be held is to the north-north-east, until you be found under 61 degrees', then west-south-west to a latitude of 58 degrees (somewhere to the west of Rockall), and thence south-west to 53 degrees (roughly level with Galway), taking 'great heed lest you fall upon the island of Ireland, for fear of the harm that may happen to you upon that coast'. From there they should make a final south-easterly run to the ports of northern Spain. Two days later the duke gave orders for all ships to make full sail: those unable to keep up would have to fend for themselves. Recalde requested permission 'to remain with the slowest ships, to accompany them. Nevertheless, His Excellency sent another order telling me to hoist full sails and follow him, and so I did'.[15]

Many mariners in 1588 were familiar with the north-about route to Spain chosen by Medina Sidonia and Flores. In 1540 James V of Scotland had led his war-fleet from the Forth, past Orkney and the Western Isles to the Clyde; and eight years later a French fleet of six warships and four galleys followed the same route to rescue the young Mary Queen of Scots, whom they brought safely from Dumbarton to Brittany. King James's chief pilot compiled a 'rutter' showing the best itinerary; and the chief pilot of the 1548 French expedition, Nicholas de Nicolay, lord of Arfeville, improved it and in 1583 published a map and rutter that showed exactly how to circumnavigate Scotland. Although the Armada's commanders apparently remained ignorant of Nicolay's priceless work, many officers aboard the Baltic *urcas* would have been familiar with the Armada's route because merchant ships sailing from the Danish Sound to Spain often went that way. The Northern Isles could usually be rounded without difficulty in the autumn with the assistance of the north-easterly Helm Wind caused by high pressure over Arctic Norway, and afterwards ships could progress southwards, even against the prevailing wind, by employing a series of long tacks.

What Medina Sidonia's ships lacked were adequate charts and pilots familiar with the North Atlantic. Published surveys of the west coast of Ireland did not exist, and it therefore remained *terra incognita* for most mariners, except for locals and those who had made a personal reconnaissance (as Recalde had done in 1580). Wagenaer's detailed charts in *The Mariner's Mirror* (Figure 94), which served as a base for those commissioned by Medina Sidonia in Lisbon, went no further than the Moray Firth in Scotland and Dursey Head in south-west Ireland. They were no use in the dangerous waters which lay between (Figure 95).

Medina Sidonia did his best to overcome this lack of knowledge. Although his repeated requests to Parma for pilots familiar with the North Sea bore no fruit, on 9 August he summoned to his flagship all the pilots 'from England, the Netherlands, Castile, Biscay and Portugal, and begged them to do their best. He also offered the foreigners 3,000 ducats, above and beyond whatever His Majesty might give them as a reward, if they saved the Armada.' A few days later the duke encountered Dutch and Scottish fishing boats, from which he 'took some pilots and mariners . . . to carry them for the coast of Ireland, and so into Spain'. On 24 August, a rare day of fine weather, the duke summoned some senior officers and pilots to his flagship to discuss their progress. According to Pedro Coco Calderón:

> I asked the duke our latitude, and he answered '58½° north'. He then consulted Diego Flores de Valdés and the [French] pilot to whom the duke had promised 2,000 ducats (who was a friend of mine). Holding a chart in our hands, we affirmed that their latitude was correct. I said that at all costs we should steer away from the coast of Ireland, but Diego Flores contradicted me. The French pilot shared my opinion, and the duke ordered a change of course.[16]

This is the first recorded example of Medina Sidonia rejecting the opinion of his principal nautical adviser. It would not be the last.

As the Helm Wind carried the fleet past Orkney, it suffered another loss. Medina Sidonia ordered the *patache Concepción de Lastero* to chase and seize a Scottish vessel of similar size, but the *patache* 'began to take on water'. The duke therefore 'ordered the transfer of the weapons and munitions' of His Majesty to the captured ship, and the *patache* sank shortly afterwards (although her crew returned safely to Spain aboard their Scottish prize).[17]

Medina Sidonia also seized at least three more Scottish craft and their crews, and purchased as much water and fish as he could, to augment the fleet's rapidly diminishing supplies. Perhaps encouraged by these unexpected windfalls, on 21 August the duke dispatched one of his staff officers, Don Balthasar de Zúñiga, in a fast vessel with orders to hasten to Spain and make sure its northern ports had enough provisions to feed his men when they arrived. Zúñiga took with him a copy of Medina Sidonia's campaign journal, and confirmation that, despite some losses, the fleet still numbered 112 vessels. The Armada may have been an expensive failure, but it was as yet by no means a disaster.

**94.** Frontispiece of the English edition of *The Mariner's Mirror*, published in 1588. A wide range of contemporary navigational instruments is shown. The sailors' dress is probably typical, although it is doubtful whether they wore fancy ruffs at sea.

# Figure 95. Navigation Aboard Armada Ships

A mariner's astrolabe. A navigator could measure the angle of the sun above the horizon by holding the instrument so it hung vertically (not always easy on a moving deck). Then, pointing it towards the sun at its zenith (noon) he rotated the sight-rule or alidade so that a ray of light passing through the hole in the upper plate fell on the centre of the lower one. The alidade's pointer would then indicate the sun's angular height above the horizon. By consulting mathematical tables for the sun's declination on that date he could convert the angle to latitude.

This example was found hidden under a rock on Valencia Island in 1845 and almost certainly comes from a survivor or victim of the Armada. The instrument is unfinished: although the scale is graduated the numbers have not been inscribed.

**Left**: Sounding lead from *Trinidad Valencera*. These were important for navigating in coastal waters. Not only did they record accurate depths but by securing a sample of the seabed in the grease-filled hollow at the head, knowledgeable mariners could often determine where they were by appearance, touch, smell and even taste.

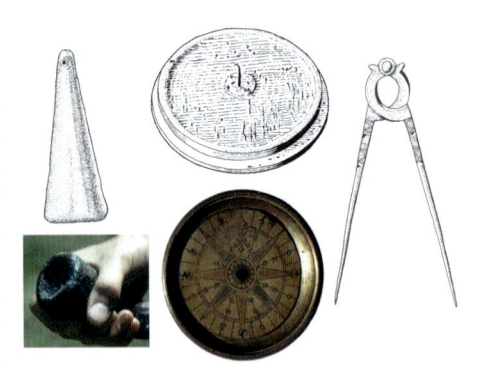

**Centre**: The wooden base of a mariner's compass from *Trinidad Valencera*. A card showing the thirty-two points of the compass with a magnetic strip glued beneath it would have swung freely on the copper pin, to indicate magnetic north. Below it is a compass from a seventeenth-century shipwreck which retains its inked and tinted card. An Armada compass would have been no different.

**Right**: Dividers, like this pair from *Trinidad Valencera*, imply the use of charts, though as we have seen, charts were not available for the final unplanned leg of the voyage.

Clearly, however, the king would want to know (as Leyva put it) exactly how 'we carried out the most important mission in the world, with the whole world watching', and why they had failed. On hearing that Zúñiga was about to leave for Spain, Don Alonso warned Recalde that 'There is reason to believe that this will be to show that you and I are the culprits and that those [on the flagship] were the only ones who fought and achieved everything. May God help us and deliver us from [their] evidence. What more could we desire than that the truth should become known, because we have performed our duty.' Still he worried. 'They say that a great reorganization is taking place aboard *San Martín*, and although they thought of you and me when they found themselves in distress, they will not do so now that they are reorganizing.' Therefore, he confided to Recalde: 'You should know that I am keeping a record of what has happened. You should do the same because if we arrive safely, I will immediately set off for the Court, since I have no position of command to detain me, and I will speak for both of us. That's all for now: nothing more until we meet.'[18]

The two commanders would never meet, because no sooner had Zúñiga left the fleet than fierce storms drove him to Shetland and dispersed the Armada. Father La Torre complained that the summer days became like winter 'and no one dared to go up to join the pilot: instead we all sheltered below.' Vanegas reported that 'because of the cold, few of the negroes and mulattos aboard the fleet survived'. A captain from Seville lamented that the men lacked clothes to withstand the cold; that they sailed 'without doctors or medicine', and that anyone who 'went down with a fever died as if they had the plague, because we had no suitable food to give them and no one to give it to them'.[19]

Four of the slower ships soon lost contact with the main fleet: the big vessel from the Levant squadron, *Trinidad Valencera*, and three *urcas*, *Gran Grifón*, *Barca de Amburg* and *Castillo Negro*. Together they struggled south-westwards for twelve days, making little headway until on 1 September *Barca de Amburg*, her pumps choked, signalled that she was about to founder. Perhaps 250 of the men aboard managed to transfer to *Gran Grifón* and *Valencera* before *Barca de Amburg* went down.

## *Trinidad Valencera*: The First Massacre

*Trinidad Valencera* was a 1,100-ton grain carrier, named after her owner, Alvise Balancer of Venice, and embargoed in Sicily to carry infantry and siege-artillery to Lisbon. Commanded by Don Alonso de Luzón, colonel of the *tercio* of Naples, in June 1588 she was one of the ships that sailed to the Scillies instead of to Corunna, but survived to play a distinguished part in the fighting until 8 August, when the English inflicted serious damage to her hull and sails. On 14 September, with the pumps no longer able to cope with increasing leaks, Luzón decided to make for the nearest land. After sighting the north coast of Donegal he headed east with the wind, perhaps intending to gain the shelter of Lough Foyle, but before he got there *Trinidad Valencera* struck a sunken reef close to the western end of Kinnagoe Bay (Figure 96). With her bow perched on a shallow rock and her stern grounded on the sand, she lay at an angle with only her forepart above water. The situation was perilous but not hopeless, and Don Alonso set off for the shore with four companions in the ship's only remaining boat.

As they approached they saw twenty or so 'savage people' standing on a rock, and when they landed on the adjacent shingle beach 'only with their rapiers in their hands' four or five of the natives helped them out of the boat and 'courteously used' them. Soon a bigger crowd of locals gathered, and the atmosphere became less cordial. The officers were roughly handled, and relieved of their valuables.

Such treatment would prove typical of the responses of the indigenous Irish. When outnumbered or injured, Armada survivors were regarded as fair game for plunder; but otherwise, with rare exceptions, they were not physically harmed and on some occasions, as on this, they were actively assisted. When *Valencera*'s boat foundered, Luzón hired another from the locals, and in due course 500 soldiers and

**96.** The wreck-site (arrowed) of *Trinidad Valencera* in Kinnagoe Bay, County Donegal.

100 seamen came safely ashore. When this boat, too, was lost in the surf, he attempted to hire another, but now the locals were more intent on salvaging what they could from the ship than on rescuing those still aboard. One soldier, attempting to swim his possessions ashore in a floating bucket containing his helmet and a pewter plate, lost them halfway across. Four centuries later, archaeologists found them where they sank (Figure 97). On 16 September the ship broke apart, taking with her the fifty Spaniards still aboard and 'more than 30 Irishmen who had come for plunder'.

On the beach Don Alonso rallied the survivors and led them inland, aiming to reach the west coast where he hoped to make contact with other returning Armada ships. He still commanded a formidable military force: most of his veterans had landed with swords, muskets, arquebuses and a few pikes; but their food and much of their ammunition remained on the wreck. One survivor recalled that 'since we could not find any food, we bought some horses and sustained ourselves by eating them' as they traversed 20 miles of boggy moorland until they reached Culmore Castle.[20]

Negotiations in Latin with the Irish bishop in charge of the castle drew an equivocal response. The bishop asked the Spaniards to make a show of force so that he might surrender, and give them assistance, without compromising his delicate relationship with English troops stationed nearby. Don Alonso viewed this offer with suspicion, and his unease was confirmed when the castle fired a gun, evidently to alert an English garrison. The Spaniards cautiously withdrew, crossed a wide bog and took up defensive positions in a ruined castle, unaware that an elaborate trap was being sprung.

97. An archaeologist with a Spanish helmet and pewter plate in a copper bucket, found between the wreck-site and the shore (*Trinidad Valencera*).

The Inishowen peninsula, on the northern shore of which they had landed, was bounded at its narrow neck by two parallel strips of boggy ground running between the sea-loughs of Foyle and Swilly. Culmore and Illagh commanded the northern crossing of the bog, while at its southern exit stood the much stronger Burt Castle, garrisoned by English soldiers commanded by Major John Kelly and 'affected' Irish troops under the Gaelic chieftain Hugh O'Donnell. Through their ignorance of the local geography the Spaniards were being lured into a killing ground from which few would escape.

Kelly emerged from Burt Castle with 200 horsemen and 200 infantry and arranged a parley. What business, he demanded, had the Spaniards in Her Majesty's dominions? Don Alonso replied that they had been shipwrecked and offered to pay handsomely if allowed to return to Spain. Kelly refused the offer, insisting that his adversaries lay down their arms and surrender as prisoners of war. Don Alonso replied that 'unless he received better terms they would rather die fighting like Spaniards' and returned to his troops; but after two nights and another day of constant skirmishing, during which they used up their ammunition and ran out of food, he realized the game was up. After consulting his captains and his sergeant-major, Balthasar López del Árbol (a veteran who had marched to the Netherlands with the duke of Alba), Don Alonso agreed that every man would lay down his arms and his best piece of clothing in return for his life.

The bargain was not honoured. First, Kelly's men stripped them all – even Don Alonso 'was left naked without his hat' – and left them in an open field, without food, for the night. Next morning, according to two survivors of the massacre that followed, the English separated some thirty men of ransomable status from the common soldiers and seamen. Then 'a line of the enemy's arquebusiers approached them on one side and a line of his cavalry on the other, killing over 300 with lance and bullet'. Only '150 Spaniards managed to escape across a bog, most of them wounded'.[21]

Eventually, some thirty Spaniards and sixteen Italians, 'naked and bare and in a most miserable estate', reached Edinburgh – though some were so ill when they arrived that they 'lie by the ways [streets] in weak case'. Although the city magistrates regarded the refugees as enemies to their faith, they were 'moved to pity their estate, and of Christian charity' gave them garments to 'clothe their nakedness', and something 'to sustain and feed their hungry bellies' until they could 'safely pass to their native countries'.[22]

For some time the fate of those reserved for ransom also hung in the balance. After a nightmare 100-mile forced march to Drogheda with little food or water and, for most, without adequate clothing or footwear, they were incarcerated while their captors haggled over the costs of their maintenance and ransoms. Only a dozen officers, including Don Alonso, lived to pay large ransoms and regain their freedom; the 500 Armada survivors ransomed and repatriated from Dartmouth in 1590 included only eleven 'other ranks' from *Trinidad Valencera*.[23]

## The Fate of *Gran Grifón*

The Spaniards aboard *Gran Grifón* fared somewhat better. The ship carried the general of the *urca* squadron, Juan Gómez de Medina, two infantry companies and a small group of priests and expatriate Irish volunteers as well as her regular crew. Like *Valencera*, in June she had sailed to the Scillies instead of Corunna, but returned safely. She suffered serious damage on 3 August, when more than twenty roundshot smashed into her hull, and the recoil of her own guns further strained the vessel's light construction, causing her seams to leak with the working of the sea. She kept company with *Valencera* until 4 September, the day after the two ships rescued survivors from *Barca de Amburg*. Now alone, *Gran Grifón* beat south-westwards into the Atlantic until 17 September, when a violent storm drove her weakened planks further apart. Everyone on board took turns at the pumps but the following day, fearing that an oncoming sea would sink her, Gómez de Medina decided to run with the weather 'until we reached Norway, where we could repair the ship and supply our needs'.[24]

They sighted St Kilda but then the wind suddenly veered into the north-west, allowing her crew to turn once more 'towards our dear Spain'. The favourable wind held for three days, but then shifted to the south-west, 'driving the ship back to where we were before; but this time we thought we would die because the wind was so strong and the waves reached to the sky, tearing the ship apart. When we could not expel all the water coming in, everyone stopped trying.' The next day was calm, which allowed the crew to 'patch up the worst of the leaks with ox-hides and planks until just one pump could clear the rest of the water inside'; but when the sea and wind rose again, destroying all their repairs, Gómez decided to make for the nearest land.

Somehow the ship negotiated the Orkney archipelago by night, aided by the glow of the Northern Lights – 'God in His mercy at that moment sent us a sudden gleam of light through the dark night, and so enabled us to avoid the danger' – but waves continued to batter the ship. 'Our only thought was that we would all die, and so each of us placed ourselves in God's hands' until at 2 p.m. on 27 September, with ten feet of water in the hold, they espied tiny Fair Isle, midway between Orkney and Shetland. At dusk Gómez de Medina dropped anchor on its sheltered eastern side, and at dawn they drove the ship ashore (Figure 98).

98. The south-east corner of Fair Isle, Shetland. The arrow indicates Stroms Hellier.

99. Stroms Hellier, where the wreck of *Gran Grifón* lies, in the gully to the left of the central spine of rock. The survivors escaped onto the overhanging cliff (left), where some of the team's equipment can be seen.

The *urca* fetched up in the triangular inlet of Stroms Hellier (Figure 99), close to the south-east corner of the island, wedged between the overhanging cliffs and the rocky spine in its middle. Most of those on board escaped by climbing the foremast, which leant against the overhang, but seven perished in the attempt and little could be saved from the ship apart from personal possessions and the squadron's pay-chest.

The situation of the 300 survivors, though improved, was still fraught with danger. Fair Isle was small (less than three square miles) and storm-bound, and there was no immediate prospect of escape. They had salvaged no food from the ship (probably because she was waterlogged). An anonymous survivor, although relieved to be on dry land again, was appalled by what he found:

> The island was inhabited by seventeen families living in hovels, more like shacks than anything else. They are savage people whose usual food is fish, without bread, except for a few barley-meal bannocks cooked over the embers of a fuel which they make or extract from the earth and call turf [peat]. They have livestock – cattle, sheep, pigs – enough for themselves, for they rarely eat meat. They depend mainly on their cows, which produce milk and butter, and use their sheep principally to produce wool for clothing. They are a filthy people, neither Catholics nor altogether heretics. They freely admit that they do not like the preaching of those who come once a year from another island, nine leagues off, but they say they dare not contradict it, which is a pity.

The situation deteriorated as winter approached, because the seventeen crofting families had little to spare for the hungry castaways who (to their credit) made no attempt to seize the islanders' provisions by force. A report later sent to Philip II stated that 'a gentleman of rank [Gómez de Medina] was in the Scottish islands, where the people were very much pleased with him, as he paid well for everything he had of them'. Seabirds and fish were plentiful but could not wholly alleviate the weakness and disease brought on by two months of malnutrition and unimaginable living conditions aboard the overcrowded vessel. Fifty of those who came ashore soon died on the island, 'most through starvation'. They included the ship's master and owner, Burgat Querquerman of Rostock. According to local tradition their bodies were buried in a mass grave: 'Spainnart's Grave', later lost to the sea.

Six weeks passed before they made contact with Fair Isle's landlord on Shetland, Malcolm Sinclair of Quendale, who arranged for a local skipper to collect Gómez de Medina for the short but dangerous crossing to Quendale, where the two men spent a month negotiating for the castaways to be rescued and ferried to the

Scottish mainland. An Orkney chronicle written four decades later provided a graphic (though perhaps apocryphal) account of the last meeting between Sinclair and Gómez de Medina. The latter, 'imagining the people did admire him', made his interpreter ask his host "'if ever he had seen such a man [as himself]?" To which Malcolm replied disdainfully "I have seen many prettier men hanging in the Burrow-Moor'" – site of a public gallows in Edinburgh.[25]

Sinclair arranged for two fishing boats to bring the survivors of *Gran Grifón* to Anstruther in Fife, a journey of 350 miles. Panic gripped those who saw 'a ship full of Spaniards' enter the harbour on the morning of 6 December, since fears of large-scale Spanish landings were still strong. However, tensions eased when Gómez de Medina explained their circumstances and friendly intentions to James Melville, the local Protestant minister. In contrast to Sinclair's insulting assessment, Melville deemed Gómez de Medina 'a very reverend man of big stature, and grave and stout countenance, grey haired, and very humble like, who', after bowing low many times, 'began his harangue in the Spanish tongue, whereof I understood the substance'. Melville was about to reply in Latin, but Gómez had brought 'a young man with him to be his interpreter', who repeated the harangue 'in good English'. He explained how King Philip 'had fitted out a navy and army to land in England for just causes, to be avenged of many intolerable wrongs he had received from that nation', and requested assistance in feeding his men and getting them back to Spain.

Melville showed the strangers 'Christian pity, and works of mercy and alms' – although he could not resist pointing out to Gómez how Scots in Spain 'were violently taken and cast in prison, their goods and gear confiscated, and their bodies committed to the cruel flaming fire for the cause of religion'. The Scots, he continued, 'were better Christians', because they allowed the Spaniards, all in a 'most miserable and pitiful' state, 'to come ashore, and lie all together, for the most part young beardless men, silly, trauchled [distressed] and hungered, to whom for a day or two kale, porridge and fish was given'.

Melville then visited nearby St Andrews, where he found a pamphlet hot from the London presses which gloatingly reported the catastrophes that had befallen the Armada in Ireland, naming the ships and noblemen who had perished (Figure 100). As he returned to Anstruther, Melville brooded on 'the prideful and cruel nature of those people, and how they would have used us in case they had landed with their forces among us', and decided to show the pamphlet to Gómez de Medina, who 'cried out for grief', and wept. Shortly afterwards the survivors, now reduced to barely 250, boarded a ship that took them across the Firth of Forth to Leith, where negotiations for their repatriation began. Technically they were free men, because Scotland remained neutral throughout the conflict and its aftermath.[26]

> # CERTAINE AD-
> ## VERTISEMENTS OVT
> ### OF IRELAND, CONCER-
> NING THE LOSSES AND
> distresses happened to the Spanish Na-
> uie, vpon the VVest coastes of Ire-
> land, in their voyage intended
> from the Northerne Isles
> beyond Scotland, to-
> wards Spaine.
>
> PSALME. 118.
> *This vvas the Lords doing, and it is maruellous in our eyes.*

100. The title page of *Certaine Advertisements Out of Ireland*, 1588, a pamphlet printed (and updated) by Elizabeth's official printer, using information supplied by Burghley. When Gómez de Medina read a copy, he burst into tears.

## Ireland: The Massacres Continue

It was not so in Ireland. Even though there had been no declaration of war, the scattered English garrisons there feared that King Philip might still intend a direct assault. According to an Irish student aboard a ship seized by Howard just before the battle off Gravelines: 'The English greatly fear that the Armada would make for the coast of Ireland and join the Irish, and there they could stay at their ease, awaiting reinforcements from Spain.' It was the same in Dublin, where (according to an apprehensive royal official) rumours of 'the approach of the Spanish fleet doth work wonderful uncertain yet calm humours in the people of this country, who stand agaze until the game be played, not daring to discover their real intentions'. Then, in September, over twenty Spanish ships *did* 'approach' the coasts of all six western counties – Donegal, Sligo, Mayo, Galway, Clare and Kerry – 'well-furnished with men, artillery and munition'; and many Spaniards came ashore.[27]

A letter from Sir Richard Bingham, a veteran of the Smerwick operation and now governor of Connacht, caught the mood of uncertainty and fear. On 18 September he wrote that he had just received 'some further news of strange ships':

Whether they be of the dispersed fleet which are fled from the supposed overthrow in the Narrow Seas, or new forces come from Spain directly, no man is able to advertise otherwise than by guess, which doth rather show their coming from Spain ... I expect very present news either from one place or the other, for by all likelihoods they mind to land. I look this night for my horses to be here, and upon receipt of further intelligence I will make towards the sea coast.[28]

That same day, in London, the Privy Council also received news that 'certain of the Spanish ships being driven upon the coasts of that Realm [Ireland] have of late, by force of tempest and foul weather, made shipwreck' (Figure 101). They instructed Sir William Fitzwilliam, Elizabeth's new Lord Deputy in Ireland, that if 'any ordnance can be recovered, that he should take special care for the safe custody thereof'; and that since they heard that 'diverse Spanish prisoners are taken, their Lordships' pleasure is that great care be had of their safe custody and keeping in some convenient place' until they could issue further orders.[29]

Unfortunately for thousands of Spaniards aboard the Armada, before this letter arrived Fitzwilliam had already initiated a very different course. On 20 September he reported to London that seven Spanish ships had appeared 'which we cannot otherwise judge than to be a force sent of purpose to infest this land'. That afternoon further reports warned him that nine more Spanish ships had been sighted off the west coast, 'which we take to be a force of itself addressed to that place to take landing there'. With the Irish 'so universally ill affected' towards the English, and with fewer than 750 troops at his disposal, Fitzwilliam decided to take no chances. He instructed his officers in the western provinces to locate and seize all 'ordnance, munitions, armour and other goods' salvaged from Armada wrecks, and 'to make diligent search and enquiry' for any 'Spanish enemies', who must 'be executed to the death, of what quality soever he or they may be, and without any respect of favour to be shown to any of them'. To locate them, Fitzwilliam authorized his officers, if 'necessity shall so require, to use any torture upon any person or persons whatsoever as to your discretion shall seem good'.[30]

Some of his agents had already anticipated this grim order. On 15 September leaks forced the *patache Concepción de Castro* into Barrow harbour near Tralee. 'Three of the company swam ashore, and being apprehended confessed themselves to be Spaniards' from the Armada. 'The ship being greatly distressed', the other twenty-four men aboard 'yielded themselves' and were taken to the stronghold of Sir Edward Denny, an English plantation landlord who owned half of County Kerry. They were unlucky. Eight years before, Sir Edward had held a Spanish prisoner taken at Smerwick for ransom, but he had inconsiderately escaped, and Denny swore that thereafter he would kill any Spaniard he encountered. Although he was not at home when the prisoners were delivered, his formidable wife took charge, and after a brief interrogation she had them summarily 'executed because there was no safe keeping for them'. Three tried to save themselves by claiming that they had friends in Waterford who would ransom them, but when pressed they could not, or would not, name them. So they too perished.[31]

On 20 September a large vessel, probably *San Esteban* (Guipúzcoa), came ashore near Doonbeg on the Clare coast. Three hundred men were reported drowned and sixty captured. On the same day, a few miles to the north, another vessel, probably the *urca Santa Bárbara* (once captained by the ill-fated Don Cristóbal de Ávila), was wrecked near Mutton Island. Only four survivors reached the shore. The prisoners from both ships were brought before Boetius Clancy, sheriff of Clare, and after a brief incarceration he had them publicly hanged at or near Doonagore Castle and buried nearby. An adjacent hillock is still called *Croc na Crocaire* (Gallows Hill). Even the noble Don Diego de Córdoba, whose safe return would have commanded a considerable ransom, perished. Tradition asserts that Clancy's name was thereafter formally cursed in the church of Don Diego's home town every seventh year, to ensure that his soul would never escape from purgatory.[32]

A little to the south *Anunciada*, a clumsy Ragusan argosy from the Levant squadron, was also in trouble. In the fight off the Isle of Wight and the battle off Gravelines 'many cannon balls hit her masts and rigging, and some hit below the waterline, so that the sea entered the ship through them, and through the ship's prow, and she started to sink'. Medina Sidonia ordered five *pataches* to escort *Anunciada* out of danger, but on 10 September storms forced them all to take shelter in Scattery Roads, off Kilrush at the mouth of the Shannon. A few days later another vessel joined them: the 450-ton *urca Barca de Danzig*, also in danger of foundering because 'she carried no ballast, but instead carried salt' which clogged the pumps. When the commander of the Portuguese infantry aboard accused 'her Flemish sailors of having sabotaged the pumps, so that the vessel would remain there', the master, the pilot and 'seven or eight of the said Flemings got into the ship's boat and headed for the shore', watched by '300 or 400 Irish savages'. An English official among them noted that the boat flew 'a small white flag in their stern', and when he challenged them in Spanish 'they confessed openly that they were of the king's army coming from Flanders and from Spain. We have kept them yet from the land although they promised us to do no harm to the country.' Observing this drama, the Armada officers sent over *pataches* which brought the fugitives back.

Since the ship's carpenters could not make *Anunciada* seaworthy, Captain Stefan Olisti Tasovčić sent them to *Barca de Danzig*. No doubt realizing that salt, not sabotage, had compromised the pumps, they managed to patch up the ship while the *pataches* transferred the soldiers, munitions and victuals, as well as the ballast, from *Anunciada*. The operation took a week, and when it was completed Olisti set fire to his ship to prevent her falling into English hands. The officers then paid the bosun of the *urca* 60 crowns, with a promise of 400 more if he could bring the vessel back to Spain. *Barca de Danzig* and the *pataches* left the Shannon on 19 September 1588. They escaped just in time.[33]

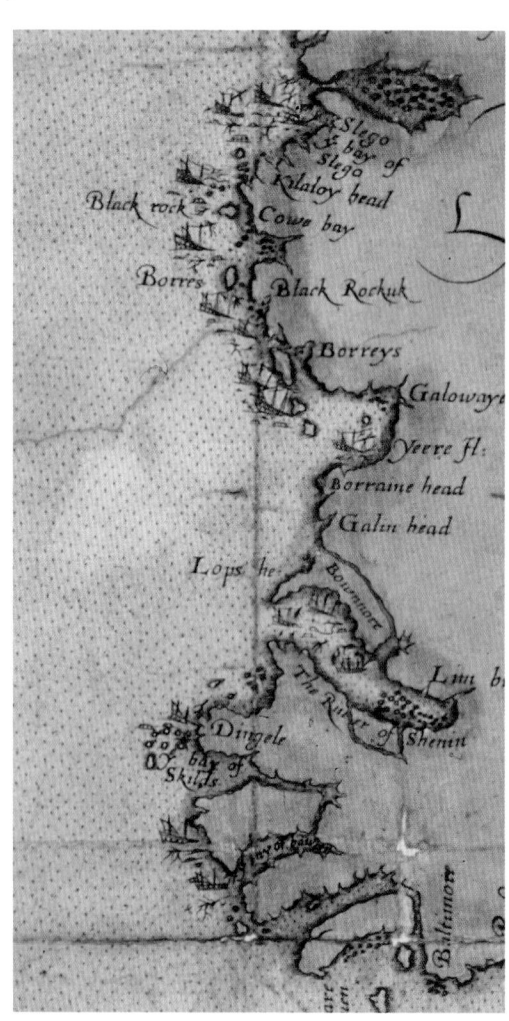

101. Detail from Figure 1, showing a string of wrecks along the west coast of Ireland from Counties Sligo (top) to Kerry.

# 15

# From Dispersal to Disaster

——≪≪✤≫≫——

## Blasket Sound

DUTCH, ENGLISH, ITALIAN AND SPANISH contemporaries all agreed that the Armada campaign took place amid highly unusual climatic conditions, probably reflecting a strong El Niño event combined with high volcanic activity at lower latitudes which affected normal weather patterns. Perhaps they contributed to the formation of two Atlantic depressions, spawned by tropical storms in the Caribbean, which battered the coasts of Europe on 18 September. Three days later they merged into a single deep depression centred off north-west Scotland, drawing in great masses of cold Arctic air. The resultant gale was described by an English official in the west of Ireland as 'a most extreme wind and cruel storm, the like whereof has not been seen a long time, which put us in very good hope' that many of the Spanish ships 'should be beaten up and cast away upon the rocks'. He would not be disappointed (Figure 102).[1]

One of the most vivid accounts of the consequences of the 'cruel storm' for the Armada comes from the Castilian galleon *San Juan Bautista*, commanded by Marcos de Aramburu, a Basque mariner with extensive experience of Atlantic navigation and a veteran of the expedition to the Strait of Magellan. Aramburu kept a journal where he recorded not only weather conditions, but also how he and the other officers calculated their ship's position. On 30 August they used an astrolabe to measure the sun's altitude at midday and so determined their latitude as '58 degrees north'. Calculating longitude proved more difficult. They dropped a sounding lead that registered '125 *brazos*' (about 120 fathoms or 720 feet) and examined the tallowed end closely when it was hauled aboard (see Figure 95). Seeing 'neither gravel nor sand', Aramburu concluded that they had reached a rocky shelf '95 leagues from the Irish coast', almost certainly the Rockall Bank, 57½ degrees north and some 300 miles north-west of Ireland – remarkably close to Aramburu's calculations. But, like other contemporary navigators, he was unaware of the North Atlantic Drift, a gentle current that slowly and invisibly pushed ships ever further east.[2]

By then Aramburu had lost sight of other Armada ships except for *Trinidad*, one of four merchantmen attached to the Castilian galleons. In zigzag legs, making use

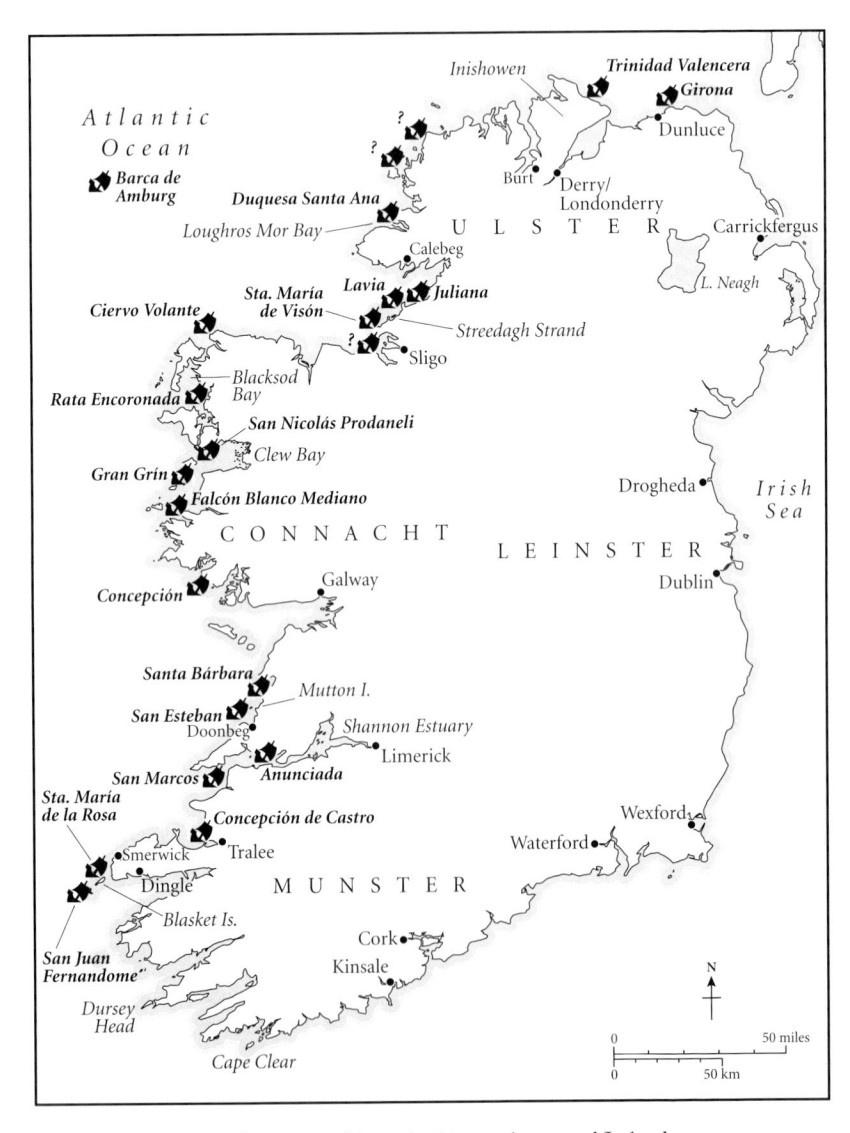

102. Location of Armada shipwrecks around Ireland.

of every remotely favourable wind, the two ships tacked southwards. On 9 September Aramburu calculated they were at 54 degrees and 100 leagues away from the coast of Ireland; but just before dawn on 11 September, to their horror, the lookouts saw land only a league (about two and a half miles) to their east. Although the pilots could not identify the location, they knew they must avoid it, so steered west. The following night, after another storm, *Trinidad* disappeared, but on 15 September Aramburu's lookouts again saw land: the Blaskets, a cluster of islands off the most westerly tip of Europe. They also saw, to their surprise, two other Armada ships: Recalde's flagship, *San Juan de Portugal*, and a *patache*, probably *San Esteban*.

On 15 August Medina Sidonia had ordered all ships to put on full sail and follow him, and had refused Recalde's request to protect those that could not keep up. Recalde disobeyed and soon fell behind the main body to escort a group of twenty-two lame ducks; but storms dispersed the ships until by 8 September they numbered only eight. Another storm four days later scattered further vessels until only the *patache* remained with Recalde. On 14 September, according to his journal, *San Juan* 'almost ran up upon some islands' and 'nearly lost the ship because we came so close under full sail in the darkness and with a strong gale. And so we turned seaward and in the morning landward again, trying to clear the headland, which we were unable to do; so we remained in great confusion as to whether we should turn seaward or search for a harbour to carry out repairs.' The following day, in the teeth of a strong westerly wind that made it impossible to make any headway out to sea, Recalde decided to 'search for a harbour'.

It was here that Aramburu joined him, 'not knowing the coast, and despairing of any remedy'. Not so Recalde – even though he and his ship were both in desperate straits. He later reported that he had suffered eleven attacks of 'tertian fever' (malaria) since the battle off Gravelines and each time 'I was bled because we had no purges, truly a cause for regret'. A sailor from *San Juan de Portugal*, captured when he came ashore in search of drinking water, confirmed that Recalde 'came not out of his bed' until 'the morning that they came upon this shore'. Some of his shipmates, when captured and interrogated by the English, stated that of the 500 soldiers on the ship (including survivors picked up from other vessels), 'there are 200 dead'; and that of the 110 Portuguese and Biscayan seamen who manned the ship when she left Lisbon, only eighty-five were left. They reported that English gunfire had killed fifteen men on 31 July, and twenty-five more in other Channel fights, with 'the rest dead of sickness'. Now, four or five men died every day from hunger and thirst despite the ship being 'one of the best furnished with victuals'. They complained that all the water aboard 'stinketh marvellously' and that 'the best that be in the admiral's ship are scarce able to stand, and if they tarry where they are any time, they will perish'.

As for their ship, she was 'many times shot through, and a shot in the mast, and the deck of the prow spoiled'. One 'mast is so weak, by reason of the shot in it, as they dare not abide any storm, nor to bear such sails as otherwise they might do'.[3]

Despite these defects, on 15 September Recalde turned his great galleon to run with the wind straight towards the shore, where a white line of breaking water ran from the northern point of Great Blasket Island to the neighbouring islets of Young and Beginish. Aramburu and the *patache* followed in blind faith, close on his stern. They had few options: either the admiral had taken leave of his senses and was leading them all to certain destruction among the crashing reefs, or he knew something about this landfall that they did not.

In the lee of Great Blasket and its adjacent islets and reefs lies a broad stretch of sheltered water, protected from the Atlantic rollers. It is marked on modern charts as a storm anchorage, and the entrance from the north-east side is wide and easy; but a maze of reefs blocks all entrances from seaward save a narrow channel difficult to negotiate. Recalde's journal states that he passed 'between two rocks through such an extremely narrow place (no wider than the yardarm of the ship), as to defy belief'. Aramburu later described it as 'wide as a ship is long'. Even today small powered craft only negotiate it in calm weather. In a heavy westerly sea, the reefs that break the force of the rollers and create the shelter beyond become themselves a terrifying maelstrom of mountainous waves and rocketing spume.

It was through this passage, and under such conditions, that Recalde conned his 1,050-ton damaged flagship – and at speed, too, for otherwise the ship would have had insufficient steerage for her inefficient whipstaff-operated rudder to bite. *San Juan*'s massive keel, 20 feet or more below the surface, must have scraped the bottom (Figures 103, 104). Once through, the galleon dropped anchor and held

103. Blasket Sound and Islands, looking south-west. Great Blasket Island looms left of centre, and to its right the fringing reefs extend northwards, with the islands of Beginish and Young fronting them. These combine to shelter from the west to north-west quarter the anchorage off Great Blasket's beach which Recalde and his followers reached by negotiating a narrow passage through the reefs.

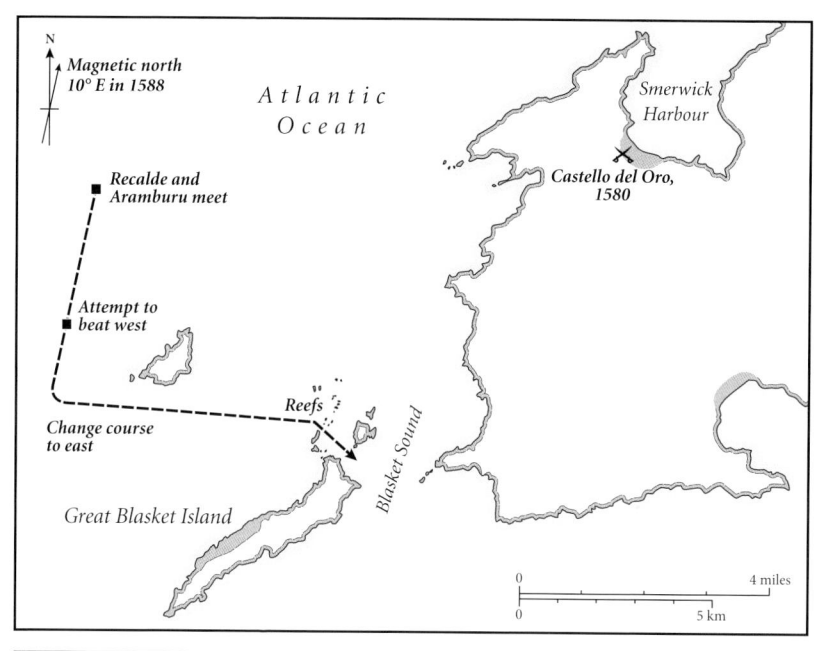

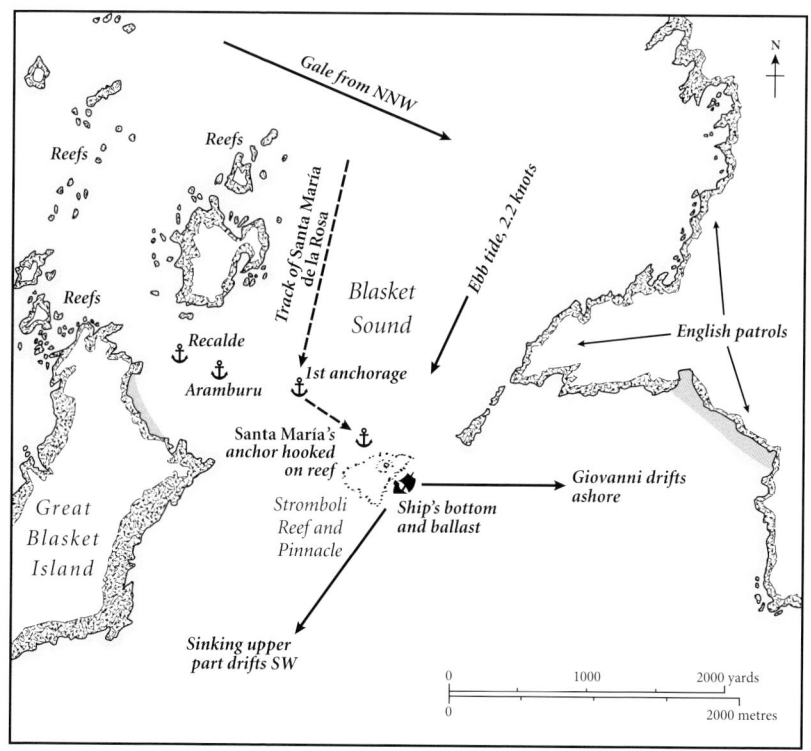

**104.** Top: route followed by Recalde and Aramburu into Blasket Sound. Bottom: location of the wreck of *Santa María de la Rosa*, and the sequence of events of 21 September 1588.

firm just off the clean white beach that curves at the foot of Great Blasket Island's north-eastern slope. Further north, off Beginish, Aramburu's *San Juan Bautista* likewise loosed her ground tackle and rode safe, and the *patache* moored clear of the big galleons. Thanks to Recalde's detailed knowledge and outstanding seamanship the three vessels were now sheltered from all quarters except the north-east, the direction from which would blow a fair wind for Spain.

How had Recalde known of this remote anchorage, and its terrifying entrance from seaward? In his journal Recalde acknowledged 'the advice of some of the Scots who we had brought on board', but he also drew on first-hand knowledge – the only way a seaman could familiarize himself with a strange shore in the days before adequate charts. By an extraordinary coincidence, Recalde had explored the adjacent coastline for two weeks in 1580 after depositing troops, artillery and stores at nearby Smerwick (see chapter 4). While searching for lost members of his scattered fleet it would be strange if a seaman of his calibre had not observed that the lee of Great Blasket Island – only six sea-miles from Smerwick – might shelter a ship caught in a westerly gale. Professional curiosity would surely have prompted him to reconnoitre the hazardous passage through the reefs by which such shelter could be gained. Eight years later, filed in the vast mental bank of Recalde's sea experience, this knowledge would save both him and his ship.

Recalde would also know what had happened to the men he left at Smerwick, and realized that a similar fate might await anyone from his ships who landed on the forbidding shore opposite. Nevertheless, since he desperately needed food and water, he had little choice. On 16 September he sent a launch containing 'a Spanish-speaking Flemish sailor, a Burgundian, and a Scot ashore' with a letter to 'the commander or governor of that land', informing them that 'we were merchantmen bound for Flanders, that we had been driven there by the storm, and that we were willing to pay for fresh stores'. He added a reminder that Irishmen had always received good treatment in Spain, and that providing him with supplies 'would further our ancient friendship'. The launch pulled away into the tossing waters of Blasket Sound and vanished from sight against the dark mainland cliffs two miles to leeward.[4]

Unknown to Recalde local officials captured and incarcerated his men in the little walled town of Dingle and forwarded the admiral's letter offering friendly trade to the nearest English garrison, pleading for immediate assistance. Next day, 17 September, Recalde dispatched his longboat with a landing party of fifty soldiers to negotiate with the local population for supplies, but 'they found only large rugged rocks against which the sea pounded, and ashore marched some 100 arquebusiers, bearing a white standard with a red cross. We feared they were

English.' They were indeed. A few days later, looking down on the Spanish ships from the Dunquin cliffs, Captain James Traunte assured his superiors that 'They are in a most wild road [anchorage], and themselves in a miserable state. We have 200 men watching them upon the shore every day ... We stand here in no fear of them, for they are too much afraid of themselves.'[5] Despite this bold statement, whether the bedraggled soldiers reported to be coming ashore from Spanish ships were survivors of the dispersed Armada or a fresh invasion force from Spain, the sparse, ill-equipped and disorganized English troops stationed in the wild mountains and western coasts of Ireland could not afford to let them get inland and rally the disaffected Celtic clans.

In the event, Recalde made no further attempts to reach the mainland. Instead, every day he sent men in the ships' boats to the uninhabited Great Blasket Island 'to refresh themselves and to take on water' from the tiny spring that still wells above the beach. They also found 'some pigs and many rabbits' which provided much-needed fresh meat. The admiral also worked hard to make his ships seaworthy. Aramburu stood in need of cables, for he had only the one attached to his anchor, so Recalde gave him two of his. In return Aramburu sent over a 30-quintal bow anchor, which Recalde lacked.

Lope de Vega, soon to become Spain's most prolific playwright, later claimed that he had started to write his epic poem *La hermosura de Angélica* while serving as an arquebusier 'at sea, surrounded by the rigging of the galleon *San Juan*, beneath the banners of the Catholic King'. If true, then the first few days anchored in Blasket Sound may have provided the leisure he needed 'to take up his pen'.[6] It did not last. On 21 September the worst gale of that whole wild autumn came howling out of the north-west, and like many sudden Atlantic gales spawned by cyclonic conditions in mid-ocean it arrived without warning out of a clear sky. According to Aramburu the 'wind came with the most terrible fury, but cloudless and with little rain. The flagship of Juan Martínez [de Recalde] drifted down on our ship, but having smashed our great lantern and damaged our mizzen-tackle and rigging, she used another cable to secure herself.' Then, around noon, Aramburu watched in horror as *Santa María de la Rosa* (Guipúzcoa) struggled into Blasket Sound by the wider northern entrance nearer the mainland:

> She fired a shot on entering, as if seeking help, and another soon afterwards. All her sails were in tatters except the main foresail. She cast a single anchor, because that was all she had, and with the tide coming in from the south-east and pounding her stern she stayed there until two o'clock, when the tide began to ebb. As the tide turned [to flow in the opposite direction], the

ship began to swing on her anchor and dragged to within two cable-lengths from us, and we dragged with her. We could see that she was going to sink. They tried to hoist the main foresail, but she sank with all on board, not a person being saved, a most extraordinary and terrifying thing.

Recalde, too, looked on helplessly as *Santa María* suddenly 'sank without a single man out of the more than four hundred that we knew she carried escaping or being seen'.[7]

There was in fact one survivor: Giovanni Manona from Genoa, son of the ship's pilot, reached the shore at Coumenoule Strand 'naked upon a board', where Traunte's men captured him. Manona described the disaster to his captors in vivid terms. *Santa María* was already badly damaged: 'shot through four times, and one of the shots was between the wind and the water, whereof they thought she would have sunk; and most of her tackle was spoiled with shot'. When she 'broke against the rocks in the Sound', chaos broke out, with 'the gentlemen thinking to save themselves by the boat, [but] it was so fast tied as they could not get her loose, thereby they were drowned'. Then 'one of the captains slew this examinate's father [the pilot] saying he did it by treason'.[8]

The brutal slaying of the ship's pilot by 'one of the captains' – that is, one of the infantry officers aboard – presumably reflected the underlying tension between soldiers and seamen on the Armada. Two pieces of evidence support this. The first is Aramburu's statement that after striking the rock *Santa María* attempted to hoist her foresail. The second is the discovery, in 1968, of *Santa María*'s anchor hooked foul on the northern edge of the reef on which she had been impaled. Taken together these details suggest that someone on board – probably the pilot Manona – gave orders to raise the foresail and cut the anchor cable in a bid to bring the ship's head round so that the gale might carry her towards the mainland shore and relative safety (just as it bore his son Giovanni) before she sank. Did an argument break out between Manona, as he tried to get the ship off the reef, and the panic-stricken soldiers, who may have hoped for rescue from one of the other ships? They probably also feared the treatment they would receive from the English troops on shore.

Giovanni Manona gave his interrogators the names of some of the officers and noblemen who perished in the ship, starting with the prince of Ascoli, whom Manona asserted was 'the king's base son', who had boarded *Santa María* off Calais with ten other 'gentlemen of accompt'. We now know that the prince remained in Calais and returned safely to Spain, so perhaps Giovanni's claim arose from a mistranslation or misunderstanding by his captors. Or perhaps the lowly son of a foreign pilot saw the corpse of one of the 'gentlemen of accompt' aboard *Santa María* washed ashore in his fine clothes and misidentified him as Ascoli? Whatever the reason, Manona's story has survived in local legend: a tall stone on a green mound above Dunquin is still known as *Uaig Mhic Rí na Spaínne*: 'Grave of the son of the king of Spain' (Figure 105).⁹

By contrast we can confirm the presence on the ship of three individuals named by Manona. One was the ship's master and owner, Martín de Villafranca, scion of a noted whaling family from San Sebastián. His father had built the ship the year before the Armada sailed, almost certainly to serve as a mother-ship for the Newfoundland whale fishery, and he remained in command after she was embargoed in Lisbon. When he died there, his son took over until he drowned in Blasket Sound. The others were Francisco Ruiz Matute and his brother, company officers in the *tercio* of Sicily. Their surname is inscribed on two pewter plates recovered from the wreck. These, now in the Ulster Museum, are their only monument (Figure 106).

105. The standing stone overlooking Blasket Sound, traditionally the grave of the king of Spain's son.

106. Pewter plate inscribed 'Matute'. Captain Francisco Ruiz Matute and his brother sailed aboard *Santa María de la Rosa*.

*Santa María de La Rosa* was not the only ship to enter Blasket Sound on 21 September. A few hours later the *patache Isabella* (Vizcaya) and *San Juan Fernandome* (Castile) joined them. The latter arrived 'with her mainmast sprung and her hull opening'; and 'as she came in, her foresail was torn to pieces'. The next day Recalde sent his pilots and other experts 'to inspect the ship to determine whether she was seaworthy'. After they reported that 'she was not fit to sail', Recalde oversaw the evacuation of the two infantry companies (one led by Don Diego de Bazan, son of the marquis of Santa Cruz) and some of the powder, artillery and victuals aboard. Gunpowder was brought out first: as always, Recalde's primary concern was for the fighting efficiency of his ships, and he personally supervised its removal. Next came artillery and victuals, including bread and wine. At a moment like this, when he and his comrades were half dead from privation and sickness, and all seemed hopeless, to transfer heavy guns from a sinking to a damaged ship in difficult sea conditions in order to bring them back to Spain to fight another day speaks volumes for the indomitable will and unbreakable spirit of Recalde and his men.[10]

On 26 September Recalde ordered *San Juan Fernandome* to be burned. By then Aramburu had used ropes and spars to extract his *San Juan Bautista* from the Blasket anchorage by the hazardous passage through which he had come, between the western reefs. Recalde and the two *pataches* made their exit on 28 September, sailing 'so close to a promontory that at one point it was possible to jump ashore from the galleon, and our deliverance from that was one of the greatest miracles ever seen'. All four ships got safely back to Spain.

## The Galleass *Zúñiga*

Another Armada ship had an equally miraculous return to Spain, although it took much longer. *Zúñiga* managed to keep up with *San Martín* until 2 September, when her rudder broke yet again and she fell behind. Although those aboard were desperately short of food and water, Medina Sidonia could offer no assistance and simply told them to 'do the best they could'. Five days later they encountered Recalde and his group of lame ducks, but were advised to head straight for Corunna or any other port they could find.

On 15 September, still at the mercy of the wind because of her broken rudder, 'for want of meat and water, and partly through error for lack of pilots', the galleass sought shelter in Liscannor Bay (County Clare), 'such a perilous place that it is hard to escape'. After riding out the great gale of 21 September, two men came ashore 'feigning themselves to be merchants, in the hope the rather to get flesh and water for money without suspicion'. They found the inhabitants to be 'savages devoted to England' who would not allow them to 'obtain water; nor would they sell us food; so by necessity we took up arms and obtained supplies by force' – the only known example of Armada soldiers using violence against the Irish. Some of the men were captured and executed. One carried a copy of Medina Sidonia's sailing instructions for the return to Spain, which his captors translated and sent to London (see chapter 14).[11]

After spending a week replenishing supplies and repairing the rudder, the galleass was rowed back to the open sea and headed south, until a week later contrary winds in the latitude of the Scillies carried her far to the east. On 4 October, 'with not a drop of water and no more victuals, so that if we had delayed one more day we would all have died', *Zúñiga* approached the French port of Le Havre; but 'without sails or rudder', and 'taking in water because the ship was open at both bow and stern', she ran aground on the harbour bar.

She was not the first Armada ship to do so. Four days after leaving Corunna, *Santa Ana*, flagship of the Vizcaya squadron, lost contact with the main fleet and eventually anchored in the roadstead off Le Havre. When the duke of Parma became aware of their situation, he ordered the disembarkation of the 50,000 ducats in gold that she carried and her immediate departure for Corunna; but before she could leave a flotilla of eight English warships, resupplied after the battle off Gravelines, arrived. On 11 September they bombarded her 'from dawn until 2 p.m.', causing so much damage that she could no longer manoeuvre. A week later a storm drove *Santa Ana* ashore and she was wrecked.

A month later local boats saved *Zúñiga* from this fate, dragging her to safety, and she spent six months in Le Havre making repairs. A muster of those present on her arrival showed 204 soldiers, 85 sailors and 175 oarsmen – but their number soon dwindled. First, the rowers staged a mass escape, and although most were recaptured and placed under guard on the ship, the town's governor insisted that sixteen Frenchmen among them should remain free. Then more than twenty soldiers, led by their lieutenant and two sergeants, deserted and headed home. Misfortune continued to dog the ship: two of the captains appropriated money intended for their men, and storms thwarted three attempts to leave for Spain. Only in August 1589, having jettisoned twelve guns and most of her munitions, did the galleass make it home.

## More Armada Wrecks in Ireland

The gale of 21 September wrecked other Armada ships in Irish waters (see Figure 101). *Gran Grín* was driven into Clew Bay, County Mayo. She sank off Clare Island and although 200 men aboard drowned, the senior officers managed to bring 100 ashore. For a time they remained on the island, virtual prisoners of Dowdarra Roe O'Malley, and when some made a spirited attempt to escape by stealing their captors' boats the O'Malleys killed them. A few gentlemen 'were spared from the sword till order might be had from the Lord Deputy how to proceed against them'. No doubt this reprieve temporarily raised their spirits, but Sir William Fitzwilliam sent 'special direction' that they should be 'executed as the rest were', so they too perished.[12]

The Ragusan *San Nicolás Prodaneli* probably went down nearby at Toorglass on the Curraun Peninsula. Only ninety of the 300 men aboard got ashore, and most were immediately executed. Their captors initially spared two Spanish infantry captains 'and some five or six Dutch boys and young men', taken 'after the fury and heat of justice was past . . . in respect they were pressed into the fleet against their wills'; but on Fitzwilliam's express order they too were executed. When some 500 Armada prisoners were ransomed and repatriated from Dartmouth in 1590, only two came from *San Nicolás Prodaneli*.[13]

The fate of those aboard three other Armada vessels wrecked in Connacht was equally grim. The *urca Ciervo Volante* sank on the north coast of County Mayo, perhaps at Inver in Broad Haven; *Falcón Blanco Mediano*, another *urca*, foundered on a small island near Inishbofin (County Galway); and *Concepción* (Vizcaya) sank near Mace Head (County Galway) at or near a spot traditionally named *Duirling na Spainneach* (Spanish Landing). A local chieftain initially helped the twenty survivors but later, mindful of his own survival, he handed them over to Sir Richard Bingham, governor of Connacht. Most of those aboard these three ships drowned, and the rest were killed – some instantly: one Melaghlin McCabb butchered eighty survivors on the beach with his gallowglass axe. Bingham rounded up other survivors and imprisoned them in Galway town until in early October, having spared just 'ten of the best' for ransom, he marched the remainder – perhaps 300 men – to an Augustinian priory on the outskirts of the town, where they were all executed and thrown into a common grave. The final testament left by one of these unfortunate prisoners has survived. Don Antonio de Ulloa y Sandoval specified in detail the Masses to be said for his soul over the next twenty years in various churches in his home town before making a single legacy: 100 ducats to his cousin 'whom I beg to forgive me for my offences against him'. Chillingly, his testament stopped in mid-sentence: 'The hangman will not allow me more time to . . .' (Figure 107).[14]

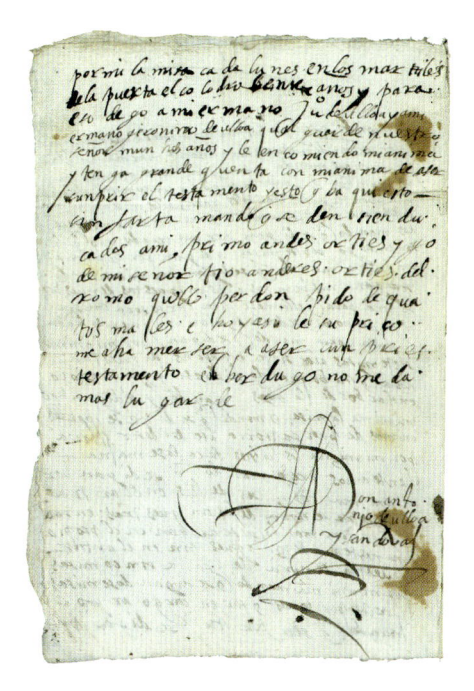

107. The last will and testament of Don Antonio de Ulloa y Sandoval from Córdoba, written in his own hand as the hangman waited impatiently to dispatch him ('*el verdugo no me da más lugar de . . .*').

Don Luis de Córdoba, who had proudly carried the campaign banner through the streets of Lisbon on 25 April, was one of the few who managed to save himself from the massacre (perhaps because he failed to mention his role as standard-bearer and lied about his elder brother, the marquis of Ayamonte, whom he told his captors was merely 'a gentleman of 1,000 ducats a year'). Don Luis was luckier than he knew. Bingham boasted that of the '15 or 16 ships cast away on the coast' of Connacht 'there have perished 6,000 or 7,000 men, of which there have been put to the sword . . . and executed one way or other about 700 or 800 or upwards'. The Armada prisoners ransomed and repatriated in 1590 included only five survivors from *Falcón Blanco* (three Spanish soldiers, a German sailor and a twelve-year-old cabin boy from Danzig), and only two men from *Ciervo Volante*.[35]

Catastrophe also befell three merchantmen from Bertendona's Levant squadron: *Juliana*, *Lavia* and *Santa María de Visón*. After parting company with the flagship as they rounded Scotland they joined Recalde's lame ducks, but on 7 September lost contact. A week later all three anchored close to Inishmurray Island, at the southern end of Donegal Bay, to make repairs, replenish stores and 'transfer men on *Juliana* to the other two ships, because she was sinking'. It was a hazardous location, without shelter and open to all winds except an easterly. Erris Head, which they would have to clear before heading south, stood fifty miles to the west.[16]

The Armada's Judge Advocate, Don Martín de Aranda, sailed aboard *Lavia* with Francisco de Cuéllar, deprived of his command and under arrest after the debacle off Gravelines. Of all the accounts written by Armada survivors, by far the most detailed and dramatic is Cuéllar's long letter to a friend after he reached safety in Antwerp more than a year later.

The three ships were still trapped in their exposed anchorage when on 21 September:

> A great gale hit us broadside on, with the waves reaching the sky, so that the [anchor] cables could not hold and the sails could not be set. We found ourselves driven ashore on a beach of very fine sand, hemmed in at either end by huge rocks. The likes of this had never been seen, for within an hour all three ships were smashed to pieces. Fewer than three hundred men escaped. More than a thousand drowned, among them many important people.

The gale had driven the ships onto Streedagh Strand, a two-mile-long beach backed by wind-blown dunes and a lagoon, ten miles north of Sligo (Figures 108, 109). They grounded on the unyielding sand a couple of hundred yards from shore, where the surf pummelled and smashed their hulls. Many of those aboard desperately attempted to escape but the deep draught of the ships meant they had grounded in 20 feet or more of wind-whipped water, with massive pieces of debris dropping and swirling all around. Don Diego Tellez Enríquez, a senior infantry officer on one of the other two ships, whom Cuéllar called 'the hunchback [*el corcovado*]', had himself battened below the deck of the ship's boat together with three companions and 16,000 ducats in jewels and coin. The boat was cast adrift in the hope of being blown ashore, but when seventy panic-stricken survivors scrambled aboard she capsized. The boat came ashore upside down, and the wreckers on the beach hacked her open. By then three of her occupants were dead, and Don Diego expired as his clothes and valuables were ripped from him.

Cuéllar was torn by indecision. He could not swim, and death seemed certain if he stayed on the disintegrating *Lavia*, but his prospects if he reached land seemed no less dreadful. The beach, he observed, 'was full of enemies who went about dancing and skipping with glee at our misfortunes. Indeed, when any of our men reached the shore, two hundred savages and other enemies fell upon him and stripped him of what he had on until he was left stark naked … All of this could be plainly seen from the battered ships.'

108. Detail of a map depicting the three Streedagh wrecks, sent by Sir Richard Bingham to Lord Burghley, who endorsed and dated it 20 April 1589.

109. Streedagh Strand in a gale. The wreck on the beach is of eighteenth-century date.

In an instinctive bid for survival Cuéllar and Aranda grasped a loose hatch-cover and launched themselves into the surf. Almost immediately a wave swept over their makeshift raft and Cuéllar went under, colliding with a piece of timber that gashed his legs. But he struggled to the surface and regained the hatch-cover. Aranda, however, weighed down by coins sewn into his clothes, lost his grip. Like many others he sank to the bottom and drowned.

Cuéllar reached the beach covered in blood, but somehow escaped the attentions of the ghouls ambling among the bodies that littered the strand, stripping them of whatever they possessed and clubbing them down if they offered the slightest resistance. Inch by inch, and in acute pain, Cuéllar dragged himself into the comparative shelter of the dunes. Soon afterwards:

> A very nice young gentleman, quite naked, came up to me. He was so dazed that he could not speak, not even to tell me who he was; and at that time, which would be about nine o'clock at night, the wind was calm and the sea subsiding. I was then wet through to the skin, dying with pain and hunger, when up came two men – one of them armed and the other with a great iron axe in his hands. We remained silent, as if there was nothing wrong. They grieved to see us, and without speaking a word they cut a quantity of rushes and hay, covered us well, and then went off to the shore to ransack and break open money-chests and whatever they might find, together with more than two thousand savages and Englishmen from garrisons nearby.

Cuéllar now fell into a deep sleep, from which he woke during the night to find his companion dead, and English cavalry galloping along the beach to pillage the wreckage and kill any survivors. He lay undiscovered until the following morning, when he slipped inland to start his long and perilous journey to safety.

Some weeks later Lord Deputy Fitzwilliam rode along the strand and viewed 'the bay where some of those ships wrecked, and where, as I heard, lay not long before 1,200 or 1,300 of the dead'. Scattered along the beach he observed timber from the three wrecks more 'than would have built five of the greatest ships I ever saw, besides mighty great boats, cables, and other cordage answerable thereunto, and some such masts, for bigness and length, as in mine judgement I never saw any two could make the like'. The lord deputy did not exaggerate. *Juliana*'s great rudder, discovered in 1985 by underwater archaeologists in the shifting sands off Streedagh, was 36 feet long.[17]

Cuéllar first sought sanctuary at Staad Abbey, a small religious foundation two miles inland, but as he came close he 'found it deserted, the church and its images of saints burned, everything destroyed, and inside the church twelve Spaniards hanged there by the English Lutherans'. Hurrying from this awful place he entered a large wood, where he found a 'rough savage woman' hiding her cows from the English troops quartered in her village. Confused, he returned to the beach in search of food, where he found and buried the body of Don Diego Tellez Enríquez *el corcovado*. Then, barefoot and in great pain he hobbled inland until three men and 'an extremely beautiful young woman of about twenty' relieved him of 'a gold chain worth more than a thousand *reales* [100 ducats]' and shredded his doublet to find the forty-five gold coins hidden there. After that they treated him more kindly and dressed his wounds. Somewhat recovered, he headed further into the mountainous interior 'where lay a good country belonging to a great savage chief who was a friend of the King of Spain'. On the way he sheltered in a deserted village by a lake (almost certainly Glencar), where he found other fugitive Spaniards. The group made their way to the territory of another 'great savage chief', Sir Brian O'Rourke, a sworn enemy of the English. Here Cuéllar stayed for some days before heading towards the castle of another 'great enemy of the queen of England and all that belonged to her': the MacGlannahie [McClancy], whose main stronghold was the reputably impregnable island tower at Rossclogher in Lough Melvin.

Cuéllar had chosen well. Not only did his Spanish manners and penchant for fortune-telling enchant the ladies, including McClancy's wife ('very beautiful in the extreme and especially kind to me'), but the weapons and ammunition he and his comrades had gathered from the wrecks, not to mention their professional expertise, provided a welcome boost to McClancy's military resources. The timing was fortuitous. Goaded by years of McClancy cattle-raiding and generally rebellious behaviour (now aggravated by the succouring of Spaniards), Lord Deputy Fitzwilliam was at this moment assembling a task force of 1,800 men in Dublin to extirpate the troublesome clan. McClancy's proposed defensive response was simple. He and his people would vanish into the hills they knew so well and re-emerge only after the English went home for the winter (it was now November). Cuéllar was more bullish: fill Rossclogher with muskets, ammunition and supplies for six months, and he and eight comrades could hold out almost indefinitely. They did. Lacking artillery and with a 200-yard stretch of open water to cross in full view of the nine sharpshooters on Rossclogher's commanding battlements, the Lord Deputy could do little apart from hang two Spanish prisoners in view of the defenders, an atrocity that only strengthened the latter's resolve. Winter snows fell early that year, and after seventeen miserable days thre frozen and bedraggled English army trudged back empty-handed to Dublin. The delighted McClancy emerged from the hills and offered Cuéllar his sister's hand in marriage. Though no doubt flattered by the gesture, the Spanish captain tactfully declined and next morning slipped quietly away.

The rest of Cuéllar's journey was less adventurous. Three weeks later he reached Ireland's north coast where, helped by the O'Cahan chief (in whose village he once again became friendly with 'some exceedingly beautiful girls'), he arranged a passage to Scotland. He made the crossing in April 1589 in what he describes as '*una pobre barca*' – probably a skin-covered *curragh*, which despite its fragile appearance was an excellent sea-boat.

Few others survived the wrecks on Streedagh Strand. Perhaps a dozen escaped to Scotland; two captains paid a ransom of 600 ducats each; and the Armada prisoners ransomed in Dartmouth in 1590 included only seven men from *Lavia*, five from *Juliana* and three from *Santa María de Visón*. Almost all these prisoners had 'a large wound in the face', probably acquired as they came ashore, but were lucky to survive at all given that the three ships had left Corunna with over 1,000 men aboard.[18]

Nevertheless, they fared better than the men aboard three ships successively commanded by Don Alonso de Leyva. His unofficial flagship, the Genoese merchantman *Rata Santa María Encoronada*, had been in the thick of the fighting throughout the Channel battles, but now, like her Levantine sisters, she could not keep up with the flagship. Moreover, like the other Mediterranean merchantmen, she had been severely strained by the recoil of her own artillery.

On 17 September the damaged *Rata* lay off Blacksod Bay in County Mayo. Leyva had decided to enter this wide haven to make repairs and take on fresh water; and after sending a reconnaissance party ashore he anchored off Fahy, a creek at the south-eastern end of a bay notorious for dangerous tide-rips. Four days later the storm that wrecked so many other Armada vessels drove *Rata* towards the sands of Tullaghan Bay, where she grounded immovably. At this point Giovanni Avancini, the ship's master, and fourteen Italian mariners selfishly seized the ship's boat to get ashore, where they abandoned it and fled inland. This forced Don Alonso 'to set men aland upon empty casks to fetch her again, whereby they saved themselves from drowning when the ship was distressed'.

After he had ferried his men and their weapons ashore in good order, Leyva set fire to *Rata* and started to fortify nearby Doona Castle while he took stock of the situation. Shortly afterwards news arrived that the *urca Duquesa Santa Ana* had anchored on the other side of Blacksod Bay. She, too, had suffered serious damage in action and needed repairs, as well as food and water. Leyva and his men abandoned Doona and marched twenty-five miles overland to reach *Duquesa*, with portable goods 'of any value, as plate, apparel, money, jewels, weapons and armour, leaving behind victual, ordnance, and much other stuff'. Overloaded and leaking she set sail, but contrary winds blew her northwards and after four days Leyva decided to make for Scotland. When another storm threatened, the ship anchored in Loughros Mor Bay, Donegal. But the gale 'broke asunder all their cables, and struck them upon ground, whereby Don Alonso and all his company were enforced to go on shore taking all their goods and armour with them' once more.

In the process Leyva was seriously injured by a capstan bar, 'in such sort as he was neither able to go nor ride'; instead, from a sedan chair he directed efforts to find a defensible location, choosing a ruined castle on an island in Kiltooris Lough. He probably hoped to hold out there until aid arrived from Spain, but food soon ran short, and when news arrived a week later that the galleass *Girona* was at

'Calebeg', known today as McSween's Bay, Leyva decided to lead his men almost twenty-five miles overland to reach it.[19]

For the next two weeks Calebeg bustled with activity as the 1,300 survivors stripped another Armada ship which had grounded nearby for materials to repair *Girona*. Once again, with so many mouths to feed in a barren land, victuals soon ran short. Don Alonso may have considered negotiating a ceasefire but then survivors from *Trinidad Valencera* arrived and described in lurid detail 'the great treachery towards Don Alonso de Luzón and his men' after they surrendered. 'Some of his captains told him that they would starve to death if they all embarked on the galleass', because the overloaded and crank vessel was unlikely to survive the perils of the open Atlantic, but Leyva declared that 'he would rather die at sea like a knight than let his king know that he had surrendered to such vile people'. On 26 October *Girona* therefore set out for neutral Scotland instead of Spain.

Since *Girona* could not accommodate the full complements of three ships, Leyva decided to leave some men behind to fend for themselves. A Greek seaman from *Girona*, 'a poor wretched creature', said that he 'with many such like were thrust out of the galleass when Don Alonso de Leyva was received into her' – but they were the lucky ones. Off the north coast of Antrim *Girona*'s poorly designed rudder failed, and she smashed onto the rocky fang of Lacada Point, close to the Giant's Causeway (Figure 110). All but nine of the 1,300 men crammed aboard

110. Lacada Point, Co. Antrim (centre), where the galleass *Girona* was wrecked.

perished among the kelp-covered rocks. The survivors – eight Spaniards and one Italian – later visited the beaches nearest to the wreck 'to see if they recognized any of the drowned men; and although many bodies lay there, we could not identify any of them'.[20]

We now know from artefacts recovered from the wreck-site, as well as from the testimony of the survivors, that the dead included Leyva and the thirty-six gentlemen who formed part of his entourage; Thomas Perrenot, nephew of Cardinal Granvelle, and thirteen followers; and the count of Paredes with his twelve retainers.

Giovanni Avancini and the other Italians who had abandoned Leyva in Tullaghan Bay and fled inland fared no better. A local landowner 'took them prisoners and spoiled them of all they had' before murdering them in cold blood.

## The 'Tobermory galleon'

A week after *Girona* sank, most of the 300 or so men aboard *San Juan de Sicilia* (yet another member of the ill-fated Levant squadron) perished 100 miles away in Scotland. The ship had served with distinction until the final battle off Gravelines when she collided with *María Juan*, after which a group of English warships surrounded both vessels and bombarded them. *María Juan* sank that evening, and *San Juan de Sicilia* almost foundered because 'the enemy flotilla fired their guns with such terrible effect that only Divine Providence kept her afloat', despite some hits 'high and low, and from prow to poop'. In addition, 'the enemy did so much damage that we had to replace all her sails'.

Even with new sails *San Juan de Sicilia* could not keep up with the flagship, and in late September she dropped anchor in Tobermory Bay, a sheltered natural harbour on the island of Mull, off the west coast of Scotland (Figure 111), to take on water and provisions, and carry out urgent repairs. Sir Lachlan Maclean of Duart, the local clan chief, agreed to help the Spaniards in return for a modest if unconventional price: the loan of a company of Spanish infantry and a couple of field guns to settle his outstanding feuds. The ship's officers readily agreed, though they demanded five Maclean hostages as surety. For more than a month the ship lay at Tobermory, making repairs and taking on supplies (later valued at 8,000 ducats), while 100 Spanish veterans made short work of Sir Lachlan's enemies ashore. They 'looted, wrecked and spoiled' the adjacent isles, 'treasonably raised fire, and in most barbarous, shameful and cruel manner, burnt the same isles, with all the men, women and children inside'. Meanwhile, trouble was brewing elsewhere.

111. The sheltered natural harbour at Tobermory on the Isle of Mull, Scotland, where *San Juan de Sicilia* sank (arrowed).

To hedge his bets Maclean had reported *San Juan*'s arrival to King James in Edinburgh. The English ambassador in Scotland, William Asheby, immediately relayed this news to London, suggesting that one of the queen's ships 'might have a great prize of this ship for she is thought to be very rich'. Two weeks later he received electrifying news: 'The Spanish ship' had been 'burnt, as it is reported here, by the treachery of the Irish [Gaelic-speaking Scots], and almost all the men within it consumed by fire.' Another informant soon confirmed the news: an explosion had killed Maclean's five pledges, two captains, and all the soldiers and seamen aboard. 'Nothing was saved that was in her at that instant; and what was unburned is now sunk under water.' Only the men who had come ashore to fight Maclean's enemies survived.[21]

Mystery surrounds the cause of the devastating explosion on 5 November 1588. A subsequent Spanish account blamed the accidental ignition of gunpowder spread on the deck to dry, but an English account written a few months after the event reported that 'John Smollett, a man that had great trust among the Spaniards, entered the ship and cast in the powder a piece of lint and so departed.' Smollett was apparently a Dumbarton merchant who may also have been an English undercover agent. Asheby suggested as much when he informed Walsingham enigmatically of 'the party that laid the [explosive] train, whom we hear say be come into England: the man known to Your Honour and called Smallet'.

In December, Asheby reported the arrival in Edinburgh of '18 Spaniards that were saved out of the ship burnt in the Isle of Mull'. One was Juan de Soranguren, who had served on *María Juan* and just before she sank transferred to *San Juan de Sicilia*. He was on deck when her powder exploded 'and the force of the explosion threw me into the air. I fell into the sea, and since I received no injury, I swam to shore'. Six months later he obtained a passage to Norway where he joined another group of Armada survivors.[22]

**Table 15.1.** *Relative survival rates of the Armada's squadrons.*
The loss of Armada vessels off Ireland and Scotland was greater among the galleasses and merchant ships than the fighting galleons, and grreater among Mediterranean merchantmen than those built on the Atlantic seaboard.

| SQUADRON | Total ships left Corunna | Failed to reach Channel | Captured/aground/sunk in Channel | Wrecked or disappeared on return voyage | Returned | % lost | Lost/damaged on or soon after return | % lost by end of 1588 |
|---|---|---|---|---|---|---|---|---|
| Portugal | 11 | -- | 2 | 1 | 8 | 27% | -- | 27% |
| Castile | 16 | -- | -- | 4 | 12 | 25% | -- | 25% |
| Galleys | 4 | 4 | -- | -- | 4 | 0% | 1 | 25% |
| Galleasses | 4 | -- | 1 | 1 | 2 | 50% | -- | 50% |
| Vizcaya | 14 | 1 | 1 | 1 | 11 | 21% | -- | 21% |
| Andalucia | 11 | -- | 1 | 1 | 9 | 18% | -- | 18% |
| Guipúzcoa | 14 | -- | 1 | 2 | 11 | 21% | 1 | 29% |
| Levant | 11/12 | -- | -- | 8 | 3/4 | 73/75% | 1 | 82% |
| Urcas | 22 | 1 | -- | 9 | 12 | 45% | 1 | 50% |
| Pataches & zabras | 23/26 | 1 | -- | 4 | 18/21 | 22/19% | -- | 22/19% |
| Total | 128/132 | 7 | 6 | 31 | 91 | | 4 | |

## Getting the Survivors Back to Spain

At least two Armada ships ended up in Norway. One, unnamed, was apparently wrecked near Trondheim; another, *Santiago*, an elderly Flemish *urca*, came ashore near Bergen (Figure 112). *Santiago* had carried mules to haul the siege-guns, their handlers, and thirty-two married Spanish soldiers and their wives.

Storms forced *Santiago* to 'run towards Norway, because it was closest', but her hull 'had come open, so that even though we worked the pumps day and night' the ship took on so much water that she no longer responded to the rudder. As she approached the narrow fjords leading to Bergen she ran onto rocks and sank. A hundred Spaniards scrambled ashore and salvaged ten barrels of powder and other munitions, which they offered for 'the hire of a ship which would carry us to the lands of King Philip'; but the ship's captain refused to transport them. Some survivors left in December and sailed round Scotland and Ireland to reach Lisbon in January 1589; the rest hired another ship to take them to Spain, but she foundered on the coast of Denmark. The senior infantry officer, Alonso de Olmos, led thirty-two soldiers, their wives, three seamen and twelve young muleteers overland to Hamburg, but there 'they were forced to separate, each travelling by himself for greater safety, since some of the territories on our route seemed dangerous'. Olmos himself headed for Genoa, where he found a ship that landed him at Alicante in July 1589, a year after his departure from Corunna. The plaintive petitions to the government for their wage arrears and travel costs record the individual odysseys of other survivors of *Santiago*, the 'ship of the women'.[23]

Only one Armada vessel was wrecked on the coast of England: the hospital-ship *San Pedro Mayor*. Storms in the Tagus and again off Corunna had caused

112. Detail from Figure 1, showing two Armada ships wrecked on the coast of Norway.

serious damage, and when she anchored off Calais the master, pilot and several sailors jumped ship under cover of darkness. After the battle off Gravelines *San Pedro* lost contact with the flagship and sailed on alone. On 28 September, desperate for food and water, her crew anchored off Kilrush near the mouth of the Shannon, where they saw *Anunciada*'s burned-out hull. The next day ten men went ashore and met 'some people in savage costume who received them under a flag of truce'. Some of the 'savages' had mastered Latin, and so 'five of them came aboard the ship' to negotiate a price for supplying water and food. The process went smoothly until two companies of English soldiers arrived. They seized and stripped ten of the Spaniards ashore and marched them towards Galway. A Catholic landowner arranged a ransom of 200 ducats for four of the prisoners, and did his best to save the rest, but their captors insisted on taking them to Galway town, where Sir Richard Bingham executed them along with the survivors of other wrecks.

After two weeks buying food and taking on water *San Pedro* departed for Spain, but storms soon forced her to anchor again. Once the weather improved her crew found they could not recover the anchor – their last one, since they had abandoned the others off Calais – so they rashly cut the cable and again set sail for Spain. Once more storms drove them eastwards 'until we were within sight of Plymouth'. On 6 November they approached Hope Cove, near Salcombe in Devon, where 'we struck some rocks because we had no anchors left'.

English boats swiftly 'got the men ashore, perhaps 200 in all, whom they stripped but otherwise did not harm'. After that, locals ransacked the ship. A magistrate later reported that *San Pedro* 'lies on a rock, and full of water to her upper decks ... There hath been some plate and certain ducats rifled and spoiled at their first landing, both from their persons and out of their chests.' He predicted that the ship itself 'will prove of no great value; the ordnance is all iron, and no brass; their ground tackle all spent'; and although she had left Spain with 'drugs and pothecary stuff as came to 6,000 ducats', seawater had ruined most of it. In any case, soon afterwards the ship was 'through tempestuous weather broken in pieces and scattered on the seashore'.

At first the Privy Council ordered the local magistrates to separate the 'persons of quality' and cause the rest, 'being Spaniards born, to be executed and destroyed, and dealt with by martial law, as most pernicious enemies to Her Majesty and the realm'; but before these draconian measures could be carried out the Council relented. They authorized the release of the French, Dutch and German prisoners, and later the Portuguese on condition that they enlisted with the forces of Dom Antonio, the Pretender. They also declared that since the Spanish soldiers and seamen 'were driven into this realm by chance, and came not of any set purpose', they should be treated as shipwrecked mariners. Therefore the local authorities, not the Crown, must shoulder the cost of their upkeep.

This delayed their release. The Council had already indicated to Parma that the queen would accept a ransom of '15 ducats a man, one with another', for rank-and-file prisoners held in England, but their envoy became trapped behind enemy lines and could not deliver his offer for several weeks. Parma considered the price excessive and made a counter-offer: the equivalent of one month's wages per man, plus reimbursement of reasonable expenses (the norm for ransoming prisoners in the Low Countries Wars). The Privy Council refused, and Parma eventually agreed to pay 17 ducats a man, plus expenses, because (he reasoned) although it seemed excessive, 'it is right to relieve and help the soldiers and vassals who have risked their lives, with such love and loyalty, for the service of God and His Majesty'. Not everyone in the Low Countries shared this benevolent attitude. The prisoners from *San Pedro* suffered a final humiliation when the officers who had deserted the ship off Calais happened to visit England, 'and when they heard that we were in prison they came to jeer at us'.[24]

In all, more than 2,000 soldiers aboard the Armada escaped to the Spanish Netherlands from England and Ireland, and a further 800 from Scotland.[25] In December 1589 three ships left Dunkirk under a flag of truce to pick up more prisoners whom their English captors had assembled at Dartmouth. The following month a special commissioner, Carlos Longin, compiled a list of 494 men and boys from the Armada whom he repatriated to Spain. To demonstrate exactly how he had spent the money entrusted to him, Longin compiled a register that detailed how much each prisoner received from him in ransom, daily food allowance and new clothes for the bracing voyage home. He also recorded each man's age, place of birth, ship (and unit for the soldiers), as well as any distinguishing marks. The largest contingent (almost half) came from *Rosario*, and the next largest (at least sixty-five men) from *San Pedro*, including some survivors from *San Salvador*, many still showing burns (Longin referred to them as '*los quemados*'). They arrived at Corunna in February 1590.

Longin did not manage to free all the Armada prisoners in England. One captive presented himself as an ordinary soldier named 'Emanuel Alfonso, tall and handsome', but someone must have recognized and denounced him, because Longin crossed through his original entry in the register and wrote in the margin: 'He's called Don Melchor de Pereda', a staff officer. The English now demanded 1,000 ducats for his ransom, and Longin noted that 'He was left behind because of his offence.'[26]

Most of the Armada prisoners in Scotland also languished for several months. Although technically neutral in the conflict between England and Spain, King James had no wish to antagonize Elizabeth and jeopardize her subsidies. Moreover, as he told the envoy who delivered the queen's thanks for his support, if Philip prevailed in England, Scotland would be next – or in James's colourful phrase: 'The king of Spain's favours towards him would [have] been like Polyphemus to Ulysses: that he should be the last man he would eat.'[27] The situation was complicated by a strong pro-Spanish faction in Scotland and Gómez de Medina of *Gran Grifón*, as the highest-ranking Armada officer in the country, became a target for intrigue soon after he reached Edinburgh. On the one hand Elizabeth demanded his extradition on the grounds that he possessed detailed knowledge of the South Atlantic; on the other hand a group of Scottish Catholics saw him as a means of securing Spanish assistance for their cause. Early in 1589 an English agent reported that 'Don John de Medina and diverse captains of the Spaniards' enjoyed great credit with 'diverse of the nobility here ... On Sunday last I dined with [the earl of] Bothwell, where I found four Spanish captains whom he entertained.' Many suspected Bothwell's loyalty to the king even before he provided Gómez de Medina with a small vessel and an exhortation to 'let the Spanish king know how many well-wishers he hath in this country, and to procure but 4,000 Spaniards, good shot, and leaders, with a sum of money to be brought hither by his conduct with speed'. Gómez also took with him in Bothwell's vessel twenty-eight survivors from *Grifón*, including the Irish priests and expatriates who had come with him from Spain – men who could expect no mercy if they fell into enemy hands.[28]

Despite a close encounter with English ships, Gómez de Medina eventually reached Cadiz, where he showed himself to be a man of honour. A merchant ship from Anstruther, the town where he and his men had landed after their misadventures in the Northern Isles, had been impounded by the port authorities, and her crew imprisoned by the Inquisition. Mindful of the succour that *Grifón*'s survivors had received in this small Scottish seaport, he set about securing their release. Although Philip rarely interfered with the work of the Inquisition, he now urged Inquisitor-General Quiroga to investigate the reason for the detention of any Scots in his cells and, unless they had committed an offence on Spanish soil, ordered their release. Otherwise, he reasoned, 'Armada prisoners in Scotland might suffer if the Scots here should suffer'. Gómez de Medina eventually sent the ship from Anstruther home with kindly messages to his Protestant benefactors.[29]

Gómez also worked hard to secure the repatriation of his own ship's company still stranded in Scotland. He had not shared his escape strategy with the two infantry captains who had sailed with him aboard *Grifón*, and when they learned of his stealthy departure they denounced his conduct. In a bitter letter to the king they complained that Gómez, 'forgetting his duty and his obligation to your Majesty's colours, secretly seized a vessel which he had promised would transport one of our infantry companies, and departed on her alone'. They also pleaded with Parma to send ships large enough to transport the Spanish troops now scattered among the towns of Lothian and Fife. According to William Asheby, apart from the *Grifón* men, most were survivors from the Irish shipwrecks (including Cuéllar), with some recently arrived from Norway, but he reckoned that only 'about 400 are serviceable men. The rest, some sick, some lame, [are] such miserable wretches as they will never be able to do any service.' In addition, 'many are dead since their arrival here', and others were 'better entertained here in noblemen's houses than they look to be in following the wars, so as some will be loath to part from hence'.[30]

At this point two English galleons, *Vanguard* and *Tiger*, anchored off Leith. In less troubled times King James might have regarded this as a high-handed act by his powerful neighbour, but now he welcomed the English officers to his Court at Holyrood and issued passes for the crews to come ashore and sample the pleasures of the Scottish capital. Trouble soon followed. After carousing fraternally with Scots and Spaniards in a dockside tavern, harsh words were exchanged and in the ensuing fracas a Spanish soldier fatally stabbed an English trumpeter. The diplomatic turmoil that followed threatened to subvert the delicate process of negotiating the Spaniards' repatriation.

Then Elizabeth unexpectedly granted safe conduct to Dunkirk for all Spaniards in Scotland, and money arrived from Parma for their passage. As Asheby had predicted, a few Armada survivors stayed put, 'sprinkled about in noblemen's houses, choosing rather to lead a serving man's life at ease in this country than to follow the wars in Flanders in want and danger'; and Maclean of Duart held back the Spanish troops still in the west. But on 4 August 1589 the bulk of the survivors set sail for Flanders in four chartered Scottish ships.[31]

At first all went well. Elizabeth's guarantee was scrupulously observed as the transports sailed along the English coast, but as Cuéllar was to discover:

> A treaty had been made with the ships of Holland and Zeeland, by which it was agreed that they should put to sea and lie in wait for us off the bar of Dunkirk and put us all to the sword to the last man. The Dutch carried out this order and waited for us for a month and a half at the said port of Dunkirk, and there they would have caught us all but for God's help.

In the event, the Dutch captured only one ship and peremptorily threw everyone on board, Scotsman and Spaniard alike, over the side. The three other vessels ran ashore in an effort to escape and broke up in the surf under heavy fire from the gunboats. More than half the Spaniards perished. But once again Cuéllar survived.

## The Laws of War

The stark variations in the treatment of Armada prisoners by their captors require explanation. Against the savagery of this episode in autumn 1589 we must set the cordial negotiations between Parma and the Dutch for the ransom of some 200 Armada survivors six months earlier. Likewise the massacre of over a thousand Armada survivors in Ireland in September and October 1588 is mitigated by the orderly ransom of 500 others in Dartmouth in January 1590.

Initially, Elizabeth herself rejoiced that God had 'of his mercy delivered some of our enemies upon that part of the coast of Ireland where (not many years since) they had as good payment as now they have had'. She referred, of course, to the massacre in 1580 of the garrison of the Castello del Oro at Smerwick, who had also landed without a declaration of war and whose fate had been publicized by pamphlets issued by her government's printer (see chapter 4). Since Bingham feared that the Armada ships approaching Connacht in 1588 carried an invasion force, just as Recalde's ships had done eight years before, he made haste to kill them before they could recover, join together and overwhelm the isolated English garrisons under his command.[32]

To justify his brutal conduct Bingham could cite the prevailing Laws of War, which allowed lethal force against the surprise attack by an enemy, especially when (as in 1580 and again in 1588) that enemy had made no formal declaration of war. Executing those captured 'after the fury and heat of justice was past', by contrast, was deemed a war crime. Even Bingham felt that such men should be spared and ransomed, but Lord Deputy Fitzwilliam overruled him and hanged them as he made his way through Connacht. Fitzwilliam also sent a posse from Dublin with orders 'to make diligent search and enquiry for such of the Spaniards and Italians of the dispersed fleet as came with purpose to invade her Majesty's kingdom, and to apprehend and take them, and thereupon to execute them to the death by martial law without respect of person'.[33]

The military historian Cyril Falls explained these extreme actions as follows: 'If the Spaniards, after resting and being fed, had broken out of captivity or been rescued by Irish sympathisers, they would have become a deadly menace to English power.' Fitzwilliam himself feared that if Leyva received reinforcements from Spain, 'I see not how but that before I could have given your Lordships advertisement, Her Majesty might have been dispossessed of Ireland.' His attitude only softened nine months later, when he paid £10 to 'Signior Aurelia Sappa' for conducting 'all such Italians as remained in Dublin and were of the late Spanish fleet, having nothing to pay their expenses or transportation, to supply their wants at Her Majesty's charge'.[34]

In England, too, attitudes towards Armada prisoners softened with time. When the Spaniards aboard *Rosario* arrived, one of their captors reported that 'We would have been very glad they had been made water-spaniels when they first were taken', because 'the peoples' charity unto them (coming with so wicked an intent) is very cold'. The local magistrates incarcerated almost 400 prisoners in a building in the grounds of Torre Abbey, still called the Spanish Barn, before returning them to *Rosario* under guard to await ransom.[35]

These men were lucky because they escaped the privations of those who kept up with Medina Sidonia. On 8 September, 'off the Irish coast, the soldiers on the ships with the duke received a new issue of powder, match and ball for their arquebuses so that they would be ready in case the enemy attacked'; but they escaped this peril and on 21 September (the day of the great storm in the North Atlantic) the flagship, her hull frapped with three great hawsers, and the few ships still in her company sighted the Spanish coast. Those aboard 'were so pleased that they behaved like children, but their joy did not last (because the joys of this world seldom last long) because the pilots did not know where we were'. They therefore sailed along the coast until the next day someone recognized Santander. The duke fired his guns to summon help, and two *pataches* came out with pilots. The duke unchivalrously leapt into one *patache* while 'most of the gentlemen aboard the flagship' leaped into the other and they all headed for the shore. Eight other warships managed to follow *San Martín*, but (according to a Portuguese Jesuit) 'all of us who entered the port of Santander were sick and disfigured [*doentes e desfigurados*]' from hunger and thirst – no doubt because on the last forty-five days of the voyage some had received only thirty days' rations, and a few received less. Several ships had run out of drinking water before they reached Spain.[36]

Diego Flores also tried to jump into a *patache* and escape to shore, like the duke, but his brother officers forced him to re-embark and take command. Almost immediately another storm struck, but on 23 September Flores led twenty-five large ships into Laredo. There was just one casualty: the *urca Doncella*, which had bravely rescued men from *San Felipe* under fire during the battle off Gravelines, sank just as she entered the harbour 'because Diego Flores would not send assistance'. That same day 100 miles to the east Miguel de Oquendo led eight ships and two *pataches* into the adjacent harbours of Pasajes and San Sebastián 'in such a state that God only knows how we got here', with his men 'dying like flies [*mueren como chinches*]'. Another vessel, the *zabra Nuestra Señora de Castro*, sank with all hands within sight of the coast. On 7 October Recalde's *San Juan* and two *pataches* entered Corunna; three days later Bertendona's *Regazona* anchored at Muros (Galicia); and on 14 October Aramburu's *San Juan Bautista* reached Santander.[37]

Juan Gómez de Medina no doubt spoke for many survivors when he told the duke of Medina Sidonia: 'If I wanted to tell Your Grace the calamities which have befallen me since we parted company, I would fill a large book.' The master of Recalde's *San Juan* struck a similar note when he concluded his brief account of the voyage: 'I won't say any more, because I don't have enough paper to narrate all the terrible things which happened to us.' What had gone wrong?[38]

# 16

# Analysis of Failure

⋘❀⋙

> *'There's some say that we wan, some say that they wan, some say that nane wan at a', man.'*
>
> Murdoch McLennan, describing the inconclusive battle of Sherrifmuir during the Jacobite Rising in 1715

Philip's Grand Design had failed – his Armada never managed to 'join hands' with Parma's troops, still less get any of them ashore – but Elizabeth's navy had also demonstrated weaknesses. It managed to prevent the planned invasion but proved unable to cripple the Armada so badly that it could never return. What explains the failures on both sides?

## The Nature of Failure in War

In their seminal 1990 study, *Military Misfortunes*, Eliot Cohen and John Gooch distinguished three categories of failure in war: failure to learn from the past; failure to anticipate future developments; and failure to adapt to the immediate circumstances on the battlefield. They further suggested that if only the first or the second occurs, which they termed a 'simple failure', it can often be overcome by skilful adaptation. A simultaneous failure in learning and anticipation, which they termed an 'aggregate failure', is more difficult but not impossible to surmount; but a failure to adapt can produce a disaster of such scope that recovery is impossible. Let us apply their framework to the protagonists in the Armada campaign.

As Cohen and Gooch noted: 'Some people never learn. Having experienced disaster once, they continue to indulge in exactly the same patterns of foolhardy behaviour until they are visited by disaster once more.'[1] This was certainly true of Philip II after 1588 (see chapter 18), but not before. On the contrary, his Armada strategy drew upon important lessons learned from recent amphibious operations. In 1580 his ships and his troops had carried out a joint assault with spectacular success: a fleet composed mostly of embargoed merchantmen 'joined hands' with an army at Setubal on the Atlantic coast just south of the Tagus and transported 15,000 soldiers and twenty-two siege-guns safely to Cascais on the other side of the estuary, a distance of 70 miles. Soon after it landed, the army won a battle and went on to capture first Lisbon and then the rest of Portugal. Only the Azores archipelago, 1,000 miles west of Lisbon, defied him and in each of the next three years Philip sent an amphibious expedition to conquer them. According to the king, who carried out a personal inspection, the first task force comprised 'a fleet of fourteen or fifteen galleons, ships and caravels with 1,000 Spanish and 1,000 German infantry' commanded by Don Pedro de Valdés. Their attempt to capture Terceira island failed ignominiously because of insufficient strength.

Santa Cruz led the second expedition in 1582 but left before a squadron of Vizcayan ships under Recalde and a squadron of galleys from Cadiz could join him. His thirty warships therefore faced an enemy fleet twice its size, and although the marquis prevailed in a battle fought off the island of São Miguel, 224 of his men perished, with another 550 injured. Extensive damage inflicted on the vice-flagship *San Mateo* prevented her from serving in the third expedition the following year, which saw Santa Cruz lead 15,000 men on ninety-eight ships (including twelve galleys, two galleasses, five Portuguese galleons and seventeen embargoed Mediterranean merchantmen) to Terceira. They overcame a spirited defence, gained control of the entire island and returned to Lisbon in triumph. The obvious lesson for a future amphibious operation, therefore, was to neutralize or defeat any naval opposition so as to land an army safely and in overwhelming strength. That is precisely what Philip instructed the Armada to do.[2]

His English opponents had fewer lessons from which to learn, since the last full fleet deployment had occurred in 1559 when, after scarcely a year on the throne, Elizabeth had instructed William Winter to prevent the pro-French regime in Scotland from overwhelming her Protestant allies. Winter led a fleet of twenty-nine vessels (fourteen of them the queen's ships) to the Firth of Forth with orders that if 'he may conveniently surprise and defeat the French navy' he might attack them 'to the uttermost, either by shot, fire or otherwise' – clear evidence that England's naval experts already saw stand-off gunnery and fireships as standard operating procedures.[3] Although Winter did none of these things, he managed to keep his fleet on station for seven months – a remarkable feat. Two decades later he sailed to south-west Ireland, directed an artillery bombardment by six of the queen's ships until the garrison of the Castello del Oro at Smerwick surrendered, and then kept his fleet on station continuously for nine months – another remarkable feat (see Figure 39).

Other captains of the queen's ships in 1588 besides Winter had commanded expeditionary forces for prolonged periods, sometimes under fire. Edward Fenton had used two galleons to fight and win an artillery duel on his troublesome voyage to the South Atlantic in 1582; Sir Francis Drake led a fleet of thirty-three vessels (two of them the queen's ships) to Spain and across the Atlantic to the Caribbean in a journey that lasted ten months in 1585–6; and John Hawkins maintained a blockade of the Iberian coast with a fleet of eighteen warships for three months in 1586. The following year Drake led twenty-four vessels, including six of the queen's ships, to raid Cadiz, Lagos and Sagres before sailing to the Azores and back: a total of three months at sea. Admittedly, few of these ventures involved protracted combat – many of the Armada's senior officers could claim greater fighting experience: Recalde and Bertendona in the Netherlands; many others in the Azores – but the English commanders learned logistical and tactical lessons that would prove vital when the protracted Spanish invasion scare kept the entire Tudor navy at sea for seven months. There was thus no 'failure to learn' on either side.

## Failure to Anticipate

It is harder to grade the protagonists in 1588 on the second category of failure in war identified by Cohen and Gooch: a failure to anticipate. It would be unfair to fault the Spaniards for their lack of pilots and charts to guide them in the North Atlantic. Although a printed map of the waters around Scotland had existed since 1583 (see p. 327), none existed for the west coast of Ireland. The expertise of the captains and masters of the Baltic *urcas* which sometimes sailed to Spain that way was probably the best available. To be sure, Admiral Howard could consult pilots familiar with the ports and hazards of the south and east coasts of England, and he may well have drawn on local knowledge to prevent the Armada from entering the Solent; but Medina Sidonia could also consult pilots familiar with the Narrow Seas (for example, in 1587 *Lavia* spent two months at Margate, the designated landing-zone, delivering wine and loading lead and tin). We cannot fairly blame the duke for failing to anticipate the need to circumnavigate Britain and Ireland.

Medina Sidonia certainly foresaw the tactics his enemies might deploy. He received Francisco de Guevara's warning that the English 'have adapted their gunports for heavy artillery, so that once they deploy each piece they can raise the breech and fire low at the side of an enemy ship', so that 'if it comes to an artillery duel Your Majesty's Armada will lose', and 'it would be better to board the enemy ships immediately'. The duke therefore ordered his carpenters to extend the castles on some of his ships to improve their boarding capacity (see chapter 11). Although this was the opposite of the structural changes implemented by Hawkins and others to produce England's 'race-built' galleons, Medina Sidonia could not have known that. On the contrary, he had evidence from an apparently impeccable source that the rival warships were virtually identical.

While he blockaded the Iberian coast in 1586 Hawkins captured three Portuguese ships, interrogated their officers and then released them. On his return to Lisbon one of the pilots filed a report on meeting Hawkins aboard his flagship, *Nonpareil* (ironically the ship launched in 1557 as *Philip and Mary*). He correctly identified his captor as 'the man who escaped from San Juan de Ulúa' and 'the fleet commanded by Don Martín Enríquez, viceroy of New Spain'; and he paid close attention as 'Hawkins showed me his ship'. The pilot deemed her 'very well armed and equipped, with 44 large bronze guns, and 300 men; and John Hawkins told me that his fleet carried 1,200 musketeers apart from the arquebusiers and archers'. The English fleet, he said, included 'four large galleons of the queen, each of them about 800 tons, and they resembled the great galleons' of Portugal. Confirmation of this comparison came from the master of another Portuguese ship whom Hawkins questioned aboard his vice-flagship, *Hope*. The master deemed her the largest of Hawkins's ships and 'only slightly less than the galleon *San Martín* in size. 'She was very well armed and carried 54 bronze guns, all very large, and 350 men; and like the other royal galleons, the outside of her stern was lavishly gilded with the arms of the queen of England.' These experienced and observant mariners thus detected no significant differences between the queen's ships and the galleons of Portugal. The only possible grounds for disquiet were that 'the four royal galleons all carried the same armament, and the other ships and pinnaces also carried many guns and men'.[4]

We therefore cannot fault Medina Sidonia for believing that his fighting ships were a match for those they would meet; but we must censure him for disregarding two pieces of intelligence – both correct – about likely English tactics. On 14 May 1588 the king sent an express courier to him with a warning that the English might attempt a fireship attack. He insisted that Medina Sidonia must ensure that 'our enemies cannot set fire to any of our ships, something that people willing to do anything, and possessed of abundant artifices for it, might try'. The duke apparently dismissed not only this insight but also a more detailed warning sent by Don Juan de Idiáquez two months later:

> The more the enemy fears our strength, the more likely he is to use stratagems and artifices, as the Dutch did in the river of Antwerp with those hellburners, and again more recently in Dunkirk ... We have now received some intelligence, albeit vague and uncertain, that the English may attempt something similar, sending a couple of ships from their fleet with the same devices, timed to explode later; so you must let them pass and do not try to board them so that they will explode without effect, and concentrate on boarding the rest.

The duke's response provides a classic example of a 'failure to anticipate'. He assured Idiáquez that 'if such ships travel in the middle of their fleet, they run the same risk as we do', and 'should the English send them out ahead alone, if we move away slightly we will avoid damage. Moreover, since the currents at sea are not as strong as those in rivers, it seems very unlikely that such vessels could get to the places the English might desire.' His orders for 'the defence of this flagship' therefore made no mention of fireships.[5]

Medina Sidonia likewise dismissed the interrogation of the captain of a German *urca*, intercepted first by the English in the Channel and then by Don Alonso de Luzón, which brought sensational news: 'Asked about the size and location of the English navy, he said that they now had only 35 ships between Dover and Calais, with more at Plymouth, so there were now 160 ships in all.' The duke forwarded the document to Philip, 'even though it contains nothing of importance', and he ignored its contents – just as he ignored Gómez de Medina's detailed account of the same interrogation, which included the crucial intelligence that the German captain had seen 'warships of the queen deployed between Dover and Calais expressly to prevent the passage of the prince of Parma, while the rest of the English fleet is at Plymouth, awaiting by the hour news about us'.[6]

The duke was not alone in ignoring vital intelligence that could have allowed him to anticipate what his enemies might do, however: Elizabeth, her ministers and her commanders did the same. The repeated changes to Philip's Grand Design, combined with the shifting weather patterns of July 1588, meant that Howard at Plymouth received virtually no advance warning of the Armada's approach. Only Medina Sidonia's ill-advised decision to take in sail while off the Lizard deprived the Armada of the critical advantage of surprise – but at least the tight secrecy surrounding the 'agreed place' prevented the English from divining the designated landing-zone. Thanks to the capture and interrogation of high-value prisoners before the campaign (above all Oda Colonna) and during it (above all Don Pedro de Valdés), the queen learned that the Armada planned to 'join hands' with Parma as the prelude to a march on London, but she remained firmly convinced that the invaders would land in Essex. She therefore moved her assets there. No warships, no modern fortifications and virtually no troops defended the Isle of Thanet and north-east Kent (see chapter 19).

The failure of each protagonist to achieve its goal in 1588 cannot therefore be ascribed to the first two categories proposed by Cohen and Gooch: both learned from past experience and both failed to anticipate future developments. So what of a failure to adapt? The role of heavy artillery in the outcome of the campaign justifies a close examination of its use by both sides.

## Big Guns I: The Armada

During the naval encounters between 31 July and 8 August 1588 some Spanish eyewitnesses thought it 'rained shot', and some who 'were in the fight at Lepanto' claimed they saw 'twenty times as much great shot . . . plied as they had there'. Admiral Howard concurred. 'It may well be said,' he wrote, that 'there was never seen more terrible value of great shot, nor more hot fight than this was.' Moreover, at least on the last day, the English delivered their 'great shot' at very close range because eyewitnesses on both sides spoke of firing the big guns 'within half-musket shot', 'within arquebus shot' and 'within speech of one another'. At one point two ships came close enough for an intrepid Englishman to leap aboard his Spanish foe.[7]

Yet even at such close range the Armada apparently inflicted little damage on its adversary. Admittedly stories circulated about the supposed ferocity of the Spanish bombardment and, perhaps predictably, several came from sources close to Drake. In one version his ship 'was pierced with shot above forty times, and his very cabin was twice shot through; and about the conclusion of the fight, the bed of a certain gentleman lying weary thereupon was taken quite from under him with the force of a bullet'. A little later, while two noblemen aboard another vessel were at dinner, 'the bullet of a demi-culverin broke through the midst of their cabin, touched their feet, and struck down two of the standers by'.[8]

Perhaps the ships' carpenters swiftly and silently repaired the damage, because it has left little documentary trace. The 'Dockyard Survey' of the queen's ships, carried out in September 1588 after they returned from campaign, revealed only a few unserviceable components – variously described as 'worn', 'cracked' and 'decayed' – which required replacement. Perhaps some of these terms were euphemisms for battle damage, although the frequency with which they occur is little greater than one might expect in ships that had spent several months at sea. In a few cases damage was directly attributed to enemy action – a smashed (or lost) ship's boat; *Revenge*'s mainmast 'decayed and perished with shot' – but the Dockyard Survey made no mention of substantial combat damage to the hull of any of the thirty-four royal warships.[9]

It is always dangerous to argue from absence of evidence, however, and this is especially true of the Tudor navy because in 1588 officials from several different organs of government each submitted separate accounts. The Dockyard Survey mentioned no damage to the hulls because the royal dockyards were responsible for masts, sails and other fittings: the cost of repairing hulls fell to the Treasurer of the Navy. Now the accounts of Treasurer Hawkins for 1588 do indeed include substantial payments for 'the grounding, repairing and preparing at Chatham of all her highness's ships' after the Armada campaign, which required over 12,000 feet of planking in thicknesses ranging from 1 to 4 inches, almost 100,000 nails and 1,000 trenails (wooden dowels), plus more than 15,000 pounds of ironwork, 85 loads of oak and elm timber, and wages for 948 'shipwrights, sawyers and pulley-makers' who worked an average of thirty-five days each. This total, one of the largest repair bills found in any of the annual accounts submitted by the Treasurer of the Navy during the entire conflict with Spain between 1585 and 1604, proves that Elizabeth's warships returned to port after the Armada campaign in need of considerable repair.

Nevertheless, this expenditure must be seen in perspective. First, the total amounted to only £3,500, slightly less than the cost of building just one new warship. Second, although Hawkins's accounts did not specify which ships underwent what repairs, the scale and nature of the operation can be deduced from the materials purchased. The majority of the planking required after the fleet's return was 1 and 2 inches thick (11,000 feet), suitable only for light superstructures, while the 3-inch planking (1,500 feet) was probably required for internal decking. Repairing damage to a ship's lower hull would require 4-inch planking, and of that Hawkins purchased only 500 feet. Likewise the iron nails would have been used mainly for the decks and superstructures, because in England hull planking was almost exclusively fastened to the frames with wooden trenails, of which relatively few were ordered. Finally, 85 loads of timber would not go far, since constructing an Elizabethan galleon required approximately 500 loads.[10]

The same accounts reveal that far more extensive repairs took place just before the Armada campaign. In spring 1588 naval contractors supplied almost 29,000 feet of planking (almost 4,000 feet of it 4-inch), 9,000 trenails, 56 'great beams', and 262 loads of oak, elm and maple. In other words the queen's ships required far more repairs before they fought the Armada than they did afterwards. The explanation is simple: wooden ships are in a constant state of decay whether at sea or ashore. They need frequent refurbishment and occasional rebuilding. Hawkins's accounts for 1588 show expenditure on routine maintenance in both spring and autumn, but no evidence of battle damage. They therefore provide evidence of absence, not just absence of evidence: the Armada did not inflict serious damage on the queen's ships. Why?[11]

Although the Spanish fleet carried 2,431 guns, only eighty-eight fired a 16-pound shot or above. Moreover fourteen (16 per cent) of these big guns were not intended for use at sea: they formed part of a siege-train intended for the land campaign.[12] Nevertheless, at least a dozen vessels carried artillery capable of inflicting serious damage on an enemy vessel. Above all each of the four galleasses from Naples, and also the Tuscan *San Francisco* (normally known as the *Florencia* and rated a galleass), carried two 50-pounder *cañones de batir*, four 35- and 36-pounder *cañones*, and eight *cañones pedreros*. The big guns on the fore- and aftercastles fired 'a great bullet almost of a height of four or five inches', and all were 'mounted on sea carriages'. Several eyewitnesses recorded that the galleasses inflicted some serious damage on their adversaries, including the shot which damaged the mainmast of *Revenge*, and that at other times their approach led the English to pull back.[13]

Other eyewitnesses, however, including Medina Sidonia, complained that the galleasses 'did not perform as we had hoped'. This may reflect some last-minute personnel changes. Don Hugo de Moncada received his commission as squadron commander only in January 1588, when he replaced another officer who 'although an upstanding gentleman, lacks the experience required and necessary in case they have to fight'. Two months later Medina Sidonia asked the king to remove Paolo Ghislieri from command of *Zúñiga* in view of 'the complaints I have received about him'. The king complied on the bizarre grounds that Ghislieri, a veteran of Lepanto, 'is more of a soldier than a sailor'. These and other personnel changes may have impaired the ships' fighting potential. It is notable that Captain Perucho Morán of *Napolitana*, the only galleass to return to Spain intact, had commanded her since at least the Terceira campaign in 1583.[14]

Two vessels in the squadron of Portugal also carried formidable ordnance. *San Juan de Portugal*, built in 1586 and reputed 'the best-gunned ship in the Armada', carried fifty-eight pieces, including one 40- and six 35-pounder *pedreros*, with seven more pieces throwing iron shot of 16 pounds or more. *San Martín* carried forty-six bronze guns – including six *cañones gruesos*, six *pedreros* and four *medios cañones*. Several Spanish eyewitnesses reported that the approach of either vessel, ably and aggressively commanded by Recalde and Medina Sidonia respectively, caused the English to withdraw. The other Portuguese warships carried far fewer big guns: eighteen aboard *San Luis* (nine *pedreros* and nine *medias culebrinas*); twelve on *Santiago* (seven *pedreros* and five *medias culebrinas*); seven on *San Bernardo* (four *pedreros* and three *medias culebrinas*); and six on *San Cristóbal* (two *pedreros* and four *medias culebrinas*). The remainder of their ordnance fired 12-pound balls or lighter – often much lighter.[15]

Eight other Armada ships carried heavy artillery. Each of the four galleys carried a 50-pounder centreline gun mounted on a sled, so that the recoil brought the gun inboard where reloading could take place in relative safety. Some manuals on Mediterranean naval warfare recommended keeping part of a galley fleet 'out of battle, so that they can fire 10 or even 15 times at the sides and sterns of enemy vessels'.[16] The other well-gunned ships were Oquendo's *Santa Ana*, with forty-seven guns (including one *cañón*, three *pedreros*, one *medio cañón*, two *culebrinas* and nine *medias culebrinas*); his vice-flagship *San Salvador* with twenty-four guns (including two *cañones*, four *pedreros*, and four *culebrinas* or *medias culebrinas*); *Nuestra Señora del Rosario* with forty-six guns (including two *pedreros*, six *medios cañones*, two *culebrinas* and two *medias culebrinas*); and *Santa Ana*, flagship of the Vizcayan squadron, with thirty-one guns (including two *medios cañones* and four *pedreros*). But of these eight powerful vessels, only Oquendo's flagship managed to get to Calais: *Santa Ana* and all four galleys lost contact with the fleet in the Bay of Biscay; and the English captured both *San Salvador* and *Rosario* after the first day's fight.[17]

Spain's naval experts struggled with the operational problems of working such big guns at sea. In July 1587 Don Juan de Acuña Vela, Captain-General of Artillery, submitted to the king a scale drawing of three designs for a *media culebrina* (Figure 113). The gun on top was of a pattern recommended by the marquis of Santa Cruz, but Don Juan considered its walls too thin for safety and too long for handling on shipboard. The bottom gun had been suitably beefed up but, according to Acuña, it was still too long and now too heavy as well. He presented his solution at the centre: a gun shortened to bring it to manageable length with the weight of metal saved used to make the barrel thicker. His sound judgement evidently took time to filter through the system, however: a *media culebrina* cast at Lisbon on his instructions over the winter of 1587–8 and recovered from the wreck of *Gran Grifón* was made to the outdated 'Santa Cruz' proportions.

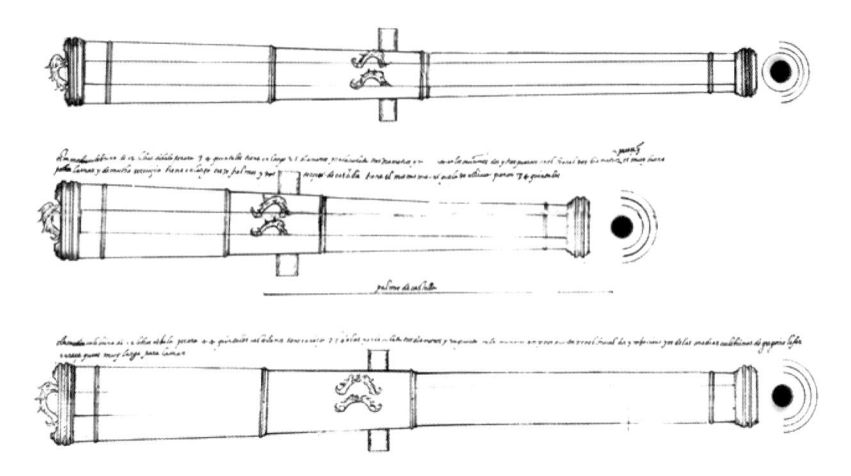

113. Three designs for a *media culebrina* by Don Juan de Acuña Vela, July 1587. Although Don Juan probably did not realize it, his ideal design (middle) brought the gun to a calibre-to-length ratio of optimum ballistic efficiency (about 1:25).

## Comparative Seamanship

Despite such defects, the Armada carried almost 2,500 artillery pieces and nearly 130,000 rounds for them to fire: why did they fail to inflict more damage?

The surviving sources suggest a variety of reasons. First, everyone agreed that the English ships sailed faster and better than their adversaries. After the fight on 4 August a Spanish observer lamented that 'two of the fastest ships in the Armada gave chase' to an English vessel 'but in comparison they seemed as if they were at anchor' – a fine tribute to the superior 'race-built' design of many English galleons.[18]

Inferior seamanship accentuated the structural discrepancies. On 26 July the galleon *Santiago* (Portugal) collided with *San Cristobal* (Castile) 'and our sails were locked together for more than an hour, which placed both ships in peril'. Although they eventually separated, 'the initial impact broke two anchors and several spars on the capstan' of *Santiago*.[19] Five days later *Rosario* ran into another vessel, breaking her bowsprit and bringing down her foremast; and the following day the duke's efforts to scuttle *San Salvador*, and thus prevent her from falling into English hands, failed because the crews sent to do it could not find any tools 'able to sink her'. On the night of 7 August *Rata Encoronada* collided with the galleass *San Lorenzo*, breaking her rudder so she could not steer.

In addition, careless handling of the powder aboard caused explosions that destroyed three of the embargoed merchantmen: *San Salvador* in the Channel; *San Juan de Sicilia* in Tobermory Bay; and Oquendo's *Santa Ana* in Pasajes. Similar disasters were only narrowly averted. During a chance encounter with an English 'pirate' in July 1588, the powder-flask of a soldier aboard the *urca Paloma Blanca* 'blew up and caused the explosion of several cartridges of powder' prepared for the big guns: the ship was lucky to make port again. During the fight on 2 August two gunners aboard *San Juan Fernandome* received serious burns 'because they had not cleaned the piece carefully' before firing it.[20]

Admittedly English ships and crews occasionally suffered similar mishaps. In January 1588, while Drake's men practised firing their artillery, 'a piece broke and killed a man, with some others hurt'. On 7 August, at anchor off Calais, five ships (including *Ark Royal*) became 'all tangled together, so as there was some hurt done by breaking of yards and spoil of tackle'; but their crews managed to disentangle them without impairing their fighting capacity.[21] Perhaps this was just good luck, but it may also reflect the familiarity of English officers and crews with their ships. Most had spent several months aboard their vessels and twice sailed on them almost to Spain and back before the Armada entered the Channel. In contrast Medina Sidonia did not board his flagship *San Martín* until May and Recalde, who had as much naval experience as anyone, transferred to *San Juan de Portugal* on 26 March. Of the other commanders of Portuguese galleons, Mexía, Pimentel and Toledo only boarded their ships in Lisbon, and the marquis of Peñafiel did not take command of *San Marcos* until Corunna when Bobadilla moved to the flagship. Although the quartet fought heroically throughout the Channel battles, none had prior experience of sailing – let alone of combat – on their vessels in Atlantic waters.

*Maestre de campo* Don Alonso de Luzón also boarded his ship for the first time at Lisbon, and when his English captors later asked him about the dimensions of the vessel he commanded, he replied that *Trinidad Valencera* was 'a very great ship but of what certain burthen he knows not'; and when questioned about the guns she carried, he replied: '32 pieces of brass and iron, whereof 4 were cannons of brass but of what kinds the rest were, how many of brass or how many of iron, he knows not'. It is hard to imagine any English captain not knowing the precise displacement and armament of his vessel.[22]

Some Armada commanders also displayed striking operational incompetence. When Diego Flores led the squadron of Castile from the ports of Andalucia into the Tagus on 28 April 1588 the king reprimanded him because his ships arrived with virtually no water, few anchors and insufficient ballast for stability.[23] The commander of the Venetian *Trinidad de Escala* displayed incompetence throughout the campaign. He fired his big guns 'to ask for help' on 2 June 'when the masts broke'; on 25 and 26 June 'because we didn't know where we were'; on 9 August 'because we were falling behind the flagship'; on 12 and 13 September, 'asking for help from the fleet because we were taking in so much water'; and on 22 September, requesting help in entering the port of Santander. Once again, it is hard to imagine similar behaviour among English captains.[24]

The presence of many officers apparently promoted solely because of their social rank also played a part in the Armada's failure. A list of 'experienced officers' in the Armada drawn up in February 1588 included the names of seventy-one infantry captains – but since more than 150 captains sailed with the fleet, the list implied that more than half had never previously held command. An evaluation of surviving officers after the campaign noted several who were 'young': one who was 'young, and this was his first campaign' (Bobadilla's nephew), and another who had 'been a captain for only one year' (Paredes's brother).[25] Recalde blamed such men, 'the courtiers and others who always want to enjoy their usual comforts', for persuading the duke to put into Corunna in June instead of pressing on to the Channel; and his analysis of 'The reasons for the Armada's failure', composed after his return in October, devoted three paragraphs to the baleful influence of inexperienced military officers. 'If another armada should be assembled,' he wrote, 'His Majesty should not permit young gentlemen or persons who have recently acquired a title of nobility to join the general's council or to serve in any other post of command.' Instead, 'young gentlemen should be distributed among the companies of veteran captains, and no more than two or three in each one, because the manner in which they went on this voyage caused much anger and fear among the sailors aboard the ships in which they went'. He continued: 'The companies commanded by young inexperienced captains should be dissolved and strict measures should be taken that only proven soldiers should command, because the masters of the ships failed to do their duty for fear of them.'[26]

The hybrid composition of the fleet, with vessels and crews from many different ports of western Europe, could also produce interpersonal problems. Pimentel complained to his Dutch captors that the pilot of *San Mateo* 'was a Portuguese, whom he could not always understand'; the gunner suspected of sabotaging *San Salvador* was German (or Flemish, according to some accounts); the pilot of *Santa María de la Rosa* was Italian, and the Spanish infantry captain aboard who killed him just before she sank may have suspected his loyalty. Some of those aboard other Armada ships left no doubt on this score. No sooner had *San Pedro Mayor*, the hospital ship, anchored off Calais than the 'master, bosun and several other officers and sailors' (all apparently Dutch) deserted. Shortly afterwards two more Dutch sailors slipped into 'the boat tied behind the ship' and rowed ashore to Holland. When *San Lorenzo* ran aground off Calais, 'the Italian gunners and sailors were the first to jump ashore and flee'.

Later on, when *Barca de Danzig* took refuge in the Shannon, a dozen Flemish crew members 'got into the ship's boat and headed for the shore'; and when *Rata Encoronada* ran aground her master Giovanni Avancini 'and fourteen Italian mariners went ashore in the cockboat', leaving their shipmates in the lurch. The French prisoners condemned to row two of the galleys mutinied as soon as storms forced their vessels ashore; and when the galleass *Zúñiga* reached temporary safety in Le Havre twelve of the Italians aboard deserted.[27] Some of the survivors who got back to Spain behaved no better. As soon as the remnants of the Castile squadron reached Cantabria, 184 sailors abandoned their vessels and headed for their homes in Andalucia. When Bertendona went to the prow of *Regazona* to try and get her off the rocks near Ferrol, 'two local pilots, three of their colleagues, the bosun and master of the ship, as well as eleven sailors, went to the stern and abandoned me: a total of sixteen men.'[28]

## Powder and Shot

Contemporaries advanced two further explanations for the Armada's failure: poor powder and a shortage of experienced gunners. In March 1588, on the eve of their departure from Lisbon, the masters of some Armada ships declared that 'the powder and match aboard was not fit for purpose, because it is too old for a campaign like the one we understand is planned'. Six months later, the Tuscan ambassador in Madrid echoed this complaint in a dispatch composed after speaking with Don Balthasar de Zúñiga and other Armada survivors: 'They say the gunpowder supplied to the fleet was very poor, composed primarily of charcoal [*carbone*] so that the artillery rounds travelled more slowly and some did not reach their target at all.' Alonso Vanegas, the chief gunnery officer aboard the flagship, stated that his adversaries 'enjoyed an advantage in artillery and in powder, which was certainly much better than ours'. A Portuguese Jesuit who sailed with him echoed that the English 'ships carried more and better artillery than we did, and better powder'.[29]

Although no English source made this comparison in 1588, a decade earlier William Bourne began his *Art of Shooting in Great Ordnance* with a list of 'Ten principal things [that] are to be considered in the shooting of Ordnance . . . to make a perfect shot at any mark assigned', including a chapter on 'How to know the goodness and badness of powder'. An Italian eyewitness of the Cadiz raid in

1587 observed that not only was the English artillery 'better than ours, but so was their powder, because ours (they say) is very weak and is often what comes off the fleets from America, mixed with a little that is more fresh'.[30] The following year Armada vessels apparently used arquebus-grade powder in their big guns, which would have put undue pressure on the metal (see Appendix 4).

A royal decree in November 1589 documented a second important technical weakness. The king began by noting that 'when the Armada returned to Santander' a government inspector commented on 'the shortage of trained Spanish gunners'. He therefore created 'a school where gunners could practise and acquire expertise'. Now, 'in view of the current scarcity of gunners in Spain, and how much they are needed for both sea and land service', the king commanded the magistrates of Corunna to establish a second gunnery school. Moreover, as 'to this end there must be good gunpowder, since one cannot practise without it, you must tell me how much you think will be used and where we might find it – assuming practice will only take place on holidays and on the weekdays that you consider appropriate'.[31] These were remarkable admissions. Even allowing for Philip's irresistible urge to micromanage, the need to detail so many defects is eloquent testimony to the scale of the problem.

Data from the fleet itself support his analysis. An inventory of the forty-eight surviving Armada vessels in Santander in November 1588 listed 1,744 naval personnel, of whom 196 were described as gunners (*artilleros*); and a similar inventory of their seven sister ships in the ports of Galicia revealed 304 naval personnel of whom 67 were gunners – an average of five per ship. Even these figures are exaggerated, because several men were *artilleros de campaña*, embarked to serve the field-pieces aboard the Armada after the expeditionary force had landed.[32]

The administrative dossiers at Simancas indicate that the big guns aboard the hired ships only fired celebratory salvoes until they reached the Channel. Even those events were rare: on 15 April at the hoisting of the royal standard; in May when the duke inspected the fleet (twice) and to salute the major fortresses as they sailed down the Tagus (four times); on entering and leaving Corunna; and on 30 July 'on entering the Channel between England and France'. Only on the last occasion did the quartermasters 'work out the weight of powder' required for each gun. This left no time for artillery practice because battle commenced the next day.[33]

Here was a striking contrast. The following year, in his account of 'how it happened that the English were able to chase the enemy from their seas', Petruccio Ubaldini singled out the gunners whose proficiency in their profession required 'not only manual practice, which is one of the most important parts of soldiering, but also the judgement of the eye and mind'. He noted with approval that 'among the artillery it had been absolutely decided by the English that all should be of one nationality, one language, and therefore one constant disposition to serve well'. Moreover, according to Ubaldini, Howard 'made good use of the most reliable quality of his excellent and speedy ships, not crowded out with useless soldiers, but with decks clear for the use of artillery, so they could safely play it at any hour to harm the enemy, at any moment which it suited them best to do so'. William Bourne agreed: his *Art of Shooting in Great Ordnance* stated that 'the chief cause that Englishmen are thought to be good gunners is this: for that they are handsome about their ordnance in ships, on the sea', and he devoted two chapters to how to handle naval guns effectively. A little later Sir Arthur Gorgas, who had fought against the Armada, attributed the outcome unequivocally to the ability of the English to discharge 'our broadsides of ordnance double for their single, we carrying as good and great artillery as they do and to better proof, and having far better gunners'.[34]

## Lack of Ammunition?

Medina Sidonia and his entourage disagreed. They did not attribute their failure to shortcomings in their big guns, powder or gunners: instead, they claimed repeatedly and vociferously that they had run out of shot. The duke's own campaign diary stated that he had begged Parma to send powder and shot and – since they did not arrive – the day after the battle he informed his Council of War that the commanders of all the fighting ships 'had begged him to supply them with munitions, because they had used up all their own, and even the supplies aboard the *urcas*'. Several others among the fleet agreed. A Portuguese Jesuit on the flagship confirmed that by then most of the fighting ships 'had no rounds left to fire'; Bobadilla later complained about 'the few artillery rounds we carried, so that scarcely none of the fighting ships had anything left to fire'; and when Ambassador Khevenhüller asked Don Balthasar de Zúñiga, back in Madrid, 'why the fleet did not make its way back through the Channel, he answered that they had absolutely no ammunition left, not even two cannon balls, with which to withstand the enemy'.[35]

Despite this unanimity, we now know that – for whatever reason – they all erred. Medina Sidonia's request to Parma revealed that he was not short of heavy-calibre shot: what he requested was '4-, 6- and 10-pound rounds, because we have fired so many in the skirmishes'. He did not ask for ammunition for his big guns, presumably because they had fired less frequently. This impression is confirmed by administrative dossiers at Simancas, which show that most of the ships that returned to Spain still carried large stocks of powder and shot. The inventory of munitions aboard the forty-three Armada vessels anchored at Santander on 1 November 1588, compiled by Coco Calderón, listed 14,816 iron, 2,468 stone and 300 lead shot for artillery, and almost 800 quintals of powder. The inventory of the four ships that returned to Corunna listed at least 1,000 shot and 700 quintals of powder (Figure 114).[36]

The dossiers at Simancas show a similar situation for some of the embargoed merchantmen but provide more detail because the clerk of each ship had received instructions to 'record the powder, shot and match expended, noting down how much is used every day and for what reason, with what effects and by whose order. Take particular note of the artillery pieces fired, and of their calibre and weight, and of the powder and shot consumed in firing them.' Where they survive, these accounts provide a day-to-day record of the gunnery performance of individual ships throughout the fighting. The results are remarkable.[37]

Of the 1,640 rounds fired by nine hired Armada ships, only 175 (11 per cent) exceeded 9 pounds and none was greater than 20 pounds. Each ship brought back to Spain vast quantities of unused munitions. *Concepción Menor* received 1,521 projectiles at Lisbon and handed back 1,256 (83 per cent); *San Francisco* received the exceptionally large quota of 8,731 rounds and returned 8,489 (97 per cent).[38]

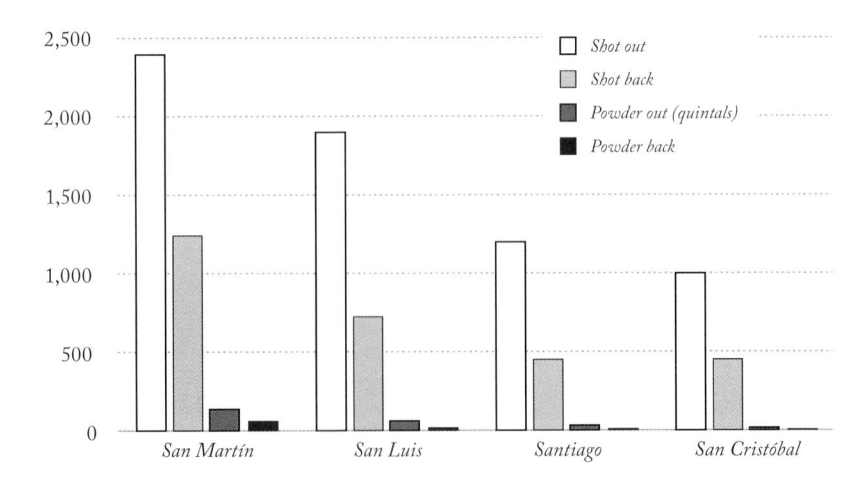

114. Shot and powder supplied to and returned by four Portuguese galleons.

**Table 16.1.** *Roundshot fired by selected Armada ships*

| Ship | Squadron | Guns (Corunna) | Date | Shots fired | Rounds per gun | Comments |
|---|---|---|---|---|---|---|
| *Santa Bárbara* | Guipúzcoa | 28 | 31 July | 22 | 0.8 | |
| | | | 1 Aug | 28 | 1 | |
| | | | 2 Aug | 47 | 1.7 | |
| | | | 8 Aug | 167 | 6 | 'after they left Calais and fought with the enemy, serving in the vanguard beside the flagship' |
| *Concepción Menor* | Vizcaya | 18 | 31 July | 17 | 0.9 | |
| | | | 2 Aug | 33 | 1.8 | |
| | | | 4 Aug | 35 | 1.9 | |
| | | | 8 Aug | 71 | 3.9 | |
| *San Francisco* | Andalucia | 21 | 4 days | 242 | 11.5 | |
| *Santa Catalina* | Andalucia | 23 | 4 days | 300 | 13 | |
| *San Juan Bautista de la Esperanza* | Levant | | 4 days | 314 iron, 41 x 5-lb, 13 x 3/4-lb, 260 x <2-lb | | 'in the fight with the English vice-flagship as well as in others' |
| *Trinidad de Escala* | Levant | 4 *medios cañones* | 2 Aug | 20 | 5 | |
| | | | 4 Aug | 14 | 3.5 | |
| | | | 8 Aug | 19 | 4.75 | |
| | | 15 others | | 41 | 2.7 | |

Admittedly none of these ships belonged to the 'troubleshooting' elite: most were invasion transports ordered to maintain strict formation discipline, and would not normally have engaged an enemy that consistently avoided coming to close quarters, but the galleons of Portugal also returned with many munitions unused (Figure 114).

We can provide more details for the two most powerful ships in the squadron. Recalde's campaign journal stated that *San Juan*'s fifty-eight guns fired 140 rounds on 31 July; 130 on 3 August; and 300 on 8 August. Vanegas recorded that *San Martín*'s forty-eight guns fired 120 rounds on 31 July; 120 on 2 August; 130 on 3 August; and 300 on 8 August, when 'the flagship sailed to wherever the fighting was hottest'. Despite sending munitions to other fighting ships, she still returned to Spain with 650 iron, 450 stone and 100 lead rounds, and 70 quintals of powder.[39]

The only exception to this pattern appears to be nine ships of Oquendo's squadron. An inventory in November 1588, just after their return to the port of Pasajes, listed 3,366 iron and 184 stone shot – but specified that 'most of these were for the smaller guns, which were not fired because the smaller guns fired few rounds. There are few rounds for the larger calibre pieces, because they had been fired at the enemy.' It is possible that the galleasses, which carried heavy ordnance in their bow- and stern-castles, did the same, but the surviving records do not support this view. *Napolitana*, the only galleass to return to Spain intact, brought back 6,000 iron and 800 stone rounds. Finally, *San Lorenzo*, noted by both sides as being involved in all the fleet actions in the Channel, sank with at least 3,000 roundshot (including over 700 for the *cañones gruesos*) and 37 quintals of powder.[40]

The archaeological record tells the same story. Shot of all calibres, and especially the larger calibres, has been found in abundance on every Armada shipwreck so far excavated. *Gran Grifón*, heavily engaged in the Channel battles and wrecked on Fair Isle, received four *medias culebrinas* at Lisbon, and these long 10-pounders were the heaviest pieces she carried; yet of the 200 balls of this calibre originally issued, 97 were recovered from the wreck. At the very least, therefore, almost half her most effective firepower was not used against the enemy (and the true figure is certainly higher because the wreck has been only partially excavated). The picture for *Grifón*'s thirty-four lighter guns, 6-pounders and less, is very different. For these 273 rounds of ammunition were recovered, only 16 per cent of the total allocation. This substantial sampling strongly suggests that *Grifón*'s lighter guns were fired on average three times more frequently than her *medias culebrinas*, even though the latter were the only pieces heavy enough to inflict serious damage on an enemy vessel (Figure 115).

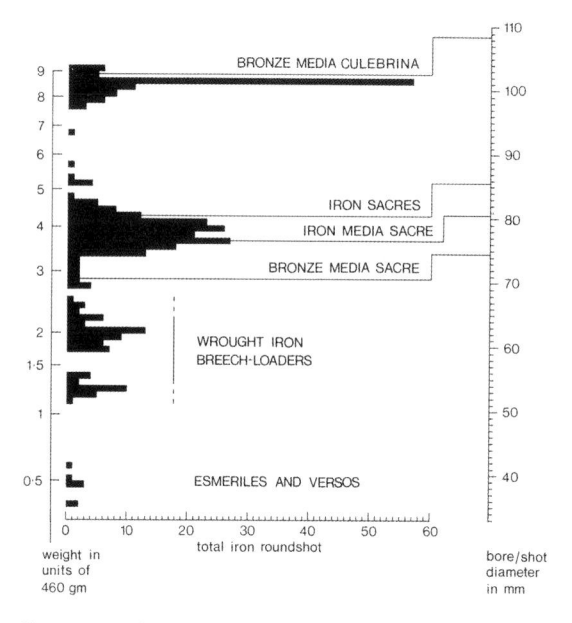

**115.** Shot sizes and quantities remaining on the wreck of *Gran Grifón*.

Here at last is a full and sufficient explanation for the Armada's failure to inflict serious damage on the English fleet, and thus perhaps keep it at bay: the Spaniards simply did not fire their guns, especially their heavier guns often enough at close range. But again we must ask why.

## Reloading

The kind of warfare the English had developed, and applied so successfully at Gravelines, involved a sustained close-range bombardment intended to neutralize an enemy by the attrition of gunfire alone. The Spaniards, however, given their inferior sailing qualities, were prevented from closing and boarding as they would have liked. The Armada's only effective response was to reply in kind; but to do this their ships needed to reload their guns repeatedly during the course of an engagement. This was more easily said than done. Not only was such a practice outside the training and tactical experience of Spanish commanders and their crews, it was also one for which their equipment was fundamentally unsuited.

The instructions issued by Diego Flores to the fleet sailing to the Strait of Magellan in 1581 read: 'See that all artillery is loaded and ready, even when it is not run out, so that if it were necessary to have use of it quickly, they have to do no more than run it out of its gunport. And next to the artillery there should be with each gun a box where they keep the shot for that same piece, without mixing some shots with others.' Flores said not a word about reloading, or about tactics in case of attack. Medina Sidonia's fighting instructions for his flagship, supported by evidence from the wrecks, shows that naval battle-drills had not changed in 1588.[41]

No doubt, as it became apparent that the English ships could not be grappled and boarded as the Spaniards wished, efforts were made to continue working the guns after the first salvo had been discharged. This was almost certainly the case with the smaller pieces – a conclusion reinforced by Medina Sidonia's statement that *San Martín* had run out of smaller-calibre shot – but improvising effective reloading drills for the larger-calibre guns was not so easy.

During the sixteenth century muzzle-loading artillery aboard sailing ships could be reloaded in two ways. The guns could either be hauled inboard after firing, and the necessary procedures carried out within the ship, or they could be left in the run-out position and reloaded outboard. The much more efficient process of allowing a gun's recoil to bring it inboard under the restraint of a breeching rope and the friction of its tackles does not appear to have been adopted until after the Armada campaign. Normally, it seems, each piece was unhitched after firing and hauled back manually. This was laborious but reasonably efficient, and during the process the crew would be covered from the view, and to some extent the fire, of the enemy. Outboard loading, although it required a smaller crew, was far more awkward and perilous, for it required the loader to straddle the barrel of the gun outside the port and carry out the clearing and charging operations from this exposed and uncomfortable position.

Both fleets almost certainly used inboard loading, but the recoil stresses were better absorbed by the English galleons that Hawkins had strengthened for this very reason. Most Spanish ships, in contrast, were less able to absorb such strains. Surviving accounts specify the damage done 'by the recoil of her own artillery' in the case of at least three ships – *San Mateo* (Portugal), *Gran Grifón* (*urca*) and *Rata* (Levant) – and an inspection of the vessels that returned to Santander in October revealed 'some vessels whose decks had been weakened by carrying too much heavy artillery'. This may well have induced some Armada captains to fire only their lighter guns.[42]

But there was more. The two large-diameter wheels and long trails of many Armada gun carriages limited the working space on the gun-decks, making it impracticable for the pieces to be reloaded inboard during an action. It seems more likely that once combat began most Spanish ships only managed to fire off their pre-prepared salvo. This does not of course mean that no further firing was possible – the *medios cañones* aboard *Trinidad de Escala* each fired five times on 2 and 8 August, and at least three times on 4 August – but both documentary and archaeological evidence suggests that overall rates of fire were generally slow.

The Dutch traveller Jan Huyghen van Linschoten, aboard a large Portuguese carrack, described an Iberian gun-deck in action. In 1589 English privateers attacked his ship and 'Whenever we shot off a piece,' Linschoten wrote, 'we had at least an hour's work to lade it in again, whereby we had so great a noise and cry aboard the ship as if we had all been cast away.' A similar confusion had probably occurred on at least some Armada ships the previous year.[43]

## 'Some are crooked in their chase, other of unequal bores'

Some of the Armada's big guns were safer left unfired. When one of the guns cast by Don Juan de Acuña Vela 'in great haste' was proofed at the new foundry in Lisbon in February 1588 it exploded, killing three men.[44] *Gran Grifón* received eight bronze pieces from the same crash gun-founding programme just before the fleet sailed: four *medias culebrinas* and four *medios sacres*. One of the *medias culebrinas* recovered from the wreck had a bore so far off-centre that its breech would have been eccentrically thin. In all probability it could never have been safely fired, and certainly not with a full charge (Figure 116). Nor was this an isolated case. An Italian *sacre* recovered from the wreck of *Juliana*, off Streedagh Strand, had suffered just such a mishap near the muzzle, rendering it useless (Figure 117). The English gunnery expert Robert Norton may not have been wide of the mark when he wrote disparagingly in 1628 of Spanish and Italian gun-founding techniques:

> It is apparent that they commit great and absurd faults therein. Some of their pieces (and not a few) are bored awry ... Some are crooked in their chase, other of unequal bores ... and a great many are come forth of the furnace spongy, or full of honeycombs or flaws ... [Such guns] will either break, split, or blowingly spring their metals and (besides that mischief they do) they will be utterly unserviceable ever after.[45]

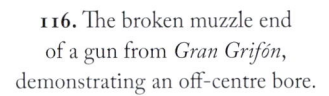

116. The broken muzzle end of a gun from *Gran Grifón*, demonstrating an off-centre bore.

117. A gun from *Juliana* that has suffered a blow-out.

## Figure 118. Measuring shot

The hybrid nature of the Armada meant that there was no common standard of weights and measures, and consequently the apparently simple process of matching guns to shot of the right size was fraught with problems. Gunners used a simple ruler to measure the bore of a piece, expressed as the weight of the required ball. A corresponding gauge was then used to select the correct size of shot. *Trinidad Valencera* has yielded a wooden gunner's rule (b), marked to measure calibres of 1- to 120-pound iron shot. Associated with it were three circular gauges (c) that matched the 1-, 12- and 16-pound calibrations on the rule. Working from the specific mass of iron (itself a variable factor), it ought to have been possible to establish the value and hence the origin of the weight unit involved and test its consistency across the multiples on the scale. Unfortunately, the values thus derived proved wildly and inexplicably erratic. Both rule and gauges were calibrated according to the same graduations, so the errors on this particular set would be avoided because the ball selected using the appropriate gauge would fit the barrel, even if its nominal weight was wrong. But this would only work across the fleet as a whole if all gunners' measuring instruments carried identical errors. They did not. Another gunner's rule from *San Juan de Sicilia* (a) carries errors as idiosyncratic as those on the *Valencera* rule but different.

Had Philip II commissioned a rigorous 'After Action Report', the mismatching of gun-bores and shot-diameters would surely have been high on the list of criticisms. Wide inconsistencies in gun-bores throughout the Armada (except perhaps for royal guns) were exacerbated by widespread innumeracy at all levels from the ordering, specifying, manufacturing and supplying processes of shot production and its allocation and delivery to the right guns.

A gunner aboard *Trinidad Valencera* took his own steps to deal with the problem. The guns on his ship were calibrated in much lighter Venetian pounds, his wooden gauge indicating that the diameter of a 16-lb ball equated to only 12 lbs by the Castilian standard. He had corrected the anomaly by roughly incising the Roman numeral XII on the gauge, adding twelve notches on its rim, no doubt so the figure could be identified by touch in the dimly lit magazine (below, right).

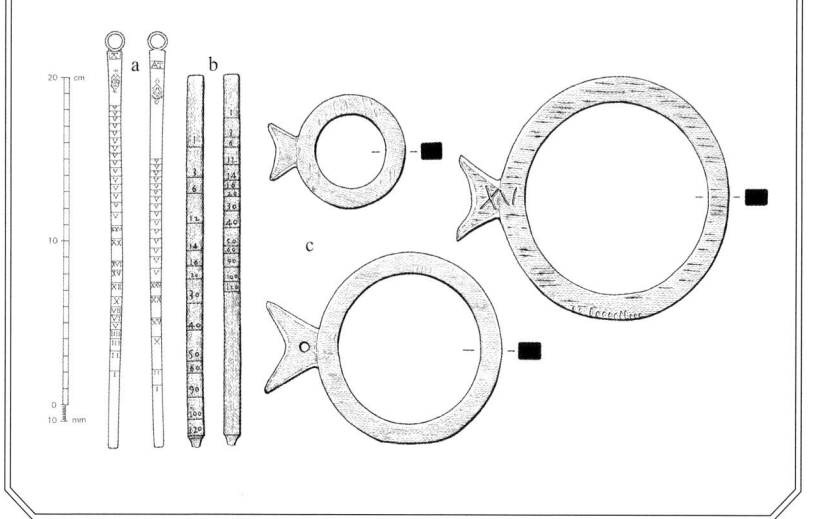

A further insidious difficulty was heaped upon the unfortunate men working the Armada's guns. Because the fleet was not a 'Spanish' Armada at all, but one drawn from the length and breadth of Europe, its guns and projectiles came from foundries and arsenals scattered from the Adriatic to the Baltic, and sometimes beyond. Not a few came from England. Even within individual foundries there was little enough standardization of proportions and bore, while each country (and often individual cities and regions within a country) employed its own often widely differing standards of weights and measures. The Iberian Peninsula employed at least eight regional pound standards, ranging from 345 to 575 grams, while a similar number of Italian standards varied between 301 and 891 grams.[46] The confusion engendered was immense, not least in the apparently simple process of matching projectiles to guns. A further difficulty arose from the traditional practice of expressing gun calibres not as simple diameters of the bore less windage, but in terms of the weight of shot appropriate to them. Thus variations in the specific gravities of stone and cast iron (which may be considerable) might determine whether or not shot of a particular weight ('calibre', or *qua libre*) would actually fit the intended piece. In short, not all 40-pound balls were of the same diameter (Figure 118 and Appendix 4).

## Big Guns II: The English Fleet

What, then, of the other side? Writing shortly after the battle off Gravelines, the English master-gunner William Thomas saw only a lost opportunity:

> If it had pleased God that Her Majesty's ships had been manned with a full supply of good gunners, according to the forces they carry ... it would have been the woefullest time or enterprise that ever the Spaniard took in hand; and not otherwise to be thought or doubted of, but that the most noblest victory by the sea that ever was heard of would have fallen to Her Majesty. What can be said but our sins was the cause that so much powder and shot [were] spent, and so long time in fight, and, in comparison thereof, so little harm?[47]

There was some truth in this. Throughout the campaign Howard and his captains complained that they did not have enough ammunition; and as night fell on 8 August, according to Winter, 'When every man was weary with labour, and our cartridges spent, and munitions wasted – I think in some altogether – we ceased and followed the enemy.' Sir Walter Raleigh agreed: 'In the sea-battle with the

Spaniards in the year 88, when it so nearly concerned the defence and preservation of the kingdom ... many of those great guns, wanting powder and shot, stood but as cyphers and scarecrows.' Had full replenishment of powder and shot arrived at this point, it might indeed have been, as William Thomas speculated, the 'woefullest time' for Spain.[48]

And yet it was woeful enough. The English seem to have surmounted the problem of working ship-killing artillery in close engagements, whereas their adversaries had not. On 31 July, when Recalde's *San Juan* fired 140 rounds, he thought the English fired 300 rounds at his ship, and on 8 August he thought the ratio was 300 outgoing rounds against 1,000 incoming. Aboard *San Martín*, Vanegas thought that on 31 July the Armada ships fired 600 rounds whereas the English fired more than 2,000, and he expressed surprise at 'the speed and rapidity with which they reloaded their guns'. On 8 August he opined that the English 'fired their big guns at the same speed that we fired our muskets', and he recorded that *San Martín* received '107 direct hits on the hull, masts and sails by cannon shot' (see chapter 13).

Several reasons explain this disparity. First, the English fleet carried at least 250 'ship-smashing' guns, almost triple the number aboard the Armada (even counting those intended for use on land), and they were served by far more gunners: 521 aboard the twenty-one larger queen's ships, compared with 196 aboard the forty-eight Armada ships that returned to Santander. The overall ratio between English and Spanish gunners may have been as high as 4:1.[49] Furthermore, the English gunners were all mariners, thoroughly familiar with the guns aboard their own vessels and conversant with the tasks of operating them at sea. Those detailed to work the guns were not expected, like the Spaniards, to double as soldiers, so they were not encumbered with military clothing and accoutrements and could continue to work their guns throughout an action. Drake's men had even undergone training with precious live ammunition (although Howard disapproved of such prodigality: see chapter 3).

In addition, a common mensuration standard was enforced throughout the realm (in 1588 a control Avoirdupois pound of 453.6 grams was placed in the cellars of the Exchequer: this remains the standard today). And while there was no absolute conformity of gun-types, the common values of weights and measures suggest that little mismatching of ammunition and gun calibres occurred on English gun-decks.

England's shipboard artillery enjoyed a final advantage: its compact four-wheeled truck carriage (see chapter 11). Its superiority was decisively demonstrated in 1988, when Alan Ereira produced a BBC documentary trilogy about the Armada. He decided to test the relative efficiency of Spanish and English naval gun carriages by building replicas and conducting a comparative test (Figures 119, 120).

119. A six-man Portsmouth gun crew in 1988 working a replica culverin from *Mary Rose* on a replica Spanish sea-carriage based on one from *Trinidad Valencera*.

120. The same gun mounted on a replica four-wheeled truck carriage based on one from *Mary Rose*. Only four members of the Portsmouth team were needed to operate it, and they performed the drills in half the time.

In each case the same gun was used – a replica culverin from *Mary Rose* – served by a six-strong crew and a gun-captain from the Portsmouth field-gun team – that year's champions in the Royal Navy's thrilling field-gun race at the Royal Tournament (sadly discontinued in 1999). It would be invidious to compare these fit, highly motivated, superbly trained and intensely competitive young men with either the Spanish or English gun crews of 1588; moreover, the Portsmouth team was working under ideal conditions on a ship moored in harbour and not under fire at sea. Even the awkward Spanish gun-rig took them only five minutes to load, haul into position, fire and haul inboard for reloading; but, significantly, a crew of only four took only half that time to perform the drill with the same gun mounted on a truck carriage. In comparative terms, the latter was therefore 100 per cent more efficient than the two-wheeled trailed version used on at least some Armada ships, and it also required fewer men.

This decisive advantage, combined with all the rest (more big guns; more gunners with more experience; better powder) fully explains why the English gunners fired more often than their adversaries. This increased their fighting capability by the equivalent factors.

The ability of English ships to fire at close quarters and then swiftly disengage and reload, thanks to their superior sailing qualities, was also critical. And firing at close quarters was essential. In 2015 another BBC programme about the Armada demonstrated this by a further experiment. The test firing of a replica 4-pounder against timber similar in thickness to the hull of an Armada ship was arranged. It was ineffective at 200 yards, either missing the target or failing to penetrate, but at a range of 100 yards it proved devastating – and in 1588 the Tudor navy fired not just 4-pounders but many 40-pounders.[50]

## The Pathway to Victory

The events of 8 August confirmed Philip's worst fears that the dastardly English would fire low, and so inflict damage on the vulnerable belt 'between wind and water' – but this had not been the case at first. They had shown extreme caution during their first encounters – mere 'feather-plucking', in Howard's words; 'More coldly done than became the value of our nation,' thought one of his more outspoken subordinates – and when they closed for the kill off Gravelines it was almost too late, for by then their ammunition stocks were running low.

Why had they delayed so long? Numerous senior officers had already used their big guns in combat – Hawkins at San Juan de Ulúa; Winter at Smerwick; Fenton in the South Atlantic; Drake and Frobisher in the West Indies; Drake again at Cadiz in 1587 – but (except for Hawkins) they had faced only ill-prepared opponents, and had operated only in relatively small squadrons. As the vast Spanish fleet entered the Channel in battle-array, none of Elizabeth's sea-captains knew in advance either its strengths or its weaknesses. It certainly *looked* impregnable, and there seemed no obvious avenue of attack.

So what were they to do? Go in close and risk disablement from those rows of gleaming bronze muzzles? Attempt to board the Spanish ships and be annihilated by their massed companies of troops? At first Howard's colleagues in the Privy Council failed to grasp his predicament. When on 31 July the Lord Admiral begged 'for the love of God and our country let us have with some speed some great shot sent to us of all bigness', the Council responded by sending a contingent of musketeers. Howard angrily sent them back. Sir Francis Walsingham, at least, knew better and on 3 August ordered the commander of the Portsmouth garrison to 'see the Lord Admiral provided, though we lack by land, for that all his fight consists in powder and bullet'. But two days later the Council interfered again: 'Her Majesty, seeing the enemy disposed to continue a lingering fight, has found it most fit to have her ships double-manned' and therefore ordered musketeers to assemble in Kent 'to be embarked as the service shall require'. She also recalled from the English regiments in the Netherlands '1,000 of their best shot for the furnishing of the ships'. Even on 10 August, when thanks to Howard's efforts the Armada was in full retreat, the Council sent a messenger to demand of him:

> What causes are there that the Spanish navy hath not been boarded by the queen's ships? And though some of the ships of Spain may be thought too huge to be boarded by the English, yet some of the queen's ships are thought very able to have boarded divers of the meaner ships of the Spanish navy.

Howard's reply, perhaps fortunately, has not been preserved.[51]

Nevertheless, until they anchored off Calais on 6 August the two fleets were locked in a tactical stalemate. The Spaniards could neither sink nor get close enough to board the English, but the English could not sink and dared not board the Spaniards either. If the Armada had been a self-contained force, as Santa Cruz intended, Howard could not have prevented it from landing.

Then on 8 August, in the wake of the dislocation caused by the fireships to the Armada's hitherto tight and steadfastly maintained defensive formation, the queen's ships finally launched an aggressive close-range gunnery assault on the retreating but fast-reforming Spanish fleet – a tactic that required remarkable fire discipline. But why had they not done this from the beginning? What changed their initial caution to the vigorous and confident close action off Gravelines?

It is here that what Cohen and Gooch call the 'ability to adapt' came into play. Somehow the bubble of the Armada's apparent invincibility had been pricked, and its shortcomings in sailing performance and gunnery recognized. This realization evidently dawned at some point between the first encounter on 31 July and the battle off Gravelines nine days later. We do not know for certain how or why it dawned on them, but Howard and his captains had clearly perceived the Armada's underlying vulnerability by the time they reached Calais. After the battles off the Isle of Wight on 3 and 4 August, fighting ceased for three days, as Medina Sidonia progressed nervously towards his rendezvous with Parma. This suggests that on or before 4 August Howard and his lieutenants had decided to conserve their dwindling ammunition stocks for a decisive attack on the Armada after they had been reinforced by Winter and Seymour in the Narrow Seas. It seems they now believed that they could come close enough to the Spaniards to inflict damage without risking serious retaliation, so long as they used their decisive sailing advantages to avoid being grappled and boarded.

Who first made this momentous discovery, and when, we do not know for sure. Perhaps it was a gradual realization as events unfolded, in the minds and conversations of Howard and his Council of War; but Sir Francis Drake seems a likely candidate, and we can discern a number of incidents that may have helped him towards this vital realization.

First was his capture, on the morning of 1 August, of Don Pedro de Valdés and *Rosario*. Here was one of the largest and best-gunned ships in the Armada, and yet she put up only a token resistance. As soon as they boarded their prize, Drake and his officers saw that 'they are not in such good order in their putting themselves in battle' – no doubt a reference to the striking contrast between their own compact truck gun carriages and the cumbersome carriages of their adversary, making it difficult to fire accurately and reload in battle.[52] With his revolutionary ideas about comradely teamwork under a single naval officer who wielded absolute authority, Drake would also have taken note of the scratch crews of soldiers who tended *Rosario*'s guns, the inefficient and divisive structures of command, and the vast reserves of unspent powder and shot. Perhaps Sir Francis exploited his ready wit, infectious charm and fluent Spanish to extract further information from the disgruntled Don Pedro. Emanuel van Meteren did not doubt it, writing in his *History* that 'Valdés began to recount to Drake details of his voyage as soon as he came on board' *Revenge*, where 'he ate at Drake's table and slept in Drake's cabin'. In this relaxed atmosphere Don Pedro may also have revealed the fleet's strategy: a junction with Parma as the essential prelude to the invasion and the capture of London. Some in Spain suspected as much: shortly after the remnants of the Armada returned, one of Elizabeth's spies reported that Don Pedro was 'now in great suspicion with the king and nobles of Spain to have revealed some great things of their counsels and pretences, by reason of his good usage and entertainment' by Drake.[53]

No one was better qualified than Sir Francis to appreciate the significance of these revelations, both seen and heard, and it may be that his capture of *Rosario*, though bitterly criticized by his contemporaries, was in retrospect one of the most significant episodes of the campaign.

It is tempting to link the dawn attack on *Gran Grifón* off the Solent on 3 August with the conclusions Drake had drawn from his inspection of *Rosario* and his conversations with Don Pedro. Here, for the first time, we hear of a really close ship-to-ship action in which English tactics involved mobility and firepower. Is it a coincidence that the aggressor seems to have been *Revenge*? Was Drake perhaps testing a developing theory about the Spaniards' inability to fight a mobile artillery action, and wisely choosing one of the less-well-armed troubleshooters for his experiment? If so, he must have found the result deeply gratifying, for (according to Gómez de Medina) 'he fired more than 20 rounds into the bowels of my ship, which ruined her and was the main reason for her loss on Fair Isle', while *Grifón*'s four bronze *medias culebrinas* – the biggest guns she carried – remained virtually silent.[54]

A day later, off the Isle of Wight, someone (was it Drake again?) repeated this experiment in full squadron strength. An observer aboard *San Martín* noted that 'today our enemies came closer than before, firing their heaviest guns from the lower deck', and they managed to break the Armada's right wing.[55] Howard and his officers now had all the information they needed to identify the Armada's fundamental weakness, and it was at this point that they resolved to conserve their ammunition for a final decisive battle. Even if the Armada could not be defeated or broken at sea, it might be deflected irretrievably from its junction with Parma and sent on its perilous voyage home. That was the measure of England's success at Calais and Gravelines.

It nevertheless remained a close-run thing. Even at the last, the Armada retained a sting in its tail. Some of the troubleshooters were still able to fire, reload and fire again. According to Captain Vanegas, on 7 August one of the English ships stationed off Dover 'came up behind the Armada and when it was close, she fired all the guns on her port side; but fire from the *culebrinas* on the stern of two galleasses returned the compliment and the English ship soon rejoined her own fleet.' According to his jaundiced critic Sir Martin Frobisher, Drake also made a serious tactical error when he came 'bragging up at the first, indeed, and gave them his prow and his broadside', but this time his Spanish adversary was ready and gave him powerful return fire. Thereafter, Frobisher reported with relish, Drake was 'glad he was gone again, like a cowardly knave or traitor'. By the end of the day *Revenge* was 'pierced with shot above forty times', probably also from the heavy guns of a galleass, and her mainmast was 'perished with shot'. But this remained the exception: few other Armada ships could administer punishment this severe.[56]

A terrifying scenario for Tudor England had been averted, and in the process a new era of naval warfare was born. A few days after the battle off Gravelines, Winter (the same admiral who thirty years before had instructed that 'no ordnance to be shot but by the captain's licence and that not in vain': see chapter 3) claimed that 'out of my ship', *Vanguard*, 'there was shot 500 shot of demi-cannon, culverin and demi-culverin'. Although the absence of Ordnance Office records for 1588 prevents us from establishing whether this fearsome rate of fire was typical, its records for 1596 reveal that by then it was standard operating procedure. Not only did the 308 heavy guns aboard seventeen of the queen's ships discharge almost 4,000 rounds in a second raid on Cadiz, they fired most of them on a single day (1 July 1596) when, according to a contemporary account, 'infinite store of shot was spent between our ships, the town and galleys, much to their damage and nothing to our loss' (Figure 121).[57]

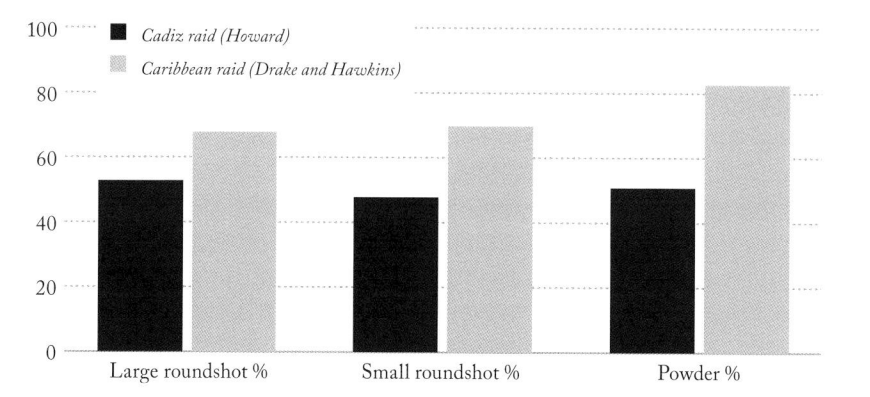

121. Percentage of shot and powder used by the navy royal, 1595–6.

All the evidence suggests that the English fleet employed the same tactics on 8 August 1588, because by the end of the action Howard's ships had apparently run out of shot, and he was reduced to bluff. 'We put on a brag countenance and gave chase,' he noted, as the Armada disappeared into the northern seas, 'as if we had wanted nothing.' In fact, they wanted everything: not only were their shot-lockers empty but their crews were exhausted and close to starvation. Many were mortally ill. If the Armada at this point had been entering the Thames estuary, its ships impregnable because the soldiers crowding their decks precluded close combat, with Parma's barges sheltered in their midst, the queen's almost impotent navy could have done little to stop them.

Instead, however, in defiant if somewhat ragged array, the great Armada departed England's shores. It had fought and failed but it had not suffered outright defeat. Medina Sidonia and his men had lost much, but they had not lost their honour.

**(Overleaf) 122.** *The Spanish Armada off the coast of England.* This miniature painting done *c.* 1600 by an unknown artist in the Flemish style shows the climax of the Armada campaign on 7 and 8 August 1588. Elizabeth I (on horseback, far right) watches from the shore as her navy (right) attacks the Spanish Armada (left) with both fireships (centre) and artillery (front). A chain of beacons burn in the background.

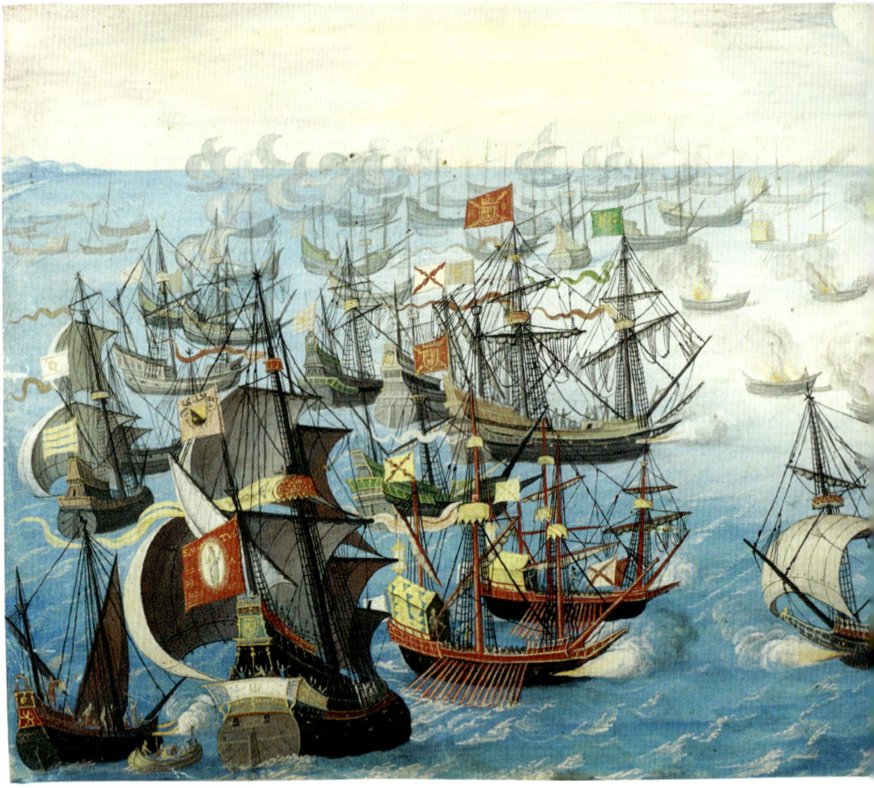

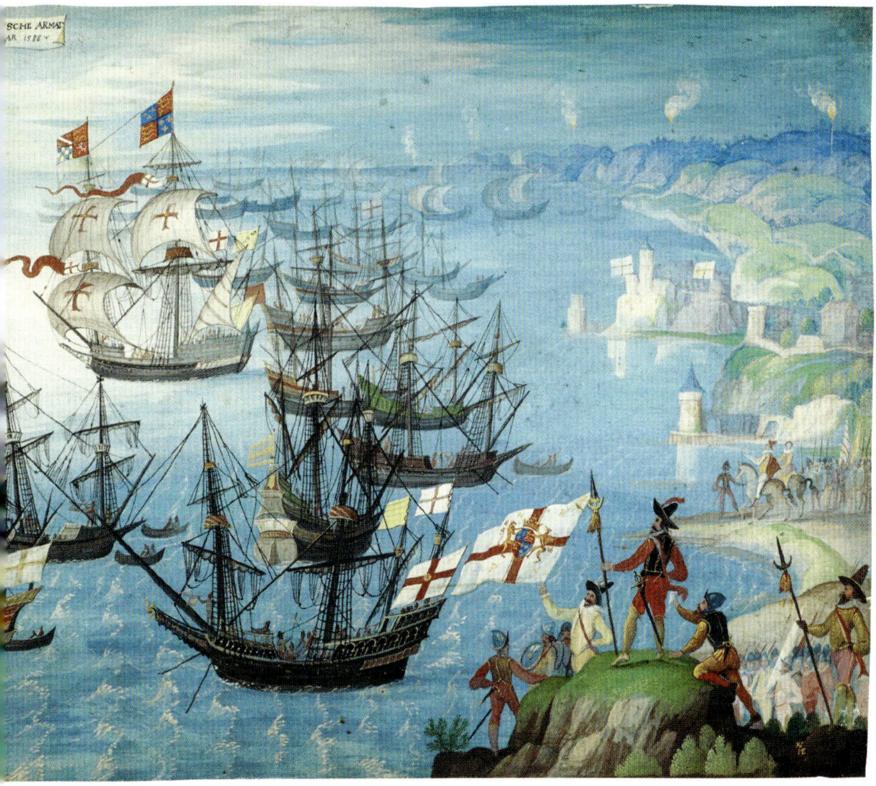
SCHE ARMAD
AR 1588

## Part IV
# The Aftermath

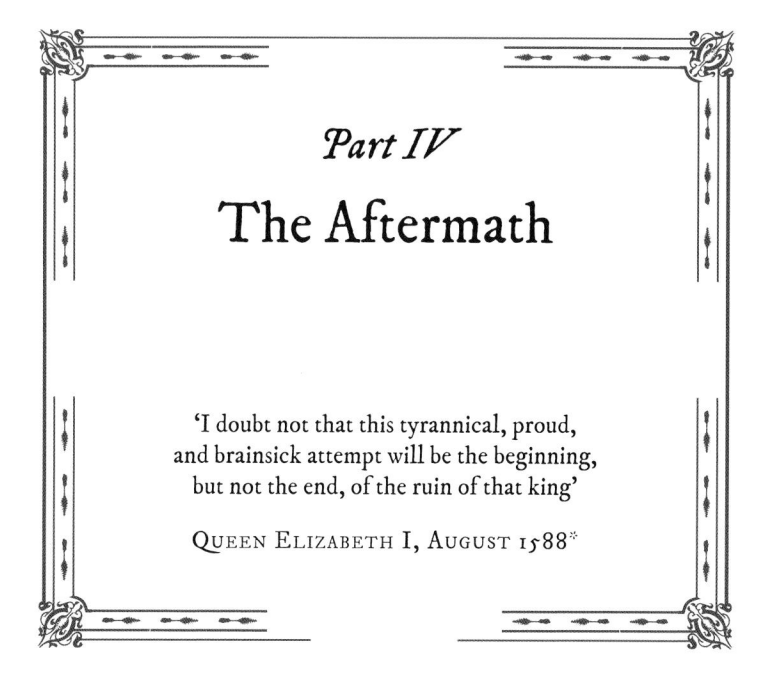

'I doubt not that this tyrannical, proud, and brainsick attempt will be the beginning, but not the end, of the ruin of that king'

QUEEN ELIZABETH I, AUGUST 1588[*]

# 17

# The Bitterness of Defeat

~~~~~<<<✿>>>~~~~~

## Good News, Bad News

After news arrived that the Armada had left Lisbon, Philip turned his attention to other matters. On 27 June 1588 he asked the count of Olivares, his ambassador in Rome, to assess the chances of securing a papal dispensation for his daughter Isabella Clara Eugenia, now twenty-two, to marry her cousin Emperor Rudolf II or one of his brothers: Ernest, Matthias, Maximilian or Albert. This would form the prelude to investing her and her new husband with the kingdoms of England and Ireland.[1]

On learning on 25 July that the Armada had left Corunna, Philip authorized and took part in a procession of thanksgiving. He did the same the following day, 'the feast of St Anne, since in the past God had granted him victories on that day' (a reference to Santa Cruz's successes in the Azores in 1582 and 1583), but the effort seems to have exhausted him. The next day he sent a dossier back to his secretary Mateo Vázquez unopened because 'it's ten o'clock and I have not dined or lifted my head all day'. Since 'I now have neither eyes nor concentration' to read any more, Vázquez must 'send it back to me tomorrow'.[2] The king's spirits had evidently recovered on the feast of St Dominic, 4 August, because he left the Escorial with his children, the Infanta Isabella and the future Philip III, 'to hunt rabbits, and he seemed very happy when he returned late having killed many of them with his crossbow'. After celebrating the festival of St Lawrence, patron saint of the Escorial, on 10 August he even managed a joke. When Vázquez reminded him that he needed to review and resolve 800 *consultas*, Philip jested that matters were not so bad because the unread *consultas* on and around his desk numbered 'only'

300. A few days later, however, one of the officials responsible for managing the flow of dossiers to and from the king's desk implored a colleague in desperation: 'Please stop sending papers until His Majesty is able to deal with them. It is torture for some of us here to read the letters and other papers that come from so many sources, and to write, write, write!'[3]

Excitement mounted when a report arrived that the Armada had been sighted 'off Le Conquet' – but where was that? The king consulted his copies of Medina Sidonia's *Derrotero*, Ortelius's *Atlas*, and two charts, rather like Salanio in Shakespeare's *Merchant of Venice*:

> Peering in maps for ports and piers and roads;
> And every object that might make me fear
> Misfortune to my ventures, out of doubt
> Would make me sad.

But 'peering' did not make Philip sad. 'I could not find Le Conquet on the smaller map,' he reported, 'but the larger one' showed that it was in Brittany. The Armada was therefore approaching its objective.[4]

The letters written by Medina Sidonia and others aboard the Armada on 30 and 31 July, which arrived at the Escorial in record time, maintained this optimism. Don Juan de Idiáquez immediately noted that 'the good news started to arrive here on the vigil of the Assumption [14 August]. May God be pleased to let news of victory arrive within the *novena* [the nine-day period of devotion that Catholics observe after major religious events].' A report from Dieppe in Normandy dated 7 August, entitled 'A letter about the encounter of the English and Spanish fleets, and of the Spanish victory', duly followed, together with details from Ambassador Mendoza in Paris which confirmed the good news.[5]

Everything changed on 31 August. The Tuscan ambassador in Madrid began a letter that day complaining about the secrecy surrounding the Armada's fate caused by a government-imposed news blackout, so that 'even if we learn anything through friendship with the royal secretaries, it is embargoed' because no couriers were allowed to leave. But that night irrefutable evidence arrived from Mendoza that the fleet had failed to 'join hands' with the duke of Parma.[6]

As usual Philip and his entourage initially saw the setback as another case of God testing their fortitude. Idiáquez forwarded the bad news to the king with a covering note that began: 'The doubt and anguish in which we find ourselves is great'; but, he continued, 'It is possible that God will grant us victory after this setback so that we may see His hand more clearly. And even if He should allow something else, for His secret reasons, such a great enterprise cannot fail to earn a great reward [in heaven].'[7]

Next, again as usual, the king and his staff sought to control the situation by pen. Idiáquez prepared a long memorandum telling Medina Sidonia what to do. If the Armada had taken refuge in Scotland it must refit and prepare to invade England the following year; and if the duke had decided to return to Spain, he should put troops ashore near Waterford in Ireland to form a bridgehead for operations the following year. This was absurdly unrealistic, but at least the minister and his master had recognized – albeit too late – the need for a 'Plan B'. Philip even recognized the need for delegation. At the end of his letter to the duke he conceded that 'after you have discussed the matter with your advisers and others on the fleet, you must do what seems best to you, because since you are on the spot you can see matters more clearly'.[8]

The king's departure from his usual style of micromanagement reveals, perhaps more eloquently than anything else, the shattering blow dealt to his self-confidence. When he read a reply to Parma drafted by Idiáquez, expressing the hope 'that God will have allowed some improvement, and that the reputation of everyone (which is now so compromised) may be recovered', the king underlined the passage. 'It might be better,' he told Idiáquez, 'to delete what I have underlined, because in what God does, and in what we do for God, there is no gain or loss of reputation. It is better not to speak of such things. So take it out.'[9]

Idiáquez, for his part, confided to Parma that:

> I cannot exaggerate the grief caused by seeing something that cost so much time, money and trouble – and is so important to the service of God and His Majesty – placed in jeopardy, just at the point when it was about to bear fruit. His Majesty has felt it more than you would believe possible, and if there were not some remaining hope in God that all this might still achieve something for His cause . . . I do not know how he could bear such a great blow. Certainly this business leaves no time to think about anything else, nor to think of it without excessive grief.[10]

Time brought no relief. Instead, on 3 September, a courier from France brought confirmation of the Armada's northward flight. The cipher-clerks and ministers blenched and debated which of them should break the news to the king. The choice fell on Mateo Vázquez, but even he did so with great trepidation and indirectly, by forwarding a tactless parallel drawn by a courtier. 'If we consider', it ran, 'the case of King Louis IX of France, who was a saint and was engaged on a saintly enterprise [the Seventh Crusade in 1250], and yet saw his army die of plague, with himself defeated and captured, we certainly cannot fail to fear greatly for the success of our Armada.' To avert this fate, Vázquez suggested offering more prayers for success. This proved too much for the king: 'I hope that God has not permitted so much evil,' he scribbled angrily, 'for everything has been done for His service.'[11]

Once more the king reluctantly decided to delegate. He signed another letter authorizing Parma to decide what to do next 'since you are on the spot' – although 'I hope that with God's help you will achieve something that brings consolation for what is happening now, which is so different from what – with good reason – we expected.' Idiáquez's letter to Parma was more blunt:

> His Majesty regretted your news from the start, and his regret increases every day. It does not affect his health, because (God be praised) he is doing well, and his spirits suffice to absorb any reverse; but as a Christian who undertook this enterprise with such holy zeal, the failure to complete such an important service to God causes him extreme pain – especially having come so close to success and having done more himself than anyone could expect or imagine.[12]

For the next two weeks no further reliable information about the Armada arrived in Spain and hopes began to rise once more. On 5 September a printer in Seville issued a cheerful newsletter entitled *What has happened to the Most Happy Armada so far*: after noting the losses of *Rosario*, *San Salvador* and *San Lorenzo*, it described the subsequent victory won by the Spanish fleet. Two weeks later, a papal agent in Madrid relayed back to Rome rumours that:

> The Armada has landed in some Scottish port. Although we sustained some damage in the battle, we ended up victorious and the enemy fleet is severely damaged. We hear that we sank some of their ships and captured others, and that the English admiral returned to the Thames with no more than 25 badly damaged ships. Everyone is sure that Drake has been captured or killed.

A royal minister told Cesare Speciano, the papal nuncio, that 'we are obliged to believe in the victory of our Armada. Therefore,' he added, 'raising doubts about its fate is unhelpful' because so much depended on a favourable outcome. This did not convince Speciano. He interpreted the silence to mean that the Enterprise of England had failed, and that Medina Sidonia had 'decided to return home by circumnavigating England and Ireland, just as many German merchant ships do, to avoid the English Channel'. He predicted that 'one morning we will get news that the Armada is back in Portugal or Galicia'.[13]

Although remarkably prescient, this too remained speculation. Parma sent pinnaces from Dunkirk to Scotland and to Devon with messages and munitions for Medina Sidonia, but they found no trace of the fleet; and although Mendoza, in Paris, accumulated an abundance of information, he dismissed it as propaganda because it came from England. In contrast, Mendoza believed intelligence from England suggesting that the queen's ships were regrouping, perhaps in preparation for a counter-attack on Spain. He dispatched a warning via an express courier who arrived in Madrid on 20 September. The king's ministers promptly sent out orders to all major ports with instructions that, whenever the Armada got home, its soldiers and mariners must not disembark but instead remain at their posts, come what may, ready to meet any emergency. The folly of all this became apparent four days later, with the arrival at Court of a bedraggled Don Balthasar de Zúñiga (Figure 123).

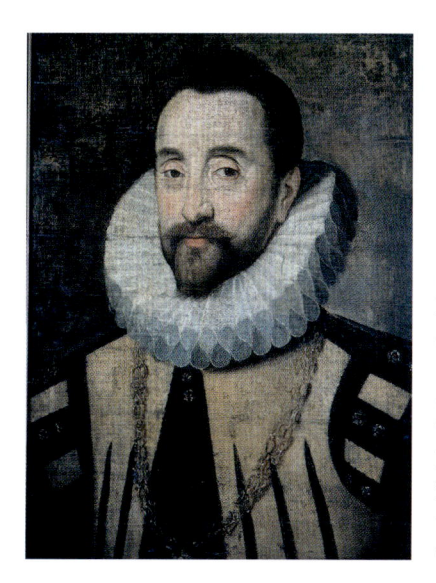

123. Don Balthasar de Zúñiga, *c.* 1615. Medina Sidonia chose Zúñiga, a staff officer on his flagship, to return to Spain and explain to Philip the failure of the Armada and Parma's army to 'join hands'. Zúñiga subsequently held important diplomatic posts until in 1618 he became chief minister of the Spanish monarchy, a post he held until his death four years later.

## Bad News, Worse News

Don Balthasar had left the fleet off Shetland on 21 August 'at 61 degrees north and 300 leagues from Spain'. He took with him letters and reports from Medina Sidonia, Bobadilla and others aboard the flagship *San Martín* detailing the Armada's voyage since leaving Corunna and explaining why it had failed to 'join hands' with Parma. But the same storms that delayed and damaged the main fleet also afflicted Zúñiga, who only reached Spain on 21 September – the same day as the duke. He immediately rode to the Escorial, which he reached in just three days, and then 'spent several hours with His Majesty explaining what had happened' up to the point when he left the fleet.[14]

The situation had become incomparably worse since then. Medina Sidonia had shamelessly abandoned his flagship as soon as it came within sight of Santander, and spent the next two days convalescing ashore before he found the courage to update the king on the state of his fleet. 'I am unable to describe to Your Majesty the misfortunes and miseries which have befallen us,' he wrote, 'because they are the worst that have been known on any voyage. Some of the ships which put into this port have spent the last fourteen days without a single drop of water.' During the voyage, Medina Sidonia continued, he had given his two warm cloaks to a frozen priest and a wounded boy, leaving him with only a thin short cloak; and of the 500 men who had left Lisbon on his flagship, '180 are already dead of sickness, as well as three of the four pilots'. (This loss may explain why, having set course for Cape Finisterre, 'when we first espied land, we all believed it was Corunna' when 'in fact we were 100 leagues away from that harbour, without knowing where we were at all'.) 'Of the 60 members of my own household, so many have sickened or died that only two are left.' Many of the survivors who came ashore were ill with dysentery or typhus, and the duke himself suffered from what might be called today post-traumatic stress disorder. 'I arrived very close to death, and so I am in bed and cannot cope with everything, even though I want to,' he told the king. His letter to Don Juan de Idiáquez was shorter but no less bitter. 'I wish I could write more now, but I am in no state to do so because illness prevents me, and so I am in bed suffering from extreme weakness, and my head hurts so much because of the lack of sleep. I have not had a wink of sleep, day or night, for 31 days except for yesterday and last night. No, none' (a strangely eloquent construction). He closed with a reminder that 'I find myself in this situation only because I have obeyed His Majesty', and he pleaded for permission to go home at once.[15]

We may excuse the duke's defeatism, but it is hard to forgive his delay in arranging emergency measures for his fellow survivors. Not until 24 September did he sign letters to the towns of northern Castile appealing for medical supplies, food and 'beds and blankets for the wounded' – although he found time to arrange the disembarkation of his personal possessions from the flagship and to purchase four packs of playing cards. He bought another four packs on 27 September, just after sending Idiáquez another pathetic plea for permission to go home, 'since I know nothing about the sea or about fighting'. The duke continued:

> I did not volunteer for this job, because Our Lord did not call me to this vocation and also because (as I have told you countless times) I cannot satisfy either my conscience or my duty in trying to do it. Under no circumstances and in no way will I handle maritime affairs any further, even if the king should chop off my head, because that would be easier than persevering in a command that I neither know nor understand, compelled to believe those who advised me, without knowing their motive.[16]

News of the disaster soon spread. On 26 September the magistrates of Burgos received Medina Sidonia's appeal for emergency supplies, and immediately sent thirty mules carrying food and medicines. A few weeks later wounded soldiers from the fleet arrived in the city 'in such a state that it is a shame to see them and hear them'. One of the most upsetting stories was that of Francisco de Montenegro, a soldier who had served the king for twenty years before he embarked on Oquendo's flagship *Santa Ana*. Although the vessel got back to San Sebastián relatively intact, soon afterwards a spark ignited the powder magazine, destroying the ship, killing several members of her crew and maiming many more – including Montenegro, who was left 'blind in both eyes and lacking both hands'. He made a partial recovery in the Burgos hospital, and in November the city magistrates gave him two ducats for his journey to Madrid, where he planned to ask the king to reward his services and his suffering.[17]

He did not travel alone. According to one Irish eyewitness, to every port along the Cantabrian coast 'there came daily people out of divers parts of Spain to inquire for ships and their friends who were missing, with great lamentation for divers [persons] of account who were lost'. One of his compatriots who had been imprisoned in Corunna as a spy reported that 'people there do nothing but lament, mourn and weep, both openly and privately, for the loss of their parents, husbands, children, brethren, and friends, with open exclamation, and cursing the time that the said Armada was made'.[18]

It would be easy to dismiss such statements as exaggeration, but in October 1588 a royal proclamation forbade subjects to cover their houses in black or compel their whole household to wear mourning; henceforth only the immediate family could wear black. Offenders would be fined (and forfeit their mourning clothes). The preamble to the proclamation claimed that such excessive expressions of grief 'do not please Our Lord, or help or heal the souls of the dead, and they are and appear vain and superstitious'. Such verbosity did not fool Nuncio Speciano. 'The proclamation was issued to prevent people here from getting depressed,' he reported to Rome, 'because the number of those aboard the Armada reported dead increases every day, and so you see more courtiers in mourning.' It did not fool Ambassador Khevenhüller either, who reported that 'at this point over 60 ships are missing'. Should they 'be permanently lost – and they number half of those that set forth – we may speculate on the impact on those whose children, brothers, fathers and friends sailed with the Armada and are now lost'. In short, 'This has been a shameful, terrible enterprise.'[19]

The king now ordered prayers for the fleet's success to cease, to be replaced by a solemn Mass in each diocese to give thanks that not everything had been lost. He also called for a new round of devotions 'by all clerics, and other suitably devout persons ... entrusting to Our Lord most sincerely in their private and secret prayers all my actions, so that his Divine Majesty may direct and guide them to whatever may serve Him, the exaltation of His church, and the good and conservation of Christendom – which is what I desire'. A few days later he grumbled that 'I have got a terrible cough and cold, and I am convinced it comes from my papers because as soon as I pick them up, I start to cough.'[20]

November brought no relief. Khevenhüller opined that 'This venture has failed to such an extent that I truly believe that even if one wanted to imagine the most disagreeable outcome, it would still be better than what has actually happened. At present fifty ships are still missing, and no one knows where they are.' An Italian diplomat likewise reported that 'half the Armada is missing, taking into account those captured or sunk by bombardment or by storms', and that 'more than 12,000 soldiers, the flower of Spain (as one might say), have perished'. A member of the Council of War told Speciano that 'sixty ships, great and small, are missing, and two-thirds of the men aboard the Armada are dead, so that of the 30,000 who sailed only 10,000 remain'. According to the nuncio: 'Everyone is now agitated, seeing that God has almost certainly turned His hand against us.'[21]

Even the king briefly shared these negative feelings. On 10 November, in anguish and despair, he confided to Vázquez that he longed for death because:

> If God does not send us a miracle (which is what I hope from Him), I hope to die and go to Him before all this happens – which is what I pray for, so as

not to see so many misfortunes and reverses. All this is for your eyes alone. Please God, let me be mistaken, but I do not think so: rather, we shall have to witness, sooner than anyone thinks, what we so much fear – unless God returns to fight for His cause . . . Very soon we shall find ourselves in such a state that we shall wish that we had never been born.[22]

This was an extraordinary admission for a monarch who prided himself on his Catholic faith, but it reflected a depressing census of the fleet just received from his naval officials, which showed eight Armada ships definitely lost and fifty-nine more missing. The rest lay scattered in sundry ports along 500 miles of coast: nine at San Sebastián, six at Corunna, one each at Ribadeo and Muros, and forty-four at Santander. Of the latter, 'every vessel needs to be careened and some need repairs to their decks, damaged by so many heavy guns'. All of them also needed anchors – two or three per ship, on average – and more ship's boats. Efforts to concentrate all the surviving vessels at Santander led to the wreck of three more vessels before the year ended: the *urcas Barca de Danzig* and *Casa de Paz Grande*, and Bertendona's *Regazona* – the sixth squadron flagship to be lost.[23]

Equally dangerous for Spain's defensive posture was the loss of artillery, especially the great siege-guns cast by Gregorio Loeffler and Remigy de Halut, and the loss of senior officers. By the end of 1588 Santa Cruz, Recalde, Leyva, Moncada and Oquendo were dead; Medina Sidonia and Bobadilla wrote each other 'sick notes' and left the fleet at the earliest opportunity; both Don Pedro and Diego Flores de Valdés languished in gaol. Of the five *maestres de campo*, Luzón and Pimentel were also prisoners; Isla died in Le Havre when a mast fell on his head; and Toledo remained in Flanders. Only Mexía returned to Spain aboard the fleet, but (he claimed two weeks later) 'I arrived so ill – and remain so – that I have not yet got out of bed'.[24]

We may never know the exact total of those lost on the Armada campaign, even though royal officials did their best to ascertain them. The chief magistrate of Guipúzcoa, for example, toured the province and noted the number and rank of the fallen, the ship on which they had sailed, their home, and the number of dependants they had left. The list of the dead included 502 names, almost all mariners. Of these no fewer than 221 died in Lisbon before the fleet sailed; forty-nine perished in the explosion of *San Salvador*; and 102 were lost in Ireland. Only twenty-three died in combat. Almost half the dead left widows and children (most of them young). The campaign almost wiped out some families. Three brothers of the Iriarte family of Zumaya died, 'leaving their parents in great poverty'. Not only did Martín de Aranda, Captain Cuéllar's gaoler, die – so did all his nine cousins aboard the 'Most Happy Armada'.

Philip did his best to care for the bereaved. He made the brother of Don Felipe de Córdoba, killed by a cannonball on the flagship, a gentleman of the royal bedchamber. He wrote letters of condolence to afflicted noble families, assuring them that the death of their loved one 'was the will of God, and so you must accept it, and console yourself that he is with Him in glory'. He also paid for services rendered by the dead. Recalde's nephew received the admiral's pay arrears in full in December 1588; Leyva's widow received Don Alonso's arrears in March 1590, and the king petitioned the pope to allow their young son to succeed him as Knight Commander of Alcántara.[25]

The king also did his best to ensure that the soldiers and seamen who survived received their dues. When he discovered in December 1588 that his officials had discharged some Armada veterans without a full settlement of their wages he immediately protested that: 'This is contrary to Christian charity and also very much alien to my desire, which has been (and is) that those who have served (and are still serving) me should not only be paid what they are owed but also rewarded as far as our resources permit.' Henceforth, before any veteran left the king's service, the Council of War must review his service record, and his arrears, and then recommend an appropriate recompense. The king created a special fund 'to pay the wages of dead and discharged soldiers' who had served aboard his Armada. He also took steps to ascertain who was to blame for the failure of the Enterprise.[26]

## The Search for Scapegoats I: The Duke of Parma

As soon as the Armada sailed into the North Sea arguments began over how and where the venture had gone wrong. 'There is nobody aboard this fleet,' Bobadilla informed Idiáquez from the flagship on 20 August, 'who is not now saying "I told you so" or "I knew this would happen." But it's just like trying to lock the stable door after the horse has bolted.' Bobadilla nevertheless went on to propound his own explanation of the debacle. 'The most important thing,' he asserted, 'was that we found that many of the enemy's ships held great advantages over us in combat, both in their design and in their guns, gunners and crews, and they used their sails to steer so that they could do whatever they wanted.' In contrast, 'we carried very few cannonballs' and soon either ran low or ran out. 'But despite everything,' he continued, 'the duke [of Medina Sidonia] managed to bring his fleet to anchor in Calais roads, just seven leagues from Dunkirk . . . and if, on the day that we arrived there, Parma had come out [with his forces], we would have carried out the invasion'. If only, he repeated a few lines later, 'Parma had been at Dunkirk, as

Your Lordship told me he would be, with his eyes open and ready to sail as soon as he saw our fleet, we would have done it'.[27]

This analysis of failure – the earliest one to survive – accords with most of the known facts. Despite all the defects in supply, design, organization and leadership, the Armada had indeed reached Calais with its order unimpaired and relatively few losses; and it managed to stay there for thirty-six hours. If the English fireships and close-range artillery fire had not broken the fleet's disciplined formation, so that it could wait a few more days, Philip II's Grand Design might have succeeded.

Bobadilla was not alone in blaming Parma for the failure. Why had he not been ready, despite the repeated messages that reported the fleet's progress from Corunna? Why had he not at least attempted a sortie? A Spanish nobleman who arrived in Dunkirk from the Armada 'said openly' that if Parma 'were in Spain he would lose his head'. According to Don Bernardino de Mendoza in Paris, many French observers believed that Parma had deliberately sabotaged the Armada. In Italy the duke of Savoy (Philip's son-in-law) offered to take command of the Army of Flanders because 'in view of the accounts, which seem worse every day, of how badly Parma has carried out his orders (whether through malice or carelessness) to be ready and to aid Medina Sidonia, it seems impossible . . . that Your Majesty can leave him in the Netherlands'. After learning of the fleet's losses, a Venetian military expert surmised that 'Parma has reason to be, after King Philip, the most desperate man in the world'.[28]

Criticisms of the duke also spread in Spain. Don Balthasar de Zúñiga told a Tuscan diplomat in Madrid that 'Medina Sidonia placed all the blame on the duke of Parma', because 'Don Rodrigo Tello had reached [Parma] with news of the Armada's arrival in the Channel soon after the first of August' (a blatant lie: although Tello did indeed reach Parma late on 1 August, Medina Sidonia dispatched him on 25 July, almost a week before the Armada entered the Channel). A few days later another diplomat in Madrid reported that 'all the Spaniards, and especially those who returned on the Armada' blamed its failure 'almost entirely on the delays of the duke of Parma' – adding 'so the poor gentleman will need a good excuse'.[29]

Parma had anticipated this. In the town square of Dunkirk, surrounded by his principal officers, he issued a public challenge 'not as Captain General of the armies of Philip II, his uncle, but as Alexander Farnese, to satisfy anyone who blamed him for the failure of the Enterprise of England'. No one present replied.[30] Although this challenge silenced his local critics for a time, it had little effect elsewhere. Parma had anticipated this too. Hardly had the Armada sailed away than he wrote to urge his uncle, Cardinal Farnese, who watched over the family's interests in Rome, to provide immediate refutation 'if it should happen that, either to exculpate the duke of Medina Sidonia or for some other reason, the Spaniards wish to blame me for these reverses'. He also sent a special envoy to Italy to defend his conduct: Count Niccolò Cesi, who had fought at Parma's side for twenty years. Cesi seems to have blamed Medina Sidonia for the disaster and the outraged Spanish ambassador in Rome, who happened to be Medina's cousin, wrote to chide Parma for his disloyalty and pettiness: 'It was God's will, not your fault – and not Medina's either.' In any case, the ambassador added tartly, 'explanations of how each commander behaved are due to His Majesty and to nobody else'.[31]

Parma had anticipated this, too. Giovanni de' Medici, a brother of the grand duke of Tuscany stationed at Bruges, reported that when Don Rodrigo Tello arrived on the night of 1 August with news that the Armada was on the move, Parma summoned his leading experts – including Giovanni Battista Piatti, who had brought the royal Masterplan back from Spain – and asked for their advice: 'They all said that His Highness should do nothing until he knew that the Armada was very close, or at least had entered the Channel.' On 7 August Medici reported the arrival of a letter from Bobadilla 'stating that, given the danger and the weakness of his commander [Medina Sidonia], the service of His Majesty' required Parma to sail out and 'join the Armada to give its commander advice and courage [*consiglio et animo*]. His Highness replied that he was obliged to obey the commands of the king and he would not sail out until the appointed time.' Medici confirmed that 'all our infantry had embarked' on 8 August, 'leaving only the cavalry to go aboard at the opportune moment' and that Parma, together with Piatti and the commander of the Flanders fleet, were ready to board as they listened to the ominous sound of the naval guns just over the horizon. Although the duke then allowed the troops to disembark he did not give up: 'Parma has ordered some of the soldiers at Nieuwpoort to re-embark, either to have them ready in case the Armada returns, or because (as some say) he intends to attack Ostend by sea.'[32]

Inspector-General Don Jorge Manrique, marooned at Dunkirk, confirmed that Parma began the process of embarkation as soon as he learned of the Armada's imminent approach:

> The German, Italian, and Walloon troops, to the number of 18,000 were embarked, and the Spanish infantry together with the cavalry were at Dunkirk ready for embarkation. As they were boarding news arrived that the Armada had gone away; but everything remains in the same state, and the duke of Parma is present in person and will make no changes until there is certain news of our fleet.

The Dutch, too, did not doubt that the fate of the Enterprise hung in the balance. On 10 August the States of Zeeland reported that their small blockading squadron 'heard shouting last night from Dunkirk, and so we presume that the duke of Parma is ready to come out, having embarked (they say) 25,000 infantry aboard the barges at Nieuwpoort and the ships at Dunkirk'. That same day Parma reassured his master that:

> Those who came here off the fleet and have tried to give the impression that we were not ready – because they could not see guns and munitions on my ships, nor the troops aboard – are mistaken. Everything was prepared as it should have been for the Channel crossing . . . We would have gained nothing by embarking things in advance, because the ships are so small that there is not even room to turn round in. Undoubtedly the men would have sickened, the food would have rotted, and everything would have perished.[33]

Gradually the diplomatic corps in Madrid began to pin the outcome of the Enterprise of England on the failure of Medina Sidonia's messengers from the fleet to reach Flanders in time. After reporting that the duke himself now blamed Don Rodrigo Tello for taking too long to inform Parma of the Armada's approach, the Tuscan ambassador added perceptively that it seemed more likely that the duke had sent the messenger too late. Khevenhüller reached the same conclusion: 'I believe this happened because he [Parma] could not have known anything about the Armada' in advance. Sir Francis Drake agreed: had Medina's messengers arrived slightly sooner, or had the duke taken longer to advance up the Channel, the rendezvous might have become a reality because the Armada 'came to the place appointed, which was at Calais, and there stayed [i.e. awaited] the duke of Parma's coming above 24 hours, yea, and until they were fired thence'.[34]

Philip and his senior advisers nevertheless continued to harbour doubts about Parma. When Idiáquez replied to the duke's explanatory letter of 10 August, he began by noting acerbically that it had been written at Bruges 'which is a long way from Dunkirk' (see Figure 88). In November Idiáquez became more direct. Having assured the duke that 'you have no truer servant in any country than me', and after dismissing 'the lies sowed by the ignorant, the malignant, and those who are looking for an excuse', he regretted that there remained a 'cloud to dispel' because some people continued to assert that Parma's forces would have needed two weeks to embark. Therefore, Idiáquez continued disarmingly but firmly: 'So that we, your servants, can (when occasion arises) counter with confidence and with substance the confusion over whether your army and its transports were or were not ready when the Armada arrived, please will Your Excellency tell me clearly on which day of August you intended to cross, had the fleet not sailed away?'[35]

This time Parma's reply was more cautious. He devoted several paragraphs to disowning the conduct of Niccolò Cesi, who (he claimed unconvincingly) had been sent to Rome only because Cardinal Farnese had fallen ill, and it seemed important to have someone at the papal court to protect his reputation; he had never authorized Cesi to blame others. Next he defended the readiness of his forces. 'On Monday 7 August, which was the day that Secretary Arceo arrived' with the news that the Armada had reached Calais:

> I had 16,000 infantry embarked in Nieuwpoort and when I arrived at Dunkirk, which was on Tuesday the 8th, the troops who were to embark there had arrived before dawn and were beginning to board, and they finished that same day together with the munitions and all the other things which were ready and prepared. We were embarking at top speed [*a furia*], and we would certainly have finished. Had we not called a halt in view of the news we received of the Armada, we could well have begun to sail out that same night and joined the Nieuwpoort contingent together with that from Dunkirk in order to effect their task [sc. the invasion] that night and part of the next day, because they lacked nothing that they needed.

He concluded defiantly: 'My statement that we needed no more than three days to embark and be ready to sail forth was not made without justification.'[36]

In June 1589, suspecting that the king and his advisers still harboured doubts about his conduct, Parma sent copies of all the relevant Armada documents to Court – nine letters from Medina Sidonia and six replies; memoranda of the artillery, munitions and food prepared for the embarkation; and all his major letters to the king – together with another attempt at exculpation. Perhaps unwisely, Parma also added some barbed comments about the flaws in the Grand Design, provoking a long response from the king which (in effect) told him to stop complaining and concentrate instead on current matters. After a brief spell under a cloud, Parma thus managed to convince the king that he had indeed been 'ready and prepared' for the Enterprise.[37]

## The Search for Scapegoats II: The Duke of Medina Sidonia

Medina Sidonia experienced more difficulty in explaining his conduct. Although he had shown great skill in getting the Armada to sea, and great courage under fire, he had abandoned his fleet as soon as he sighted Santander on 21 September, and early on 5 October, having loaded his personal effects onto twenty-eight pack animals, he set off for home. The accounts of his household treasurer show that the duke made generous donations to clerics and paupers along the way until he reached Sanlúcar de Barrameda three weeks later. There was just one ugly moment. As Medina Sidonia tried to snatch a night's rest in Valladolid, youths surrounded his lodgings until dawn chanting 'Drake, Drake, Drake is coming', and taunted him with the offensive sobriquet 'duke of Gallina' (chicken duke). By mid-October, according to an ambassador, most people at Court blamed Medina Sidonia for the Armada's failure, 'because he lacked both experience and courage; because he abandoned Don Pedro de Valdés; because he fled too quickly and too fearfully from the fireships; and because he was later the first to come ashore, leaving the majority of his fleet scattered'.[38]

The king himself never openly criticized Medina Sidonia. Perhaps he recalled the duke's reluctance to accept the command, and his warning that the operation was doomed and should be aborted. Philip may also have taken into account the praise bestowed on Medina's leadership by Bobadilla, normally a stern judge of others, who wrote just after disembarking: 'Even our enemies will admit, although it may grieve them, that no commander in the world has done more than this one.'[39] Bobadilla had sailed on the flagship, however, and so protecting the duke's reputation also protected his own. Recalde, the duke's deputy and commander of the rearguard, and Leyva, the duke's designated successor and commander of the vanguard, had no such reservations.

A few days after the Armada began its long voyage home Leyva confided to Recalde 'I am keeping a record of what has happened', which he planned to deliver to the king, but his 'record' presumably perished when he drowned off the Irish coast.[40] Recalde kept a 'Diary' of the journey and the day after he got back to Spain he sent it to Court together with two letters from Leyva and part of his correspondence with the flagship during the campaign. Each one of these documents criticized Medina Sidonia, but Recalde reserved special condemnation for six of the duke's decisions: failing to attack the English fleet at Plymouth; abandoning *Rosario*; anchoring off Calais; refusing to make a good-faith effort to return to Flanders after the battle off Gravelines; considering the surrender of the fleet; and abandoning any ship unable to keep up. He urged the king not to 'leave unpunished the errors made in the fleet' or 'the misconduct of individuals, because if they are overlooked similar things will recur in future ventures'.[41]

Illness prevented Recalde from presenting his views in person but he sent a dossier to one of his relatives at Court, who duly forwarded it without comment to the king's desk. Although Philip wrote on the file 'I have seen all this, although I think it would have been better not to see it, because it hurts so much', he never received the incriminating letters from Leyva and may not have studied the rest of Recalde's dossier (certainly he did not annotate it).[42] Nevertheless he did punish Medina Sidonia – albeit in a characteristically underhand way. Back in March the duke had requested the grant of large estates (*encomiendas*) to two of his sons 'before I embark', and although the king turned him down he told his secretary in confidence that he intended to confer those *encomiendas* 'when he returns, or if he falls' (see chapter 8). He never followed through.

## The Search for Scapegoats III:
## Diego Flores de Valdés and the Plaza Prophets

In contrast the king soon took steps to ascertain whether others had contributed to the failure of the Enterprise, as well as to advise him what to do next. He ordered Don Rodrigo de Santillán, a criminal judge in the appeal court in Valladolid, to go to Santander and assemble all the fleet's surviving senior officials to discuss remedies. Santillán arrived on 19 October. Finding both Flores and Mexía in church, attending Mass, he hauled them out to meet Coco Calderón, Aramburu and the city magistrates. They formed a committee of inquiry and began by inspecting every warship in the harbour, concluding that it would cost over 100,000 ducats to replace the missing anchors, hawsers, ship's boats, rigging, sails and masts, and to careen and repair the decks of vessels that 'had been weakened by carrying too much heavy artillery'.[43]

A few days later Philip sent to Santander Don Juan de Cardona, a member of his Council of War who had extensive naval experience, with instructions to 'use secrecy and dissimulation to get to the bottom of who had done their duty in the past campaign, both soldiers and sailors, and those who had not'.[44] Cardona found many willing whistle-blowers. One senior official reported that 'the disillusion and discontent' of the Armada survivors, 'and what they are saying about each other, is causing greater damage than our enemies did'. According to a second official, 'everyone says that Diego Flores carried out his tasks badly' and should be relieved of his command, adding that 'it is also not in Your Majesty's interests that Don Francisco de Bobadilla should continue to serve for now'. A third called for an investigation of 'the conduct of some ships under fire, about which there are many complaints'.[45]

In the end Cardona singled out only two officers for censure: Diego Flores, mainly because he had insisted that the duke abandon *Rosario*, which Cardona identified as the 'origin and cause of all subsequent events' because it discouraged all aboard the fleet even as it encouraged the enemy; and Pedro Coco Calderón, the senior accountant still with the fleet, who had authorized some payments from the royal treasury without obtaining a counter-signature. Beyond that, Cardona reported, 'I have not found enough hard evidence to identify anyone else' who had conducted themselves badly, and he therefore advised his master to be merciful. 'I don't know what to tell Your Majesty, except that this Armada lacks so much, including many of its senior commanders, with more soldiers and mariners dying since they got back, that Your Majesty should not single out others to punish among those who remain.'[46]

Judge Santillán now swung into action. Just before Christmas he arrested Flores and sent him to Burgos Castle under guard, with orders 'that he should not be allowed to speak or write to anyone'. The guards intercepted his incoming letters and sent them to Madrid, where government ministers read them – including one from a relative who cited a careless remark by Bobadilla about the decision to abandon *Rosario*: 'If Diego Flores is guilty, so is the duke and so am I – because we were all of the same opinion.' The relative went on to suggest to Flores that 'even if you are not guilty, perhaps you are going to prison to frighten others'. A further humiliation soon reinforced this speculation. Shortly before Easter 1589 Flores complained to the king that he had been unable to hear Mass since he entered Burgos Castle and asked for permission to attend a local parish church during Holy Week. Philip refused. 'It is not appropriate at the moment that he should be allowed to leave the castle,' he informed the archbishop of Burgos, 'so I order you to designate a room in the said castle where Mass can be said during Holy Week and on other religious holidays.' A few months later Flores complained that the cost of paying for his captivity (mainly the salaries of his guards) was ruining him and noted that 'my son-in-law sailed with me on the campaign and died in it, as did many other relatives'. He also begged 'Your Majesty to hear' his explanation of the disaster, adding 'My voice was only one among many, yet only I suffer.' Philip relented somewhat in December, removing the guards and allowing Flores to remain in the castle on parole, and a month later he was freed.[47]

By then the king had appointed a 'commission to examine the conduct of the officers of my royal Armada', starting with those in charge of its medical services; and in February 1589 Judge Santillán seized all Coco Calderón's papers and sent him to Madrid to answer charges of corruption. Three months later, however, a thorough examination of the accountant's records revealed no irregularities and Santillán withdrew all charges. Diego Flores was apparently the only official to be publicly sanctioned for the failure of the Enterprise.[48]

Nevertheless, a few others received punishment in the wake of the Armada's defeat. The Inquisition moved against some of the Plaza Prophets denounced in *The treatise of true and false prophecy* for predicting (correctly) the fate of the Armada in 'the year of 88' (see chapter 1). Acting on Philip's express orders, the Inquisitors of Toledo condemned Miguel de Piedrola, one of the prophets of doom, to two years' seclusion in a remote location (chosen to make sure he would lack followers) and forbade him ever to visit Madrid, write letters, speak about religious matters or read the Bible. In Portugal, when news of the Armada's defeat arrived, the dreams and visions of the 'nun of Lisbon' turned nationalist, and she claimed that 'the kingdom of Portugal does not belong to Philip II but to the Braganza family'. The Inquisitors started to investigate and in mid-October they supervised the scrubbing of her hands with soap and hot water for half an hour, which removed her 'stigmata'. In December an ecclesiastical commission headed by Cardinal Albert (once Sor María's staunchest supporter) condemned her to solitary confinement in perpetuity in another convent. Luis de Granada's eulogy of her remained unpublished for four centuries.[49]

## The Search for Scapegoats IV: The King

For some, responsibility for the Armada's failure lay not with Parma, the fleet's principal officers or the Plaza Prophets, but with the supreme commander in the Escorial. On 5 August, at Bruges, Giovanni de' Medici probably expressed the misgivings circulating at Parma's headquarters when he wrote:

> As I see it, the matter comes down to this: how can the Armada keep together in a storm once it enters the Channel, since there are no harbours. And even if the Channel were filled with suitable harbours, as some maintain, how could the fleet sail in safety after passing through the Strait of Dover, because heaps of sand or reefs . . . are everywhere? It seems impossible that such a large fleet with so many big ships could avoid them. And if the fleet

does pass the Strait, it is hard to see what use it could be unless it provides an escort to cover our passage or protect us from the enemy fleet – because clearly the ships in which the duke [of Parma] needs to embark with his troops can withstand neither the sea nor the enemy, as they have low sides and lack artillery, so that even a modest warship could destroy them. And if they take too long to cross from Dunkirk to England, the sea could swallow them.

Medici drew the obvious conclusion: 'If we want the landing to take place, the Armada must provide an escort, so that we can cross immediately and get ashore; but with all these obstacles it is hard to see how it could do that . . . And yet the king nevertheless persists with his original plan for the Enterprise.'[50]

Similar criticisms soon multiplied. According to the Tuscan ambassador in Madrid, writing in October, some people 'go so far as to reproach the king with being imprudent and careless, and say that he is fit only to live among friars'. The papal nuncio was even more critical. The following month he reported that the loss of so many ships and men, coupled with the failure of the Enterprise, 'troubles everyone, since they can see the hand of God almost openly raised against us'.[51]

The Jesuit Pedro de Ribadeneira, once the foremost Armada-enthusiast, now shared this pessimistic assessment (Figure 124). 'After some prayer and much thought', in December 1588 he warned Idiáquez that:

> The judgements of God are most secret, so that we cannot know for certain the purpose of His Divine Majesty in the extraordinary fate he has decreed for the king's powerful fleet. Nevertheless, seeing that the cause was so much His, and was undertaken with such a holy intent, and was so much desired and assisted by the whole Catholic church, the fact that He was not moved by the pious prayers and tears of so many and such great devotees makes us fearful that there are serious reasons why Our Lord has sent us this affliction . . . So that it is both necessary and advisable to seek and consider the causes which may have moved God to punish us in this way.

Ribadeneira went on to offer six reasons why God might have allowed 'the damned souls of the English' to administer such a 'blow and punishment' to Spain in general and her king in particular. They ranged from the corruption and incompetence of some royal officials (notably in Andalucia), through the prevalence of 'sin and scandal' throughout Spain, to Philip's 'failure to protect the Catholics of England to avoid offending the queen who persecutes them'. He urged Idiáquez to present this analysis 'to His Majesty in whatever way you deem appropriate'.[52]

**124.** Pedro de Ribadeneira, holding an image of Ignatius Loyola, founder of the Jesuit Order. Ribadeneira's best-known work was a life of the saint, which went through numerous editions in Spanish and Latin, but he also wrote best-selling books about the fate of Catholicism in England, where he served in the 1550s.

PETRVS RIBADENEIRA TOLETANVS
SOCIETATIS IESV PRESBYTER THEOLOGVS:

## Lessons Learned

His Majesty nevertheless took some immediate steps to remedy the defects revealed by the failure of the Armada. In November 1588 he authorized Don Juan de Cardona, in Cantabria, to convene a committee of twenty-five shipwrights, ship masters and captains to determine the best dimensions for twelve new galleons of 500, 600 and 800 *toneladas*, four ships in each class. The committee included Agustín de Ojeda, commander of the squadron of *pataches* and *zabras* on the Armada campaign, who oversaw the construction of half the twelve new galleons, which Cardona decided to name after the twelve Apostles. Each boasted a more streamlined design and a 22-gun broadside consisting of 'guns which are appropriate to its size and weight, and of a sort which can do damage from a distance because of their good range, and from close range wreak notable destruction on the enemy fleet'. The hulls of the new-style galleons were launched in record time, between October 1589 and June 1590, and half took part in naval operations in summer 1591 (Figure 125).[53]

**125.** A drawing of a post-Armada Spanish galleon, presumably made by an English spy. Note the main and fore topmasts in 'struck' position, shear-hooks on the mainyard and foreyard, and a horizontal boarding ram (like a galleass). These arrangements imply that the designer still envisaged boarding as the principal tactic in battle. A Santiago cross decorates the stern. The main gun-deck mounts four big guns on each side, pointing ahead and astern, plus two each at bow and stern. The second deck has five guns on each broadside and two at each end, while the castle-works have a total of ten (total armament thirty-six).

The king also took measures to improve the fighting potential of the ships that survived the Armada campaign. Apart from creating two gunnery schools (see chapter 16), Cardona sent the king a set of technical drawings on 'How to affix the rudders of galleasses' and thus address a weakness observed repeatedly on the Armada campaign (Figure 126).[54] In 1590 Philip sent Sir William Stanley, 'given his prowess and experience of how other nations fight', to inspect his Atlantic fleet and 'provide advice on the way to equip them with artillery'. According to Don Alonso de Bazán, Santa Cruz's brother and now commander of the fleet, Stanley recommended adding 'a lot more artillery, placing at least six guns at the bow and stern of each ship, because that is what Queen Elizabeth's ships do'. Bazán dismissed this as totally unrealistic for Spain: 'I hope Your Majesty will send me a lot of big guns,' he told Philip, 'but since most of the ships in this fleet are merchantmen they lack the gunports in the prow and stern to accommodate them'.[55]

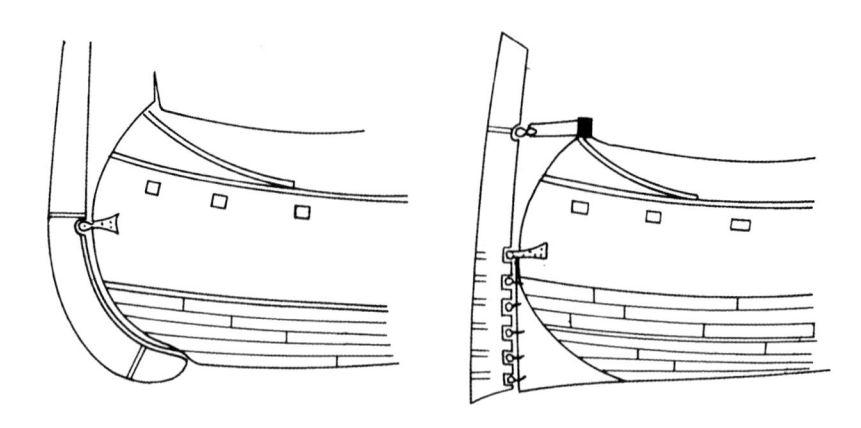

**126.** Because of her bulbous stern, a galleass's rudder hung on a curved post (left), an awkward and weak configuration that contributed to the loss of the flag galleass *San Lorenzo* off Calais, *Girona* off Antrim, and almost *Zúñiga* off Le Havre. The drawing on the right is a proposal for a new, better way, allowing for a vertically hung rudder.

Meanwhile Don Juan de Acuña Vela strove to standardize the munitions aboard the fleet. When in January 1590 he placed an order for 9,000 iron roundshot for each of the 3-, 7-, 12- and 16-pounder calibres, he included a sheet of paper on which he inscribed with compasses (the holes at the centres can still be seen) eight carefully measured circles. These show the size of each iron ball with its weight marked, together with a slightly larger circle indicating the diameter of the bore into which it would be fitted, again expressed in terms of a theoretical iron shot-weight. A note was appended to the effect that from now on these sizes were to be *exactly* as set out in the diagram, irrespective of variations in their supposed weights (Figure 127).

Initially, it seemed that these measures succeeded. In 1590 the galleasses *Zúñiga* and *Napolitana* managed to land an expeditionary force in Brittany, which built a fortified base for future operations against the Tudor state; and the following year Bazán, Aramburu and Bertendona led a powerful fleet that included three of the new galleons to the Azores, which met the annual transatlantic convoy and drove off an English squadron sent to intercept it. They even managed to isolate *Revenge* and forced her to surrender after an artillery duel so intense that the ship sank shortly afterwards – the first of the queen's ships to fall into enemy hands since *Jesus of Lübeck* (see chapter 4) and the only one that had fought the Armada to perish in action. Although this success occasioned great rejoicing in Spain, a few months later both the galleasses were wrecked off the coast of Galicia.[56]

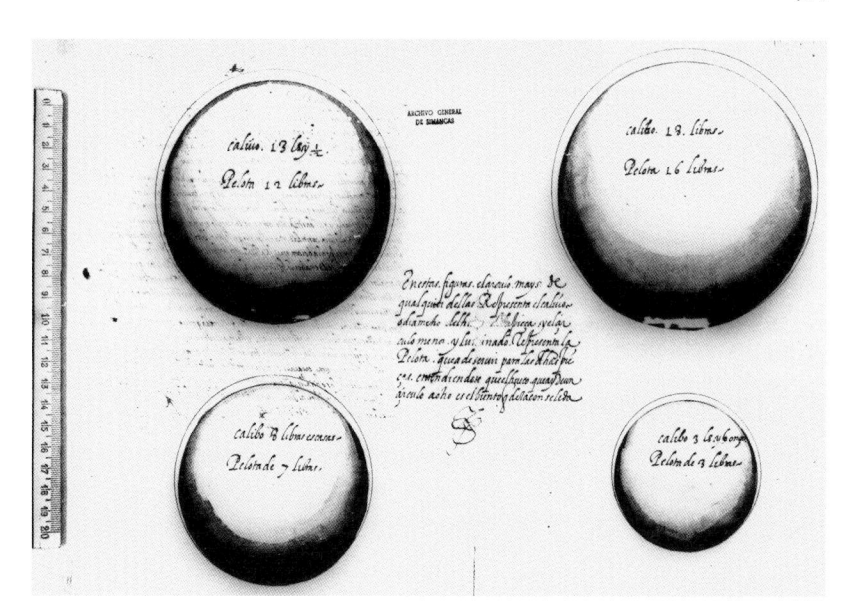

**127.** After the Armada the Captain-General of Artillery, Don Juan de Acuña Vela, attempted to standardize gun calibres and shot sizes, and to impose the Castilian pound as the standard for shot-weight. He drew a diagram with circles to represent the diameters of specified guns and the appropriate size of shot, allowing for windage, defining them by circles appropriate to the various diameters. Unfortunately, his calculations were questionable, and the problem remained unresolved for many years.

Perhaps the 'Twelve Apostles' had been constructed too fast. When they joined the main fleet in 1591, the gunports on three were deemed too low to be opened in rough weather; and five years later, during the Cadiz raid, the English easily overcame the four that they encountered, capturing two: *San Mateo* and *San Andrés*. Both sailed with the queen's ships in 1597 on the 'Islands Voyage' to the Azores, but the English intended to sacrifice these 'two great carts' (as the earl of Essex, their captor, termed them) in a pre-emptive attack on the Spanish fleet anchored in Ferrol. In the event, *San Mateo* lost her foremast (and almost her mainmast as well) five days out from Plymouth and had to be escorted home, while *San Andrés* also spent her main topmast and got lost twice on the expedition. The English never used them again.[57]

Perhaps poetry best expressed the mood of desperation and despondency caused throughout the Iberian Peninsula by the fate of the Armada. One of the first literary works in Spanish that manifested a sense of *desengaño* (disillusion) with empire was the verse *Farewell of the ladies of the Court to the gallants sailing on the Armada*, which urged the courtiers aboard the fleet to abandon their mission because all they would gain from the venture was injury, discomfort and disease. Soon afterwards, a satire in the form of awkward questions and answers began to circulate in Portugal:

>Q: Which ships have arrived?
>A: Those that the English allowed to escape.
>Q: And what happened to the rest?
>A: The sailors will tell you.
>Q: So what happened?
>A: It's said that they were lost.
>Q: Do we know their names?
>A: They are well known in London.

A host of similar works soon followed. Miguel de Cervantes, Spain's greatest novelist (and according to some, one of the world's worst poets), who in 1587 had helped to organize supplies for the fleet that Leyva led from Cadiz to Lisbon, now composed a 'Song about the loss of the Armada which sailed against England', celebrating the valiant soldiers ('*los valientes de la guerra*') who had 'returned confused but unbowed' and predicting:

>The pirates may have triumphed for now,
>Holding celebrations and festivals
>Because the seas and the winds
>Worked in their favour,
>Without recalling that one day
>All debtors must pay.

In the long run Cervantes was correct, but for several months the triumphant 'pirates' held spectacular 'celebrations and festivals'.[58]

# 18

# The Counter-Armada

## Let the Gloating Commence

When the States of Zeeland heard on 11 August 1588 that the Spanish fleet was sailing north with the English in pursuit, with enough food for only two weeks, they crowed to Maurice of Nassau about 'the victory that Our Lord God has granted us'. Soon afterwards Maurice commissioned a medal with the triumphalist motto: GOD BLEW AND THEY WERE SCATTERED. Similar medals followed (see Figure 92). According to an Italian diplomat in the Spanish Netherlands, 'in all the enemy cities we heard great artillery salvoes and other signs of rejoicing'. In Leiden the great battle-pennant of the captured Portuguese galleon *San Mateo* (Figure 128) was hung in the choir of St Peter's church and inspired a local bard to compose a patriotic treatise in Latin entitled *Oration on the Fleet of the Spanish Xerxes*, declaimed for the first time on 21 August and soon published with a dedication to Elizabeth. Several translations appeared.[1]

At first English rejoicing was more muted. When Admiral Howard ordered his fleet to disengage off the Firth of Forth on 12 August the Armada still numbered over 100 ships in good formation, and (he wrote in frustration) 'God knows whether they go either to the Naze of Norway or into Denmark or to the Isles of Orkney to refresh themselves, and so to return.' Drake also felt apprehensive. In Norway or Denmark the Armada might find 'great anchors, cables, masts, ropes and victuals; and what the king of Spain's hot crowns will do in cold countries for mariners and men, I leave to your good lordship.' He feared that afterwards Medina Sidonia might make a second attempt to join up with the duke of Parma;

**128.** All that remains of the standard of *San Mateo*. Her Dutch captors presented it to St Peter's church, Leiden, where it hung from the roof as a trophy. It was so long that its lower part was rolled up on the floor where it rotted.

or perhaps, while the English fleet was far away in the North Sea, Parma might attempt an invasion on his own, because 'I take him to be as a bear robbed of her whelps; and no doubt but, being so great a soldier as he is, that he will presently, if he may, undertake some great matter.' Two weeks later, Drake still believed that 'We ought much more to have regard to the duke of Parma and his soldiers than to the duke of Sidonia and his ships.'[2]

Such fears were well founded. Although Parma disembarked his troops from their cramped barges after a couple of days, he did not stand them down for three more weeks. The earl of Leicester was therefore horrified to learn on 6 August that Elizabeth planned to join him at Tilbury camp, and he forbade her to come. After praising her 'princely courage to transport yourself to the uttermost confines of your realm to meet your enemies and to defend your subjects, I cannot, most dear queen, consent to that, for upon your well doing consists all'. Instead, he instructed her to shelter at Havering House, five miles north of London, concluding with a command that no one else would dare to utter: 'This far, but no further, can I consent to adventure your person.' It worked. The queen meekly retired to Havering House and was out hunting nearby when she received news of the Armada's retreat after the battle off Gravelines. According to local tradition, in a burst of exultation she galloped her horse up the stairway of a nearby hunting lodge, after which she returned to St James's Palace.[3]

The Privy Council continued to oppose the queen's desire to 'repair to the camp' at Tilbury because of the 'misadventure that may fall out' should some disaffected English Catholic or a desperate Spanish hireling try to kill the last Tudor, but on 18 August Elizabeth defied them and travelled on a barge down the Thames to Tilbury. There Leicester escorted her as she rode among the 3,000 tents to inspect 17,000 soldiers deployed according to 'their counties, lodged and quartered in their several camps'. She declined the earl's invitation to spend the night 'in your poor lieutenant's cabin', and instead slept in the house of Edward Rich, a courtier who lived nearby.[4]

When the queen returned to Tilbury camp the next day, Leicester had drawn up his troops in 'battalions, ready as it were to fight with any enemy. She rode round about them, and did view them curiously', before delivering the short speech that became 'the iconic moment of her reign' (Figure 129):

> Let tyrants fear; but I have always so behaved myself that, under God, I have placed my chiefest strength and safeguard in the loyal hearts and goodwill of my subjects. And therefore I am come amongst you as you see at this time not for my recreation and disport, being resolved, in the midst and heat of the battle to live or die amongst you all, to lay down for my God and for my kingdom and for my people, my honour and my blood even in the dust. I know I have the body but of a weak and feeble woman, but I have the heart and stomach of a king, and of a king of England too, and think foul scorn that Parma, or Spain, or any prince of Europe should dare to invade the borders of my realm.[5]

Shortly after making her speech, while lunching with Leicester in his tent, a courier arrived with the alarming news that 'Parma was embarked with 50,000 men foot and 6,000 horse, and that he put to sea yesterday, and it was surely expected he would land here'. Elizabeth declared 'that in honour she could not return [to London], in case there were any likelihood that the enemy would attempt anything'; but when it became clear later that day that it was a false alarm, Leicester persuaded her to board her barge and depart.[6]

Some of her ministers still worried that 'the heat of the battle' had not yet passed. According to Walsingham, 'it were not wisdom, until we see what will become of the Spanish fleet, to disarm too fast, seeing Her Majesty is to fight for a kingdom'. He therefore summoned Leicester and Howard to Court, 'there to confer with the rest of her Council what were fit to be done therein, whereunto Her Majesty assented' (a revealing insight into Elizabethan decision-making: the secretary of state decided, the queen later concurred). On 24 August the Council decided to

**129.** *Allegory of the Spanish Armada* in St Faith's church, Gaywood, Norfolk. This panel painting measuring more than five feet square, said to be done on wood from an Armada ship, shows Elizabeth surrounded by courtiers and soldiers at Tilbury as Armada ships burn in the background. An angel hovers above the queen holding a laurel crown and a Latin inscription proclaims 'Favoured by God, the winds changed for you'. The lengthy legend below includes the text of her speech to the troops. The church also contains a matching panel painting of the Gunpowder Plot.

send home all but the cavalry and 6,000 infantry at Tilbury. Three days later, on learning that Parma had moved his troops away from Dunkirk and Nieuwpoort, it ordered 'the dissolution and total discharge' of the army, save only the officers.[7]

By then Elizabeth felt sure of her victory. In a letter to her cousin James VI of Scotland she predicted that 'For my part I doubt not that this tyrannical, proud, and brainsick attempt will be the beginning, but not the end, of the ruin' of King Philip, whose unsuccessful assault had 'dimmed the light of his sunshine'. The return of Thomas Cavendish a few weeks later after circumnavigating the world, bringing Spanish plunder worth perhaps £100,000, occasioned another round of royal gloating. As his ship sailed past Greenwich Palace – 'his mariners clothed in silk, his sails of damask, his top-masts cloth-of-gold' – the queen jested that 'The king of Spain barks a good deal but does not bite. We care nothing for the Spaniards because their ships loaded with American gold and silver come here anyway.' She now turned to demobilizing her fleet.[8]

In a macabre sense, the 16,000 men crowded aboard the English ships had already started the process themselves, for death and sickness took a heavy toll. Of the 500 men aboard *Elizabeth Bonaventure* when she left Plymouth in July some 200 were dead of disease a month later. Admiral Howard feared that 'the like infection will grow throughout the most part of our fleet, for they have been so long at sea, and have so little shift of apparel and so [few] places to provide them of such wants, and no money wherewith to buy it, for some have been – yea, the most part – eight months at sea'. By early September Howard claimed that it 'would grieve any man's heart to see them that have served so valiantly die so miserably', and to see almost all the ships 'foul and unsavoury' with many 'so weakly manned that they have not mariners to weigh their anchors'.[9]

But the hearts of the men at Court did not grieve. Instead, Burghley callously expressed the hope that 'by death, by discharging of sick men, and such like . . . there may be spared something in the general pay'. He clearly intended that such unfortunates should receive nothing for their part in defeating the Spanish Armada. Howard was appalled. 'It were too pitiful to have men starve after such a service,' he remonstrated, and persuaded Drake to part with 3,000 gold ducats from the treasure captured on *Nuestra Señora del Rosario*, which Howard promptly spent on feeding and clothing his men. He assured the queen that 'had it not been mere necessity, I would not have touched [the money]; but if I had not a sum to have bestowed upon some poor and miserable men, I should have wished myself out of the world.' Fearing that moral blackmail would not work on his sovereign, the Lord Admiral fell back on self-interest: 'If men should not be cared for better than to let them starve and die miserably, we should very hardly get men to serve.'[10]

He was wasting his time. When Howard sent an emissary to London to discuss arrangements for discharging the fleet, he found everyone at the windows of St James's Palace, watching a victory parade, and could get no guidance or instruction. When the government later calculated the exact cost of the defensive effort against

Spain, which totalled nearly £400,000 on the fleet alone, 'rewards to the injured' accounted for a mere £180. By comparison Elizabeth paid £130 to prepare Edward Rich's house for her overnight stay on 18/19 August.[11]

In the end the commanders took responsibility for the welfare of their men – although for a while some of them also seemed preoccupied by other matters. No sooner had the queen's ships returned to port than Sir Martin Frobisher threatened to disembowel Drake for cowardice and desertion (see p. 289); shortly afterwards Lord Henry Seymour abandoned his command of the Narrow Seas squadron rather than resume his boring vigil on the Flemish coast; and three months later Sir Walter Raleigh (a stalwart defender of Howard's strategy during the campaign) fought a duel with the earl of Essex (an ally of Drake). Eventually Sir John Hawkins, Drake and Howard set up a special fund for 'poor sailors maimed in the navy', which operated like an insurance scheme: a small deduction was made from the wages paid to each seaman, and the balance deposited in a large locked chest at Chatham dockyard. As need arose, the 'Chatham Chest' issued burial money for the dead, pensions for the old, and compensation payments for the injured or disabled. But these benefits only became available after 1590. Those who had fallen ill or suffered wounds fighting the Armada had to rely on the individual charity of their officers (and here again Howard set a noble example), or of the towns in which they were discharged. Perhaps only half the men who fought for England in 1588 lived to celebrate the following Christmas.

## England's Deliverance

The Privy Council arranged a service of thanksgiving in St Paul's Cathedral in London on 18 September, when 'eleven of the Spanish ensigns (once the badges of their bravery but now of their vanity and ignominy) were hung on the lower battlements of that church, as palms of praise for England's deliverance'. Two months later the Council appointed 29 November as a day of national thanksgiving for God's 'gracious favour extended towards us in our deliverance and defence in the wonderful overthrow [and] destruction shewed by His mighty hand on our malicious enemies, the Spaniards, who had sought to invade and make a conquest of the realm'. To add to the solemnity, the Council instructed the magistrates in each city to attend the service 'in your most comely and decent manner', and make sure that all 'well-affected citizens' – meaning Protestants – participated in 'a general communion'. They must also 'cause all shops, taverns, and tippling houses to be shut up all that day (as they were and will be in London) lest through any worldly occasion those who are not fully grounded in good heal might withdraw themselves from that most godly action'.¹²

Originally, Elizabeth planned to attend the service of thanksgiving at St Paul's Cathedral that same day, but she postponed it – perhaps for security reasons because, according to the Jesuit Henry Garnet, an order went out 'that in every single household along the route no-one should be allowed to look out from the windows while she was passing, unless the householder was prepared to stake his life and entire fortune on his trustworthiness'. Not until 4 December did the queen travel down Fleet Street and Ludgate Hill 'in a gilded chair' drawn by two horses, 'covered with a royal awning; it hung down behind but was open in front and on both sides', amid 'the unceasing uproar of the vast crowds' as she passed (Figure 130). After entering St Paul's, Elizabeth knelt to say some prayers and then mounted 'a raised platform [where] she heard the sermon. From time to time, in the course of it, she applauded the preacher in a loud voice' (it is hard to imagine Philip II doing this).¹³

130. A Royal Progress. Queen Elizabeth being carried through the streets, *c.* 1600. In 1588 she was drawn by two horses, but descriptions of her open 'chariot' match this one. Note the presence of several Armada commanders in the front row, including from the left, Lord Sheffield, Howard of Effingham, Lord Cumberland, Lord Hunsdon (the queen's cousin, commander of the army assembled to protect her and her capital) and Lord Shrewsbury (Mary Stuart's gaoler).

Her subjects celebrated their deliverance in various ways. In Bristol, after attending a special communion service in the cathedral, the magistrates, in scarlet robes, distributed alms to the poor. The churchwardens of St Margaret's Westminster paid two shillings (ten pence) to those who rang the bells as the queen travelled to and from St Paul's, noting that this was double what they had 'paid for ringing at the beheading of the queen of Scots'. (The bellringers were so energetic that the next day the churchwardens had to pay 'for mending of the ropes'.) Many churchwardens elsewhere recorded similar payments to those who rang bells at 'the triumph for the safe deliverance of our Queen and the Realm from our enemies'. Lord Shrewsbury, Mary Stuart's gaoler, presented a bell to the church of St Mary the Virgin at Handsworth (now a suburb of Sheffield) to commemorate the victory. It is still rung to this day.[14]

No fewer than twenty-four contemporary popular songs about the Armada have survived, including the (wisely) anonymous 'A Skeltonicall Salutation or condign gratulation and just vexation of the Spanish Nation', which plumbed the depths of bad taste by assuring its readers that those who ate a fish that had feasted on drowned Spaniards could not acquire their venereal diseases. Its title page bears the proud imprint of the recently founded Oxford University Press.

131. The first use of the term 'Invincible Armada'. Lord Burghley sarcastically applied the term 'invincible' to the Armada in the earliest manuscript drafts of his polemic *Copie of a letter*, purporting to be a report by an English Jesuit on the losses suffered. The epilogue of the Italian translation read: 'Here ends the account of the misfortunes of the Spanish Armada that they called INVINCIBLE, sent to conquer the most powerful and most fortunate kingdom of England.'

The most successful work of propaganda appeared shortly afterwards: a pamphlet known somewhat inelegantly as *The copie of a letter sent out of England to Don Bernardin Mendoza*. Burghley himself composed it in the guise of a bitter reproach from an English Jesuit to the Spanish ambassador in France, because all his bold promises and boasts had come to nothing. The pamphlet rehearsed in detail Spain's (unjust) reasons for attacking England; Elizabeth's (laudable) countermeasures; the course of the campaign; the names of the Spanish ships and officers who perished; and the eventual safe return of the English fleet. Further printings soon appeared, as well as Dutch, French, German and Italian translations, each with updates to the list of Armada ships known to have sunk and other 'misfortunes of the Spanish Armada which they called INVINCIBLE'. The word was capitalized – even though no Spaniard had ever used it (Figure 131).[15]

Burghley's clever epithet soon passed into the vocabulary of all Europe. The following year even Pedro de Ribadeneira used the term in his *Treatise on Tribulation*, dedicated to Philip's sister Empress María, which sought to explain how adversity can sometimes be salutary. Ribadeneira marvelled that:

> A great and powerful fleet, which seemed invincible [*que parecía invencible*], prepared to advance the cause of God and His Holy Catholic faith, and accompanied by so many prayers, processions and penances from His faithful servants, should be undone and lost in a manner so unusual as to allow no denial that it was a scourge and severe punishment from the hand of the Most High.

Even more remarkable, Ribadeneira continued, 'is that God should forsake us in a cause that was so much His own, and that the heretics are left to gloat and the Catholics to weep and suffer'.[16]

## The Counter-Armada

The heretics did not merely gloat: they had tasted Spanish blood and wanted more. So how best could they obtain it? After he accompanied Elizabeth to Tilbury, Burghley realized that the Armada would 'pass about Ireland' and suggested 'that four good ships well manned and conducted, might follow them to their ports, where they might distress a great number of them'. Walsingham poured cold water on the idea: 'If it had been thought of in time, they might have been very well employed, but I fear it will now be too late.' Nothing daunted, two weeks later the queen instructed Howard to lead his warships back to sea 'for the intercepting of the king's treasure from the Indies', but the Lord Admiral poured cold water on that idea too. He saw no 'ships here in the fleet any ways able to go such a voyage before they have been aground [careened]'; and it would take two weeks to get his warships to the dockyards at Chatham, the only place where that operation could take place. Fearing that the queen might not believe him, Howard entrusted delivery of his warning to Drake, 'a man of judgment and best acquainted with it, [who] will tell you what must be done for such a journey'.[17] The queen knew that she must authorize some counterstroke. As Henry of Navarre reminded her:

> The Spanish fleet became scattered on the high seas so that each ship returned to her own home port. We share your view of the peril that faced England, and rejoice that everyone can see the hand of God in the outcome; but it is crucial that the queen should keep her foot on the king of Spain's throat because if she does not, and he recovers, we have no guarantee of a similar success a second time.

Elizabeth drew the same conclusion. In October 1588 she authorized Drake and Sir John Norris to start mobilizing ships and troops 'to invade and destroy the powers, forces and preparations' of those who 'have this last year both by sea and by land with their hostile and warlike powers and armadas sought and attempted the invasion of our realm of England'.[18] The plan was both ambitious and expensive – but since her treasury was empty Elizabeth limited her contribution to six warships and £20,000 in cash. She expected Drake and Norris to raise funds from investors in England and the Dutch Republic to cover all other necessary items.

Before they left, the queen's naval experts conducted what military organizations today call 'After-Action Reports'. Howard commissioned John Mountgomerie to update his 'Treatise concerning the navy of England' to incorporate lessons learned from the 'huge and mighty navy' of Spain. His twenty-eight-page report devoted special attention to the design and fighting potential of the galleasses, because of reports that the 'four galleasses made the most answer and offer of fight against us'. In November 1588 the Navy Board – which included Howard, Drake, Winter, Hawkins and other commanders, together with the shipwrights Matthew Baker and Richard Chapman, with Lord Treasurer Burghley in the chair – approved a 'device' to build eight new warships: two just like *Revenge*; another 'in the form of the *Revenge* but exceeding her in burthen 200 tons'; a fourth 'betwixt a galleass and a galleon'; and four cromsters 'of musket proof' like the Dutch blockade ships.[19] No fewer than sixteen new warships were built for the navy between 1590 and 1596. Five were capital ships of 650 tons or more and by 1595, when the building programme was almost complete, the thirty-eight ships of the queen's navy carried a total of 1,059 guns (628 of them 9-pounders and above).[20]

These achievements lay in the future. Late in 1588 Norris left for the Netherlands to gain support for the Counter-Armada, while Drake agreed to take with him Dom Antonio, the 'Portuguese Pretender', to make a further bid to regain his ancestors' throne. This caused consternation among some English clerics, who debated whether Protestants 'may without offence to God aid a popish prince to recover his kingdom'. They eventually approved restoring Dom Antonio 'not for any love we bear unto him, but only to weaken the arm of our capital enemy the king of Spain'.[21] The English clerics erred, however, because by trying to do too much the expedition achieved virtually nothing.

The Venetian ambassador in Madrid stressed to his government the potential damage of a descent by Drake 'on the shores of Spain, where he would find no obstacle to his depredations, and might even burn a part of the ships which have come back for they are lying scattered in various places along the coast, without any troops to guard them as all the soldiers reach home sick and in the bad plight I have reported; besides which some of these ships are in harbours which have no forts.' And indeed in May 1589 the Anglo-Dutch force achieved total surprise when it entered Corunna harbour, where it destroyed Recalde's *San Juan de Portugal* and burned down much of the town – but since both the queen and the Dutch had refused to provide siege-guns, the citadel held out. The 'Counter-Armada' should now have sailed east to the ports of Cantabria where (according to an English spy) Spain's warships still 'did ride all unrigged, and their ordnance on the shore'. Instead, after three weeks of looting in Galicia, Drake sailed south to Portugal.[22]

At first things looked promising. On 26 May the governor of the port of Peniche, 50 miles north of Lisbon, welcomed Dom Antonio when he came ashore with Norris at the head of 12,000 English troops. Meanwhile Drake led his fleet into the Tagus, where the governor of Cascais soon surrendered. Many other Portuguese expressed enthusiasm for 'King Antonio', as he and the English army advanced until it set up camp just outside the walls of the enemy capital – something the Armada had conspicuously failed to do. For a time the outcome hung in the balance. To improve Lisbon's defences Philip had ordered all buildings adjacent to the walls to be levelled, but his officials spared churches, convents and the houses of those prepared to pay a bribe, providing valuable cover to the besiegers. According to a diarist in the city: 'All the principal people fled and those who remained had their escape planned, with their horses and boats ready to use in an instant.' A Spanish general lamented that 'the soldiers under my command are of such a sort that

I cannot decide if it would be better for us if they were armed or disarmed'. Two things saved Portugal for King Philip: as at Corunna, the English lacked siege-guns and so could not breach the walls of Lisbon, while Dom Antonio's return to his native land at the head of heretics alienated many of his Catholic supporters.[23]

After another month on enemy soil Norris and Dom Antonio retreated to Cascais, where they embarked on Drake's ships and set sail for the Azores in the hope of injuring Philip by the 'method of Jason, by fetching away his golden fleece'; but storms drove them back to England empty-handed. They took few prizes and inflicted only minimal losses. Moreover, the elements inflicted considerable damage to the queen's ships and some 10,000 of the men aboard either died or became too sick to serve further: £100,000 had been spent with little to show for it. Elizabeth banished both Drake and Norris from her Court.

The Counter-Armada had been England's best opportunity to turn the deliverance of 1588 into a lasting victory, but instead the queen had to spend heavily on defending her realms for the rest of her reign. In August 1589 even Walsingham, who had once eagerly embraced the cause, longed to find a way out of the Dutch alliance: 'I wish that our fortune and theirs were not so straitly tied as it is, so as we cannot well untie it without great hazard, and then there would be safely found some way to free us from them without peril.'[24]

## 'We are in a state of open war'

Philip also fretted about the future. As soon as he had heard Don Balthasar de Zúñiga's description of how the Enterprise had failed, he summoned delegates from the Cortes of Castile to the Escorial and gave a short speech reminding them that 'what led me to undertake this campaign' against England 'was the service of God, and the good and security of Christendom. That's why I sent my Armada. You will see the results from the *Diario* which the duke of Medina Sidonia has sent me.' Now, the king continued, 'we are in a state of open war' and 'our enemies are well defended; so we fear that they might come here to do some damage, which obliges us to make great and excessive expenditures, or risk terrible harm'. The delegates returned to Madrid with a memorial 'entirely written in His Majesty's hand', which repeated these details, as well as a copy of Medina Sidonia's *Diario* and a request for more taxes to cover the cost of re-arming Spain.[25]

The king's decision to communicate his wishes 'orally and in his own handwriting (an extraordinary and unprecedented thing)' failed to impress the Cortes, and they asked him to provide an estimate of the cost. The king replied – again in his own hand – that 'he would be glad to tell them the exact amount required to achieve our objectives; but we do not know, precisely, what sum we would need'. Nevertheless, since the failed campaign had 'cost more than ten million ducats', and 'since we need to supply what we lack, and undertake an offensive war', Philip suggested that mobilizing against a Counter-Armada would cost no less.[26]

In February 1589, by twenty-four votes to twelve, the Cortes agreed to provide Philip with taxes worth 8 million ducats – soon known as the *Millones* – 'for the defence of the faith and of his realms'. The deputies also endorsed his view that the best strategy was to attempt another invasion of England, because 'if we defeat this enemy it will end the war in the Netherlands, which has been and still is so expensive for Your Majesty and these kingdoms, because England provides them with the means to carry on'. Therefore, they hoped, 'the army and navy that you send on this campaign will aim to attack and conquer England, and in achieving its goal will recover past losses and the reputation of our nation'.[27]

Unfortunately for Spain the king ignored the warnings of Bobadilla, Recalde and others about the risks inherent in any combined operation. In May 1589 he sent money to Parma with orders to prepare men and ships for a surprise attack on the Isle of Wight, which would create a diversion while a new Armada from Spain sailed up the Channel to deliver the *coup de grâce*. He only abandoned this plan when the Counter-Armada arrived – but he still refused to change his style of decision-making. When Bertendona went to Court in June 1589 and requested an audience at which he could impart some advice 'in case there should be a campaign against England next year', Philip characteristically replied: 'You can tell me about it in writing, since there is no opportunity to do it in person.' A few months later he asked Bertendona to send him detailed information on naval affairs, 'because I would like to be informed of what occurs to you for when we take a decision on the matters you raise' – but once again he insisted that it must be submitted in writing.[28]

Philip also continued to believe that he was executing God's will, despite the reverses, although now he sometimes looked more carefully for any indication of divine disfavour. Thus in May 1589, bowing to intense pressure from his confessor (a Dominican), Philip agreed to initiate a thorough *visita* (judicial inquiry) concerning alleged abuses among the Spanish Jesuits; but the draft of the order landed on his desk just as news arrived of the Anglo-Dutch descent on Corunna. The king immediately saw a connection. 'You will have heard of the report which came today from Corunna,' he told Mateo Vázquez. 'The English fleet has arrived there and put troops ashore; so I am not sure that this is the right time to proceed against the Society of Jesus ... I think that what has already been done must suffice for now'. No *visita* ever took place. The role of Sir Francis Drake in the survival of the Jesuit Order in Spain has seldom received the attention it deserves.[29]

Only in Ireland did the Armada manage to advance Philip's religious and political goals. Lord Deputy Fitzwilliam ordered a special service to be held in the principal church of every county on 25 January 1589 'to celebrate Her Majesty's happy success against the Spaniards' but reported that 'very few or none almost resorted thereunto'. In Dublin even the lawyers 'took occasion to leave the town, of purpose to absent themselves from that godly exercise' – a clear sign of widespread sympathy for the Spanish cause. More signs followed. In March 1589 the mayor of Galway warned Fitzwilliam that those opposed to English rule in Munster now mustered 'Two thousand able men and have more munition and armour than ever we saw them to have, by means of the wrecks of the Spanish ships that chanced in their countries' as well as 'the great ordnance that was in two or three ships'. In addition, they had 'about 20 of the Spaniards with them yet alive', who had begun to train Irish recruits.[30]

Further north, in Connacht, the Burkes reportedly had 'many good musketeers among them'; Sir Brian O'Rourke had 'some 24 Spaniards who train his kerns [native infantry] daily [and] serve with pikes and armour such as was found in the country of the last Spanish fleet's furniture'; and Captain Cuéllar and other Armada survivors fought for O'Rourke's ally, Tadhg óg McClancy (see chapter 15). In Ulster Hugh O'Neill, earl of Tyrone, also sheltered many of the Spanish soldiers who came his way and used them to train his own troops in the arts of modern warfare, which helped his cause when in 1594 he rebelled against Elizabeth. One of those who escaped from the wrecked *Juliana* at Streedagh Strand, Pedro Blanco, became the earl's personal bodyguard and, after the rebellion's collapse, Blanco fled with his master to Flanders and thence to Rome. Just before he died in 1616, Tyrone wrote a glowing testimonial for Blanco who has 'fought so valiantly that I never wanted to be parted from him'. He begged Philip III to bestow some reward on this faithful warrior for the Catholic cause.[31]

The *Compendium of the History of Catholic Ireland*, written in exile a few years later by Philip O'Sullivan Beare, portrayed the Armada as a turning point, because it revealed the fragility of English rule. The author began his account of what he called 'The Fifteen Years War' with the landing and deployment of the surviving Spanish troops by the Irish Catholic lords in 1588, and ended it with the surrender of Tyrone to Elizabeth's forces in 1603.[32]

Elsewhere, however, the failure of the Armada called into question the power of Spain, and those who feared or resented Spanish hegemony now raised their heads. In Italy, in November, the mathematician and astrologer Giorgio Rizzacasa daringly dedicated a book to Elizabeth, whom he compared with the biblical Judith. He also poked fun at 'the king of Spain, who had recently tried to make himself ruler of the whole world' and sent his fleet 'to defend himself from the bold attacks by the glorious Drake [*del Drago glorioso*]'. Rizzacasa rejoiced that the queen's 'most happy fleet' (a cruel parody of the term usually applied by Catholics to the Armada) had 'miraculously defeated and destroyed' its adversaries.[33] In Germany a Cologne newsletter covering March–September 1588 included details on how 'Drake and his English fleet' had chased the Armada into the North Sea; and a print circulated widely entitled 'The pedlar with the latest newspaper', which showed a travelling salesman with pamphlets about the defeat of the Armada. An English diplomat returning that winter from a mission to the Ottoman sultan reported that in one Baltic port city after another the magistrates 'presented me sundry sorts of their best wine and fresh fish, every one of them with a long discourse, congratulating, in the names of their whole Senate, her Majesty's victory over the Spaniard'.[34]

In France, just before Christmas, Henry III and his supporters isolated and murdered the duke of Guise and demanded the recall of Ambassador Mendoza. In Moscow, Elizabeth's envoy reported that the tsar had abandoned his plan to form a league with the Habsburgs against the Turks 'after your Highness's victory against the King of Spain was well known there (which I understood by letters sent me by Sir Francis Drake, which I caused to be translated into the Russian tongue, together with your Highness's oration made to the army in Essex)'. In Portuguese India, which had welcomed Philip II's accession as king of Portugal, the spirits of royal officials sagged as 'confusion about the fate of the Armada Your Majesty sent against England' gave way in November 1589 to confirmation of its defeat. They now feared that the news might encourage his enemies in the region to mount an attack.[35]

The failure of the Enterprise also compromised Philip's position in the Netherlands. An Italian at Parma's headquarters reported that although his troops 'had been happy to embark for England without thinking about their wages, now that they have no hope of the Enterprise they insist that they want to be paid, so that there is a risk of mutiny'. After some diversionary manoeuvres Parma laid siege to the Dutch town of Bergen-op-Zoom, but to no avail: after six inconclusive weeks in the trenches he gave up, having received (as Walsingham gleefully noted) 'no less blemish (through the goodness of Almighty God) by land than he hath done by sea'. A cycle of mutinies that paralysed the Army of Flanders began the next year. Those voices in the young Republic that had called for a compromise peace with the king now fell silent.[36]

Faced by so many setbacks Philip sometimes despaired over what to do next. The affairs of his monarchy, he reflected on one occasion, 'do not depend on my will, or on my wanting it, but rather on many other matters which are hard to arrange. Everything is in a terrible state unless God remedies it.' But such moments of uncertainty did not last long. In 1590, after expressing his regret for the taxes imposed in 'the defence of our holy faith and the conservation of my kingdoms and lordships', he warned his subjects that they would have to pay more because 'I have such a special obligation to God and the world to act; and also because if the heretics prevail (which I hope God will not permit), it might open the door to worse damage and danger, and to war at home.' The following year, when Vázquez warned his master that 'if God had placed Your Majesty under an obligation to remedy all the troubles of the world, He would have given you the money and the strength to do so', Philip replied sharply: 'I know you are moved by the great zeal you have for my service to say what you did, but you must also understand that these are not matters which can be abandoned by a person who is as conscientious about his responsibilities as you know me to be, even though they depress me and matter to me more than to anyone. Above all,' he concluded, 'these issues involve the cause of religion, which must take precedence over everything.'[37]

Occasionally the king's perseverance paid off. In 1595 a small force operating from a forward base in Brittany succeeded where the Armada had failed: it landed troops on English soil, burning down Penzance and some surrounding Cornish villages, creating widespread panic; but this could not compare with the panic caused in Spain by Elizabeth's reaction to the raid. Drake and Hawkins led an expeditionary force of twenty-seven vessels (six of them royal warships) to the Caribbean, where they captured Nombre de Dios; and Howard led an Anglo-Dutch fleet of over 100 vessels (seventeen of them royal warships) to Cadiz, which they captured, held for two weeks and then burned. They then sailed to Faro in the Portuguese Algarve, which they also captured and burned, returning to England with vast booty, numerous hostages and two of the new galleons built to replace those lost in the Armada campaign (see chapter 17). In all, the task force destroyed ships and property worth 4 million ducats. According to historian Guillermo Céspedes del Castillo everyone in Spain saw these events 'as a national disgrace and an irreparable humiliation which produced a wave of pessimism and sadness'.[38]

It could have been even worse. Don Juan de Silva, charged with the defence of Portugal, observed bitterly that 'A king of Spain can preserve his reputation without capturing London' but 'he cannot preserve or recover it if we lose Lisbon in the same way we lost Cadiz.' He also reported that the Portuguese refused to serve under the Castilian commander appointed by the king.[39] Philip was lucky that the English troops landed at Faro, not Lisbon, and then sailed for home. He was also lucky that England's Caribbean expedition failed, withdrawing with few gains and leaving behind many dead, including both Hawkins and Drake.

Nevertheless, the Spanish monarchy now faced financial collapse. Shortly before the sack of Cadiz, Don Cristóbal de Moura confided to a colleague: 'The more we acquire, the more we must defend, and the more our enemies want to take from us.' His colleague, who as head of the treasury shared his pessimism, responded:

> His Majesty must see that it is impossible to carry on as we are, because although we have already spent all His Majesty's revenues until the year 1599, his expenses continue and even increase, so that even if his revenues were unencumbered, we could not carry on. To do this, one only needs to know what I know: that His Majesty must either reduce his expenditure voluntarily until things improve, or else find a way to achieve the impossible.

When news of the sack of Cadiz arrived, Moura protested that 'here we are drowning tied back-to-back' (a particularly graphic phrase), and a few months later the king signed another Decree of Bankruptcy which, like the one signed in 1575 (see chapter 2), suspended all interest payments and confiscated the capital of all outstanding loans. Castile had become the world's first serial defaulter on sovereign debt and Philip had become, in the phrase of a modern monograph, 'the borrower from hell'.[40]

Despite these setbacks, Philip refused to change either his policies or his perspective. To avenge the sack of Cadiz he determined to send a new Armada to Ireland, where it would occupy a town or two in the south; and when its commander failed to get it to sea, he deployed precisely the same arsenal of spiritual blackmail that he had used against Santa Cruz and Medina Sidonia:

> Leave in the name of God and do what I have ordered in the voyage and in the whole campaign. Although I see that the season is advanced, and the risks that this poses, we have to trust in God (who has done so much for us) in this. To stop what we have begun now would be to show weakness in His service, to spend money without profit, and to find ourselves without troops in time of need. Since these are definite disadvantages, it would not be sensible to allow them.[41]

The venture proved another disaster: frustrated that the fleet had still not set sail by mid-October 1596, the king suddenly changed his mind: he ordered it to capture a port in Brittany instead and spend the winter there – but the fleet set forth too late, as usual, storms destroyed a quarter of its ships, and some 2,000 of its men never returned.

Philip's death in 1598 at first changed nothing. Three years later his son, Philip III, launched another Armada that captured Kinsale and some other ports on Ireland's south coast, far away from Tyrone's rebel strongholds in Ulster. English forces foiled a desperate attempt by the earl to 'join hands' with the Spaniards, who surrendered the following year; and in April 1603 Tyrone did the same – obtaining generous terms in part because Elizabeth had died a few days earlier.

The queen's death transformed both the international and domestic situation. James VI of Scotland, who succeeded her in England and Ireland, had remained at peace with Spain and he immediately revoked all 'letters of marque' issued by Elizabeth to legalize attacks on Spanish shipping and indicated his willingness to negotiate an end to the costly conflict: between 1585 and 1603 Elizabeth had spent over £1 million in subsidies to the Dutch, over £1.5 million on the navy and £2 million in Ireland – all to prevent Spain winning the conflict she herself had provoked.[42]

Philip III sent a team of negotiators to London, and even permitted them to attend James's coronation. The peace treaty agreed the following year brought significant political gains for both sides. Each granted a general amnesty and promised to end all attacks on the other's shipping and possessions; James also agreed to end all financial and military aid to the Dutch Republic (although English troops would continue to garrison certain towns until the Dutch repaid the subsidies received from Elizabeth); Philip recognized the legitimacy of the Protestant regime in Britain and Ireland. This in essence restored the pre-war political situation, but the clauses of the treaty that concerned religion, initially kept secret, favoured James. His subjects received guarantees of toleration in both Spain and the southern Netherlands – they were not obliged to attend Catholic worship, nor could the Inquisition proceed against them for the private exercise of their faith – but British Catholics received no reciprocal concessions. Philip III thus abandoned all the goals his father had intended the Armada to achieve.[43]

## The Stories of the 1588 Survivors

Not surprisingly, several prominent Spanish Catholics, including the hawkish Jesuit Pedro de Ribadeneira, condemned the peace; and a poem attributed to Cervantes also condemned the welcome extended to the British delegation led by Admiral Howard, whose arrival to ratify the peace coincided with the birth of a prince of Spain:

> The queen gave birth; the Lutheran came
> With six hundred heretics and their heresies;

> In two weeks we spent a million
> On jewels, hospitality and wine for them.[44]

How the Armada's surviving senior officers reacted to the presence of Howard and his 'six hundred heretics' on Spanish soil remains unknown; but we know a lot about their subsequent careers.

Don Pedro de Valdés, the first and most senior officer to be taken prisoner, had been well treated immediately after his surrender, eating at Sir Francis Drake's table and sleeping in his cabin for some days before being sent to prison in London for interrogation. His situation improved somewhat after Drake came to Court and plucked him from gaol to see the queen in St James's Park. Although Elizabeth refused to speak to the Spaniard, she looked meaningfully in Drake's direction and said, 'Drake, God give you joy of this prisoner.' For almost five years Valdés and the principal officers captured with him on *Rosario* resided in the house of Drake's cousin in Surrey, where Sir Francis and others visited them frequently. On such occasions music and dancing were provided, and the Spaniards would emerge to view, and be viewed by, the assembled audience. Don Pedro also spent some time revising the first Spanish–English dictionary, prepared by his interpreter, Richard Percyvall, and published in 1591 (Figure 132).[45]

Early in 1593 Valdés regained his freedom in return for a ransom of £1,500, plus the exchange of a notable English prisoner, but no sooner had he reached the relative safety of Brussels than the king demanded to know the fate of the 50,000 ducats from the royal treasury embarked on *Nuestra Señora del Rosario*. Don Pedro evidently provided a satisfactory answer because in

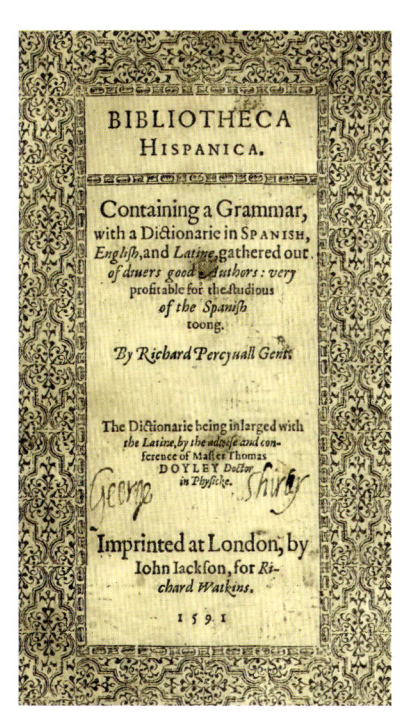

**132.** Title page of Percyvall's *Bibliotheca Hispanica* (1591). The first Spanish–English dictionary, it has 12,500 entries, and Percyvall acknowledged his debt to two illustrious Armada prisoners: 'I ran it over twice with Don Pedro de Valdés and Don Vasco de Silva, to whom I had access.'

1595 he received payment of his salary arrears as commander of the squadron of Andalucia until the day of his surrender, and he later served for eight years as governor of Cuba. Then in 1615 Don Pedro dramatically changed the story of how and why he had surrendered *Rosario*, asserting that he had only done so 'after a day and a night of bombardment' and against a promise that he and his crew 'would be given free passage to Spain or Flanders, whichever they preferred, and they would receive back their arms and insignia'. He died shortly afterwards at the age of seventy.[46]

Don Alonso de Luzón also received a cool welcome after he was ransomed and returned home. He did not receive his pay arrears until 1595, and even then only until 31 July 1588 although he had continued to command *Trinidad Valencera* for six more weeks. The king nominated him for a knighthood in 1597 (apparently after the rejection of earlier requests), but those appointed to examine Don Alonso's pedigree encountered a witness who stated that one of his ancestors had been burned at the stake as a Jew in 1500. This testimony was eventually discredited as a smear by a rival of the Luzón family, but clearing Don Alonso's name – and therefore securing his knighthood – took eighteen months.[47]

Don Diego Pimentel regained his freedom after six months in a Dutch gaol, thanks to a hefty ransom arranged by the duke of Parma, and served for a decade in the Army of Flanders. He then held a number of prominent positions in Spain and Italy until in 1621 (now marquis of Los Gelves) he was appointed viceroy of New Spain. His rule proved a disaster: three years after his arrival he provoked a major rebellion. The insurgents imprisoned him and secured his replacement and recall. A Dutch fleet intercepted him as he sailed back to Spain and almost took him prisoner a second time, but he escaped and served on the Council of State in Madrid until his death in 1636, aged seventy-six. He was by then the last surviving senior Armada officer. He was also the only one to leave a self-portrait (Figure 133).

Apart from Diego Flores de Valdés the other general officers who survived to spend Christmas 1588 in Spain fared rather better. Although Philip never granted the *encomiendas* he had promised to Medina Sidonia's sons, from his palace at Sanlúcar de Barrameda the duke continued to oversee the assembly and dispatch of the annual transatlantic convoys. Then in 1596 he again led an army to save Cadiz – albeit only after the English had withdrawn. This prompted another bitter sonnet from Cervantes that ended:

> And in Cadiz, at last, at stately pace,
> At no risk since the English had already left,
> The great duke of Medina made his triumphal entrance.

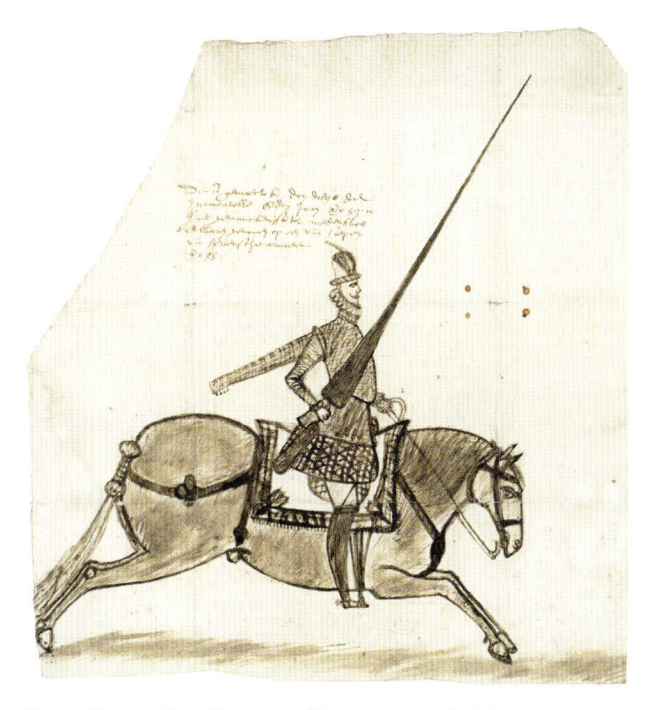

**133.** Don Diego Pimentel's self-portrait. Pimentel scratched this escapist image on the wall of the cell where he languished as a prisoner in Medemblik Castle (Holland) in 1589, following the surrender of his galleon *San Mateo*.

Despite this smear, the duke served as one of the pallbearers at Philip II's funeral and then returned to Sanlúcar to continue his work on the convoys until he died there in 1615.[48]

Martín de Bertendona also died in harness. After the wreck of his flagship *Regazona* in December 1588 he replaced Recalde as general of the squadron of Vizcaya, which he led to the Azores in 1591, to Brittany the following year, and in the Armadas sent against England in 1596 and 1597. In 1604, as he led his squadron to Lisbon, the king at last proposed him for a knighthood in the Order of Santiago; but ill-health forced him ashore and he died after a few days, aged eighty-two. The investigation into his merits for knighthood died with him.[49]

Don Balthasar de Zúñiga (see Figure 123) enjoyed the most successful career of all Armada survivors. After a series of distinguished diplomatic postings he returned to Spain and became chief minister in 1618, serving until his death in 1622 when he was succeeded by his nephew Don Gaspar de Guzmán, count of Olivares, son of Philip's ambassador in Rome. Like Don Balthasar, the count needed a special papal dispensation to receive a knighthood in the Order of Santiago because his ancestors included an archbishop. Despite this 'stain', he served as chief minister for two decades.[50]

Don Francisco de Bobadilla also prospered. In 1591 Philip tasked him with suppressing a rebellion in Aragon, and he headed the army of occupation afterwards. Five years later he went to Lisbon to coordinate its defence against a possible Anglo-Dutch attack, and in 1597 (now count of Puñonrostro) he became chief magistrate of Seville, where his draconian rule gained him immortality as a character in the novella *La ilustre fregona* (*The Illustrious Serving Maid*), published in 1613 by Cervantes.[51]

Don Agustín Mexía also played a prominent part in the pacification of Aragon, and between 1609 and 1611 commanded the troops deployed to expel all Moriscos from Spain (the task assigned to Leyva a generation before, but never executed: see chapter 6). Until his death in 1629 Mexía served beside Pimentel on the Council of State, a rare distinction for a career soldier.

The prince of Ascoli had a less successful subsequent career. When the fireships approached the Armada off Calais in the early hours of 8 August 1588, he was one of those whom Medina Sidonia sent round the fleet in feluccas to give instructions on the appropriate evasive action, but when dawn broke the prince found himself isolated between the two fleets. Unable to rejoin the flagship he took refuge in Calais and from there travelled to Dunkirk, ready to embark on Parma's flotilla. Once it became clear that the Enterprise had failed, Ascoli returned to Court where in 1596 he was accused of sodomy, arrested, threatened with torture, and sentenced to another term of banishment 'to set an example that will extirpate this abomination in Spain, and ensure that noblemen do not indulge in it'. Ascoli left to serve with the Army of Lombardy and died in Italy around 1610.[52]

Of those who had helped to prepare the Armada but did not sail with it, Archduke Albert remained viceroy of Portugal until 1593, when he returned to Spain to give audiences and receive ambassadors in the king's name and sat on the Junta de Gobierno (equivalent to the English Privy Council). Two years later he led an army up the Spanish Road and took command in the Netherlands, returning to Spain in 1598 to marry Philip II's daughter, Infanta Isabella. Together they returned to the Netherlands as sovereign rulers until Albert's death in 1621.

The count of Fuentes, whom Philip had sent to Lisbon bearing an ultimatum that the marquis of Santa Cruz must either immediately lead the Armada to sea or be replaced, remained in Portugal until 1591, when Philip selected him for a similar task. This time he would replace Parma as commander of all Spanish forces in France, to ensure the execution of the king's priorities: upholding the French

Catholic League must take precedence over defeating the Dutch Protestants. The following year Philip lost patience with his nephew. 'If I could have you in more than one place at the same time, my load would be lighter,' he wrote soothingly, but 'since this cannot be ... I want to have you here [in Spain] for a time.' Parma died before he learned of his recall, and Fuentes replaced him in command of the Army of Flanders until Albert arrived. The count then served as an aggressive governor of Lombardy until his death in 1610.[53]

Of those who had helped the king to shape his disastrous Masterplan, Mateo Vázquez died in 1591, after serving as the king's personal secretary for eighteen years. Bernardino de Escalante sent his last known paper of advice to Court from the headquarters of the Seville Inquisition in 1605, where he served, and probably died shortly afterwards. Don Cristóbal de Moura eventually became Philip II's alter ego, taking decisions and signing documents in his name until the king's death. Although the new regime appointed him viceroy of his native Portugal and elevated him to the rank of grandee, he never again influenced central policy. He died in 1613. By contrast, his colleague Don Juan de Idiáquez retained his position at the heart of government and continued to advise Philip III until his own death in 1614.

Don Bernardino de Mendoza, who had provided so much of the intelligence on which Philip relied as he formed and changed his foreign policies, also survived his master. After the assassination of Henry III in 1589 (an event that afforded him enormous satisfaction) he successfully directed the defence of Paris against the forces of the Protestant claimant to the French throne, Henry of Navarre, before returning to Spain. There, although totally blind, he committed his military and diplomatic experience to books. Despite Burghley's ridicule in *The Copie of a letter*, the former ambassador even gained a following in England: a participant in the Cadiz expedition in 1596 looted a copy of Mendoza's *Theory and Practice of War* and later that year, 'with the aid of two hostages lodged in my house, and the excellent and helpful dictionary compiled by Richard Percyvall', he published an English translation. By then Mendoza had purchased a house adjacent to a Cistercian convent in Madrid, so that with his door open he could follow the services within; and when he died in 1604 he bequeathed his house to the convent.[54]

We can piece together the fate of a few other Armada survivors. Marcos de Aramburu returned to command transatlantic convoys until 1606, when he was sixty-two, but after that no more is known. Pedro Coco Calderón, who in July 1588 asked Philip to appoint him 'Chief Accountant in England' after the conquest, fell under suspicion of corruption after his return to Spain. Exonerated, in 1594 he set sail for Mexico with his wife, children, servants and three slaves to become treasurer of the entrepôt city of Veracruz. He was still there in 1607 after half a century of royal service but then, like Aramburu, he disappears from the record. Captain Francisco de Cuéllar requested and received permission to sail to Mexico in 1606, after serving as a staff officer in the Netherlands under Parma, Fuentes and Albert, and also in Italy and on the transatlantic guardships. Then, like Aramburu and Coco Calderón, he too disappears from the record.

We know a lot more about the later career of Lope de Vega. After his ship, *San Juan de Portugal*, limped back to Corunna, he complied with the terms of his exile and joined his new wife first in Valencia and then in Toledo, improving the quality and increasing the quantity of his verse. He survived an assassination attempt, and by the time of his death in 1635 he had sired about fifteen children (some after he became a priest in 1614) and written seven novels and novellas, nine epic poems, at least 500 plays and some 3,000 sonnets. Like Mendoza, some of Lope's work also gained a following in England: by the 1660s his plays were being performed on the London stage.

Tristram Winslade, one of the English Catholics captured when *Rosario* surrendered, also survived. In September 1588 the Privy Council sent him to the Tower with orders for their officials to place him 'upon the rack, using torture to him at their pleasure'; but after eighteen months of enhanced interrogation the Council accepted his claim that 'he was brought hither against his will; and so taking bonds of him for his appearance at all times upon ten days' warning' they set him free. Winslade immediately fled to Brussels where he received a Spanish pension and composed a treatise on how best to conquer England and convert it back to Catholicism. He died in 1605.[55]

Gerónimo de Vera from Córdoba, aged thirty in 1588, was one of twenty-three Jesuits who sailed with the Armada, and one of six who survived – but only just. After the battle off Gravelines his vessel took on water and began to sink so he tried to transfer to another, but 'because it was already full of men, they refused to accept anyone else'. He was saved only because he had cured one of the ship's boys, who recognized him and persuaded his shipmates to let him come aboard. Afterwards he served first in the regional headquarters of the Order in Madrid, and then in the small Jesuit College in Huete (Castile) where he died in 1631 aged seventy-three.[56]

The Jesuit Order also assisted fourteen English and Irish exiled priests and students who had assembled in Valladolid while they waited for news that it was safe for them to return home. In 1589 they admitted defeat and begged the city council to provide a permanent home and a stipend. Don Francisco de Bobadilla became their 'Protector', and the English College of St Alban stands on the spot granted to the exiles by the city magistrates: Calle de Don Sancho, 17, Valladolid.

The king of Spain still appoints its rector: one of the last living legacies of the Armada campaign.[57]

Some Armada survivors who joined the Army of Flanders were even luckier. The service record for 133 soldiers, compiled after they mutinied for their wage arrears, reveals that many had enlisted in 1586 and started to serve aboard either the transatlantic guardships or Recalde's Vizcaya squadron. Although each man had received almost all his wages in either cash or goods when he left Lisbon for England, after the mutiny they received their unpaid arrears in cash – often enough to make them rich in the towns and villages from which they came, and to which many now clandestinely returned.[58]

These men were the exception. In January 1589 Diego Felipe de Espinosa, a physician and professor of medicine at the university of Salamanca, informed the king that although he had cured more than fifty of the sick soldiers brought to the city hospital from the Armada, 'none regained their former strength'. He also performed an autopsy on nine who died and in all he found atrophied and discoloured internal organs, 'without doubt because of the foul food and contaminated water on which they had subsisted' on the long voyage. Espinosa reported that before they died, many had 'vomited contagious substances which infected all the hospital staff as well as the students and citizens who cared for them'.[59] Another unlucky Armada survivor arrived in Salamanca early in 1589. 'A man named Alonso Requena' soon 'committed some outrages which led to his arrest. When he was tortured, he confessed' that he had been condemned to ten years as a galley-slave for a previous crime and served aboard the flag galley as it accompanied the Grand Fleet. After the vessel ran aground off Bayonne in France, like his fellow oarsmen Requena mutinied and fled, 'stealing the royal treasure and other goods aboard' worth at least 11,000 ducats before returning overland to Spain. The magistrates of Salamanca condemned him to death.[60]

---

So many lives lost, and so much suffering, and all for nothing. Could it have been otherwise? In 1888, the tercentenary of the Armada, the historian and naval officer John Knox Laughton posed that counterfactual question, apparently for the first time. Might the Armada have somehow managed to 'join hands' with Parma, land its veteran troops and siege-train in Kent, and then capture London as planned? In short, as he put it: 'What would have happened had the Armada succeeded?'[61]

# 19

# If the Armada had Landed

In December 1923 Edward P. Cheyney, a historian of Tudor England, began his presidential address to the American Historical Association with a counterfactual exercise. He claimed that 'On the morning of the 10th of August 1588, the last and most eventful day of the running fight of the English fleet with the Spanish Armada, the wind blew steadily from the south-west.' Nevertheless, he continued: 'If the wind on that critical day had blown from some other quarter, the Invincible Armada might have justified its name and effected the invasion of England.' Then, abruptly, Cheyney changed tack:

> Although the wind blew from the south-west on the tenth of August, 1588, it did not blow adversely for the Spaniards through the whole twenty years of the Elizabethan war. Yet Spain never successfully invaded England. Moreover, as we compare the two countries it becomes doubtful whether, even if Spanish troops had landed on the shores of England, any serious influence would have been exerted on the general course of the history of the two countries.

To him, the reason was obvious:

> Spain, overstrained by too ambitious undertakings, unsupported by adequate economic resources, deficient in statesmanship, was an anaemic giant, holding her predominance in Europe with a constantly slackening hand. England, of youthful vigor, hardening Protestantism, rapidly increasing wealth, an exhilarating sense of her own nationality, was of almost unlimited, if undisciplined, powers and was especially resistant to all forms of foreign control.[1]

It is hard to know which of Cheyney's errors to correct first. He misstated both the date of the crucial battle (8 August) and the prevailing wind direction (which shifted from south-south-west to north-west). Above all, he forgot that foreign troops 'landed on the shores of England' exactly a century later and placed the entire kingdom, as well as Scotland and Ireland, under 'foreign control'.

## 1688 and All That

'To contemporaries and foreigners alike,' Clare Jackson has written, Stuart England (like its Tudor predecessor) 'was a failed state: a discomfiting byword for seditious rebellion, religious extremism and regime change.' The last successful invasion of England in 1688, like the attempted invasion a century earlier, arose from a similar combination of religious, dynastic and commercial disputes; and it likewise triggered a prolonged war on land and sea that almost bankrupted the victors.[2]

In 1685 James II, a Catholic, became king of England, Ireland and Scotland and soon took steps to undermine Protestantism in all three kingdoms, appointing Catholics to offices in the Court, the country, the army and the navy. Although many of his Protestant subjects resented these moves, they consoled themselves that James could not live for ever and would be succeeded by his Protestant daughter Mary, married to the equally Protestant Prince William of Orange, commander of the armed forces of the Dutch Republic. Then in June 1688, after numerous miscarriages, James's second wife (a Catholic) gave birth to a healthy son and heir. Almost immediately a group of Protestant nobles sent a formal appeal for William to come to England and save them from Catholicism and absolutism. The prince hastened to accept, in part because the previous year Louis XIV of France had banned certain Dutch imports and doubled the tariffs on many more, and in September 1688 he embargoed all Dutch ships in French ports. The leaders of the Republic reluctantly concluded that a war with France was now both inevitable and imminent; and since James seemed likely to support Louis in the coming conflict, they authorized Prince William to invade England and create an anti-French regime in London.

Whereas Philip II took three years to create his Armada, William of Orange took less than three months to assemble 460 ships (including fifty-three warships) to transport to England 23,000 infantry and 5,000 cavalry, together with fifty siege-guns, copious munitions, a printing press, £100,000 in cash, and dies with which to strike fresh coins. Aged thirty-eight and without previous experience of naval command (like Medina Sidonia a century before), the prince nevertheless insisted on planning and leading the invasion in person. In July 1688 he drew up a list of 'Necessary preparations for the Design' (even using the same term as Philip) and discussed them in secret with a select group of advisers. His list left some important issues unresolved – above all: 'Whether to land in one place or several? Should we make a landing in Scotland at the same time?' – but, he concluded crisply: 'Act according to events.'[3]

Although the prince thus retained full tactical flexibility, he took two critical strategic decisions. First, as with Philip's Enterprise of England, success depended on getting a large expeditionary force ashore relatively unscathed. The prince therefore instructed his admirals to 'avoid combat as much as possible' until they had shepherded the troop-transports safely to the landing-zone, because 'if our fleet should meet with a mishap, everything will be lost'. Second, although William's ultimate goal was to capture London, he knew that James had stationed the bulk of his fleet and his troops in Kent and Essex, which made it imperative to avoid them and instead land either in Yorkshire or in Devon. But which? His admirals warned that 'it is by the winds that in a great measure the descent must be governed', so the prince made plans for both possibilities, accumulating data on all promising landing-zones in England from Tynemouth in the north-east to Falmouth in the south-west.[4]

For a time this information was irrelevant, because westerly winds confined the invasion fleet to port. According to the British ambassador in The Hague on 28 September: 'The Catholics pray ardently for [James's] preservation and for the success of his army against his enemies. The wind continuing contrary all this while they call it a "popish wind". God continue it one month longer.' And apparently He did: 'I see God Almighty continues his protection to me by bringing the wind westerly,' James rejoiced on 30 October. His Protestant opponents also solicited divine favour. Clergymen led public prayers each day for a favourable wind: in Dutch at 9 and 2 o'clock, in English at 10 and 3 o'clock, and in French at 11 and 4 o'clock. The prince himself spent hours 'in his prayers here, upon his bended knees, after a most devout manner'. These prayers were answered on 9 November, when the wind changed to easterly.[5]

The prince's ships now weighed anchor and three days later, with his entire fleet gathered off the coast, William 'gave a signal that the admirals should come aboard him'. After some discussion they resolved to sail through the Channel to one of three possible landing-zones: the Isle of Wight, Poole in Dorset, or Exmouth in Devon – although with the proviso that if, 'after sailing, the wind should alter and run south-west, then we are to follow a course to the north' and land in Yorkshire. That night William sent a trusted envoy to England to gather last-minute intelligence.

He returned with two important details. First, the Royal Navy lay at the Gunfleet anchorage off Harwich in Essex, an excellent position from which to intercept an enemy trying to enter the Thames, or to pursue a fleet sailing north, but probably ineffective against one sailing south-west through the Channel. Second, James had sent reinforcements to Yorkshire but not to Dorset or Devon. Since the easterly wind continued to blow, the prince took what in American football is known as a 'game-time decision': only now did he make the irrevocable choice to lead his vast Armada towards the west of England.[6]

It was a dangerous gamble, because sandbanks presented the same hazard to a large fleet of sailing ships in 1688 as they had done a century before. Therefore, 'through fear that such a numerous fleet, which occupied a great expanse of sea, should not be damaged by the banks of Flanders', the prince ordered all his ships to take in sail on the night of 12–13 November. Then, after consulting his senior officers again the prince gave a prearranged signal, 'stretching the whole fleet in a line, from Dover to Calais, twenty-five deep, so that our fleet reached within a league of each place', and 'the trumpets and drums play[ed] various tunes to rejoice our hearts'. A 'gentle east wind' allowed the fleet to sail on throughout the night. At dawn on 14 November they sighted the Isle of Wight and that evening reached

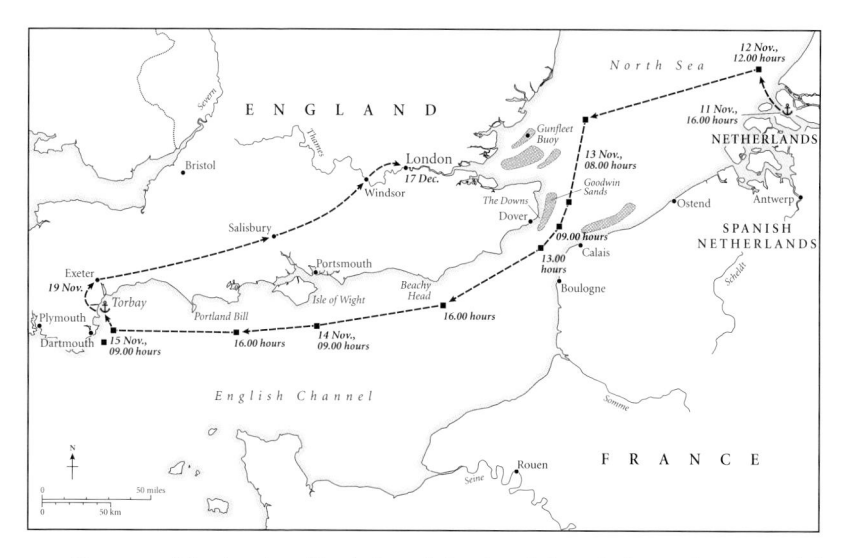

134. The route of the victorious Dutch Armada in 1688. A fleet of 460 vessels commanded by Prince William of Orange left port on 11 November 1688 and started landing its 28,000 troops and fifty siege-guns at Torbay in Devon a mere four days later. Just over a month later they took control of London and the surrounding counties.

Portland Bill, where the prince consulted his pilots about the best landing-zone. They insisted that 'the sea is too great for the fleet to go to Exmouth', and so in another game-time decision William resolved to land his forces at both Torbay and Dartmouth (Figure 134).[7]

The rest of the Dutch Armada now 'made all the sail that our ships could bear' until at dawn on 15 November 'the vanguard swung round, followed by the rearguard and battle. Nothing could seem finer at that time than this manoeuvre, carried out under a clear sky so everyone could watch, bringing the whole fleet together' in Torbay. The prince again signalled that his admirals should join him for consultation, 'which they did; and then [he] ordered that the whole fleet should come to anchor, and immediately land'. Once more, William himself noted the orders given: 'Land as many cavalry troopers here as possible and find somewhere else to land the rest. March tomorrow towards Exeter with some or all of the infantry. Take enough bread for four days.'[8]

On 15 November, as a participant noted, 'the sea was so calm that it seemed like a great lake', allowing the small vessels which had accompanied the fleet to ferry the infantry ashore, followed by the prince, his entourage and the cavalry. This was easier said than done. Some 600 horses perished as they swam ashore, and many of the rest were 'sorely bruised and not able to find their legs for some days'; moreover, after disembarking, many soldiers 'would stumble and sometimes fall, because of a dizziness in their heads after they had been so long tossed at sea'. Nevertheless, after a brief rest William led his army on forced marches, sleeping in tents or 'in their campaign coats' in the 'cold frosty night'. As the invaders entered Exeter (25 miles away) on 19 November 1688 the troops looked 'sorely weather-beaten' and 'very pale'. One exhausted officer considered that 'The poor state of our troops, and especially of the cavalry, most of whom lacked horses', offered King James 'the means to prevent our advance, if he had dared to attack us'. Some of his comrades agreed: 'It was the Lord's goodness that our foes did not come upon us in this juncture and unfit condition.'[9]

## The Conquest of England

The prince and his 460 vessels had covered the 200 nautical miles that separate Calais from Dartmouth in just forty-eight hours – three times faster than Medina Sidonia and his 130 vessels a century before – and they did so in mid-November with the loss of only one ship (a troop-transport captured after she lost her rudder). In part this reflected the superb sailing qualities of William's ships and the superior calibre of his mariners and pilots; but it also reflected the failure of the Royal Navy to intercept them. As naval historian David Davies observed: 'James fell because William was able to land, and he was able to land only because James's fleet did not intercept William's fleet.' So why did James's fleet not fight?[10]

The most obvious answer to this counterfactual question is that the fleet's commander, Lord Dartmouth, failed to anticipate where William would strike. The king, who had extensive experience of naval command, was horrified when Dartmouth announced in October 1688 that he would lead his warships from the Downs to the Gunfleet, because they might 'be surprised while there by the sudden coming of the Dutch fleet, as being a place he cannot well get out to sea from, while the wind remains easterly'. Unlike Philip, however, James refused to micromanage operations and tell Dartmouth what he must do. Instead, he 'resolved to put no restraints upon' his admiral, 'committing [the fleet] entirely to your prudence'.[11]

It proved a critical error. By the time he learned that William's fleet was at sea Dartmouth's warships had 'their yards and topsails down' and 'could not stir'. Adverse winds and tides 'kept him at anchor all day and night', but the next day twenty-eight warships and twelve fireships left the Gunfleet and on 15 November, as they drew level with Beachy Head, they deployed in line of battle – only to learn that the invaders had already landed. Dartmouth convened a Council of War at which, believing that forty-five Dutch capital ships ('almost double our force') opposed them, the senior captains voted unanimously that 'it was not thought fit to hazard the fleet at such odds and to no purpose'. They therefore returned to the Downs without firing a shot.[12]

In seeking to explain this 'comprehensive admission of defeat', Davies blamed Dartmouth's inexperience. Whereas 'a bold and experienced admiral' might have convinced his senior officers to persevere and fight 'by force of personality', Dartmouth took command of the fleet on 12 October after serving only twenty-two months as a ship's captain. His surviving correspondence reveals that he 'was naturally indecisive, alternated between self-doubt and exaggerated self-belief, and was unable to impose himself on a divided, factious fleet' – all fatal flaws when confronted by the massive Dutch Armada.[13]

Davies largely overlooked a further reason for the Royal Navy's failure to prevent the Dutch invasion: inferior ships and seamanship. Although the deployment of sailing warships in the Channel in November was a high-risk enterprise for all protagonists – as the English commander observed, 'It is strange that such mad proceedings should have such success at this time of year' – the Dutch Armada suffered only one loss before reaching its destination. By contrast, on 16 November two English warships 'fell foul of each other' off the Isle of Wight; the next day the flagship sprang her foremast and another warship made a signal of distress; and when Dartmouth led his fleet back to the Downs, two ships ran aground. He set forth again on 26 November intending to locate and engage the Dutch, but two of his ships had to take refuge in Portsmouth for repair, and the main and mizzen sails of the flagship split and blew away. By the time he sighted the Dutch fleet at Torbay on 29 November, two weeks after the landing, Dartmouth commanded only twenty-two ships. Once again he decided to withdraw without firing a shot.[14]

William exploited these advantages to the full. He spent almost two weeks in Exeter, resting his men, purchasing horses and provisions, and preparing his artillery and baggage-train to meet James's army in battle. As in 1588, the invasion fleet had been spotted as it approached the English coast, triggering rapid countermeasures ashore. A courier from Dover arrived at Court on the night of 13 November with news that the Dutch fleet had passed by that morning, 'so thick that there is no telling of them, but 'tis judged about 300 sails, others say 400'. James immediately dispatched troops towards Portsmouth; but two days later another courier left Devon at 5 a.m. and staggered into James's presence at 3 p.m. on 16 November, bringing news of the enemy fleet's true destination almost as fast as the beacons had done a century before – but, unlike the beacons, the courier 'imparted something of his own knowledge to His Majesty'. James now correctly anticipated that the prince would head to Exeter and thence towards London, and he deployed his troops in a strong defensive position on Salisbury Plain, midway between the two cities. But as William's army advanced, so many English nobles and officers deserted James that he lost his nerve and on 3 December retreated to London, provoking another wave of defections.[15]

The first Dutch troops entered the capital virtually unopposed on 17 December, and James abandoned his capital – creating a vacuum of power and a widespread fear of chaos. Four days later, James gave orders that all the troops under his command 'to make no opposition' to William and instead lay down their arms and thus avoid 'the misfortune of effusion of blood'.[16]

Shortly afterwards the prince stationed units of his army in and around the capital, culminating with Dutch dragoons moving into Hornchurch, Ilford, Romford and Ingatestone in Essex on 28 December. That same day the prince made his ceremonial entry into London, advancing at the head of his elite foreign troops up Knightsbridge and via Hyde Park Corner to St James's Palace amid cheering crowds, many wearing orange ribbons and some waving oranges on the ends of their walking sticks to show their support of the invaders. It was six weeks and a day since they had landed on English soil.

For the next sixteen months William's Dutch, German and Scandinavian troops stood guard over the principal government buildings in and around the capital: an unmistakable sign that England had come under 'foreign control'. In February

1689 they surrounded the Palace of Westminster while the House of Lords debated whether to offer the crown jointly to William and his wife Mary; and again while the House of Commons voted unanimously to pay the Dutch States-General £600,000 'for their assistance to the king at his late coming into this kingdom for its deliverance from popery and arbitrary power', plus 6 per cent interest on the indemnity, backdated to October 1688. In April 1689, as William and Mary travelled to Westminster Abbey for their coronation, an eyewitness reported something that 'never happened since William the Conqueror's time, which was that a king and queen of England should make their procession at the coronation through a treble rank of armed horse and foot, *all foreigners*'.[17]

In the words of an amazed Jesuit living in London:

A new prince has arrived with a foreign army, without encountering the least resistance. It is something never before seen, heard of, or recorded in History: a king in peaceful possession of his realm, with an army of thirty thousand soldiers and forty warships, has left his kingdom without firing a shot. Even the victorious foreigners are astonished at their own success and laugh at the English for their cowardice and disloyalty to their prince. It seems as if heaven and earth have conspired against us.

He added a terse postscript: 'This time we are really screwed.'[18]

## Parma Comes Ashore

Would Tudor England have been 'really screwed' if Parma had come ashore a century before? He certainly had some encouraging precedents to hand. Besides the successful invasions of England in 1471 (by Edward IV) and 1485 (by Henry Tudor), in 1580 an expeditionary force that included several of those who would serve on the Armada had marched 120 miles through the heart of Portugal to Setubal, sailed across the mouth of the Tagus for two days before landing at Cascais, and then marched another 20 miles before routing in battle an enthusiastic but untrained army beneath the walls of Lisbon (see chapter 4). In 1583 many of the same men had sailed 1,000 miles from Lisbon to Terceira and stormed ashore, where they again routed the enthusiastic but untrained defenders before sailing back with few losses (see chapter 5).

Philip II's Instructions charged Parma to advance from Margate through Kent to London, where he should capture Elizabeth and her ministers. Perhaps the queen's discontented subjects in the north, in the west, and in Ireland, would rise in rebellion and aid the invaders, but the success of Philip's design did not hinge on domestic support. He expected few English Catholics to provide active support to his troops, despite the propaganda directed towards them by Cardinal Allen and other exiled pamphleteers; and the English Catholic exiles, including Allen, would serve as important props for the Enterprise only *after* the conquest.

Parma seems to have envisaged a battle with Elizabeth's troops soon after he landed, because when at an audience in July 1588 Dr Valentine Dale pressed the duke about his intentions he shot back: 'Her Majesty had more need to be desirous of peace than they, for if the king lost a battle he could recover it well because he was in Spain far enough off; [but] if the queen lost a battle it was the loss of her crown.' According to Dale, 'they persuade themselves that no man can withstand them if they could set footing in England'.[19]

Many of those who would have faced Parma's troops shared this assessment. When Queen Elizabeth visited Tilbury camp, she met a member of the Vere family with experience of the Low Countries Wars, and asked him 'what he thought of the army'. Vere replied that 'He was the only coward there. *They* were all wishing to have the Spaniards land, and every man was telling what feats he would then do; *he* was the only man that was trembling for fear of it.' The earl of Leicester agreed. Outmanoeuvred by Parma on campaign in the Netherlands and now in command of England's land defences, he warned the Privy Council on 3 August 1588: 'Let no hope or other supposition abuse you or carry you from presently and most speedy providing to defend this mighty enemy now knocking in a manner at the gate.' Two days later he repeated that 'Her Majesty cannot be strong enough too soon' and so 'I beseech you assemble your forces and play not away this kingdom by delays'. Looking back, Sir Walter Raleigh believed that if Parma had 'joined the army which he commanded with that of Spain, and landed it on the south coast', it was 'easy to divine what had become of the liberty of England', because its defences by land were 'of no such force as to encounter an army like unto that, wherewith it was intended that the prince of Parma should have landed in England'.[20]

Although Parma lacked a siege-train, the Armada carried one ready for immediate assembly and use (see Appendix 4). This would have provided a critical advantage, because even Elizabeth's military experts lamented 'not only how weak and how unfortified our towns are, but also how unprovided of all necessities to abide a siege'. Admittedly, Henry VIII had improved the coastal defences of Kent by building five forts between the Downs and Rye, and five more along the Thames estuary; but, as a visit to the still-extant castles of Camber and Walmer shows, their defences consisted of thin circular walls and curved, hollow bulwarks. They possessed poor defensive capability. In November 1587 the defenders of Sandgate Castle numbered only a captain, his deputy, five soldiers and ten gunners, serving one demi-culverin; at Walmer Castle a similarly small crew served one demi-cannon, one saker and one falcon; at Sandown Castle a captain, his deputy, five soldiers, two gunners and 'one gunner more to be supplied' served one saker and one falcon. 'Margate in the isle of Thanet' had a small, ancient castle with one falcon and one falconet. The Armada's artillery and Parma's assault squads would have swiftly overcome them.[21]

Since Thanet was an island, advancing beyond their landing-zone required the invaders to cross the Wantsum channel, spanned by a single bridge (see Figure 79). Perhaps Parma hoped to capture the bridge intact amid the confusion caused by his surprise attack; but if not, the Armada carried plenty of small boats that could either serve as ferries or form a bridge of boats to convey his troops and their siege-guns onto the Kentish mainland. His engineers and sappers had plenty of experience of throwing improvised bridges across the rivers and canals of Flanders and Brabant.

Recent continental wars had demonstrated that only angular earth-backed bastions protected by a wide moat could withstand bombardment by heavy artillery, and Parma would have encountered few of them. The only large towns between Margate and London – Canterbury and Rochester – still relied on their antiquated medieval walls. In 1639 a visitor to Rochester, commanding the main crossing over the Medway, commented that it had a fine bridge but 'a ruined castle and ancient walls about the city'. Admittedly the small castle of Upnor, built to defend the new naval dockyard at Chatham, included a bastion, but it seems unlikely that it alone could have halted Parma's advance – especially since on 2 August 1588 the Privy Council ordered the keeper of Upnor to send as much 'ordnance, powder and other munition' as possible to Essex (Figure 135).[22]

With so few physical obstacles in his path Parma would have been able to move fast. When he invaded Normandy in 1592 with 22,000 men, they covered 65 miles in six days despite tenacious opposition from numerically superior forces. In 1588 a similar force might have covered the 80 miles between Margate and London in a week – but not at once because (as William of Orange and his invading army discovered a century later) both men and animals need time to recover from a sea voyage.

Consider the experience of the French embassy sent to persuade Elizabeth to spare the life of Mary Queen of Scots in November 1586: they embarked at Calais at midnight and 'arrived at Dover the next day about 9 o'clock in the morning, not without having endured somewhat of the usual sea-sickness'. The ambassador spent the whole day at Dover 'to allow the gentlemen who had accompanied him

135. Upnor Castle, on the Medway. A single bastion projects into the river, but otherwise the castle retains medieval-style fortifications. In 1667 it failed to prevent the Dutch navy from sailing up the Medway to Chatham, where it captured two warships and burned several more. There is little reason to suppose Upnor would have performed any better in 1588.

to rest, who were much shaken by the sea'.[23] The men and animals embarked upon Parma's barges would have fared no better, and those who sailed with Medina Sidonia would have fared far worse because they had been aboard their ships for almost three months, and under sail for more than two weeks, when they reached Calais. They, like the mules and horses they brought with them, would have needed several days to recover, and (as in 1688) no doubt many animals would have died when coming ashore.

Nevertheless, the invaders would still have achieved strategic surprise and perhaps swiftly gained access to copious food supplies and draught animals, because in August 1588 the Kent harvest would have been in full swing. Even Elizabeth's capital represented a soft target. As an English military expert reflected wistfully that summer, London could only withstand a siege if it 'were trenched about as Paris was' with bastions, because bastions were 'the only way thought by good soldiers to break all the enemy's designs to his utter ruin'. Sir William Winter shared this view. The Tudor state would always remain at risk, he warned Walsingham, unless 'London be fortified as it may be able to make resistance for a time against an army, and that also certain points of the shore lying in the river of Thames may have sconces [forts] made on them'.[24]

Parma, however, knew from experience that the state of a town's physical defences did not always prove decisive. Thanks to the determination of their besieged populations, several places in the Netherlands with poor, outdated fortifications had defied capture. Conversely, other strongholds surrounded by the latest defensive systems had surrendered to him because their citizens, garrisons or commanders had succumbed to bribes – including some of the troops sent by Elizabeth to defend the Dutch. In 1584 the English garrison of Aalst sold their town to Parma for 45,000 ducats; and three years later Sir William Stanley and Captain Roland Yorke, with over 700 men under their command, betrayed the places entrusted to their care to Parma and turned against their former comrades and allies. In July 1588 the commander of the English garrison of Ostend raged about 'the baseness of our countrymen's minds, that now they hear the enemy is said to intend to come hither, [they] do run away daily, five and six together'.[25]

Admittedly, many of these defectors were Irish or Anglo-Irish Catholics, and thus of questionable loyalty to Elizabeth; but all had been recruited and sent to the Low Countries specifically to fight for the Protestant cause. Moreover, the queen relied on the comrades of these traitors, recalling 4,000 men from her expeditionary force in Holland to form the nucleus of the army intended to defend her person and her capital. Its quartermaster-general was Edmund Yorke, brother of Roland, and its third-in-command, Sir Roger Williams, had fought in the Spanish Army of Flanders for four years in the 1570s. How resolutely would they fight for her now?

Elizabeth had few options: she relied on the veterans from Holland because they were the only experienced troops she could call on. In December 1587 she complained that the militia in Essex was not 'better trained and disciplined, for to be more able to encounter with an enemy that is exercised, than hath been possible to be done by certain short musters and trainings, which have served more, as it is thought, for fashion than for substance of discipline'. Six months later a government census to ascertain how many 'martial men' (i.e. military veterans) resided in England listed only a hundred – some of whom, with service going back to the 1540s, would now be too old. At least one was described as 'a papist obstinate'. In Yorkshire, the largest county in the land, the Lord Lieutenant could identify only seven gentlemen with military experience, and although he felt sure there were 'divers others' who had previously served as junior officers, he admitted that 'as yet I have not knowledge of their names'.[26]

The 6,000 men in the London Trained Bands (militias), who had been drilling twice weekly since March, might have put up an effective resistance (although some doubted it), but little could be expected from the county militias. Most were expected to conscript a large contingent of archers – on 7 August the Privy Council 'in this dangerous time have thought it very requisite that a collection of archers should be made in every shire of the realm' – even though it took a lifetime to train a man to draw a longbow with lethal effect.[27] Many militiamen were poorly equipped. A survey of the 9,000 men mobilized in Hampshire revealed many 'very rawly furnished, some whereof lack a headpiece, some a sword, some with one thing or another that is evil, unfit or unbeseeming about him' (and even those 'reasonably well armed' were 'much unperfected in training'). The commander of the Dorset levies believed his men 'will sooner kill one another than annoy the enemy'. The Yorkshire militiamen equipped with firearms received only one pound of powder for each fortnight's training, so that 'they have been driven hitherto for the most part to train with false fires' (that is to say, they could prime their firearms but lacked charge and bullet for target practice).

The recruits raised to defend the queen herself were little better. From May they trained for three days every fortnight, but even this ceased on 1 August, because 'soon after that time harvest will begin'. The royal bodyguard would thus have received a grand total of fifteen days' training before they faced Parma's hardened troops. The Kent militia, which would have borne the brunt of the invasion, was equally weak. It numbered some 7,000 men, including 567 archers and 1,172 'shot'. This, as J. J. McGurk observed in his survey of the county's defensive state in 1588, might seem 'a formidable force indeed, if we did not remember that only about 300 of them would have been trained soldiers'.[28]

Elizabeth and her ministers also failed to develop an adequate defensive plan for these imperfect assets. Part of the problem was structural: invaders by sea always hold the initiative. As an eighteenth-century English strategist eloquently put it, an amphibious attack:

> Goes against the enemy like an arrow from a bow. It gives no warning where it is to come and leaves no traces where it has passed. It must wound, too, where it hits, if rightly pointed at a vulnerable part . . . [The defender] in the meantime, like a man in the dark labouring under the weight of an unwieldy shield, moves slowly to and fro, distracted and at a loss which way to go, to guard against the stroke of an invisible hand.[29]

In the case of England, geography reinforced this inherent disadvantage: the south-eastern shires, closest to the continent, formed a perennial 'vulnerable part'. In 1940, threatened with a major cross-Channel invasion, the commander-in-chief of Britain's Home Forces lamented that 'the extent of coast to be defended by Eastern Command is approximately 320 miles, 160 miles north of the Thames, and 160 miles south of the Thames', and 'that there are few places in which a German landing can be opposed in strength quickly'. Moreover, the ability to shift assets to repel any landing 'was greatly hampered by the River Thames and London, which cut right through my front; and to move formations across that area there for an attack was a slow business.'[30]

The situation was slightly better in 1588. Thanks to the premature distribution of Cardinal Allen's *Admonition* and *Declaration*, the London government knew in June that 'the duke of Parma is expressly named and chosen by the pope and the king of Spain to be a principal executioner' of the planned invasion. They therefore correctly deduced that he would land in either Essex or Kent. But which?

On 27 July the Privy Council learned 'that the duke of Parma resolutely purposes to attempt London, however he may' and summoned some military experts to discuss ways of 'withstanding the attempt'. Four days later they made their fateful choice: they decided that 'the enemy will attempt to land in some part of Essex'. Leicester continued to believe this fiction long after the crisis had passed. In late August he told a French ally that Spain's 'plan was that the duke of Parma should sail from Dunkirk with an army, intending to disembark and land it, while the fleet from Spain attacked' the navy. Elizabeth had ordered him to command 'a fine and fair army' in Essex ready to attack the invaders there as they disembarked.[31]

Leicester's error is easily explained: Essex made better strategic sense. As William Monson, who had fought against the Armada, later wrote:

> If an enemy land in Kent he is kept by the river of Thames from coming to London, unless it be by the bridge of London, or of Kingston, which may be prevented by breaking them down; whereas if an enemy land on [the] Essex side, he may march directly to London without let, impeachment, or other impediment, but by the encounter of an army.

The same logic led the Privy Council in July 1588 to withdraw 2,500 soldiers from Kent 'to attend Her Majesty', leaving only 4,000 behind 'to make head against the enemy' should they land there. On 4 August the Council further ordered 'a good number of the best and choicest' musketeers in Kent to go 'forthwith to the seaside' ready to reinforce Admiral Howard's men aboard the fleet.[32]

Worse still, when the first 4,000 men from the county militias arrived at Tilbury camp on 5 August they did so with 'not so much as one meal's provision of victual with them, so that, at their arrival here, there was not a barrel of beer nor loaf of bread for them'. They also lacked basic weapons. On 7 August, when the Armada lay anchored off Calais, the Privy Council ordered 2,000 pikes and as many helmets to be sent 'into Essex to arm such able men there as are not furnished with armour nor weapon'. Two days later the Council learned that the pioneers they had sent to fortify Tilbury included 'artificers and handicraft men, which are not so fit for those works' and ordered Leicester 'to make choice of labouring men that use the spade and the pickaxe, as men more fit for such labours'. They also ordered the urgent dispatch of twelve artillery pieces from the Tower of London to Tilbury but found that only seven were available.[33]

Sir John Smythe later recalled that 'In the camp and army at Tilbury' in 1588 'I did see and observe so great disorder and deformity ... Many did wear their armours very uncomely and uneasily.' But Smythe, who a decade before in Madrid had valiantly traded insults with the Inquisitor-General (see chapter 4), did not 'see and observe' at Tilbury for very long. According to Leicester, 'You would laugh to see how Sir John Smythe hath dealt, since my coming. He came to me and told me that his disease so grew upon him as he must needs to go to the baths' – in other words, Smythe was a coward and fled. He was not alone. On 13 August Leicester complained that many cavalry troopers 'have failed [sc. deserted] and surely some punishment must follow. I have written to my lords of some of the offenders, which are too many at such a time.'[34]

Defensive preparations elsewhere were little better. In May 1588 Sir John Norris rode along the coast of Dorset, noting places suitable to 'disembark men and other provisions that necessarily must follow an army', but he identified so many vulnerable places that he recommended garrisons for only the larger locations. In July a royal official informed the Privy Council that there was 'no militia organization and no beacon system between Newcastle and Berwick', and requested funds to rectify this dangerous situation. A floating boom across the Thames – an improvised affair of masts, chains and cables designed by Federico Giambelli to keep out enemy shipping – broke on the first flood tide; and a bridge of boats across the river, intended to link the queen's forces in Kent and Essex, remained incomplete.[35]

At first glance the defences of Norfolk offered an exception. In May 1588 Edmund Yorke (brother of Roland) completed a bird's-eye sketch of the fortifications at Weybourne Hope, which offered an ideal landing-zone because deep water comes very close to the shore. Although Yorke endorsed his sketch 'Reason would a scale, but time permits not', because it was 'made in haste', his sketch showed bastions, flanks and even a small citadel in the modern style (Figure 136).

**136.** Edmund Yorke's sketch of Weybourne Hope, Norfolk, in 1588. Weybourne Hope offered an ideal landing-zone for an amphibious operation, because deep-draught ships can come close to the shore. The fortifications depicted by Yorke would have made a landing difficult there – assuming they were actually constructed, rather than merely recommended – but of course the invaders intended to land in Kent, not Norfolk.

At the same time Sir Thomas Leighton, a veteran who later served at Tilbury camp with Leicester, drew up a sensible contingency plan for the defence of Norfolk in case of invasion. He began with the assumption that 'upon any alarum or firing of [the] beacon, the multitude will assemble themselves in some disorderly sort'. Therefore, 'for avoiding of confusion, which may happen upon the rudeness of the people', the local magistrates must identify in advance 'some choice and discreet persons' to lead the rest of the 'able men' back to prearranged strongholds. For example, if 'the enemy shall make his descent' at Weybourne Hope, the local forces must retreat to Norwich, 25 miles to the south, 'at all times [giving] them alarum, and keep them waking'. If possible, Leighton opined, the harvest should be 'burned and spoiled' and no 'carts or carthorses left behind, for the aid of the enemy'. Upon reaching Norwich, the militiamen must entrench 'the chief part of their forces upon the hill of Mount Surrey . . . disposing the rest in fortifying the castle and town'.[36]

Leighton's plan contained three flaws. First, according to an eyewitness, instead of an orderly retreat, 'myself can remember when upon the firing of the beacons (whereby an alarum was given) the country people forthwith ran down to the seaside, some with clubs, some with piked staves and pitchforks, all unarmed, and they that were best appointed were but with a bill, a bow, and a sheaf of arrows, no captain or commander appointed to direct, lead or order them'. In Essex, the Puritan parson Richard Rogers recorded similar scenes of chaos in his diary entry for 9 August 1588:

> When our neighbours were gone to [militia] training three mile hence, on a sudden there was proclaimed ... that they must with all speed depart to the seacoast more than twenty miles off ... never seeing wife nor taking order about their goods and business, which sudden thing frightened many, and yet we know not the end of their going.

Second, Leighton apparently forgot that Norwich's fortifications had improved little since 1549, when a rebel army made Mount Surrey their headquarters, seized the town, and held it for a month until its recapture by a royal army commanded by Leicester's father, spearheaded (ironically) by Spanish and German soldiers. Third and most important, Parma intended to land in Kent, not in Norfolk.[37]

Elizabeth's military commanders in the proposed landing-zone also miscalculated. The local commander in Kent, Sir Thomas Scott, wanted to deploy all his troops along the seashore, 'either keeping the enemy from landing, by disordering or diminishing some part of his forces, or at the least by staying of him for a time'. This would, he hoped, 'stay the enemy from speedy passage to London or the heart of the realm'. Scott, like Leighton, reckoned without the panic caused by the approach of the Spanish fleet. He ordered 'all of our forces that lay in camp within two miles of the shore to make a show upon the Downs to the enemy', but when they saw the Armada anchor off Calais the following day many of his men deserted.[38] Norris, the senior officer commanding in the south-east, opposed Scott's plan. Instead, he wished to leave just a skeleton force to defend the beaches and withdraw the rest inland ready to give battle to the invaders. He therefore 'caused all the forces appointed for the defence of the Downs' to encamp near Dover and breathed a sigh of relief that the only place lacking adequate defences was the Isle of Thanet – precisely the landing-zone chosen by Philip.[39]

Much of England's unpreparedness and confusion stemmed from poverty and isolation. Elizabeth could raise no loans at home because hostilities with Spain had caused a trade recession; nor could she do so abroad, because most continental bankers thought Spain would win. This forced her to delay every stage of her counter-invasion plans until the last possible moment to save money. On 29 July Lord Treasurer Burghley complained that outstanding bills totalling £40,000 lay on his desk 'with no probability how to get money' to pay them. 'A man would wish,' he concluded sourly, 'if peace cannot be had, that the enemy would no longer delay, but prove, as I trust, his evil fortune.' Apart from the Dutch, England stood entirely alone.[40]

In contrast, Philip managed to mobilize huge sums of money for the Enterprise of England. He later claimed that he had spent 10 million ducats (£2.5 million) on the Armada itself, including 250,000 ducats in cash carried aboard the fleet. Between 1587 and 1590 he also sent 1.5 million ducats to the French Catholic League, and 21 million more to the Army of Flanders. At the same time his diplomats managed either to win over or to neutralize every other state in Europe. In July 1588, just before the Armada left Corunna, Ambassador Khevenhüller noted with admiration that:

> At the moment, the Catholic King [Philip II] is safe: France cannot threaten him, and the Turks can do little; neither can the king of Scots, who is offended at Queen Elizabeth on account of the death of his mother. The one [monarch] who could have made trouble was the king of Denmark, who has just died, and his son is young and so has other things to deal with. In addition, the Protestant princes of the Holy Roman Empire will do nothing to help the queen; and the king can be assured that the Swiss cantons will not move against him; nor will they allow others to do so, since they are now his allies.

In short, Khevenhüller concluded, no foreign power could prevent the execution of the king's Grand Design.[41]

It therefore seems reasonable to conjecture, like Khevenhüller, that had the 27,000 veterans from Flanders landed at Margate in August 1588, supported by the siege-train, munitions and reinforcements aboard the fleet, and had they marched towards London after a brief period of recuperation, they would have encountered inferior numbers of largely untrained troops, acting without clear orders, backed up by a few poorly fortified towns.

The invasion's success would therefore have hinged mainly upon the spirit of the ordinary citizens of south-east England. Would Elizabeth's subjects there have committed to 'defend our Island, whatever the cost may be?' Would they have declared: 'We shall fight on the beaches, we shall fight on the landing grounds, we shall fight in the fields and in the streets, we shall fight in the hills; we shall never surrender'?[42]

Without doubt many Englishmen hated the Spaniards, especially in the staunchly Protestant south-eastern shires, their hatred stoked by memories of the hundreds of their fellows burned to death during the reign of Philip and Mary, and by evocative propaganda concerning Spanish cruelty such as George Gascoigne's *The Spoyle of Antwerp* (1576). But could hate alone have kept the English fighting on the beaches and in the streets for Elizabeth Tudor, an ageing monarch with no acknowledged successor, and for her compromise Church which (according to a contemporary) 'the common people for the greater part' still called 'the new religion'?

On 24 July, as the Armada advanced through the Bay of Biscay, the Privy Council heard that many wealthy citizens of London 'refuse to contribute to the general charge of victualling' the navy; and two weeks later, with the Armada off the coast of Sussex, they learned that 'certain inhabitants of Lyme House and Ratcliff have denied to deliver certain anchors and other things' demanded by the queen's master-shipwrights because 'they doubted to be paid for the same'.[43]

On 'being told of the repulse' of the Armada, a citizen of Kent 'said it was lies and we should hear other news shortly, rejoicing when any report was of their good success and sorrowing for the contrary'. Shortly afterwards another citizen declared that the Spaniards 'were better than the people of this land, and therefore he … had rather that they were here than the rich men of this country'. From Portsmouth, another place of great strategic importance, the royal commander relayed to the Privy Council in December 1587 the response of the well-to-do: 'We are much charged many ways, and when the enemy comes we will provide for him, but he will not come yet.' In Norfolk a military veteran warned the Council that he found 'the country people generally in that untowardness and disorder in martial actions, and so unfurnished and unable, as I thought our case most desperate to match and encounter with our mighty enemies'. In Essex Parson Rogers wrote in his diary: 'We are now in peril of goods, liberty, life by our enemies the Spaniards, and at home papists in multitudes ready to come upon us unawares.'[44]

Rogers wrote on 23 August 1588, almost a week after Elizabeth gave her rousing speech a few miles away at Tilbury. How would he have felt if the childless queen had died that month, whether through natural causes or by an assassin's hand (like her cousins Darnley and Moray in Scotland before, and Guise and Henry III in France shortly afterwards), when the task of defending the Tudor state would have fallen to a Council of Regency which lacked parliamentary warrant?

## The Limits of Counterfactuals

To be credible, 'alternative history' – the study of what could easily have happened but did not – must satisfy two protocols. The first is the 'minimum rewrite rule': the historical record should be tweaked as little as possible to secure a different but plausible outcome. We cannot give Parma cruise missiles; and perhaps even postulating that he could capture London, as William of Orange would do one century later, is a counterfactual too far. But what if the invaders came ashore at Margate and got across the Wantsum channel with all their equipment, but then encountered stiff opposition and became bogged down in Kent? Even then, they might have achieved some of Philip's contingent goals, exploiting their occupation of Kent, together with the fear of another Catholic uprising in the north or in Ireland, to force the English government to pay a hefty indemnity (as its successors would pay to the Dutch a century later) and pull its troops out of the Netherlands. After all, alarmed by Spain's preparations for invasion, English commissioners had conducted negotiations with Parma at Bourbourg throughout the spring of 1588 on this very issue. With the duke on English soil, this key concession might have seemed unavoidable.

After the English expeditionary force withdrew, perhaps surrendering to Spain the strategic towns it held, the Dutch Republic might have been unable to prolong its resistance. A vociferous peace party already existed there: when, at Elizabeth's insistence, the States-General of the Republic debated at length in December 1587 whether they should send a delegation to the peace talks at Bourbourg, several voices called for compromise. Although most deputies from Holland, Zeeland and Utrecht firmly opposed talks with Spain, some towns dissented, and the inland provinces that had to bear the brunt of the war against Spain (Gelderland, Overijssel, the Ommelanden around Groningen and most of Friesland) lobbied strongly in favour of a settlement. A few months earlier, according to one of Elizabeth's special envoys to the Dutch, given that 'the Commonwealth of these provinces [consists] of divers parts and professions as, namely, Protestants, Puritans, Anabaptists and Spanish Hearts, which are no small number, it is most certain that dividing these in five parts, the Protestants and the Puritans do hardly contain even one part of five'. Moreover, the envoy continued, only the 'Protestants and Puritans' favoured a continuation of the war. The Republic's Council of State in The Hague agreed: it reported that 'the people – or most of them – strongly favour peace'. Had the Enterprise of England succeeded the pressure on the States-General to compromise might have become irresistible.[45]

Finally, ending the Dutch Revolt would have profoundly affected the balance of power in Europe. Without a costly army to maintain in the Netherlands, Philip would have been free to intervene decisively to assist the Catholic cause in both France and Germany, and to extend Spain's authority (as well as its language and culture) all around the globe. In the words of Ambassador Khevenhüller:

> If matters had turned out according to the preparations and plans, it would have made [Philip] lord of the whole of Europe. Where would the parts of the Low Countries in rebellion have found the power to resist such a powerful king, so well-armed and prepared, just across their frontier? As for the rest, who could have resisted him – ruler of so many parts of Africa and Asia, and ruler of all America – if he had become ruler of England? ... Certainly, if this monarch had achieved his goals, he would have become absolute ruler of the seas, and that would have brought him absolute control of the land.[46]

Khevenhüller's scenario almost happened, and historians should give Philip credit for the selection of an ideal landing-zone, for the concentration of immense resources, for the successful diplomacy that left the Tudor state isolated abroad, and for the fact that against all the odds his irresistible fleet from Spain came almost within sight of his invincible army in the Netherlands. Despite all the flaws and deficiencies, if in August 1588 Parma had landed at Margate with his troops and siege-train and begun his march on London, posterity would have regarded Philip II's Masterplan as his masterpiece.

Or would they? Another protocol of sound alternative histories is to postulate a 'second order' or 'reversionary' counterfactual. The clock of history does not stop if and when a single hypothetical change occurs: although some things might have happened differently in the short term, the long-term outcome might remain the same. Two of Philip's fundamental policies might well have prevented him from achieving lasting gains even had the Enterprise succeeded.

The king regarded himself as both omniscient and divinely inspired where English affairs were concerned, believing that 'I can give better information and advice on that kingdom and on its affairs and people than anyone else'. Such assurance helps to explain his insistence on micromanaging every aspect of the Armada campaign, starting with the creation of a Masterplan predicated on the junction of a fleet from Spain with an army in Flanders, separated by 700 miles of ocean, as the ineluctable preliminary to invasion. It also helps to explain why he refused to allow anyone – whether councillor, general or admiral – to challenge the wisdom of his Grand Design, instead urging them to 'believe me as one who has complete information on the present state of affairs in all areas'.

So even had Don Alonso de Levya taken over from Medina Sidonia and attacked Plymouth, and even had Medina managed to avoid the fireships and escorted Parma's barges to Margate, Philip's desire to meddle would surely have continued unabated. If Parma's forces became bogged down in Kent, the king would no doubt have insisted that his nephew reject all offers of compromise and instead strive for total victory. The results of such inflexibility would have been disastrous: with Parma and his troops fully committed in England, continued Dutch resistance could have prevented Spanish intervention in France after the assassination of Henry III in 1589, thus allowing Henry of Navarre to triumph much earlier.

A second reversionary counterfactual involves genetics. The rulers of Spain had long pursued a policy of intermarriage in the hope of uniting the entire peninsula under a single sceptre. Although in 1580 these incestuous unions achieved their goal when Philip became king of Portugal, they dramatically reduced the dynasty's gene pool. Philip's son Don Carlos (d. 1568) and his great-grandson Carlos II (d. 1700) each had only six great-grandparents instead of the normal sixteen, with an 'inbreeding coefficient' much the same as the incestuous offspring of siblings, or of a parent and child: 0.25. Both manifested physical and mental handicaps; both died childless. In 1570 Philip married one of his nieces and they produced seven children with an 'inbreeding coefficient' of 0.22. Only one, Philip III, survived his father, and during his reign (1598–1621) Spain lost ground both in Europe (notably in Italy) and overseas (notably in India and the Caribbean). Bankruptcy and military failure forced him to make peace with Elizabeth's successor in 1604 and three years later to conclude a ceasefire with the Dutch Republic which in effect recognized its sovereignty. It seems unlikely that Philip III would have proved more successful in retaining any gains made in England in 1588.

Perhaps Edward P. Cheyney was correct after all. It is 'doubtful whether, even if Spanish troops had landed on the shores of England, any serious influence would have been exerted on the general course of the history of the two countries'.

# 20

# The Armada in History and Legend

## The Armada Remembered in England

Some of those who defended England in 1588 did not enjoy their deliverance for long. Leicester and Seymour died that same year; Winter and Dale followed in 1589; Walsingham and Croft in 1590. Frobisher was mortally wounded while trying to dislodge Spanish troops from Brittany in 1594; Hawkins and Drake both died on their unsuccessful voyage to the Caribbean, in 1595 and 1596 respectively.

Howard, in contrast, enjoyed a long and successful career. In 1596, while he briefly occupied Cadiz, he addressed a courteous letter in Latin 'To the most illustrious duke of Medina Sidonia', which began: 'I presume I am not unknown to you, since in the year 1588 my lady, the Queen's Majesty, entrusted me with sole command against you and your troops.' He declared himself ready to negotiate an exchange of prisoners 'according to the laws of war'. The duke accepted, and even though Howard's men sacked and torched Cadiz a few days later, Medina Sidonia kept his word and delivered 'a galley full of English prisoners, with a flag of truce': a gracious gesture.[1] On Howard's return Elizabeth created him earl of Nottingham, and he probably profited more than anyone else in England from loot and piracy at Spain's expense. Despite all this, in 1605 James I chose him to lead the spectacular embassy sent to ratify the treaty of London with Philip III. During his visit he entered the English College in Valladolid and afterwards accepted a Spanish pension. Nevertheless, his magnificent full-length portrait done in 1620 (see Figure 27) showed the Armada battles in the background: evidence that he still regarded his service then as the high point of his career. He died four years later, aged eighty-eight.[2]

Other English women and men remembered the Armada year in different ways. The mother of Thomas Hobbes, England's greatest political philosopher, 'fell in labour with him upon the fright of the invasion of the Spaniards'; whereas the High Court Judge James Whitelocke later recalled 'the terrible show of the sea Armada from Spain' as just 'a little distemper to the quiet course of [his] studies' as a freshman at Oxford. As early as November 1588 Parson Rogers in Essex considered 'our late deliverance from the rage of Spain as memorable a work of God as ever was any in my remembrance'.[3]

Many others, like Rogers, recalled the Armada summer as England's finest hour. A survey of London and its suburbs in 1633 transcribed numerous commemorative inscriptions. The memorial in St Margaret's church, Westminster, to Lady Mary Dudley, who died in 1600, noted that she was the sister of Lord Admiral Howard 'by whose prosperous direction, through the goodness of God in defending his handmaid, Queen Elizabeth, the whole fleet of Spain was defeated and discomfited'. The tomb in Deptford church of Edward Fenton, who died in 1603, recorded his command of one of the queen's ships fifteen years before. A spectacular stained-glass window in St Mildred's church, Bread Street, installed in the 1620s, included 'a very artful and curious representation of the Spaniards' great Armado, and the battle in 1588' with a verse rejoicing that 'Both ships and men / We did see flee and drown'd'. An officer of the Norfolk militia who visited Tilbury in 1635 met 'a little old man' who regaled him with:

> A long and tedious relation of that great Camp, how the men were billeted, drilled, ordered, and quartered. 'There stood,' quoth he, 'her Majesty's tent; there she viewed her troops of horse, with their warlike riders; here her regiment of foot; there rode the Navy Royal; in this place she encouraged her brave commanders, in another place her private soldiers.' And all [this] my host so pathetically and punctually related as if it had been but the other day.

To Martin Bond, who when young had commanded a company in 'that great camp', the events of 1588 also seemed like 'but the other day', because in 1643 he chose for his tombstone a scene in high relief that showed him seated in full armour, flanked by two musketeers, with a page holding his horse, awaiting the call to defend his country (Figure 137).[4]

137. The tomb of Martin Bond, 1643. Although he was a prosperous merchant twice elected a Member of Parliament, when he died aged eighty-five Martin Bond chose for his tombstone a high relief which showed him seated at the entrance to his tent, with two sentries, above the inscription that reminded the world of his proudest achievement: 'he was Captaine in ye yeare 1588 at ye campe at Tilbury'.

Artists, as well as 'little old men' and veterans, strove to perpetuate such memories. George Gower and other painters soon started work on a special 'Armada portrait' of Elizabeth. Three copies survive today (there were once perhaps ten), with the queen life-sized at the centre wearing clothes covered in pearls (a sign of chastity) and her right hand on a globe oriented towards North America. Her fingers rest on Panama, the principal artery of the Spanish Empire. Behind her, the left 'window' shows two scenes from the naval actions of 1588 – the English fleet pursuing the Spaniards in the background and the battle off Gravelines in the foreground – and the right window depicts Armada ships wrecked by storms (Figure 138).

Other pictorial representations of the Armada soon followed. Early in the seventeenth century an unknown artist (probably Dutch or Dutch-trained) completed an enormous canvas that showed two events: at lower left, Elizabeth reviews her troops at Tilbury, wearing her crown and sceptre, with beacons blazing out behind her on an exotic rocky landscape; at centre and right Howard's *Ark Royal*, a galleass and other ships fight the battle off Gravelines (Figure 155). Another Dutch artist, Hendrik Corneliszoon Vroom of Haarlem, painted a powerful canvas that also showed two events: the fireship attack and the battle off Gravelines (see Figure 66).

**138.** Elizabeth: The Armada Portrait. Elizabeth maintained close control over her image, and this one – painted soon after the Armada – would have followed a 'pattern' that she had approved. This explains why her image is almost identical in two other surviving versions of this portrait: one, seriously cut down, in the National Portrait Gallery; the other acquired in 2016 by the National Maritime Museum from descendants of Sir Francis Drake. This one is 41 x 52 in. (104.1 x 132.1 cm).

Vroom was already familiar with his subject. Not long after returning to port, Howard of Effingham commissioned the map-maker Robert Adams to compose a record of the Armada campaign in eleven charts. One showed the route of the fleet's return to Spain (including the presumed sites of wrecked vessels) (see Figure 1); the rest showed the different 'actions' between 31 July and 8 August, two per chart in a bird's-eye view. Howard then paid Augustine Ryther to engrave each chart on copper plates, published in 1590 together with a narrative composed (almost certainly from material supplied by the Lord Admiral) by the exiled Italian humanist Petruccio Ubaldini as *A true description of the Spanish descent on England in the year 1588.* More ambitiously, Howard also celebrated his achievements in the most expensive medium available: tapestry. He commissioned a series of hangings from the master weaver François Spierincx of Delft, who asked Vroom to compose the 'cartoons' (rough drawings) to guide his weavers. Vroom visited Howard, who evidently showed him the Adams charts because the ten giant tapestries – each one 14½ feet (4.4 m) high and up to 28½ feet (8.7 m) wide – likewise combined the episodes portrayed in the charts with a bird's-eye view to create a panoramic overview of the two fleets in action. Each tapestry included Howard's coat of arms and his portrait in the centre of the border right above the royal arms. On completion he paid Spierincx £1,582 and displayed the hangings in his home until 1616, when he sold them to the Crown.[5]

Others commemorated the Armada's defeat on a more modest scale. The register of the Stationers' Company of London included twenty-four songs and ballads on the subject licensed between July and December 1588. At least seven commemorative wall paintings once existed: one in a 'pleasure house' belonging to Sir Francis Carew, who had taken part in the campaign, and the rest in churches. One at Gaywood (Norfolk) (see Figure 129) shows Elizabeth visiting the camp at Tilbury, together with the text of her speech there. Another, 50 miles away at Bratoft (Lincolnshire), shows a fleet encircled by a huge red dragon, with an inscription that records the destruction of the Spanish ships 'like Pharaoh's scattered host' which 'came gaping to devour England' (Figure 139).[6]

139. Allegory of the Spanish Armada in the church of Bratoft, Lincolnshire. This huge panel painting (more than 5 x 7 feet; 1.5 x 2.1 m), executed in 1610, depicts a huge red dragon destroying Armada ships with its fiery breath. The presence of Irish warships (flying the flag of St Patrick: top left) suggests Irish involvement: a reminder to Protestant congregations of the constant Catholic threat against England.

It is surely no accident that both these Armada paintings appeared in parishes where Protestantism had put down deep roots, because the events of 1588 soon became an integral part of Protestant rhetoric. In 1601 William Leigh, a Lancashire preacher, delivered a sermon on the anniversary of Elizabeth's accession which proclaimed that the 'Mirabilis annus of 88 will never be forgotten so long as the sun and moon endure; when the stars fought for our Deborah, as the sun and moon did then for Joshua.' Even the 'seas, rocks and shelves fought for England,' Leigh continued triumphantly, and 'their armies were discomforted, the great Armada was scattered, beaten and broken'.[7]

Individual successes, starting with the capture of *Rosario* on 31 July 1588, also provoked rejoicing. The accounts of several churchwardens record payments to the bellringers on 5 August 'for drink when Don Pedro [de Valdés] was taken'; and ten days later Thomas Deloney registered with the Stationers' Company *A joyful new Ballad, declaring the happy obtaining of the great galleazzo, wherein Don Pedro de Valdes was the chief*. Eleven flags and pennants captured with the ship were taken to the capital and displayed first on London Bridge and then in St Paul's Cathedral (where they perished in the Great Fire of 1666). The ship itself became a trophy exhibited at Deptford.[8]

The accession of James VI of Scotland to the English throne on the death of Elizabeth in 1603 briefly put an end to such triumphalism because he desired peace with Spain. His accession also ended another policy of his predecessor. Just one hour after Elizabeth's death, the 'Great Council of the Realm' proclaimed James king because he was 'lineally and lawfully descended from the body of Margaret', Henry VII's older daughter, through her granddaughter Mary Queen of Scots. This legitimized Mary's steadfast claim to be Elizabeth's lawful successor. Lest anyone doubt this, James commissioned two new tombs in Henry VII's chapel in Westminster Abbey: in one, which cost £2,000, he interred his mother; in the other, which cost £765, he interred Elizabeth next to her sister Mary Tudor.[9]

English triumphalism revived after the Gunpowder Plot: an unsuccessful attempt by a group of English Catholics in November 1605 to blow up the royal family and parliament. England's 'double deliverance' immediately took a place of honour in Protestant rhetoric: a large print devised by the preacher Samuel Ward showed the Devil presiding over a meeting of pope, cardinals and the king of Spain to plot the destruction of England, flanked by cameos of the discovery of the Gunpowder Plot and the defeat of the Armada (Figure 140). The appended verse ran:

In EIGHTY EIGHT Spain, armed with potent might,
Against our peaceful land came on to fight

> The winds and waves and fire in one conspire
> To help the ENGLISH frustrate SPAIN'S desire.

At the request of the Spanish ambassador in England, the Privy Council arrested, interrogated and imprisoned Ward; but it was too late to silence him. The printer of another of Ward's works reminded readers that he 'has lately published a most remarkable monument of the Invincible navy of 88 and the unmatchable powder treason of 1605, necessary to be had in the house of every good Christian, to show God's loving and wonderful providence over this kingdom'. Whether or not the print hung 'in the house of every good Christian', it soon appeared on funeral monuments, brass plates and even embroidered cushions throughout England.[10]

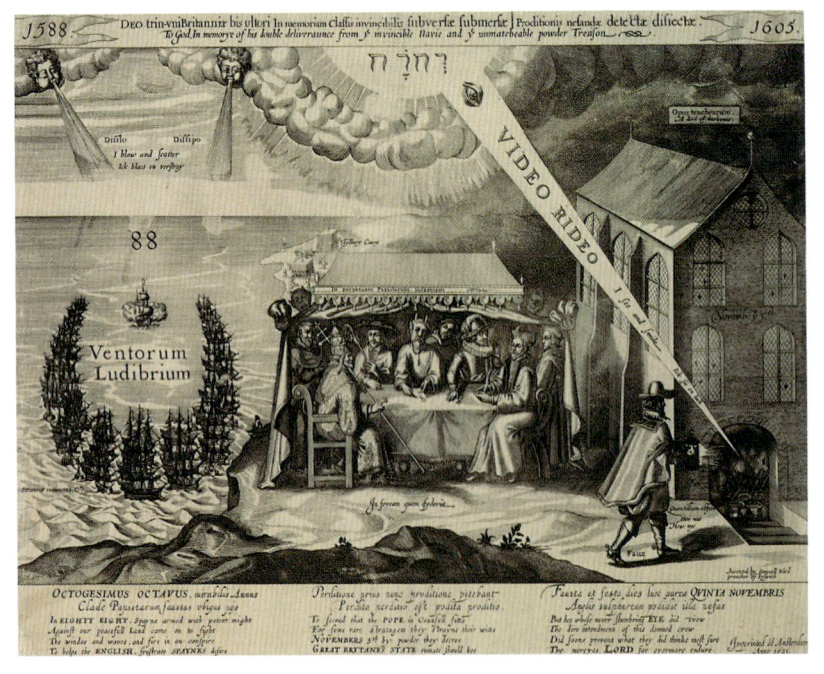

140. Samuel Ward, 'The double deliverance' (Amsterdam, 1621). The left of the engraving shows the Armada in its crescent formation sailing towards 'Tilbury Camp'. In the centre, Philip III (in a ruff) sits next to the Devil as he consults leading Catholic clerics as Guy Fawkes ('Faux') sneaks into the basement of Westminster Hall. Only divine intervention preserves Protestant England.

The voyage of the future Charles I to Madrid in 1623, in the hope of bringing back Philip II's granddaughter as his wife, provoked another outpouring of anti-Spanish rhetoric. Lionel Sharpe, Leicester's chaplain at Tilbury, now released the text of Elizabeth's speech there; and during the ensuing war with Spain (1624–30) patriotic donors in many parts of England endowed annual sermons of thanksgiving, including one 'upon the last day of July, in remembrance of the Lord's gracious deliverance from the Spanish Armada in 88' at Alcester (Warwickshire), and another in 1630 'to be preached in St Peter's church in the town of Nottingham on 28th July' each year, 'acknowledging God's mercy and giving thanks for the deliverance of this land and people'. In his annual *Almanac and Prognostication* Richard Allestree integrated the Armada into a 'Compendious Chronology' which calculated the passage of each year under multiple headings: 'Since the creation of the world'; 'Since the destruction of Sodom with fire and brimstone'; 'Since the beginning of Blessed Queen Elizabeth's reign'; and '*Since the camp at Tilbury*'.[11]

Similar rhetoric reappeared whenever England's Protestant elite sought past examples of how God's intervention had saved their cause. In 1644, in the grip of rebellion against Charles I, Parliament ordered 'the suit of hangings of the story of Eighty-eight' – Howard's tapestries – 'to be put on display in the House of Lords. Five years later, having executed the king, England's new rulers decreed 'the hangings containing the story of 88 to be reserved for the use of the state' and hung in the chamber where they 'would give audience' so that all visitors would know of England's finest hour.[12]

## Legends and Myths

The Armada unleashed not only history and polemics but also legends and myths. Thomas Deloney led the field with *A new Ballad of the strange and most cruel Whips, which the Spaniards had prepared to whip and torment English men and women: which were found and taken at the overthrow of certain of the Spanish ships in July last past 1588*. Its sixteen verses asserted that 'one sort of whips they had for the men', which could 'pluck the spreading sinews from the hardened bloody bone', and another for 'our silly women' to be used after raping them:

> Although their bodies sweet and fair
> Their spoil they meant to make,
> And on them first their filthy lust
> And pleasure for to take.

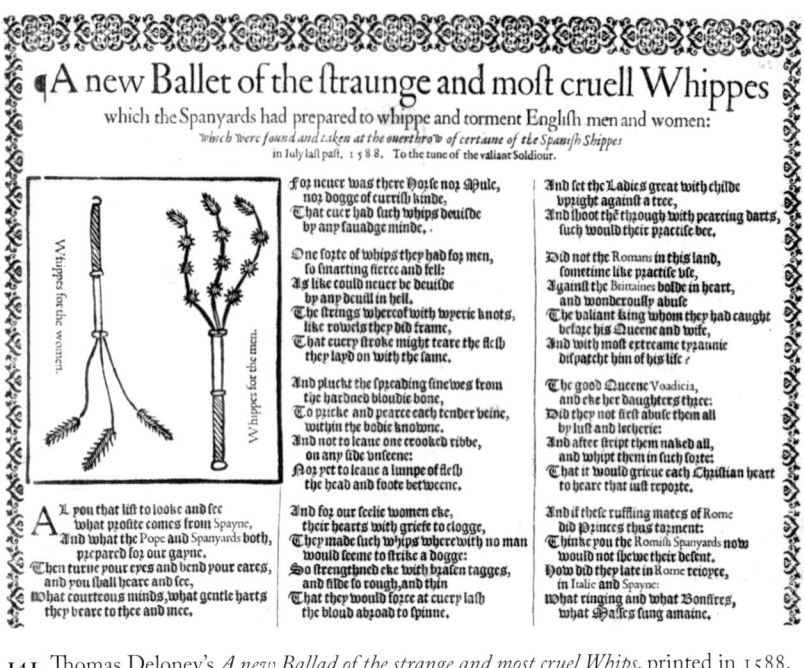

141. Thomas Deloney's *A new Ballad of the strange and most cruel Whips*, printed in 1588.

He included an image of the scourge destined for each gender and noted the tune to which his vicious verses should be sung (Figure 141).[13]

Deloney's myth enjoyed a long life. By the eighteenth century, for just one shilling (five pence) the patriotic visitor could enter 'The Spanish Armoury' in the Tower of London and admire not only the whips but also an 'abundance' of thumbscrews 'designed to extort a confession from the English where they had hid their money', as well as some 'Spanish cravats: engines of torture, made of iron, intended to lock together the heads, arms and feet of English heretics.' The author of the guidebook hoped that these gruesome artefacts would 'perpetuate the memory of that signal victory by England over Spain and render the glorious name of queen Elizabeth dear to every Briton'. A book on the Armada published in 1840 mentioned that visitors to 'the Tower of London are aware that a number of instruments of torture are exhibited as having been found on board the Spanish fleet'; and in 1888 some of them featured in an exhibition celebrating the tercentenary of the Armada, including the manacles, thumbscrews and other instruments of torture – even though the catalogue itself specified that they all came from a cell operated by the Inquisition of Cuenca, and were dated 1679, which meant that they had nothing to do with the Armada.[14]

Other myths and legends stemmed from the anti-Spanish backlash provoked by Prince Charles's trip to Spain in 1623. One also involved whips. Dr Lionel Sharpe wrote a memoir describing what 'I remember in 88, waiting upon the earl of Leicester at Tilbury Camp', which included the text of an interrogation of Don Pedro de Valdés by Elizabeth's Privy Council. Sharpe claimed that Burghley gave it to him, and that on Leicester's orders he read it out to the English soldiers there assembled:

> *Don Pedro* being asked what was the intent of their coming, stoutly answered the Lords: What? But to subdue your Nation, and root it out.
>
> Good, said the Lords, and what meant you then to do with the Catholics? He answered: We meant to send them (good men) directly unto Heaven, as all you that are Heretics to hell.
>
> Yea but, said the Lords, what meant you to do with your whips of cord, and wire? (whereof they had great store in their ships).
>
> What? said he, We meant to whip you heretics to death, that have assisted my master's rebels, and done such dishonours to our Catholic King [Philip] and people.
>
> Yea, but what would you have done (said they) with their young children? They (said he) which were above seven years old, should have gone the way their fathers went, the rest should have lived, branded in the forehead with the letter *L*. for *Lutheran* to perpetual bondage.

The transcript of Don Pedro's actual interrogation by the Council contains no such questions and answers: Sharpe is the sole source for the story. He may well have read out this exchange (or something similar) at Tilbury, but if so (like *The copie of a letter*) it formed part of Burghley's anti-Spanish propaganda.[15]

In 1624 Thomas Scott, a Protestant minister in exile in the Dutch Republic, published a pamphlet which contained the first known version of another enduring legend: that Elizabeth's 'commanders and captains were at bowls upon the hoe of Plymouth' when they heard of the Armada's approach. Admittedly, Scott (like Sharpe) published this anecdote when some protagonists in those events were still alive, so it may have been true; but this was not the case with later embellishments. Thus an account first published in 1736 had Drake deliver his famous (and surely apocryphal) bon mot: 'There is time to finish the game and beat the Spaniards too.' Countless subsequent accounts and several paintings perpetuated the myth (Figure 142).[16]

**142.** *The Armada in sight. Plymouth Hoe.* John Seymour Lucas's painting of 1880 shows Drake intent on finishing his game of bowls despite the beacon warning of the Armada's approach.

The Armada also generated local legends. Some were blatantly false, such as the claim that the ship which sank in Tobermory Bay, on the Isle of Mull in Scotland, carried '30 millions of money'; or that an illegitimate son of the king of Spain drowned on one of the vessels which sank in Blasket Sound; or that anyone with dark hair living in the west of Scotland and Ireland is necessarily descended from an Armada survivor. Other legends had a basis in fact, however: at least three of the excavated Armada wrecks were located because a local tradition or place name encouraged underwater archaeologists to dive and find them (see chapter 21).

## The Armada Remembered in Iberia

Not surprisingly, Spanish and Portuguese memories of the Armada were overwhelmingly negative. Perhaps the most devastating verdicts came from two Portuguese survivors, who compared its impact with the battle of Alcázarquivir in Morocco just ten years earlier in which King Sebastian perished and most of the nation's nobles also died or fell prisoner (see chapter 4). Both writers were clerics.

'The damage and losses of the Armada were so great that everyone considered them worse than what we lost in Africa,' wrote one; 'Those who consider this outcome without prejudice will rate it so grave and great that it eclipses the losses suffered by this kingdom in Africa,' echoed the other.[17]

Some of their Spanish colleagues felt equally devastated. According to the chronicle kept by Fray Jerónimo de Sepúlveda at the Escorial, 'People talked of nothing else' except the fate of the Armada. 'The grief it caused in all of Spain was extraordinary: almost the entire country went into mourning.' It was a misfortune 'worthy to be wept over for ever,' he continued, 'because it lost us the respect and good reputation that we used to have among warlike people'. Fray José de Sigüenza, librarian and custodian of the relics at the Escorial, who saw Philip II on a regular basis, echoed this verdict in his history of the monastery, published in 1605. The Armada, he wrote, 'was the greatest disaster to strike Spain in over six hundred years'.[18]

Several Spaniards sought scapegoats. In his tract *Consolation for Spaniards because a sudden tempest sank the fleet sent against England*, the Jesuit Melchor de la Cerda blamed the weather for the disaster; and a play by Juan Pérez de Montalbán emphasized Philip II's stoic insouciance when he first heard the news that the Armada had failed. 'I sent my fleet against men,' Montalbán made the king say, 'not against the wind and the waves.'[19] Fray Juan de Vitoria, a Dominican who jotted down what he heard and read for future use in a *History of the Kings of Spain*, characterized Medina Sidonia as 'the most cowardly captain ever seen in the world'. Vitoria is our sole source suggesting that young men filled the street outside the duke's lodgings in Valladolid as he returned home, 'chanting "Drake, Drake, Drake is coming" all night long' (see chapter 17). He is also our sole source stating that when Don Francisco de Bobadilla came to Court for an audience with Philip and 'praised the duke for his outstanding conduct and for obeying in all things the orders he had received, as had his Council of War, the king replied: "I did not issue orders for the duke and his council to run away."'[20]

Another Jesuit, Juan de Mariana, went even further. His notes for a *General History of Spain* attributed the failure of the Armada to a combination of human and supernatural factors. Among the former he cited the superior English artillery performance, which led to 'the capture of some ships, most of them damaged by the shot that rained down on them', and the long voyage back to Spain during which 'many ships ran aground and sank and many soldiers died of cold and hunger'. Mariana also portrayed the outcome as an example of 'how the plans of humans are destroyed by a Higher Power. Without doubt the flower of Spain's manhood perished in this venture, and through this disaster God punished our many and grave sins.' In 1599 Mariana expanded on this bold claim in his Latin treatise *Of Kings and the Education of Kings*: disaster had struck because of Philip's lifestyle:

> A few years ago we lost a great Armada on the shores of England, a defeat and shame that we will not efface for many years; but it was merely God's revenge for grave offences committed by our nation and, unless my memory fails, also because of the barely disguised lusts of a certain prince who, having forgotten the dignity of his position and his advanced age, was rumoured at that time to have given himself over to unbridled licentiousness.[21]

Other Spanish writers continued to blame Parma. As Antonio de Herrera y Tordesillas prepared the third and final volume of his semi-official *History of the World in the Reign of Philip II*, covering the years 1585–98, he composed a list of 'Points' critical of Parma's actions (the first five concerned 'Why the duke promoted the Enterprise of England and then undermined it'). When he presented his list to the Madrid agent of Alexander Farnese's son and heir, Ranuccio, the agent suggested to his master that a payment of 150 ducats might produce a positive evaluation. This Ranuccio agreed to pay, but then Herrera indicated that sanitizing his account would cost 1,000 ducats. Perhaps Ranuccio paid the bribe in full because when it appeared, the third volume of Herrera's history eulogized Alexander and asserted that 'if the duke failed to achieve all his goals, the fault lay with his advisers who deceived him'.[22]

Eight years later another historian, Luis Cabrera de Córdoba, asked Ranuccio's agent in Madrid to provide material on Alexander's conduct for his projected *History of Philip II*. This time the agent passed on the request to his master in a ciphered letter and warned that Cabrera had served in the Army of Flanders between 1586 and 1588 and so had personal knowledge of what had happened; but in the event Cabrera, too, exonerated the duke. He even claimed that Parma had chosen him as a messenger to explain to Philip in person that 'it was not possible for the fleet in Flanders to join the one from Spain'. Cabrera also vehemently criticized the argument of Sigüenza, Mariana and others that the Armada's failure was God's way of punishing Spain for its sins. Instead, Cabrera opined, by their nature 'Great enterprises are subject to major misfortunes, especially those that need prudence and luck. Friars should stick to writing the history of their religious orders.'[23]

The arrival in 1623 of the future Charles I reawakened memories in Spain as well as in England. A team of Jesuits at Santander preached sermons beneath the windows of his entourage, condemning the wickedness of Elizabeth and both her parents (declaiming their diatribe in Latin, to be better understood); but such hostility remained isolated. On their way to Madrid, as the English passed by a village 'belonging to the great Don Pedro [de Valdés], son to him who was chief commander in 88, [he] sent us excellent wine'.[24]

## Lessons not Learned

After war broke out again with England in 1624, Spain's most experienced naval commander, Don Diego Brochero, urged the king 'to imitate the way our enemies operate their fleets, seeing the successes they have and how few ships they lose'. Brochero continued: 'It is a matter for regret that after regularly losing so many fleets and ships we do not make any changes', and he singled out 'having two commanders on the same ship, which is unique to our Atlantic fleet, because the transatlantic guardships and the Portuguese warships have only one commander for everyone aboard, and it is the same for the English, Dutch, Turks, Venetians, and others'. The Spanish Council of State roundly dismissed this logic. The count-duke of Olivares, son of the Spanish ambassador in Rome in the 1580s and now the king's chief minister, conceded that 'our enemies – the Danes, the Dutch and the English – understand these matters better than we do', but still argued that making soldiers obey orders given by sailors would undermine Spain's entire social fabric, which exalted the military.[25]

Perhaps the resounding defeat of another Anglo-Dutch descent on Cadiz reassured Olivares that Spain had, after all, nothing to learn from her enemies, but three years later the topic reappeared in connection with thirteen royal warships under construction in Spanish shipyards. The Council of War pondered whether to appoint two captains – one for naval and one for military matters – or just one captain for each ship. This time the king sought the opinion of an unusually wide range of advisers including two veteran Armada commanders, Pimentel and Mexía. He ordered each adviser to give his reasons alone and in secret. Their rationales covered almost eighty manuscript pages.

Almost everyone recognized that English warships performed superbly with a naval officer in overall command but (like Olivares) feared that making the infantry ('in which many younger sons of noblemen serve') take orders from low-born sailors might undermine Spain's distinctive military culture. Two councillors opined that each warship could be entrusted to a naval officer if 'we could find today men like Menéndez, Valdés, Recalde, Oquendo' or 'like Bertendona and

Aramburu'; but in the absence of such heroes they argued that the senior infantry officer aboard should continue to command Spain's Atlantic warships. One councillor went further, conceding that 'in both sailing and equipment, and in their use of artillery, our enemies have obvious advantages', which explained why the English 'almost always beat us' in naval engagements; but, he continued, this did not matter because Spain's naval operations always aimed to put an army ashore, not to prevail in combat afloat. Therefore, a warship needed either two captains, or else the senior infantry captain should command. Faced by such conflicting advice, the king vacillated. 'The example set by our enemies is compelling,' he decreed, 'so let's try entrusting some ships to the same man, who will command both soldiers and sailors, but not in all of them. Then we can see how it works out.'[26] It did not work out well. In summer 1639 Olivares assembled a large fleet of warships, which he entrusted to Don Antonio de Oquendo (son of Miguel), and packed them with infantry companies, but the Dutch navy destroyed or captured perhaps forty of his ships and killed or captured some 7,000 of his soldiers and sailors (see the Epilogue).

The most balanced evaluations of the Enterprise of England by Spanish participants came from two officers who had served under Parma. *The Wars of the Low Countries* (Antwerp, 1624) by Don Carlos Coloma began in 1588 when he joined the Army of Flanders and ended in 1599 when he left it. By the time he published, Coloma had served as viceroy, general and ambassador, and so his account alternated between the perspectives of a subaltern and a commander. Coloma wrote like a subaltern when he described the frantic measures taken by Parma to embark his army when he heard the Armada had reached Calais, causing 'a lot of laughter among the soldiers' because their ships did not appear seaworthy (see Figure 25); but he insisted that they could still have got to sea 'if the duke of Medina had managed to interpose his fleet between the English and the coast of Flanders'. Then Coloma switched to the viewpoint of a commander. He insisted that Parma had been correct to insist on capturing Flushing, or another Dutch deep-water port, before attempting the invasion; and he criticized Philip's Grand Design because, if it were to succeed, 'so many factors had to align – the time, the tides, the currents, the sandbanks – to say nothing of the need to do everything at top speed', in the teeth of English and Dutch opposition. This, Coloma continued, was not reasonable:

> In plans made so far away, however much diligence and prudence one devotes to foreseeing the dangers, rarely does execution fail to reveal something that shows how difficult it is to predict the future. It is therefore essential to leave room for the prudence and ability of those charged with executing the plans,

allowing them to make changes according to circumstances to the orders received from their prince, who cannot be consulted in time.[27]

Antonio Carnero, who had served as chief accountant of the Army of Flanders, offered a remarkably similar (and sensible) assessment in his *History of the Civil Wars of the Netherlands* (Brussels, 1625). He informed his readers that 'I was present at most of the events' described, 'and perhaps I saw things more clearly than those directly involved, because I was not in danger like them'. He also cited testimony provided by other eyewitnesses, including Balthasar López del Árbol, who had sailed on *Trinidad Valencera* and survived shipwreck in Ireland before serving in the Netherlands. Like Coloma, Carnero insisted that Parma's troops were fully prepared for the Enterprise by the time the Armada arrived. He also condemned the failure to secure Flushing and argued that the fatal defect lay in the Grand Design itself: 'Such was the fate of the Spanish Armada, whose strength was considered irresistible. But there is nothing in the world in which we should place less trust and confidence than in military affairs, in which something you never considered makes the difference between victory and defeat.' In any case, Carnero continued: 'Plans do not fail because of poor advice or imprudence, but because of the special providence of heaven that no human brain can fathom or understand. For His own secret reasons, God did not wish to punish the queen and her lands at that time. We should leave the matter there.'[28]

## Rule Britannia

In northern Europe the Armada attracted widespread interest a century later as evidence mounted that William of Orange planned to invade England and depose his uncle James II. In October 1688, according to the French ambassador in The Hague: 'With the impressive forces he has mobilized, and the support he enjoys in England, the prince of Orange may succeed in his enterprise, unless God intervenes – as he did with the Invincible Armada that Philip II launched against England exactly a century ago.' His Polish colleague reported that:

> The Dutch are convinced that they will be as fortunate in their plan to attack England as Philip II was unfortunate, when he sent his fearful fleet against Elizabeth in the month of August in the year 1588. There are few among them who are unaware of this period of history and who do not know by heart the inscriptions on the medals which were struck at that time.[29]

In the event, the prince led his Armada into the Channel in mid-November (far later in the year than in 1588), got all his men and munitions safely ashore, captured London, and effected a 'Glorious Revolution' that guaranteed a Protestant ascendancy in England, Scotland, Ireland and their American colonies (see chapter 19).

Four years later Protestant preachers hailed the defeat of the French at the battle of Barfleur as 'such a victory over our enemies at sea as has not been known since the vanquishing of the Spanish Armada'. Then in 1719, during another war with Spain, Bishop White Kennett delivered a sermon to the City of London magistrates, which encouraged their charitable work by pointing to the numerous benevolent foundations created 'one hundred and thirty years since' when 'our forefathers had a mighty surprise upon them by a pretended Spanish invasion with an Armada which they called invincible'. Kennett also stressed the role of practical planning in securing a 'victory so great that it stands in our annals as a wonderful year' and continued rhetorically: 'Amidst the rumours of that invasion, what was the preparation made against it? The wisdom of the queen and ministry was taking all proper measures for defence of the commonwealth.'[30]

Twenty years later, amid agitation about yet another war with Spain, some again looked to the Armada for inspiration. It was 'the most glorious victory that was ever obtained at sea, and the most important to the British nation,' John Pine claimed in his preface to *The tapestry hangings of the House of Lords representing the several engagements between the English and Spanish fleets, in the ever memorable year MDLXXXVIII.* It contained engravings of Howard's tapestries by Pine, at a scale of one inch to one foot, together with the charts by Adams and a commentary. In 1759, when France planned a massive surprise invasion of England from Brittany, the government of William Pitt produced a short pamphlet with a long title: *The History of the Spanish Armada, which had been preparing three years for the invasion and conquest of England, and which in the year 1588 came upon the English Coast to effect it.* Its sixty pages included lists of England's preparations by land and sea, copied from the Harleian Manuscripts acquired by the British Museum (the first publication of original Armada documents). It also included a map of the beacons and concluded with 'a summary account of the defeat and distress of that mighty armament, which the Spaniards boasted to be invincible'.

A generation later, a bitter debate about a new war with Spain saw Pitt, now earl of Chatham, use the Armada tapestries hanging in the House of Lords as a rhetorical device to criticize the policy of appeasement proposed by the earl of Suffolk, secretary of state and a descendant of Howard of Effingham:

From the tapestry that adorns these walls the immortal ancestor of this noble lord [Suffolk] frowns with indignation at the disgrace of his country. In vain he led your victorious fleets against the boasted Armada of Spain; in vain he defended and established the honour, the liberties, the religion, the Protestant religion of this country, against the arbitrary cruelties of Popery and the Inquisition.[31]

One might have expected the bicentenary of the Armada in 1788 to provoke celebrations, but they were eclipsed by the commemoration of William of Orange's landing in England. According to *The Times* of London, 'the second hundredth anniversary of the defeat of the Spanish Armada affords an additional cause of rejoicing' to the celebration of the Glorious Revolution, and it printed the 'patriotic stanzas' sung in a Westminster tavern, which made clear the hierarchy of events:

In Fifteen hundred and eighty-eight
Th'Armada was defeated;
In Sixteen hundred and eighty-eight
Our freedom was completed.[32]

Ten years later the threat of a French invasion changed the focus. The British government asked John Bruce, keeper of the State Papers, to prepare a *Report on the arrangements which were made for the internal defence of these kingdoms when Spain, by its Armada, projected the invasion and conquest of England*. Bruce embraced the task because although 'the menaced evil' in 1588 might seem to some 'less in degree' than in his day, 'it is precisely the same in kind; hence the measures adopted in the one period, having experience and success to recommend them, may furnish useful lessons in the other'. His *Report*, published in a limited edition, included an appendix of over 300 pages of documents transcribed for the first time from the State Paper Office.[33]

The threat also inspired a series of satirical prints designed by James Gillray entitled 'Consequences of a successful French invasion'. One of them showed French revolutionaries destroying the Armada tapestries in the House of Lords; but in 1834 a fire at the Palace of Westminster succeeded where the French revolutionaries had failed, burning all the tapestries exhibited there. Although replacing them formed part of the plans for redecorating the new edifice, only one painting (based on Tapestry 2) was ever completed. Instead, the Armada fell prey to jingoistic Victorians like Charles Kingsley, Regius Professor of Modern History at Cambridge, who began his anti-Catholic historical novel about Elizabethan privateers, *Westward*

*Ho!* (1855), with a homage to 'Britain's Salamis, the Glorious Fight of 1588'. It proved a best-seller, and in 1925 was the first novel to be adapted for a radio broadcast.[34]

## The Tercentenary in England

Some Victorians continued down the path of jingoism. Although an appeal in 1881 for funds to erect a national monument to mark the tercentenary of Drake's circumnavigation raised scarcely £500, the duke of Bedford agreed to pay for a statue in Tavistock (Drake's birthplace) as well as a replica at Plymouth. Three years later, before a large crowd, a member of the Drake family unveiled a 10-foot-tall bronze statue of Sir Francis on Plymouth Hoe. In 1888 William Wright, 'Honorary Secretary of the Committee of the National Armada Tercentenary Commemoration', seized upon Charles Kingsley's conceit and 'at various places in the west of England' gave a 'historical lecture' entitled *Britain's Salamis: or, The Glorious Fight of 1588*. Wright also organized an exhibition in Plymouth that included many artefacts from private collections, 'as well as some remains of the Armada itself'. He published an appeal in *The Times* of London for readers to make him aware of other memorabilia, stating that 'The experience gained in the late exhibition at Peterborough in memory of Mary Queen of Scots will serve to guide those who are organizing this one' (an admission that surely made Elizabeth and her leading ministers turn in their graves). The following month, at a meeting of the Tercentenary Commemoration committee, the duke of Norfolk – Admiral Howard's descendant and England's principal Catholic peer – made two proposals: that 'a suitable national monument' be erected on Plymouth Hoe, and 'that politics and religion are to be ignored' in the commemoration. The second suggestion provoked a furious backlash. The 'Protestant Alliance' of England announced the establishment of a rival Armada Commemoration Council 'altogether independent of the Plymouth committee'. It organized a three-day celebration of the 'providential deliverance of this country from despotic rule and papal superstition by the defeat of the Spanish Armada and by the accession of a Protestant dynasty' a century later.[35]

Similar sectarian sentiments prevailed in Scotland and Ireland. In April 1888 the Free Presbytery of Dunoon noted that 'The year 1888 is suggestive of great historical deliverance wrought by God on behalf of our nation from the menaces and miseries of Popish tyranny', and unanimously approved a motion desiring the General Assembly of the Church of Scotland to 'appoint a day for the suitable commemoration throughout our church of the Providential interposition of 1588 and 1688'. Two months later, the 'Scottish Commemoration Convention 1588–1688' held a three-day event in Edinburgh that included speeches castigating the celebration planned at Plymouth because it omitted the religious aspects both of the Armada's origins ('the papacy was the main instigator of the expedition') and of its outcome (God's role in preventing a Catholic triumph). The following month, in Ireland, the Loyal Orange Order incorporated the double centenary into their annual 12 July parades, thanking God 'for destroying the Spanish Armada in 1588 and by that means saving England and this country from eternal wrong'. Later that year a speaker in Belfast mentioned, by way of example, 'one of the great ships' wrecked by storms at Port na Spaniagh near Dunluce Castle – apparently the first attempt to link archaeology with history in telling the Armada story.[36]

These rival events failed to halt the preparations at Plymouth. Special excursion trains brought some 20,000 people to the Hoe on 19 July 1888 to witness the positioning of a huge foundation stone of Dartmouth granite for a 'national monument' in the presence of several 'descendants of Armada heroes' including a Howard, a Raleigh, a Hawkins, a Frobisher and three men called Drake. The distinguished guests then watched a game of bowls, 'played on the citadel green by the members of the Leeds and Torrington bowling clubs, in Elizabethan costume'. They also visited the Tercentenary Exhibition in the Plymouth Guildhall, full of 'Armada relics' contributed by patriotic citizens. According to *The Times* correspondent: 'The exhibition is not large in extent or in number of articles shown; but it is certainly unique and only to be compared to the Mary Stuart Tercentenary Exhibition held at Peterborough in July 1887' (another admission that surely made Elizabeth and her leading ministers turn in their graves).[37]

In October 1888 another Tercentenary Exhibition opened in the Grand Salon of the Drury Lane Theatre. *The Times* correspondent noted some 700 exhibits, including sundry portraits; items from the 'Spanish Armoury' in the Tower; memorabilia contributed by the Drake family; and a flag captured from an Armada ship presented by a descendant of Howard's chaplain.[38] The driving force behind the London exhibition was Augustus Harris, owner of the theatre and co-author of 'a great spectacular drama' entitled *The Armada*, described by Harris himself as 'a romance of 1588'. It enjoyed a limited run. The 'selection of music' played at the opening of the exhibition, composed by Walter Slaughter, musical director of the Drury Lane Theatre, also proved short-lived – probably because (as George Bernard Shaw observed of another of Slaughter's compositions) it did 'not contain a single novel, or even passably fresh point, either in melody, harmony, or orchestration'.[39] A special brass entry token to the 'spectacular drama' fared somewhat better: in 2021, an example sold on eBay for £11 – half as much as a pewter Armada tercentenary medal with a bronze finish (Figure 143).

143. An Armada tercentenary medal, 1888. The obverse shows the busts of Queen Elizabeth and Queen Victoria; on the reverse, Fame inscribes the names of Howard, Seymour, Drake, Hawkins, Winter and Frobisher on a victory column. Made by J. Carter of Birmingham.

Some of Britain's overseas Dominions also celebrated. In Canada the Reverend James Little of Toronto published *The Tercentenary of England's Great Victory Over Spain and the Armada*, which concluded with 'A lesson from the fathers of 1588 to their Canadian children': a twelve-page diatribe against the rise of Catholic power in the Dominion, notably in Quebec. In Australia Douglas Sladen, lecturer in modern history at the University of Sydney, composed *The Spanish Armada: a ballad of 1588*, with seventeen stanzas and an 'Envoi', to be read aloud at Plymouth in celebration of the fact that the Armada's defeat 'gave England religious freedom, once for all, and caused our colonies, past and present, to be to-day what they are, instead of like Cuba and Mexico'.[40]

## The Tercentenary in Spain

When news arrived in Spain that England intended to mount a major tercentenary celebration of the 'Invincible Armada' (the term then in common use by Spanish as well as English writers) the reactions ranged from incredulity through outrage to a desire to compete. Some ridiculed the idea that the Armada's fate owed anything 'to the proficiency or naval advantages of our then enemies', when 'everyone knows' that the weather had determined the outcome. Others preferred to exalt the marquis of Santa Cruz. The Madrid newspaper *El Liberal* suggested naming a naval cruiser after the marquis and then sending it to represent Spain in the Columbian quatercentenary in 1892. It also called for a 'commission to celebrate the tercentenary' of the marquis's death, which would offer prizes for the best biography and the best epic poem honouring the hero. Then the minister of war, representing the Spanish army, voiced vehement opposition to any public commemoration of Santa Cruz and the government withdrew its sponsorship. Nevertheless, a public concert in the presence of the royal family, and a public subscription, raised enough money to commission a heroic statue of the marquis from the noted sculptor Mariano Benlliure. It was inaugurated three years later, again in the presence of the royal family, and still stands before the City Hall in Madrid.[41]

Some patriotic Spaniards promoted alternative events designed to counterbalance Britain's tercentenary festivities. In July 1888 Santa Cruz de Tenerife celebrated 'with great pomp the anniversary of the defeat of Nelson's attempt to capture the town, in which he lost an arm'. The following month a popular Sunday paper asserted that no one outside Great Britain cared about the Armada anyway. 'In Spain, such spectacles produce the same reaction as watching a distinguished old man, whom one had considered sane and sensible, performing circus pirouettes. England may have brought us our admirable Parliamentary system, but it has also brought us the clowns.'[42]

## Back to the Archives

Some of the 'clowns' performed their Armada pirouettes in a different circus. In 1823 John Lingard, a Catholic priest, published the fifth volume of his *History of England from the invasion by the Romans to the accession of James I*, with a chapter on the Armada that drew for the first time on documents from the Archives of Simancas. He combined them with English printed sources to present a more balanced picture of the main protagonists, arguing (for example) that Drake's great raid in 1585 'was equivalent to a declaration of war, which Philip could not refuse to notice without the imputation of cowardice'. In a public lecture delivered in 1845 Sir Henry Ellis, Principal Librarian of the British Museum, reminded his audience that: 'There are many papers of high historical interest preserved in our manuscript repositories which have not yet seen the light of a later day to explain all the circumstances attending the formation and defeat of the Spanish Armada.'[43]

Cesáreo Fernández Duro, a distinguished officer in the Spanish navy and author of many historical publications, came to the same conclusion. In 1884–5 he published two volumes entitled *La Armada Invencible* containing 200 documents from various Spanish archives and libraries. His preface announced that:

> In my opinion, reading these documents will do more than satisfy historical curiosity. Weapons change, and so do the qualities of the men who wield them; but the basic principles of the art of war on both land and sea remain the same, and knowing what factors led to a disaster will always make profitable reading for a warrior.[44]

Duro's work inspired John Knox Laughton, a retired naval officer who held the chair of modern history at King's College London. In May 1888 Laughton gave a lecture entitled 'The Invincible Armada: a tercentenary retrospective', which combined Duro's documents with his own research in the State Paper Office to compare the fighting potential of the two sides, concluding that they were more evenly matched than previously thought. Laughton condemned those who believed that 'in past years Britannia ruled the waves . . . by some special and exceptional favour of Providence, rather than by the wise provisions of her government and by the skill and discipline of her seamen'. His lecture concluded by suggesting that the 1588 campaign offered several 'most useful and important lessons' for Victorian Britain. First, Queen Elizabeth should have spent more money on building 'a few more *Arks*' and less 'on useless shore defences in England or in the equipment of troops for Flanders'. Second, England owed her deliverance to the sustained investment in ships and artillery, and the government of his own day should do the same. Laughton was surely the author of a letter that appeared in *The Times* the following month, which provided a detailed account of the campaign and its aftermath and mentioned excavations on the Armada wreck in Tobermory Bay – another early attempt to link archaeology and history. An article in *The Times* on 20 July, also probably by Laughton, described the ceremony in Plymouth the previous day but then noted (correctly) that 'there was less difference between [Drake's] fleet and Nelson's than there is between Nelson's' and that of the Royal Navy in 1888. Like White Kennett in 1719, he warned that 'the history of the Armada is proof enough' of the need 'to have our ships and guns as efficient as human skill can make them'.[45]

In 1891 James Anthony Froude, Regius Professor of Modern History at Oxford and perhaps Britain's most famous historian, published a long essay entitled 'The Spanish Story of the Armada', which again underlined the importance of Duro's work for English readers:

The five days' battle in the English Channel in August 1588 was fought out between men on both sides of a signally gallant and noble nature; and when the asperities of theology have mellowed down at last, Spanish and English authorities together will furnish materials for a great epic poem ... Until that happy and far-distant time shall arrive, we must appropriate and take up into the story Captain Duro's contribution. With innocent necromancy he calls the dead out of their graves, and makes them play their drama over again.

Froude contributed some 'innocent necromancy' of his own, based on his extensive research in English archives and on the manuscripts he had transcribed on a visit to Simancas, and he stressed that historians must consult the 'unusually excellent' materials left by protagonists on both sides in explaining 'the most dramatic incident in our national history'. After all, he mused, 'The "Iliad" would lose half of its interest if we knew only Agamemnon and Achilles, and knew nothing of Priam and Hector.'[46]

The American scholar William F. Tilton went further in his doctoral dissertation, published by the University of Freiburg-in-Breisgau in 1894, which constructed the first detailed narrative of the crucial encounters between 31 July and 8 August 1588 based on sources from both sides. For England he used the documents published by Bruce and Laughton, as well as his own research among the manuscripts of the British Library and the State Paper Office. For Spain he drew upon the transcripts from Simancas made by Duro and Froude, as well as printed sources in Italian, Latin and Spanish. His thesis provided by far the best account of the Armada battles to that date – although few paid heed, no doubt because Tilton published it in German.[47]

In contrast, a publication by Laughton that same year permanently transformed the English story of the Armada: *State Papers relating to the Defeat of the Spanish Armada*, two volumes filled with documents transcribed from British archives. Laughton's 'Introduction' stated that 'Captain Duro has done from the Spanish point of view, what is now attempted in the following pages from the English. The two works are, in a measure, complementary of each other, and both must be studied for a full understanding of the events of the year.' In 1898 the eminent naval historian Julian S. Corbett published a 'prequel' volume: *Papers relating to the Navy during the Spanish War, 1585–1587*.

Marrying the two sets of data became far easier after 1899 thanks to the publication of the *Calendar of Letters and State Papers Relating to English affairs preserved in, or originally belonging to, the Archives of Simancas. Volume IV. Elizabeth, 1587–1603*. The editor, Martin Hume, printed either integral translations or lengthy summaries in English of almost 500 documents from the years 1587 and 1588, and for almost a century almost all Anglo-Saxon historians of the Armada have relied upon them, without feeling the need to visit Simancas either to verify Hume's translations or to seek out other sources. Some continue to do so.[48]

Interest in the Armada revived in 1940. On 11 September, in one of his celebrated wartime radio broadcasts, Prime Minister Winston Churchill claimed that the Battle of Britain 'ranks with the days when the Spanish Armada was approaching the Channel, and Drake was finishing his game of bowls'. Churchill was not alone in drawing this comparison. That same year, at a cost of $1.7 million, Warner Brothers made and distributed a film entitled *The Sea Hawk*, a thinly disguised allegory set in England at the time of the Armada, in which Philip II resembled Hitler and the hero looked like Drake. The print of the film released in Britain in summer 1940 ended with a rousing speech by 'Elizabeth':

> Freedom is the deed and title to the soil on which we exist. Firm in this faith, we shall now make ready to meet the great armada that Philip sends against us. To this end, I pledge you ships worthy of our seamen – a sturdy fleet, hewn out of the forests of England. A navy foremost in the world – not only in our time, but in generations to come.

In the closing visual, a forest of wooden mastheads flying the English flag transitioned to the steel superstructures of 'Britain's battle fleet in majestic parade'.[49]

The parallel also caught the imagination of a young American historian. In his preface to *The defeat of the Spanish Armada*, first published in 1959, Garrett Mattingly wrote: 'The idea of writing a book about the defeat of the Spanish Armada first came to me, as it must have come to others, in June 1940, when the eyes of the world were again turned to the shores of England and their surrounding seas.' Mattingly set a new standard in historical scholarship about the Armada, not least because he had served in the United States Navy during World War II, which gave him precious insight into naval warfare, and because he learned the foreign languages and palaeography that allowed him to integrate British, Dutch, French, Italian and Spanish sources.[50]

## The Quatercentenary and Beyond

The approach of the quatercentenary of the Armada led to another important advance in Armada studies, this time in Spain. In 1980 the Instituto de Historia y Cultura Naval, created four years earlier, received funding from the Ministry of Defence for an ambitious 'Plan of historical research': seven teams composed of civilian historians and naval officers would locate and transcribe documents concerning the Enterprise of England, and publish a corpus of them as well as a monograph series based on them. In 1988 nine volumes appeared in the 'Colección Gran Armada', all based on extensive archival research on both the Armada itself and Parma's army in Flanders. That same year the first volume of *La batalla del Mar Océano. Corpus documental de las hostilidades entre España e Inglaterra (1568–1604)* came out, and by 2015 four volumes in nine parts had appeared, containing full transcripts of more than 7,000 documents written between June 1568 and December 1588, with a few later outliers. Each volume contained a masterful introduction. A fifth volume contained appendices examining technical points (for example, tide-tables for the Channel in August 1588) and a 'biography' of every ship in the Armada (compiled from material published in earlier volumes). Although some documents in the series had already appeared in print, the majority were new to most researchers. The original plan was 'to continue with a second part containing documents from the period between the return of the Armada and the signature of a lasting peace in 1604. But after the passage of so many years, we abandoned the idea because we lacked the strength to carry out such a demanding task.' Sadly, Rear-Admiral José Ignacio González-Aller Hierro, the driving force behind the venture, died in October 2014, just before publication of the last volume.[51]

In England the Armada quatercentenary saw the appearance of almost 100 books, including the original version of this volume, and the broadcast of several television programmes, including the prize-winning trilogy *Armada* written, directed and produced by Alan Ereira jointly for Spanish Television and the British Broadcasting Corporation. Museums also played their part. Visitors to Brussels in the winter of 1985–6 could admire artefacts from the Ulster Museum in an exhibition entitled *Trésors de l'Armada*. England's National Maritime Museum at Greenwich teamed up with the Ulster Museum and organizations across Europe to bring together the international exhibition curated by María José Rodríguez-Salgado, *Armada 1588–1988*, which ran from April to September 1988 at Greenwich and from October 1988 to January 1989 in Belfast. Several conferences also took place in 1988 in Britain, Spain, Ireland, Australia, North America and elsewhere, but pride of place goes to those organized by Rodríguez-Salgado and Simon Adams in London and Madrid (papers published in *England, Spain and the Great Armada*), and by D. W. Cruickshank and P. Gallagher in Sligo (papers published in *God's Obvious Design*).

Interest scarcely abated after the Millennium. Apart from several more books in English and Spanish, in 2007 Universal Pictures released the film *Elizabeth: The Golden Age*, made at a cost of $55 million, in which Howard of Effingham complained during the battle with the Armada that 'We're losing too many ships', and the queen (played by Cate Blanchett) delivered a speech to her troops at Tilbury that sounded far less rousing than the surviving transcripts of the real thing. That same year a generous private donation allowed a team of artists to scale up the images in John Pine's engravings and paint five canvases modelled on Admiral Howard's tapestries. Three years later they went on display and now hang in the Prince's Chamber in the House of Lords.

In 2013 June Armstrong completed her 'Girona suite: eight evocations for piano', including 'No tengo más que darte' (the inscription on a ring found when the wreck of *Girona* was excavated: see Figure 9) and 'Don Alonso Martínez de Leyva', in honour of its last commander. Two years later, BBC television broadcast a documentary trilogy entitled *Armada: Twelve days to save England*; and Spanish television screened an episode of their *Ministry of Time* series, set in Lisbon in 1588, in which Lope de Vega almost misses his chance to sail on *San Juan de Portugal* because 'the crew-lists arrived at the last minute', prompting a royal official to remark: 'What kind of Spaniards would we be if we could not get the job done at the last minute?' Old stereotypes die hard.[52]

The enduring fascination of 1588 has manifested itself in other ways. In 2016 Royal Museums Greenwich paid more than £10 million to acquire from a member of the Drake family one of the three surviving 'Armada portraits' of Queen Elizabeth (even though significant parts had been overpainted in the eighteenth century). Two years later a table allegedly made from timbers salvaged from two Armada wrecks sold at auction in Drogheda for more than £400,000; and a portrait by an unknown artist allegedly of Drake (but more probably of Sir William Winter) sold at auction in London for more than £350,000. In 2020 the BBC devoted an episode of the series *Royal History's Biggest Fibs* to 'how the history of the Spanish Armada has been manipulated and mythologised by politicians and artists for generations'.[53]

The year 2020 also brought a major new visual source into the public domain: the 'Astor Armada drawings', a set of ten numbered ink and watercolour maps of the Armada campaign. The date and the artist remain unknown, but their style closely resembles the Ryther engravings and most of the names and features appear in both. The biggest difference is scale: the drawings are substantially smaller and show notably less coastline, suggesting that the drawings were copied either from Ryther's engravings or from the lost drawings by Robert Adams on which they were based. They were surely made by a Dutch artist because the first drawing contains an explanatory caption in Dutch and some maps give the compass cardinal points in Dutch ('Oost', 'Zuid'). An overseas buyer offered to pay £600,000 for the set at auction, but the British government immediately imposed an export ban, and the National Museum of the Royal Navy at Portsmouth raised enough money to save them for the nation and to display them there (see Figures 89, 90, 91).[54]

The 'Black Lives Matter' movement that summer shed a harsh spotlight on two of Elizabeth's naval commanders, Drake and Hawkins, both of whom had grown rich from capturing slaves in Africa and selling them in the Caribbean. At Plymouth thousands of people agitated to remove Drake's statue from the Hoe, and one night protesters placed shackles round his effigy and added a sign reading 'Decolonize history'. Although the city council refused to remove the statue, they agreed to rename Sir John Hawkins Square and promised to remove a plaque containing Hawkins's coat of arms, which prominently featured a bound African slave.

In Spain, too, polemics returned with the publication in 2011 of Luis Gorrochategui Santos, *The English Armada: The Greatest Naval Disaster in English History* (an English translation with some revisions appeared in 2018). This compared the human and material losses of the Spanish Armada in 1588 and the English Counter-Armada the following year in order to support two assertions: that the Anglo-Dutch expeditionary force sustained greater losses than the Spanish Armada; and that English historians have systematically underplayed the scale of that 'disaster'. Unfortunately for his first assertion, although Gorrochategui Santos carried out research in Spanish archives to reconstruct Philip's response to the Counter-Armada, he consulted only printed documents for England, and largely ignored Dutch and Portuguese sources. This rendered an accurate comparison of the cost of the two campaigns impossible. As for the second assertion, almost every English historical account of the 1589 expedition known to us concluded (as we do) that it proved a costly failure.

In Scotland and Ireland the overwhelming perception of the Armada today is of human tragedy, stripped of enmity or prejudice: of the futility of war and empathy with its victims, whose suffering is not eradicated by the years that have passed since their dreadful ordeals. Their remains may have dissipated in the oceans or lie buried in unknown graves on once-hostile shores, but they are not forgotten. A monument has been erected on Fair Isle to commemorate those aboard *Gran Grifón* who perished there; and a similar monument now stands on

Dunquin cliffs overlooking Blasket Sound, where *Santa María de la Rosa* and *San Juan Fernandome* sank. In Antrim the North Coast Armada Connection Group organizes commemorations near the site of the *Girona* wreck and has erected a commemorative stone in the nearby St Cuthbert's churchyard featuring the salamander jewel (see Figure 9).

Along the curving strand at Streedagh, where 1,100 men perished and bones are still sometimes revealed in the shifting dunes, in 1988 (the 400th anniversary) a simple ceremony was held to honour those who died. This annual remembrance has continued and grown. In 2017, 1,100 crosses were inscribed in the sand; the following year wooden ones were erected on the day as a form of time-based art. A stone-built memorial in the form of a ship's prow has been erected. Locals in traditional dress parade with banners. Re-enactment enthusiasts in *tercio* garb tote muskets and pikes. Visitors, many from Spain and England, are welcomed. Dignitaries, who have included Spanish ambassadors to Ireland and senior officers and ratings of today's *Armada española*, are honoured guests. Friendly Spanish warships have anchored near the site of the wrecks to drop wreaths. The occasion is solemn, joyous, respectful and fun – a mix that only perhaps the Irish and Spanish can fully appreciate (Figures 144, 145).

144. Officers of the Spanish navy on OPV *Centinela* in 2016 drop a wreath at sea off Streedagh Strand, as part of the annual commemoration.

145. Every year in September a commemoration ceremony is held on Streedagh Strand, remembering the 1,100 dead from *Juliana*, *Lavia* and *Santa María de Visón*.

And more than friendship has been generated. The long Atlantic seaboard that links Ireland and Spain has made Sligo the focus of a 'Remembering the Armada' heritage weekend held to coincide with the anniversary date of the wreckings at Streedagh in September every year. Armada-related conferences and lecture series have been included in the programme. All of this is coordinated by the Grange and Armada Development Association and Spanish Armada Ireland, locally based organizations that run events, tours and guided visits. They have also created a Spanish Armada Visitor Centre with the eventual goal of acquiring museum accreditation so that it can display items from the adjacent wrecks on loan from the core collections. In the meantime it curates visual displays that tell visitors about the Armada, and how it is hoped the Streedagh project will develop. Especially popular is the 'de Cuéllar Trail', which follows that doughty survivor's adventures through the local landscape.[55]

The proceedings of an international conference held at Spain's National Museum for Underwater Archaeology in Cartagena in 2019 and published in 2021 – *The Spanish Armada of 1588 and the English Counter Armada of 1589* – provided the most balanced view of these events to appear so far. The volume included papers by Croatian, Irish, Italian, Portuguese, Scandinavian, Scottish and Spanish scholars. Disciplines included history, underwater archaeology, and preservation of the underwater cultural heritage. Their integration is welcome and significant, because the Armada wrecks have already provided some of the most significant new discoveries about the campaign and the best hope of more to come.

# The Armada Shipwrecks

## Early Salvage

THE SEARCH FOR ARMADA SHIPWRECKS is not new. In October 1588 Lord Deputy Fitzwilliam fretted about 'the great store of ordnance, munitions, armour and other goods of several kinds' aboard the 'Spanish ships that have been lost or wrecked upon the coast' of Ireland, 'which ought to be preserved for the use of her Majesty'. He therefore established a commission 'to make diligent search and inquiry' for 'the hulls of the ships', and to seize their contents. The results proved disappointing. From Shrule Castle near Galway, Sir Richard Bingham reported that most of the wrecks in Connacht 'are now all broken in pieces, and the ordnance and everything else utterly lost, I fear me. Treasure and great wealth hath been taken no doubt, but that by such unworthy persons, as it will hardly be ever any thereof come by at all.'[1]

The situation elsewhere was similar. Wrecks lying in shallow water or driven ashore offered an irresistible target for looters. Richard Burke, picturesquely named 'the Devil's Hook', rifled Leyva's first wreck, *Rata Encoronada*, as she lay aground and burning in Blacksod Bay, County Mayo. After executing the survivors from *Gran Grin* on Clare Island, the local chieftain Dowdarra Roe O'Malley 'brought a great quantity of treasure to the island' and refused to part with it. So enthusiastic were the people of Dunbeg and Troma in County Clare in their efforts to strip the two ships wrecked there that Nicholas Kahane, a local official, was only able 'by much ado' and a hefty bribe to persuade a local youth to break off plundering and carry news of the wrecks to the Mayor of Limerick.[2]

Sir Geoffrey Fenton, secretary of the Irish Privy Council, spent two days at Streedagh Strand in October 'finding and digging out of the sands only three pieces of brass, though I employed 50 labourers, and myself there to oversee them. Yet it cannot be but many more lies hidden in the sands for that three great ships of 800 tons apiece perished here.' The problem, Fenton continued, was that 'for the great ordnance, it will be a most difficult matter in this season of the year to dig them out of the sands, wherein in some place they are sunk . . . [without] great labour of workmen with shovels and pickaxes to uncover them, and dig them up'. He feared that 'the like difficulty will be in other places till the summer come on, that the weather will give men leave to labour'. His hopes rose two months later when news arrived of the wreck of *Girona* on the Antrim coast, together with a report that 'three fair pieces of brass [which] lie among the rocks of Bunboys, where Don Alonso [de Leyva] was drowned, will also be recovered'. Once again he was disappointed: when his men came to retrieve them, they found that Sorley Boy MacDonnell had already mounted the guns on his castle at Dunluce. A secretary's summary of Fitzwilliam's report to London in February 1589 said it all: 'No ordnance of account recovered from the Spaniards.'[3]

As Fenton predicted, serious salvage in Ireland had to wait for warmer weather. In June 1589, near Galway, Sir George Carew, Master of the Ordnance in Ireland, located *San Esteban* (Guipúzcoa) and reported that 'we have spent our time to good purpose, for already we have weighed three pieces of artillery of brass': two cannon periers (7½-inch calibre) and a culverin (5½-inch calibre), all about seven feet long. He also tried to raise 'a cannon of battery or basilisk, as we suppose by the length, for they lie at four fathom and a half of water; which was so huge that it brake our cables.' His diver, who did his best with 'plain swimming', was 'so near drowned' that Carew feared he would die, 'but Irish *aqua vitae* hath such virtue as I hope of his recovery'. He added, 'if I be not deceived out of our boats we did plainly see four pieces more' and begged for 'an oyster dredge or two, in hope to scrape somewhat out of the seas'. The operation evidently met with some success because shortly afterwards Carew salvaged another culverin and a demi-culverin. In April 1589 Bingham commissioned a map showing the exact location of 'the wreck of the three Spanish ships' on Streedagh Strand, but his salvage effort there had limited success (see Figure 108).[4]

Of the three vessels captured in English coastal waters, *Rosario* surrendered with her contents intact. The Privy Council ordered her captors to send all available munitions 'to Dover to be employed in Her Majesty's service' against the Armada. Under interrogation, some servants of Don Pedro de Valdés revealed that 'certain coffers, to the number of fourteen or fifteen, appertaining to the Duke of Medina, wherein was cloth of gold and other rich furniture . . . came to the hands of some of those in the *Roebuck*, a ship belonging to Sir Walter Raleigh'.

The Council interrogated the captain and men of *Roebuck*, hoping 'to recover the same, or so much as may be had'. *Rosario*'s flags and banners went on display in London and the ship herself became a tourist attraction at Deptford until 1622 when she was broken up. The Council also attempted to salvage munitions from *San Salvador*, ordering a 'convenient bark' to collect 'all the brass pieces hither for the furnishing of Her Majesty's ships, together with such great shot and match as is belonging to the same'; but the vessel sank 'by force of foul weather upon the Isle of Wight'. Not much seems to have survived this catastrophe: the cost of 'saving of diverse things . . . to Her Majesty's use' the following year amounted to only £19.[5]

*San Pedro Mayor*, wrecked near Salcombe, Devon, in November 1588 yielded little more. She 'struck some rocks because we had no anchors left' and lay 'full of water to her upper decks'. According to the local magistrates, 'there hath been some plate and certain ducats rifled and spoiled' by the locals from the survivors, 'both from their persons and out of their chests'. Soon afterwards the ship was 'through tempestuous weather broken in pieces and scattered on the seashore'.[6]

As for the other Armada wrecks, salvors sent by the duke of Parma recovered fourteen large and two small anchors, two large cables, and 2,650 roundshot from the flag galleass *San Lorenzo*, sacked by Howard's men off Calais. The French retained her big guns. Further north, salvors from Flushing started to bring ashore munitions from the Portuguese galleon *San Mateo* as early as 22 August, and eventually she and her sister ship *San Felipe* yielded 1,700 pounds of gunpowder and fifty-six guns. The authorities redistributed them to Dutch fortresses and ships, sending a few to their French Protestant allies, and the local commander presented one of the galleon's standards to St Peter's church in Leiden 'where it hung down to the ground' (see Figure 128). In January 1589 a local merchant bought the remaining timbers of the wreck for £40.[7]

By then salvage had begun on Oquendo's flagship *Santa Ana*, which blew up and sank on 24 October, shortly after returning to Pasajes. Divers soon recovered seven guns supplied by the king – one iron and six bronze ('including one which had exploded and is in pieces') – at the price of eight ducats per gun recovered. Even though the local magistrates found the divers 'very expensive and tiresome people' who refused to work unless they were paid the agreed rate, salvage operations continued because 'if we stop our effort to find these guns it will be difficult to locate them later, because with the strong tides the sand and mud will cover them up'. The ship also carried eight guns belonging to Oquendo, the ship's owner, and within a year the divers had recovered five (a sixth had shattered when the ship blew up). Two more iron guns were salvaged in 1880 and are today in the

Naval Museum in Madrid, together with the ship's royal standard – the only other Armada flag to survive.[8]

*Regazona* sank in December 1588 on her way from the Galician port of Muros to Corunna. Winter storms forced the ship to seek refuge on the way, leading to the loss of all her remaining anchors, so she ran aground as she entered the port of Ferrol and eventually broke up. Over the next month everything on her upper deck was salvaged, and the artillery and munitions were installed on the newly fortified island of San Antón in Corunna harbour – just in time to protect it from the Anglo-Dutch Counter-Armada. In March 1589, for a payment of 4,000 ducats, her owner Giacomo Ragazzoni signed over to the consortium of the ship's insurers all claim to anything else they might salvage in future – an excellent bargain for him, especially as the Spanish treasury agreed to pay the agreed monthly hire for the ship during the entire period she was embargoed. He was probably the only owner of an embargoed vessel who made a profit from participation in the Armada.[9]

*Regazona*'s guns did not suffice to save Recalde's flagship *San Juan*, now commanded by Bertendona. She required extensive repairs after the Armada campaign, and the carpenters and shipwrights of Corunna had almost completed their work when the Counter-Armada surprised them on 4 May 1589. Even though most of her artillery was ashore, her men put up a brave defence, but two days later they set fire to the ship to prevent her falling into enemy hands. They then retreated to San Antón, abandoning all the guns and gear already ashore.[10]

Bertendona got a measure of satisfaction two years later. Off Flores in the Azores, the fleet he commanded captured *Revenge*. After a prolonged artillery duel the victors managed to salvage thirteen guns from her upper deck before she sank, and over the next thirty years divers recovered a considerable number more.[11]

## The Tobermory Wreck. Act I: The Seventeenth Century

The optimistic and largely erroneous belief that many Armada wrecks were filled with treasure has inspired fruitless salvage attempts which have continued into modern times. The most spectacular example, and by far the best documented, is the wreck of the Ragusan argosy *San Juan de Sicilia* in Tobermory Bay on the Isle of Mull, off the west coast of Scotland. The legend that she had carried vast wealth apparently originated with the seventh earl of Argyll, who in 1618 fled Scotland to enter Spanish service. He claimed to have seen a 'paper of Latin extracts out of the Spanish records that there were thirty millions of money on board of the said ship'.[12]

No remotely similar sum, in any currency or on any Armada ship, has been identified in the Spanish records, but the claim in the 'paper of Latin extracts' has triggered wild expectations and thwarted dreams since 1641, when the eighth earl requested and received from the Lord Admiral of Scotland a grant of the exclusive right to recover all 'ornaments, munition, goods, and gear, which were thought to be of great worth, cast away, and sunk to the sea ground on the coast of Mull, near Tobermory'. The grant said that the earl had heard some divers 'state that they had considered it possible to recover some of the ships and their valuables'. He therefore intended to 'cause pains to be taken thereupon at his own charges and hazard', paying the Lord Admiral one per cent of the spoils.[13]

Since the Tobermory wreck lay only 60 feet down, almost immediately James Colquhoun of Glasgow, 'a man of singular knowledge, and skill, in all mechanical arts and sciences ... went down several times' and managed to 'buoy up' some iron guns; but Argyll neglected the wreck after he became involved in the civil wars that ravaged Scotland. Soon after his execution for treason in 1661 his heir resumed salvage operations, this time with the aid of a diving bell.[14]

Diving bells had been known since ancient times (Alexander the Great is reputed to have gone down in one), and in 1662 George Sinclair, sometime lecturer at the University of St Andrews (and thus a spiritual colleague of the authors of this book), completed a manuscript entitled 'The new and great art of gravitie and levitie', which described and illustrated an 'engine for diving'. When his manuscript failed to find a printer, in 1669 Sinclair published a Latin translation, with the same illustrations. Book II, dialogue 5 devoted nineteen pages and an illustration of what he termed a *Campana Urinatoria*, operated by a *Urinator*. He suggested that the Urinator might play a role in recovering Armada wrecks. Three years later Sinclair offered more details in *The Hydrostaticks; or, the weight, force, and pressure of fluid bodies: made evident by physical and sensible experiments*, in which he described 'a wooden Ark' made of oak planks sealed with pitch in the form of a box, open at the bottom with a leaden footstool 'on which the diver's feet might stand, while he is going down'. The device, Sinclair specified, 'is for diving, a most excellent art, for lifting guns, ships, or any other things that are drowned below the water', especially when equipped with glass portholes, so the diver 'may see at a distance'. He also recommended a 'little chamber bell' with 'a small cord' linked to the surface 'whereby the persons above, might by so many tingles, speak such and such words to the diver'; and 'a little shelf' on which the diver should 'hang a little bottle with some excellent spirits, for refreshing the stomach under water' (Figure 146).[15]

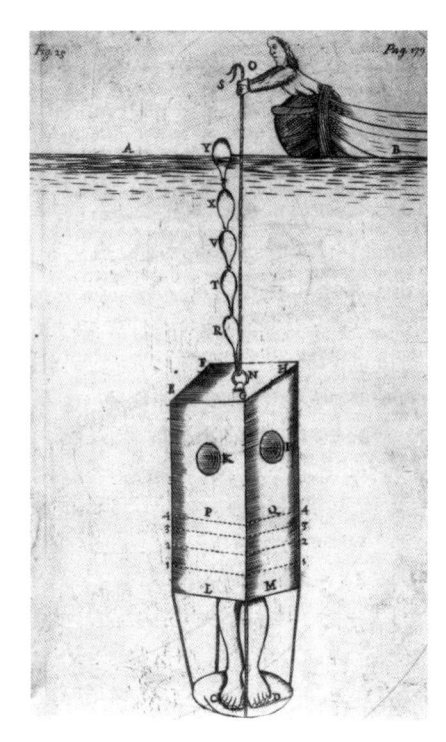

**146.** A diving bell from George Sinclair's *The Hydrostaticks* (1672). The buoys added to the rope while it descends compensate for the decrease in buoyancy as air compresses in the bell during its descent, and make it easier to haul up in an emergency.

Sinclair's invention soon attracted ridicule. In 1672 James Gregory, Regius Professor of Mathematics at St Andrews (and thus another spiritual colleague of the authors), published *The great and new art of weighing vanity*, which belittled Sinclair as 'a pitiful ignorant fellow' and argued that his 'Diving Ark' was no better than a traditional diving bell. Gregory specifically mentioned using a diving bell to recover guns and other items from the Tobermory wreck.

Soon afterwards the earl of Argyll incorrectly identified this wreck as *Florencia*, 'a ship of fifty-six guns, with 30,000,000 of money on board'. According to Argyll the wreck:

> Lay in a very good road, land-locked betwixt a little island and a bay in the Isle of Mull, a place where vessels ordinarily anchored free of any violent tide, with hardly any stream, upon ten fathom at high water and about eight at ground ebb. The fore part of the ship above water was quite burned, so that from the mizzen mast to the foreship no deck was left.

Above the stern lay 'a heap of great timber, which it would be difficult to remove, but under this is the main expectation': namely the '30,000,000 of money'.[16]

No doubt Argyll drew encouragement from news that most guns aboard the Swedish warship *Vasa*, which sank during her maiden voyage in 1628, were brought up from a depth of over 100 feet using diving bells, and he commissioned James Mauld of Melgum, 'who had learned the art of the bell in Sweden, and had made a considerable fortune by it', to take over recovery operations at Tobermory at his own expense, giving the earl one-fifth of all he found. Mauld did not find much: indeed, Argyll later complained, he 'wrought only three months, and most of this time was spent in mending his bells and sending for materials he needed'. Having raised only 'a great iron gun' and 'two brass cannon of a large calibre', each 'eight foot long and eight inches in diameter [bore]', Mauld left for England 'thinking his trade a secret, and that the Spanish ship would wait for him'. Instead, the earl undertook the work 'without the aid of any who had ever seen diving', and 'recovered six cannon, one of which weighed near six hundredweight'. In 1675 Argyll engaged Hans Albrecht van Treleben, who (like Mauld) had helped to recover guns from *Vasa* a decade before, but he 'recovered only one anchor, going away soon after, taking his gold with him, and leaving some debt behind'. Perhaps Treleben was deterred by the actions of the Macleans, still a dominant force on Mull. Furious that rivals seemed on the brink of recovering a fortune in treasure, they mobilized 100 men who dug trenches onshore from which to 'shoot guns, muskets and pistols' at the divers.[17]

The earl tried again, using 'a vessel, bells, ropes, and tongs', but 'found nothing but a great heap of cannon balls about the mainmast, and some kettles and tankers of copper', and so in 1680 he invited Archibald Millar of Greenock, one of Mauld's divers, to his castle at Inveraray. There he shared all the documents about the wreck and agreed to pay Millar £40 a month 'to attend his service at Tobermory and give advice and assistance in the work of diving, &c'.[18]

The agreement fell through the following year because James, duke of York and Lord Admiral of Scotland, had Argyll arrested and tried for treason. Nothing daunted, Millar now prepared the first known 'diving prospectus'. 'Though I be an old man,' he asserted, 'I am willing yet to go alone upon due consideration, for it is a pity that such a great business should be lost where it may be recovered by industry.' His assessment of the site provides an excellent contemporary diver's-eye view of the wreck:

> There is no deck upon her except in the hinder part, where is one great heap of timber which I take to be the cabin. I did see one door there

which I take to be the steerage door [leading into the aftercastle], and within that door I did see a number of dishes great and small of a white blueish colour, but whether they are pewter or plate I know not. Near this place I did see one great gun and her muzzle upright on end, as big or bigger than the gun I lifted, which would carry a 48 lb. ball. There is a great heap of cannon shot about midship, and upon the shot lie three iron guns. In the fore part of the ship lie many great ballast stones and some shot amongst them, and there we found one silver bell about 4 lb weight. We got within the ship at a pretty distance the said great gun with other two (all brass guns). The great gun is eleven feet length and seven and one fourth part of measure in the bore; the other two were minions. We also got two demi-culverins, two falcons, two slings all brass. We lifted three anchors whereof one was eighteen feet of length, the other was fifteen and the third ten. I got two brass sheaves [pulley wheels] weighing sixty pounds. I lifted the rudder and took eight iron pikes [hinges] of it. It was twenty-eight feet of length.

Like all the best treasure-hunting prospectuses, Millar ended with a cliff-hanging come-on. During his final dive, he claimed, 'I saw something like a coat of arms but could not reach it being entangled. I saw gilding upon several standing pieces of the ship' and also 'a crown or diadem and had hooked the same, but being chained it fell amongst the timbers'.[19]

Most of Millar's description carries a ring of authenticity. The 'great gun' standing upright among the wreckage, with its length of 11 feet and bore of 7¼ inches, was surely one of the *cañones de batir* cast by Gregorio Loeffler and carried aboard *San Juan de Sicilia*, because the specifications match exactly (see Appendix 4). The ballast stones and associated piles of roundshot in the bow are parallelled on the wreck of *Santa María de la Rosa* in Blasket Sound; and her massive 28-foot rudder was comparable with that of her Levantine sister *Juliana*, off Streedagh Strand, which was 35 feet long.

The duke of York apparently rejected Millar's offer, and instead awarded a contract in 1686 for four London merchants to salvage all 'guns and treasures' below the surface of Scotland's western seas. Over the next three summers they recovered twelve bronze guns. It was probably these divers whom a visitor watched on a visit to Tobermory in July 1688, 'sinking threescore foot under water, and stay[ing] sometimes an hour, and at last returning with the spoils of the ocean; whether it were plate or money, it convinced us of the riches and splendour of the once-thought invincible Armada.' A decade later another visitor to Mull saw 'some brass cannon, some pieces of eight, teeth, beads, and pins, that had been taken out of that ship', as well as 'some pieces of gold, and money, and a gold chain'.[20]

## The Tobermory Wreck. Act II: The Eighteenth Century

In 1720 Captain Jacob Rowe of London took out a patent for a remarkable diving 'engine' consisting of a cylindrical vessel of copper (some versions were built of wooden staves like a barrel) within which the diver was encapsulated in a prone position (Figure 147). His arms protruded through copper sleeves with leather seals, and he peered downwards through a small glass porthole. A watertight lid provided entry. Condensation on the glass (which must have been considerable) was cleared by a judicious waggling of the nose. Although unpleasant and disorientating the device was used effectively at depths of up to 60 feet, but this was close to a diver's physiological limits. One of Rowe's men experienced a strong stricture in his arms at 66 feet (representing two additional atmospheres of pressure), and 'venturing two fathom [12 feet] lower to take up a lump of earth with Pieces of Eight sticking together; the circulation of his blood was so far stopped, and he suffered so much, that he was forced to keep to his bed six weeks.' Another diver died after reaching 84 feet.[21]

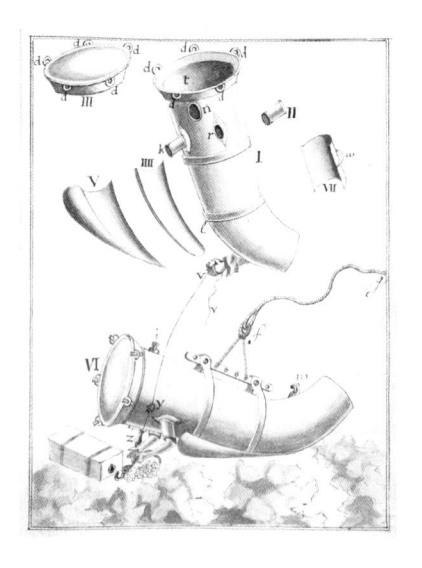

147. Jacob Rowe's 'Diving Engine'. The apparatus operated in a head-up attitude to improve the diver's view, provide arm space when working on the bottom, and prevent leaking water from gathering around his face. A saddle between his back and the top of the engine held down the upper part of his body, countering the external pressure that squeezed his arms inwards. The rear of the cylinder was angled to allow him to bend his legs more comfortably. The engine was suspended from the mothercraft, and a block of lead underneath provided slightly negative buoyancy, and could be jettisoned in emergency. A lifeline provided communication with the surface.

In 1727 Rowe and his partner William Evans took their engine to Fair Isle where the *urca Gran Grifón* had been wrecked. The similarity of her commander's name, Gómez de Medina, and 'Medina Sidonia' convinced them that she was the flagship of the whole Armada and they expected to recover a vast treasure. In fact, the survivors of the wreck had brought ashore what little she had carried (see chapter 14); and after recovering two bronze guns and losing a man in the process they were persuaded to move to Barra to salvage treasure from a recently wrecked Dutch East Indiaman. This time the site was shallow, the treasure genuine and prolific, and they recovered most of it. However, the complicated and acrimonious litigation that followed swallowed most of the profit and in 1729 Rowe decided to try his luck again – where else? – at Tobermory.[22]

John Campbell, duke of Argyll, not only agreed to share the profits with Rowe and his associates but also offered to put up the starter capital himself. From the descriptions left by earlier salvors they knew that much collapsed debris would have to be removed to gain access to the still intact parts of the wreck, while its deeper recesses – where they were confident the treasure lay – would best be reached by ripping the hull apart. This gargantuan task of demolition was accomplished with ingenuity and determination. Loose timbers were hauled clear by the divers, and either dragged aside or lifted to the surface. The shingle and mud that filled the wreck was removed with buckets and dredges. The divers then attacked the main structure. Timbers were wrenched free by attaching them to rafts of barrels that rose with the tide, and the remaining structure was dragged apart by cables pulled by windlasses onshore. Barrels of gunpowder, reinforced and sealed, were set among the wreckage and detonated either by internal clockwork timers that activated flint-and-steel strikers, or by red-hot balls dropped from the surface through waterproofed leather tubes reinforced with coiled wire (Figure 148).

Several months of this drastic treatment reduced what was left of the Ragusan argosy to little more than piles of timber around the bottom of the hull. Now, surely, the treasure would be found. On 20 November 1729 Rowe wrote confidently to his backers that he and his associates had:

> Been making as large a progress by way of dragging or clearing the wreck as if it had been summer season, so that in the spring season when the water is most clear and fittest for diving we shall have nothing more to do than clearing of wood and taking up guns and treasure. The drags under the platform ... hath broken off considerable quantities of cemented cakes of ballast ... but by the hardness and smoothness thereof we have not been able to penetrate the same so far as to take up a specimen, but I am continually endeavouring to undermine it with our drag.[23]

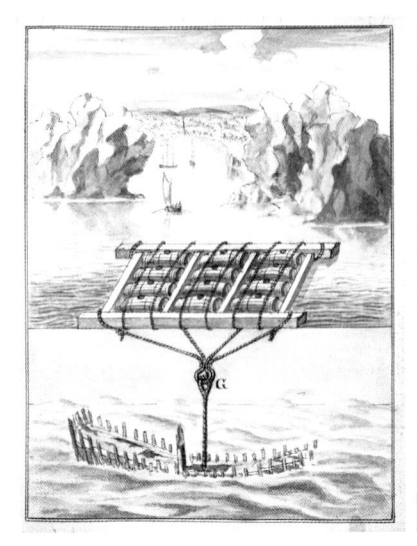

**148.** Left: Jacob Rowe's diagram of lifting a shipwreck using barrels. Right: his drawing of how to use explosives on a wreck.

They found little except the debris left by earlier expeditions. Rowe continued until 1731, by which time it was clear that the wreck had little to yield. He then departed for another unproductive venture on the Clyde.

## The Tobermory Wreck. Act III: Modern Times

So where is the legendary Tobermory treasure? It never existed. *San Juan de Sicilia* was an invasion transport: like other merchantmen in the Armada she carried troops and munitions, not treasure. She was not one of the five vessels chosen by Medina Sidonia to carry 50,000 gold escudos. True, she had wealthy people on board who would have possessed cash and personal valuables, and no doubt some of these have been recovered over the years, together with most of the ship's guns, but after Rowe's efforts almost everything had probably been either recovered or lost in the destructive processes of treasure-seeking.

Fruitless attempts nevertheless continued, especially after the invention of the closed diving suit in the mid-nineteenth century. In 1871 a diver called James Gush investigated the site but nearly came to grief when his air-line parted. Thirty years later his son participated in an expedition sponsored by the Glasgow Salvage Association, which brought to the presumed site both a steam dredger and two 'diviners' who claimed the ability not only to locate precious metals underwater but also to tell whether they were gold, silver or copper. Although they found several artefacts among the tons of seabed brought to the surface, according to the duke of Argyll these included only 'cannon balls, timber, a few pieces of plate, small articles – about 70 dollars' (roughly £20 sterling at the prevailing exchange rate). Several of these modest items survive in private hands, and a few can be viewed in the West Highland Museum at Fort William and the Mull Museum in Tobermory.[24]

Kenneth Mackenzie Foss, a retired lieutenant colonel in the Indian Army, then did his best to excavate the wreck in its entirety. With considerable backing, and a sound practical approach to the engineering aspects of the enterprise, starting in 1909 he systematically removed more of the silt that had accumulated since Jacob Rowe's efforts. Like his predecessors Foss recovered only a few items – coins, pottery, pewter plates and a silver medallion – and sold them at auction. World War I curtailed his work, but he began again in 1922 with fresh backing. A trickle of small finds continued, many broken by the brutal recovery methods employed, but of the expected treasure there was not a sign.[25]

In 1912 Andrew Lang, poet, collector of fairy tales and sometime rector of St Andrews University, published an article that correctly identified the Tobermory galleon as *San Juan de Sicilia*, but not everyone, particularly Colonel Foss, was convinced. Instead, Foss persuaded his feisty twenty-six-year-old secretary, Margaret Naylor, to go down herself (Figure 149). Her venture into what had been an exclusively male preserve caused a sensation in the press, but she was no more successful than her fellow divers. By 1927 Foss had become deranged by his obsession and was advocating impossible schemes to raise the ship (which he believed to be still

149. Publicity photo of Margaret Naylor, the 'lady diver' on the Tobermory wreck, 1924.

largely intact) and then convey her around the world as a floating exhibit. His backers became increasingly disenchanted, and five years later the duke of Argyll informed him tartly that he did not 'wish any further correspondence as to the Tobermory galleon'.[26]

Several others have tried their luck since then. In the 1950s a noted naval diver, Commander Lionel 'Buster' Crabb, negotiated an arrangement between the duke of Argyll and the Admiralty whereby two naval vessels came to Tobermory to search for the wreck. The operation proved a fiasco that ended in awkward parliamentary questions about why taxpayers' money had been used to sponsor a private treasure-hunt. Another naval officer, Commander John Grattan, led the next expedition. Grattan had coordinated the search for *Santa María de la Rosa* (see below), and in 1975 arrived at Tobermory with an underwater blowing device that located what appears to have been the 'cemented cakes of ballast' identified as the bottom of the ship by Jacob Rowe in the 1720s. Contrary to all the evidence, Grattan believed that the ship was still intact, sunk into the seabed in her entirety (a sedimentary impossibility), and that the concreted layer was the poop deck at the highest part of the sterncastle. The treasure must therefore lie immediately below it, just as Archibald Millar had asserted in 1683 when he wrote that the elusive 'thirty millions in money' lay 'under the sill of the gunroom'. Like Foss before him, Grattan claimed that the ship could be raised as a largely intact hull and restored to a seaworthy condition – if only sufficient money could be raised. This time, it appears, no investment was forthcoming.

The next attempt took place in 1982 and actually achieved what it set out to do: to establish whether profitable salvage could be achieved at Tobermory. It was mounted by a major company, Wharton Williams Taylor, which had recently located the wreck of HMS *Edinburgh* and recovered 431 gold bars valued at £45 million in 1942 when she was torpedoed in the Barents Sea and sank. After five weeks of cutting-edge geophysical survey and some limited dredging (during which a solitary cannonball was found), the company concluded that little of value remained in Tobermory Bay and prudently withdrew.[27]

This logical decision did not deter hardcore believers. John Grattan's conviction that he had identified the intact stern superstructure of the wreck in 1975 led some years later to the creation of the delightfully named Poop Company. Its goal was to recover the Tobermory ship together with all her treasure, and investment was sought in the City of London to support the work. A prospectus offered subscribers 'A rare opportunity ... to invest in what can be described as a unique wreck recovery with the potential for excellent returns'. Tempting blandishments followed. 'Due to the reports of a considerable treasure on board, both in the form of coinage and other artefacts, there have been various attempts to salvage the wreck and, more specifically, the treasure therein. All these attempts were unsuccessful mainly due to fraud or incompetence.' This time things would be different. Returns on investment, it implied, would be enormous: 'Whilst it is impossible to estimate the total value of what will be recovered with certainty', ran the prospectus, 'it is likely to be in the £10M–£50M range, and possibly as high as £100M.' The sum of £504,000 was sought from investors to cover setting-up costs: once salvage began, the operation would become self-funding and there would be plenty left over for everyone involved.[28]

Just how the anticipated profits were to be distributed is unclear, but after deducting operating costs a proportion would go to the duke of Argyll as the supposedly exclusive owner of the wreck (a dubious proposition in law), with handsome rewards for the Poop Company, its associates and shareholders. John Grattan was involved (though his stake in the venture is unclear) and the Company's CEO was Matthew French, who listed his normal activities as a 'healer of sick buildings, water divining and spirit release' – unusual qualifications, it might be thought, for the task in hand. Work began in February 2014 with eight divers and expensive equipment contracted from North-West Marine, a coastal and offshore diving company based in Oban.

A serious snag soon emerged. Grattan's positioning of his supposed 'poop' discovery had been based on 'transits': lining up intersecting bearings with identifiable features on land, an ancient and accurate method of position-fixing in coastal waters. However, changes made to the Tobermory waterfront since 1975 rendered Grattan's transits ambiguous. Although the team airlifted many tons of seabed from the area around the presumed upstanding 'poop', they failed to locate any signs of ship structure, and payments to North-West Marine ceased after the first month. Matthew French fled on the ferry to Oban, where representatives of North-West Marine awaited him. Soon afterwards work stopped and the Poop Company was dissolved.[29]

Readers beware! No treasure of the conventional kind will ever be found in Tobermory Bay because *San Juan de Sicilia* did not carry any. The real treasure would have been the ship herself, frozen as a sixteenth-century time-capsule with her buried contents wonderfully preserved in a sheltered oxygen-free environment. Had the wreck remained untouched, vast sums of money would have been saved, and dozens of enterprising and capable individuals (and not a few charlatans) spared disillusionment and ruin. Such a survival would rank today as a national treasure, comparable with *Vasa* and *Mary Rose*. Alas little now remains of the Tobermory wreck save perhaps parts of her lower hull – but even these, as the rare remains of a sixteenth-century Ragusan argosy, deserve preservation, study and protection from predatory treasure-hunters.

## Enter the Archaeologists

William Spotswood Green (1847–1919) was the first person to conduct a detailed professional survey of Armada wrecks. He was an unlikely pioneer: an ordained clergyman of a seaside parish in County Kerry, Ireland, who scaled mountains in Europe, New Zealand and North America, and developed expertise in sea-fishing and boat-handling before becoming an inspector (later chief inspector) of Irish Fisheries. In 1890 and again in 1891 he hired a steam trawler to inspect the types and quantities of fish as well as the facilities for distributing them ashore in the 'wild western bays' of Ireland. He came ashore on Great Blasket Island, inhabited by 'about twenty families', and recorded local traditions of the Armada wrecks. From Spanish sources he deduced that both *Santa María de la Rosa* and *San Juan Fernandome* had sunk there and produced a map which showed the route taken by Recalde and Aramburu between the islands to relative safety in the Sound. He speculated that 'For those who have time and means at their disposal this part of the Blasket Sound would be an interesting field for discovery.' Spotswood Green also anchored in Blacksod Bay where he 'talked to the peasantry' about the 'great ship' that had sunk there some centuries ago, and took away with him a 'large piece of a rib of Italian live oak which I found supporting a hay-stack with the trenail holes in it and the top showing unmistakable signs of fire', which he felt sure came from *Rata Encoronada*. In 1906 he read a paper to the Royal Geographical Society entitled 'The Wrecks of the Spanish Armada on the Coast of Ireland', and used his personal observations from the trawler (supported by photographs) combined with contemporary documents and local knowledge gleaned from 'the peasantry' to locate the sites of some twenty-five wrecks, many of which he correctly identified. After the lecture Spotswood Green received questions from some well-informed members of the audience: first Martin Hume ('just arrived from Madrid'), followed by John Knox Laughton and Julian Corbett – the British historians who knew most about the Armada campaign. All three recognized the importance of Spotswood Green's information, based on geography and local knowledge; but unfortunately neither they nor anyone else in the audience found the 'time and means' to follow up his admirable suggestions.[30]

The post-war invention of the aqualung opened up coastal waters to free-swimming divers, and while much activity was recreational some was of a more acquisitive nature, ranging from casual souvenir-hunting to the legitimate commercial salvage of modern wrecks. Unfortunately, some divers began to engage in the indiscriminate destruction of historic shipwrecks, particularly those believed to contain treasure. Dutch East Indiamen carrying bullion with which to purchase return cargoes of spices and porcelain from Asia were the main targets, sometimes leading to mayhem in which shots were exchanged by rival groups of treasure-hunters. Little archaeological evidence was recognized or recorded beyond listings in saleroom catalogues.

Without government or academic funding, and with no protective legislation, pioneering underwater archaeological projects had to raise support elsewhere. Some argued that selling recovered artefacts to cover costs would be a solution, but this fundamentally breaches archaeological ethics because it denies access to the finds to scholars who might subsequently wish to examine them, and excludes a public for whom such relics are parts of a common heritage. It is also incompatible with academic rigour and objectivity. No treasure-hunting venture has ever demonstrably conducted archaeology to peer-reviewable standards because the approaches are mutually exclusive: profit-seeking investors are unlikely to underwrite the ongoing and open-ended costs of conservation, research and permanent curation if many of the objects found have no intrinsic value. It is easy to ignore or dispatch up the suction pipe any fragile or 'uninteresting' items, and these are suspiciously absent from auction catalogues.

Another possibility might be to persuade a museum to purchase and conserve all the finds for permanent curation, but this too can create conflicts of interest. What if nothing of monetary value is recovered? Or if no museum wants the material? Fortunately, the six Armada wrecks so far discovered in Irish and UK waters have been treated sensitively, thanks to the professionalism of the divers who found and excavated them, and the support of far-sighted museum staff. Archaeological evidence from them has therefore made a massive contribution to complement the already rich documentary resources for the events of 1588.

## *Girona*

In the 1960s Robert Sténuit, a Belgian professional diver with scholarly leanings and a driving interest in historic shipwrecks, became fascinated by the idea of finding and investigating an Armada wreck. His research led him to *Girona*, off Ireland's Antrim coast. Local tradition and unambiguous place-name evidence (*Port na Spaniagh*) pointed him to the spot. With start-up funding from COMEX, a diving company with which he was associated, Sténuit found the site in 1967 and over the following two years he and a small team painstakingly surveyed and excavated the wreck.

The ship had smashed onto a fang of rock in a highly exposed location, and no trace of her structure survived. There was little archaeological cohesion to the wreck: on discovery the only visible artefacts were two guns, an anchor and many lead ingots. The site was a shallow jumble of rocks and gullies, the latter filled with constantly mobile shingle. Systematic excavation under rocks and through gullies revealed that heavy items had trended downwards until they stabilized on bedrock. Gold tended to accumulate in the deepest cracks. In all Sténuit and his team recovered hundreds of gold and silver coins, together with twelve gold rings, six gold chains and thirty-five other items of gold jewellery (Figure 150).

Just as valuable in archaeological terms were armament-related items, navigational instruments, domestic wares and personal possessions. Recognizing that the material required careful cleaning and conservation, Sténuit approached the Ulster Museum in Belfast whose Keeper of Antiquities, Laurence Flanagan, offered the services of his conservation laboratory without commitment on either side. On his own initiative, Flanagan then set about raising funds to purchase the entire collection (including the 'valueless' items) on behalf of the museum. He succeeded triumphantly, enabling Sténuit's costs to be covered, the items to be expertly conserved and studied, and the collection put on show and made available to researchers (ourselves among them). It is now a major attraction in Belfast's Ulster Museum.[31]

**150.** Coins, jewellery and two religious items from the *Girona* excavation. Heavy gold chains surround them (see Figures 9, 11 and 20).

## Santa María de la Rosa

Sydney Wignall was another pioneer who recognized the archaeological potential of Armada shipwrecks. Though his research objectives were at first ill-defined, since nobody then knew how well such a site might be preserved and what kind of evidence it might yield, he believed passionately that the discovery and rigorous investigation of a wreck would add to our understanding of that great historical event. The past half-century has amply justified his faith.

In 1968 Wignall mounted an expedition to locate the wreck of *Santa María de la Rosa* in Blasket Sound, County Kerry (see chapter 15). Marcos de Aramburu's eyewitness account of the incident, read in conjunction with charts and tidal configurations, suggested that the wreck lay somewhere within an area of about four square miles. Today, side-scan sonar and other geophysical techniques might pick up indications of such a wreck in a matter of hours, but these technologies were then in their infancies and the costs would have been beyond Wignall's resources. However, he had business interests in Malta in the course of which he had come to know John Grattan (see above), who at the time commanded the Royal Navy's Clearance Diving Team there.

The unit's main task was to find and make safe unexploded ordnance, and although they used various remote-sensing techniques, systematic diver search was often the best way of locating small objects on the seabed. To this end Grattan had developed a 'swim-line' technique whereby a number of divers strung at regular intervals along a line could progress in formation above the seabed, navigating by signals transmitted from a controller on the surface via buoyed vertical lines through a combination of 'pulls' and 'bells'. The basic vocabulary was 'start', 'stop', 'go right', 'go left', 'come up' and 'I have found something'. In the last event the line would be halted and the find buoyed for further investigation. As well as directing the progress of each search the controller marked its start and finish points with buoys which defined blocks of coverage. These could accurately be positioned on the surface and plotted on a chart. In this way blocks of covered ground could be built up, with overlaps to ensure that there were no gaps (Figure 151).

This was the technique with which Wignall set out to search Blasket Sound. Between April and August 1968 forty-three volunteer divers took part (Colin Martin among them), trained and supported by off-duty naval clearance divers led by Grattan. Within ten weeks the divers had identified not only the wreck (or rather part of it) but also anchors lost during incidents recorded by the Spaniards, helping to merge eyewitness accounts of the events with the topography above and below water, and local tides and currents.

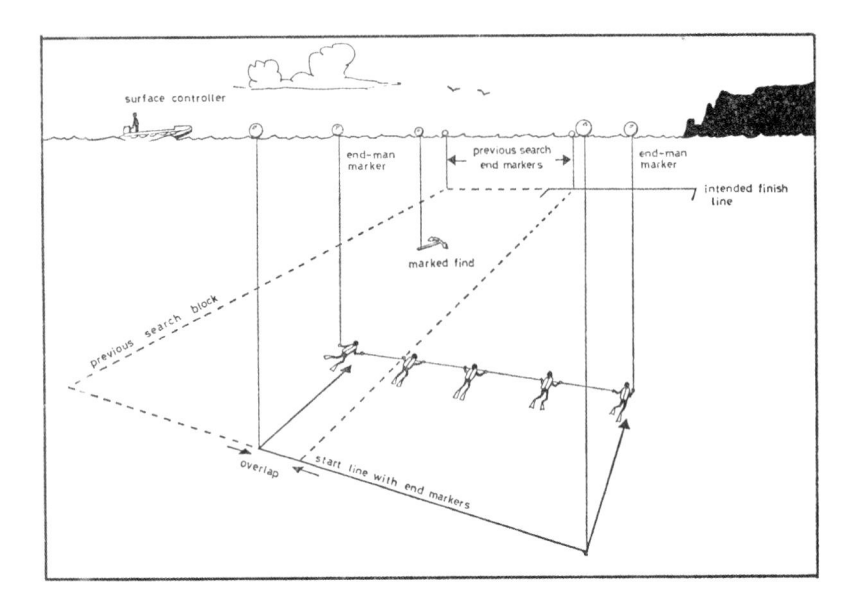

151. Diagram showing swim-line technique used in the search for the wreck of *Santa María de la Rosa*.

As described in chapter 15, having been dragged by the fiercely ebbing tide, *Santa María* hooked her anchor on the northern edge of a reef that towers close to the surface in the eye of a tide-race at the Sound's narrow neck. The ship, swinging on her fouled anchor, impaled herself on Stromboli Rock, a pinnacle only a few feet from the surface. Then her cable broke or was deliberately cut and the smashed hull sank in a matter of seconds. Still carried by the tide the wreck hit bottom 120 feet down and 150 yards from Stromboli. The anchor is still lodged on the far side of the reef, freezing for more than four centuries the moment of catastrophe.

The remainder of the 1968 season was spent surveying the wreck. The main feature was a mound of packed limestone ballast 100 feet long and 40 feet at its widest. Excavation showed that the average depth of ballast was two and a half feet, indicating a mass of about 200 tons. The northern edge was wide and blunt, and piled on it were massive concretions of iron shot, while seven lead ingots lay strewn across it. Towards the south of the mound its eastern and western sides drew together to form a distinctive tail. These features recall Archibald Millar's observation on the Tobermory wreck (see above) that 'in the fore part of the ship lie many great ballast stones and some shot amongst them'. Factors involved in ballasting a ship of this kind suggest a reason for the tadpole-like configuration. The high castle-works at the stern, with their associated armament, would have upset the trim of the vessel. Ballast concentrated forward, tapering aft with the run of the hull, would correct this imbalance, leaving a spread of ballast of the kind noted here and by Millar at Tobermory. There was no sign of guns, and none was revealed by a metal-detector survey on either side of the ballast.

In 1969 a smaller team directed by Martin returned to conduct limited excavations. An area beyond the north-western edge of the ballast revealed scattered roundshot, concreted muskets and arquebuses, lead bullets, and two pewter plates inscribed 'Matute' (see Figure 106). An infantry captain and his lieutenant with that surname sailed on *Santa María*, confirming the identity of the wreck beyond doubt.

A small excavation at the southern end of the wreck, where a metal-detector contact had been recorded, yielded human bones, two coins, and a pewter plate with the initials 'AH'. The excavations revealed that only the bottom part – perhaps only the forward bottom part – of *Santa María de la Rosa* remains at the foot of Stromboli. The paucity of finds everywhere on the site, particularly the lack of guns (of which she had carried twenty-six), suggested that the upper forward section may have remained attached to the stern when it drifted to the south-west. The seabed in this direction was too deep for safe diving with the resources then available, but with Ireland's enlightened laws now protecting historic shipwrecks, together with the strong nautical archaeological resources and expertise which exist in both state and community institutions, we may be confident that the ambitious goals set by Sydney Wignall in 1968 will one day be achieved. Until then, the main section of *Santa María de la Rosa* lies undiscovered somewhere in deep water.[32]

The few artefacts recovered were acquired and preserved by the Ulster Museum to complement the *Girona* collection. They include samples of lead, iron and stone shot. Many hundreds more were left *in situ* on and around *Santa María*'s forward ballast where they would have been stowed. The quantity of munitions on the wreck came as a total surprise, because Medina Sidonia, followed by many historians, had asserted that the primary reason for the Armada's failure was that it ran out of ammunition (see chapter 16). The wreck of *Santa María* provided the first clue that this was not entirely true.

## *Gran Grifón*

Following the Blasket project Wignall and Martin resolved to search for another Armada wreck that might provide examples of guns and perhaps explain why they had not been used to better effect. The *urca Gran Grifón*, wrecked on Fair Isle, seemed the best prospect. In the eighteenth century Jacob Rowe had recovered two bronze guns 'of a large size'; but there were surely others left. The site was not difficult to find. Tradition pointed to a rocky cleft called Stroms Hellier Geo close to the south-east end of the island. The geo is a triangular inlet penetrating an overhanging cliff, narrowing to a point at its head from a 100-yard-wide mouth – no swim-line would be needed here. The inlet is split by a reef with deep gullies on either side and a local crofter informed us that the wreck lay in the southern one. He was right: a brief dive by Martin in May 1970 was rewarded within minutes by the green glow of a bronze gun 60 feet down at the base of an underwater cliff, exactly where our informant said it would be.

A three-month season of survey and trial excavation followed, with generous support from sponsors including the Shetland Museum, which also provided conservation facilities. Though no part of the ship itself had survived, the distribution of finds indicated that she had lodged between the central reef and the geo's southern side where she broke up, depositing her heavy contents on the sea-floor (Figure 152). The gully was steep-sided and filled with shingle and stones rounded by water movement in storms. Up to six feet of these stones lay above the bedrock. Lighter

**152.** An archaeologist with an air-lift removing shingle to reveal a buried bronze gun from the wreck of *Gran Grifón*.

material that fell on it, including wooden parts of the ship, would therefore move with the shingle over time and ultimately become abraded to nothing, but heavy items would trend ever downwards until they stabilized on the bedrock. There they amalgamated in the gully bottom as a concreted stratum of guns, iron and lead shot, and lead ingots. It was exactly what the team had come to find.

To expose the buried stratum some 300 tons of overlying shingle had to be removed, a task accomplished in 1977 by a small team from the recently established Institute of Maritime Archaeology at the University of St Andrews. An air-lift (suction pipe) was positioned in the gully, powered by a compressor mounted on the ledge against which the ship's foremast had leaned, allowing the shipwrecked Spaniards to scramble ashore. The air-lift discharged spoil into the northern gully, where no wreckage had been identified during the initial survey. Three months completed the gully's excavation, and the recovered finds were deposited in the Shetland Museum.

A wide sampling of ordnance was made, including one each of the newly cast bronze *medias culebrinas* and *medias sacres* issued to the ship at Lisbon, together with examples of the wrought- and cast-iron pieces that had belonged to the ship as a Hanseatic merchantman. The surprising quantity of roundshot recorded supported the evidence from *Santa María de la Rosa* that the Spaniards had not run out of ammunition.[33]

## *Trinidad Valencera*

In 1971 members of the City of Derry Sub-Aqua Club discovered the wreck of *Trinidad Valencera* in Kinnagoe Bay, County Donegal. They found bronze guns, anchors and wooden gun-carriage wheels partly buried in a flat sandy seabed beside the shallow reef on which the ship had grounded and broken up. Two of the guns were 40-pounder *cañones de batir* cast by Remigy de Halut of Mechelen: the descriptions and weight-marks of these guns matched those recorded in the ship's lading manifest at Simancas, identifying the wreck beyond doubt.

From the outset the Club members were determined to treat their find with archaeological rigour and ensure that any finds would be conserved and eventually lodged in a suitable museum. At their invitation a survey and partial excavation of the site was directed by Martin in association with Club members in a series of summer campaigns between 1971 and 1983. In addition to the voluntary (and crucial) input given throughout by the Club, support was provided by the Ulster Museum and the Institute of Maritime Archaeology at the University of St

Andrews. Through the good offices of Laurence Flanagan the finds were treated in the conservation laboratories of the Ulster Museum. Magee College of the University of Ulster provided storage facilities and other support. The wreck is now protected under the Republic of Ireland's historic shipwreck legislation, and the Underwater Archaeology Unit of the country's National Monuments Service routinely monitors the site. A permanent exhibition of artefacts from *Trinidad Valencera* opened in the Tower Museum, Derry/Londonderry in 2005.

Although the wreck is broken up and dispersed, a wide range of objects, including many organic items, have been preserved, often in remarkably good condition. It appears that while the hull remained partially intact on the sandy seabed, scour-pits formed, triggered by water movement around the ship's intrusive bulk, which trapped many objects. Thereafter the ship seems to have disintegrated relatively rapidly, allowing the natural seabed to reassert itself, filling the scoured depressions and encapsulating and preserving anything that had fallen into them (Figure 153).

Several isolated hull-components were identified among the debris, though no articulated structure. This can be explained by the exclusive use of iron bolts in the ship's construction, a feature noted in other contemporary Mediterranean carracks. The technique minimized maintenance over a short but intensive working

153. Preparing to lift a heavy gun-carriage wheel from *Trinidad Valencera*, using air-filled barrels. The combination of fragility and weight demands padded robust support.

life – such hulls were easier to build and remained tight so long as the iron remained sound – but when the bolts began to corrode, typically within ten years or so, the vessels were discarded and replaced (rather like the Liberty Ships of World War II). This may explain why *Trinidad Valencera* broke apart so quickly, ensuring the random burial and preservation of so much associated material.[34]

*Trinidad Valencera* yielded not only a representative sample of naval and military equipment, but wide evidence of her contemporary world (Figure 154). It was

### Figure 154. Life on Board

The survival of organic materials on *Trinidad Valencera*, particularly everyday objects, has allowed us rare glimpses of life on board, bringing us into direct contact with the Armada's people. These examples show (top left) a wooden bowl and salt cellar; (below, from left) a pair of bellows, a hand-brush made of rushes, above it a fragment of esparto matting, and a heddle, used for weaving narrow fabrics, probably for protecting ropes.

Ordinary folk ate off pottery. Most of the Armada's 'other ranks' were issued with mass-produced crockery. Each man was issued with a set of four – jug, plate, small bowl and pot. The green-glazed jug shown here was made at Lisbon; the plate at Seville, of a type produced in vast quantities for the annual Indies fleets. Better-off participants often brought pewter, examples of which are shown below.

the quantity and variety of everyday items rarely found in most land contexts that awoke much interest among the general public and provided so much to present in museum displays.

## The Wrecks on Streedagh Strand

In 1985 a group of English divers led by Steven Birch, Alan King and Harry Chapman arrived at Streedagh Strand, a long curving beach north of Sligo in western Ireland where three Armada ships had been driven ashore with great loss of life (see chapter 15). They secured permission from the state authorities to look for the wrecks and arrived with inflatable boats, depth sounders and proton magnetometers. Basing their search pattern on the draught of the ships and the state of tide when the ships ran aground, they followed a line parallel to the shore and identified three targets about 100 yards from the beach spaced some 300 yards apart. With so few survivors, the identity of these vessels was not generally known. *Juliana* was identified by her guns, while surviving historical sources enabled Dr I. A. A. Thompson and the authors to determine that the other two ships were *Lavia* from Venice and *Santa María de Visón* from Ragusa. Parts of *Juliana*'s hull and enormous rudder were visible, exposed by recent storms. To establish title as 'salvor in possession' – a necessity under the law which then applied – the group conducted a detailed survey of *Juliana*'s remains and raised three guns from *Juliana* and one from the *Lavia* site.

The finders established themselves as the Streedagh Armada Group with the intention of conducting an archaeological investigation over the coming years. This spurred the Republic of Ireland to look more closely at its shipwreck legislation which, up to this point, had been formulated to regulate commercial salvage rather than archaeology. Apart from routine monitoring, the Streedagh sites lay dormant during two decades of legal arguments, which were less of a contest between the parties than a concerted attempt by the State to establish legal protocols whereby historic shipwrecks could be protected as national heritage assets. The outcome was as amicable as these things can be: the Streedagh Armada Group were commended for their responsible behaviour, and generously rewarded for their work, while the State was able to formulate the legislation that now automatically protects all wrecks in its waters more than 100 years old. In support of this enlightened policy an Underwater Archaeology Unit (UAU) was established to identify, inspect and monitor sites, and actively engage in their management.[35]

In recent years the UAU has been heavily involved with the Streedagh sites. Winter gales in 2013 and 2014 again exposed parts of *Juliana*, revealing nine more guns and other artefacts. A rescue operation was mounted, directed by the UAU and involving other stakeholders, and the nine guns were recovered, together with a massive bronze pot still containing traces of pitch. All the finds are currently undergoing conservation in the National Museum of Ireland, and the sites continue to be monitored.

# *Epilogue*

*'Defeat teaches you how to win.'*
Simón Bolívar

What lessons did the three protagonists learn from the Armada campaign? In two cases, less than one might think. In the first half of the seventeenth century both the Spanish and English navies fell short of all three categories proposed by John Gooch and Eliot Cohen (see chapter 16): they failed to learn from the past; they failed to anticipate future developments; and they failed to adapt to the immediate circumstances on the battlefield – as the naval campaign of 1639 spectacularly demonstrated.

In September of that year Don Antonio de Oquendo, son of Miguel, led another Armada from Corunna consisting of forty-five royal warships and thirty embargoed merchantmen from various Mediterranean and Atlantic ports, carrying 14,000 men, of whom 6,000 were Spanish and Italian infantry destined to reinforce the Army of Flanders, still striving to suppress the Dutch Revolt. Oquendo's principal mission was to land these reinforcements at Dunkirk, but his instructions allowed him to offer battle to the Dutch if they stood in his way. Spain's chief minister, the count-duke of Olivares, assured Oquendo that his ships were 'of such quality that I do not believe we have seen their equal since the Armada that sailed against England' – hardly an inspiring parallel, especially for Oquendo who, aged eleven in 1588, would have remembered the disaster clearly. Nevertheless, unlike Philip II, Olivares considered a Plan B: he requested permission from King Charles of England, Scotland and Ireland, son of James and rejected suitor of the Spanish princess (see chapter 20), to allow the Armada to take refuge in an English port if necessary (albeit he only requested it after the fleet had set sail).[1]

Like Medina Sidonia, just before leaving Corunna, Oquendo ordered all aboard his fleet to confess and take communion and 'to avoid all type of public sins, especially blasphemy and swearing during the voyage'. Again like Medina Sidonia, he instructed the fleet to sail 'in a half-moon formation, according to the place allotted' to each ship. If a battle ensued, 'no ship must engage the enemy flagship, which I reserve for myself', confident that the numerous soldiers on his decks would prevail when it came to boarding.[2]

Oquendo's first opportunity came on 16 September, when a small Dutch fleet under Maarten Harpertszoon Tromp intercepted the Armada off Beachy Head. According to a Portuguese officer, Oquendo's 'whole idea was to board the enemy flagship without discharging a single cannon or musket shot' and so he 'bore down upon the Hollanders so that when the two flagships were level he could clap that of the enemy on board'. Tromp, however, attacked in line ahead, the first recorded use of the tactic, firing broadsides from a distance until he forced Oquendo to break off the action. Two days later Tromp attacked at night (another innovation), again in line ahead, instructing his captains to 'keep out of musket-shot', given Oquendo's advantage 'in musketry fire'. The Dutch bombardment lasted fourteen hours during which, according to a Jesuit priest, 'he could not reach the third word of the Lord's Prayer which he was continuously saying without hearing the echo of some cannon'. Eventually Tromp ran out of ammunition and put into Calais for replacements (including a thousand 18- and 33-pounder rounds). Oquendo now decided that he could not reach Dunkirk without putting his troop-transports at risk: he therefore sailed into the anchorage of the Downs hoping that Charles's forts and fleet would protect him. The king agreed – but only if Spain paid him £150,000.[3]

Peter Mundy, an Englishman who had travelled the world, went aboard some of the Spanish ships and reported that they had an 'abundance of men in their fleet, but most part sickly, tattered and questionless inexpert either for soldiers or sailors . . . They have now a sickness amongst them, and many die, whose bodies being flung overboard, some of them are washed ashore along the beach.'[4] Oquendo managed to send some of his troops across to Dunkirk in English ships, while Tromp received reinforcements that increased his strength to 103 vessels, including sixteen fireships. He now far outnumbered not only Oquendo but also England's Narrow Seas fleet: Sir John Pennington commanded only nineteen ships at the Downs. Too late, King Charles realized that if Tromp attacked, 'no man in the world' could expect the Royal Navy to prevail, and so he ordered Pennington 'to make a show of assisting them, but not run yourself or his Majesty's ships in danger where there is no hope of victory nor expectation of anything but blows and hazard'. On 18

October the Lord Admiral, the earl of Northumberland, told Pennington that 'if when the Hollanders assault the others you see the Spaniards defend themselves' effectively, 'then are you to give them your best assistance; otherwise you must make as handsome a retreat as you can in so unlucky a business.' It was a far cry from Admiral Howard's bravura stance just over fifty years before.[5]

Three days later Tromp closed for the kill. 'Before daybreak we said prayers' and at dawn 'opened fire on the enemy, who cut their cables and made sail'. Dense fog led to a brief pause in the action, but when it cleared Tromp used a lethal combination of artillery broadsides and fireships to drive twenty-three Spanish vessels ashore. In the end he captured fourteen Spanish ships and destroyed twenty-four more, losing only one vessel in the battle, burned by one of his own fireships while entangled with a Spanish opponent.[6]

In the melee that followed Pennington boasted that '[we] shot many guns from all our ships' at the Dutch, 'shooting many of them through' and thus maintaining the honour of England; and a broadsheet ballad published in London a few days later celebrated Spain's defeat as if it rivalled that of Medina Sidonia:

> I think there have not been
> Since eighty-eight the like sea fight
> Near unto England seen.

The comparison was false. Whereas Howard's success raised England's reputation all over Europe, Pennington's impotence demolished it. A British agent in Brussels opined that 'His Majesty has lost more than the king of Spain'; while another claimed that 'The loss of the Spanish fleet has injured the king's reputation extremely, even among neutrals and well-wishers.' Pennington agreed. Allowing two foreign powers to fight a battle 'in the king's chamber,' he wrote, was 'to the dishonour of our king and kingdom'. The historian Kevin Sharpe was surely correct that 'what had looked like a splendid opportunity for the reassertion of England's capacity to tip the balance of power had turned into a disastrous demonstration of her weakness'.[7]

How had the balance of naval power changed so drastically since 1588? The Armada campaign triggered a naval arms race in the North Atlantic. Before the year was out, Philip II ordered the construction of twelve large galleons, to be known as the 'Twelve Apostles' – the largest shipbuilding programme undertaken in Spain to that date – and by 1598 his High Seas Fleet included twenty-seven purpose-built warships. The Dutch, too, embarked on a crash programme of naval construction, following the enactment by the States-General of an 'Order for maritime protecting' in 1589, and the establishment of five provincial Admiralties reporting to Maurice of Nassau, son of William and commander of the Republic's armed forces. In 1599 an all-Dutch expeditionary force of seventy-three ships attacked the Azores and the island of São Tomé; and by 1621 the Republic's navy included nine capital ships of 500 tons or more.[8]

By then the Royal Navy had also expanded: as of 1596 the thirty-eight ships of the queen's navy carried a total of 1,059 guns (628 of them 9-pounders and above); but thereafter England's shipwrights strove to build larger and more powerful battleships, which produced vessels that were slow to manoeuvre and expensive to maintain. The 1,200-ton *Prince Royal*, launched in 1610 with fifty-five guns weighing just over 83 tons, was probably the largest warship in the world until 1637, when the 1,500-ton three-deck *Sovereign of the Seas* was launched, her 104 guns weighing over 153 tons. According to Nicholas Rodger, 'Then and for at least twenty years after, she was easily the most powerful ship in the world'; indeed, *Sovereign of the Seas* was only one-third smaller than *Victory*, Nelson's flagship at Trafalgar, fought on 21 October 1805 – the same day as the battle of the Downs.[9]

But *Sovereign of the Seas* was nowhere near the Downs on the day of the battle: a few days earlier Peter Mundy had admired her at anchor at Chatham. Meanwhile the great ships built in Elizabeth's reign became decrepit. Although *Ark Royal* served as the English flagship in a raid on Cadiz in 1625, her commander considered her 'very unfit by reason her lower deck lieth so low as the water comes in'. Indeed all 'such great ships, and especially the old ones, that are so over-loaden with ordnance' that their 'own burden did [them] more harm than anything else, and had we not put much of the ordnance into the hold' they would have sunk.[10]

Nevertheless, the building and maintenance of such ships still served an important purpose: they created the world's first naval-industrial complex. A battleship was the same size as many a country house and carried more guns than many a fortress. The construction of each one took two to three years and required an immense infrastructure. After admiring *Sovereign of the Seas* in 1639, Peter Mundy visited the adjacent royal dockyard at Chatham and noted that the edifice which housed the naval ropeworks had 'the longest roof that ever I saw', allowing the ropemakers to toil 'in time of rain'.[11] Fifty years later the manufacture of ropes, sails, ordnance and munitions as well as ships for the Royal Navy employed almost 6,500 men at a time when the largest private shipyard employed just thirty-two men. In the words of Nicholas Rodger, 'The dockyards had entered the industrial age a hundred years before the rest of the country.' Meanwhile Britain's ships-of-the-line – each one armed with advanced weapons-systems composed of standardized, interchangeable parts – increased from 46 in 1650 to 112 in 1695, making the Royal Navy (in the words of John Ehrman) 'the most comprehensive and in some respects the largest industry in the country'.[12]

As in Tudor times, achieving the status of a first-class naval power at least in part reflected fear of enemies real and imagined: an arms race with the Dutch, Spain and increasingly France led successive governments in London to invest heavily in creating the 'many movable forts' vaunted by Sir Walter Raleigh. It also led to other important and lasting changes. Between 1660 and 1688 the navy was closely controlled by Charles II and his brother James II, both of whom knew more about naval affairs than any monarch before or since: the former designed yachts and in effect invented yachting as a sport; the latter commanded the navy in several major battles; both were expert pilots for the Thames estuary; both wanted a navy that was capable of defeating all possible foes at sea. To this end in 1661 Charles created a new pathway to promotion for 'such young gentlemen as are willing to apply themselves to the learning of navigation, and fitting themselves or the service of the sea', known as 'volunteers per order' (equivalent to the rank of midshipman), until 'almost all the rising generation of English sea officers were gentlemen who had entered as volunteers per order'. In 1677 Charles decreed that in future all candidates for the rank of lieutenant must have served at least three years at sea, including one as a midshipman, and then pass an examination in seamanship conducted by senior officers. As Rodger observed: 'The concept of a qualifying exam was extremely rare, and the social implications of forcing gentlemen's sons to serve alongside seamen petty officers were bound to be extremely controversial', but it created an established career structure that remains the staple of the Royal Navy.[13]

This combination of quantitative and qualitative strengths allowed Britannia, despite her small size, to rule the waves; and it is appropriate to trace their origins back to the innovations introduced by Drake and Hawkins a century before, despite the reverses that followed. The failure at Cadiz in 1625 and the humiliation at the Downs in 1639 demonstrated as clearly as the fate of the Spanish Armada that successful navies require constant innovation and investment. Naval experts learn from examples of failure as well as success. 'The misfortune and vice of our country is to believe ourselves better than other men,' wrote Admiral Sir Cloudesley Shovell in 1702:

> But experience has taught me that, where men are equally inured and disciplined in war, 'tis, without a miracle, number that gains the victory; for both in fleets, squadrons and single ships of near equal force, by the time one is beaten and ready to retreat the other is also beaten and glad the enemy has left him. To fight, beat and chase an enemy of the same strength I have

sometimes seen; but have rarely seen at sea any victory worth boasting when the strength has been near equal.

Captain Cesáreo Fernández Duro came to a similar conclusion in 1884: 'Weapons change, and so do the qualities of the men who wield them; but the basic principles of the art of war on both land and sea remain the same, and knowing what factors led to a disaster will always make profitable reading for a warrior.' That is why the fascination of the Armada campaign will endure.[14]

## The Future

Who knows what other new Armada material may be located in the future? On the documentary front, the major collections in public archives will remain the foundation of Armada historical studies, although some more new sources may yet come to light – like Recalde's correspondence with Medina Sidonia, Bobadilla and Leyva, located in 1994 in a box labelled 'Miscellaneous Papers' hidden among the papers of Spain's Military Orders in Madrid, or the register of payments made in Dartmouth to ransom 500 Armada sailors and soldiers, found while cataloguing the archive of a Belgian aristocrat in 2006. The archive of the counts of Revillagigedo contains the papers of both Diego Flores de Valdés and his cousin Don Pedro, but only a few Armada documents from that collection have entered the public domain.[15]

Much the same is true on the archaeological front. One of the two Armada ships known to have foundered off the coast of Norway has been located, though not yet excavated: Torbjørn Ødegaard has tentatively identified it as the *urca Santiago*, known as 'the ship of the women'. Excavation on a wreck which may be that of *Regazona* began in 2010 near Ferrol in Galicia and yielded some artillery pieces; but the absence of other finds makes it difficult to establish a date, let alone an Armada connection. Several attempts have been made to link other wrecks in the waters off western Ireland with the Armada. Several bronze guns were brought up from a presumed Armada wreck near Burtonport in Donegal in the early nineteenth century, and sold as scrap. Recent excavations in the area by the UAU have located a wreck that dates from slightly after 1588. The 'San Marcos Project', founded in 2014 as a community group with the goal of locating and identifying the remains of the galleon *San Marcos* (Portugal), carried out a marine geophysical survey near Mutton Island, but no results have yet been published.[16]

# EPILOGUE

As with documents, there is always the potential for further archaeological discoveries, especially with the ever-developing science of remote investigation underwater. Above all, however, we believe – and we hope this book has shown – that the most fruitful future lies in close cooperation between archaeologists and historians. Because the documentary and archaeological resources are both so full and complementary, they present rich opportunities for integrated research. Few past events, of any period, lend themselves so completely to these levels of interdisciplinary approach as the campaign of the Spanish Armada.

**(Overleaf) 155.** Presented to the Society of Apothecaries of London in 1846 by John Nussey, apothecary to Queen Victoria, this painting in oil on three pieces of linen canvas is unusually large: 121 x 285 cm (48 x 112 inches). At lower left Elizabeth reviews her troops at Tilbury, with beacons burning amid the rocky landscape behind her. On the far right an English galleon, perhaps *Ark Royal* since she flies the Royal Standard, exchanges fire with a galleass. Although neither the commission nor the artist has been identified, the work was almost certainly executed between 1600 and 1610 by a Dutch or Flemish trained artist (or, given its size, by a team of artists).

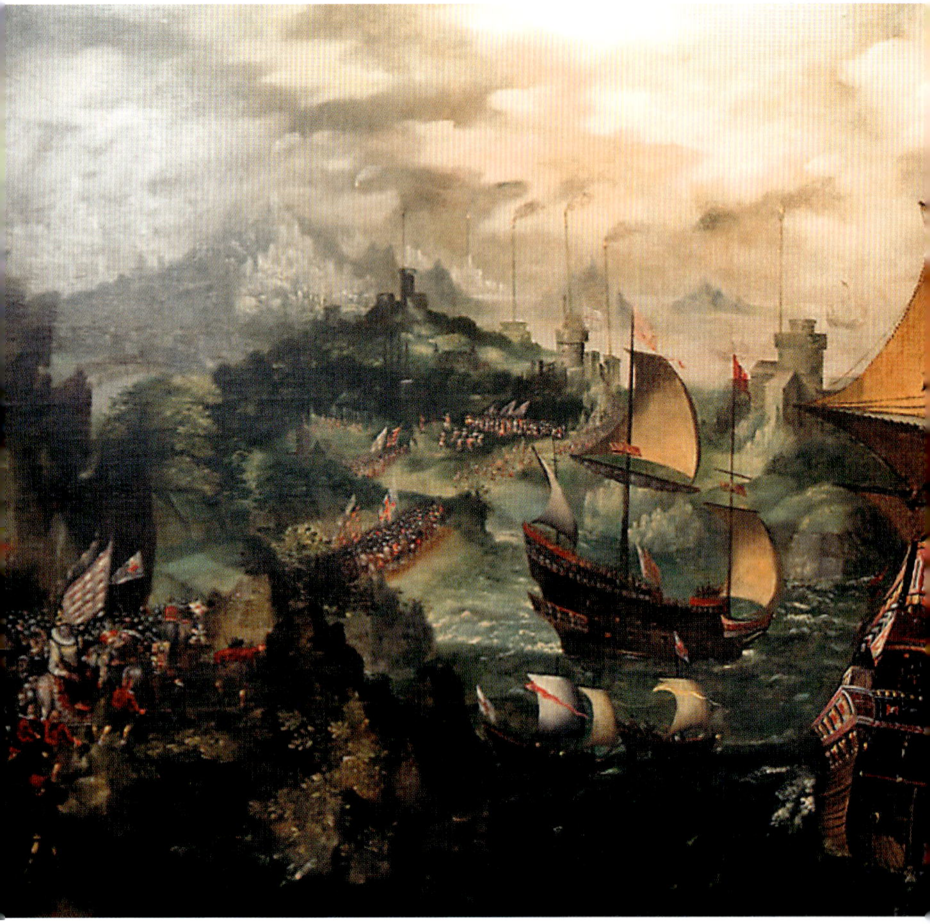

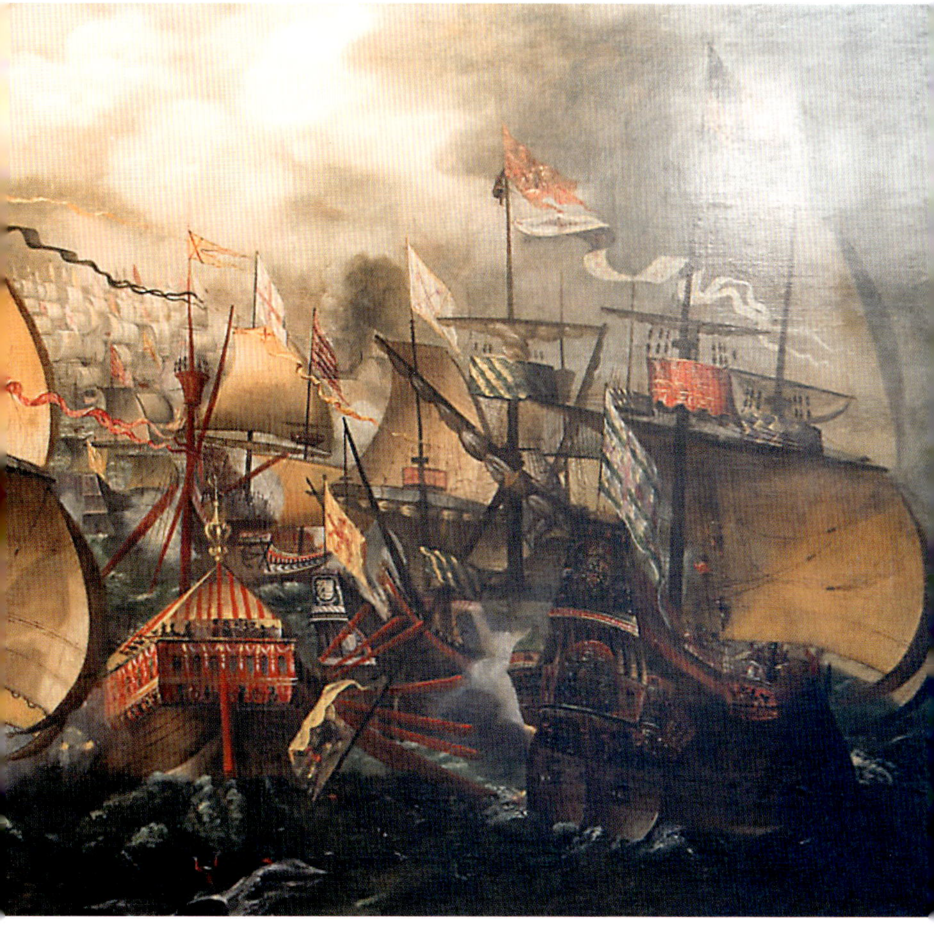

# *Glossary*

*For names of Spanish and English gun-types see also Appendix 4.*

| | |
|---|---|
| **acertar** | get it right (one of Philip II's favourite words) |
| **almiranta** | vice-flagship |
| **almirante general** | deputy commander of the Armada (Juan Martínez de Recalde) |
| **argosy** | a large merchant ship from Ragusa (Dubrovnik) |
| **astrolabe** | navigational instrument used for calculating latitude |
| **aventurero** | gentleman volunteer, usually with military experience, who served as an ordinary soldier in the Spanish infantry |
| **bark** | general term for smaller three-masted, square-rigged, sea-going vessel |
| **bastion** | projecting fortification providing for defensive crossfire |
| **billete** | comments or instructions written by one Spanish official to another |
| **bowsprit** | pole projecting forward from the stem of a vessel, usually carrying a sail |
| **capitana** | flagship, or flag-officer in overall command |
| **carabela** | caravel |
| **caravel** | a general term for merchant ships, but in terms of the Armada applied to a small vessel-type |
| **careening** | heeling a ship over under controlled conditions to clean or repair the parts of the hull normally underwater |
| **case-shot** | small projectiles within a case made of four or more pieces of wood tied together, which would disintegrate after being fired |

| | |
|---|---|
| **caulking** | a mixture of tar and unpicked rope forced in between a ship's planks to make it watertight |
| **chase-piece** | forward-firing gun |
| **cognitive dissonance** | twisting evidence inappropriately to fit a preconceived idea or theory |
| *compañias sueltas* | infantry companies not incorporated in *tercios* |
| **concretion** | the corrosion products from iron immersed in seawater for any length of time combine with the surrounding sand to form a crust which reduces the rate of corrosion; this hard crust can encapsulate other small objects within it, and if the iron object inside corrodes to extinction it can form a mould from which a cast of the original object can be made |
| *consulta* | paper forwarded to Philip II by one of his councils, containing a summary of incoming documents and suggested actions |
| **cromster** | type of small warship used by the Dutch Republic during the sixteenth and seventeenth centuries |
| **culverin** | a large gun, long in relation to its bore (Sp. *culebrina*) |
| **demi-culverin** | a smaller version of a culverin (Sp. *media culebrina*) |
| *entretenidos* | gentlemen with military experience, for whom there was initially no official position, but who were paid, and appointed as officers when vacancies arose |
| **falcon** | small gun firing 2-lb to 4-lb shot |
| **falconet** | smaller version of falcon (Sp. *falconete*) |
| *falua* | felucca |
| **felucca** | small boat propelled by oars and lateen sail |
| **fish (a mast)** | 'a fish is any piece of timber or plank which we make fast either to mast or yard, to succour and strengthen it when it is in danger to break. Then we command the carpenter *to fish* the mast or yard; which is done, first hollowing it fit for the place, and then nailing it with spikes and woolding it about with ropes' (Mainwaring, 'The seaman's dictionary') |
| **frapping** | passing cables under a ship and tightening them to hold the hull together |
| *galeaza* | galleass, a hybrid vessel combining the attributes of a galleon and a galley, and carrying heavy guns at bow and stern |
| *galera* | galley, an oared fighting vessel, usually with two masts and lateen sails, and her main armament at the bow |
| **gallowglass** | mercenary or armed retainer of an Irish chieftain |

| | |
|---|---|
| **grandee** | Spanish nobleman of the highest rank |
| **ground tackle** | anchors and their cables |
| **holograph** | handwritten by the author |
| **hoy** | small boat employed in harbours |
| **indulgence** | remission of punishment in the Roman Catholic Church |
| **Inquisition** | a network of twenty-two tribunals in the Spanish Monarchy created to investigate and punish heresy, reporting to the Inquisitor-General in Madrid (appointed by the king of Spain) |
| **Jesuit** | a member of the Society of Jesus |
| ***maestre de campo*** | colonel of a Spanish or Italian *tercio* |
| **mizzen mast** | the mast astern of the mainmast |
| **Morisco** | convert from Islam to Christianity |
| ***nao*** | ship, interchangeable with *nave* |
| ***nave*** | ship, interchangeable with *nao* |
| ***patache*** | vessel with three masts, generally of between 70 and 100 tons |
| **perier** | any gun designed to fire stone shot (Sp. *pedrero*) |
| ***pinaza*** | pinnace |
| **pinnace** | small single-masted boat with both oars and sail |
| **pirate** | seaman who plunders ships at sea |
| **privateer** | armed vessel licensed by the state to plunder enemy ships at sea |
| **quintal** | 100 Castilian pounds (broadly equivalent to 'hundredweight') |
| **relic** | bodily part of, or object associated with, Christ or a saint |
| **roundshot** | cannon balls |
| **saker** | a gun slightly larger than a falcon (Sp. *sacre*) |
| **Salamis** | decisive naval defeat of the Persian invasion of Greece in 480 BC |
| **shallop** | small coastal sailing boat |
| **shear-hook** | a curved blade fixed to the ends of the yards of a vessel so that if two ships got very close they would damage each other's rigging |
| **spritsail** | square sail carried below the bowsprit |
| **stockfish** | fish, usually cod, air-dried but not salted |
| **storm-canvas** | reduced sail to accommodate bad weather |
| ***tercio*** | regiment of Spanish or Italian infantry |
| **tonelada** | Spanish measure of ship tonnage (Eng. tons burden) |

| | |
|---|---|
| **tonnages** | there are various ways of calculating the tonnage of vessels, but the only complete set of data we have is the 'Lisbon Muster'. While some of the figures may be guesswork, what they provide is comparative sizes. English tonnage measurements were probably different, and while they too can be used as a general indication of sizes within the fleet, no direct comparison can be made between the two fleets |
| *urca* | northern European seagoing merchant ship |
| **warp** | using ropes and anchors, carried by a ship's boats, safely to extract a ship from a harbour or other confined situation, until it was safe to set sail |
| *zabra* | vessel with two masts, usually from Vizcaya or Guipúzcoa (smaller than a patache: about 40–50 tons) |

# Chronology

### All dates New Style after 1582

| | | |
|---|---|---|
| 1580 | *August* | Philip II's forces, commanded by the marquis of Santa Cruz and the duke of Alba, invade Portugal and capture Lisbon |
| | *September* | Francis Drake returns from circumnavigation; Philip II authorizes Juan Martínez de Recalde to transport a papal expeditionary force to Smerwick (Ireland) |
| 1581 | *January* | The duke of Parma begins reconquest of South Netherlands |
| | *April* | Elizabeth knights Drake; Philip acclaimed as king of Portugal |
| | *July* | Don Pedro de Valdés leads unsuccessful attempt to conquer Terceira; Dutch States-General declares Philip II deposed |
| | *November* | Diego Flores de Valdés leads fleet to Strait of Magellan (returns May 1583) |
| 1582 | *February* | Duke of Anjou becomes duke of Brabant |
| | *26 July* | Santa Cruz wins naval victory off São Miguel in the Azores |
| 1583 | *July* | Conquest of Terceira; Santa Cruz suggests follow-up attack on England |

| | | |
|---|---|---|
| 1584 | June | Santa Cruz appointed Captain-General of the Ocean Sea; death of duke of Anjou |
| | July | Assassination of William of Orange |
| | December | Spain signs treaty of Joinville with duke of Guise and French Catholic League |
| 1585 | March | Henry III signs treaty of Nemours with French Catholic League |
| | May | Philip II embargoes all foreign ships in Iberian ports; Sixtus V elected Pope |
| | August | Anglo-Dutch treaty of Nonsuch; fall of Antwerp to Spain |
| | 7 October | Francis Drake occupies ports in Galicia (to 17th), and goes on to sack Spanish possessions in the Canaries and the Caribbean |
| | 24 October | Philip declares readiness to invade England |
| | December | Philip invites Parma to prepare invasion plan (reply sent April 1586); earl of Leicester arrives to govern the Dutch Republic |
| 1586 | February | Philip II accepts Santa Cruz's offer to prepare invasion plan (sent March) |
| | June | Recalde appointed to command new squadron of Vizcaya; Hawkins begins three-month blockade of Iberian waters |
| | 20 June | Giovanni Battista Piatti arrives at Court with Parma's invasion plan |
| | 26 July | Piatti leaves Court with Masterplan for Parma |
| | 17 November | Philip orders viceroys of Naples and Sicily to send ships, munitions and troops to Spain |
| 1587 | February | Execution of Mary Queen of Scots; English garrison betrays Deventer to Parma |
| | March | Duke of Medina Sidonia embargoes *urcas* in Andalusian ports |
| | 12 April | Drake leaves Plymouth to 'singe the king of Spain's beard' |

# CHRONOLOGY

| | | |
|---|---|---|
| **1587** | *29 April* | Drake raids Cadiz and prevents Spanish shipping from leaving the Mediterranean |
| | *2 May* | Recalde and Vizcaya ships arrive in Lisbon |
| | *18 June* | Drake captures Portuguese East Indiaman *São Felipe* off Azores and returns to England |
| | *16 July* | Santa Cruz and Recalde lead Armada from Lisbon to Azores to meet treasure-fleets |
| | *29 July* | Papal–Spanish treaty on future government of Catholic England; Sixtus V deposits one million ducats in a Rome bank, payable when Spanish troops land in England |
| | *4 August* | Don Alonso de Leyva arrives in Lisbon with ships gathered in Andalucia; Parma captures Sluys |
| | *4 September* | Philip issues new Instructions for invasion of England |
| | *25 September* | Santa Cruz brings Indies treasure-fleet safely to Seville |
| | *29 September* | Santa Cruz returns to Lisbon; Armada begins to refit |
| | *10 October* | Recalde's squadron returns to Lisbon |
| | *16 November* | Storm damage to ships in Lisbon |
| | *December* | Dutch blockade squadron assumes permanent guard off Dunkirk |
| **1588** | *January* | Division of Armada into squadrons: Portugal (Medina Sidonia), Vizcaya (Recalde), Andalucia (Valdés), Guipúzcoa (Oquendo), Levant (Bertendona), *urcas* (Gómez de Medina), galleasses (Moncada), galleys (Medrano) and *pataches* and *zabras* (Mendoza, later Ojeda). |
| | *9 February* | Death of Santa Cruz |
| | *26 February* | Medina Sidonia reluctantly accepts appointment to command Armada |
| | *8 March* | Anglo-Spanish peace talks begin in Flanders |
| | *14 March* | Medina Sidonia arrives in Lisbon |
| | *1 April* | Philip signs Instructions for Medina Sidonia and Parma |
| | *23 April* | Philip signs secret patent for Don Alonso de Leyva to replace Medina Sidonia if necessary |

**1588**

| | |
|---|---|
| 28 April | Diego Flores de Valdés and squadron of Castile arrive at Lisbon |
| 29 April | Duke of Guise agrees to engineer Catholic rebellion in France |
| 7 May | Medina Sidonia draws up battle plan |
| 9 May | Medina Sidonia publishes the 'Lisbon Muster' |
| 12 May | 'Day of the Barricades' in Paris: Guise takes control |
| 23 May | Anglo-Spanish peace talks move to Bourbourg; English fleet concentrates at Plymouth |
| 28 May | Armada leaves Lisbon and heads towards England |
| 30 May | Howard leads English fleet out of Plymouth and heads towards Spain |
| 7 June | Medina Sidonia issues orders for defence of his flagship in battle |
| 13 June | First issue of powder, lead and match to soldiers aboard Armada 'for practice' |
| 14 June | Armada arrives off Cape Finisterre and waits for victuals |
| 16 June | English fleet returns to Plymouth |
| 19 June | Medina Sidonia leads part of the Armada into Corunna; storm scatters the rest of the fleet |
| 24 June | Medina Sidonia urges Philip to abandon Enterprise |
| 4 July | English navy sails for Spain |
| 5 July | Parma inspects his fleet at Dunkirk; Dutch blockade fleet reinforced |
| 18 July | At an audience in Bruges, Valentine Dale asks Parma if he plans to invade England |
| 19 July | Medina Sidonia and his Council of War at Corunna decide to try again |
| 21 July | Armada sets sail against England |
| 22 July | English fleet returns to Plymouth |
| 25 July | Medina Sidonia advises Parma of his approach |

| | | |
|---|---|---|
| 1588 | *29 July* | Armada sights Lizard and takes in sail; Council of War aboard *San Martín*; English sight the Armada |
| | *30 July* | Armada enters Channel and takes in sail again; English fleet puts to sea from Plymouth |
| | *31 July* | Second issue of powder, lead and match to soldiers aboard Armada 'to fight the English'; first blood: loss of *Rosario* and *San Salvador*; Medina Sidonia sends second messenger to Parma |
| | *1 August* | No hostilities; Armada continues its advance |
| | *2 August* | Second fight: off Portland Bill; English Privy Council orders full mobilization |
| | *3 August* | Howard divides English fleet into squadrons; Medina Sidonia's letter of 25 July reaches Parma |
| | *4 August* | Third fight: off Isle of Wight; Armada re-forms into 'roundel'; duke of Guise named 'lieutenant-general of the kingdom' in France |
| | *6 August* | Armada anchors off Calais; Parma receives news of Armada's approach; Elizabeth breaks off talks at Bourbourg; Seymour's squadron joins Howard |
| | *7/8 August* | Fireships attack |
| | *8 August* | Battle off Gravelines |
| | *9 August* | Medina Sidonia and Howard both hold a Council of War to discuss options; Seymour's squadron returns to Channel |
| | *10 August* | Parma completes embarkation of invasion forces; Medina Sidonia orders Armada to return to Spain by sailing around Scotland and Ireland, and reduces daily rations |
| | *12 August* | Armada off Firth of Forth: English fleet disengages |
| | *18 August* | Elizabeth's 'Tilbury speech' |
| | *20 August* | Armada passes into Atlantic |
| | *21 August* | Medina Sidonia sends Don Balthasar de Zúñiga to Court |
| | *27 August* | English Privy Council orders demobilization of army |
| | *31 August* | Parma stands down fleet |

| 1588 | 8 September | Final issue of powder, lead and match to soldiers aboard Armada off the Irish coast 'in case the enemy comes' |
|---|---|---|
| | 11 September | English flotilla bombards *Santa Ana* (Vizcaya) in Le Havre; she sinks a week later |
| | 12 September | Parma lays siege to Bergen-op-Zoom (to 30 October) |
| | 14/16 September | *Trinidad Valencera* wrecked off Donegal |
| | 20/22 September | Medina Sidonia returns to Santander; *San Esteban, San Nicolás Prodaneli, Ciervo Blano, Falcón Blanco Mediano, Concepción, Santa Bárbara, Gran Grín, Santa María de la Rosa, Anunciada, Lavia, Juliana, Santa María de Visón* and *Rata Encoronada* all wrecked off Ireland |
| | 23 September | Diego Flores returns to Laredo; Oquendo returns to Pasajes |
| | 24 September | *Zúñiga* arrives at the Escorial and spends several hours briefing Philip; *Duquesa Santa Ana* wrecked off Donegal |
| | 26 September | Recalde orders *San Juan Fernandome* to be burned in Blasket Sound |
| | 28 September | *Gran Grifón* wrecked off Fair Isle |
| | 7 October | Recalde returns to Corunna |
| | 10 October | Bertendona returns to Muros |
| | 13 October | Philip orders Spanish clergy to cease prayers for Armada's success and pray instead for divine guidance |
| | 14 October | Aramburu returns to Santander |
| | 21 October | Elizabeth orders Drake and Norris to prepare a Counter-Armada |
| | 28 October | *Girona* wrecked off Antrim |
| | 5 November | 'Tobermory galleon' (*San Juan de Sicilia*) destroyed |
| | 6 November | *San Pedro* wrecked off Devon |
| | 10 November | Philip wishes he were dead |
| | 12 November | Spanish Council of State advises Philip to continue war with England |
| | 22 November | Philip orders construction of twelve new galleons (the 'Twelve Apostles') |

| | | |
|---|---|---|
| **1588** | *24 November* | Thanksgiving Service at St Paul's Cathedral in London |
| | *30 November* | Elizabeth's Navy Board approves 'Device' to build eight new warships |
| | *8 December* | *Regazona* wrecked trying to enter Ferrol |
| | *4 December* | Elizabeth travels through the streets of London to give thanks in St Paul's Cathedral |
| | *23 December* | Diego Flores de Valdés arrested and imprisoned in Burgos Castle |

# Abbreviations

| | |
|---|---|
| AA | Archivo de la Casa de los Duques de Alba, Biblioteca de Liria, Madrid (with caja and folio) |
| ABB *VC* | Archief de Bergeyck, Beveren-Waas, Belgium, *sub-fonds De Visscher de Celles* |
| *ACC* | *Actas de las Cortes de Castilla*, 17 vols (Madrid, 1861–91) |
| AGI | Archivo General de Indias, Seville (with series, libro or legajo, and folio) |
|   *IG* | *Indiferente General* |
|   *Justicia* | *Papeles de Justicia* |
| AGRB | Archives Générales de Royaume/Algemeen Rijksarchief (Brussels) |
|   *Audience* | *Papiers d'État et d'Audience* (with liasse and folio) |
|   *CC* | *Chambre des Comptes* (with liasse and folio) |
|   *SEG* | *Secrétairerie d'État et de Guerre* (with register and folio) |
| AGS | Archivo General de Simancas |
|   *CJH* | *Consejos y Juntas de Hacienda* (with legajo and folio) |
|   *CMC* | *Contaduría Mayor de Cuentas* (with época and legajo) |
|   *CS* | *Contaduría del Sueldo* (with época and legajo) |
|   *Estado* | *Negociación de Estado* (with legajo and folio) |
|   *GyM* | *Guerra y Marina* (formerly *Guerra Antigua*, with legajo and folio) |
|   *MPyD* | *Mapas, Planos y Dibujos* |
|   *SP* | *Secretarías provinciales* (with legajo or libro and folio) |

| | |
|---|---|
| AHN | Archivo Histórico Nacional, Madrid |
|   *AEESS* | *Archivo de la Embajada Española cerca la Santa Sede* |
|   *OM* | *Sección Órdenes Militares* (with legajo and folio) |
|   *Inq* | *Sección Inquisición* (with legajo or libro and folio) |
| AHR | *American Historical Review* |
| AMAE *MDFDE* | Archives du Ministère des Affaires Étrangères, Paris, *Mémoires et documents: fonds divers, Espagne* |
| *APC* | *Acts of the Privy Council of England,* ed. J. R. Dasent et al., 41 vols (London, 1890–1964) |
| ARA | Algemene Rijksarchief, The Hague (with collection, loketkas and folio) |
| ASC | Archivo de la Casa de los marqueses de Santa Cruz, Madrid |
| ASF *MdP* | Archivio di Stato, Florence, *Mediceo del Principato* |
| ASG *AS* | Archivio di Stato, Genoa, *Archivio Segreto* |
| ASL *OSD* | Archivio di Stato, Lucca, *Officio sopra le differenze* |
| ASMa *AGS* | Archivio di Stato, Mantua, *Archivio Gonzaga: Spagna* |
| ASMo *AS* | Archivio di Stato, Modena, *Cancellaria ducale, sezione estero: ambasciatori Spagna* |
| ASN *CF* | Archivio di Stato, Naples, *Sezione diplomatico-politico: Carte Farnesiane* |
| ASP *CF* | Archivio di Stato, Parma, *Carteggio Farnesiano* |
| ASV | Archivio Segreto Vaticano, Vatican City |
|   *LP* | *Lettere Principi* |
|   *NS* | *Nunziatura Spagna* |
| ASVe *SDS* | Archivio di Stato, Venice, *Senato: Dispacci Spagna* |
| BAV | Biblioteca Apostolica Vaticana, Vatican City, Manuscript Collection |
|   *UL* | *Urbinate Latini* |
|   *VL* | *Vaticani Latini* |
| BCR *Ms.* | Biblioteca Casanatense, Rome, Manuscript Collection |
| *BCRH* | *Bulletin de la Commission Royale d'Histoire* |
| BL | British Library, London, Department of Western Manuscripts (with collection, volume and folio) |
| *BMO* | J. Calvar Gross, J. I. González-Aller Hierro, M. de Dueñas Fontán and M. del C. Mérida Valverde, *La batalla del Mar Océano,* 5 vols (Madrid, 1988–2015) |
| BNE *Ms.* | Biblioteca Nacional de España, Madrid, Manuscript Section |

| | |
|---|---|
| BNF | Bibliothèque Nationale de France, Paris, with Manuscript Collection, volume and folio |
| Bod | Bodleian Library, Oxford, Department of Western Manuscripts, with Manuscript Collection, volume and folio |
| BPU *Favre* | Bibliothèque Publique et Universitaire, Geneva, *Collection Manuscrite Édouard Favre* |
| BR | Biblioteca Real, Madrid (formerly Biblioteca del Palacio Real), Manuscript Section |
| BRB | Bibliothèque Royale, Brussels, Manuscript Section |
| Brugmans | H. Brugmans, ed., *Correspondence van Robert Dudley, graaf van Leycester, en andere documenten betreffende zijn gouvernement-generaal in de Nederlanden 1585–88*, 3 vols (Utrecht, 1931) |
| BZ | Biblioteca de Zabálburu, Madrid (formerly known as the Archivo de la Casa de Heredía Spínola), with caja and folio |
| *CCG* | *Correspondance du Cardinal de Granvelle, 1565–1586*, ed. E. Poullet and C. Piot, 12 vols (Brussels, 1877–96) |
| *Co.Do.In.* | *Colección de documentos inéditos para la historia de España*, 112 vols (Madrid, 1842–95) |
| *CSPD* | *Calendar of State Papers Domestic*, arranged by reign |
| *CSPF* | *Calendar of State Papers, Foreign series, of the reign of Elizabeth*, vol. XXI (in 4 parts), ed. S. C. Lomas and A. B. Hinds; and vol. XXII, ed. R. B. Wernham (London, 1927–36) |
| *CSPI* | *Calendar of State Papers relating to Ireland in the reign of Elizabeth, vol. IV: 1588–1592*, ed. H. C. Hamilton (London, 1885) |
| *CSP Rome* | *Calendar of State Papers relating to English affairs preserved principally at Rome*, ed. J. M. Rigg, 2 vols (London, 1916–26) |
| *CSPSc* | *Calendar of State Papers relating to Scotland*, ed. J. Bain, W. K. Boyd, A. I. Dunlop and J. D. Mackie, 13 vols (Edinburgh, 1898–1969) |
| *CSPSp* | *Calendar of State Papers relating to English affairs preserved … in the archives of Simancas. Elizabeth*, ed. M. A. S. Hume, 4 vols (London, 1892–9) |
| *CSPV* | *Calendar of State Papers and manuscripts relating to English affairs existing in the archives and collections of Venice*, ed. H. F. Brown, vol. VIII (London, 1894) |

| | |
|---|---|
| *DHME* | *Documentos para la historia del monasterio de San Lorenzo El Real de El Escorial*, ed. J. Zarco Cuevas, G. de Andrés et al., 8 vols (Madrid, 1917–62) |
| Duro | C. Fernández Duro, ed., *La Armada Invencible*, 2 vols (Madrid, 1884–5) |
| *EHR* | *English Historical Review* |
| *FBD* | G. Parker, *Felipe II. La biografía definitiva* (Barcelona, 2010) |
| FCDM *AH* | Fundación Casa Ducal de Medinaceli, Toledo, *Archivo Histórico* |
| Folger *Ms.* | Folger Shakespeare Library, Washington, DC, Manuscript Collection |
| HHStA | Haus-, Hof- und Staatsarchiv, Vienna, with series, Konvolut and folio |
| *HMC* | *Historical Manuscripts Commission: Reports* (with description) |
| *HMC Foljambe* | Historical Manuscripts Commission, *Fifteenth report, Appendix, Part V: The manuscripts of the Right Honourable F. J. Savile Foljambe of Osberton* (London, 1897) |
| *HMC Hatfield House* | Historical Manuscripts Commission, *Calendar of the Manuscripts of the Most Honourable the Marquess of Salisbury, preserved at Hatfield House*, 24 vols (London, 1883–1976) |
| HSA | Hispanic Society of America, New York, Manuscript Collection |
|   *Altamira* |   *Altamira papers* (with document number) |
|   *HC* |   *Hiersemann catalogue* (with catalogue and document number) |
| Hunt | The Huntington Library, Art Collections, and Botanical Gardens, San Marino, California, Manuscript Collection |
|   *HA* |   *Hastings Manuscripts* |
|   *Ms.* |   *Manuscript* |
| IVdeDJ | Instituto de Valencia de Don Juan, Madrid (with envío and folio) |
| Japikse | N. Japikse, *Resolutien der Staten Generaal van 1576 tot 1609*, 14 vols (The Hague, 1917–70) |
| KB *Ms.* | Koninklijke Bibliotheek, The Hague, Manuscript Section |
| KML *MSP* | Karpeles Manuscript Library, Santa Barbara, California, *Medina Sidonia Papers* |
|   *CC* |   *Casa de la Contratación* |
|   *CG: C* |   *Capitanía General: Cuentas* |
|   *CR* |   *Cartas de Reyes* |

| | |
|---|---|
| Laughton | J. K. Laughton, *State Papers relating to the defeat of the Spanish Armada, anno 1588*, Navy Records Society I–II (London, 1895) |
| LCP | J. Lefèvre, ed., *Correspondance de Philippe II sur les affaires des Pays-Bas*, vol. III (Brussels, 1956) |
| LL | Lilly Library, Bloomington, Indiana |
| LoC | Library of Congress, Washington, DC, Manuscript Collection |
| LPL | Lambeth Palace Library, Manuscript Collection of the archbishops of Canterbury |
| Lyell | J. P. R. Lyell, 'A commentary on certain aspects of the Spanish Armada drawn from contemporary sources' (two copies exist: Oxford University B.Litt. thesis, 1932; and Houghton Library, Harvard, fMs Eng.714. Harvard also owns the contemporary sources purchased and used by Lyell) |
| MLM | The Morgan Library and Museum, New York |
| *MM* | *The Mariner's Mirror* |
| NMM *Ms.* | National Maritime Museum, Greenwich (now part of Royal Museums Greenwich), Manuscript Library |
| *Nueva Co.Do.In* | *Nueva Colección de documentos inéditos para la historia de España y de sus Indias*, 6 vols (Madrid, 1892–6) |
| OÖLA *KB* | Oberösterreichisches Landesarchiv, Linz, *Khevenhüller Briefbücher* |
| Oria | E. Herrera Oria, *La Armada Invencible. Documentos procedentes del Archivo General de Simancas* (Valladolid, 1929: Archivo Histórico Español, II) |
| Pepys *Ms.* | Pepys Library, Magdalene College, Cambridge, Manuscript Collection |
| RAH, *Ms.* | Real Academia de la Historia, Madrid, Manuscript Collection |
| RAZ | Rijksarchief Zeeland, Middelburg (since 2000 part of the Zeeuws Archief, Middelburg), with series and volume |
| *SCJ* | *Sixteenth Century Journal* |
| SLEE *Ms.* | San Lorenzo El Real de El Escorial, Library, Manuscript Collection |
| TNA | The National Archives, Kew (formerly the Public Record Office) |
|    AO |    *Audit Office Papers* |
|    E |    *Exchequer Papers* |
|    HCA |    *High Court of Admiralty* |

| | |
|---|---|
| *PRO* | *Public Record Office* (transcripts of documents in European archives relating to British history made in the nineteenth century for *CSP* series) |
| *SP* | *State Papers* |
| *WO* | *War Office Papers* |
| Vázquez | A. Vázquez, 'Los sucesos de Flandes y Francia del tiempo de Alejandro Farnesio', *Co.Do.In.*, LXXII–LXXIV (Madrid, 1879–80) |

# Notes

## Introduction

1 Parker, 'Anatomy', 320–2, Don Alonso de Leyva to Juan Martínez de Recalde, 12 August 1588.
2 Laughton, I, 358–61, Hawkins to Walsingham, 31 July 1588 OS.
3 Laughton, II, 59–61 and 97–100, Howard and Drake to Walsingham, 8 and 10 August 1588 OS.
4 KML *MSP CH: C* 9/146–7v, Medina Sidonia's Instructions to Juan de Escandón, *escrivano de raciones* on the *urca San Bartolomé*, 29 June 1587.
5 Keegan, *The face of battle*, 303; Parshall and Tully, *Shattered sword*, 71; *BMO*, IV/1, p. XIX.

## PART I

\* Canestrini and Desjardins, *Négociations*, IV, 737, Tuscan ambassador Cavriana to Vinta, Paris, postscript dated 22 November 1587.

### 1. 'Arise O Lord and Avenge Thy Cause'

1 'Exsurge domine et judica causam tuam' is the Latin text of Psalm 74.
2 AGS *CS* 2a/284/43–4, Leyva's *pliego de asiento* records the 'armas doradas con todas sus piezas' supplied by the king and charged against Don Alonso's salary of 500 ducats a month.
3 Burghley scrawled those words on his annotated copy of *Relación de la Felicíssima Armada*: BL 192.f.17 (i). He may have picked up the smear from William of Orange's *Apology* in 1581 (Duke, 'William of Orange', 29), but he also read the interrogations of several Armada prisoners who asserted that Ascoli was 'the base son of the king of Spain'.

4 Huerga, 'La vida', 60, count of Olivares, Spanish ambassador in Rome, to Albert, 1584; Bouza, *Cartas*, 75, Philip to his daughters, 5 March 1582.
5 *BMO*, IV/1, 41 and 126, Don Francisco de Melo to Philip, and Philip to Medina Sidonia, 20 and 28 February 1588; Gracia Rivas, *Los tercios*, 151, patent of Medina Sidonia, 19 April 1588. Pedro Luis de Andrade apparently raised a second company of Moriscos: *BMO*, IV/2, 117, Philip to Medina Sidonia, 5 April 1588.
6 *BMO*, IV/4, 229, 'Relación' of Alonso Vanegas, aboard the flagship; TNA *SP* 12/218/23–5, list of prisoners from *San Pedro Mayor*, November 1588 ('three others dead since they landed, whereof one was a negro'); *BMO*, IV/4, 210, Account of the explosion aboard *Santa Ana*, October 1588 ('un negro del general', so probably the African slave mentioned in Oquendo's will: Tellechea Idígoras, *Otra cara*, 545–6).
7 *BMO*, IV/1, 291–2, and IV/2, 87–8, Medina Sidonia to Philip, 23 March and 2 April 1588; ibid., 151, Philip's reply, 11 April 1588.
8 AGS *CMC* 2a/31, unfol., Antolínez to Contador Lucas de la Cruz, Brussels, 4 February 1595, holograph, about the service of the 21 men from his former company involved in the mutiny of La Chapelle.
9 AGS *GyM* 81/422, Matute's service record 1567–76; AGS *CMC* 2a/29 and 31, settlement with the mutineers of La Chapelle, 10 July 1596, when Blanco alias Ortega was 34.
10 *BMO*, IV/2, 239, Medina Sidonia to Philip, 29 April 1588 (thus four days after the parade); AGS *CMC* 2a/772, 'Libro tercero de quentas', dossier of *San Francisco*, unfol., distribution of 'pólvora, cuerda y plomo' to the infantry on 13 June 1588.
11 TNA *SP* 63/137/99, interrogation of Balthasar López del Árbol, sergeant-major of the *tercio* of Naples, Drogheda, 13 October 1588, answer to question 4.
12 Martin, *Spanish Armada prisoners*, 25. Several of those interrogated said that there had been two chests of silver vessels belonging to Don Pedro de Valdés and to Medina Sidonia, and another mentioned a 'great store of apparel for the Duke of Medina'. Alonso Vanegas on *San Martín* also said that some of the duke's possessions were on board *Rosario*.
13 AGS *GyM* 216, unfol., muster of six companies recruited in July and August 1587 (we thank Tony Thompson for this information); Vermeir, 'The ransoming of prisoners', 60–1 (deducting two years from the ages of the prisoners in January 1590); ABB *VC*, nr 1214, 'Lista'.
14 AGS *CMC* 2a/29, 31 and 47, 'fenescimientos de cuentas' with 52 Armada veterans among the mutineers at La Chapelle and 81 among those at St Pol.
15 *BMO*, IV/1, p. LX; 'Hermano perico', a popular Spanish ballad from 1588, quoted in Jérez-Gómez, 'Elizabeth I', 151–2.
16 Tellechea Idígoras, *Otra cara*, 397 (global figures), 409 (widows and orphans), and 411–92 (list of the dead from Guipúzcoa, with details on how and where they died); García de Palacio, *Instrucción*, ff. 119v–20.
17 Tellechea Idígoras, *Otra cara*, 425 (the Iriarte brothers) and 481 (Villafranca: both men left an illegitimate son to mourn them).

18 ABB *VC* 1214, 'Lista' by Carlos Longin, January 1590 (noting that the English had already released many captured seamen from France, Italy, the Netherlands and Portugal). See also KML *MSP: CC* 8/1–170, list of the crews aboard 11 Baltic *urcas* embargoed in July 1587. They would later join the squadron of Andalucia.
19 HSA *Altamira* 7/I/16, Santa Cruz to Medina Sidonia, 24 January 1582, forwarded to Philip on 8 February, with his irate comment in a *billete* to Mateo Vázquez on the 16th; HSA *Altamira* 5/III/9, Vázquez to Santa Cruz, 18 February 1582, minute.
20 AGI *IG* 740/223, *consulta* of the Council of the Indies, 8 February 1584.
21 *BMO*, II, 473–4, and III/3, 1932–3, Recalde to Philip, 13 December 1586 and 13 February 1588; idem, IV/1, 227, Medina Sidonia to Philip, 12 March 1588.
22 There can be no doubt about the personal briefing: see *BMO*, III/1, 427–8, Iñigo de Aranza, agent of Guipúzcoa at Court, to the Diputación, 26 May 1587; ibid., III/2, 684–5, Oquendo to the Diputación, 8 July 1588. Tellechea Idígoras, *Otra cara*, published both documents with the correct recipients (pp. 254–6), and also Oquendo's will (pp. 533–72).
23 On Valdés's botched raid, and its consequences, see Fernández Duro, *La conquista*, 11–17.
24 *BMO*, IV/2, 310–11, Philip to Don Jorge Manrique, 9 May 1588, in answer to his complaint that Flores and his fleet arrived 'without anchors and ballast' and with little drinking water – presumably because of their hasty departure.
25 Parker, 'Anatomy', 322 and 340 n. 48, argued that Leyva referred to Luis de León's poem, 'A la salida de la Cárcel'; Tellechea Idígoras, *Otra cara*, 533–72, Oquendo's will. Of the other squadron generals, we have located only the will of Diego Flores, and it mentioned no books.
26 *BMO*, IV/1, Fuentes to Idiáquez and Moura, 16 February 1588; *BMO*, IV/2, 592, Medina Sidonia to Philip, 28 June 1588.
27 Phillips, *The struggle*, 29 n. 5, Cristobal de Eraso to Juan Delgado, secretary of state for war, 27 September 1581; *BMO*, IV/1, 59–60, denunciation of Flores to Philip, 21 February 1588, anonymous but certainly by an officer on the Straits expedition. Phillips, *The struggle*, 46, noted that Pedro de Sarmiento also accused Flores of 'cowardice, dishonesty, dereliction of duty [and] greed' during the operation.
28 AGI *IG* 740/223, *consulta* of the Council of the Indies, 8 February 1584 (Gómez had also crossed swords with Diego Flores, who deprived him of command of his ship in 1574, but he appealed successfully: AGI *Justicia* 1167 N. 6 R. 3); *FBD*, 341–2 (Acuña in 1561–2); AHN *OM Santiago* 5930, *pruebas*, unfol., testimony of Licenciados Masa and Cortés (the Inquisitors had summoned and fined Oquendo in 1579 for attempting to suborn a witness in a case against his brother-in-law).
29 AHN *OM Santiago* 8435, Valdés *pruebas* begun in April 1565 and concluded in March 1566, information taken in Gijón, 21 May 1565. In his defence, other witnesses asserted that 'everybody' in Asturias bought and sold produce, and numbered fornicating priests among their ancestors 'without anyone thinking it disqualified them for a knighthood'.

30 Tellechea Idígoras, *Otra cara*, 299–301 (royal warrants for Oquendo to carry arms, 6 February 1562) and 89–130; AHN *OM Santiago* 5930, Oquendo *pruebas* begun October 1582 and concluded December 1584, unfol., including evidence from García de Arce: ('los que le tienen mala boluntad, que son muchos en esta villa') and a memorial of Oquendo, 19 October 1583 ('mis enemigos [me] han hecho guerra en mi ausencia').

31 AHN *OM Santiago* 4715, Luzón *pruebas* begun January 1597 and concluded July 1598, another huge folder because of the 'tachas' against Don Alonso, and papers about revoking the knighthood of his father, Don Francisco: therefore despite 'auer seruido mucho al Rey y sido su maestre de campo y auer pedido áuito mucho tiempo a su Magestad, no se le a dado' to Don Alonso because of his alleged Jewish ancestor, and because a 'vando contrario suyo, an querido poner mácula en su linpieza, así por las enemistades que con ellos tenían' (testimony of Juan Aldrete, 20 February 1597, ff. 1, 7).

32 AHN *OM Santiago* 9232 (Zúñiga) is somewhat unclear, but clarity emerges from AHN *AEESS* 11/36, Philip to the duke of Sessa, 15 June 1592, requesting a dispensation so that Zúñiga's nephew, the future count-duke of Olivares, could obtain a knighthood despite the 'stain'. Although we could not find the *pruebas* of Ascoli, those of his son in 1631 cover several hundred folios because Doña Eufrasia de Guzmán was descended from 'Bishop Paul, a Jew' (AHN *OM Santiago* 4428).

33 ASF *MdP* 3254, unfol., 'Avviso' from Madrid, 26 April 1581; HSA *Altamira* 7/II/32–4, count of Barajas to Philip, and the sentences on Ascoli, Enríquez and others, 3, 10 and 17 September 1587; ASF *MdP* 4918/163–5, Vincenzo Alemanni to the grand duke, 19 September 1587.

34 BAV *UL* 1115/178–9, Avviso dated 6 February 1588, noted that Philip approved Ascoli's appeal to suspend his exile so that he could join the Armada; *BMO*, IV/2, 34, Philip to Medina Sidonia, 28 March 1588.

35 ASP *CF* 150, unfol., Juan del Monte Pichardo to Cardinal Farnese, 7 March 1587, on the decision to imprison the marquis in Turégano Castle.

36 BZ 152/41, Leyva to Medina Sidonia, Barcelona, 22 January 1582, copy (the duke had married the daughter of the princess of Eboli, who was widely suspected of having an affair with Secretary of State Antonio Pérez; Leyva asked the duke to help him regain Philip's favour); *BMO*, III/3, 506–7, Philip to Antonio de Guevara, 9 June 1587; *BMO*, IV/2, 204–5, Philip patent to Leyva, 22 April 1588.

37 *BMO*, II, 116–17, Francisco de Estrada to Philip, 13 April 1586; *BMO*, III/2, 875, Diego Maldonado to Philip, 8 August 1587.

38 *BMO*, III/3, 1406–7, Santa Cruz to Philip, 14 November 1587 (the king approved on the 24th: ibid., 1449–50). Our reading of this document differs from Kelly, *Captain Francisco*, 114.

39 HHStA *Staatenabteilung Spanien: Diplomatische Korrespondenz*, Karton 11/375–6v, list of *aventureros* aboard the Armada dated 10 May 1588 sent to the emperor by Ambassador Khevenhüller, reproduced in Parker, 'Lope de Vega'.

40 *BMO*, IV/1, 243–5, 'Relación de la visita', 19 March 1588; ibid., 251, Oquendo to Philip, 19 March 1588 ('El duque, luego que llegó, visitó toda la Armada y entró en todas las naves y mandó que luego envergasen las velas').

41 *La felicíssima Armada*, Lisbon, 9 May 1588 (printed in *BMO*, IV/2, 298–308); BZ 143/77, Philip to Mateo Vázquez, and rescript, 3 June 1588 (Vázquez described the document as 'bien curiosa', which means both 'curious' and 'detailed'). When detailed statements of the Armada's strength at Corunna reached the Escorial, Philip refused to share them with his ministers in Madrid for fear 'someone will print them like the rest': *BMO*, IV/3, 172, Idiáquez to Philip and rescript, 16 July 1588.

42 These figures are derived from documents in *BMO*. Our higher totals include vessels not included therein but for which there is documentary evidence that they joined the Armada at the last minute: three *pataches* from Castro Urdiales, and *San Bautista de la Esperanza*, also from Castro Urdiales, a *nave* in the Levant squadron. We have found no figures for the soldiers or seamen aboard these four vessels.

43 IVdeDJ 53/5/15, Philip to Vázquez, 27 January 1576; Maura, *El designio*, 38, Philip to Medina Sidonia, 29 October 1578. See also TNA *SP* 70/143/29, Sir John Smythe to Walsingham, Madrid, 5 February 1577, reporting a conversation in which Secretary of State Zayas told him 'the king having infinite matters of great importance, that *he could not well remember the particularities of things delivered unto him by speech*' (our italics).

44 *Co.Do.In.*, XXXV, 61, Philip to Alba, 2 August 1580, holograph postscript; *BMO*, IV/3, 256, Philip to Don Bernardino de Mendoza, 28 July 1588, italics added.

45 TNA *SP* 70/136/38, Sir Henry Cobham to Burghley, Madrid, 14 November 1575; ASVe *SDS* 20/68–72, Lippomano to Venice, 14 April 1587 (partial precis in *CSPV*, VIII, 266).

46 IVdeDJ 61/130, Philip to Pedro de Hoyo, April 1567; IVdeDJ 51/162, 180 and 181, Vázquez to Philip and reply, 11 April and 15 October 1578, and 26 January 1581.

47 IVdeDJ 53/3/56 and 144/36, Vázquez to Philip and reply, 13 May and 11 December 1574.

48 *BMO*, III, 1006–7, Philip to Parma, 4 September 1587 (compare Naish, 'Documents', 7–11, royal assurances to Santa Cruz, 14 September 1587, quoted in ch. 8 below); *BMO*, IV/1, 172–3, same to same, 6 March 1588; ibid., 275, Philip to Medina Sidonia, 21 March 1588.

49 Rizzacasa, *Predittioni*, sig. D1; RAH *Ms.* 9–2320/5v, Creswell to Philip III, 1602: 'el santo varón … me dixó que aquella Armada iría en humo' – so perhaps he did indeed enjoy a hotline to Heaven.

50 Kagan, *Lucrecia's dreams*, 75–6, dreams of 14 December 1587 and 16 January 1588 (the marquis died on 9 February); AHN *Inq* 3712/4, f. 19, dream of 1 May 1588; Horozco y Covarrubias, *Tratado*, ff. 37–8: the 'particular engaño desta donzella que no se nombra'. Calderón Calderón, 'Memoria e imagen', 514–17, gives more examples of prophecies of doom recorded over the winter of 1587–8 by the Lisbon chronicler Pero Roiz Soares.

51 Ribadeneira, *Exhortación* (although this is undated, the author sent a copy to Medina

Sidonia in mid-May 1588: *BMO*, IV/2, 395–6); ASV *LP* 46/121, 'Breve instrucción para todos los que huvieren de ganar el Santíssimo Iubileo'; BAV *UL* 1115/199–206, 'Avvisi' of 28 May and 25 June 1588 (on the processions and the royal family at prayer).

52  ASF *MdP* 4919/88, Alemanni to Tuscany, 6 February 1588. See the similar sentiments of the ambassadors of Lucca (ASL *Anziani*, 644, Compagni to Republic, 26 June 1588) and Ferrara (ASMo *AS* 15, unfol., Ripa to Ferrara, 5 March, 30 April, 25 June and 23 July 1588).

53  *BMO*, IV/2, 430–2, Medina Sidonia's General Orders, 21 May 1588 (TNA *SP* 12/210/19–23 is an original copy, signed by Medina Sidonia and endorsed by Lord Burghley, presumably captured on *Rosario*; *CSPSp*, IV, 290–4, prints a partial English translation, but without a date); von Klarwill, *Fugger-Zeitungen*, I, 117, Madrid, 18 May 1588 (news forwarded from Lisbon); *BMO*, IV/2, 181, memorandum by Medina Sidonia's confessor, 17 April 1588 (advance absolution).

54  *BMO*, IV/2, 395–6, Ribadeneira to Ana Félix de Guzmán, Madrid, *c.* 15 May 1588; ibid., 338–9, Medina Sidonia to Philip, 14 May 1588.

55  *BMO*, IV/3, 71 and 123–4, Recalde to Martín de Idiáquez, 6 and 11 July 88; Génard, 'Index', *Antwerpsch Archievenblad*, I, 332, and III, 140, entries for 25 February and 2 March 1577; *BMO*, II, 473–4, Recalde to Philip, 13 December 1586.

56  Last Will of Flores, 6 January 1595, https://investigadoresrb.patrimonionacional.es/node/8323; *BMO*, III/3, 1643, and IV/1, 251, Oquendo to Philip, 2 January and 19 March 1588.

57  *BMO*, III/3, 648–9, Leyva to Philip, 3 July 1587; IV/2, 261, Leyva to Idiáquez, 7 May 1588: Parker, 'Anatomy', 320–2, Leyva to Recalde, 12 and 17 August 1588.

58  Mattingly, *The defeat*, 223, quoting a letter from Muzio Buongiovanni, papal collector in Lisbon, to Cardinal Montalto. Mattingly speculated that the 'highest and most experienced officer' quoted was Recalde; but we believe similar remarks by Bertendona (ch. 8) make him a more likely source. Mattingly did not provide a date or call number for the letter, and we could not find it among Buongiovanni's letters in ASV *NS* 36/404–69. Neither could Tellechea Idígoras, who published the rest of the collector's letters in *'La Invencible'*, 99–108.

59  *BMO*, IV/3, 307–10, 'Relación' by an anonymous Portuguese Jesuit; *BMO*, IV/2, 338, Medina Sidonia to Philip, and 384–5, 'Relación' of someone aboard *Annunciata*, both dated 14 May 1588.

60  *BMO*, IV/2, 450–1, Medina Sidonia to Philip, 28 May 1588; Canestrini and Desjardins, *Négociations*, IV, 737, Tuscan ambassador Cavriana to Vinta, Paris, postscript dated 22 November 1587.

## 2. 'The great bog of Europe'

1  Feltham, *A brief character of the Low Countries* (written in the 1620s), 1, 5.
2  *Nueva Co.Do.In.*, V, 368, Don Luis de Requesens to Philip, 6 October 1574; IVdeDJ 53/3/87 and 77, Philip to Mateo Vázquez, 4 and 18 July 1574. See similar statements in ch. 1.

3   TNA *SP* 77/2/201–3, Robert Spencer to Burghley, 15 March 1588 NS. On Parma's apprenticeship at the Court of Spain (which included German lessons), see Rodríguez-Salgado, 'Kinship', 61–7.
4   Bianchi, 'Una riserva', 332–3, instructions to Amadeo from his brother Duke Charles Emanuel, Philip II's son-in-law, September 1587; BAV *VL* 7750/7, 'Advertimientos' of Idiáquez for his son, 13 February 1587.
5   Lincoln Record Office, *Ancaster Muniments*, X, fo. 1, Lord Willoughby to (?) Cristóbal de Mondragón, June 1586.
6   Lodge, *Illustrations*, II, 400, Burghley to the earl of Shrewsbury, 27 May 1589 OS. The 'French king' was Henry III; the 'king of Scots' was James VI.
7   *CSPF 1581–2*, 346 and 406, Thomas Stokes to Walsingham, 22 October 1581 and 28 January 1582.
8   Strada, *De bello Belgico*, II, 325–6.
9   Bertini, 'La nazione italiana', 270–1; Biblioteca Nazionale Centrale, Rome, *Fondo Gesuitico* Ms. 371/96–v, mentions the games (we thank Giampiero Brunelli for this reference); Rinaldi, quoted by van der Essen, *Alexandre Farnèse*, V, 295.
10  Gascoigne, *The complete works*, II, 599; Evans, *The works of Sir Roger Williams*, 14 (from his *Art of Warre*, 1590); Brugmans, III, 284–6, Leicester to Burghley, 15 November 1587 NS.
11  Moryson, *Itinerary*, I, 47 (he visited in 1592). The magnificent monument which stands today in the Nieuwe Kerk at Delft was built by Hendrik de Keyser between 1614 and 1622.
12  AGS *Estado* 590/22, Parma to Philip, 28 February 1586.
13  BNF *Ms. Espagnol* 182/212, Parma to (?) Don Juan de Zúñiga, 16 September 1585; AGS *SP* 2534/212, Parma to Philip, 30 September 1585; AGS *Estado* 589/120, same to same, 31 December 1585.
14  *Co.Do.In.*, LXXIII, 323 (from Vázquez, 'Los sucesos'); *BMO*, III/1, 231, Parma to Idiáquez, 28 April 1587. More details on this unit in O'Donnell, *La fuerza*, 36–9.
15  AGS *Estado* 592/141, Parma to Philip, 14 November 1587.
16  AGRB *Audience* 189/153–7, Parma to Philip, 3 February 1588, minute ('ilz sont diminuez d'ung ters pour le moings de ce qu'ilz estoient auparavant, oultre ung million de malades'); BL *Sloane Ms.* 262/81v–2, from 'An ephemeris or diarie', almost certainly written by Dr Valentine Dale (one of Elizabeth's peace commissioners).
17  Tamalio, 'I Gonzaga', 149–50, Ercole Gonzaga to the duke of Mantua. Although this is undated, Gonzaga mentioned that 'Captain Moresin arrived 15 days ago' with news from Medina Sidonia. Since Moresin arrived on 22 June, Gonzaga must have written his letter on or about 7 July 1588.
18  Tamalio, 'I Gonzaga', 149–50, Ercole Gonzaga to the duke of Mantua, c. 7 July 1588.
19  ASN *CF* 1722/II, unfol., Queralt to Parma, 17 July 1588, holograph.
20  Laughton, I, 213, Winter to Walsingham, 20 June 1588 OS. Winter based his estimate on his recollections of the English expedition to Scotland in 1544, which

had involved 260 vessels. Note that Winter used 'tons burthen': tons displacement would be approximately 50 per cent higher (see p. 555 above).

21 AGS *CMC* 2a/8, 12, 16, 885, 1077 and 3a/692 and 713, the fragmented accounts of the paymaster of the Flanders Fleet, Thorivio Martinez, for 1587–8 (Riaño Lozano, *Los medios navales*, 168–78, quoted some extracts, not always accurately); BAV *UL* 1056/304, 'Aviso' from Antwerp, 18 June 1588; *CSPF* XXI.4, 511, 'Advertisements' of 22 June 1588 OS; Laughton, I, 321–2, Leicester to Walsingham, 26 July 1588 OS, holograph.

22 AGS *CMC* 2a/885, Cuenta of Thorivio Martínez, pliego 145 (400 florins paid to Artus Estamelart); and 2a/1077, unfol. (2,400 florins paid to Hans Smit for painting almost 200 flags); TNA *SP* 101/9/85, 'Advertisements' sent to Burghley in September 1588; *Co.Do.In.*, LXXIII, 347 (Vázquez, *Sucesos*); Piot, *Chroniques*, 672 (from an anonymous 'Vlaemsche Kronyk' composed in Dunkirk); Brugmans, III, 284–6, Leicester to Burghley, 5 November 1587 OS; BL *Harleian Ms.* 287/86, 'Advertisements' of March/April 1588; TNA *SP* 101/9/80, '1588 occurents' (undated but probably June 1588); van Meteren, *Historia*, 178–9; RAZ *Notulen van de Staten van Zeeland 1588*, letters to Count Maurice of Nassau and Queen Elizabeth, 13 July 1588 NS.

23 ASN *CF* 2125/I, 'Registro di contabilità, 1588'; van der Essen, 'De auteur'.

24 AGRB *SEG* 11/54v, Order to pay 600 escudos for the salaries of the 'congregación de padres de diversas naciones' involved 'en la jornada que se trae entre manos', 17 August 1588; van Meteren, *Belgische ofte Nederlandtsche historie*, f. 287v (English text in Hakluyt, *The principal navigations*, I, 388).

25 TNA *SP* 77/4/231–3, Dale to Elizabeth, 12 July 1588 OS; BL *Sloane Ms.* 262/67v, from the 'Ephemeris or diarie' (almost certainly written by Dale); Bertini, *Militari italiani*, 239–42, Parma's instructions to Count Niccolò Cesi, going to Rome, August 1588.

26 *BMO*, IV/2, 105–6, Philip to Parma, 5 April 1588, drafted when 'estamos en 3 de abril' but 'por un día o dos o tres esperemos' before sending it.

27 Examples from Soen, '*Reconquista*'; quotation from p. 21. She argues plausibly that Parma's demand that the magistrates of Ghent 'humiliate' themselves reflected a desire to repeat the punishment imposed on the city in 1540 by his grandfather Charles V after an earlier rebellion: see pp. 13–14.

28 *BMO*, III/3, Philip to Olivares, 7 February 1588; *BMO*, IV/2, 1056, Philip to Parma, 5 April 1588; AGRB *SEG* 11 ff. 2 (Westmoreland, 7 August 1588) and 9 (Archbishop MacShamhradháin, 3 May 1588). BRB *Ms.* II.1155/214 (Rinaldi) and Bianchi, 'Una riserva', 332–3, listed other illustrious Catholics who came to join Parma for the invasion.

29 *BMO*, II, 254–5, Philip to Parma, 18 July 1586, minute; Japikse, V, 541–4 (Lord Buckhurst's explanation to the States-General, 14 April) and 580–4 (on the Danish peace plan, 26 May 1587); *CSPF*, XXI.3, 83, letter of Buckhurst to the towns of the United Provinces, May 1587; Brugmans II, 236–41, Buckhurst to Elizabeth, 10 May 1587; and *BMO*, III/1, 413, Frederick of Denmark to Parma, 14 May 1587 OS.

30 Cadoppi, 'Un "macello di huomini da bene"', 163, Livio Podocattaro to Ferrara, Bruges, 29 July 1588.

## 3. 'A fleet to impeach it'

1  *HMC Seventh Report, Appendix Part V*, 45, Privy Council to the Lords Lieutenant of England, 27 June 1588 OS.
2  Ibid., 48–9, same to same, 23 July 1588 OS.
3  Raleigh, *The Historie*, 101, 105 (bk. V, ch. 1, section ix).
4  Laughton, I, 83–6 and 201, Howard to Walsingham, 29 February and 14 June 1588 (both dates OS); Rodger, *The safeguard*, 327.
5  Hildred, *Weapons of Warre*, 856–61, 883–5; Knighton and Loades, *The Anthony Roll*, 42–3.
6  *CSPV*, II, 105, Antonio Bavarin to the Pesaro company, London, 4 July 1513.
7  TNA *SP* 11/6/16 and 17, 'Memoria', August/September 1555 (English translation in Knighton and Loades, *The navy*, 306). Philip and Mary also persuaded parliament to pass legislation overhauling the militia: 4 and 5 Philip and Mary c 2, 'Act for taking of musters', and c 3, 'Act for horse, armour and weapons'.
8  TNA *SP* 11/10/1, Privy Council order, 6 January 1557 (partly printed in Oppenheim, *A history*, 112); TNA *SP* 11/10/2, Philip and Mary warrant dormant to the Lord Treasurer, 10 January 1557.
9  TNA *SP* 12/2/107, untitled list of the queen's ships, including the plaintive plea about 'continuance', 20 February 1559 (although unsigned, such detailed information can only have come from the navy's principal officers); TNA *SP* 12/3/131–5, 'A boke for see causes', 24 March 1559. Hattendorf, *British naval documents*, 62–70, printed part of this important document; Glasgow, 'Maturing', 12–14 and 23–4, and Redding, 'English naval expansion', 647–8, discussed it and other position papers prepared at the same time.
10  Oppenheim, *A history*, 122, quoting the Commonplace book of Robert Commaundre, a Chester cleric; Nichols, *Diary of Henry Machyn*, 203 (entry for 3 July 1559).
11  TNA *SP* 70/13/225–36, Throckmorton to Elizabeth, heavily ciphered, and Forbes, *A full view*, I, 415–18, Throckmorton to Cecil, both written on 28 April 1560. Throckmorton was related to Katherine Parr, the sixth wife of Henry VIII, and served in her household where he would have met Princess Elizabeth. Queen Mary imprisoned both her half-sister and Throckmorton in the Tower.
12  TNA *SP* 12/15/4–5, Ordinance 'for the office of our Admiraltie and maryn affaires', undated but filed with 'Letters and papers 1560 undated' (mostly printed in *MM*, XIII [1927], 48–50).
13  Corbett, *Fighting instructions*, 42; and idem, *Signals and instructions*, 364–71, Winter's 'Orders to be observed at the seas in the queen's majesty's ships', 31 March 1558; TNA *SP* 12/3/136–42, 'The state and report of the officers of the ordenaunce' presented by Winter to the queen on 24 March 1559; Parker, 'The *Dreadnought*

revolution', 287 (artillery carried in 1596 by those of the queen's ships which had fought in 1588, adding *Revenge*, lost in 1591).
14 Hunt, *Ellesmere Ms.* 6206B/15v–16, 'The names of Her Majesty's shipps with the nomber of men, and furniture requisite for the setting forth of the same', 1574; BL *Additional Ms.* 69,892/5, 'A note', 24 May 1574.
15 Kemp, *The Papers of Admiral Sir John Fisher*, I, 40, Fisher to the Committee of Seven, May 1904.
16 Laughton, I, 34–7, 'The bargain of John Hawkyns', 1579; Adams, 'New light', 107–11, schedule of ships to be 'new built' between 1584 and 1599.
17 McElvogue, 'The hull', 98–9. Knighton and Fontana, 'More documents', and Knighton, 'Overgunning', present evidence of plans to improve the ability of *Mary Rose* and two other ships to fire their big guns forward.
18 Raleigh, *The works*, II, 78.
19 Rodger, *The safeguard*, 331–2.
20 Corbett, *Papers*, 207–10, Winter to Burghley, 8 April 1585 OS; ibid., 224–31, statement by Pett and Baker, 12 October 1587 OS; ibid., 242–7, 'Articles of discovery', 1587 (anonymous but probably by George Fenner).
21 Laughton, I, 79–80, Howard to Burghley, 21 February 1588; ibid., 199–202, Howard to Walsingham, 14 June 1588 (both dates OS).
22 Rodger, *The safeguard*, 332.
23 TNA *SP* 12/215/77, Seymour to Walsingham, 23 August 1588 (our reading differs slightly from Laughton, II, 145–6); TNA *PROB* 11/87/268, Will of Hawkins, 3 March 1595 (both dates OS). On the shouting match, see ch. 16.
24 Maclean, *The life*, 33–4, except that Maclean has 'marines' instead of 'mariners': see the correct text in Brewer and Bullen, *Calendar of Carew Manuscripts*, I, pp. lxxx–lxxxi.
25 Hellowes, *A booke of the inuention of the art of navigation*, dedication to Howard; Rodger, *The safeguard*, 302, quoted Drake's declaration and pointed out that it appeared in a hostile account intended to discredit him.
26 Corbett, *Papers*, 291–9, printed the list (6 of the 76 were named Drake, 4 were named Winter, and 4 more were named Raleigh). The annotations on the original (TNA *SP* 12/186/15) show that Burghley took a personal interest.
27 Laughton, I, 96–102, Howard to Burghley, 9 March 1588; ibid., 224, Seymour to Howard, 23 June 1588 (both dates OS).
28 BL *Sloane Ms.* 226/11v and 14v–15, 'A breefe and a true discourse of the late honorable voyage' to Cadiz by Roger Marbeck, Howard's personal physician, italics added.
29 Details from Keeler, *Sir Francis Drake's West Indian voyage*, 12–16; and Andrews, *Elizabethan privateering*, 89–94.
30 Maclean, *The life*, 32–3 (Henry in the Solent); Nichols, *The diary of Henry Machyn*, 203 and 232; Johnson, 'Making mathematical practice', 135, quoting a letter from the Navy Board in November 1588, referring to the new 'ships, galeasses and crompsters' commissioned by the Board: see ch. 18.

31 Nichols, *The progresses*, I, 354; ibid., III, 56–7 and 117; TNA *E* 351/2218 and AO1/1684/17, accounts of Hawkins as Treasurer of the Navy, 1582. For Philip's presence at the launch of *San Felipe* in January 1582, see ch. 1.
32 Hartley, *Proceedings*, I, 538, speech of Sir Walter Mildmay, Chancellor of the Exchequer, to the House of Commons, January 1581.
33 Maclean, *The life*, 31; *ODNB* entries for the relationships between survivors of the 1545 campaign. Corbett, *Papers*, 242–7, 'Articles of discovery', stated that Winter had 'knowledge of my Lord [Leicester] since infancy'.
34 Hammer, 'Sex and the Virgin Queen', 80–1 (Elizabeth 'bitch-slapping' Mary Shelton in 1574 and Essex in 1598).
35 Cole, *The portable queen*, 38 (see also pp. 29–31, on the queen's visits to Cecil and Leicester); *Co.Do.In.*, XC, 98–101, Guzmán de Silva to Philip, 10 July 1568; Nichols, *The progresses*, III, 57 (the next morning, the queen sent magistrates to Islington, where they arrested and imprisoned 74 'begging rogues': Islington has clearly gone downhill since then).
36 Parker, 'Queen Elizabeth's Instructions', 205–6, Instructions to Howard, 20 December 1587; *APC*, XVI, 221–2, Privy Council to Leicester, 5 August 1588 (both dates OS).
37 BL *Harleian Ms.* 6994/120, Howard to Burghley, 'from Hackney', 13 April 1588, holograph (heavily corrected: Laughton, I, 150–1, did not indicate the corrections); Laughton, I, 159, Howard to Burghley, 'from my house in Deptford', 17 April 1588 (both dates OS; italics added). We note an interesting parallel here with the conduct of the Falklands War in 1982 by Prime Minister Margaret Thatcher: on the advice of one of her predecessors, Harold Macmillan, she excluded all Treasury ministers from her 'War Cabinet': Thatcher, *The Downing Street years*, 188.
38 *HMC 15th Report, Appendix Part V*, 116, Instructions to Howard, 13 May 1588 OS; Rodger, *The safeguard*, 263.
39 *HMC Hatfield House*, VI, 101–2, Thomas Windebank, clerk of the signet, to Robert Cecil, 17 March 1596 OS (two letters, with postscripts). The original commission, signed the following day, was sold at Sotheby's in 2011: https://www.sothebys.com/en/auctions/ecatalogue/2011/english-literature-history-childrens-books-illustrations-l11404/lot.1.html
40 Laughton, I, 192–3, Walsingham to Howard, 9 June 1588; ibid., 202–5, reply, 15 June 1588; ibid., Howard to the Privy Council, 22 June 1588, in reply to their letter of the 17th. Elizabeth continued to question Howard's strategic decisions: see his aggrieved letter to Walsingham dated 13 July 1588: ibid., I, 256–8. All dates OS.
41 Laughton, I, 65–7, Howard to Walsingham, 11 February 1588 OS, holograph (his flagship was then *White Bear*).
42 Hakluyt, *The principal navigations*, I, xxxiv (Epistle dedicatory to Howard, 1598); Corbett, 'Relation', 51–8, Instructions to Howard and Essex, May 1596; TNA *E* 351/2225 (and, more legibly, TNA *AO* 1/1686/23), Hawkins accounts for 1588.
43 Laughton, I, 217–19, Howard to the Privy Council, 22 June 1588; ibid., 48–50, Howard to Walsingham, 27 January 1588 (both dates OS).

44 Laughton, I, 147–9, Drake to Elizabeth, 13 April 1588; ibid., 274–5, Hawkins to Burghley, 17 July 1588, holograph; Taylor, 'Sir William Monson' (he consulted Forman before undertaking at least three other voyages); Laughton, II, 68, Drake to Elizabeth, 18 August 1588 (all dates OS).

45 Brayshay, 'Plymouth's coastal defences', 192–3, proclamation by the town council, 29 August 1587 OS; TNA SP 12/205/118, earl of Sussex to the Privy Council, Portsmouth, 30 November 1587 OS, with annotations by Burghley (printed with some errors in Bruce, *Report*, appendix V).

46 Harvey, *An astrological discourse*, 44–5; Muller, *The excommunication*, 160 (the Canterbury yeoman, with other similar examples); TNA SP 12/194/87–9, Arthur Herrys to Lord Chancellor Bromley, 22 October 1586 OS (examination of John White); BL *Lansdowne Ms.* 54/19–20, examination of Ralph Durdan, June 1587.

47 McGrath, 'The Bloody Questions', 305, 310–12.

48 Sanchez, 'Anti-Spanish sentiment', 160, with quotations from Thomas Stocker, *A tragicall history of the Civile warres of the Lowe Countries* (1583), George Whetstone, *The Honourable Reputation of a Souldier* (1586), and other similar works about events in the Spanish Netherlands.

49 Mears, *National prayers*, 177–81, Whitgift's Injunction of 10 July and Privy Council order of 23 July 1588 (both OS).

50 Churchill, *The world crisis*, III, pt. 1, 106.

# PART II

* Mattingly, *The defeat*, 40, quoting a letter from Mendoza to Philip, Paris, 28 February 1587, upon hearing of the execution of Mary Queen of Scots. *BMO*, II, 636–7, printed the original.

## 4. Armed Neutrality, 1558–80

1 Guy, *My heart*, 95–6 and 468; TNA SP 12/7/169–72v, Elizabeth's Instructions to Winter, 16 December 1559, two drafts in Cecil's hand; TNA SP 52/2/15.I, duke of Norfolk to Winter, 23 January 1560.

2 BL *Cotton Ms.* Caligula B.X/89, Petition of the Privy Council to Elizabeth, 23 March 1560, draft in Cecil's hand; TNA SP 15/21/237, Henry Hastings, earl of Huntingdon, to Cecil, York, 28 December 1572.

3 Marcus, *Elizabeth I*, 65–9, 'Queen Elizabeth's conversations' with Maitland of Lethington, September–October 1561, as reported by Maitland.

4 Duffy, *Fires of faith*, 7.

5 Wernham, *Before the Armada*, 208; Stow, *The chronicles*, 1085.

6 SLEE *Ms.* &-III-23/68a–73a, *Diarium . . . in rebellione Thomae Wyort*, printed in Latin (English translation in Malfatti, *The accession*, 65–75 and 132–8); Knighton, *Calendar*, 172 and 211–12, depositions of Thomas White in the Tower, March 1556, and charges against John Dethicke in May 1556. The conspirators probably

intended to carry out their plot during the 'Cane Game' and tournament staged before the monarchs in February 1555.

7   AGS *Estado* 128/378, Philip to Juan Vázquez de Molina, 9 December 1558, holograph postscript (he had learned he was a widower two days before); AGS *Estado* 811/93, Elizabeth to Philip, 22 November 1558, copy; TNA *SP* 70/2/49, Philip to Elizabeth, 20 January 1559 (one example among others). The parliamentary act that ratified the marriage contract between Philip and Mary in 1554 (1 Mar. Sess. 3 c 2) prohibited Philip from exercising the titles 'king of England and Ireland' should the queen predecease him.

8   The semi-official letter offering marriage is relatively well known (*CSPSp*, I, 22–3, Philip to Feria, 10 January 1559), but the king's secret letters on the subject are not: FCDM *AH* R7–1 and R7–21, Philip to Feria, 10 and 28 January 1559, both holographs. For the humiliating terms of his marriage treaty to Mary, which left Philip 'constitutionally cuckolded', see Samson, 'Changing places'.

9   FCDM *AH* R7–23, Philip to Feria, 21 March 1559, holograph. Poor little king.

10  Fernández Álvarez, *Tres embajadores*, 242–6, Philip's instruction to M. de Glajon, March [?] 1560. See also ASP *CF* 107, unfol., Tomás de Armenteros to Margaret of Parma, 26 February 1560; and AGRB *Audience* 778/34, minutes of the Council of State, Brussels, 25 October 1560 (note that all these sources contradict the account presented by Wernham, *Before the Armada*, 256, based exclusively on English records).

11  *Co.Do.In.*, XC, 14–15, Philip to Guzmán de Silva, [19] February 1568. *CSPSp*, II, 3, dated his English summary 4 February 1568, but Guzmán's reply gave the date 19 February: *Co.Do.In.*, XC, 38.

12  Serrano, *Correspondencia*, II, 360, Philip to Don Juan de Zúñiga, his ambassador in Rome, 8 March 1568; *Co.Do.In.*, XC, 70–1, Philip to Guzmán de Silva, 23 May 1568. Illescas, *Historia pontifical*, soon became a best-seller in both Spain and Spanish America, and Medina Sidonia took a copy with him when he boarded the Armada. See three offending passages sent to Elizabeth in TNA *SP* 70/98/5.

13  BMO, I, 1–4, Philip's Instructions to Spes, 23 June 1568; Brunetti and Vitale, *La corrispondenza*, I, 445, Ambassador Donà to Venice, 11 March 1572. Guy, *My heart*, 173–4, documents Mary's contact with Spain in 1563–5.

14  Green, 'Letters', 438–9, Pedro Menéndez de Avilés to Philip, 15 October 1565, a report brought to the king by Diego Flores de Valdés. See Philip's endorsement on p. 459, verified from Massachusetts Historical Society, Francis Parkman Papers, vol. XXVIII, p. 60.

15  Unwin, *The defeat of John Hawkins*, 186–200.

16  *Archivo Documental Español*, XVI (*Negociaciones con Francia*, XI), 394–6, Mary to Philip, 30 November 1568, received 6 February 1569, Spanish translation (Labanoff, *Lettres*, II, 237–41, printed a French re-translation of a Spanish version of Mary's French original); Rodríguez, *Don Francés de Álava*, 301–2, Philip to Álava, his ambassador in France, 18 February 1569; idem, 310–11, Philip to Mary, 28 February 1568 (signed 'Your good brother and ally').

17 *CSPSp*, II, 109, Philip to Alba, 18 February 1569; Rodríguez, *Don Francés de Álava*, 317, Philip to Álava, 20 March 1569.
18 Sharp, *Memorials*, 38–9 and 78–82, Robert Bowes to the earl of Sussex, 12 and 29 November 1569; TNA *SP* 53/4/64, earl of Shrewsbury to Cecil, Tutbury, 21 November 1569.
19 *CSPSp*, II, 254, Philip to Spes, 30 June 1570.
20 *BMO*, I, 42, Philip to Alba, 22 January 1570: a remarkably convoluted letter. The king did not yet know that Alba had not only arranged the return of the treasure confiscated by Elizabeth but also sent an agent to England to receive it: see AA 159/19, Alba's patent to Tommaso Fieschi, 24 December 1569.
21 *BMO*, I, 43–7, Alba to Philip, 23 and 24 February 1570.
22 *Sotheby's Auctions e-Catalogue, 2014*, item 403, Elizabeth's Instructions to Howard, 1 September 1570. This seems to have been Howard's first experience of naval command.
23 *BMO*, I, 52–3, Elizabeth to Philip, 20 March 1571, and ibid., 54–5, account of a meeting between Elizabeth's envoy (Sir Henry Cobham) and Feria, 8 June 1571. These documents make clear that the queen wished Cobham to settle the trade dispute and arrange a new exchange of ambassadors. The account in Wernham, *Before the Armada*, 308, based on English sources, seems misleading.
24 LPL *Ms.* 3197/33, Burghley to Shrewsbury, Mary's custodian, 5 September 1571, holograph; details of this aspect of the plot from *CSPSc*, IV, 30–2, bishop of Ross to Burghley, 9 November 1571. If Mary had somehow managed to reach Hawkins, he would presumably have 'conveyed' her back to gaol because he was almost certainly a double agent: see Parker, 'The place of Tudor England', 217–19.
25 HSA *HC* 380/98 folder 50, unfol., Spes to Zúñiga, London, 25 March 1571, was explicit about this: 'For his own security, the letter from the duke of Norfolk is written in the cypher that I recently sent to you.' Reliance by all protagonists on the same cipher fatally compromised the plot.
26 Rodríguez, *Don Francés de Álava*, 257 and 291, Gabriel de Zayas, Philip's secretary of state, to Álava, 10 September 1568 and 12 January 1569 (need for haste); ibid., 316–18 and 341–2, Philip to Álava, 20 March and 25 June 1569 (resort to foot couriers).
27 Serrano, *Correspondencia*, IV, 382, Castagna to Rusticucci, 9 July 1571.
28 BL *Additional Ms.* 28,336/70 and AGS *Estado* 153/68, Dr Martín de Velasco to Cardinal Espinosa and to Secretary of State Zayas, both from the Escorial on 27 July 1571.
29 Serrano, *Correspondencia*, IV, 382, Castagna to Rusticucci, 9 July 1571; AGS *Estado* 823/150–8, *consulta* of the Council of State, 7 July 1571 (a remarkable document, which recorded a further interview with Ridolfi and the substance of each minister's views at two meetings of the council, all on the same day). Ridolfi's intelligence was correct in at least one detail: Elizabeth did indeed make a progress through Essex in August and September 1571, where she would have been more vulnerable to capture or assassination: see Nichols, *The progresses*, I, 279–82.

30 AA 7/58, Philip to Alba, 14 July 1571, ciphered with decrypt. The king's letter repeated three times that Elizabeth would be 'either killed or captured' (in that order), and in another paragraph used the word 'dispatched' (which, as in English, could mean 'killed'). Throughout the letter he referred to Elizabeth Tudor as 'la Isabel' instead of 'the queen'.
31 *BMO*, I, 57–9, Philip to Alba, 4 August 1571.
32 ARA *Staten Generaal* 12548, loketkas 14B/14, Philip to Alba, 30 August 1571, telling the duke to send money to Mary's supporters in Scotland (some of this money did arrive: see *CSPSc*, IV, 60–1, 168–9 and 226–8); and *Co.Do.In.*, XC, 493–5 (precis in *CSPSp*, II, 333–4), Philip to Spes, 30 August 1571, announcing Hawkins's involvement. For proof that Hawkins's shipmates imprisoned in Seville had by then gained their freedom, see AGS *Estado* 153/75–8, Velasco to Zayas, 5, 9 and 11 August 1571; and AGI *Justicia* 908/2/10v–12, royal pardon for Hawkins and others involved in the events at San Juan de Ulúa, issued 10 August 1571 (register copy).
33 *BMO*, I, 59–62, Alba to Philip, 27 August 1571, in answer to Philip's 'further instructions' sent on 4 August.
34 *BMO*, I, 62–4, Philip to Alba, 14 September 1571.
35 LPL *Ms.* 3197/33, Burghley to Shrewsbury, 5 September 1571, holograph, written in response to information from Hawkins: Williamson, *Hawkins*, 185–6, Hawkins to Burghley, 4 September 1571. Endorsements on Burghley's letter show that the courier did his job well, covering 125 miles in 23 hours.
36 Murdin, *A collection of state papers*, 57, Dr Thomas Wilson to Burghley, 8 November 1571.
37 Alba, *Epistolario*, II, 760, royal apostil on Alba to Philip, 19 October 1571.
38 Cooper, *Recueil*, IV, 315–17, La Mothe to Charles IX, 22 December 1571, relating a conversation 'tout bas' with Elizabeth at dinner three days before. Five months later the queen again told him that Philip's plots to overthrow her justified England's support for the Dutch rebels: ibid., 453–5, La Mothe to Charles IX, 13 May 1572.
39 Pizarro Llorente, *Un gran patrón*, 352–4, citing *consultas* of the Councils of State and of the Inquisition in November 1575; BL *Harleian Ms.* 288/72, Elizabeth's Instructions to Sir Henry Cobham, July 1575.
40 TNA *SP* 15/22, 'Marchant shipps in England, A. 1572', discussed in Pollitt, 'Contingency planning'. See ch. 3 above for *Dreadnought* and her successors.
41 IVdeDJ 88/378, 'Presupuestos y advertencias en caso que se aya de ymbiar a Flandes Armada esta primavera de 1575' prepared by the count of Olivares, who had accompanied Philip to England and the Netherlands in 1554–5, and would later serve as Spanish ambassador in Rome while Philip and the pope planned the Armada; TNA *SP* 12/105/51, Walsingham to Burghley, 6 October 1575, reporting the arrival of '48 sail of Spanish men of war' off the south coast requesting shelter, and noting that 'the General of them is Don Pedro de Valdés, who married Pedro Malenda's [i.e. Menéndez's] daughter'.
42 TNA *SP* 70/136/36, Sir Henry Cobham to Elizabeth, Madrid, 13 November 1575 (about Valdés); TNA *SP* 70/139/123, Philip to Elizabeth, 1 September 1576 (with

a holograph postscript in French); TNA *SP* 70/145/49–50, 'The speech that passed betweene Sir John Smithe and the Archbishop of Toledo, and the evill usage of him', 19 May 1577, in Spanish; BL *Egerton Ms.* 1506/54, Quiroga to Philip, 6 May 1577, with rescript.

43  Details from *The true reporte*, Sig. Aiiiv; TNA *SP* 63/78/59–65, Grey to Elizabeth, 12 November 1580 (in the beautiful handwriting of Grey's secretary, Edmund Spenser), with additions; ibid., ff. 66–8, Grey to Walsingham, 12 November 1580; Wright, *Queen Elizabeth*, II, 120–2, Bingham to Leicester, 12 November 1580.
44  Bouza, *Cartas*, 50–1, Philip to his daughters, Isabella and Catalina, Lisbon, 10 July 1581; *BMO*, I, 409, anonymous account of the failed Terceira landing in 1581.
45  Phillips, *The struggle*, 100 (the account of Pedro de Rada, also consulted in the original: Hunt *Ms.* 59,416/27–8v) and 131–4, Diego Flores's Instructions, 24 September 1581. Other officers in the expedition to the South Atlantic would also sail with the Armada, including Marcos de Aramburu and Gregorio de las Alas.
46  Phillips, *The struggle*, 22.

## 5. Cold War, 1581–5

1  *BMO*, I, 296–7, Mendoza to Philip, 20 October 1581, an account of Mendoza's audience a week before, quotes three sentences by Elizabeth in Italian (although the transcript is incorrect – see *CSPSp*, III, 155–62, for the correct text. Both *CSPSp* and *Co.Do.In.*, XCII, 155–62, incorrectly dated the letter 30 October). See also *BMO*, I, 426–7, same to same, 26 January 1584, reporting his 'exit interview' with the Privy Council at which 'Walsingham said that because he was more fluent in Italian, he would serve as interpreter'.
2  *BMO*, I, 212–13 and 296–7, Mendoza to Philip, 23 March 1580 and 20 October 1581; TNA *SP* 46/17/19, records the payment on 13 September 1581 (thus before Mendoza's audience) of £1,000 to 'the king of Portingale' by a goldsmith who handled secret cash transactions for the English government. For another example of Mendoza's misogyny, see *Co.Do.In.*, XCII, 69–72, same to same, 4 July 1581: he told Elizabeth to her face that she was behaving 'como dama, cuya condición era mostrar de ordinario pesar y desagradecimiento de las cosas en que les hacían mayor servicio'.
3  Fernández Duro, *La conquista*, 396–9, Instruction for Santa Cruz, 6 June 1582.
4  Freitas de Meneses, *Os Açores e o domínio filipino*, I, 150–1, II, 59–61 and 83, Cristóbal de Erasso and Rodrigo de Vargas to Antonio de Erasso, 1 August 1582, and Don Lope de Figueroa to Philip, 3 October 1582.
5  HSA *Altamira* 1/I/6, ff. 189–95, Mateo Vázquez to Philip and rescripts, Lisbon, 6 and 7 September 1582 (this no doubt inspired the similarly outrageous demands of the duke of Medina Sidonia six years later: see ch. 8); BNF *Fonds français* 16,108/365 and 425–7, Ambassador St Gouard to Catherine de Medici, 20 August 1582, and to Henry III, 7 October 1582.
6  Guilmartin, *Gunpowder and galleys*, 228–9, quoting a report by Santa Cruz.

7  *CCG*, X, 331–2, Granvelle to Idiáquez, 21 August 1583; IVdeDJ 51/105, Vázquez to Philip, 22 August 1583.
8  Bouza, *Imagen y propaganda*, 85–6; Keeler, *Sir Francis Drake's West Indian voyage*, 245–6 and 315, 'A summarie and true discourse of Sir Francis Drake's West Indian Voyage'.
9  For a discussion among Philip's ministers of new ways of portraying St James at precisely this time, see IVdeDJ 62/917, Duarte Nunes de Leão to Gabriel de Zayas, 17 August 1585.
10  BNF *Cinq Cents Colbert* 473/589, Catherine de Medici to Michel de Castelnau, French ambassador in London, 25 July 1584 (we thank Mack Holt for this reference). See also *CCG*, XI, 617–19, Zúñiga's first paper of advice to Philip on French policy in the wake of Anjou's death, 27–28 June 1584, based on the assumption that Parma could henceforth concentrate on fighting the Dutch without fear of further French intervention.
11  *CCG*, XI, 621–32, Zúñiga's second and third papers of advice, together with a cover note to Don Juan de Idiáquez, 28 June 1584 (quotation from p. 622). Zúñiga also recommended partitioning France in order to prevent a Huguenot succession: see AGS *Estado* 2855, unfol., 'Para mayor declaración de lo que se ha respondido a los puntos que vinieron en la memoria', June 1584.
12  AGS *Estado* K 1448/38a, Philip to Juan Bautista de Tassis, his special envoy to the League, 4 January 1585. On 4 May 1585 Guise signed a receipt for 300,000 ducats in gold delivered by a courier from Spain: AGS *Estado* K 1573/40.
13  BL *Harleian Ms.* 168/102–5, 'A consultacion touchinge an aide to be sent in to Hollande againste the king of Spaine', 8 March 1585 OS; and *Harleian Ms.* 285/123–4, 'A memorial for Burnham of things to be communicated to Mr Davison and Mr Gilpin', 9 March 1585 OS.
14  TNA *SP* 12/48/165, Walsingham to Cecil, London, 20 December 1568 OS; *ODNB*, 'Elizabeth I' by Patrick Collinson.
15  Digges, *The compleat ambassador*, 216, Walsingham to Leicester, Paris, 28 May 1572, referring to the French Protestants' plan to invade the Netherlands to support Orange; Vaux, *The world encompassed*, quoting Drake's account of his meeting with the queen, facilitated by Walsingham (recorded by John Cooke).
16  BNF *Fonds français* 15,970/15v–16, M. de Vulcob to his uncle, French Ambassador Jacques de la Forest, Stamford, 6 August 1566; TNA *SP* 12/182/41, Leicester to Walsingham, 28 September 1585 OS (the earl eventually set sail for Holland on 9 December). We have put both documents into the first person. See also Leicester's peremptory order forbidding Elizabeth to join him at Tilbury camp in August 1588: ch. 17.
17  Aylmer, *An harborowe*, sig. N3v, published in April 1559. The queen herself may have been Aylmer's source for this chilling anecdote.
18  TNA *SP* 12/193/75–6v, Burghley to Walsingham, Windsor, 10 September 1586, 'at night', holograph. See also *APC*, XIV, 216–20, Privy Council to various officials in southern England and Ireland, 9–10 September 1586, warning that a Spanish fleet lay off Brittany and might 'make descent on some coast of this land'.

19 Anon., *A discouerie of the treasons*, published by the queen's printer, sig. Aiii; *BMO*, I, 426–7 and 428–9, Mendoza to Philip and to Don Juan de Idiáquez, 26 January 1584 (*CSPSp*, III, 513–17, printed a translation of both letters, but incorrectly dated the second one 30 January).

20 TNA *SP* 12/168/8–10, 'A memoryall', 3 February 1584 OS, written entirely in Burghley's hand; BL *Cotton Ms. Galba* C.VII/267–75, naval treaty signed by Orange, Delft, 4 March 1584 (French original, with an English translation of each article in the margin).

21 TNA *SP* 12/274, a volume composed entirely of papers concerning 'The Instrument of an Association for preservation of the Queen's Majesty's Royal Person', starting with the originals, signed and sealed by a dozen Privy Councillors and a score of senior prelates at Hampton Court Palace on 19 October 1584 (ff. 8–9), italics added. The volume also contains copies of the Instrument sent to individual towns and counties, and returned with the signatures of leading subjects. The document from Devon includes the bold signature of Francis Drake. TNA *SP* 12/173/128–33, contains drafts of the Instrument with corrections by Walsingham and others. The verdict comes from Guy, *My heart*, 474.

22 See TNA *SP* 83/23/59–61, 'The resolution of ye conference had upon the question of whyther hir Majesty shuld presently releve the States of ye Low Countryes of Holland and Zelland or no', holograph notes by Burghley rehearsing Spain's past aggression against Elizabeth, 20 October 1584 OS (summary in *CSPF*, XIX, 95–8, and *HMC Salisbury*, III, 67–70); MacCaffrey, *Queen Elizabeth*, 338–9 (citing Camden's *Annals*); Scott, *The Somers Collection*, I, 164–70 (Burghley's argument).

23 BL *Lansdowne Ms.* 43/20–1, Hawkins to Burghley, 20 July 1584 OS, on how to 'strongly annoy and offend the king of Spain'.

24 TNA *SP* 46/17/190, 202 and 205, royal writs dated 29 and 30 July 1584 OS, and TNA *AO* 1/1685/20A, document the issue of £10,000 to Drake for his expedition 'to the Moluccas', starting with £3,500 paid in August 1584. See also BL *Lansdowne Ms.* 41/5, Burghley's memorandum entitled 'The charge of the voyage to the Moluccas', 20 November 1584 OS.

25 TNA *SP* 46/17/183, Elizabeth's warrant dated 23 December 1584, reassuring those who had invested in Drake's voyage that 'if upon any consideration we shall stay their enterprise, to promise hereby that the adventurers shall bear no loss'. Spanish spies soon got wind of Elizabeth's plan to send another expedition to the Moluccas (*CCG*, XII, 58, Granvelle to Margaret of Parma, 29 May 1585), probably via intelligence from Mendoza, now Philip's ambassador in Paris (*CSPSp*, III, 531–2 and 537). For further details on Drake's preparations, see Adams, 'The outbreak', 50–8.

26 *CCG*, XI, 177–9 and 204–5, Granvelle to Idiáquez, 1 and 6 September 1584; ibid., 367–8, Granvelle to Charles de Mansfeld, 27 October 1584. See other letters on the same subject – Granvelle was nothing if not persistent – in *CCG*, XI, 336–8, 340–1, 347–9 and 354–5, all to Idiáquez, 14, 17, 18 and 21 October 1584; and *CCG*, XII, 58 and 70, to Margaret of Parma, 29 May and 22 June 1585.

27 *BMO*, I, 476–7, Philip's order of 25 May 1585. It is worth stressing those words 'with the pretence [*con color*]', because some scholars have argued that the embargo was indeed intended to provide ships for naval operations (like the embargoes of vessels ordered by Philip in 1582, 1583 and 1586–8); but this does not appear to have been the case on this occasion. For contrary views, see Rodríguez-Salgado and Adams, *England, Spain and the Gran Armada*, 6, 56 and 241.

28 *BMO*, I, 490–1, order of 3 July 1585; AGS *GyM* 80/125, 'Copia del apuntamiento que Antonio de Erasso dio a Don Cristóbal de Moura', 20 July 1585; KML *MSP: CC* 7, 'Cuentas del valor de las urcas de estrangeros que por mandado de Su Magestad se arrestaron'.

29 TNA *SP* 12/179/15, earl of Sussex to the Privy Council, 9 June 1585 OS, and ff. 32–3v, interrogation of Guevara, 13 June OS; and TNA *SP* 94/2/78–84, Philip to the *corregidor* of Bilbao, 29 May 1585 NS, received by Guevara on 5 June, original with two distinct English translations. Mote, *The Primrose*, a pamphlet published in 1585, contained a copy of the royal letter.

30 *CCG*, IV, 420, Granvelle to Margaret of Parma, 11 September 1572, expressing his contempt for the English.

31 Bain, *The Hamilton Papers*, II, 650–1, Walsingham to Edward Wotton, 11 June 1585 OS.

32 TNA *SP* 12/179/36–8, Examination of the well-informed Bilbao merchant Pedro de Villareal, 13 June 1585 OS (he also confirmed that Spain sent regular subsidies to the French Catholic League: someone later underlined all information in his testimony concerning France); and TNA *SP* 12/180/59A, captured letter from Juan del Hoyo, a Spanish merchant, 5 July 1585 NS.

33 TNA *SP* 12/177/153–4, 'A plott', spring 1585, draft; Durand-Lapié, 'Un roi détroné', 640, Leicester to Dom Antonio, 24 May 1585 OS; Read, *Mr. Secretary Walsingham*, III, 226–8, Walsingham to Harborne, 8 October 1585 OS, referring to his instructions 'about six months since'; TNA *SP* 12/179/48, Commission to Bernard Drake, 20 June 1585 OS, copy.

34 Corbett, *Papers*, 36–8, 'Articles set down for the merchants, owners of ships and others whose goods have been arrested in Spain, and have licence from the Lord Admiral to reprise upon the Spaniards', 9 July 1585 OS (Adams, 'The outbreak', 46, notes that the issue of letters of reprisal began three days later); TNA *SP* 46/17/184, Elizabeth's warrant, 1 July 1585 OS, and ff. 196 and 200, Privy Council warrants, 11 July 1585 OS.

35 Strype, *The life*, I, 437–40 (collated with LPL *Ms.* 178/15), date established by a message from Leicester to Whitgift, 19 July 1585 OS, asking why he and other prelates had not 'declared their minds unto Her Majesty; the rather to stir Her Highness to the enterprising of so honourable an action'. See also the advice of Bishop John Piers, the queen's almoner, in Strype, op. cit., III, 165–70.

36 Read, *Mr. Secretary Walsingham*, III, 226–8, Walsingham to Harborne, 8 October 1585 OS (Read himself deciphered the original).

37 Details from the English side in Corbett, *Papers*, 39–49, Christopher Carleill to Walsingham, 4–11 October 1585 OS; and from the Spanish side in *BMO*, I,

518–19 and 539, Pedro Bermudez to the Court, 7 October 1585, and Licenciado Antolinez to Philip, 14 November 1585. Almost all foreign ambassadors in Madrid obtained and forwarded to their governments a copy of Bermudez's letter. Mousset, *Dépêches*, 192, Longlée to Henry III, 28 October 1585, and ASVe *SDS* 18, unfol., Gradinegro to the Doge, 25 October 1585, detailed the damage done by Drake.

38  TNA *SP* 12/183/22–4v, Carleill to Walsingham, 4–11 October 1585 OS (Corbett, *Papers*, 42, printed this passage with some errors); *Breeder Verclaringhe vande Vloote van Spaegnien*, unfol.; TNA *SP* 63/137/99, deposition of Sergeant-Major López, 13 October 1588. See also the discussion of motives and sources in Rodríguez-Salgado and Adams, *England, Spain and the Gran Armada*, 59.

39  Kinney, *Elizabethan backgrounds*, 197–211, 'A declaration of the causes moouing the queene of England to giue aide to the defence of the people afflicted and oppressed in the Lowe Countries', 1 October 1585 OS; Kouri, *Elizabethan England*, 49–50, Elizabeth to Hamburg, 5 November 1585 OS.

40  OÖLA *KB* 4/137, Khevenhüller to Rudolf II, 13 October 1585; *CSPF*, XIX, 705, 'Certain things to be considered', 23 July 1585.

## 6. The Grand Design and its Architect

1  Salazar, *Política española*, 24; González Dávila, *Teatro*, 1; Feltham, *A brief character*, 84–5; Camden, *Historie*, bk. IV, 131.

2  Bratli, *Philippe II*, 222, Relation of Philippe de Caverel, Lisbon, 1582; Mousset, *Dépêches*, 366–7, M. de Longlée to Henry III, Madrid, 30 April 1588; BL *Additional Ms.* 28,362/1, count of Barajas to Mateo Vázquez, 1 January 1584.

3  TNA *SP* 70/6/15, Challoner to Elizabeth, Ghent, 3 August 1559, draft; *DHME*, IV, 4 (Sepúlveda, 'Historia'); Cock, *Relación*, 47, 52.

4  AGS *CJH* 27/214, duchess of Francavilla to Ruy Gómez da Silva, her son-in-law, 21 November 1557 (commenting on the king's decision to nominate Fray Bartolomé de Carranza as the next archbishop of Toledo); Santullano, *Obras completas de Teresa de Jesús*, 1394, Teresa to Doña Inés Nieto, undated but 1576–7; Iñiguez de Lequerica, *Sermones funerales*, Sermon by Dr Terrones, 1598, f. 12.

5  AHN *Inquisición Libro* 100/242, 243 and 294, Philip to Quiroga, 26 July, 16 February and October 1576, all holographs.

6  CCG, XI, 272, Granvelle to Margaret of Parma, 21 September 1584; ASV *NS* 19/192, Novara to Rusticucci, 3 May 1587.

7  BCR *Ms.* 2417/39, Silva to Esteban de Ibarra, 13 August 1589.

8  Lhermite, *Passetemps*, II, 130, quoting Juan Ruiz de Velasco as well as his own observation.

9  SLEE, *Ms.* A-1-5 #1, statement by Philip and attestation by Sigüenza, 17 October 1591.

10  BPU *Favre* 30/73v, Philip to Don Luis de Requesens, 20 October 1573, copy of holograph original; AHN *Inquisición libro* 101/325, Philip rescript to a *consulta* from Quiroga, 11 January 1592, italics added.

11 BZ 166/92 and 100, rescripts on Hernando de Vega to Philip, 9 and 11 November 1586; IVdeDJ 51/31, Mateo Vázquez to Philip, 31 May 1574.
12 Brunetti and Vitale, *La corrispondenza*, 340, Leonardo Donà to Venice, 1 August 1571.
13 Firpo, *Relazioni*, VIII, 670, Final Relation of Donà, January 1574.
14 Ugolini, 'Le comunicazioni postali', 321.
15 AA 5/69, Philip to Alba, 7 August 1567, holograph; AGS *Estado* 561/122, Philip to Requesens, 22 October 1574, minute.
16 HSA *Altamira* 5/III/4, Mateo Vázquez apostil on a letter from Juan Fernández de Espinosa, 9 December 1585; *BMO*, III, 1274 and 1225, Philip to Santa Cruz, 21 October and 10 October 1587, italics added.
17 Watts, 'Friction in future war', 91; and Jablonsky, *The owl of Minerva*, 33–6.
18 AHN *OM* 3511/10, Thomas Stukeley to Philip, 15 March [1572]. Parker, *Grand strategy*, ch. 5, discusses other plots against the Tudor regime in the 1570s.
19 *BMO*, I, 395–6, Santa Cruz to Philip, 9 August 1583. See also the poems and other triumphalist commemorations in Fernández Duro, *La conquista*, 94–175.
20 ASC 48/3, Philip to Santa Cruz, 23 September 1583 (partially printed in *BMO*, I, 406).
21 Benítez Sánchez-Blanco, 'De moriscos', 115–19, quoted the debates about expelling the Moriscos in the 1580s, revealed by Don Juan de Idiáquez when the government of Philip III planned the successful operation that took place in 1609–14.
22 *BMO*, II, 315–17, Mendoza to Philip, 13 August 1586, with numerous royal apostils. The ambassador expressed the hope that Howard 'might support the queen of Scotland' if Elizabeth died, and bring over to her side the navy royal. Philip scrawled beside this passage: 'This is the most important thing of all. Howard was very young when I was there [in England].' (*CSPSp*, III, 607, provides a spectacularly inaccurate English translation of this passage.)
23 *BMO*, I, 405–6, Philip to Parma, 12 September 1583, asking his urgent advice about a possible invasion; ibid., 411–12 and 420–1, Parma to Philip, 11 October and 30 November 1583, forwarding a careful survey of the English coasts. In a rare breach of security, four years later Don Bernardino de Mendoza identified the author as Robert Heighington, a Catholic who went into exile after the failure of the Northern Rising in 1569. He had prepared the survey for William Allen: *BMO*, III, 1459. At just this time a search of the lodgings of Francis Throckmorton, who sought Spanish aid for his plot to murder Elizabeth, uncovered a list of ports and havens that an invading army could use. This was probably a copy of Heighington's survey.
24 NMM *Ms.* PHB 1B/435, Olivares to Zúñiga, 24 October 1583, deciphered with royal apostil.
25 *BMO*, I, 478, royal apostil on a letter from the count of Olivares to Philip, 4 June 1585.
26 AGS *Estado* 946/85–8 and 103–4, Olivares to Philip, 4 June and 13 and 28 July 1585; and *BMO*, I, 496, and AGS *Estado* 946/229, Philip to Olivares, 2 and 22

August 1585; Altadonna, 'Cartas de Felipe II a Carlos Manuel', 157, Philip to Savoy, 23 August 1585; AGS *Estado* 1260/211, Philip to Count Sfondrato, his ambassador to Savoy; and idem, 1261/90, to the duke of Terranova, governor of Milan, 22 August 1585. To please the pope, all these royal letters expressed approval for an assault on Geneva.

27 The documentation is complex: see ASF *MdP* 2636/123-4, Instruction from the grand duke to Luigi Dovara, 28 February 1585, sent to Rome to secure support from Pope Gregory XIII for a Spanish invasion of England. The initiative thus came from Tuscany, but the promise of papal support formed the critical element.

28 BR *Ms* II-1670/180, Philip to Licenciado Antolinez, 31 October 1585. News of Drake's landing reached the king, then at Monzón in Aragon, on 11 October 1585, and his leading ministers immediately met in Zúñiga's lodgings to discuss 'the excesses committed by the English ships' (*BMO*, I, 521).

29 Villari and Parker, *La política de Felipe II*, 110-15, Zúñiga to Philip, undated but probably prepared soon after the meeting in Zúñiga's lodgings on 11 October 1585.

30 *CCG*, XII, 133-5, Granvelle to Charles de Mansfelt, 29 November 1585; *BMO*, I, 529-31, Memorial sent by Santa Cruz to Philip, 26 October 1585. News of the build-up of English forces in Holland reached Philip in two letters from Parma dated 30 September 1585 (AGS *Estado* 589/81 and AGS *SP* 2534/212). Although the duke did not yet know that Elizabeth had signed a formal treaty with the Dutch, he intercepted letters between them revealing that these troops formed part of a new commitment by England. News of Drake's destructive progress through the Caribbean arrived in Spain at regular intervals, maintaining the general sense of panic there: see *BMO*, I, 533-4, 539-40, 547-8 and 551-2.

31 IVdeDJ 23/385, Don Rodrigo de Castro to Hernando de Vega, president of the Council of the Indies, Seville, 15 November 1585, together with the council's *consulta* and the royal rescript.

32 *BMO*, I, 536-7, 'Lo que se responde a Su Santidad', undated but entrusted to Luis Dovara on 24 October 1584 (ibid., 528). Philip evidently referred to the 'Enterprise of England', and not to an attack on Algiers (as the editors of *BMO* suggest: ibid., 536). The assertion of Rodríguez Salgado, 'The Anglo-Spanish war', 7-8 and 34-5, that at this stage Philip only agreed to 'some enterprise' (perhaps Algiers, perhaps England) likewise seems incorrect. Although the document 'Lo que se responde' does not include the word 'Inglaterra' (or, for that matter, 'Argel'), an attack on England was the only 'Enterprise' for which Dovara had authority to secure Philip's support: see ASF *MdP* 2636/123-4, Instructions of the grand duke to Dovara, 28 February 1585, and also AGS *Estado* 1452/20, Philip to the grand duke, 27 July 1585.

33 *BMO*, I, 550, Philip to Parma, 29 December 1585; ibid., I, 553-4, Philip to Olivares, 2 January 1586. The hiatus between the king's decision on 24 October 1585 and his letter of commitment on 2 January 1586 led Rodríguez Salgado to

suggest that he changed his mind in the interim ('The Anglo-Spanish war', 7–8). However, two obvious considerations explain the delay: first, the need to assess the strategic implications for the king's other policies, above all in France and the Netherlands; and, second, the need to make sure of the new pope's enthusiastic support – something that could only be established after Dovara, who carried the king's response of 24 October 1585, reached Rome. (The king initially forbade Olivares to discuss the 'Enterprise' with the pope until after Dovara arrived: *BMO*, I, 535.)

34  We thank Paul C. Allen for discussing this point with us. See the surprisingly long list of successful invasions in Rodger, *The Safeguard*, 429.
35  *BMO*, I, 564–7, Santa Cruz to Philip, 13 February 1586, and Philip and Idiáquez to Santa Cruz, 26 February 1586 (February is the correct month, not 'January' as the volume states).
36  The marquis showed commendable wisdom in keeping the proposed landing-zone to himself: copies of his 'Relación' fell into the hands of several foreign agents – including those of France, Urbino, Venice and, most dangerous of all, England: see Parker, *Grand strategy*, 209–10.
37  *BMO*, II, 44–74, Santa Cruz to Philip and to Idiáquez, with the detailed 'Relación' compiled by the marquis and Bernabé de Pedroso, victualler-general of the fleet, 22 March 1586 (a document only recovered for the Archives of Simancas in 1983: see the endorsement on AGS *GyM* 221/1bis).
38  Maura, *El designio*, 168–72, Medina Sidonia to Don Juan de Idiáquez, 5 March 1587, relating 'what I heard from certain councillors in Madrid last year'.
39  *HMC Bath*, V, 71–2, Thomas Bayly to the earl of Shrewsbury, 27 July 1586 OS; *BMO* II, 95–7 and 98, Philip and Idiáquez to Santa Cruz, 2 April, and to the Council of the Indies, 3 April 1586. Idiáquez's postscript appears in the original of his letter to the marquis: ASC legajo 11 expediente 18, 1º cuaderno.
40  *BMO*, II, 103–4 and 119–20, Santa Cruz to Philip, 9 April, and the king's reply 20 April 1586.
41  *BMO*, II, 108–11, Parma to Philip, 20 April 1586, and 195–6, 'Lo que dixo Juan Bautista Piata de palabra'.
42  OÖLA *KB* 4/173v, Khevenhüller to Rudolf, 3 May 1586, register copy.
43  HSA *Altamira* 7/II/24 'Memoria de algunas de las cosas que se han avisado passan estos días en Madrid', Mateo Vázquez (at the Escorial with the king) to the count of Barajas (in Madrid), undated but 18 July 1586, with the count's reply.
44  Casado Soto, *Discursos*, 110–27, Escalante's 'Discurso' of June 1586, composed at the Escorial (see ibid., 52, 79–80, 82, 147 and 157 for evidence of Escalante's 'hot-line' to the king and his ministers); *BMO*, II, 212, 'Parecer' of Zúñiga, undated but June/July 1586.
45  https://www.youtube.com/watch?v=Qhx4z4jGroA, a revealing interview with Field Marshal Viscount Alanbrooke in February 1957, referring to the Allied conferences at Casablanca (January 1943), Cairo and Tehran (November 1943), and Yalta (February 1945). Italics added.

46 ASF *MdP* 4919/496–7, Giulio Battaglione to Venta, 12 October 1588; ibid., 499–501, Alemanni to grand duke, 15 October 1588, both letters partially ciphered. Granvelle died on 21 September and Zúñiga on 17 November 1586.

47 Lapèyre, *Une famille des marchands*, 422–3; Pérez Mínguez, *Reivindicación del siglo XVI*, 308, two letters from Vega to Philip in March 1586; LoC *Sir Francis Drake Collection* #3, Medina Sidonia to Philip, 25 October 1586, holograph minute, point 13. See also the bellicose views of one of Parma's advisers: *CCG*, XII, 161, Richardot to Granvelle, 30 March 1586.

48 AGS *Estado* 1261/87, Philip to the governor of Milan, 7 August 1586, ordering him to send Spanish troops to the Army of Flanders. On 7 October 1586 he ordered the towns of Spain to raise troops (AGS *GyM* 189/119 and replies 189/120–68). The following month he commanded the viceroys of Naples and Sicily to dispatch galleasses, artillery and troops 'to chase the pirates from the coasts of Portugal and make safe the seas around us': *BMO*, II, 414, Philip to the viceroys, 12 November 1586.

## 7. Phoney War

1 *BMO*, II, 315–17, Mendoza to Philip, 13 August 1586, with numerous royal apostils (*CSPSp*, III, 607, provides a spectacularly inaccurate English precis). The absence of Leicester's name from the 'death list' forwarded by Mendoza is intriguing: perhaps he regarded the earl, who had fought for Philip at St Quentin and managed to visit Mary Stuart with suspicious frequency, as a potential ally?

2 *CSPSc*, IX, 417, account of an audience (which Elizabeth conducted in French) on 7 December 1586.

3 Morris, *The letter-books*, 459–62, Walsingham and Davison to Paulet, 1 February 1587, and Paulet's reply the following day; LPL *Fairhurst Ms* 4287/19–20, Privy Council to the earl of Kent, 3 February 1587, copy. Davison's subsequent account of the events of 11 February 1587 emphasized Howard's crucial role in convincing the queen that she must sign the warrant: Nicholas, *Life*, 231–4. All dates OS.

4 BL *Cotton Ms. Galba* C/IX/290–3, Walsingham to Leicester, 'from the coort', 9 July 1586 (a letter with several compromising passages partially erased, no doubt by the earl); Hall, *Society*, 258–60, Marmaduke Darrell to his cousin, Fotheringhay, 8 February 1587 (both dates OS).

5 Teulet, *Relations politiques*, IV, 169–173, Châteauneuf to Henry III of France, 27 February 1587; Goodman, *The court*, I, 131.

6 TNA *SP* 12/202/1, [Maliverny Catlyn] to Walsingham, 1 June 1587 OS. Jackson, *Devil-Land*, 37–46, gives an excellent account of the continental reaction to the regicide.

7 Wright, *Queen Elizabeth*, II, 335–6, Walsingham to Leicester, 3 April 1587 OS; *CSPF*, XXI/3, 18, Walsingham to Thomas Wilkes, 13 April 1587 OS. Elizabeth had evidently forgiven Burghley by July, when she stayed in his country house for two weeks.

8   *CSPV*, 241–2, Lippomano to Venice, 9 February 1587.
9   The Knights of Malta, Christendom's first line of defence in the Mediterranean, remained on 'red alert' against a possible Turkish attack throughout the spring of 1588: AGS *Estado* 1089/288, Grand Master to Philip, 16 June 1588.
10  *HMC Bath*, V, 84–5, Elizabeth to Shrewsbury, 3 November 1587; and Hunt *HA* 30881/87v–88 and 120, Lord Huntingdon to Privy Council, 23 June and 11 August 1588 (all dates OS).
11  Cimber and Danjou, *Archives curieuses*, 1ère série XI, 296, report of Nicholas Poulain. The forces of the Catholic League made another attempt to take Boulogne in spring 1588, but again they failed: see Constant, *Les Guise*, 164–5, and BL *Additional Ms.* 35,841/69, Stafford to Walsingham, 18 June 1588 OS.
12  *BMO*, II, 135–6, royal *cédula* of 5 May 1586 (see also a copy in the archives of the English government: TNA *SP* 94/2/142); ibid., 273–4 and 282–4, *provisão* of 30 July 1586; KML *MSP: CR* 4/51 and 325, Philip to Medina Sidonia, 10 March and 25 August 1587.
13  Heredía Herrera, *Catálogo*, I, 597, royal apostil on a *consulta* of the Council of the Indies dated 3 September 1586; Cunha Rivara, *Arquivo Português Oriental*, III, 130–1, Philip to Viceroy Dom Duarte de Meneses, 23 February and 14 March 1588; Headley, 'Spain's Asian presence', 638–45.
14  ASF *MdP* 2636/124, Instruction to Dovara; ch. 6 above (estimate by Santa Cruz and Pedrosa); IVdeDJ 101/99–104, *consulta* of 31 January–5 February 1587 (2 million for the fleet and 5 million for the Army of Flanders).
15  *BMO*, II, 26–7, 329 and 345, Olivares to Philip, 24 February, 29 August and 9 September 1586; ibid., 420, Philip to Olivares, 18 November 1586.
16  *BMO*, II, 420–3, Philip to Olivares, 18–19 November 1586; ibid., 487–8, Olivares to Philip, 22 December 1586; and AGS *Estado* 949/86, declaration on 29 July 1587 by the Rome bankers, G. A. Pinelli and G. Gentili, that papal agents had just deposited in their vaults 1 million ducats for the Armada.
17  TNA *SP* 84/19/149–52v, interrogation of Oda Colonna, nephew of Cardinal Marco Antonio Colonna, by Maurice of Nassau on 9 December 1587, forwarded by him to Walsingham that same day (summary at *CSPF*, XXI/3, 448–9); BL *Cotton Ms.* Vespasian C.VIII/95, Walsingham to Leicester, 5 May 1588 OS.
18  *BMO*, II, 305–7, Don Bernardino de Mendoza to Philip, 13 August 1586 (with copious royal apostils) and 338–9, Philip's reply, 5 September 1586; Plymouth Archives, The Box, *Drake Ms.* 277/15 (formerly Plymouth and West Devon Record Office, PCM 1963 37/15), Elizabeth's commission for Drake to command the fleet about to set sail 'for the honor and safetie of our Realmes and Domynions', 15 March 1587 OS.
19  Corbett, *Papers*, 102–4, Drake to Walsingham, 2 April 1587 OS.
20  Hopper, *Sir Francis Drake's memorable service*, 28–9, Privy Council to Drake, 9 April 1587 OS; *BMO*, III/1, 201–2, Mendoza to Philip, 19 April 1587.
21  BL *Additional Ms.* 28,376/33–4, Andrés de Prada to Don Juan de Idiáquez, 17 May 1587.

22 Details on each ship hired for the Armada in *BMO*, V, anexo 5, 'Resumen del historial'.
23 Adams, 'Armada correspondence', 55–8, Thomas Fenner to Arthur Atye (?), undated but May 1588. Corbett, *Papers*, 113–16, published parts of this letter, which served as the basis for two printed narratives of the raid (details in Adams, op. cit., 55 n. 4). Tanturri, 'La incursión', 83–8 (two Italian accounts), *CSPV*, VIII, 274–5 ('Report of Drake's operations'), and Hopper, *Sir Francis Drake's memorable service*, 35–8, 'Advis de ce qui est passé', all recorded that Drake had intended to capture and sack the town, and commented on the superior range of his naval guns.
24 Adams, 'Armada correspondence', 52–4, Drake to Leicester, 27 April and 17 May 1587 OS; Corbett, *Papers*, 131, Drake to Walsingham, 17 May 1587 OS; ASV *NS* 19/12, Novara to Rusticucci, 14 May 1587 (500,000 ducats of damage suffered by Philip, and 200,000 more by individuals). Many sources have underestimated the consequences of Drake's interdiction of sea communication between the Mediterranean and the Atlantic, but see KML *MSP: CR* 4/149, Idiáquez to Medina Sidonia, 20 May 1587, and 167–8, Philip to Medina Sidonia, 27 May 1587, about the need to detain the troops and troopships sent from Italy at Gibraltar until Drake had gone.
25 Drake intercepted a letter which expressed concern for the safe return of a carrack 'that did winter in the Indies', thus alerting him to the possible prize: Hopper, *Sir Francis Drake's memorable service*, 41–2.
26 *BMO*, III, 479, 692–4, 721–2, 773–5, 816–17 and 862. Even this oversimplifies the story. The king bombarded his various commanders with several other changes of plan over these four weeks, and of course the contents of each letter had to be shared with all others affected: see, for example, KML *MSP: CR* 4/273, 281 and 284, Philip to Medina Sidonia, 10, 14 and 23 July 1587.
27 Roiz Soares, *Memorial*, 238; ASMa *AGS* 600a, unfol., Cavriano of Mantua to the duke, 27 May 1587. Examples of other ambassadors' obsession with Drake during summer 1587 appear in the dispatches in *CSPV*; in ASG *AS* 2418/3; in ASF *MdP* 4918; and in OÖLA *KB*, IV.
28 *BMO*, III, 380 and 411, *consulta* of the Council of War on 19 May 1587, and royal resolution on the 23rd.
29 *BMO*, II, 640–1, Idiáquez to Medina Sidonia, 28 February 1587; ASV *NS* 19/256, Novara to Rusticucci, 6 May 1587, quoting Don Hernando de Toledo.

## 8. The Armada Takes Shape

1 *BMO*, II, 387–8, Parma to Philip, 30 October 1586.
2 *BMO*, II, 471, Philip to Parma, 17 December 1586 (draft with royal apostil).
3 *BMO*, II, 535–6 and 621–2, Parma to Philip, 17 January 1587, and Philip's reply of 28 February. The king had previously expressed concern about the lack of a deep-water port in the Netherlands, noting that 'it would be most useful to have some port there, somewhere like Enkhuisen, which faces Friesland, because nothing

can be done without a port' (*BMO*, I, 550, Philip to Parma, 29 December 1585). Indeed.
4   MLM *Ms*. MA 661, 'Ciertas minutas de principio del año de 1587 sobre cosas de Inglaterra' by Idiáquez, holograph and heavily corrected. Although undated, internal evidence shows that he composed it in mid-February 1587, just before learning of Mary Stuart's execution.
5   Maura, *El designio*, 167–8, Idiáquez to Medina Sidonia, 28 February 1587.
6   Ibid., 163–74, Medina Sidonia to Idiáquez, 22 February 1587; Idiáquez's reply, 28 February; Medina Sidonia again, 5 March; and *BMO*, III/1, 474–5, Philip to Medina Sidonia, 3 June 1587.
7   *BMO*, III/1, 479–80, Philip to Parma, 5 June 1587. See also ibid., III/2, 770–2, Parma's withering dismissal on 20 July 1587. On the 'enterprise of Scotland', for which the king sent 10,000 ducats to Scots conspirators, see *BMO*, II, 436–7 and 492–4, Mendoza to Philip, 28 November and 24 December 1586, and 555–6, Philip to Mendoza, 28 January 1587; ibid., III/1, 228, Parma to Philip, 27 April 1587, and 385–6, Mendoza to Philip, 20 May 1587; and III/2, 155–6, Robert Bruce to Mendoza, 2 October 1587.
8   BL *Additional Ms*. 28,700/147, 151, 155 and 156, Vázquez to Philip, 6, 7, 9 and 14 February 1587, with royal rescripts.
9   BL *Additional Ms*. 28,363/116–17, Juan Ruiz de Velasco to Vázquez, 20 June. The king began to transact business again on 1 July and got out of bed for the first time two days later (f. 128).
10  BL *Additional Ms*. 28,376/336, Andrés de Prada to Juan de Idiáquez, 17 May 1587.
11  *BMO*, III/2, 652, *consulta* of 3 July 1587; *CSPV*, 302, Lippomano to the doge of Venice, 5 August 1587 (relaying the pessimistic view of Prior Don Hernando de Toledo).
12  Naish, 'Documents', 7–11, a translation of NMM *Ms*. PHB/1B/444–7. This is the original document drawn up by Idiáquez (it bears his 'rúbrica', the equivalent of initials: a detail omitted by Naish) and sent to Archduke Albert on 14 September 1587 to be communicated to Santa Cruz as soon as he returned from the Azores. *BMO*, III/2, 1065–7, printed a minute of this document, with several amendments by Philip.
13  *BMO*, III/2, 1006–7 and 1067–8, Instructions to Parma, 4 September 1587, and to Santa Cruz, 14 September 1587, both minutes. Despite the different dates, the two documents were conceived and prepared at the same time, because in the former Philip twice mentioned the latter. He no doubt delayed the Lisbon document for ten days in the hope that both would then reach their destination at the same time.
14  *BMO*, III/2, 1069–70, Philip to Parma, 14 September 1587.
15  *BMO*, III/3, 1274, Philip to Santa Cruz, 21 October 1587; HHStA *Statenabteilung Spanien: diplomatische Korrespondenz* neu 11, Konvolut 6/319, Khevenhüller to Rudolf, 15 November 1587 ('welle Er gern als ein Particular Soldat, aber nicht als sein General mit').
16  ASVe *SDS* 20, unfol., Lippomano to the doge, 14 November 1587, enclosing a copy of Santa Cruz's letter of 4 November (see a partial precis in *CSPV*, VIII,

320–3, 'undated'); HHStA *Statenabteilung Spanien: diplomatische Korrespondenz* neu 11, Konvolut 7/344–5, Khevenhüller to Rudolf, 30 November 1587. See also the perceptive analysis by the papal nuncio of the strategic risks if Philip postponed the Enterprise to the next year: ASV *NS* 19/283–4, Novara to Rusticucci, 10 August 1587.

17  *BMO*, III/2, 1069–70, Philip to Parma, 14 September 1587, and III/3, 1274, Philip to Santa Cruz, 21 October 1587, both minutes.
18  *BMO*, IV/2, 235–8, 'Relación' of the Army of Flanders, 29 April 1588 (monthly cost = 454,315 ducats); *ACC*, X, 118 (Philip claimed on 9 June 1588 that the Armada cost 900,000 ducats per month); BZ 141/160, Philip to the count of Barajas, 18 June 1588, copy (concentrate on cash flow); IVdeDJ 55/XI/62–3, Mateo Vázquez to Philip and reply, 31 March 1588 (selling jewels).
19  *BMO*, III/3, 1398–1401, Philip to Parma, 14 November 1587, in reply to a royal letter dated 30 September 1587 (ibid., 1146).
20  *BMO*, III/3, 1391–2, 1536, 1579, 1616–17 and 1662–3, Philip to Santa Cruz, 9 November, 10, 21 and 29 December 1587 and 4 January 1588 (the verbal bombardment only ceased when the marquis announced that his spies in England had confirmed that Parma remained in Flanders); and ibid., 1538–9 and 1594, Philip to Parma, 11 and 24 December 1587.
21  *BMO*, III/3, 1834, Parma to Philip, 31 January 1588.
22  *HMC Bath*, V, 80–1 and 85, Burghley to the earl of Shrewsbury, 19 June and 26 November 1587; Parker, 'Queen Elizabeth's Instructions', Instructions prepared by Walsingham and signed by the queen, 20 December 1587 (Adams, 'The Armada', 39, and *HMC Foljambe*, 109–10, printed slightly different drafts); Stoye, 'An early letter', 527–8, John Chamberlain to Stephen Powle, 15 December 1587 (all dates OS).
23  Laughton, I, 45–6, Howard to Burghley, 23 January 1588, holograph (see the heavily corrected original at BL *Harleian Ms.* 6994/112); Adams, 'The Armada', 68–70, same to same, 23 February 1588; *HMC Bath*, V, 86, Walsingham to Shrewsbury, 27 February 1588 (all dates OS).
24  Laughton, I, 123–6, Drake to the Privy Council, 30 March 1588; ibid., 147–9, Drake to Elizabeth, 13 April 1588, in reply to her 'particular notes' (both dates OS). Laughton, I, 159, Howard to Burghley, 17 April 1588.
25  *HMC Bath*, V, 90, Lord Talbot to Shrewsbury, 7 May 1588 (both dates OS).
26  *APC*, XVI, 57–8, order of 10 May 1588 (this explains the mystery of where Drake was when Fenner and Cross wrote to him from Plymouth on 12 May: Laughton, I, 171 n. 1); *HMC Foljambe*, 116, Elizabeth to Howard, 13 May 1588 (all dates OS).
27  Laughton, I, 179–80, Howard to Burghley, 23 May 1588 OS.
28  Adams, 'Armada correspondence', 76–7, Howard to Leicester, 6 June 1588 OS; Laughton, I, 252–3, Marmaduke Darrell to the Privy Council, Plymouth, 11 July 1588 OS. Brayshay, 'Plymouth's coastal defences', estimated the population of Plymouth in 1588 at 4,000–4,500.

29 BL *Additional Ms.* 28,363 ff. 175–9v, Vázquez to Juan Ruiz de Velasco and reply, 16–20 January 1588; but f. 188, dated 12 February 1588, reported that the king was still under doctor's orders. For further health bulletins, see BZ 143 ff. 12–13 (23 January 1588), 29 (27 February), 41 (8 March) and 46 (16 March).

30 *BMO*, III/2, 1181, Leyva to Philip, 10 October 1587; *BMO*, III/3, 1732–3, *consultas* of the Council of War, 16 January 1588, endorsing suggestions made to them in person by Leyva; idem, 1801–2 and 1806, Philip to Santa Cruz, 28 January 1588. ASV *NS* 34/119–20, Novara to Montalto, 22 January 1588, noted Leyva's arrival in Madrid two days earlier, adding 'he will not return to Lisbon because he does not agree with the marquis of Santa Cruz'.

31 *BMO*, III/3, 1744, Santa Cruz to Philip, 19 January 1588; ibid., 1757, secret instruction to Fuentes, 23 January 1588.

32 *BMO*, III/3, 1822–3, Philip to Santa Cruz, 30 January 1588; and 1840–2, Instructions for Santa Cruz, draft with holograph royal corrections. *BMO* dates these instructions 'circa 30 January' but 23 January seems more likely, since on that day Philip signed his instructions for Fuentes.

33 *BMO*, III/3, 1813, Fuentes to Moura and Idiáquez, Lisbon, 30 January 1588, holograph. An English translation cannot do justice to Fuentes's insulting tone, because he addressed Santa Cruz with the imperative voice and the 'vos' form used when addressing social inferiors ('Mirad mi instrucción y veréis . . .').

34 TNA *SP* 12/211/157–62, 'The reporte of George Wood towching the Spanische preparation'.

35 *BMO*, III/3, 1255–7 and 1301–2, Juan de Acuña Vela to Philip, 17 and 24 October 1587, pointing out the need for new field carriages and the difficulties of constructing them. Problems of embarking the siege-train reconstructed from *BMO*, III/3, 1653–4, 1819 and 1865–6, and IV/1, 209–10, Acuña Vela to Philip, 2 and 30 January, 3 February and 12 March 1588.

36 Gracia Rivas, *Los tercios*, 172–3, recorded losses from the *tercios*; Tellechea Idígoras, *Otra cara*, 397, noted deaths of sailors from Guipúzcoa; AGS *CS* 2a/278/29–42, 'Sumario de los soldados y marineros que han muerto del Armada', 11 December 1587.

37 Roiz Soares, *Memorial*, 245; HHStA *Statenabteilung Spanien: diplomatische Korrespondenz* neu 11, Konvolut 7/345–8, Khevenhüller to Rudolf, 21 February 1588.

38 Fernández Duro, *Disquisiciones náuticas*, V (1880), 413–515, printed Escalante's *Itinerario de navegación* for the first time (quotation from pp. 482–3). For the fate of the manuscript (now BNE *Ms.* 3,104), see AGI *IG* 740/95, *consulta* of the Council of the Indies, 18 August 1582, with royal rescript. The council recommended a payment to Escalante of 1,000 ducats for his work; Philip granted him 500.

39 *BMO*, IV/2, 395–6, Ribadeneira to the marchioness of Camarasa, mid-May 1588. The duke's great-great-grandfather was Ferdinand the Catholic.

40 KML *MSP: CR* 4/95–6, Don Juan de Idiáquez to Medina Sidonia, 31 May 1587, saying that Philip had asked him to repeat something contained in an earlier royal

missive; HHStA *Spanien Varia* fasz 2/347v, Ibañez de la Cruz, 'Discurso en que se condena al gobierno', 1599.
41 HSA *Altamira* 7/1/9, Medina Sidonia to Mateo Vázquez, 20 May 1580, asking for the Milan posting; Biblioteca Bartolomé March, Madrid, *Medina Sidonia Papers*, royal patents as governor of Milan dated 27 March and 15 May 1581.
42 *BMO*, IV/1, 3–4, Medina Sidonia to Don Juan de Idiáquez (two letters), 16 February 1588. Duro, I, 414–17, also printed the first letter but with some serious errors of transcription, repeated in *CSPSp*, IV, 207–8.
43 Like the editors of *BMO*, we failed to locate the duke's letter of 18 February 1588 and have therefore reconstructed its contents from the reply written by Idiáquez and Moura four days later: *BMO*, IV/1, 65, italics added. See also ibid., 36–7, Philip, Idiáquez and Moura to Medina Sidonia, 20 February 1588, all attributing the duke's earlier disclaimers 'to your great modesty' – although Moura cruelly added: 'May I remind you how much some people have sacrificed to achieve at their deaths what Your Lordship brings to this venture at the outset.' *BMO*, IV/1, 3–4, Medina Sidonia to Idiáquez, 16 February 1588, blamed the two ministers for arranging his unwelcome appointment.
44 HSA *Altamira* 1/I/44, Medina Sidonia to Vázquez, 29 February 1588, holograph (*BMO*, IV/1, 138, printed only part of this remarkable letter). ASMa *AGS* 601, unfol., Cavriano to the duke of Mantua, 2 March 1588, recorded the royal rejection of Medina Sidonia's request to 'kiss the king's hands' on his way from Sanlúcar to Lisbon. The king had rejected a similar request nine months before: KML *MSP: CR* 4/288–9, Don Juan de Idiáquez to Medina Sidonia, 24 July 1587.
45 HSA *Altamira* 1/I/46, Vázquez to Philip, 8 March 1588, with a heavily corrected rescript (*BMO*, IV/1, 192, printed only part of this remarkable rescript). KML *MSP: CR* 5/82, Philip to Medina Sidonia, 11 March 1588, is the original of Philip's 'soothing letter', drafted by Vázquez who did indeed 'take what you like from what I have written'; *BMO*, IV/1, 198, printed the minute.
46 *BMO*, III/3, 1964, Bertendona to Philip, 15 February 1588, italics added.
47 Campbell, *Grammatical man*, 73, summarizing von Neumann's brilliant work on 'redundancy'.

## 9. Medina Sidonia Takes Charge

1 *BMO*, IV/1, 151–2, Fuentes to Philip, 2 March 1588 (hanging deserters, approved by Philip on the 7th: ibid., 181); ibid., 7–8, Fuentes to Idiáquez and Moura, 16 February 1588.
2 *BMO*, IV/1, 226, and IV/2, 14–15, Medina Sidonia to Philip, 15 and 26 March 1588; *BMO*, IV/1, 243–5, 'Relación de la visita que en particular hizo el duque', 19 March 1588; *BMO*, IV/3, 453, Bobadilla to Idiáquez, 20 August 1588. On 26 March, Acuña Vela protested to the king that 'Two or three months ago, thirty rounds per gun seemed more than enough to everyone', but 'now the duke of Medina insists on providing fifty rounds per gun'. He urged Philip to overrule

his overzealous new commander, but the king refused (although he forbade the duke to delay his departure to take on more munitions): *BMO*, IV/2, 22–3, Acuña Vela to Philip, 26 March 1588; ibid., 95–6, Philip to Medina Sidonia, 3 April 1588.

3  *BMO*, IV/1, 172–3 and 275, Philip to Parma, 6 March 1588, and to Medina Sidonia, 21 March 1588, italics added.
4  Mousset, *Dépêches*, 380, Longlée to Henry III, 5 June 1588.
5  BL *Additional Ms.* 35,841/88–9v, Sir Edward Stafford to Walsingham, 7 July 1588 OS.
6  Brugmans, II, 447, 'Discours' of Thomas Wilkes, 1587.
7  Dutch strength by land taken from *CSPF*, XXI pt. 3, 14–15; and by sea from ARA *Staten-General* 12561.3 ff. 1–2, and Bor, *Oorspronck*, III, pt. 2, bk. 25, ff. 6–7.
8  *BMO*, IV/2, 105–6, Philip to Parma, 5 April 1588.
9  ASN *CF* 1690, unfol., 'Relación de los baxeles que se hallan oy lunes 2 de noviembre [1587] en este puerto de Dunckerque' (recording only nine boats of 150–200 tons burthen). See also the accounts of the Paymaster of the 'Armada de los Estados de Flandes', Thorivio Martinez, preserved in fragmentary form in AGS *CMC* 2a/1077, 3a/692 and 3a/713. On the phantom Scottish vessels see *BMO*, III/1, 80–1 and 228, Parma to Philip, 22 March and 28 April 1587; ibid., 182, Parma to Mendoza, 13 April 1587; ibid., 385–6, Mendoza to Philip, 20 May 1587; and ibid., III/3, 1155–7, Robert Bruce to Mendoza, 2 October 1587.
10  *BMO*, III/3, 1579–81, 1617–19 and 1834–5, Parma to Philip, 21 and 29 December 1587, and 31 January 1588; *BMO*, IV/1, 257–9, and IV/2, 107–8, same to same, 20 March and 5 April 1588.
11  *BMO*, IV/2, 38, Corregidor of Vizcaya to Andrés de Alva, 28 March 1588, with royal apostils.
12  *BMO*, III/1, 174–6, Medina Sidonia to Philip, 31 March 1587, a remarkably perceptive letter.
13  *BMO*, IV/2, 14–17, Medina Sidonia to Philip, 26 March 1588 (2 letters).
14  *BMO*, III/3, 1799, Philip to Santa Cruz, 28 January 1588; *BMO*, IV/1, 90, Medina Sidonia to Philip, 25 February 1588; ibid., 227–8, same to same, 15 March 1588; ibid., 178, Philip to Medina Sidonia, 7 March 1588; *BMO*, IV/2, 13, Medina Sidonia to Martín de Idiáquez, 26 March 1588.
15  *BMO*, IV/1, 137, Acuña Vela to Philip, 10 April 1588, about the production of utility ordnance 'sin ningún follaje ni labor'. Details on the Lisbon foundries, and the extreme production pressures of early 1588, from *BMO*, IV/1, 94–5 and 208–10, Acuña Vela to Philip, 25 February and 12 March 1588 (2 letters); *BMO*, IV/1, 202, Fuentes to Philip, 12 March 1588; and Salgado, *Os navios*, 34–6.
16  *BMO*, IV/2, 134, Medina Sidonia to Martín de Idiáquez, 9 April 1588.
17  Fernández Duro, *Disquisiciones náuticas*, II, 194, letter of Eugenio de Salazar, 1573.
18  *BMO*, I, 420–1, Parma to Philip, 30 November 1583; ibid., III, 1112–16, Idiáquez to Santa Cruz, 25 September 1587, enclosing the 'Relación' prepared by Robert Heighington, an English Catholic exile (see p. 586 n. 23).

19 *BMO*, IV/1, 291–2, Medina Sidonia to Philip, 23 March 1588. The king approved these decisions and asked to see a copy of both the map and the *Derrotero*; the duke complied on 2 April (*BMO*, IV/2, 87–8). The duke received praise for both innovations: see *BMO*, IV/2, 36, Idiáquez to Medina Sidonia, 28 March 1588: 'Lo de la carta y derrotero que Vuestra Señoría ha mandado hazer para su viaje, se ha tenido por cosa acertadíssima'.

20 *BMO*, IV/2, 42–8, printed the copy of the *Derrotero* published by 'Antonio Álvarez, printer to His Excellency' and dated 30 March 1588, now at AGS *E* 431/17. This is presumably the copy sent to Philip by the duke. Rodríguez-Salgado, 'Pilots', 148–51, noted the haphazard nature of the data in the *Derrotero* and speculated that its authors recycled outdated commercial sources.

21 AGS *CS* 2a/283, unfol. (a large *legajo* arranged by Christian name), final payment on 12 May 1588 to 'Ceprián Sánchez, maestre de hazer cartas de marear' of 297 escudos and 5 reals for 85 'quarterones de cartas de marear con sus braxeajes [i.e. braceajes, soundings]'.

22 *BMO*, IV/2, 324, Barnabé de Pedroso to Philip, 12 May 1588.

23 *BMO*, IV/2, 395–6, Ribadeneira, *Exhortación* (sent to Medina Sidonia in mid-May 1588); Weinrich, *Pedro de Ribadeneyra's Ecclesiastical History*, 751–2, published simultaneously in June 1588 in Madrid, Zaragoza, Valencia, Barcelona, Naples and Antwerp (date from ASF *MdP* 4919/408–11, Alemanni to the grand duke, 23 July 1588, noting that he had sent a copy of the book on 7 July). Ribadeneira himself mentioned Drake's role: *MHSI Ribadeneira*, II, 77, letter to Alonso Deza, 22 August 1587.

24 Laughton, I, 186–9, Howard to Burghley, Plymouth, 28 May 1588 OS.

25 Hughes and Larkin, *Tudor royal proclamations*, III, 14–15, proclamation of 1 July 1588; TNA *SP* 12/211/93, Burghley to Walsingham, 24 June 1588; TNA *SP* 77/4/171–3, Elizabeth to her peace commissioners, 29 June 1588, copy (and ibid., ff. 177–80v, a draft of this letter with Burghley's numerous corrections, undated but between 24 and 28 June). All dates OS.

26 TNA *SP* 77/4/231–3, Dale to Elizabeth, 12 July 1588 OS (underline in the original). Dale boldly reminded Parma that one battle rarely sufficed 'to conquer a kingdom in another country'.

27 Wright, *Queen Elizabeth*, II, 378, Sir Thomas Heneage to Leicester, from the Court, 17 July 1588; KML 'Dr Valentine Dale: letters on talks with the duke of Parma', no. 2, Dale to Robert Beale, Bourbourg, 25 July 1588, with similarly acerbic letters to Leicester, Walsingham, Burghley and Hatton on the same day (all dates OS). Camden, *Annales*, 262–3, printed an account of Dale's audience with Parma clearly based on his letters.

28 *BMO*, IV/2, 338, Medina Sidonia to Philip, 14 May 1588.

29 *BMO*, III/3, 1576, Philip to Oquendo, 21 December 1587; *BMO*, IV/2, 430–2, Medina Sidonia's general orders, 21 May 1588.

30 Robres and Ortolá, *La monja*, 70–4, Granada to Patriarch Juan de Ribera, 22 and 27 May 1588; *BMO*, IV/2, 424, Acuña Vela to Philip, 21 May 1588.

31 *BMO*, IV/2, 449–51, Medina Sidonia to Philip, 28 May 1588.
32 *BMO*, IV/2, 470, Medina Sidonia to Philip, 30 May 1588; ibid., 464, Bobadilla to Idiáquez, 29 May 1588.
33 San Gerónimo, 'Memorias', 428; BL *Additional Ms.* 28,263/469, Philip to Vázquez, 25 May 1588 (Philip's use of 'su pueblo' is notable). Philip's younger daughter, Catalina, had left for Savoy immediately after her marriage in 1585. She died in 1597 and Philip never saw her again.
34 Pérez Bustamente, 'El cronista', 755 n. 1, Moura to Parma, 17 June 1588.
35 BZ 143/97, Philip to Vázquez, 18 June 1588.
36 BZ 143/111, Vázquez to Philip and reply, 28 June 1588, about a letter from the duke of Infantado (Vázquez first brought the duke's letter to Philip's attention on 14 June, but the king replied that 'I dare not read papers as long as this just now': BZ 143/88); AGS *Estado* 595/32, Idiáquez to Philip and reply, undated but August 1588.

## 10. Advance to Contact

1 BZ 142/171ª, Philip's address to the Cortes of Castile, January 1588, holograph; *BMO*, IV/1, 65, Idiáquez and Moura to Medina Sidonia, 22 February 1588.
2 *BMO*, IV/2, 522, Medina Sidonia to Philip, 14 June 1588, mentioned that he had dispatched Captain Moresin back to Parma four days before.
3 *BMO*, IV/2, 522–3, Medina Sidonia to Philip and Idiáquez, 14 June 1588.
4 *BMO*, IV/3, 64–5, 'Relación del viaje' by Miguel de Esquivel listing the Armada ships that he found in the Isles of Scilly; ibid., 243, Medina Sidonia to Parma, 25 July 1588, stated that the storms of the previous month had scattered 'two thirds of the fleet'.
5 *BMO*, IV/2, 551–5, Medina Sidonia to Philip and Idiáquez, 24 June 1588, together with supporting material. Unusually, Medina Sidonia wrote the entire draft of his letter to the king, as well as the original, in his own hand – presumably because, given its contents, he did not dare to employ a secretary. He also prudently wrote 'Keep this safe [*guárdesse*]' and 'Take care [*Ojo*]' on the back of the draft, since its contents could both ruin him and disgrace his family: KML *MSP: CR* 5/280–2.
6 OÖLA *KB* 4/311–12, Khevenhüller to Rudolf II, 13 July 1588; Tellechea Idígoras, '*La Invencible*', 79, Novara to Montalto, 6 July 1588.
7 *BMO*, IV/2, 603, Recalde to Martín de Idiáquez, 28 June 1588; ibid., 581–2, minutes of the council debate on 27 June by the duke's secretary, Arceo (a fascinating document); ibid., 592, Medina Sidonia to Philip, 28 June 1588.
8 *BMO*, IV/2, 602, Medina Sidonia to Don Juan de Idiáquez, 28 June 1588.
9 *BMO*, IV/3, 123–4, Recalde to Martín de Idiáquez, 11 July 1588. On re-stepping *Santa María*'s mast, see *BMO*, IV/3, 113–14 and 123–4, Medina Sidonia and Recalde to Philip, both dated 11 July 1588. Oquendo also praised this achievement 'because everyone said the ship would not be able to sail with the rest of the fleet': ibid., 161, Oquendo to Philip, 15 July 1588.

10 BZ 143/97 and 111, Philip to Mateo Vázquez, 18 and 28 June 1588; *BMO*, IV/3, 62–3, Idiáquez to Philip, and rescript, 6 July 1588.
11 *BMO*, IV/3, 10–11, Philip to Medina Sidonia, 1 July 1588, together with a document entitled 'The rationale for overcoming the obstacles to completing the campaign already begun, and the reasons why His Majesty remains committed to persevere with it'.
12 *BMO*, IV/3, 17–18, Moura and Idiáquez to Medina Sidonia, 1 July 1588; and ibid., 53–4, Philip to Medina Sidonia, 5 July 1588 ('espero en Nuestro Señor que ha de *trocar* todas estas dificultades del principio en mayor gloria suya al cabo'). Compare the king's desire to '*granjear*' divine favour in ch. 9.
13 *BMO*, IV/2, 513, Medina Sidonia to Parma, 10 June 1588, copy sent to (and annotated by) Philip. See also KML *MSP: CR* 5/264–7, minute of the same letter, listing *en clair* the three anchorages where the Armada could wait while Parma completed his preparations: 'Euchep' (Beachy Head), 'Hislaga' (Hastings) and 'Rromaneos' (Romney) – precisely the anchorages indicated on the surviving 'Armada map' of the south coast and in Wagenaer's *Speculum*.
14 *BMO*, IV/2, 541, Philip to Medina Sidonia, 21 June 1588, minute. Some have suggested that the duke never received this letter, originally sent to him by way of Flanders, but documents in his archive prove that a duplicate reached him in Corunna: KML *MSP: CR* 5/278–9, 289, Philip's note of 26 June, enclosing a copy of the preceding; and *BMO*, IV/3, 66, Medina Sidonia to Philip, 6 July, acknowledging its receipt.
15 *BMO*, IV/3, 71, Recalde to Martín de Idiáquez, Corunna, 6 July 1588 (first letter).
16 *BMO*, IV/3, 71–2, Recalde to Martín de Idiáquez, Corunna, 6 July 1588 (second letter); ibid., 79–80 and 89, *consulta* of the Council of War, 6 July 1588, with the king's rescript the following day; Naish, 'Documents', 29, Philip's instructions to Andrés de Alva, 9 July 1588. When the duke refused to accept Bobadilla, Alva overruled him (*BMO*, IV/3, 115, Medina Sidonia to Don Juan de Idiáquez, 11 July, and ibid., 202–3, Alva to Philip, 19 July 1588). The duke probably chose to summon Flores to the flagship on 6 July because the two had worked together when the latter commanded transatlantic fleets and when he led the Strait expedition (IV/3, 68, Medina Sidonia to Don Juan de Idiáquez, 6 July 1588).
17 *BMO*, IV/3, 68 and 115–16, Medina Sidonia to Don Juan de Idiáquez, 6 and 11 July 1588, and 166, to Archduke Albert, 15 July 1588.
18 *BMO*, IV/3, 123–4, Recalde to Don Juan and to Don Martín de Idiáquez ('My letter is very long and, I fear, somewhat impertinent'), 11 July 1588.
19 Adams, 'Armada correspondence', 75–6, Howard to Leicester, 23 May and 6 June 1588; Strype, *Annals*, III, pt. II, 545, Drake to Burghley, 7 June 1588. See also Laughton, I, 179–80, Howard to Burghley, 6 June 1588; and McDermott, *England and the Spanish Armada*, 209–13. All dates OS.
20 *Calendar of the Manuscripts of the Marquis of Bath*, II, 28, Drake to Burghley, 6 June 1588 OS; Laughton, I, 288–9, Howard to Walsingham, 21 July 1588 OS. *BMO*, IV/1, p. LXXXIV, includes a map of Howard's journey, 15–22 July 1588.

21 *BMO*, IV/3, 123–4, Recalde to Martín de Idiáquez, 11 July 1588.
22 TNA *SP* 12/214/49–60v, interrogation in Bridewell prison of those taken on *Rosario*, London, 12 August 1588 NS, testimony of Vicente Álvarez, captain of the ship, Dr Góngora, and Gregorio de Sotomayor (some parts published in Laughton, II, 17–24); and Hyland, *A century of persecution*, 194–5, interrogation of Winslade, 9 August 1588 NS. In Holland, Don Diego Pimentel told his captors that he had received instructions 'to take the queen prisoner, but to treat her as a queen until they received further orders' from Philip: [Pimentel,] *Breeder verclaringhe*.
23 *BMO*, IV/3, 202–4, Andrés de Alva and Medina Sidonia to Philip, Corunna, both dated 19 July 1588.
24 *BMO*, IV/3, 217, Bernabé de Pedroso, victualler-general of the fleet, to Andrés de Alva, Corunna, 20 July 1588; AGS *CMC* 2a/772, unfol., papers of the *San Francisco*, pre-printed order reducing rations, 9 July 1588.
25 *BMO*, IV/3, 209–10 and 220, minutes of meetings on 20 and 21 July 1588, signed by Medina Sidonia; and ibid., 220, statement signed by all present at the meeting of pilots, Corunna, 21 July 1588, at 7 a.m. See also the original record of these debates retained by Medina Sidonia and filed in his archive, no doubt for his protection in case the venture failed: KML *MSP: CR* 5/338–40.
26 *BMO*, IV/3, 222 and 229, Medina Sidonia to Philip, 22 and 23 July 1588; ibid., 243, Medina Sidonia to Parma, 25 July 1588.
27 *BMO*, IV/1, p. CIX; ibid., IV/3, 265–6, Medina Sidonia to Philip, 29 July 1588, sent on the 30th (with additional material in the minute in KML *MSP: CR* 5/369–70); *BMO*, IV/3, 262, Recalde to Martín de Idiáquez, 29 July 1588; Tellechea Idígoras, '*La Invencible*', 84, Novara to Montalto, 15 August 1588, quoting a letter received from Leyva; *BMO*, IV/3, 266, Medina Sidonia to Martín de Idiáquez, 30 July 1588.
28 *BMO*, IV/3, 468–71, 'Relación de lo sucedido', 30 July 1588.
29 TNA *SP* 12/200/14, earl of Bath (Lord Lieutenant) to the Privy Council, 14 December 1587 OS; BL *Lansdowne Ms.* 65/40–1v, Francis Drake and William Hawkins petition, 3 May 1590 OS; *BMO*, IV/4 224–9, account of Alonso Vanegas for 30 July. The only advantage gained by the duke from this delay was the opportunity to repair the damaged rudder of the flag galleass *San Lorenzo*.

# PART III

* The motto on a Dutch medal of 1588: VENIT, VIDIT, FUIT. https://www.alamy.com/medal-on-the-downfall-of-the-invincible-fleet-jeton-utility-medal-medal-exchange-copper-battle-between-two-ships-omschrift-met-hetje-text-in-cut-cut-classis-hisp-omschrift-venit-x-fvit-x-15-fortress-88-x-the-spanish-fleet-has-come-and-has-been-1588-armada-invincible-fleet-spain-image228081194.html; Harvard, Houghton Library, *Ms.* Typ. 16, John Mountgomerie, 'A treatise concerning the navie of England', Addition dated 1589.

## 11. Battle Stations

1. Naish, 'Documents', 7–11, a translation of NMM *Ms.* PHB/1B/444–7, a memorandum drawn up by Idiáquez and endorsed 'Communicated by His Highness [Archduke Albert] to the duke of Medina Sidonia on behalf of His Majesty, in view of the marquis of Santa Cruz's death'. We know that the duke received this document, because he filed it with the royal instructions of 1 April: *BMO*, IV/2, 73–4.
2. *BMO*, IV/2, 75, Secret Instructions, 1 April 1588, minute, italics added. An earlier draft of this document had authorized Medina Sidonia to capture Southampton as well, but then the king had second thoughts, scribbling in the margin: 'It will be enough to capture and fortify the Isle of Wight, because if we take a place on the mainland the whole kingdom [of England] will rally to it – which they cannot do with Wight, because it is an island': NMM *Ms* PHB/1B/441. Philip himself had sailed up the Solent to Southampton in 1554.
3. *BMO*, IV/2, 76, Instructions for Parma, 1 April 1588, 'to be sent with the Armada'. *CSPSp*, IV, 251–2, provided a good English translation but omitted the holograph postscript.
4. *BMO*, IV/2, 92, Philip to Medina Sidonia, 3 April 1588.
5. *BMO*, IV/2, 204–5, sealed patent for Leyva, and cover note for Recalde, 23 April 1588 (in the event, Recalde sent the commission back unopened when he returned to Corunna in October); ibid., 209–10, Philip to Medina Sidonia, 23 April 1588, minute.
6. *BMO*, IV/2, 261–2, Medina Sidonia to Idiáquez, 7 May 1588, stating that 'envío a Su Majestad la forma que tengo dada para la batalla, y tan mal dibujada y a prisa como V. S. verá'; KML *MSP: CR* 5/142–3, 'La forma de cómo se avía de pelear con los galeones' (printed with numerous errors in *BMO*, IV/2, 276–7).
7. ASF *MdP* 4919/340 and 5037/615, two slightly different sketches sent by the Tuscan ambassador in Madrid to the grand duke, probably on 28 May 1588, together with other documents about the Armada. We believe that Ambassador Vicenzo Alemanni saw and made copies from the duke's original, because the disposition of the ships in the 'wings' is the same as that in KML *MSP: CR* 5/142–3, 'La forma' (preceding note).
8. Chaves, *Espejo de navigantes*, 'De la guerra o batalla que se da en la mar', a manuscript of *c.* 1540 published in Fernández Duro, *Armada Española*, I, 379–91; Oliveira, *A arte da guerra do mar*, f. lxxii.
9. *BMO*, IV/2, 415, Bertendona to Philip, 19 May 1588; *BMO*, IV/3, 161–2, Valdés to Philip, 15 July 1588, recalling what he had advocated in Lisbon two months earlier; *BMO*, IV/2, 449–51, Medina Sidonia to Philip, 28 May 1588.
10. *BMO*, IV/3, 310, 'Relación' of an anonymous Jesuit on the flagship, entry for 4 August 1588. Don Diego should not be confused with Don Diego Téllez Enríquez, the senior officer aboard *San Juan de Sicilia*.
11. Naish, 'Documents', 13–20, Philip's Secret Instructions to Medina Sidonia, 1 April 1588.

12 *BMO*, III, 1750, Guevara to Philip, 22 January 1588. Ironically, Guevara largely repeated something Medina Sidonia already knew: see his Instructions to the fleet leaving for America, 31 March 1587, in Maura, *El designio*, 175–7. The other reports ('avisos') mentioned by the king probably included a description in 1586 of English naval superiority and the need to use different (smaller) ships in order to counter it: AGS *SP* libro 1550/569, Cardinal Albert to Philip, 25 October 1586.

13 The following paragraphs are based on BMO IV/2, 500–2, 'La orden que ordeno y mando se tenga en la defensa de este galeón real', 7 June 1588, italics added, and BMO IV/4, 225, 'Relación' of Captain Vanegas, chief gunnery officer aboard the flagship, entry for 30 July 1588. The details in the two accounts differ because Vanegas wrote later and recorded the dispositions as the Armada entered the Channel.

14 More details in Martin, 'Incendiary weapons', passim.

15 *BMO*, IV/4, 224, description of gun protocols in the 'Relación' of Vanegas.

16 *BMO*, IV/2, 523 Medina Sidonia to Philip, off Cape Finisterre, 14 June 1588; AGS *CMC* 2a/772 (i) Papers of *San Francisco* (Andalucia), issue of powder, cord and lead on 13 June 1588.

17 *BMO*, IV/2, 522, Medina Sidonia to Philip, off Cape Finisterre, 14 June 1588.

18 *BMO*, III/3, 648–9, Leyva to Philip, 3 July 1587; IV/2, 261, Leyva to Idiáquez, 7 May 1588.

19 *BMO*, IV/3, 204–5, Medina Sidonia to Philip, 19 July 1588, confirmed by ibid., 206, a jubilant Valdés to Philip, 19 July 1588.

20 *BMO*, IV/3, 137–8, Idiáquez to Medina Sidonia, 12 July 1588; ibid., 205–6, Medina Sidonia's dismissive reply, 19 July 1588.

21 *BMO*, IV/3, 136, Philip to Medina Sidonia, 12 July 1588; Hyland, *A century*, 194–5, examination of Winslade, London, 30 July 1588 OS.

22 *BMO*, IV/3, 468–71, 'Relación de lo sucedido', 31 July 1588. Rodger, 'The development of broadside gunnery', 301, attributes the origin of this misconception to Julian Corbett, *Drake and the Tudor navy*, II, 207, with other historians following faithfully astern.

23 Lewis, *The Spanish Armada*, 114.

24 BL *Cotton Ms. Galba C.V*/32, Fogaza to Don Luis de Requesens, 10 May 1574, copy. *CSPSp*, II, 480, provides a somewhat inaccurate English translation but its editor, Martin Hume, identified the author as Fogaza: ibid., p. xli. Francisco Guevara confirmed every detail of Fogaza's analysis.

25 Dr Tom Glasgow first alerted us to the importance of this contemporary sketch. See also his article, 'Elizabethan ships'. The map underestimated the number of naval guns brought ashore – two culverins each from *Revenge*, *Swiftsure* and *Tiger*, and a saker each from *Aid* and *Achates*: see Wright, *Queen Elizabeth*, II, 120–2, Bingham to Leicester, 11 November 1580 OS; and TNA *SP* 63/78/59–72, letters from Bingham and Lord Deputy Grey to Elizabeth and Walsingham, 11–12 November 1580 OS.

26 Bourne, *The art*, 57–8 (we cite the second edition of 1587 because no copies survive of an earlier edition printed in 1578 and still available in 1581: Taylor, *A regiment*,

442–4); Mainwaring, 'The seaman's dictionary' (written between 1620 and 1623), 119 ('carriage'), 241–2 ('tackles') and 249 ('trucks').

27  AGS *CMC* 2a/1210, Miscellaneous accounts, order of Valdés dated 22 April 1588; a second copy at *CMC* 1a/1718 fo. 759, noted that the gun (a 9-pounder) was exchanged for a much smaller *medio sacre* – one more example of Valdés 'gunning up' his own ship.

28  *BMO*, IV/4, 288–9, accounts of Pietro Pauber for salvaging *San Lorenzo*; García de Palacio *Instrucción naúthica*, ch. 33; KML *MSP CC* 8/30–41 (ff. 171–236), accounts of ordnance and munitions supplied to embargoed ships by Medina Sidonia in July 1587: details on the 'ruedas nuevas de pino' in #30 (*Gran Grín*), #32 (*Santa Catalina*) and #38 (*San Bartolomé*). We thank John F. Guilmartin for pointing out to us the design flaws in the Portuguese drawing of a 'sea carriage'.

29  Laughton, II, 44–7, Seymour, Winter and Palmer to the Privy Council, the Downs, 6 August 1588 OS. The trio nevertheless prepared to join Howard, and only his return forestalled them.

30  Crone, 'The Mariners Mirrour', noted the differences between the Dutch, Latin and English editions of Wagenaer.

31  TNA *SP* 12/186/142–4, Report on the defensive state of Essex, February 1586; BL *Additional Ms.* 62,935, 'Carde of the beacons of Kent', August 1585; *BMO*, IV/4, 468, 'Relación' by Stukeley, 30 July 1588; *APC*, XVI, 169, 171, Privy Council minutes for 23 and 24 July 1588 OS.

32  *APC*, XVI, 176 and 183–5, Privy Council minutes for 24 and 26 July 1588; Laughton, I, 289–90 and 300, Drake to Seymour, 21 July, and Seymour to the Privy Council, 23 July 1588. All dates OS.

33  *APC*, XVI, 178, 187, 211 and 302, Privy Council minutes for 26 July (Sussex), 2 August (Newcastle and Berwick) and 6 October 1588 (Topsham) (all dates OS). Each last was 24 barrels, or 2,400 lbs, or just over 1,000 kilos.

34  Harvard, Houghton Library, *Ms. Typ.* 16, John Mountgomerie, 'A treatise concerning the navie of England', Addition dated 1589 (partly published in Brydges, *Censura literaria*, V, 139–40).

## 12. Stalemate in the Channel

1  KML *MSP: CR* 5/369–70, Medina Sidonia to Philip, 30 July 1588, corrected copy. *BMO*, IV/3, 265–6, also prints this letter, but from another text which lacks some crucial parts of the KML version.

2  TNA *SP* 63/136/153–5v, Examination of Emanuel Fremoso, 12 September 1588 (copies at ibid., ff. 141–2v and 178); *BMO*, IV/3, 262, Recalde to Idiáquez, 29 July 1588 (evidently written before the Council of War held that day); Parker, 'Anatomy', 328, Recalde's journal; *BMO*, IV/4, 436, petition of Juan Gil de la Salde, 13 February 1589; ibid., IV/3, 267, Medina Sidonia to Parma, 31 July/1 August 1588; ibid., 468–71, 'Relación de lo sucedido', 30/31 July 1588.

3  Parker, 'Anatomy', 328; *BMO*, IV/3, 468–71, 'Relación de lo sucedido', 31 July 1588; *BMO*, IV/4, 224–9, account of Alonso Vanegas for 30 July; Laughton, II, 28,

interrogation of Don Pedro de Valdés (who opposed the assault); and ibid., 133, Valdés to Philip, 31 August 1588 (an English translation made for Walsingham).

4   *BMO*, IV/4, 20–4, 'Relación de lo sucedido' by Pedro Coco Calderón, entry for 30 July 1588.
5   *BMO*, IV/3, 468–71, 'Relación de lo sucedido', 31 July 1588.
6   Parker, 'Anatomy', 328, 'Diario' entry for 31 July. Some accounts reported that *Gran Grín* stood by Recalde, but the admiral himself stated unequivocally that the ship 'never took up her position' (ibid., 325, to Medina Sidonia, 1 August 1588).
7   Adams, 'Armada correspondence', 78, Howard to the earl of Sussex, 22 July 1588 (inferior copy in Laughton, I, 299); Laughton, I, 288–90, Howard to Walsingham, and Drake to Seymour, 21 July 1588; and 358, Hawkins to Walsingham, 31 July 1588 (all dates OS).
8   Laughton, I, 301–2, Nicholas Oseley to Walsingham, 2 August 1588; ibid., II, 63–5, White to Walsingham, 8 August 1588 (both dates OS).
9   Parker, 'Anatomy', 324–5, Recalde to Bobadilla and Medina Sidonia, 1 August 1588, holograph, each returned with responses in the margin. Howard confirmed the perception that the English were trying to sap the Armada's strength gradually: 'we pluck their feathers by little and little' (p. 295).
10  ASF *MdP* 4919/532–3, 'Relazione cavata d'una lettera d'un Raguzeo'. *BMO*, IV/1, p. CCL n. 57, printed and evaluated the contradictory explanations of how *San Salvador* came to explode. Tellechea Idígoras, *Otra cara*, 520–5, listed the Basque sailors who died aboard the ship.
11  *BMO*, IV/3, 468, 'Relación de lo sucedido', 31 July 1588.
12  *BMO*, IV/3, 468, 'Relación de lo sucedido', 31 July 1588; ibid., 372, Don Jorge Manrique to Philip, 11 August 1588; ASF *MdP* 4919/532–3, 'Relazione cavata d'una lettera d'un Raguzeo'; Borja de Medina, 'Jesuitas', 30–4, 'Imformação'. Martin, *Spanish Armada prisoners*, and *BMO*, IV/1, pp. CXIX–CXXI, tried to reconcile the numerous accounts of *Rosario*'s fate.
13  *BMO*, IV/3, 415–16, Góngora to Fray Martín de Los Angeles, 15 August 1588; *BMO*, IV/4, 279–80, Don Juan de Cardona to Philip, 20 November 1588. For others who saw abandoning *Rosario* as a critical error, see *BMO*, IV/3, 431–3, Luis de Miranda to 'Your Honour' 18 August 1588; IV/4, 77–8, Gonzalo de Eraso to Philip, 1 October 1588; and Parker, 'Anatomy', 328 (Recalde).
14  *BMO*, IV/3, 463–7, Medina Sidonia's *Diario* gave broadly the same story. Two weeks earlier, Valdés complained that the duke 'has treated me worse than any of the other squadron commanders': *BMO*, IV/3, 161–2, Valdés to Philip, 15 July 1588 – and he did not exaggerate: see the duke's snide comment about him in a letter to the king: p. 29.
15  Laughton, II, 102, 'A note of certain speeches spoken by Sir Martin Frobisher at Harwich' on 11 August 1588 OS by an eyewitness.
16  Laughton, II, 134–6, interrogation of Valdés by his English captors. On this occasion, Don Pedro stated that he surrendered his flagship when Drake offered 'the safety of our lives and courteous entertainment'. Years later, he changed his story: see ch. 18.

17 TNA *E* 133/47/3, 'Drake versus Drake, 1605': depositions of George Hughes, Wood and Evan Owen; Nuttall, *New light*, 207, Zárate (coincidentally a cousin of Medina Sidonia) to Viceroy Don Martín Enríquez, 16 April 1579. One of the two English captives, Tristram Winslade, was later tortured on the rack: *APC*, XVI, 200 and 273.

18 Laughton, II, 29, 'Examination' of Valdés, 14 August 1588 NS; TNA *SP* 12/215/105, Drake's statement on 6 September 1588: 'This I confess to have: 25,300' ducats.'

19 *BMO*, IV/4, 77–8, Gonzalo de Eraso to Philip, 1 October 1588; *BMO*, IV/3, 499–500, Medina Sidonia to Philip, 30 July 1589; ibid., 468, 'Relación de lo sucedido', 31 July 1588. Vanegas also blamed Flores for failing to scupper the *San Salvador* 'while it travelled in the middle of the fleet', and so did a Portuguese Jesuit aboard the flagship: *BMO*, IV/4, 224–9, and *BMO*, IV/3, 307–10.

20 Kempe, *The Loseley Manuscripts*, 300–2, Privy Council to the deputy lieutenants of Surrey, 23 July 1588 OS (minute in *HMC Foljambe*, 48); Adams, 'Armada correspondence', 78, Howard to the earl of Sussex, 22 July 1588 OS.

21 *BMO*, IV/3, 469, 'Relación de lo sucedido', and *BMO*, IV/4, 226, 'Relación' of Vanegas, entries for 2 August 1588.

22 *BMO*, IV/3, 469, 'Relación de lo sucedido', 2 August 1588.

23 *BMO*, IV/4, 521, account by Diego López, 10 November 1589, who claimed to have heard the story from Frobisher himself ('le habían rompido el timón las galeazas'); Recalde stated that 'we noticed that the enemy flagship [presumably *Triumph*] had lost her rudder, and so all our fleet gave chase to her' (Parker, 'Anatomy', 329); *BMO*, IV/4, 141–4, 'Comentarios' of Fernando de Ayala, aboard *San Lorenzo*. Ayala set the story on 'the second day of combat, the 5th of August', but the second day of combat was 2 August and Ayala clearly described the fight on that day with *Triumph*, which he correctly identified as the largest ship in the English fleet (so large that he thought it might be the Portuguese carrack captured by Drake the previous year). Moncada's advance also probably faltered because he had to cross the tide race that runs between Portland Bill and the Shambles reef towards which, no doubt, the wily Frobisher had purposely lured him.

24 TNA *SP* 94/3/11, Medina Sidonia to Moncada, 2 August 1588, copy. (The precis of this important document in *CSPSp*, IV, 359, contained some serious errors of translation; *BMO*, IV/3, 297, printed a Spanish translation of the *CSPSp* precis, not the Spanish original.)

25 Laughton, I, 11–12, Howard's 'Relation'; Plymouth Archives, The Box, 2103/3, 'Accompte of soundrye monyes disbursed by Sir Ffrancis Drake', f. 4v; Parker, 'Anatomy', 329, Recalde's Diary for 2 August 1588, confirmed by Bertendona's account: LL *Bertendona Papers*, 171, 'Relación de servicios'.

26 *BMO*, IV/3, 469, 'Relación de lo sucedido', 2 August 1588.

27 TNA *SP* 94/3/11, Medina Sidonia to Moncada, 2 August 1588, copy (see also *BMO*, IV/3, 463–7, Medina Sidonia's 'Diario'); Parker, 'Anatomy', 324, Bobadilla to Recalde, 1 August, suggesting precisely this formation; *BMO*, IV/3, 307–10, 'Relación' by a Portuguese Jesuit travelling on the flagship.

28 Laughton, I, 301–2, Nicholas Oseley to Walsingham, 23 July 1588 OS; *BMO*, IV/3, 224–9, 'Relación' of Vanegas, entry for 2 August 1588.
29 Four Spanish accounts specified that the gun of a galleass struck a mast on 'la capitana enemiga', presumably *Revenge*: *BMO*, IV/3, 309–10 (Portuguese Jesuit), 372 (Don Jorge Manrique), 463–7 (Medina Sidonia's *Diario*) and 468–71 (Stukeley).
30 Parker, 'Anatomy', 329.
31 *BMO*, IV/4, 31, 'Relación' of Captain Alonso de Tauste, 22 September 1588.
32 *BMO*, IV/3, 305–6, Medina Sidonia to Parma, 4 August 1588, copy.
33 Recalde, 'Anatomy', 329, entry for 5 August 1588.
34 *BMO*, IV/3, 463–7, Medina Sidonia's 'Diario'; ibid., 392–5, 'Cartas dos padres'; ibid., 321, Medina Sidonia to Parma, 6 August 1588, copy (his second letter of the day). Adams, 'The battle that never was', 187, correctly pointed out that the duke can only have meant a port in England.
35 Nash, *Pierce penilesse*, unfol.; HMC *Seventh Report*, pt. I, 645, the countess of Lincoln (one of the queen's ladies-in-waiting) to Sir William More, 30 July 1588 OS, reporting the reaction at Court two days earlier when the young earl of Essex delivered news of what he had 'discerned' from Dover cliffs.

## 13. The Test of Battle

1 *BMO*, IV/3, 285, Medina Sidonia to Parma, 31 July/1 August 1588, copy; ASP *CF* 129 (*Spagna* 6), folder 1, unfol., Bobadilla to Parma, 1 August 1588.
2 *BMO*, IV/3, 305–6 and 314, Medina Sidonia to Parma, 4 and 5 August 1588, copies.
3 *BMO*, IV/3, 321 and 329–30, Medina Sidonia to Parma, 6 and 7 August 1588 (two letters), copies sent to the king, often with Parma's holograph hostile annotations. (The transcription of the second letter of 7 August in *BMO* contains a small error: both the copies in ASP *CF* 129 read 'campeando' and not 'capeando'.)
4 *BMO*, IV/3, 328–9, Parma to Philip, 7 August 1588, detailed the time each letter had arrived, and his response. The delays are corroborated by ASP *CF* 129 (*Spagna* 6), folder 1, Bobadilla to Parma, 25 July 1588, endorsed 'received on 2 August'; and loc. cit., same to same, 1 August 1588, endorsed 'received on 6 August'.
5 *BMO*, IV/3, 392–5, 'Cartas dos padres', entry for 7 August 1588.
6 *Breeder verclaringhe*, 9, a transcript of Pimentel's interrogation by his Dutch captors.
7 BL *Sloane Ms.* 262/62 ('Diarie' of the English commissioners); and HHStA *Belgien PC* 43/1, Spanish delegates to Parma, Bourbourg, 6 August 1588.
8 *BMO*, IV/3, 354–5, Parma to Philip, 10 August 1588, stating that Don Jorge Manrique suggested a landing on the Isle of Wight when he arrived at Parma's headquarters on 8 August (Parma repeated the statement in his letter to Juan de Cernosa, Spanish consul in Venice, 10 August 1588: Malfatti, *Cuatro documentos*, 34–8); BRB *Ms.* II.1155/216–216v, 'Liber relationum' of Paolo Rinaldi, Parma's chamberlain, recorded the discussion of these suggestions by Parma's council.

9 *BMO*, IV/2, 541, Philip to Medina Sidonia, 21 June 1588. See also ibid., 36, Idiáquez to Medina Sidonia, 28 March 1588, reminding him that Parma's ships 'are not strong enough for combat, which is why they must remain where they are until the Armada arrives and protects their crossing'. How could the message have been clearer?

10 *BMO*, IV/2, 513, Medina Sidonia to Parma, 10 June 1588, copy sent to (and annotated by) Philip (see also KML *MSP: CR* 5/264–7, minute of the same letter); ibid., 541 and 573–4, Philip to Medina Sidonia, 21 and 26 June 1588.

11 *BMO*, IV/3, 266, Medina Sidonia to Philip, 30 July 1588.

12 *BMO*, IV/2, 513, Medina Sidonia to Parma, 10 June 1588, copy. Medina Sidonia also announced that he had consulted his pilots, 'men who are very familiar with the coast of England, and asked them in which ports on that coast this Armada might anchor'. They supplied a list of south coast ports, which Medina Sidonia entrusted to Captain Moresin, together with their recommendation that the fleet should not pass beyond Beachy Head. It seems strange that Moresin apparently did not point out the duke's error. Philip's comment appears on the copy of this letter sent to him by Parma, and he wrote his 21 June letter in response (ibid., 541). See also ibid., 544, Parma's letter of protest to Philip, dated 22 June 1588, with the king's forlorn annotation on 7 August.

13 *BMO*, IV/3, 219–20, Parma to Philip, 21 July 1588, rehearsed what he had instructed Moresin to say to correct Medina Sidonia's misconceptions; ibid., 363, 'Lo que refiere Don Rodrigo de Avilés' (on Moresin's delayed arrival); and ibid., 192–4, Parma to Philip, 18 July 1588, which only reached Philip on 7 August (ibid., 326, Philip to Parma, 7 August 1588).

14 TNA *SP* 84/26/54–5, James Digges to Walsingham, Middelburg, [6] August 1588.

15 Piot, *Chroniques*, 672–3, 'Vlaemsche Kronyk', whose author was present, offers the best account of the incident. The triumphant report by David Cabreth to Walsingham, printed in Rodríguez-Salgado, *Armada*, 121, appears to be totally false.

16 BL *Cotton Ms.* Vespasian C.VIII/12–16v, an account of the ships and stores at Dunkirk, 13 June 1588 OS; ibid., f. 106, 'A note of what shipping the king hath in the Lowe Countreys'; *BMO*, IV/3, 328, Parma to Philip, 7 August 1588; Laughton, I, 321–2, Leicester to Walsingham, 26 July 1588 OS.

17 Laughton, I, 331 and 341, Seymour to the Privy Council, 6 August 1588 NS, and Howard to Walsingham, 8 August 1588 NS; ARA *Raad van State*, 7, unfol., council decision on 9 August 1588 to send more ships to blockade Dunkirk. According to the duke of Urbino's agent four days later, 45 Dutch warships stood off the Flemish coast, and a further 40 had joined Howard in pursuit of the Armada: BAV *UL* 1056/422–v, Gratioso Gratiosi to the duke of Urbino, Antwerp, 13 August 1588.

18 AGRB *Chambre des Comptes* 26,136/88–91, Account of Michel Fourlaux, recorded the departure of 10 boats from Dunkirk 'to locate the royal fleet from Spain' between 17 February and 30 July 1588; subsequent departures were reported in TNA *SP* 101/9/85, 'Advertisement' sent to Burghley in September 1588 (precis in *CSPF*,

XXII, 171–2); and Piot, *Chroniques*, 682. ASV *LP* 46/240, 'Relatione d'un grumete', narrated the journey of a seaman who sailed on one of these vessels, returned to Dunkirk and sailed thence back to Corunna and Lisbon, arriving on 5 October 1588. The safe arrival of two Armada vessels appears in AGS *CMC* 3a/2761 (the *zabras Santa Ana* and *Magdalena* arrived on 17 and 25 August respectively).

19 Laughton, I, 344–50, Richard Thomson to Walsingham, 30 July 1588; and II, 7–14, Winter to Walsingham, 1 August 1588 (both dates OS). Perhaps the English ships became untangled without 'destruction' because, unlike their adversaries, many of their officers and crew boasted long familiarity with the ships on which they served.

20 Oppenheim, *History*, 163. Three of the fireships (*Barks Talbot* and *Bond*, and *Hope*) had sailed with Drake to the Caribbean in 1585 (Keeler, *Drake's West Indian voyage*, 45–6); and Drake provided one more fireship himself (*Bark Thomas*). Captain Vanegas and an officer aboard *Gran Grifón* both described the attack by one of Seymour's ships: *BMO*, IV/4, 224–9 and 303–5, entries for 7 August.

21 *BMO*, IV/3, 372, Report of Manrique and Marolín, Dunkirk, 11 August 1588; ibid., 392–5, 'Cartas dos padres' (La Torre attributed the opinion that the Armada should remain at anchor and use its boats to steer the fireships away to Oquendo, not to Recalde: *BMO*, IV/4, 66–8).

22 Parker, 'Anatomy', 330 (when dawn broke, the felucca carrying Ascoli and Marolín de Juan, the chief pilot of the fleet, had strayed into the midst of the English fleet and so they took refuge in Calais: *BMO*, IV/3, 387, Ascoli to Philip, 12 August 1588); *BMO*, IV/4, 224–9, 'Relación' of Alonso Vanegas, entries for 7 and 8 August; ibid., 141–4, 'Comentario' by Fernando de Ayala.

23 *BMO*, IV/4, 20–4, 'Relación' of Coco Calderón, entry for 9 August 1588; Admiral González-Aller Hierro (*BMO*, IV/1, p. CCLX n. 3) found confirmation for the veracity of Oquendo's insolent comment in the contempt for Medina Sidonia shown in his last letter, written when he knew he was dying: *BMO*, IV/4, 60, Oquendo to Andrés de Alva, 29 September 1588.

24 Laughton, II, 7–14, Winter to Walsingham, 1 August 1588 OS.

25 *BMO*, IV/4, 141–4, 'Comentario' by Ayala, aboard *San Lorenzo*.

26 Details from Laughton, I, 344–50, Richard Thomson (one of the 100 men who boarded the galleass) to Walsingham, 30 July 1588 OS; and Borja de Medina, 'Jesuítas', 30–4, 'Imformação' (the priest was Father Antonio Crespo, who survived to become a chaplain in the Army of Flanders).

27 *BMO*, IV/3, 431–3, letter of Luis de Miranda, 18 August 1588; *BMO*, IV/4, 31–2, Anonymous 'Relación', probably by Captain Alonso de Tauste of *Asunción*, 22 September 1588, entry for 7 August. See also TNA *SP* 63/136/175–6v, Examination of Pietro Baptista, soldier and purser from the galleass *Zuñiga*, 9 September 1588.

28 *BMO*, IV/4, 20–4, 'Relación' by Pedro Coco Calderón, collated with the original: AGS *GA* 221/189–90. ASF *MP* 4919/476–7, Giulio Battaglione to the grand duke of Tuscany, 27 September 1588, recalled the distinguished role of *San Mateo* six years before.

29 Laughton, II, 7–14, Winter to Walsingham, 1 August 1588 OS; *BMO*, IV/4, 66–8, La Torre to Alonso de Deza, 30 September 1588; ibid., 20–4, 'Relación' by Pedro Coco Calderón; ibid., 224–9, 'Relación' of Vanegas, and *BMO*, IV/3, 392–5, 'Cartas dos padres', entries for 8 August 1588.
30 *BMO*, IV/4, 66–8, La Torre to Deza; ibid., IV/3, 441, Don Jorge Manrique to Philip, 19 August 1588; *BMO*, IV/3, 468–71, 'Relación de lo sucedido', 8 August 1588.
31 *BMO*, IV/3, 468–71, 'Relación de lo sucedido', 8 August 1588; *BMO*, IV/4, 20–4, 'Relación' by Pedro Coco Calderón; BAV *UL* 1113/619, Don Jusepe de Acuña to Olivares, Turin, 27 August 1588, copy.
32 Parker, 'Anatomy', 330. Gonzalo de Eraso, a staff officer aboard the flagship, also later condemned Medina Sidonia for failing to tow the two galleons and prevent them falling into enemy hands: *BMO*, IV/4, 77–8, Eraso to Philip, Santander, 1 October 1588. Howard's 'Relation of proceedings' credited the destruction of the two galleons to the squadron led by Seymour and Winter (Laughton, I, 17).
33 RAZ *Register van Acten en Brieven*, portfeuille 1625/257v–8, States of Zeeland to Count Maurice, 10 August 1588; Laughton, II, 29–30, William Borlas (the senior officer) to Walsingham, 3 August 1588 OS; TNA SP 101/45/22, Richard Eshertone to Richard Saltonstall, 7 August 1588 OS.
34 *BMO*, IV/4, testimony of Marco di Pietro (Marko Petrov), Ferrol, 14 June 1590, Spanish translation of an Italian original. Kostić, 'Ragusa', 214–16, identified the gunner and provided both a partial facsimile and a translation of his deposition.
35 TNA SP 63/136/146–7, examination of Giovanni Antonio Manona, on *Santa Maria*; Tellechea Idígoras, *Otra cara*, 359, on *Santa Ana*; Gallagher and Cruickshank, *God's obvious design*, 224, on *San Pedro*. See also *BMO*, IV/4, 66–8, La Torre to Deza.
36 Rodger, *The Armada*, 58–9, Drake to Walsingham, 29 July/8 August 1588, holograph, facsimile and transcript.
37 *BMO*, IV/3, 468–71, 'Relación de lo sucedido', 9 August 1588; *BMO*, IV/4, 66–8, La Torre to Deza; ibid., 224–9, 'Relación' of Vanegas.
38 Parker, 'Anatomy', 321, Leyva to Recalde, 12 August 1588; and 319, Recalde to Don Martín de Idiáquez, 8 October 1588.

## 14. 'God blew and they were scattered'

1 *BMO*, IV/3, 470, 'Relación de lo sucedido', 9 August 1588.
2 *BMO*, IV/4, 66–8, La Torre to Deza.
3 *BMO*, IV/4, 229, 'Relación' of Vanegas; ibid., 304, 'Relación' by someone aboard *Gran Grifón*. According to Cuéllar, Don Francisco de Bobadilla condemned all twenty officers to death, but the duke upheld only the sentence on Ávila: see Gallagher and Cruickshank, *God's obvious design*, 225. Hanging was regarded as a particularly degrading punishment: gentlemen condemned to death were normally beheaded. AGS *CS* 2a/286/51 contains the 'pliego de asiento' for Ávila, captain of *Santa Bárbara*.

4 *BMO*, IV/3, 468–71, 'Relación de lo sucedido', entry for 9 August 1588 (changing the past to the present tense).
5 Parker, 'Anatomy', 321, Leyva to Recalde, 17 August 1588, holograph; *BMO*, IV/4, 228, Vanegas, entry for 9 August 1588; ibid., 66–8, La Torre to Deza; ibid., 141–4, 'Comentario' by Fernando de Ayala (changing the past to the present tense).
6 Parker, 'Anatomy', 320–2, Leyva to Recalde, 12 and 17 August 1588, both holographs.
7 Parker, 'Anatomy', 331. AGS *CMC* 2a/772, file concerning *San Francisco* (Castile), contains a copy of the order of 10 August reducing rations.
8 Parker, 'Anatomy', 327, Recalde to the duke, 11/12 August 1588.
9 *BMO*, IV/4, 10, Medina Sidonia to Don Juan de Idiáquez, 23 September 1588; Gallagher and Cruickshank, *God's obvious design*, 202; RAZ *Register van Acten en Brieven*, portefeuille 1625/258v, States of Zeeland to Count Maurice, 11 August 1588; *BMO*, IV/4, 66–8, La Torre to Deza; Borja de Medina, 'Jesuitas', 30–4, 'Imformação'.
10 *BMO*, IV/4, 303–5, account of someone on *Gran Grifón*, entry for 12 August; Gallagher and Cruickshank, *God's obvious design*, 202; TNA *SP* 63/136/157–8, second Examination of Piet O'Carr from *San Juan de Portugal*, 12 September 1588 OS ('the Admiral … came not out of his bed until this day sennight [i.e. a week ago, 5 September] in the morning that they came upon this shore').
11 Laughton, II, 11–13, Winter to Walsingham, 1 August 1588; ibid., 6, 'Resolution at a Council of War', 1 August 1588; ibid., 53–4, Howard to Walsingham, 7 August 1588 (all dates OS).
12 Parker, 'Anatomy', 331, entry for 10 August 1588; Laughton, II, 95, Sir Thomas Heneage to Walsingham, 9 August 1588 OS; TNA *SP* 63/137/5, Examination of Don Luis de Córdoba, late September 1588, annotated by Burghley (the 'great volley').
13 Parker, 'Anatomy', 326–7, Recalde's exchanges with the duke on 10 and 11/12 August 1588; TNA *SP* 63/136/143 and 156, examination of Emanuel Francisc from *San Juan*, 12 September 1588 OS.
14 Parker, 'Anatomy', 327, Recalde to Medina Sidonia, 11/12 August 1588; idem, 320–2, Leyva to Recalde, 12 August (in reply to a lost letter from the latter which evidently suggested the same 'Finisterre option' as the extant letter to the duke) and 17 August 1588.
15 *CSPI*, 49–50, prints the only known example of Medina Sidonia's sailing orders, taken from the purser of the galleass *Zúñiga* when he was captured, translated into English (perhaps inaccurately in parts) and sent on to London. Although it is undated, Coco Calderón stated that the orders were issued on 13 August. Recalde had reminded Medina Sidonia of the need to issue sailing orders the day before (Parker, 'Anatomy', 327). Recalde's log recorded with obvious disapproval the duke's decision to abandon those who could not keep up (ibid., 331, entry for 15 August).
16 *BMO*, IV/4, 228–9, 'Relación' of Vanegas, entry for 9 August 1588; BL *Cotton Ms.* Caligula D.1/292 and 305–6, William Asheby to Walsingham, Edinburgh, 22

August and 8 September 1588 OS; *BMO*, IV/4, 24, 'Relación' of Coco Calderón, entry for 24 August 1588 (one wonders which chart ['*carta*'] they held in their hands). Vanegas said that one of the pilots was 'Flamenco', which we translate as 'from the Netherlands', and that the duke offered him 3,000 ducats; Coco said that 'his friend' was 'Francés', which may mean that he came from the French-speaking part of the Netherlands. Coco also stated that the duke offered him 2,000 ducats.

17 Porras Arboledas, 'La aportación', 70–1, testimony by Francisco de Lastero on the fate of his ship, *La concepción*, 20 March 1590.

18 Parker, 'Anatomy', 320–2, Leyva to Recalde, 12 and 17 August 1588.

19 *BMO*, IV/4, 68, La Torre to Deza; ibid., 229, 'Relación' of Vanegas; ibid., 31–2, 'Relación' of Captain Alonso de Tauste.

20 *BMO*, IV/4, Francisco Duarte to Andrés de Alva, Lisbon, 11 January 1589, relaying the account of a Venetian sailor who survived the wreck of *Trinidad Valencera*.

21 *BMO*, IV/4, 394–5, 'Lo que refieren Juan de Nova … y Francisco de Borja', Paris, 16 January 1589 (summarized in *CSPSp*, IV, 506–10, with the incorrect date of 21 January).

22 *CSPSc*, IX, 624, passport issued by Provost John Arnott of Edinburgh, 28 October 1588; BL *Cotton Ms.* Caligula D.I/226–7, William Asheby to Walsingham, Edinburgh, 23 October 1588. Asheby stated that *Trinidad Valencera* was 'wrecked the 6 of September', and that 50 survivors (16 of them Italians) reached Edinburgh on 10 October; five days later Provost Arnott gave the total as 46 survivors. All dates OS.

23 ABB *VC* 1214/9–11 and 28, described 10 Spanish soldiers and 1 Flemish sailor from *Trinidad Valencera*, ransomed for 51 florins each and repatriated from Dartmouth in January 1590, and in other folios named the officers who had promised to pay a 'rescate particular' in addition to the 51 florins. A few other survivors managed to escape: see their testimony in *BMO*, IV/4, 383–4, 387–91, 394–5, 444–5, 455–7 and 493–5.

24 *BMO*, IV/4, 303–5, 'Relación verdadera del suceso' by someone aboard the *Grifón*, the source of all quotations about the ship's voyage. The *relación* was clearly written by an officer, but not by Gómez de Medina because it described his departure for Shetland on 28 October and stated 'he has not yet returned'.

25 Monteith, *The Description*, Part II (Shetland), 25–7 (written in 1633, though not printed until 1711).

26 All quotations from James Melville, *The diary*, 174–6. The pamphlet that made Gómez de Medina weep was surely *Certeine advertisements ovt of Ireland concerning the losses happened to the Spanish Armie vpon the west costes of Irelande* (London, 1588): Figure 100.

27 *BMO*, IV/3, 532–3, Interrogation of Patrick Cathmhaoil [Caughwell], 3 September 1588; *Calendar of the Carew manuscripts*, II, 470, Sir George Carew to Sir Christopher Hatton, Dublin, 4 August 1588 OS; TNA *SP* 63/136/232–5, 'A discourse of the overthrow and shipwreck of the Spaniards on the coasts of Connaught' by Edward White, entry for 6 September 1588 OS.

28  *CSPI*, IV, 29, Bingham to Lord Deputy Fitzwilliam, Athlone, 8 September 1588 OS.
29  *APC*, XVI, 280–1, order of 18 September 1588 OS.
30  TNA *SP* 63/163/88, Fitzwilliam to the Privy Council, London, 10 September 1588 OS; LPL *Carew Ms* 618/83–83v, Commission of Fitzwilliam to Thomas Norris and others, Dublin, 22 September 1588 OS.
31  TNA *SP* 63/136/84, 'Examination' of 24 Spanish prisoners, forwarded to Walsingham on 9 September 1588 OS. In earlier editions of this work we identified the Tralee wreck as *Nuestra Señora de Castro*, but Porras Arboledas, 'La aportación', 78–9, cited depositions by relatives of the crew on this ship demonstrating that she foundered within sight of the Spanish coast, with the loss of all hands. He plausibly suggests that the Tralee wreck was *Concepción de Castro* (ibid., 73).
32  Some sources claim that the murdered man was Don Felipe de Córdoba, son of Philip's chamberlain, but an English cannonball killed him aboard the flagship on 8 August. The list of Armada gentlemen initially saved but later murdered in cold blood included 'Don Diego de Córdoba': TNA *SP* 63/139/5, fifth name. We suggest that this was the man whom Clancy hanged. We further suggest that the ship wrecked off Mutton Island was *Santa Bárbara* (whose fate is otherwise unknown) because the same list included an officer who sailed on her: Captain Bartolomeo Bravo.
33  AGS *CS* 2a/280/1391–458, audited accounts for *Anunciada*; *BMO*, IV/4, 101–2, testimony of Juan de los Ríos, Ordoño de Zamudio and Alonso de Porres on the fate of *Anunciada* and *Barca de Danzig*, 4 October 1588; ibid., 183–4, list of the munitions successfully salvaged from *Anunciada* and brought back to Spain; ibid., 311–12, statement of Oliste about the fate of his ship, and requesting 20,000 ducats in compensation; TNA *SP* 63/163/96, Nicholas Cahan to Boetius Clancy, 5 September 1588 OS, copy.

## 15. From Dispersal to Disaster

1  TNA *SP* 63/136/232–5, *A discourse of the overthrow and shipwreck of the Spaniards on the coasts of Connaught and Thomond*, by Richard Bingham.
2  *BMO*, IV/4, 189, 'Relación' of Marcos de Aramburu, entry for 30 August 1588.
3  TNA *SP* 63/136/141–5, examination of the Portuguese seamen Emanuel Fremoso and Emanuel Francist, and the Fleming Piet O'Carr, Cork, 12 September 1588 OS.
4  We believe that TNA *SP* 63/136/70 is a copy of Recalde's letter. It was addressed 'al illmo Señor capitán o gobernador' ashore and signed by 'Captain Pedro de Esquivel' (an *entretenido* aboard *San Juan*), to be delivered by 'this Burgundian' – a significant detail, since Recalde's log stated that he sent his letter with 'a Burgundian' (Parker, 'Anatomy', 333). Thomas Norris, vice-president of Munster, made a copy of the letter and forwarded it to Walsingham on 8 September OS (TNA *SP* 63/136/67). Although the date of the Spanish copy is almost illegible, it may read 'diez y seis

de septiembre' – viz 6 September OS – which is the day Recalde's log recorded sending it and also the day the English commander at Dingle probably received it. The date of '8 September' assigned by the TNA archivists (followed by the editor of *CSPI*, IV, 27) seems incorrect.
5   TNA *SP* 63/136/182, James Traunte to Sir Edward Denny, Dingle, 11 September 1588 OS, with copious annotations by Lord Burghley.
6   For Lope's claim see Parker, 'Lope de Vega'.
7   Aramburu stated that the storm struck on 21 September (*BMO*, IV/4, 190), but Recalde assigned the same events to the 20th (Parker, 'Anatomy', 334). We have accepted Aramburu's date.
8   TNA *SP* 63/136/146–7 and 159–60, Examination of 'John Anthony of Genova marryner', Cork, 15 September 1588 OS.
9   Ibid.
10  Bazan survived and returned to Corunna aboard Recalde's ship, but 'very few men from his original ship survived': Gracia Rivas, *Los tercios*, 187, report of the marquis of Cerralvo in October 1588. *BMO*, IV/3, 125, a muster on 8 October 1588, showed 56 men from Bazan's company.
11  TNA *SP* 63/136/175–6, Examination of Pietro Baptista, purser of *Zúñiga*, 9 September 1588 OS; *BMO*, IV/4, 96, Juan de Saavedra to Philip, 4 October 1588.
12  Laughton, II, 299–302, Bingham to Elizabeth, 3 December 1588 OS, with a list of 34 of 'some 50 gentlemen' whom he had executed in cold blood, acting on Fitzwilliam's express order. Bingham's list included Gaspar de los Reyes, master and pilot of *Gran Grín*, and at least two of the infantry captains aboard, Don Alonso Ladrón de Guevara and Don Diego Santillana.
13  Laughton, II, 299–301, Bingham to Elizabeth, 3 December 1588 OS, mentioned that his brother had spared 'one Don Graveillo de Swasso and another gentleman' but did not mention their ship. Don Gabriel de Suazo commanded an infantry company on *San Nicolás Prodaneli*, which identifies the ship. The other company captain aboard was Don Alonso de Riquelme. ABB *VC* 1214/16 named two surviving soldiers from Riquelme's company, aged 22 and 24 in 1590.
14  AGS *Estado* 166/63, Testament of Ulloa, undated, forwarded to Spain by Balthasar López del Árbol on 12 July 1589 (*BMO*, IV/4, 495, followed by an incomplete transcript of the testament). Although López speculated that Ulloa came from Toro, the names of the churches mentioned in the testament prove that he came from Córdoba. Ulloa appeared on Bingham's list of those he had executed: TNA *SP* 63/139/5, fourth name.
15  TNA *SP* 63/136/236–41, Bingham's 'True declaracon of the greate losses and overthrow received by the remnants of the Spanishe fleet', asserted that he had judged only 40 Spanish prisoners in Galway on 21 September 1588 OS and spared 10; TNA *SP* 63/137/3, Bingham to Fitzwilliam, 21 September 1588 (totals); ABB *VC* 1214/13, 14, 15, 17 and 21 (survivors ransomed in 1590). TNA *SP* 63/137/5, 'Examination of Don Lewes de Cordova', late September 1588, stated that he was in command of the 100 soldiers aboard *Falcón Blanco*, but the 'Relación' of

a captain from *Barca de Amburg*, Brussels, February 1589 (*BMO*, IV/4, 437–8), stated that Don Luis was captain of the *Ciervo Volante* – another example of the contradictions between the surviving sources. In this case we believe Córdoba.

16  *BMO*, IV/4, 521, 'Declaration' of Diego López, a soldier aboard *Lavia*, 10 November 1589. Like Cuéllar, our source for the rest of this section, he 'crossed the whole of Ireland without suffering any loss', escaped to Le Havre and got back to Spain.

17  *CSPI*, IV, 92–8, Fitzwilliam to the Privy Council, 31 December 1588 OS.

18  ABB *VC* 1214/11, 12, 13, 14, 18, 19, 21 and 27. Carlos Longin, who compiled the list of prisoners whom he ransomed in January 1590, noted visible wounds because (like the colour of each man's eyes and beard, which he also noted) they were 'distinguishing marks'. The men may have received face wounds at any point in their lives, of course, but their frequency among those from the Streedagh wrecks suggests disfiguring wounds either as they struggled ashore or soon afterwards.

19  Earlier editions of this book asserted that *Girona* had sheltered at the present harbour-town of Killibegs; but Ken Douglas has pointed out that in the sixteenth century 'Calebeg' referred to the adjacent McSween's Bay (*The downfall*, 35–6).

20  TNA *SP* 63/139/82–3, examinations of James Machary and George de Venery by Fitzwilliam, Dublin, 29 December 1588; *BMO*, IV/4, 455–7, testimony of Melchior de Sevilla and Jacomo Hescafin, Ribadeo, February 1589. AGS *CS* 2a/273, *Girona* dossier, named 16 sailors from the galleass still alive to claim their pay in the 1590s, out of 127 who left Corunna, but 10 had transferred to other ships before she sank.

21  BL *Cotton Ms.* Caligula D.I/230–1v, Asheby to Walsingham, Edinburgh, 6 November 1588; TNA *SP* 52/42/119, Asheby to Burghley, Edinburgh, 13 November 1588; and TNA *SP* 63/141/50, Report of Charles Edgerton to Fitzwilliam, Carrickfergus, January 1589, forwarded to Walsingham.

22  BL *Cotton Ms.* Caligula D.I/228–9v, Asheby to Walsingham, Edinburgh, 26 November 1588 OS; *BMO*, IV/4, 533, petition of Juan de Soranguren, 1589.

23  Ødegaard, *Alonso de Olmos*, 32–3, Testimony of Simón Uniques, master, Bergen, 15 November 1588; ibid., 37–8, Diego de la Hava to Parma, 2 April 1589; ibid., 62–4, Olmos to Philip, Alicante, 22 July 1589; and Ødegaard, *Den spanske armada*, 79–80, testimony of Juan Rayam, pilot, Lisbon, 11 January 1589.

24  AGRB *SEG* 11/163v–4, Parma's order to pay 50,000 florins to ransom 500 Armada prisoners in England, 17 March 1589; *BMO*, IV/4, 441–2, 'Relación' by three officers from *San Pedro*, 18 February 1589, one of whom reported the jeers of those who had abandoned the ship at Calais.

25  Carnero, *Historia*, 229. Since he served as senior auditor of the Army of Flanders in 1588, we may accept Carnero's figures with confidence.

26  ABB *VC* 1214/7, amended entry for Pereda.

27  *CSPSc*, IX, 607, Sir Robert Sidney to Walsingham, Edinburgh, 1 September 1588 OS, reporting on his audience with James.

28  *CSPSc*, IX, 669–70, Thomas Fowler to Walsingham, Edinburgh, 15 January 1589 OS.

29 HSA *Altamira* 2/III/15, Mateo Vázquez to Philip, 19 February 1589, with a rescript that proposed a remarkably convoluted manoeuvre to persuade Quiroga to act as the king wished, but without seeming to interfere in the work of the Inquisitors.
30 BMO, IV/4, 402, Patricio Antolinez and Esteban de Legoretta to Philip, Edinburgh, 22 January 1589; ibid., 468, Legoretta to Parma, 29 March 1589; TNA *SP* 52/44/57 and 61, Asheby to Walsingham, 14 and 22 July 1589 OS, holograph. BL *Cotton Ms.* Caligula D.I/424, Asheby to Walsingham, 1 April 1589, reported the arrival in Scotland of 300 survivors from Norway.
31 *CSPSc*, X, 122–3, Asheby to Burghley, 26 July 1589 OS. Asheby later reported that between 60 and 80 Spanish soldiers from Mull arrived in Edinburgh two days after their comrades left on their ill-fated voyage.
32 *HMC Bath*, V, 94, Elizabeth to Shrewsbury, 1588 [undated but mid-September].
33 McNeill, 'Report', 95, payment to Mathew Smythe, 8 November 1588 OS.
34 Falls, *Elizabeth's Irish wars*, 166; *CSPI*, IV, 92–8, Fitzwilliam to the Privy Council, 31 December 1588; McNeill, 'Report', 96–7, payment to Sappa, 15 September 1590, from the accounts of Sir Henry Wallop, Irish Treasurer-at-war (all dates OS).
35 Laughton, II, 186–8, George Cary to Walsingham, 29 August 1588 OS.
36 AGS *CMC* 2a/772, dossier of *San Francisco* (Andalucia), account of arquebus powder, match and ball issued; BNE *Ms.* 3556/298v, 'Relación' of a Portuguese Jesuit aboard the flagship. AGS *CMC* 2a/29 and 31, accounts settled with the mutineers from the company of Francisco de Frías at La Chapelle (1596), detailed the rations actually issued to those who had served on the Armada.
37 BMO, IV/4, 24, 'Relación' of Pedro Coco Calderón; ibid., 29–30, Oquendo to Andrés de Alva and to Philip, 24 September 1588; ibid., 77–8, Gonzalo de Erasso to Philip, 1 October 1588; ibid., 229, 'Relación' of Captain Vanegas; ibid., 403–4, Coco Calderón to Philip, 24 January 1589.
38 BMO, IV/4, 461, Gómez de Medina to the duke, 4 March 1589, copy; Pires de Lima, 'Um documento português', 100, letter from the master of *San Juan de Portugal*, Corunna, 19 October 1588.

## 16. Analysis of Failure

1 Cohen and Gooch, *Military misfortunes*, 25.
2 Bouza, *Cartas de Felipe II*, 50–1, Philip to his daughters, Lisbon, 10 July 1581, describing his inspection of Valdés's fleet in harbour that morning; Salgado, *Os navios*, 19–30, on the campaigns in 1582 and 1583.
3 TNA *SP* 12/7/169–72v, Elizabeth's Instructions to Winter, 16 December 1559, two drafts in Cecil's hand; TNA *SP* 52/2/15.I, duke of Norfolk to Winter, 23 January 1560.
4 BMO, II, 382–3, 'Lo que refiere Manuel Blanco', Lisbon, 11 October 1586 (precis in *CSPSp*, III, 632–3).

5 *BMO*, IV/2, 418–19, Philip to Medina Sidonia, 14 May 1588; *BMO*, IV/3, 137–8 and 205–6, Juan de Idiáquez to Medina Sidonia and reply, 12 and 19 July 1588.
6 *BMO*, IV/3, 65, Interrogation of 'Olvermos' by Don Alonso de Luzón in the Scilly Islands, 28 June 1588 (Medina Sidonia forwarded two copies to Philip from Corunna, on 6 July 1588 'aunque no dice nada de consideración': ibid., 63); ibid., 72, Gómez de Medina to Philip, Corunna, 6 July 1588.
7 Laughton, I, 12 (Howard's 'Relation of proceedings'); and ibid., II, 59–60, Howard to Walsingham, 8 August 1588 OS, reporting a comparison made by Spanish captives. See the similar statement made by someone on *San Martín* who had survived Lepanto: 'There was no comparison between the two in either duration or intensity' (*BMO*, IV/4, 66, 'Relación' of La Torre). Other quotations from chs 14 and 15.
8 Hakluyt, *Principal navigations*, II, 393, a translation of van Meteren's *Historia*, repeating anecdotes that first appeared in Ubaldini's 'Comentario' in 1589 (Naish, 'Documents', 96).
9 TNA *SP* 12/220, 'Survey' of the Queen's Ships carried out on 25 September 1588 OS (see extracts in Laughton, II, 241–9).
10 TNA *SP* 12/218/46–8, 'Device' of the Navy Board, 20 November 1588 OS, estimated that building four galleons and four cromsters would require '600 tons of timber': see pp. 444–5 above.
11 TNA *E* 351/2225 (and, more legibly, TNA *AO* 1/1686/23), accounts of Sir John Hawkins as Treasurer of the Navy for 1588. BL *Sloane Ms.* 2450, 'Sea causes extraordinary, A.D. 1588', also includes accounts for numerous repairs carried out in spring 1588, as well as in September (see f. 54).
12 We accept the careful computation of the Armada's big guns in *BMO*, V, anexo 5, summarized in ibid., IV/1, p. LVII and corresponding notes.
13 Data from *BMO*, IV/4, 246–53, 'Relación' of 43 Armada ships at Santander, 1 November 1588 (*Napolitana*); ibid., 288–9 and 299–300, 'Relación' of artillery salvaged from *San Lorenzo*, 22 and 29 November 1588; Harvard, Houghton Library, *Ms. Typ.* 16, John Mountgomerie, 'The nauie'; TNA *SP* 12/211/157–62, 'The reporte of George Wod', a prisoner aboard a galleass for 22 weeks, June 1588. Perhaps the other two galleasses carried similar armament, but we cannot know for sure because *Girona* foundered and *Zúñiga* only got back to Spain in August 1589 after jettisoning most of her heavy guns.
14 *BMO*, III/3, *consulta* of the Council of War, 16 January 1588; ibid., IV/2, 14 and 94–5, Medina Sidonia to Philip, 26 March 1588, and reply, 3 April 1588 (Ghislieri was also the nephew of Pope Pius V and cousin of the papal secretary of state, which raised suspicions about his loyalty). See *BMO*, III/3, 1289, 'Resultados' of an inspection of the 4 galleasses in Lisbon by Recalde, 21 October 1587, revealing serious defects.
15 Data from AGS *GA* 347/218, 'Las naves que fueron en esta última armada'; AGS *GA* 347/206, 'Relación particular'; *BMO*, IV/4, 219–20 (Corunna); and ibid., 246–53 (Santander). RAZ *Rekenkamer* C 2983, account of Pieter Willemszoon

for the 38 guns recovered from the wrecked Portuguese galleons *San Mateo* and *San Felipe*: the heaviest were nine 14-pounders.
16   Eliav, 'Tactics', 407–8, quoting Cristoforo da Canale, *Della milizia militare* (1553–4).
17   *BMO*, V, 252–5, on *Santa Ana* of Guipúzcoa; Laughton, II, 156 (armament recovered after the explosion) and *BMO*, V, 255–6, on *San Salvador*; *BMO*, V, 234–5, on *Rosario*; and ibid., 215–17, on *Santa Ana* (Vizcaya).
18   *BMO*, IV/4, 22, 'Relación' by Coco Calderón, entry for 4 August 1588. See also the 'Relación' by Captain Alonso de Tauste, entry for 7 August, quoted in ch. 13 above.
19   Borja de Medina, 30–4, 'Informação' of a Portuguese Jesuit aboard *Santiago* (Spanish translation in *BMO*, IV/4, 346–7).
20   BMO IV/3, 109–10, 'Relación' of Alférez Becerra, Corunna, 10 July 1588; BMO IV/4, 21, 'Relación' of Coco Calderón, entry for 2 August 1588.
21   Laughton, I, 48–50, Howard to Walsingham, 27 January 1588, and II, 7–14, Winter to Walsingham, 11 August 1588 (both dates OS).
22   TNA *SP* 63/137/97–8v, 'Examination' of Luzón at Drogheda, 13 October 1588 OS, answer to the 14th question. It might be objected that Don Alonso feigned ignorance in order to avoid providing his captors with useful intelligence, but since *Trinidad Valencera* had already sunk, it is hard to see what he gained by his vague answers. Moreover, he had no inhibition about telling his captors that the Armada carried 600,000 ducats in cash, part of it aboard *San Salvador*. When the imprisoned officers of *Rosario* were asked to describe the armament of their vessel, their answers were similarly vague, ranging from 40 to 58 guns: TNA *SP* 12/214/49–60v.
23   *BMO*, IV/2, 310–11, Philip to Don Jorge Manrique, Antonio de Guevara and Diego Flores, 9 May 1588. See also *BMO*, IV/4, 457–8, Petition of Simon Claes, master of *Casa de Paz*, February 1589, claiming that his ship was wrecked as she tried to enter Laredo because 'Diego Flores de Valdés ordered him to surrender the main anchor, some hawsers and other items essential to save the ship'.
24   AGS *CMC* 2a/942, accounts of *Trinidad de Escala*, ff. 109–12. The following summer, despite frequent warnings to be prepared, the officers of this ship claimed they were not ready to put to sea 'giving such feeble excuses [*escusas tan flacas*] that they deserve exemplary punishment'. The fleet commander thereupon decreed that the ship would receive no payment for her hire after 21 September 1588, when it returned with the Armada: AGS *CMC* 2a/1012, Papers of the *Trinidad Escala*, order of Don Alonso de Bazán, 5 August 1589.
25   *BMO*, III/3, 1921–2, list sent to Philip by Fuentes, 13 February 1588; Gracia Rivas, *Los tercios*, 186–8, 'Relación' by the marquis of Cerralvo of the captains aboard the Armada ships who returned to Galicia.
26   *BMO*, IV/3, 71–2 and 123–4, Recalde to Martín de Idiáquez, 6 and 11 July 1588; Parker, 'Anatomy', 320, Recalde's 'Observations' for Philip, 9 October 1588 (no doubt Recalde had in mind the prince of Ascoli, aged 24, whom Philip appointed to serve on the Council of War on the flagship).

27 *BMO*, IV/4, 20–4, 'Relación of Coco Calderón (aboard *San Salvador* but with a brother serving on *San Pedro*), stated that the master and pilot abandoned the ship off Calais; ibid., 441–2, 'Relación' by Francisco de Ledesma, 18 February 1589, stated that several more members of the crew had deserted there, and that he had later seen them again aboard a Dutch ship; *HMC Salisbury*, III, 343–6, records the defection of the other two Dutch sailors; *BMO*, IV/3, 402–3, 'Avisos' from Calais, 13 August 1588; *BMO*, IV/4, 119, Pedro de Igueldo to Bernardino de Mendoza, Le Havre, 8 October 1588; ibid., 176–8, list of fugitives from the Castile squadron at Santander and Laredo, 16 October 1588. Other details from chs 14 and 15.

28 *BMO*, IV/4, 176–8, 'Relación de la gente de mar que en este puerto de Santander y Laredo se ha huido' from the squadron of Castile, 16 October 1588; ibid., 320, Bertendona to Philip, Ferrol, 17 December 1588.

29 *BMO*, IV/2, 53–7, declaration of masters of ships from the squadrons of Vizcaya and Andalucia, 30 March 1588; ASF *MdP* 4919/484–6v, Alemanni to the Grand Duke, Madrid, 4 October 1588; *BMO* IV/4, 224–9, 'Relación' of Vanegas; ibid., 392–5, 'Relación' of a Portuguese Jesuit.

30 Bourne, *The arte*, 1; Tanturri, 'La incursión', 84, a letter written by a Jesuit in Cadiz, 21 May 1587.

31 *BMO*, IV/4, 526, Philip to the governor of Galicia, 29 November 1589.

32 *BMO*, IV/4, 274–6 and 298, 'Relación de la gente' aboard the ships at Santander and in Galicia, 18 and 28 November 1588. According to the list, the galleass *Napolitana*, at Santander, had no gunners: this is odd, because a muster of those aboard her sister ship *Zúñiga* at Le Havre the previous month revealed 28 'artilleros' (ibid., 119, Pedro de Igueldo to Bernardino de Mendoza, 8 October 1588); but perhaps all those aboard *Napolitana* died on campaign. On the presence of 'artilleros de campaña' among the total – often lumped together with the 'mozos de mulas' (the men in charge of the mules embarked to pull the siege-guns) – see ibid., 3 and 159–60). Most previous musters of the Armada lumped together 'artilleros y marineros'.

33 AGS *CMC* 2a/772, Papers of *San Francisco* (Andalucia) unfol.; ibid., papers of *Concepción Menor* (Vizcaya), ff. 128–32.

34 Naish, 'Documents', 97–8; Bourne, *The art*, sig. Aiii (preface); Glasgow, 'Gorgas' seafight', 180–1.

35 *BMO*, IV/4, 229, 'Relación' of Vanegas; *BMO*, IV/3, 394, 'Relación' of a Portuguese Jesuit; ibid., 453, Bobadilla to Idiáquez, 'from the flagship at 60 degrees', 20 August 1588; OÖLA *KB* IV/320, Khevenhüller to Rudolf, 12 October 1588.

36 *BMO*, IV/3, 463–7, Medina Sidonia 'Diario', entry for 4 August 1588; *BMO*, IV/4, 246–53, 'Relación' of 43 Armada ships at Santander, 1 November 1588; ibid., 219–20 and AGS *E* 165/323, inventory of ships at Corunna, 3 and 29 October 1588 (no total of shot recorded for Recalde's ship).

37 KML *MSP CG: C* 9/146–7v, Medina Sidonia's Instructions to Juan de Escandón, *escrivano de raciones* of *San Bartolomé* of the Andalusian squadron, 29 June 1587. See also AGS *CMC* 2a/772, Papers of *Concepción Menor*, pliego 132, statement

of Antonio del Castillo, 'persona señalada ... para el apercivimiento de la pelea y distribuyción de las municiones y armas'.
38   Details from AGS *CMC* 2a/772 (*San Francisco* and *Concepción Menor*), 2a/460 and 1a/1736 (*Santa Bárbara*), 2a/905 (*Santa Catalina*); 2a/942 (*Trinidad Escala*) and 2a/905 (*Esperanza*); and KML *MSP CC* 8/32 and 8/37. See also the tables and further statistics in Parker, 'The *Dreadnought* revolution', 279–80, and Parker, *The grand strategy*, 258.
39   Parker, 'Anatomy', 328–30 (*San Juan*); *BMO*, IV/4, 224–9, 'Relación' of Vanegas (*San Martín*).
40   *BMO*, IV/4, 267–70, 'Relación' of the Armada ships at Pasaje, 17 November 1588 (excluding the munitions aboard Oquendo's flagship, destroyed by an explosion); ibid., 246–53, 'Relación de la gente de mar y Guerra, y de los bastimentos, artillería, armas y municiones', October–November 1588 (the *Napolitana*, although she only carried 8 quintals of powder, which suggests she had fired many more rounds); *BMO*, IV/4, 288–9, and AGS *CMC* 3a/1704, no. 45, accounts of Pietro Pauber and Vicenzo de Bune for salvaging *San Lorenzo*; AGS *GA* 221/1, 'La felicíssima Armada', f. A9 (claiming that the galleass carried 2,500 rounds when it left Lisbon). On *Girona* and *Zúñiga*, see note 13 above.
41   Phillips, *The Struggle*, 131–4, 'Instrucción y orden' issued by Flores to his fleet, Sanlúcar, 24 September 1581. García de Palacio, *Instrucción naúthica* (1587), also said nothing about reloading drills.
42   *BMO*, IV/4, 198–9, Vallejo to Andrés de Prada, 21 October 1588.
43   Burnell and Tiele, *The voyage of John Huyghen van Linschoten*, II, 268–9.
44   BMO IV/1, 94–5, Archduke Albert to Philip, 25 February 1588.
45   Norton, *The Gunner*, 67–8.
46   Lewis, *Armada guns*, 205–19.
47   Laughton, II, 258–60, William Thomas to Burghley, Flushing, 30 September 1588 OS.
48   Laughton, II, 11, Winter to Walsingham, 11 August 1588; Raleigh, *Judicious and select essayes*, pt. III, 26 (part of his 'Excellent observations and notes concerning the royall navy', written in or before 1612). See the similar laments about the lack of powder and especially shot in ibid., I, 359, Hawkins to Walsingham, 10 August 1588; ibid., II, 38, Fenner to Walsingham, 14 August 1588; 54, Howard to Walsingham, 17 August 1588; 64, Whyte to Walsingham, 18 August 1588; and Oppenheim, *The naval tracts*, I, 175–6 (all dates NS).
49   Once again we accept the careful computation of the Armada's big guns and the ratio of gunners in *BMO*, V, anexo 5, summarized in ibid., IV/1, pp. LVII and CLXXXII, and corresponding notes.
50   'Armada: Twelve Days to Save England', episode 2, a demonstration supervised by Nicholas Hall, Keeper of Artillery at the Royal Armouries, London, first broadcast in June 2015.
51   Laughton, I, 289, Howard to Walsingham, 21 July 1588; Adams, 'Armada correspondence', 81–3, Walsingham to Sussex, 24 July, and to Leicester, 26 July

1588; Laughton, I, 355, Memorial for Richard Drake, 31 July 1588 (all dates OS). Admittedly on 1 August Howard asked the governor of Portsmouth to send him 'tall men' (p. 291), but this seems to have been an aberration.
52 Laughton, I, 301–2, Nicholas Oseley to Walsingham, from *Revenge* off Portland, 2 August 1588. Oseley, fluent in Spanish, had served as a spy for Walsingham. He was among the first to board *Rosario*.
53 Meteren, *Belgische ofte Nederlantsche historie*, f. 287; TNA SP 63/141/57–8, 'The report by William Herbert', December 1588. Interestingly, Elizabeth feared the opposite, ordering Drake to set ashore Valdés and other Spanish prisoners 'now kept on seaboard . . . *where either they may practise some mischief or else come to understanding of the secrets of the service*': Laughton, I, 356, Memorial for Richard Drake, 31 July 1588 OS, italics added.
54 BMO, IV/4, 500–1, Petition of Gómez de Medina, July 1589.
55 BNE *Ms.* 3556/291, 'Relação' of a Portuguese Jesuit for 4 August 1588: 'se chegaron mais perto que o outro dia, tirando as peças mais grossas da cuberta mais baixa' (partial Spanish translation in *BMO*, IV/3, 309–10). Medina Sidonia made the same point that day in his *Diario*: BMO, IV/3, 463–7.
56 BMO IV/4, 227, 'Relación' of Vanegas, entry for 7 August 1588; Laughton, II, 102, 'A note of certain speeches spoken by Sir Martin Frobisher at Harwich' on 11 August 1588 OS.
57 Laughton, II, 11, Winter to Walsingham, 11 August 1588 NS; TNA WO 55/1627, 'The booke of the remaynes of Her Majesties shippes returninge from the seas', December 1595–August 1596, section ('the waste spente at the seas'); Usherwood, *The Counter-Armada*, 77. See more details in Parker, 'The *Dreadnought* revolution'.

# PART IV

\* Marcus, *Elizabeth I*, 357–8, Elizabeth to James VI of Scotland, undated but late August 1588, holograph.

## 17. The Bitterness of Defeat

1 AMAE *MDFDE* 237/94–5, Olivares to Philip, 27 June 1588, 'en la materia secreta'. Ten years later Isabella would marry Albert, and Philip made them joint rulers of the Netherlands.
2 San Gerónimo, 'Memorias', 429–30; IVdeDJ 55/XI/121–2, Vázquez to Philip and reply, 27 July 1588.
3 IVdeDJ 55/XI/153, Vázquez to Philip and reply, 10 August 1588; Tellechea Idígoras, 'La Invencible', 82, Novara to Montalto, 4 August 1588; AHN *Inquisición Libro* 100/551, Juan Ruiz de Velasco to Vázquez, 23 August 1588.
4 William Shakespeare, *The Merchant of Venice* (written 1596–7), act 1, scene 1; *BMO*, IV/3, 264, undated royal memorandum probably written on receipt of a report dated 22 July that the Armada had been spotted off Le Conquet (ibid., 226).

5    *BMO*, IV/3, 409–10, Idiáquez to Philip, undated but 14 August 1588; [P. le Goux], *Copie d'une lettre envoyé de Dieppe* (Paris, 1588: see Lyell, nos 95–7; Spanish translation in *BMO*, IV/3, 334–5).
6    ASF *MdP* 4919/457, Camillo Guidi to the grand duke, 31 August 1588, enclosing a 'Relación' from Mendoza in Paris dated 20 August – a remarkably fast transmission by Mendoza's courier, and an outstanding feat of espionage by Guidi.
7    *BMO*, IV/3, 517–18, Idiáquez opinion, undated but 31 August 1588.
8    *BMO*, IV/3, 519–20, Idiáquez opinion, and Philip to Medina Sidonia, both composed 31 August 1588.
9    *BMO*, IV/3, 520, Philip to Parma, 31 August 1588, draft.
10   *BMO*, IV/3, 518–19, Idiáquez to Parma, 31 August 1588.
11   IVdeDJ 51/190, Vázquez to Philip, 4 September 1588, enclosing a note from Pedro Nuñez written the previous day, with the king's reply.
12   *BMO*, IV/3, 534, Philip and Idiáquez to Parma, 3 September 1588.
13   *Relaciō de lo que hasta oy a los 5 de septiembre . . . se ha sabido* (Seville, 1588: Lyell, no. 80); ASP *CF* 129 (Spagna 6) folder III, Juan de Monte Pichardo to Cardinal Farnese, Madrid, 17 September 1588; ASV *NS* 34/504–5, Cesare Speciano, bishop of Novara, to Cardinal Montalto, papal secretary of state, 17 September 1588. The minister was Francisco de Idiáquez.
14   There can be no doubt about Zúñiga's late arrival, even though most historians have assumed that he reached Spain long before: see ASF *MdP*, 4919/476–7, Giulio Battaglione to the grand duke of Tuscany, 27 September 1588 (cited here); *BMO*, IV/4, 43, Philip to Medina Sidonia, 27 September 1588; and *CSPV*, VIII, 194, Lippomano to the Doge, 29 September 1588.
15   *BMO*, IV/4, 9–10, Medina Sidonia to Philip and Idiáquez, Santander, 23 September 1588.
16   López Mata, *La ciudad*, 133, Medina Sidonia to Burgos, 24 September 1588; *BMO*, IV/4, 44–5, Medina Sidonia to Idiáquez, Santander, 27 September 1588. Saltillo, 'El duque', 174, cited the duke's household accounts for 1588 with payments for playing cards.
17   *BMO*, IV/4, 210 (the fate of *Santa Ana*); López Mata, *La ciudad*, 133 (the duke's letter to Burgos dated 24 September 1588), 200–1 (the wasted warriors) and 205 n. 10 (Montenegro).
18   TNA *SP* 63/141/47, Deposition of John Brown of Clontarf, mariner, recently escaped from Ribadeo, 28 January 1589 OS; idem, ff. 57–8, 'The Report by William Herbert of Dublin, merchant', early 1589.
19   Philip II, *Premática*, sig. a 2; Tellechea Idígoras, *'La Invencible'*, 93, Novara to Montalto, 24 October 1588; OÖLA *KB* IV/326, Khevenhüller to Rudolf, 12 October 1588.
20   ASV *LP* 46/82, Philip circular to all Spanish prelates, 13 October 1588, copy (another copy in BAV *UL* 1115/246); IVdeDJ, 55/IX/ 217, Vázquez to Philip and reply, 17 October 1588.
21   OÖLA *KB* IV/332, Khevenhüller to Rudolf, 11 November 1588; ASL *OSD*, 271,

unfol., Compagno Compagni to the Republic of Lucca, 12 November 1588; ASV *NS* 34/ 583–5, Novara to Montalto, 8 November 1588. The Ferrarese ambassador reported that 50 ships were still missing 'and of 27,000 people who boarded the Armada, only 10,000 are still alive, and more are dying because of what they suffered on the voyage': ASMo *AS* 15, unfol., bishop of Ripa to the duke, 12 November 1588.

22 BZ 145/76, Philip to Vázquez, 10 November 1588. The king added: 'This is for your eyes alone.'

23 *BMO*, IV/4, 195–8, 'Relación de los galeones ... y otros navíos que salieron de la Coruña ... y los que dellos han vuelto a España, por avisos que se han recibido en Madrid hasta 20 del mes de octubre, y en que puertos están, y los que no se sabe, y los que de cierto se han perdido'; ibid., 198–200, García de Vallejo to Andrés de Alva, Santander, 21 October 1588.

24 *BMO*, IV/4, 102–3, Mexía to Philip, Laredo, 4 October 1588.

25 *BMO*, IV/4, 123, Philip to the duke of Escalona, 8 October 1588; ibid., 434, Vázquez to Philip, 10 February 1589, and rescript (letter of condolence to Leyva's widow and *encomienda* of Alcuéscar to his son); AGS *CS* 2ª/284/43–4 and 759 (arrears to heirs of Leyva and Recalde).

26 BZ 122/120, Philip to the Captain-General of Guipúzcoa, 26 December 1588. AGS *CS* 2a/275, an unfoliated bundle of accounts paid to those who had served in the 'Armada de Yngalaterra' between 1587 and 1593, records several payments from a special fund 'consignado para pagar los sueldos de soldados muertos y despedidos'.

27 *BMO*, IV/3, 453, Bobadilla to Idiáquez, 'from the flagship at 60 degrees', 20 August 1588 (no doubt one of the documents entrusted to Zúñiga when he left the flagship for Spain the following day).

28 *HMC Bath*, V, 93, Cobham to Walsingham, Calais, 1 August 88 OS, copy (no doubt quoting either the prince of Ascoli or Don Jorge Manrique, the only Spanish noblemen on the Armada who had reached Dunkirk by then); *BMO*, IV/4, 17–18, Mendoza to Philip, Paris, 24 September 1588; AGS *Estado* 1261/115, Don Jusepe de Acuña, Spanish ambassador in Savoy, to Philip, Turin, 6 September 1588; Malfatti, *Cuatro documentos*, 43, Giulio Savorgnano to Filippo Pigafetta, Venice, 23 September 1588. Several Armada prisoners interrogated at Dover and Flushing also blamed Parma (Laughton, I, 342–3, and II, 32). So did Fray Bernardo de Góngora: *BMO*, IV/3, 415–16, letter to Fray Martín de los Ángeles from the flagship, 15 August 1588.

29 ASF *MdP* 4919/476–7, Giulio Battaglione to the grand duke of Tuscany, 27 September 1588 (citing conversations not only with Zúñiga but also with Don Pedro de Guzmán, whose name he ciphered); ASF *MdP* 4919/484v, Alemanni to the grand duke, 4 October 1588. The nuncio agreed: 'The confusion and condemnation is very great,' he wrote, with 'everyone speaking freely, according to his loyalties and passions', but the majority blamed Parma (ASV *NS* 34/510–13, Novara to Montalto, 26 September 1588).

30 Vázquez, II, 352. Alonso Vázquez gave no date for this episode, nor is it recorded in any other contemporary account, but the author – a sergeant in the *tercio* of Sicily captured by the Dutch aboard *San Mateo*, ransomed and brought to the Army of Flanders later in the year – added immediately afterwards: 'I have written faithfully what I saw and what I could find out.' See AGRB *SEG* 12/46v, Parma's warrant awarding Vázquez a pay supplement, 20 June 1589; and his service record to 1595 in AGS *CS* 2a/275, unfol., under 'A' for Alonso.

31 Fea, *Alessandro Farnese*, 308–10, Parma to Cardinal Farnese (undated but presumably 12 August 1588); Bertini, *Militari italiani*, 239–41, Parma's instructions to Cesi, undated but August 1588; *BMO*, IV/4, 215, count of Olivares to Philip, 29 October 1588; AGS *Estado* 950/229, Olivares to Parma, 15 October 1588, copy (extract in *BMO*, IV/4, 162). The chronicle compiled by Parma's chamberlain, Paolo Rinaldi, blamed Medina Sidonia for the failure of the Enterprise: in his view (which probably reflected that of other members of Parma's entourage), the outcome would have been very different had Santa Cruz remained in command of the fleet: BRB *Ms.* II.1155, 'Liber relationum', f. 217.

32 ASF *MdP* 5151/151–2v and 162–3, Giovanni de' Medici to the grand duke, his brother, Bruges, 5 and 12 August 1588. We have not found the letter from Bobadilla about Medina Sidonia's pusillanimity described by Medici, but since Giovanni was attached to the duke's headquarters at Bruges, and since the rest of his reporting was accurate, we see no reason not to believe him.

33 *BMO*, IV/3, 371–2, Manrique to Philip, 11 August 1588; RAZ *Register van Acten en Brieven*, portfeuille 1625/257–8, two letters from the States of Zeeland to Count Maurice, 10 August 1588, relaying messages received from Justinus of Nassau blockading Dunkirk; *BMO*, IV/3, 354–5, Parma to Philip, 10 August 1588.

34 ASF *MdP* 4919/477, Battaglino to the grand duke, 27 September 1588; HHStA *Statenabteilung Spanien, Diplomatische Korrespondenz* neu 11, Konvolut 7/398v, Khevenhüller to Rudolf II, 14 September 1588; Laughton, II, 99, Drake to Walsingham, 10 August 1588 OS.

35 *BMO*, IV/3, 518, and AGS *Estado* 2219/101–2, Idiáquez to Parma, 31 August and 9 November 1588, minutes (the latter heavily emended; a clean copy, probably sent by Parma to Cardinal Farnese, is at ASP *CF* 129, folder 3, unfol.).

36 *BMO*, IV/4, 331–2, Parma to Idiáquez, 30 December 1588. The duke might have added, in his defence, that he did not pay off the Flanders flotilla until the end of August (AGS *CMC* 2a/1077, accounts of Thorivio Martinez), and did not issue exeats for individuals who had arrived for the invasion until 12 September, 'attento a haverse, según paresce, alargado la ocasión de la Jornada' (AGRB *SEG* 11/40 and 46v, passports for Juan de Anaya Solís and the marquis of Favara).

37 ASP *CF* 109 folder 3, unfol., 'Memoria de los papeles que entrego oy 5 de junio 1589 al Señor Presidente Richardot'; AGS *Estado* 2855, unfol., 'Lo que Su Magestad es servido que se responda a los cuatro papeles principales que dio el Presidente Richardot' (November 1589), second point. Ironically, at precisely this moment other servants of the Crown began to question Parma's commitment to executing

Philip's policies in another area: France (see AGS *Estado* 597/128, Juan Moreo to Philip II, 18 November 1589, with interesting royal apostils).

38  Details from Saltillo, 'El duque', 174–6; Fray Juan de Vitoria, 'Noticias de la Invencible', in Tellechea Idígoras, *Otra cara*, 188 (see Tellechea Idígoras's masterful assessment of this much-quoted and much-misunderstood source: ibid., 133–47); ASF *MdP* 4919/499–502, Alemanni to the grand duke, 15 October 1588, ciphered with decrypt.

39  *BMO*, IV/4, 11, Bobadilla to Idiáquez, 28 September 1588, postscript.

40  After he landed in Ireland, Leyva may have decided to send his 'report' directly to the king. In December 1588 the Corregidor of Bilbao reported that an Irish boy had arrived in Le Croisic (Brittany) with 'a large folder of letters which he said don Alonso de Leyva gave him' in 'Drosal' or 'Drudral' (perhaps Donegal). A Spanish official in Le Croisic, Martín de Igueldo, asked to see the letters, but the boy refused, saying he had orders to deliver them only to the Corregidor of Bilbao in person; Igueldo therefore merely inspected the seals and addresses, and sent the boy on to St Jean de Luz, whence he would take another ship to Bilbao. However, although the information from Igueldo arrived, the boy (and his precious 'large folder of letters') did not: *BMO*, IV/4, 319, Corregidor of Bilbao to Philip, 16 December 1588, together with two copies of a passage from a letter of Igueldo, 29 November 1588 (ibid., 221–2). Perhaps the 'report' will turn up one day: after all, Leyva's letters to Recalde dated 12 and 17 August 1588 languished unread in the archives for more than four centuries.

41  Parker, 'Anatomy', 320, Recalde's 'Observations for Philip II on the reasons for the Armada's failure', 9 October 1588, point 1.

42  Parker, 'Anatomy', 319, Don Martín de Idiáquez to Philip, undated, together with the royal rescript. This almost certainly formed the cover sheet to AHN *OM* 3511/41, 'Armada de Inglaterra, 1588: Papeles y advertimientos de Juan Martínez de Recalde', including Recalde's letter to Idiáquez, 8 October 1588, which began: 'As you will learn from letters included here from Don Alonso de Leyva . . .' The king wrote beside this statement: 'I'm not sure that these have arrived.' We presume that Recalde referred to the two letters from Leyva now at AHN *OM* 3511/38, printed by Parker, 'Anatomy', 320–2.

43  *BMO*, IV/4, 198–9, Vallejo to Andrés de Prada, 21 October 1588.

44  *BMO*, IV/4, 175, 219 and 279–80, instructions for Cardona, 16 and 29 October 1588, and Cardona to Philip, 20 November 1588, referring to a secret royal letter apparently now lost.

45  *BMO*, IV/4, Andrés de Alva to Martín de Idiáquez, 7 October 1588; ibid., 103, García de Vallejo to Andrés de Alva, 4 October 1588; and ibid., 106, Zamudio to Philip, 5 October 1588.

46  *BMO*, IV/4, 297–80, Cardona to Philip, 20 November 1588. Many others blamed Flores for the Armada's failure: ibid., 196, Zamudio to Philip, 5 October 1588; ibid., 403–4, Coco Calderón to Philip, 24 January 1589; LL *Bertendona Ms*. no. 21, Bertendona to Philip, 23 June 1589. So did Andrés de Alva, who added that the

king should have appointed Oquendo instead as the duke's naval adviser (*BMO*, IV/4, 126, Alva to Don Martín de Idiáquez, 8 October 1588).

47 AGS *GA* 228/131, Santillán to Philip, 23 December 1588; *BMO*, IV/4, 333, Juan Fernández de Castro to Andrés de Alva, 30 December 1588; ibid., 373–4, Cristóbal Flores to Diego Flores, 3 January 1589 (these and other letters to Diego at this time are in AGS, which suggests that they were never delivered); ibid., 400–11, Luis de Arteaga to Philip, 20 January 1589; ibid., 469, Philip to the archbishop of Burgos, 29 March 1589; ibid., 488, 501–3 and 526–7, Flores to Philip, 7 May, 20 and 23 August, and 7 December 1589; and Tellechea Idígoras, *Otra cara*, 593–6.

48 *BMO*, IV/4, 491, *consulta* of the Council of War exonerating Coco Calderón, 18 May 1589.

49 Huerga, 'La vida', 77–90, described the trial and fate of Sor María, and printed the transcript of the hand-scrubbing on 14 October 1588 which revealed her fraud (p. 89 n. 64); AHN, *Inquisición libro* 100/597–610, *billetes* exchanged between Quiroga and Vázquez between 14 November 1588 and 11 January 1589, conveying the king's wishes on what to do with Piedrola ('the condemned man isn't mad: he is a great rogue'). Kagan and Dyer, *Inquisitorial inquiries*, 61–79, printed Piedrola's combative autobiography, intended to convince the Inquisitors that he was indeed a prophet; Kagan, 'Politics', discussed both Piedrola and Sor María, as well as Lucrecia de León (who remained at large until 1590).

50 ASF *MdP* 5151/151–2v, Giovanni de' Medici to the grand duke, his brother, Bruges, 5 August 1588. See also the criticisms of Bobadilla and Recalde in ch. 16.

51 ASF *MdP* 4919/499–502, Alemanni to the grand duke, 4 October 1588, ciphered (a precaution seldom taken by Alemanni, but his words came close to treason: 'Si biasima il re di poca prudenza et di spensierato, et che non sia buono ad altro che a starsi fra frati'); ASV *NS* 34/ 583–5, Novara to Montalto, 8 November 1588.

52 *BMO*, IV/4, 348–9, Ribadeneira to Idiáquez, December 1588 (also in *Monumenta historica societatis Iesu, LX: Ribadeneira*, II, 105–11). For more on this letter, see *FBD*, 856–8.

53 Casabán, 'The design and construction'; Thompson, *War and society*, VII, 79.

54 *BMO* IV/4, 451–2, 'Relación de la manera que han de ir los timones de la galeazas', February 1589.

55 AGS *GyM* 285/162, Bazán to Philip, Ferrol, 23 June 1590. Stanley had served under both the duke of Alba and the earl of Leicester in the Netherlands. In 1587 he betrayed the town of Deventer to Parma, who planned to include him and his regiment of Irish defectors in the invasion army. As far as we can tell, he had no personal experience of naval warfare.

56 See Earle, *The last fight*, on the loss of *Revenge*; see ch. 4 on the loss of *Jesus* in 1568.

57 Casabán, 'The design and construction', 399; Wernham, *The return of the Armadas*, 162, 168, 183. Nevertheless *San Mateo*, at least, bore a great deal of ordnance: 4 demi-cannon, 4 cannon periers, 14 culverins, 15 demi-culverins and 6 lighter pieces (TNA *WO*55/1626/232–3, Inventories of the two ships, 12 November 1596). Both

ships were repaired (at a cost of £1,200) in the royal dockyards in 1598 (TNA E351/2236, Account of Roger Langford).

58 'Carta de las damas de la corte' in Rosales, *El sentimiento*, 68–9; Caeiro, *O Archiduque Alberto*, 162–3; Cervantes Saavedra, *Obras completas*, II, 1592–5, 'Canción segunda, de la pérdida de la Armada que fue a Inglaterra'; Paul Archer's verdict on Cervantes's poetry.

## 18. The Counter-Armada

1   RAZ *Register van Acten en Brieven*, portfeuille 1625/258–9, States of Zeeland to Count Maurice, 11 August 1588, using the word 'victorie' twice; ASF *MdP* 5151/162–3, Giovanni de' Medici to the grand duke of Tuscany, Bruges, 12 August 1588. On Verheyden and his *In classem Xerxis Hispani Oratio*, see Scheltema, *De uitrusting*, 274–99.
2   Laughton, II, 59–61, Howard to Walsingham, Margate road, 18 August 1588; ibid., 97–100 and 146–8, Drake to Walsingham, 20 August and 2 September 1588 (all dates NS).
3   TNA *SP* 12/213/79–80, Leicester to Elizabeth, 27 July 1588 OS (printed with some differences in Kempe, *Loseley*, 286–9, from a copy).
4   Wright, *Queen Elizabeth*, II, 384, Walsingham to Leicester, 6 August 1588 OS; Folgerpedia, 'The Elizabethan court day by day' for 1588, pp. 34–41.
5   Nichols, *The progresses*, III, 422–4, the queen's speech on 9 August 1588 OS.
6   Wright, *Queen Elizabeth*, II, 384, Walsingham to Leicester, 6 August 1588; *HMC Bath*, V, 211, Thomas Fowler to John Montgomery, 11 August 1588 (both dates OS). Such fears were not unfounded: on 12 August Parma apparently re-embarked some of his troops in Nieuwpoort: ASF *MdP* 5151/166, Giovanni de' Medici to the grand duke, Bruges, 18 August 1588.
7   Wright, *Queen Elizabeth*, II, 388–9, Walsingham to Burghley, 9 August 1588 (two letters); ibid., 391–2, Leicester to Burghley, and Bodleian *Ms. St. Amand* 8/65, Leicester to Norris, both dated 18 August 1588; *HMC Foljambe*, 58–60, Privy Council to Leicester, 14 and 17 August 1588 (slightly different minutes in *APC*, XVI, 233–5 and 239). All dates OS.
8   Marcus, *Elizabeth I*, 357–8, Elizabeth to James, undated but late August 1588, holograph; LPL *Ms.* 647/122, Francis Allen to Anthony Bacon, 17 August 1589 OS; *BMO*, IV/4, 297, news from London, 27 November 1588 (English translation in *CSPSp*, IV, 491–2).
9   Laughton, II, 96–7, Howard to Burghley, 10 August 1588, and 167–9, Howard to Walsingham, 27 August 1588 (both dates OS).
10  Laughton, II, 183–5, Howard to Walsingham, 29 August 1588 OS.
11  BL *Harleian Ms.* 168/180–5, Accounts.
12  Clark, *England's Remembrancer*, 32; *APC*, XVI, 334, order of 3 November 1588; *HMC 8th Report, Appendix – Part I, section ii* (London, 1881), 374, the bishop of Chester to the mayor of Manchester, 11 November 1588. Folgerpedia, 'The

Elizabethan court day by day' for 1588, pp. 55–6, described some of the nationwide celebrations on 19 November 1588. All dates OS.
13 Caraman, *Henry Garnet*, 82–3, Garnet to Jesuit General Acquaviva, 4 December 1588. A Spanish spy in London also reported that Elizabeth decided not to attend the official thanksgiving service 'for fear that someone might shoot her': *BMO*, IV/4, 240, 'Avisos' of 5 November 1588, annotated by Philip.
14 Noble, *The names*, xxvi (on Westminster); other details from Folgerpedia, 'The Elizabethan court day by day' for 1588.
15 Whitehead, *Of brags and boasts*, ch. 10, and Brown, 'The Hearts', provided brilliant accounts of how Burghley drafted his polemic.
16 Ribadeneira, *Tratado de la tribulación*, pt. II, ff. 142–142v (licensed by the Jesuit provincial on 20 June 1589).
17 Wernham, *The expedition*, 4–5, and Wright, *Queen Elizabeth*, II, 388–9, Burghley to Walsingham, and reply, both 9 August 1588; Laughton, II, 167–8, Howard to Walsingham, 27 August 1588 (all dates OS).
18 Duplessis-Mornay, *Suite des lettres*, 270–1, letter to M. de Buzenval, 18 October 1588; Wernham, *The expedition*, 11, Burghley's notes on the 'journey', 20 September 1588; ibid., 12–14, royal commission to Norris and Drake, 11 October 1588 (all dates OS).
19 Mountgomerie, 'The nauie: A treatise concerninge the nauie of England', 1589 (the manuscript evidently circulated widely, since at least six copies survive: three in the BL, one in the Pepys Library, and two among Lyell's papers in the Houghton Library, Harvard, Ms Typ 16); TNA *SP* 12/218/46–8, 'Device' of the Navy Board, 20 November 1588 OS, written by Howard, annotated by Burghley, and signed by each member together with his estimate of the cost of implementation. Philip II created a committee of experts at the same time to oversee the construction of new warships: see ch. 17.
20 TNA *WO* 55/1672, 'A view and survey of all her Majesty's Ordinnance' in 1595, listing all ships except *Warspite* and *Repulse*; the totals for these two ships have been added from TNA *WO* 55/1627, 'The booke of the remaynes'. Parker, 'The *Dreadnought* revolution', Appendix I, gives details for the capital ships.
21 Wernham, *The expedition*, 28–31, documents concerning the religious 'disputation' between London clerics about spiritual aspects of the voyage, February 1589.
22 *CSPV*, VIII, 405–7, Lippomano to the doge and senate, 22 October 1588 (adding 'I, who am living on the spot, know full well' whereof he spoke); Wernham, *The expedition*, 217–18, Edmund Palmer to Walsingham, St Jean-de-Luz, 25 July 1589.
23 Roiz Soares, *Memorias*, 292–3; BCR *Ms.* 2417/17–22, Don Juan de Silva to Esteban de Ibarra, 19, 21 and 22 June 1589 (three letters that revealed how close the English came to victory).
24 BL *Cotton Ms.* Galba D.V/65, Walsingham to Bodley, 2 August 1589 OS, holograph postscript.
25 *ACC*, X, 233–45, Actas of 22, 23 and 30 September and 1 October 1588 (see also a draft of Philip's Memorial at IVdeDJ 45/348). The Cortes made copies of Medina Sidonia's *Diario* for each of its constituent cities.

26 *ACC*, X, 348–9, Acta of 7 December 1588.
27 Ibid., X, 397–8 and 422–3, Acta of 8 February 1589.
28 AGS *Estado* 2219/176, Philip to Parma, 11 May 1589; LL *Bertendona Ms.* 21 and 24, Philip to Bertendona, 23 June and 15 November 1589.
29 IVdeDJ 69/234A, Vázquez draft of the king's reply to a *consulta* of the Council of the Inquisition, ordering the 'Visita', 10 May 1589, with the king's rescript countermanding it.
30 TNA *SP* 63/141/118, Fitzwilliam to Walsingham, 11 February 1589; Mears, *National prayers*, 189, archbishop of Dublin to Burghley, 22 September 1590; TNA *SP* 63/143/41–3, Fitzwilliam to Burghley, 5 April 1589, forwarding a letter from Galway dated 26 March, copy; idem, ff. 8–10, Bingham to Burghley, 6 April 1589 (all dates OS). Further details in Maginn, 'After the Armada'.
31 TNA *SP* 63/159/85, Donag O'Connor Sligo to Richard Barret, archbishop of Tuam, 17 March 1590 OS, intercepted copy annotated by Burghley (TNA *SP* 63/151/228, Bingham to Fitzwilliam, 24 April 1590 OS, asserted that O'Rourke had 'great store of the Spanish wreck which fell at the Grange' – that is, one of the ships wrecked on Streedagh Strand – as well as '12 or 14 Spaniards' experienced in the use of firearms'); Walsh, *'Destruction by Peace'*, 140, 370, and idem, 'The anonymous Spaniard', 88–9 (on Blanco).
32 O'Sullivan Beare, *Historiae*, bk. III: 'De bello quindecim annorum'.
33 Rizzacasa, *La fisionomia*, dedication, Sig. Aiv (dated 10 November 1588); Dooley, 'Sources and methods', 36–41, noted that the archive of the government of Florence contains 'several hundred documents relating to the Armada'.
34 Eyzinger, *Historica*, 106–8 (pp. 74–94 of the work printed a German translation of the Lisbon Muster); Behringer, *Im Zeichen des Merkur*, 307–8, reproduced and discussed 'Der Kramer mit der newe Zeittung'; Hakluyt, *The principal navigations*, III, 368–9, 'The returne of Master William Harborne'.
35 Bond, *Russia*, 347, report by Dr Giles Fletcher, December 1588; AGS *SP libro* 1551/746–55, viceroy of India to Philip, Panjim, 12 December 1589; ibid., f. 798, magistrates of Goa to Philip, 24 November 1589.
36 ASF *MdP* 5151/166, Giovanni de' Medici to the grand duke, Bruges, 18 August 1588; TNA *SP* 84/27/33–9, 'Memorial for Sir John Norris', 6 October 1588 OS, draft, addition by Walsingham.
37 BZ 141/203, Philip to Vázquez, 29 January 1591; KML *MSP: CR* 6/174, Philip to Medina Sidonia, 15 December 1590; IVdeDJ 51/1, Vázquez to Philip and rescript, 8 February 1591.
38 Céspedes del Castillo, 'La defensa', 403.
39 BL *Additional Ms.* 20,929/104, Silva to Philip III, April 1599.
40 BL *Additional Ms.* 28,378/41–8v, rescript of Moura to the marquis of Poza, president of the Council of Finance, 15 May 1596; ibid., ff. 69–73v, 75–6 and 128–31, Poza to Moura, 9 and 13 June and 28/31 July 1596, with rescripts; Drelichman and Voth, *Lending*.
41 AGS *Estado* 176, unfol., Philip to Santa Gadea, 3 October 1596 (we thank Edward Tenace for providing a transcript of this interesting document).

42 Larkin and Hughes, *Stuart royal proclamations*, I, 30–2, proclamation dated 23 June 1603 OS, ordering the return of all goods taken from subjects of the king of Spain since 24 April, one month after James's accession, 'which time wee limit unto all men of warre at Sea as a sufficient space, within which they might have taken knowledge of the discontinuance of the said Warre'.

43 Wijffels, 'The Anglo-Spanish peace', 80–3, summarized the treaty; Thomas, 'The treaty of London', 279–85, examined the religious concessions in theory and practice (for example, they only applied to English merchants and travellers who stayed less than a year and a day). James made just one reciprocal concession: he appointed a Catholic as his first ambassador in Madrid.

44 We follow de Armas, 'Heretical stars', 95, in attributing the poem to Cervantes rather than to Góngora.

45 TNA *E* 133/47/3, deposition of Simon Wood, 1605 (Don Pedro's encounter with the queen); TNA *E* 133/47/5, deposition of Evan Owen, 1605 (Don Pedro as a celebrity); Percyvall, *Bibliotheca Hispanica*, 'To the reader'.

46 BMO, IV/4, 614, Philip to Valdés, 20 March 1593; Martínez, *Cartas*, 117, Valdés petition of *c.* 1615; AGS *CS* 2a/275, unfol., paysheet of Valdés, filed under 'Pedro' (in 1624 his heirs received government bonds – *juros* – equal to the 18,000 ducats owed to Valdés, but they were unlucky: the revenues allocated to pay interest on the bonds proved inadequate). On Don Pedro's interrogation, see ch. 9.

47 AHN *OM Santiago*, expediente 4715, begun 19 January 1597, approved 8 July 1598 (see a separate foliation after f. 35 for the accusation that Don Alonso was 'confeso y deçendiente de judíos'); AGS *CMC* 2a/275, unfol., pay sheet of Luzón (filed under 'Alonso').

48 Cervantes Saavedra, *Obras completas*, II, 1400, 'El capitán Becerra vino a Sevilla a enseñar lo que habían de hacer los soldados, y a esto, y a la entrada del Duque de Medina en Cádiz, hizo Cervantes este soneto'.

49 AHN *OM Santiago expedientillos*, esp. 107, 'Genealoxia del General Martín de Vertendona'.

50 AHN *AEESS* 11/36, Philip to the duke of Sessa, 15 June 1592, requesting a dispensation for the future count-duke of Olivares.

51 In *La ilustra fregona* two muleteers complain that Puñonrostro, when Asistente of Seville in 1597–9, had conducted a crackdown on crime, particularly crimes committed by soldiers.

52 RAH *Salazar Ms.* M-59/292, *Consulta* of Rodrigo Vázquez, president of the Council of Castile, 17 October 1596, copy.

53 Van der Essen, 'Rapport' (but note that the document was *not* addressed to Philip, because it referred to 'Su Magestad'); Rodríguez-Salgado, 'Kinship, collaboration and conflict', 89–92, quoting Philip's changing orders between May 1591 and March 1592.

54 Mendoza, *Theorique and practice*, unfoliated dedication by Edward Hoby, the translator (in Spanish). Bobadilla granted permission, on behalf of the royal council, to print the Spanish original in 1595.

55  APC, XVI, 273, and XVIII, 387, orders of the Privy Council concerning Winslade, 8 September 1588 and 24 February 1590 (both dates OS); Hayden, 'Tristram Winslade'.
56  BMO, IV/4, 619, obituary of Gerónimo de Vera, S. J., 20 August 1631; Borja de Medina, 'Jesuitas', 38.
57  Alonso Cortés, *Valladolid*, 338–9, petition of the exiles, 24 October 1588.
58  AGS *CMC* 2a/29, 31 and 47, 'Fenescimientos de cuentas', with 52 Armada veterans among the mutineers at La Chapelle and 81 mutineers at St Pol. At La Chapelle in July 1596 Francisco Blanco alias Juan Ortega, a veteran aged 34 with service stretching back to the conquest of Portugal who had sailed on *Gran Grifón*, received 246 gold escudos in pay arrears.
59  BMO, IV/4, 372–3, Dr Espinosa to Philip, Salamanca, 2 January 1589.
60  BMO, IV/4, 432, Hernando Niño de Zúñiga to Philip, Salamanca, 7 February 1589.
61  Laughton's letter in *The Times* (London), 20 July 1888.

## 19. If the Armada had Landed

1  Cheyney, 'Law in history', 231–3, presidential address delivered in (oh, the shame!) Columbus, Ohio, in December 1923. We thank Susan Mills and Margaret Wallis for help in framing the argument of this chapter, based on a paper given by Geoffrey Parker at a conference in 1974 organized by Colin Martin, who also suggested the subject. It was their first cooperation.
2  Jackson, *Devil-Land*, 1–2.
3  TNA *SP* 31/4/228–32, 'Preventions necessaires pour le dessin', July 1688, holograph notes by William. The critical entry read: 'Agir selon les occurrences.' *CSPD James II, 1687–9*, 245–6, provided more detail, with some errors of translation. The composition of the document, in the form of a list, suggests that it was either the agenda or the minutes of a meeting to determine how best to execute William's 'design'.
4  Japikse, *Correspondentie*, 1st series I, 57–8, Orange to Bentinck, 26 September 1688; ibid., II, 610–13, Advice submitted by Admiral Herbert, *c.* 1 October 1688; ibid., II, 617–18, list of suitable landing-zones.
5  BL *Additional Ms.* 41,816/202, Ignatius White, marquis of Albeville, James's ambassador in The Hague, to Secretary of State Middleton, 28 September 1688 OS; *HMC Eleventh Report, Appendix Part V*, 169–70, James to Lord Dartmouth, in command of the English fleet, 20 October 1688 OS; Whittle, *An exact diary*, 18–19 (Whittle was a chaplain serving with the English troops who sailed with William).
6  Japikse, *Correspondentie*, 1st series II, 623–4, minutes of Council of War on the afternoon of 11 November by Bentinck, and his note to William on 12 November 1688; ibid., III, 53, William to Bentinck, 1 a.m. on 13 November 1688 (we accept the date proposed by Jones, 'The Protestant wind', 213 n. 59); *HMC Eleventh Report, Appendix Part V*, 201–2, Albeville to James, 16 November 1688, copy, described the

prince's deliberations on 11 November (information presumably provided by one of the six spies whom Albeville had managed to place on William's flagship: Campana de Cavelli, *Les derniers Stuarts*, II, 318–19, Nuncio d'Adda to the papal secretary of state, London, 15 November 1688). The prince's secretary Huygens, who sailed on the flagship, also stated that the prince decided only at the last moment 'that we would not sail to the north of England but to the west': Huygens, *Journaal*, I, 12–14, entry for 13 November 1688.

7   Jones, 'Journal', 17; Whittle, *An exact diary*, 21–2; *HMC Seventh Report, Appendix*, 225, 'Relation du voyage d'Angleterre'; Burnet, *The expedition*, 3 (using OS dates); Japikse, *Correspondentie*, 2nd series III, 53–4, Orange and Admiral Russell to Herbert, both on 14 November 1688 (note that 'Mr Gilbert', the pilot who advised against landing at Exmouth, was Henry Gilbert, and not Gilbert Burnet as Japikse asserted).

8   Read and Waddington, *Mémoires*, 215; Burnet, *The expedition*, 4 (using OS dates); Burnet, *Bishop Burnet's history*, I, 789; TNA *SP* 8/2 pt. 2, ff. 148–9, 'Mémoire pour le 5/15 novembre', 1688, in William's own hand (like the 'Preventions necessaires' cited above, this is either an agenda or a minute of the meeting).

9   Burnet, *The expedition*, 4; Whittle, *An exact diary*, 29–30 and 35; Read and Waddington, *Mémoires*, 219–20 and 222.

10  Davies, 'James II', 82–3.

11  *HMC Eleventh Report, Appendix Part V*, 163–7, Samuel Pepys, secretary of the navy, to Dartmouth, 17 October 1688 OS.

12  *HMC Fifteenth Report, Appendix Part I*, 56–7, journal of Grenville Collins, master of the flagship *Resolution*; Laughton, *Memoirs*, 29, journal of Lieutenant George Byng; Davies, 'James II', 93–4, quoting the logs of several English warships. An analysis of the tides on 13 November 1688 by Powley, *The English navy*, 91–2, confirmed that Dartmouth could not have got his fleet to sea that day.

13  Davies, 'James II', 94; *ODNB*, s. v. George Legge, Viscount Dartmouth (by Davies).

14  *HMC Eleventh Report, Appendix Part V*, 267, Lord Dartmouth to James II, 11 November 1688 OS; *HMC Fifteenth Report, Appendix Part I*, 56–8, journal of Grenville Collins. His colleague George Byng agreed: the English fleet had failed 'perhaps from want of skill' (Laughton, *Memoirs*, 300).

15  *HMC Eleventh Report, Appendix Part V*, 183–4, Pepys to Dartmouth, 3 November 1688 OS, 'past midnight', enclosing the report from Dover; Campana de Cavelli, *Les derniers Stuarts*, II, 314–17, Imperial Ambassador Hoffmann to Emperor Leopold, London, 15 November 1688 (reporting James's reaction on hearing that the Dutch fleet had been spotted off the Isle of Wight the previous day); Taylor, *The entring book*, IV, 331 (the courier from Dartmouth); TNA *SP* 44/97/22, Lord Middleton to Secretary of State Preston, Salisbury, 23 November 1688 OS, register copy.

16  Japikse, *Correspondentie*, III, 82, Lord Feversham to William, Uxbridge, 11 December 1688 OS; Levillain, 'London besieged?'

17  *Journal of the House of Commons, X: 1688–1693* (London, 1802), 47–50, entries for 14–15 March 1689, 'to defray the charges laid out by the Dutch in the expedition for England'; Shaw, *Calendar of Treasury Books, IX: 1689–92*, 273–4, royal warrant

of 3 October 1689; Anon, *A letter from a gentleman in the country*, 1 (describing the coronation procession on 11 April 1689; italics added). All dates OS. Cambridge, 'The march', 169–74, detailed the distribution of William's army in and around London in December 1688.

18 *The State Letters of Henry earl of Clarendon*, II, 326–8, Father Conn, S. J., to his superiors in Rome, London, 10 December 1588 OS, copy (the postscript reads 'Siamo futti per questa volta').

19 *BMO*, IV/2, 76, Philip's instructions to Parma, signed on 1 April 1588 but entrusted to Medina Sidonia and therefore never seen by Parma himself (Duro, II, 16–18, also printed the Instructions, but without the king's holograph postscript; English precis in *CSPSp*, IV, 250–2); KML *Dr Valentine Dale: letters on talks with the duke of Parma*, #2, Dale to Robert Beale, 25 July 1588 OS, holograph. The interview took place on 8 July 1588 OS: see details in TNA *SP* 77/4/231–3, Dale to Elizabeth, 12 July 1588 OS.

20 Anon., *A collection of State Tracts*, II, 588 (from a tract printed in 1697); Brugmans, III, 284–6, Leicester to Burghley, 15 November 1587; TNA *SP* 12/213/38, Leicester to the Privy Council, Gravesend, 24 July 1588, endorsed 'Hast, hast, hast'; and ibid., ff. 64 and 39, Leicester to Walsingham, Gravesend, 26 July 1588, two letters, both holograph (all dates OS); Raleigh, *The historie*, Preface (sig. B2v) and bk. V, ch. 1, section ix (pp. 360–1), composed between 1607 and 1614.

21 Wilford, *A military discourse*, 11–12 (making an invidious comparison with the bastions that surrounded most Dutch towns); TNA *SP* 12/218/1–3, 'The scedule of the nomber of capteynes and soldiers appointed to serve in the fortes of Kent and Sussex', November 1587; TNA *SP* 12/219/6–16, 'A remaine of brasse ordinance in the castles, fforts and bulwarkes along the seacoast', November 1588. Admittedly, the castles at Camber and Dover boasted more guns – nine and fifteen respectively – but Parma planned to land at Margate.

22 Mundy, *The travels*, IV, 34; *APC*, XVI, 174–8, order of 24 July 1588 OS.

23 *CSPSc*, IX, 416, 'Proceedings of the French ambassador'.

24 TNA *SP* 84/25/165, Henry Killigrew to Walsingham, The Hague, 31 July 1588, holograph postscript (Laughton, I, 351–4, published the letter but read 'retreat' instead of 'bulwark'); Laughton, II, 309–13, Winter to Walsingham, 20 December 1588 (both dates OS).

25 TNA *SP* 84/25/68, Edward Norris to Walsingham, Ostend, 12 July 1588 OS.

26 HMC *Foljambe*, 29–31, Privy Council to Sir John Smythe and others, 10 December 1587; ibid., 40–2, 'The names of the martial men certified from the several counties', June 1588; Hunt *HA* 30,881/85v–6, Huntingdon to Walsingham, 20 June 1588 (all dates OS).

27 Goring and Wake, *Northamptonshire Lieutenancy papers*, 61, Sir Christopher Hatton, Privy Councillor and Lord Lieutenant of Northamptonshire, to his deputy, 28 July 1588 OS, wondering if the county could provide 200 trained archers.

28 TNA *SP* 12/210/70–1, Certificate of a survey by Captain Nicholas Dawtrey sent by the Privy Council to supervise the defence of Hampshire, 30 May 1588; Hunt

*HA* 30,881/76, Huntingdon to Burghley and Walsingham, 15 May 1588, and 85v–6, to Walsingham, 20 June 1588; Flower-Smith, 'The able and the willynge'; McGurk, 'Armada preparations', 87 (all dates OS).

29 Molyneux, *Conjunct expeditions* (1759) pt. II, 21 (we thank Adam Siegel for bringing this work to our attention).

30 Newbold, 'British planning', 154, Ironside to the Chief of the Imperial General Staff, 11 June 1940; https://www.youtube.com/watch?v=Qhx4z4jGroA, a BBC interview with Lord Alanbrooke (who succeeded Ironside), broadcast on 8 February 1957.

31 TNA *SP* 77/4/177–80v, Elizabeth to her peace commissioners, 29 June 1588, draft heavily corrected by Burghley; Wright, *Queen Elizabeth*, II, 378, Sir Thomas Heneage to Leicester, from the Court, 17 July 1588; *HMC Foljambe*, 48, Privy Council to Lords Lieutenants, 23 July 1588; Blok, *Correspondance inédite*, 197–8, Leicester to the duke of Montmorency, St James, 12 August 1588, holograph (all dates OS). Blok argued that Leicester wrote on 22 August OS, or 2 September NS, but this seems unlikely because the earl left Court on 27 August OS because he felt ill. He died a week later.

32 Oppenheim, *The naval tracts*, II, 283; TNA *SP* 12/212/58, Thomas Scott and Thomas Fane to Burghley, Rochester, 12 July 1588; *APC*, XVI, 185, Privy Council order on 26 July 1588. Laughton, II, 309–13, Winter to Walsingham, 20 December 1588 shows that he, too, still believed that Essex had been the intended landing-zone. All dates OS.

33 Laughton, I, 318–21, Leicester to Walsingham, 26 July 1588; *APC*, XVI, 198, 206 and 208, orders dated 28 and 31 July and 1 August 1588 (all dates OS).

34 Smythe, *Instructions* (1591), 183; TNA *SP* 12/213/92–3, Leicester to Walsingham, 28 July 1588; Folger *Ms.* X.c.126, Leicester to Elizabeth, 'in some haste from Tilbury', 3 August 1588 (both dates OS).

35 BL *Additional Ms.* 69,907A, 'The advise and answere of Sir John Norreys … uppon his view taken of the places of desent and strengthe of that countie' [Dorset], 10 May 1588; Braddick, 'Uppon this instant extraordinarie occasion', 440, report received by Lord Huntingdon in York on 27 July 1588, and 442 (all dates OS).

36 O'Neil, 'The fortifications', 252–5, printed Leighton's 'Directions' dated 30 April 1588 OS and concluded from other sources that Weybourne was indeed fortified in 1588 with 'sconces, ordinance and all manner of warlike appointment to defend the Spaniards landing there'.

37 Noble, *The names*, xvii–xviii, from a 'Military discourse' by Sir Thomas Wilford, *c.* 1595; Knappen, *Two Elizabethan Puritan diaries*, 79, entry for 31 July 1588 OS.

38 TNA *SP* 12/212/64 and 12/213/78, Scott to Burghley, 13 and 27 July 1588 OS.

39 Scott, 'Pay-list of the Kentish forces raised to resist the Spanish Armada'; Thompson, *The Twysden Lieutenancy Papers*, 70–1; NMM *Ms. PHB 1B*/444–7v, 'Lo que Su Magestad ha mandado comunicar al Señor Cardenal Archiduque', sent to Medina Sidonia together with the king's Instructions on 1 April 1588.

40 Rodger, *The Armada*, 48–9, Burghley to Walsingham, 19 July 1588 OS (facsimile and transcription).

41  OÖLA *KB* IV/311–12, Khevenhüller to Rudolf II, 13 July 1588.
42  Winston Churchill's speech to the House of Commons, 4 June 1940.
43  *APC*, XVI, 165 and 183, acts of 14 and 26 July 1588 (both dates OS).
44  Clark, *English Provincial Society*, 249, quoting Court records (see other treasonable statements at p. 454 n. 2, and in *APC*, XVI, 218 and 246); TNA *SP* 12/205/118, earl of Sussex to the Privy Council, Portsmouth, 30 November 1587 OS, with annotations by Burghley (printed with some errors in Bruce, *Report*, Appendix v); Wilford, *A discourse*, 46; Knappen, *Two Elizabethan Puritan diaries*, 80, entry for 13 August 1588 OS.
45  *Cabala* (3rd edn., London, 1691), II, 37, Lord Buckhurst to Elizabeth, 27 May 1587 OS; ARA *Raad van State* 6/19v–20, discussion on 16 June 1587.
46  Khevenhüller, *Diario*, 358.

## 20. The Armada in History and Legend

1  Hakluyt, *Principal navigations*, IV, 263–8, Howard to Medina Sidonia, 'from the English fleet before Cadiz', 30 June 1596 OS, composed in Latin by Roger Marbeck, followed by an account of the prisoner exchange.
2  AGS *Estado* 2512/16, 'Copia de la Memoria', and AGS *CMC* 2ª/42, unfol., 'Gastos Secretos' of the count of Villamediana, ambassador in London 1604–7, record the pension to Howard (we thank Paul C. Allen for these details). While in Spain Howard also visited his aunt Jane Dormer, who had married Philip II's confidant the count of Feria, the leading advocate for the Ridolfi Plot.
3  Aubrey, *Brief Lives*, I, 327 (perhaps Hobbes exaggerated: he was born on 5 April 1588 OS); Bruce, *Liber Famelicus*, 12–13 (written by Whitelocke *c.* 1610; we thank Richard Kagan for this reference); Knappen, *Two Elizabethan Puritan diaries*, 81, diary entry by Richard Rogers for 26 October 1588 OS.
4  Stow, *The survey*, 805, 813, 819, 859–60; Wickham Legg, 'A relation', 6–7, by Lieutenant Hammond from Norwich in 1635.
5  Van Mander, *The lives*, V, 234–8, and van Mander, *Het schilder-boek*, ff. 287–8v, record Vroom's visit to Howard and make clear that afterwards he prepared a large cartoon showing 'the seven days of the battle on one large canvas'. The cartoon has not survived.
6  Mears, 'Walls speak'. Hearn, 'Elizabeth I', 126 and n. 9, describes two miniatures showing the defeat of the Armada, both done in the early seventeenth century and now in private hands, and a third once possessed by Charles I in the 1630s but now apparently lost.
7  Leigh, *Queene Elizabeth*, 93 and 96 (on p. 94 Leigh provided a version of Elizabeth's speech at Tilbury).
8  Folgerpedia, 'The Elizabethan court day by day' for 1588, entries for 22 and 26 July OS; *BMO*, V, 239. Further details in Martin, *Armada prisoners*. The large standard once in St Paul's no doubt resembled those from *San Mateo* (Portugal), now in the Lakenhal, Leiden, and *Santa Ana* (Guipúzcoa), now in the Museo Naval, Madrid.

9   Larkin and Hughes, *Stuart royal proclamations*, I, 1–4, proclamation dated 24 March 1603 OS. James had already approved a draft of this document, although it did not mention his mother Mary. See also the first parliamentary statute of his reign: 1 Jac. I, c. 1. Because she married twice, Margaret Tudor was also grandmother to Henry Darnley, James VI's father: inbreeding worthy of a Habsburg.
10  Ward, *To God*; idem, *The life*, 117 ('The bookseller to the reader', dated January 1622); Walsham, 'Impolitic pictures', 318–20.
11  *Cabala*, 257–62; Edwards, *A collection*, 159–60 (sermons); Allestree, *A prognostication*, sig. C2, italics added.
12  Farrell, 'The Armada tapestries', 423–4, quoting the Lords Journal for May 1645 and the Commons Journal for 1651; Jansson, 'Remembering', 256–7, decree of the Council of State, April 1650 (both dates OS).
13  Deloney, *Thomas of Reading*, 203–9.
14  Ffoulkes, *Inventory*, 7–8, 29–31, with some items illustrated on p. 30; Anon., *A companion*, 24–8, contents of the Spanish Armoury in 1795; Lathbury, *The Spanish Armada*, 147–8; Wright, *Catalogue*, 36–7 (exhibit 318).
15  *Cabala*, 258–9, Sharpe to Buckingham, 1623 or 1624; Laughton, II, 27–9.
16  Scott, *The second part of Vox Populi*, 6; William Oldys, *The life of Sir Walter Raleigh* (1736), in his edition of *The works of Sir Walter Ralegh*, I, 104–5 (the bon mot).
17  Borja de Medina, 'Jesuitas', 33–4, campaign diary written by a Portuguese Jesuit in October 1588 (Spanish translation in *BMO*, IV/4, 346–7); *BMO*, IV/4, 411–12, Fray Ángelo de San Pablo to Madre María de San José, early 1589 (Spanish translation).
18  Sepúlveda, 'Historia' in Zarco Cuevas, *Documentos*, IV, 59; Sigüenza, *La fundación*, 120 (by 'over six hundred years' the friar no doubt meant since the Muslim conquest of Spain).
19  Cerda, *Consolatio ad Hispanos*, written in the 1590s and reprinted in 1621; Juan Pérez de Montalbán, *El Segundo Seneca de España y príncipe don Carlos*, second part (undated; first printed 1632).
20  Tellechea Idígoras, *Otra cara*, Vitoria's 'Memorias', 187 (greatest coward), 188 (the duke's humiliation in Valladolid, 'which he entered on 10 October, at 4 P.M.'), and 195 (audience).
21  Mariana, *Obras*, II, 405 (*Historiae de rebus hispaniae*), and 555 (from *De rege et regis instructione, libri III*). Mariana dedicated his book of advice on government to the new king, Philip III. This passage presumably got past the censors because the new king and his ministers initially welcomed criticisms of his father.
22  Pérez Bustamente, 'El cronista', 779–83, ('Puntos' and letter of Giovanni Canobio, 21 October 1608); Herrera y Tordesillas, *Historia del mundo*, III, bk. I, ch. 1, and bk. VIII, ch. 7.
23  Pérez Bustamente, 'El cronista', 790, Flavio Atti to Ranuccio, 4 April 1616. Cabrera de Córdoba, *Historia*, pt. II, bk. III, chs 8–9, first published from a manuscript copy in 1877.
24  Wynne, 'A brief relation', 430–4.

25 AGS *GyM* 3152, unfol., *consulta* of the Council of State, 28 April 1625, on the paper submitted by Brochero, Gran Prior de San Juan, on 'the reason for the defeats experienced by the navy of Your Majesty in the operations it has undertaken, and why your enemies, namely the English and the Dutch, have a different style of command'.

26 AGS *GyM* 3152, unfol., *consulta* of Council of War, 14 May 1628, with individual *votos* attached. Quotations from the *votos* of Bartolomé de Anaya Villanueva (who had served under Santa Cruz and lamented the lack of Oquendo, Bertendona and Aramburu), Don Luis Bravo (who praised Menéndez and the rest), Don Juan de Velasco (the English are just superior, get used to it), and the marquis of Montesclaros ('the practice of enemy navies does not count').

27 Coloma, *Las guerras*, 11. In the case of the Armada, Coloma cited the fireship attack as the 'tiny mishap [*arto pequeño accidente*]' which caused the entire Design to fail.

28 Carnero, *Historia*, 'Al lector', and 230–1. Although this was published in Brussels in 1625, Carnero said that he wrote this passage while Don Balthasar de Zúñiga was ambassador in Germany, so between 1608 and 1617.

29 Mallet, *Négociations*, VI, 281, count of Avaux to Louis XIV, 7 October 1688; BL *Additional Ms.* 38,495/28v, Moreau, Polish Resident in the United Provinces, to the king of Poland, The Hague, 12 October 1688.

30 Barton, *A Sermon*, 28; Kennett, *Charity and Restitution*, 25–32. The bishop supplied footnotes to the printed text of his sermons full of details on measures taken in 1588.

31 Hansard, *The Parliamentary History*, XIX, cols 369–70, Chatham's reply to the king's speech in November 1777.

32 *The Times*, 1 and 7 November 1788; Rogers, '1688 and 1888', 892–4. Everyone apparently forgot that Britain had changed from the Julian to the Gregorian Calendar in 1752, so that William actually landed on 15 November 1688 NS.

33 Bruce, *Report*, 1–2.

34 Kingsley, *Westward Ho!*, 8; Briggs, *The BBC*, 63.

35 *The Times* (London), 7 April and 4, 11, 17, 18 and 31 May 1888.

36 *The Glasgow Herald*, 4 April 1888; *The Belfast News-letter*, 1 June, 27 June, 14 July (Carrickfergus) and 6 August (Mountpottinger, Belfast) 1888.

37 *The Times* (London), 19 and 20 July 1888; *The Belfast News-letter*, 20 July 1888.

38 *The Times* (London), 20 August and 25 October 1888; Wright, *Catalogue*, 36–7 (exhibit 318); Lathbury, *The Spanish Armada*, 147–8; Ffoulkes, *Inventory*, 7.

39 *Programme for the opening of the Armada Tercentenary Exhibition on 24 October 1888*; *The Saturday Review of politics, literature, science and art*, LXXIX (1895), 315 (9 March 1895), scathing review of '"Gentleman Joe", a new musical farce' by 'G. B. S.'

40 Little, *The Tercentenary*, 227–38; Sladen, *The Spanish Armada*, 'to the Reader'. The copy in the State Library Victoria, Melbourne, Australia, contains a handwritten dedication by Sladen, stating that he had written his poem 'for recitation at the

great Plymouth celebration of the tercentenary of the destruction of the Spanish Armada'.
41 *La época*, 29 June 1887 (the commission) and 4 February 1888 (Cassola's opposition); *La correspondencia de España*, 15 July 1887 (prizes); *El Liberal*, 19 July 1887 (the cruiser); *La Unión*, 29 August 1887 (incorrect English interpretation).
42 *La época*, 26 July 1888 (Nelson's defeat in July 1797); *Los Dominicales del Libre Pensamiento* (Madrid), CCCIII (19 August 1888). The paper even used the English word: 'Cierto que si de Inglaterra nos viene el admirable sistema parlamentario, tambiém nos vienen los clowns'.
43 Lingard, *A history*, V, 488–9 (on how Lingard obtained copies of documents in AGS, the first foreign scholar ever to do so, see Jones, 'John Lingard'); Ellis, 'Copy', 373.
44 Duro, I, x. Most of the documents printed by Captain Duro were eighteenth-century copies now in the Archivo del Museo Naval, Madrid. He gathered materials for a third volume, but never published it.
45 Laughton, 'The Invincible Armada'; *The Times* (London), 8 June and 20 July 1888.
46 Froude, *The Spanish story*, 1–2 (pagination from the version re-published in his 1892 book). Froude spent several weeks working at Simancas in 1861, where he found (among other items) the 'Relation' of Pedro Coco Calderón, omitted by Duro.
47 Tilton, *Die Katastrophe*. In December 1895 Tilton published an English text of part of his thesis in *The Atlantic Monthly*, but it seems to have attracted little attention: Tilton, 'The defeat'.
48 Laughton, I, xxiv n. 1; *CSPSp*, IV. Hume was fluent in Spanish and, in our opinion, his translations seldom strayed far from the sense of the originals. For two exceptions see pp. 586 n.22 and 589 n.1.
49 Churchill's broadcast at https://www.nationalchurchillmuseum.org/every-man-to-his-post.html; Behlmer, *The sea hawk*, 41–2, 207–8 (scenes 267 and 268). Another major publication of Armada documents appeared in 1929 – Oria – but many were merely superior transcriptions of items already printed by Duro, using copies of the originals at AGS.
50 Mattingly, *The defeat*, 11.
51 *BMO*, IV/1, p. XV.
52 *El ministerio de tiempo*, episode 2, 'Tiempo de Gloria' (2015), exchange between 'Gil Pérez' and 'Julián Martínez'. In episode 23 of the series, 'Cambio de Tiempo' (2016), Philip II learns of the Armada's defeat and, with the permission of some sympathetic Inquisitors, travels forward to the present to secure a different outcome. Again he fails. Of course.
53 https://www.rmg.co.uk/discover/behind-the-scenes/blog/revealing-icon-conserving-armada-portrait; http://artdaily.com/news/105937/Rare-portrait-of-Sir-Francis-Drake-top-lot-at-Bonhams#.XXgc6yhKiM8; https://www.irishpost.com/news/historic-armada-table-sells-auction-e430000-centuries-spanish-armada-ships-wrecked-west-coast-ireland-160939. We doubt that this very fine portrait shows Drake, as claimed by Bonhams. It dates from the 1570s, but

Drake was only knighted in 1581: appearing in full tournament armour before being knighted seems remarkably pretentious, even for Drake. Italian armour was expensive: the 1589 Will of Sir William Winter singled out 'my Milan corslet' among his prized possessions (TNA *PROB* 11/73/383). The queen knighted Winter in 1573, the first officer to be honoured for his service to the navy, so perhaps the portrait shows Winter wearing his 'Milan corslet' shortly after that?

54 https://www.nmrn.org.uk/major-appeals/armada-maps/view-armada-maps shows the maps. https://www.artscouncil.org.uk/sites/default/files/download-file/EA%20statement_Armada%20drawings.pdf established the provenance and evaluated the relationship to the Ryther engravings.

55 In 2020 Spanish Armada Ireland commissioned a docudrama *Armada 1588 – Shipwreck & Survival*, which can be downloaded at www.SpanishArmadaIreland.com.

## 21. The Armada Shipwrecks

1 LPL *Carew Ms.* 618/83–83v, Fitzwilliam's commission to Sir George Carew, 22 September 1588, signed register copy (partial precis in *Calendar of the Carew manuscripts*, II, 490–1); *CSPI*, IV, 48–9, Richard Bingham to Fitzwilliam, 21 September 1588 (both dates OS).

2 *CSPI*, IV, xxviii, Edward White to Walsingham, 30 September 1588; ibid., 38, Nicholas Kahane to the mayor of Limerick, Kilrush, 12 September 1588 (both dates OS).

3 TNA *SP* 63/137/58, Fenton to Fitzwilliam, 'in haste at Ballymote', 9 October 1588; ibid., 97, and TNA *SP* 63/140/159–61, Fitzwilliam to the Privy Council, 30 January 1589 (all dates OS).

4 LPL *Carew Ms.* 618/25, Carew to Fitzwilliam, Dunmore, 22 June 1589; TNA *SP* 63/145/111, Fitzwilliam to Burghley, 3 July 1589 (both dates OS).

5 Martin, *Rosario*; *APC*, XVI, 189 (26 July), 192 (27 July), 309–10 (12 October) and 363 (1 December 1588, all dates OS); TNA *E* 351/2226, accounts of the Treasurer of the Navy, 1589.

6 *APC*, XVI, 328–9 (1 November), 347–8 (17 November) and 373–4 (8 December 1588, all dates OS); Laughton, II, 289–95, letters from George Carey and Anthony Ashley to the Privy Council, 5 and 12 November 1588; and *BMO*, IV/4, 441–2, 'Relación' by three officers, 18 February 1589.

7 AGS *CMC* 3a/1704 no. 45, Account of Captain Vicenzo de Bune; RAZ *Rekenkamer* C 2938, account of Pieter Willemszoen.

8 *BMO*, IV/4, 269, 'Relación de la artillería', 17 November 1588; ibid., 506, 'Información' by María de Zantátegui, Oquendo's widow, 12 September 1589. The guns salvaged in 1880 are today MNM Inv #1570.130 and 119. The Banner is MNM, Inv #4202: photo in *BMO* IV/1, p. XLVII.

9 *BMO*, IV/4, 253, Philip to Bertendona, 7 November 1588; ibid., 316, 'Relación de lo que ha sucedido a la nave *Regazona*', 11 December 1588; ibid., 549–61, list of

items salvaged from the vessel, 9 December 1588–9 January 1589, and of payment while embargoed (February–December 1588); Beltrami, 'Three Venetian ships', 200, 'Cessio' on 21 March 1589.
10 *BMO*, IV/4, 302, 'Relación sumaria del adovio y cosas que han menester los seis navíos', Corunna, 29 November 1588; ibid., 471, 'Relación del estado en que se hallan los adobios de los navios', Corunna, 15 April 1589.
11 Earle, *The last fight of the Revenge*, 144–6, 158–61.
12 Kostić, 'Ragusa', 223, 'Information' by Archibald Millar, 1683. Millar had dived on the wreck for Argyll and visited Inveraray Castle, where the earl kept his archive.
13 *HMC Sixth Report*, 625, Grant by the duke of Lennox to Argyll, 5 February 1641, precis. At this time King Charles I was offering bribes to win Argyll over to his cause. Since Lennox was the king's cousin, the grant may have been one of the bribes.
14 Sinclair, *The principles*, postscript (separate pagination), 'To buoy up a ship', 1–2.
15 Sinclair, *Ars nova*, 220–44 (drawing at p. 238); idem, *The Hydrostaticks*, 153–5, part of a 26-page description ('Experiment XVIII').
16 Gregory, *The great and new art*, 24–7, 47–9 (even the title was a cruel paraphrase of the title of Sinclair's 1669 tract); Craik, 'The hydrostatical works', 258–61; *HMC Sixth Report*, 626–7, Contract between Argyll, Captain Smith and Treleben, 26 December 1676; 627, 'Information anent the Spanish wreck, 1676'; idem, Memorandum by the ninth Earl of Argyll about the Spanish 'Wrack', 1677; Sinclair, *The principles*, 'Postscript', 1–2. Laughton, II, 51, States of Zeeland to Elizabeth, 16 August 1588, mentioned that Parma had prepared a crown and sceptre.
17 *HMC Sixth Report*, 627, Memorandum by the ninth earl of Argyll about the Spanish 'Wrack', 1677; ibid., Instrument at the instance of Captain Adolphus Smith against John McLean, 7 September 1678. On the *Vasa* guns, see Kristensen and Jørgensen, 'The mystery'.
18 *HMC Sixth Report*, 627, Agreement between Argyll and Millar, Inveraray, 6 April 1680.
19 Kostić, 'Ragusa', 223–4, 'Information' by Millar, Greenock, 20 November 1683. Lang, 'The mystery', 431–2, also published a transcript of the document (Bod *Rawlinson Ms.* A.189/423) and plausibly suggested that it was prepared for James.
20 Laing, 'Notice', 435–9, printed the 1686 warrant; Sacheverell, *An account*, 97 (July 1688); Martin, *A description*, 253–4 (describing his personal reconnaissance in 1695–7).
21 Rowe, *A demonstration*, 6–7.
22 Martin, 'The wreck of the Dutch East-Indiaman Adelaar'.
23 McLeay, *The Tobermory treasure*, 57–8, quoting a letter from Jacob Rowe to Mackenzie of Delvine.
24 Paine, *The book of buried treasure*, 220, letter of Argyll to Paine, 25 April 1910.
25 Brown and Whittaker, *A treasure lost*, 22, listed the artefacts sold at auction by Foss in 1910, mostly fragmentary and 'incrusted' with iron concretion. Foss became a lieutenant in the Indian army in 1877, rising to the rank of Lt. Colonel in 1903.

This was not his first attempt to raise money by unusual means: *Parliamentary Papers: Ceylon* (1906) contains an entire appendix filled with the correspondence in 1904–6 of the UK Colonial Office concerning Foss's offer to lease the Pearl Fisheries on the coast of Ceylon (Sri Lanka).
26 Lang, 'The mystery' (an identification finally confirmed in 1972 by research in the archives of Ragusa, now Dubrovnik, by Veselin Kostić); McLeay, *The Tobermory treasure*, 107–15.
27 McLeay, *The Tobermory treasure*, 132–3.
28 *The Q Wealth Report*, Issue 64, winter 2014, 19–23.
29 *Daily Express*, 26 April 2014.
30 Spotswood Green, 'Armada ships', 262 (map) and 269 (quote); idem, '*La Rata*', 275 (talking to 'the peasantry' and souvenir-hunting in haystacks); *Report of the inspectors* (1891), 45 (landing on Great Blasket Island). From Blasket Sound, he steamed to Smerwick harbour; and later he stopped at Moville, close to the wreck of *Trinidad Valencera*. Later he also followed Cuéllar's trail: 'The wrecks', 444–5.
31 Sténuit, *Treasures of the Armada*. Laurence Flanagan was murdered in 2001 when his Belfast home was burgled. Acquiring the *Girona* artefacts was the greatest coup of his long and distinguished tenure as Keeper of Antiquities at the Ulster Museum, and his permanent monument.
32 Martin, 'The Spanish Armada Expedition'; idem, *Full Fathom Five*; idem, '*La Santa María de la Rosa*'.
33 Martin, *Full Fathom Five*; idem, '*El Gran Grifón*'.
34 Martin, '*La Trinidad Valencera*: an Armada invasion transport'; Atherton, *La Trinidad Valencera*.
35 In 1994 the Supreme Court of the Irish Republic accepted our identification of the three wrecks but refused a licence to excavate the site 'until proper conservation facilities were available onshore': *Irish Law Reports Monthly*, CXCIV/1, 194–202, 'On the matter of the sailing vessels "La Lavia", "Juliana" and "Santa María"'. See also Birch and McElvogue, '*La Lavia*, *La Juliana* and the *Santa María de Visón*'.

# Epilogue

1 Fernández Duro, *Armada Española*, IV, 203 n. 1, Olivares to Oquendo, 27 July 1639; Ogle and Bliss, *Calendar*, I, 183, Hopton to Windebank, 19 September 1639.
2 Fernández Duro, *Armada Española*, IV, 224–6, Oquendo's Instructions to his fleet, Corunna, 31 August 1639.
3 Ogle and Bliss, *Calendar*, I, 184–5, Windebank to Gage and Hopton, 8 October 1639. Account of the battles on 16 and 18 September reconstructed from Tromp's *Journal* and Manuel de Melo's *Epanáphoras*, printed in Boxer, *The Journal*.
4 Mundy, *The travels*, IV, 38–9 (entry for 30 September 1639 OS). Mundy later reported his conversation with some of the Spanish survivors after the battle, whom he considered 'labourers, vagabonds [and] poor people' pressed into service against

their wills (ibid., 41–2). An eyewitness of the embarkation at Corunna confirmed this: Manuel de Melo, *Epanáphoras*, 308–9.
5   *CSPD Charles I*, XIV, 538–9, Thomas Smith, secretary to Lord Admiral Northumberland, 30 September 1639; ibid., XV, 18–19, Northumberland to Pennington, 8 October 1639 (both dates OS).
6   Boxer, *The Journal*, 195–6, entry for 21 October 1639; TNA *SP* 16/431/145, 'The names of the shippes that run on shore'.
7   *CSPD Charles I*, XV, 26–7, 'Relation' of the battle by Sir John Pennington and his captains, 11 October 1639 OS (they noted that Tromp did not return fire on the English warships); Price, *A new Spanish tragedy* (published on 25 October 1639); Ogle and Bliss, *Calendar*, I, 184–5, Colonel Leslie to Windebank, Brussels, 28 October 1639; TNA *SP* 77/29/402–5, Balthasar Gerbier to Secretary of State Windebank, Brussels, 29 October 1639 NS (quoting Eeryck de Putte); *CSPD Charles I*, XIV, 518, Instructions of Pennington to Captain John Whitman, September 1639 (all dates NS); Sharpe, *The personal rule*, 832.
8   On the Twelve Apostles, see Casabán, 'The design', 386–99; on the Dutch, see Elias, *De vlootbouw*, 4–7; Bruijn, *The Dutch navy*, 20–1; Schokkenbroek, 'The growth'.
9   PRO *WO* 55/1672, 'A view and survey of all her Majesty's Ordinnance', listing all ships except *Warspite* and *Repulse*; the totals for these two ships have been added from WO 55/1627, 'The booke of the remaynes'; Mundy, *The travels*, IV, 35–6; Rodger, *The safeguard*, 388 (*Sovereign of the Seas*).
10  Rodger, *The safeguard*, 389 (*Ark*, renamed *Anne Royal* in 1608; sank 1636). More details in Appendix 3.
11  Mundy, *The travels*, IV, 36.
12  Ehrman, *The navy*, 174; Rodger, *The command*, 189.
13  Rodger, *The command*, 96 and 120–2. Currently all officers in the Royal Navy begin as midshipmen and after 12 months of service rise automatically to the rank of sub-lieutenant, and normally serve a further 30 months before promotion to lieutenant.
14  *CSPD Anne*, I, 189–90, Shovell to the earl of Nottingham, secretary of state, 18 July 1702; Duro, I, p. x.
15  Parker, 'Anatomy' (on Recalde); Vermeir, 'The ransoming of prisoners' (Dartmouth).
16  Email exchanges between John Treacy and Geoffrey Parker, August 2016 and September 2021.

# Bibliography

*Actas de las Cortes de Castilla*, 17 vols (Madrid, 1861–91)
*Acts of the Privy Council of England*, ed. J. R. Dasent et al., 46 vols (London, 1890–1984)
Adams, S., 'Eliza enthroned? The court and its politics', in C. Haigh, ed., *The Reign of Elizabeth* (London, 1984), 55–77
Adams, S., 'Stanley, York and Elizabeth's Catholics', *History Today*, XXXVII/7 (July 1987), 46–50
Adams, S., 'New light on the "Reformation" of Sir John Hawkins: the Ellesmere naval survey of January 1584', *EHR*, CV (1990), 96–111
Adams, S., 'The decision to intervene: England and the United Provinces, 1584–1585', in J. Martínez Millán, ed., *Felipe II (1527–1598): Europa y la Monarquía Católica*, 5 vols (Madrid, 1999), I, 19–31
Adams, S., 'The battle that never was: the Downs and the Armada campaign', in Rodríguez-Salgado and Adams, *England, Spain and the Gran Armada*, 173–96
Adams, S., 'The outbreak of the Elizabethan naval war against the Spanish empire: the embargo of May 1585 and Sir Francis Drake's West India voyage', in Rodríguez-Salgado and Adams, *England, Spain and the Gran Armada*, 45–69
Adams, S., *Leicester and the Court: Essays on Elizabethan politics* (Manchester, 2002)
Adams, S., 'The Armada correspondence in Cotton MSS Otho E VII and E IX', in M. Duffy, ed., *The Naval Miscellany*, VI (Aldershot, 2003: Navy Records Society, CXLVI), 37–92
Alba, J. Fitz-James Stuart, 17th duke of, *Epistolario del III duque de Alba*, 3 vols (Madrid, 1952)
Alemán, M., *Primera parte de Guzmán de Alfarache* (Madrid, 1599)
Allestree, R., *A prognostication for this present yeare of grace, 1628* (London, 1628)
Alonso Cortés, N., *Valladolid y la armada invencible* (1916), reprinted in idem, *Miscelánea Vallisoletana*, I (Valladolid, 1955), 321–50
Altadonna, G., 'Cartas de Felipe II a Carlos Manuel II Duque de Saboya (1583–1596)', *Cuadernos de investigación histórica*, IX (1986), 137–90

Álvarez de Toledo, L. I., duchess of Medina Sidonia, *Alonso Pérez de Guzmán, General de la Invencible*, 2 vols (Cádiz, 1995)
Álvarez Nogal, C., 'El verdadero impacto económico de la Gran Armada: mito y realidad', in *La Armada Española de 1588*, 365–76
Alzaga García, M. et al., 'El barco genovés San Giorgio y San Telmo Buenaventura al servicio de la Gran Armada', in *La Armada Española de 1588*, 133–53
Anderson, J. L., 'Climatic change, sea-power and historical discontinuity: the Spanish Armada and the Glorious Revolution of 1688', *The Great Circle*, V/1 (1983), 13–23
Anderson, J. L., 'Combined operations and the Protestant wind: Some maritime aspects of the Glorious Revolution of 1688', *The Great Circle*, IX/2 (1987), 96–107
Anderson, J. L., 'Prince William's descent upon Devon, 1688: the environmental constraints', in S. Fisher, ed., *Lisbon as a port town, the British seaman, and other maritime themes* (Exeter, 1988), 37–55
Anderson, R. C., *Oared fighting ships: From classical times to the coming of steam* (Kings Langley, 1976)
Andrews, K. R., *Elizabethan privateering: English privateering during the Spanish War, 1585–1603* (Cambridge, 1964)
Andrews, K. R., *Drake's voyages: A reassessment of their place in Elizabethan naval expansion* (London, 1967)
Andrews, K. R., *Trade, plunder and settlement: Maritime enterprise and the genesis of the British Empire, 1480–1630* (Cambridge, 1984)
Anon., *The true reporte of the prosperous successe which God gaue vnto our English souldiours against the forraine bands of our Romaine enemies lately ariued, (but soone inough to theyr cost) in Ireland, in the yeare 1580* (London, 1581)
Anon., *A discouerie of the treasons practised and attempted against the Queenes Maiestie and the realme, by Francis Throckmorton* (London, 1584)
Anon., *A true Report of the general Imbarrement of all the English Shippes, vnder the dominion of the kinge of Spaine: and of the daungerous aduenture, & wonderfull deliuerance, of a Ship of London* (London, 1585)
Anon., *Relaciõ de lo que hasta oy a los 5 de septiembre . . . se ha sabido* (Seville, 1588)
Anon., *A letter from a gentleman in the country to his correspondent in the city, concerning the coronation medal distributed April 11, 1689* (London, [dated 16 Apr 1689])
Anon., *A collection of State Tracts publish'd in the reign of King William III*, 2 vols (London, 1706)
Anon., *The History of the Spanish Armada, which had been preparing three years for the invasion and conquest of England, and which in the year 1588 came upon the English Coast to effect it* (London, 1759)
Anon., *A companion to all the principal places of curiosity and entertainment in and about London and Westminster. Containing an historical description of London, the Tower of London . . . and other places*, 8th edn. (London, 1796)
*Archivo histórico español*, 35 vols to date (Madrid, 1950–)
Ares, N., *Éboli. Secretos de la vida de Ana de Mendoza* (Madrid, 2005)
Aske, J., *Elizabetha triumphans* (London, 1588)

Astraín, A., *Historia de la Compañía de Jesús en la asistencia de España*, III (Madrid, 1909)
Atherton, D., *La Trinidad Valencera* (Derry-Londonderry, 2013)
Aubrey, J., *Brief lives, chiefly of contemporaries, set down by John Aubrey, between the years 1669 & 1696*, ed. A. Clark, 2 vols (Oxford, 1898)
Aylmer, J., *An harborowe for faithfull and trevve subiectes agaynst the late blowne blaste, concerninge the government of Wemen* (London, 1559)
Bacon, F., 'Considerations touching a warre with Spaine' (1624), in W. Rawley, ed., *Certaine miscellany works of the Right Honourable Francis, Lord Verulam* (London, 1929), separate pagination
Bain, J., ed., *The Hamilton Papers. Letters and papers illustrating the political relations to England and Scotland in the XVIth century*, 2 vols (Edinburgh, 1890–2)
Barton, S., *A Sermon preached before the Right Honourable the Lord Mayor and Aldermen of the City of London, at St. Mary-le-Bow, Octob. 27th. 1692. Being the Day of Publick Thanksgiving for the signal victory at sea* (London, 1692)
Beck, H., 'The prince of Spain, 1588', *Journal of the Folklore Institute*, VIII (1971), 48–56
Behlmer, R., *The sea hawk* (Madison, WI, 1982)
Behringer, W., *Im Zeichen des Merkur: Reichspost und Kommunikationsrevolution in der Frühen Neuzeit* (Göttingen, 2003)
Belsey, A., and C. Belsey, 'Icons of divinity: portraits of Elizabeth', in L. Gent and N. Llewellyn, eds, *Renaissance bodies: The human figure in English culture, c. 1540–1660*, 2nd edn. (London, 1995), 11–35
Beltrame, C., 'Three Venetian ships in the Armada', *Mediterranean Historical Review*, XXXIV/2 (2019), 195–206
Benítez Sánchez-Blanco, R., 'De moriscos, papeles y archivos: el gran memorándum de 1607', in A. Marcos Martín, ed., *Hacer historia desde Simancas. Homenaje a José Luis Rodríguez de Diego* (Valladolid, 2011), 107–28
Benton, J. G., *A course of instruction of ordnance and gunnery* (New York, 1862)
Bertini, G., 'La nazione italiana nell'esercito di Alessandro Farnese nei Paesi Bassi: nuove prostettive', *Philostrato. Revista de historia y arte. Número extraordinario* (March 2018), 258–95
Bertini, G., ed., *Militari italiani dell'esercito di Alessandro Farnese nelle Fiandre* (Parma, 2013)
Bianchi, P., 'Una riserva di fedeltà. I bastardi dei Savoia fra esercito, diplomazia e cariche curiali', in Bianchi and L. C. Gentile, eds, *L'affermarsi della corte sabauda. Dinastie, poteri, élites in Piemonte e Savoia tra tardo medioevo e prima età moderna* (Turin, 2006), 305–60
Birch, S., and D. M. McElvogue, '*La Lavia*, *La Juliana* and the *Santa María de Visón*: three Spanish Armada transports lost off Streedagh Strand, Co. Sligo: an interim report', *International Journal of Nautical Archaeology*, XXVIII (1999), 265–76
Biringuccio, V., *Pirotechnia* (1540), transl. and ed. C. S. Smith and M. T. Gnudi (1990)
Blackmore, H. L., *The armouries of the Tower of London. I. Ordnance* (London, 1976)
Blok, P. J., *Correspondance inédite de Robert Dudley, comte de Leycester, et de François et Jean Hotman* (Haarlem, 1911)

Bond, E. A., ed., *Russia at the close of the sixteenth century* (London, 1856: Hakluyt Society, XX)
Bor, P. C., *Oorspronck, begin ende vervolgh der Nederlantsche Oorloghen*, 7 vols (Leiden and Amsterdam, 1621–84)
Borja de Medina, F. de, 'Jesuitas en la Armada contra Inglaterra (1588). Notas para un centenario', *Archivum historicum Societatis Iesu*, LVIII (1989), 3–42
Borman, T., 'Untying the knot? The survival of the Anglo-Dutch alliance, 1587–97', *European History Quarterly*, XXVII (1997), 307–37
Bossy, J., *Under the molehill: An Elizabethan spy story* (London and New Haven, CT, 2001)
Bourne, W., *The art of shooting in great ordnaunce* (1578; 2nd edn., London, 1587)
Bouza, F., *Cartas de Felipe II a sus hijas*, 2nd edn. (Madrid, 1998)
Bouza, F. J., *Imagen y propaganda. Capítulos de historia cultural del reinado de Felipe II* (London, 1998)
Bovill, E. W., 'Queen Elizabeth's gunpowder', *MM*, XXXIII (1947), 179–86
Boxer, C. R., 'The papers of Martín de Bertendona, a Basque admiral of Spain's Golden Age, 1584–1604', *Indiana University Bookman*, X (1969), 3–23
Boxer, C. R., ed., *The Journal of Maarten Harpertszoon Tromp, anno 1639* (Cambridge, 1930)
Braddick, M. J., '"Uppon this instant extraordinarie occasion": military mobilization in Yorkshire before and after the Armada', *Huntington Library Quarterly*, LXI (1998), 429–55
Bratli, C., *Philippe II, roi d'Espagne* (Paris, 1912)
Braudel, F., *The Mediterranean and the Mediterranean world in the age of Philip II*, 2 vols (London, 1973)
Brayshay, M., 'Plymouth's coastal defences in the year of the Spanish Armada', *Reports and Transactions of the Devonshire Association for the Advancement of Science*, CXIX (1987), 169–96
*Breeder verclaringhe vande vloote van Spaegnien. De bekentenisse van Don Diego de Piementel* (The Hague, 1588: Knuttel pamphlet nr. 847)
Briggs, A., *The BBC: The first fifty years* (Oxford, 1985)
Brown, K., 'The making of a *politique:* the Counter-Reformation and the regional policies of John, eighth Lord Maxwell', *Scottish Historical Review*, LXVI (1987), 152–75
Brown, M. J., '"The Hearts of All Sorts of People Were Enflamed": manipulating readers of Spanish Armada news', *Book History*, XVII (2014), 94–116
Brown, O., and J. Whittaker, *A treasure lost: The Spanish wreck in Tobermory Bay* (n.p., 2000)
Bruce, J., *Report on the arrangements which were made for the internal defence of these kingdoms when Spain, by its Armada, projected the invasion and conquest of England* (London, 1798)
Bruce, J., ed., *The Liber Famelicus of Sir James Whitelocke* (London, 1858: Camden Society Series, LXX)
Brugmans, H., ed., *Correspondentie van Robert Dudley graaf van Leycester en andere documenten betreffende zijn Gouvernement-Generaal in de Nederlanden, 1585–8*, 3 vols (Utrecht, 1931)

Bruijn, J. R., *The Dutch navy of the seventeenth and eighteenth centuries* (Columbia, SC, 1993)
Brunetti, M., and E. Vitale, *La corrispondenza da Madrid dell'ambasciatore Leonardo Donà (1570–1573)*, 2 vols (Venice-Rome, 1963)
Bryce, W. M., 'Mary Stuart's voyage to France in 1548', *EHR*, XXII (1907), 43–50
Brydges, S. E., *Censura Literaria. Containing titles, abstracts and opinions of Old English books*, 6 vols (London, 1805–9)
Burghley, William Cecil, Baron, *Copie of a Letter sent out of England to Don Bernardin Mendoza ambassadour in France for the King of Spaine declaring the state of England, contrary to the opinion of Don Bernardin, and of all his partizans Spaniardes and Other* (London, 1588)
Burnell, A. C., and P. A. Tiele, eds, *The voyage of John Huyghen van Linschoten to the East Indies*, 2 vols (1598; London, 1885: Hakluyt Society, LXX–LXXI)
[Burnet, G.,] *The expedition of His Highness the prince of Orange for England, giving an account of the most remarkable passages thereof, from the day of his setting sail from Holland, to the first day of this instant December, 1688: in a letter to a person of quality* [n.p., 1688]
Burnet, G., *Bishop Burnet's history of his own time*, 2 vols (1724–34; new edn., London, 1840)
*Cabala, Mysteries of State, in Letters of the Great Minister of K. James and K. Charles . . . faithfully collected by a Noble Hand* (London, 1653)
Cabrera de Córdoba, L., *Historia de Felipe II, rey de España*, 3 vols (Salamanca, 1998)
Cadoppi, A., 'Un "macello di huomini da bene". Lettere al duca d'Este dalle Fiandre di militari al servizio di Alessandro Farnese', in Bertini, *Militari italiani*, 153–70
Caeiro, F., *O Archiduque Alberto de Áustria. Vice-rei e Inquisidor-Mor de Portugal* (Lisbon, 1961)
Calderón Calderón, M., 'Memoria e imagen de la Armada y Contra Armada en Portugal (1588–1589)', in *La Armada Española de 1588*, 499–519
*Calendar of Letters and State Papers relating to English affairs preserved in, or originally belonging to, the Archives of Simancas. Elizabeth*, ed. M. A. S. Hume, 4 vols (London, 1892–9)
*Calendar of State Papers, Domestic Series: Edward VI, Mary, Elizabeth (1581–90)* (London, 1865); *see also* Knighton
*Calendar of State Papers, Foreign Series, of the reign of Elizabeth*, XIX, XXI (in 4 pts.) and XXII (London, 1916, 1927–31, 1936)
*Calendar of State Papers and manuscripts relating to English affairs existing in the archives and collections of Venice*, VIII: *1581–1591*, ed. H. F. Brown (London, 1894)
*Calendar of State Papers relating to Ireland in the reign of Elizabeth*, IV: *1588–92*, ed. H. C. Hamilton (London, 1885)
*Calendar of State Papers relating to Scotland*, ed. J. Bain, W. K. Boyd, A. I. Dunlop and J. D. Mackie, 13 vols (Edinburgh, 1898–1969)
*Calendar of the Carew Manuscripts preserved in the archiepiscopal library at Lambeth*, ed. J. S. Brewer and W. Bullen, 6 vols (London, 1867–79)

Calvar Gross, J., J. I. González-Aller Hierro, M. de Dueñas Fontán and M. del C. Mérida Valverde, *La batalla del Mar Océano. Corpus documental de las hostilidades entre España e Inglaterra (1568–1604)*, 5 vols in 10 pts. (Madrid, 1988–2015)

Cambridge, marquess of, 'The march of William of Orange from Torbay to London', *Journal of the Society for Army Historical Research*, XLIV (1966), 152–74

Camden, W., *Annales: the true and royall history of the famous empresse Elizabeth Queene of England, France and Ireland* (London, 1625)

Camden, W., *The historie of the most renowned and victorious Princesse Elizabeth* (Latin original of pt. I, London, 1615; English trans., London, 1630)

Campana de Cavelli, Emily Rowles, marquise of, *Les derniers Stuarts à Saint-Germain en Laye. Documents inédits*, 2 vols (Paris, 1871)

Campbell, J., *Grammatical man: Information, entropy, language and life* (New York, 1982)

Canestrini, G., and A. Desjardins, *Négociations diplomatiques de la France avec la Toscane*, 6 vols (Paris, 1859–86)

Caraman, P., *Henry Garnet, 1555–1606, and the Gunpowder Plot* (London, 1964)

Carey, V., 'Atrocity and history: Grey, Spenser, and the slaughter at Smerwick', in D. Edwards, P. Lenihan and C. Tait, eds, *The age of atrocity: Violence and political conflict in early modern Ireland* (Dublin, 2007), 79–94

Carnero, A., *Historia de las guerras civiles que ha avido en los estados de Flandes desde el año 1559 hasta el de 1609 y las causas de la rebelión de dichos estados* (Brussels, 1625)

Casabán, J. L., 'The design and construction of the Twelve Apostles (1588–1592)', in *La Armada Española de 1588*, 377–403

Casado Soto, J. L., *Los barcos españoles del siglo XVI y la Gran Armada de 1588* (Madrid, 1988)

Casado Soto, J. L., *Discursos de Bernardino de Escalante al rey y sus ministros, 1585–1605* (Laredo, 1995)

Casado Soto, J. L., 'Flota atlántica y tecnología naval hispana en tiempos de Felipe II', in L. M. Enciso and L. A. Ribot, eds, *Las sociedades ibéricas y el mar a finales del siglo XVI*, II (Madrid, 1998), 339–63

Cerda, M. de la, *Consolatio ad Hispanos propter classem in Angliam profectam subita tempestate submersam* (Seville, 1621)

Cerezo Martínez, R., 'La conquista de la isla Tercera (1583)', *Revista de historia naval*, I/3 (1983), 5–45

Cervantes Saavedra, M., *Obras completas*, ed. J. C. Peinado, 2 vols (Madrid, 2005)

Céspedes del Castillo, G., 'La defensa de América', in F. Ruiz Martín, *La monarquía de Felipe II* (Madrid, 2003), 381–412

Chaves, A. de, 'Espejo de navigantes', a manuscript of *c.* 1540 published in Fernández Duro, *Armada Española*, I, 379–91

Chevallier, P., *Henri III: roi shakespearien* (Paris, 1985)

Cheyney, E. P., 'Law in history', *AHR*, XXIX (1924), 231–48

Christie's, *Valuable travel, atlases and natural history books, including important portolan charts* (London, 1988)

Churchill, W. S., *The world crisis*, 6 vols (London, 1923–31)

Cimber, M., and F. Danjou, *Archives curieuses de l'histoire de la France*, 1st series, XI (Paris, 1836)
Cipolla, C. M., *Guns and sails in the early phase of European expansion, 1400–1700* (London, 1965)
Clark, P., *English provincial society from the Reformation to the Revolution: Religion, politics and society in Kent, 1500–1640* (Hassocks, 1977)
Clark, S., *England's Remembrancer, containing a true and full narrative of that never-to-be-forgotten deliverance, the Spanish invasion in 1588* (1657; reprinted London, 1819)
Clowes, W. L., *The Royal Navy: A history*, I (London, 1898)
Cock, E., *Relación del viaje hecho por Felipe II en 1585 a Zaragoza, Barcelona y Valencia*, ed. A. Morel-Fatio and A. Rodríguez Villa (Madrid, 1876)
Cock, R., and N. A. M. Rodger, *A guide to the naval records in the National Archives of the UK*, 2nd edn. (London, 2008)
Cocroft, W. D., *Dangerous Energy: The archaeology of gunpowder and military explosives manufacture* (Swindon, 2000)
Cohen, E., and J. Gooch, *Military misfortunes: The anatomy of failure in war* (New York, 1990; revised edn., 2006)
Cole, M. H., *The portable queen: Elizabeth I and the politics of ceremony* (Amherst, MA, 1999)
Collado, L., *Plática manual de artillería* (Venice, 1592)
Collinson, P., *The English captivity of Mary Queen of Scots* (Sheffield, 1987)
Collinson, P., *Elizabethan essays* (London, 1994)
Collinson, P., 'William Camden and the anti-myth of Elizabeth: setting the mould?', in S. Doran and T. S. Freeman, eds, *The Myth of Elizabeth* (Basingstoke, 2003), 79–98
Coloma, C., *Las guerras de los Estados Baxos desde el año de MDLXXXVIII hasta el de MDXCIX* (Antwerp, 1624)
Colvin, H., *The history of the king's works*, IV (London, 1982)
Constant, J. M., *Les Guise* (Paris, 1984)
Cookson, J., 'What if Napoleon had landed?', *History Today*, LIII/9 (September 2003), 10–17
Cooper, C. P., *Recueil des dépêches, rapports, instructions et mémoires des ambassadeurs de France en Angleterre: correspondance de Bertrand de Salignac de la Mothe Fénélon*, 7 vols (Paris and London, 1838–42)
Corbett, J. S., *Papers relating to the navy during the Spanish war, 1585–1587* (London, 1898: Navy Records Society, XI)
Corbett, J. S., *Drake and the Tudor navy, with a history of the rise of England as a maritime power*, 2 vols (new edn., London, 1899)
Corbett, J. S., 'Relation of the voyage to Cadiz in 1596', in J. K. Laughton, ed., *The Naval Miscellany*, I (London, 1902: Navy Records Society, XX), 24–92
Corbett, J. S., *Fighting instructions, 1530–1816* (London, 1905: Navy Records Society, XXIX)
Corbett, J. S., *Signals and instructions, 1776–1794, with addenda to volume XXIX* (London, 1908: Navy Records Society, XXXV)

Cortesão, A., and A. Teixeira de Mota, *Portugaliae monumenta cartographia*, III (Lisbon, 1960)

Craik, A. D. D., 'The hydrostatical works of George Sinclair (*c.* 1630–1696): their neglect and criticism', *Notes and records*, LXXII (2018), 239–73

Cressy, D., 'The Spanish Armada: celebration, myth and memory', in J. Doyle and B. Moore, eds, *England and the Spanish Armada* (Canberra, 1990), 157–76

Cressy, D., 'National memory in early modern England', in J. R. Gillis, ed., *Commemorations: The politics of national identity* (Princeton, NJ, 1994), 61–73

Crone, G. R., '"The Mariners Mirrour" 1588', *The Geographical Journal*, CXIX (1953), 455–8

Cruickshank, D. W., and P. Gallagher, 'A note on Cuéllar and his letter', in Gallagher and Cruickshank, *God's obvious design*, Appendix II

Cruz, A. J., ed., *Material and symbolic circulation between Spain and England, 1554–1604* (Aldershot, 2008)

Cunha Rivara, J. H. da, ed., *Arquivo Português Oriental*, III (Nova Goa, 1861)

Daultrey, S., 'The weather of north-west Europe during the summer and autumn of 1588', in Gallagher and Cruickshank, *God's obvious design*, 113–41

D'Avaux, Jean-Antoine, *Négociations de Monsieur le Comte d'Avaux en Hollande, depuis 1679 jusqu'en 1688*, 6 vols (Paris, 1752–3)

Davies, D., 'James II, William of Orange, and the Admirals', in E. Cruickshanks, ed., *By force or by default? The revolution of 1688–1689* (Edinburgh, 1989), 82–108

De Armas, F. A., 'Heretical stars: the politics of astrology in Cervantes' *La Gitanilla* and *La Española inglesa*', in Cruz, *Material and symbolic circulation*, 89–100

De Boer, M. G., *Tromp en de Armada van 1639* (Amsterdam, 1941)

Deleito y Piñuela, J., *El declinar de la monarquía española*, 2nd edn. (Madrid, 1947)

Deloney, T., *Thomas of Reading and three ballads on the Spanish Armada*, ed. C. R. Aldrich and L. Kirtland (New York, 1903)

Derks, S., 'The fruits of war: the representation of Alessandro Farnese in Paolo Rinaldi's *Liber Relationum*', in L. Geevers and M. Marini, eds, *Dynastic identities in early modern Europe: Rulers, aristocrats and the formation of identities* (Leiden, 2015), 153–78

Dickerman, E. H., 'A neglected aspect of the Spanish Armada: the Catholic League's Picardy offensive of 1587', *Canadian Journal of History*, XI (1976), 19–23

Dietz, B., 'The royal bounty and English merchant shipping', *MM*, LXXVII (1991), 5–20

Dietz, F. C., *English public finance, 1558–1641*, 2nd edn. (London, 1964)

Digges, D., *The compleat ambassador; or two treaties of the intended marriage of Queen Elizabeth of glorious memory: comprised in letters of negotiation of Sir Francis Walsingham* (London, 1655)

Donaldson, G., *All the queen's men: Power and politics in Mary Stewart's Scotland* (London, 1983)

Donno, E. S., *An Elizabethan in 1582: The diary of Richard Madox, fellow of All Souls* (London, 1976: Hakluyt Society, 2nd Series, CXLVII)

Dooley, B., 'Sources and methods in information history: the case of Medici Florence, the Armada and the siege of Ostende', in J. W. Koopmans, ed., *News and politics in early modern Europe, 1500–1800* (Leuven, 2005), 29–46

Dooley, B. M., 'Making it present', in Dooley, ed., *The dissemination of news and the emergence of contemporaneity in early modern Europe* (Farnham, 2010), 95–113

Doran, S., 'Revenge her foul and most unnatural murder? The impact of Mary Stewart's execution on Anglo-Scottish relations', *History*, LXXXV (2000), 589–612

Douglas, K., *The downfall of the Spanish Armada in Ireland* (Dublin, 2009)

Douglas, K. S., 'Navigation: the key to the Armada disaster', *Journal for Maritime Research*, V (2003), 74–120

Douglas, K. S., H. H. Lamb and C. Loader, *A meteorological study of July to October 1588: The Spanish Armada storms* (Norwich, 1978: University of East Anglia Climatic Research Unit Publications, VI)

Drelichman, M., and H.-J. Voth, *Lending to the borrower from hell: Debt, taxes and default in the reign of Philip II* (Princeton, NJ, 2014)

Duffy, E., *Fires of faith: Catholic England under Mary Tudor* (New Haven, CT, and London, 2009)

Duke, A. C., 'William of Orange's *Apologie*', *Dutch Crossing*, XXII/1 (1998), 3–96

Duplessis-Mornay, P. de., *Suite des lettres et mémoires de Messire Philippes de Mornay* (Amsterdam, 1651)

Durand-Lapié, P., 'Un roi détroné réfugié en France: Dom Antoine 1[er] de Portugal (1580–95)', *Revue d'histoire diplomatique*, XVIII (1904), 133–45, 275–307, 612–40, and XIX (1905), 113–28, 243–60

Earle, P., *The last fight of the Revenge* (London, 1992)

Edwards, H., *A collection of Old English customs, and curious bequests and charities* (London, 1842)

Edwards, J., *Mary I: England's Catholic queen* (New Haven, CT, and London, 2011)

Eguiluz, M. de, *Milicia, discurso y regla militar* (Madrid, 1592)

Ehrman, J., *The navy in the war of William III, 1689–97* (Cambridge, 1953)

Elias, J. E., *De vlootbouw in Nederland in de eerste helft der 17e eeuw, 1596–1655* (Amsterdam, 1933)

Eliav, J., 'Tactics of sixteenth-century galley artillery', *MM*, XCIX (2013), 398–409

Elizabeth, queen of England, *A declaration of the causes moouing the Queene of England* (1585); *see* Kinney

Elizabeth, queen of England, *A declaration of causes, which mooved the chief commanders of the navie . . . to take and arrest in the mouth of the river of Lisbone, certaine ships* (London, 1589)

Ellis, H., 'Copy of a short memoir on the means considered fit for putting the forces of England in order at the time the invasion from the Spaniards was expected in 1587; preserved in the Harleian Ms. 168 fol. 110', *Archaeologia: or, miscellaneous tracts related to Antiquity*, XXXII (1847), 373–8

Erikssen, N., and J. Rönnby, '*Mars* (1564): the initial archaeological investigations of a great 16th-century warship', *International Journal of Nautical Archaeology*, XLV (2017), 92–107

Estal, J. M., 'Felipe II y su archivo hagiográfico de El Escorial', *Hispania sacra*, XXIII (1970), 193–333

Evans, J. X., ed., *The works of Sir Roger Williams* (Oxford, 1972)
Eyzinger, M., *Historica postremae relationis Appendix. Das ist, Ein Historische vervolgung, der geschichten und händel, so sich, seithero des Monats Martij . . . biß auff den 15. tag jetzt ablauffenden Monats Septembris 1588* (Cologne, 1589)
Fagel, R., 'Los Juan Martínez de Recalde, de Bilbao, de mercaderes a héroe naval (1504–1588)', *Investigaciones históricas: época moderna y contemporánea*, XXIII (2003), 11–33
Fagel, R., 'Gascoigne's *The Spoyle of Antwerpe* (1576) as an Anglo-Dutch text', *Dutch Crossing*, XLI (2017), 101–10
Falconer, W., *An Universal Dictionary of the Marine* (London, 1780; reprinted Newton Abbot, 1970)
Fallon, N., *The Armada in Ireland* (London, 1978)
Falls, C., *Elizabeth's Irish wars* (London, 1950)
Farrell, S., 'The Armada tapestries in the old Palace of Westminster', *Parliamentary History*, XXIX (2010), 416–40
Fea, P., *Alessandro Farnese, duca di Parma* (Rome, 1886)
Feltham, O., *A brief character of the Low Countries* (London, 1652)
Fernández, M., *Livro de Traças de Carpintería* (1616, reprint Lisbon, 1989)
Fernández Álvarez, M., *Tres embajadores de Felipe II en Inglaterra* (Madrid, 1951)
Fernández-Armesto, F., *The Spanish Armada: The experience of war in 1588* (Oxford, 1988)
Fernández Duro, C., *La conquista de las Azores en 1583* (Madrid, 1866)
Fernández Duro, C., *Disquisiciones náuticas*, 6 vols (Madrid, 1876–81)
Fernández Duro, C., *La Armada Invencible*, 2 vols (Madrid, 1884–5)
Fernández Duro, C., *Noticia breve de las cartas y planos existentes en la biblioteca particular de S. M. el Rey* (Madrid, 1889)
Fernández Duro, C., *Armada Española desde la unión de los reinos de Castilla y Aragón*, 9 vols (Madrid, 1895–1903)
Fernández Segado, F., 'Alejandro Farnesio en las negociaciones de paz entre España y Inglaterra (1586–88)', *Hispania*, XLV (1985), 513–78
Ffoulkes, C. J., *Inventory and survey of the armouries of the Tower of London*, I (London, 1916)
Ffoulkes, C. J., *The gun-founders of England*, 2nd edn. (London, 1969)
Firpo, L., *Relazioni di ambasciatori veneti al Senato. VIII. Spagna* (Turin, 1981)
Firrufino, G. C., *El perfecto artillero: theórica y práctica* (Madrid, 1648)
Flanagan, L., *Ireland's Armada legacy* (Dublin, 1988)
Flower-Smith, A., '"The able and the willynge": the preparations of the English land forces to meet the Armada', *British Army Review*, XCV (1990), 54–91
Forbes, P., *A full view of public transactions in the reign of Q. Elizabeth*, 2 vols (London, 1740–1)
Fórmica, M., *Doña María de Mendoza. La solución a un enigma amoroso* (Madrid, 1979)
Foxcroft, H. C., *A supplement to Burnet's History of my own time* (Oxford, 1902)
Freitas de Meneses, A. de, *Os Açores e o domínio filipino (1580–1590)*, 2 vols (Angra do Heroismo, 1987)

Friel, I., 'English ships and shipping', in Rodriguez-Salgado, *Armada: 1588–1988*, 151–3, 156–8

Froude, J. A., *The Spanish story of the Armada and other essays* (London, 1892; originally published in *Longman's Magazine*, XVIII (1891), 478–503, 585–602, and XIX (1891–2), 25–42

Fruin, R. J., *Verspreide Geschriften*, III (The Hague, 1900)

Frye., S., 'The myth of Elizabeth at Tilbury', *SCJ*, XXIII (1992), 95–114

Gachard, L. P., *Correspondance de Guillaume le Taciturne, prince d'Orange*, 6 vols (Brussels, 1847–57)

Gachard, L. P., 'Les archives farnésiennes de Naples', *BCRH*, 3e série, XI (1868), 245–344

Gacto Fernández, E., 'Censura política e Inquisición: la Historia Pontifical de Gonzalo de Illescas', *Revista de la Inquisición*, 1992, no. 2, 23–40

Gainsford, T., *The Glory of England, or a true description of many excellent prerogatiues and remarkeable blessings, whereby she triumpheth ouer all the nations of the world* (London, 1618)

Gallagher, P., and D. W. Cruickshank, 'The Armada of 1588 reflected in serious and popular literature of the period', in Gallagher and Cruickshank, *God's obvious design*, 167–83

Gallagher, P., and D. W. Cruickshank, eds, *God's obvious design: Papers of the Spanish Armada symposium, Sligo, 1988* (London, 1990)

García de Palacio, D., *Instrucción náuthica para el buen uso y regimiento de las naos* (Mexico, 1587)

García Hernán, D., 'El IV centenario de la Armada contra Inglaterra. Balance historiográfico', *Cuadernos de historia moderna*, X (1989–90), 163–82

Gascoigne, G., *The complete works of George Gascoigne*, ed. J. W. Cunliffe, 2 vols (Cambridge, 1907–10)

Génard, P., 'Index der Gebodboeken, berustende ter Secretaris der stad Antwerpen [1489–1620]', *Antwerpsch Archievenblad/Bulletin des archives d'Anvers*, I (1864), 120–464, and III (1867)

Gerson, A. J., 'The English recusants and the Spanish Armada', *AHR*, XXII (1917), 589–94

Glasgow, T., 'Elizabethan ships pictured on Smerwick map, 1580', *MM*, LII (1966), 157–65

Glasgow, T., 'The navy in the French wars of Mary and Elizabeth I', *MM*, LIII (1967), 321–42; LIV (1968), 23–36 and 281–96; and LVI (1970), 3–26

Glasgow, T., 'Maturing of naval administration, 1556–1564', *MM*, LVI (1970), 3–26

Glasgow, T., 'List of ships in the Royal Navy from 1539 to 1588', *MM*, LVI (1970), 299–306

Glasgow, T., 'Gorgas' seafight', *MM*, LIX (1973), 179–85

Glete, J., *Navies and nations: Warships, navies and state-building in Europe and America, 1500–1860*, 2 vols (Stockholm, 1993)

Gómez-Centurión, C., *La Invencible y la empresa de Inglaterra* (Madrid, 1988)

González-Aller Hierro, J. I., 'La arribada de la Gran Armada a Galicia (junio-julio de 1588)', *El Museo de Pontevedra*, LI (1997), 609–47

González-Aller Hierro, J. I., 'Las galeras en la Gran Armada de 1588', *Revista de historia naval*, XXVIII (2010), 53–74

González-Aller Hierro, J. I.; *see also* Calvar Gross et al., *La batalla del Mar Océano*

González Dávila, G., *Teatro de las grandezas de la villa de Madrid* (Madrid, 1623)

Gonzalo Sánchez-Molero, J. L., *La 'Librería rica' de Felipe II. Estudio histórico y catalogación* (San Lorenzo de El Escorial, 1998)

Goodman, D., *Spanish naval power, 1589–1665: Reconstruction and defeat* (Cambridge, 1997)

Goodman, G., *The court of King James the First*, 2 vols (London, 1839)

Goring, J., and J. Wake, eds, *Northamptonshire Lieutenancy papers and other documents, 1580–1614* (Gateshead, 1975)

Gorrochategui Santos, L., *The English Armada: The greatest naval disaster in English history* (London, 2018; original Spanish edition, Madrid, 2011)

[Goux, P. le], *Copie d'une lettre envoyée de Dieppe* (Paris, 1588)

Gracia Rivas, M., 'El motín de la *Diana* y otras vicisitudes de las galeras participantes en la jornada de Inglaterra', *Revista de historia naval*, II/4 (1984), 33–45

Gracia Rivas, M., 'Aportación al estudio económico de la Gran Armada: las libranzas del pagador Juan de la Huerta, en Lisboa', *Revista de historia naval*, IV/13 (1986), 51–78

Gracia Rivas, M., *La sanidad en la jornada de Inglaterra, 1587–8* (Madrid, 1988)

Gracia Rivas, M., 'The medical services of the *Gran Armada*', in Rodríguez-Salgado and Adams, *England, Spain and the Gran Armada*, 197–215

Gracia Rivas, M., *Los tercios de la Gran Armada, 1587–8* (Madrid, 1989)

Gracia Rivas, M., 'Las banderas de la Gran Armada', *Revista de historia naval*, VII/25 (1989), 7–32

Gracia Rivas, M., 'Los Martínez de Recalde, una familia bilbaína relacionada con la mar', *Itsas Memoria. Revista de Estudios Marítimos del País Vasco*, VIII (2016), 691–723

Granada, Fray Luis de, *Historia de Sor María de la Visitación y Sermón de las Caídas Públicas*, ed. A. Huerga (Barcelona, 1962)

Grattan, J., *'How to find': The divers swimline search* (London, 1972: British Sub-Aqua Club Paper, II)

Green, J. M., '"I My Self": Queen Elizabeth's oration at Tilbury camp', *SCJ*, XXVIII (1997), 421–45

Green, S. A., 'Letters of Pero Menéndez de Avilés', *Proceedings of the Massachusetts Historical Society*, 2nd series, IX (1894), 416–68

Gregory, J., *The great and new art of weighing vanity* (Glasgow, 1672)

Grenier, R., M.-A. Bernier and W. Stevens, eds, *The underwater archaeology of Red Bay: Basque shipbuilding and whaling in the sixteenth Century*, 5 vols (Ottawa, 2007)

Groen van Prinsterer, G., *Archives ou correspondance de la maison d'Orange-Nassau*, 1st series, 8 vols (Leiden, 1835–47)

Guilmartin, J. F., *Gunpowder and galleys: Changing technology and Mediterranean warfare in the sixteenth century* (1974; revised edn., Ann Arbor, MI, 2003)

Guy, J., *My heart is my own. The life of Mary Queen of Scots* (London, 2004)
Haak, S. P., *Johan van Oldenbarnevelt. Bescheiden betreffende zijn staatkundig beleid en zijn familie. I: 1570–1601* (The Hague, 1934)
Hakluyt, R., *The principal navigations, voyages, traffiques & discoveries of the English nation*, 8 vols (London, 1910–13)
Hale, M., 'The production of history: Famiano Strada's *De Bello Belgico*', in M. Stocker and P. G. Lindley, eds, *Tributes to Jean Michel Massing: Towards a global art history* (London, 2016), 91–104
Hall, A. R., 'Military technology', in C. Singer et al., eds, *A history of technology. III: From the Renaissance to the Industrial Revolution, c. 1500 to c. 1750* (Oxford, 1957), 347–76
Hall, H., *Society in the Elizabethan age*, 2nd edn. (London, 1887)
Hammer, P. E. J., 'Sex and the Virgin Queen: aristocratic concupiscence and the court of Elizabeth I', *SCJ*, XXXI (2000), 77–97
Hansard, T. C., ed., *The Parliamentary History of England, from the earliest period to the year 1803*, 36 vols (London, 1806–20)
Hardy, E., *Survivors of the Armada* (London, 1966)
Harte, W. J., *Gleanings from the Commonplace Book of John Hooker relating to the city of Exeter, 1485–1590* (Exeter, c. 1926)
Hartley, T. E., *Proceedings in the parliaments of Elizabeth I*, 3 vols (Leicester and New York, 1981–95)
Harvey, R., *An astrological discourse vpon the great and notable Coniunction of the tvvo superiour Planets, SATVRNE & IVPITER, which shall happen the 28. day of April, 1583. With a briefe Declaration of the effectes, which the late Eclipse of the Sunne 1582. is yet heerafter to woorke* (London, 1583 [recte 1584])
Hattendorf, J. B., R. J. B. Knight, A. W. H. Pearsall and N. A. M. Rodger, eds, *British naval documents, 1204–1960* (London, 1993: Navy Records Society, CXXXI)
Hawkins, M. W. S., *Plymouth Armada heroes: The Hawkins family* (Plymouth, 1888)
Hayden, C., 'Tristram Winslade – the desperate heart of a Catholic in exile', *Cornish Studies*, XX (2012), 32–62
Headley, J. M., 'Spain's Asian presence, 1565–90: structures and aspirations', *Hispanic-American Historical Review*, LXXV (1995), 623–46
Hearn, K., 'Elizabeth I and the Spanish Armada: a painting and its afterlife', *Transactions of the Royal Historical Society*, VIth series, XIV (2004), 123–40
Hellowes, E., *A booke of the inuention of the art of nauigation and of the greate trauelles whiche they passe that saile in Gallies* (London, 1578)
Heredía Herrera, A., *Catálogo de las consultas del consejo de Indias*, I (Madrid, 1972)
Hernández, M., *Vida, martirio y translación de la gloriosa virgen y mártir santa Leocadia* (Toledo, 1591)
Herrera Oria, E., *La Armada Invencible* (Valladolid, 1929: Archivo Documental Español, II)
Herrera y Tordesillas, A., *Historia General del Mundo del tiempo del Rey Felipe II, el Prudente*, 3 vols (Madrid, 1601–12)

Hibben, C. C., *Gouda in revolt: Particularism and pacifism in the revolt of the Netherlands, 1571–1588* (Utrecht, 1983)
Hildred, A., *Weapons of Warre: The armaments of the Mary Rose* (Portsmouth, 2011: The Archaeology of the *Mary Rose*, 3.1)
Historical Manuscripts Commission, *Seventh Report, part I: Report and appendix* (London, 1879)
Historical Manuscripts Commission, *Eleventh Report, Appendix, part V: The manuscripts of the earl of Dartmouth* (London, 1887)
Historical Manuscripts Commission, *Fifteenth Report, Appendix, part V: The manuscripts of the Right Honourable F. J. Savile Foljambe of Osberton* (London, 1879)
Historical Manuscripts Commission, *Calendar of the Manuscripts of the Most Honourable the Marquess of Bath*, 5 vols (London, 1904–80)
Historical Manuscripts Commission, *Calendar of the Manuscripts of the Most Honourable the Marquess of Salisbury, preserved at Hatfield House, Hertfordshire*, 24 vols (London, 1883–1976)
Holt, M. P., *The duke of Anjou and the Politique struggle during the Wars of Religion* (Cambridge, 1986)
Hopper, C., *Sir Francis Drake's memorable service against the Spaniards in 1587* (London, 1864: The Camden Miscellany, V)
Horozco y Covarrubias, J. de, *Tratado de la verdadera y falsa prophecía* (Segovia, 1588)
Huerga, A., 'La vida seudomística y el proceso inquisitorial de Sor María de la Visitación (La monja de Lisboa)', *Hispania Sacra*, XII (1959), 35–130
Huerga, A.; *see also* Granada, Fray Luis de
Hughes, P. L., and J. S. Larkin, eds, *Tudor royal proclamations. III. The later Tudors, 1588–1603* (New Haven, CT, and London, 1969)
Huygens, C., *Journaal van Constantijn Huygens, den zoon, van 21 october 1688 tot 2 september 1696*, 3 vols (Utrecht, 1876–88: Werken van her Historisch Genootschap gevestigd te Utrecht, new series, XXIII, XXV, XLVI)
Hyland, St G. K., *A century of persecution under Tudor and Stuart sovereigns from contemporary records* (London, 1920)
Illescas, G. de, *Historia pontifical y cathólica* (Dueñas, 1566; 2nd edn., Salamanca, 1568)
Iñiguez de Lequerica, J., *Sermones funerales, en las honras del rey nuestro señor don Felipe II* (Madrid, 1599)
Ireland, J. de Courcy, 'Ragusa and the Spanish Armada of 1588', *MM*, LXIV (1978), 251–62
Israel, J. I., 'The Dutch role in the Glorious Revolution', in Israel, *The Anglo-Dutch Moment*, 105–62
Israel, J. I., ed., *The Anglo-Dutch moment: Essays on the Glorious Revolution and its world impact* (Cambridge, 1991)
Israel, J. I., and G. Parker, 'Of Providence and Protestant winds: The Spanish Armada of 1588 and the Dutch Armada of 1688', in Israel, *The Anglo-Dutch moment*, 335–63 (reprinted in Parker, *Success is never final*, 39–66)
Jablonsky, B., *The owl of Minerva flies at twilight: Doctrinal change and continuity in the revolution in military affairs* (Carlisle, PA, 1994)

Jackson, C., *Devil-Land: England under siege, 1588–1688* (London, 2021)
Jansson, M., 'Remembering Marston Moor: the politics of culture', in S. D. Amussen and M. A. Kishlansky, eds, *Political culture and cultural politics in early modern England: Essays presented to David Underdown* (Manchester, 1995), 255–76
Japikse, N. et al., *Resolutiën der Staten Generaal van 1576 tot 1609*, 14 vols (The Hague, 1917–70)
Japikse, N., *Correspondentie van Willem III en Hans Willem Bentinck, eersten graf van Portland*, 5 vols in 2 series (The Hague, 1927–37)
Jardine, L., *The awful end of Prince William the Silent: The first assassination of a head of state with a handgun* (New York and London, 2004)
Jardine, L., 'Gloriana rules the waves: or, the advantage of being excommunicated (and a woman)', *Transactions of the Royal Historical Society*, VI, series XIV (2004), 209–22
Jensen, J. de Lamar, *Diplomacy and dogmatism: Bernardino de Mendoza and the French Catholic League* (Cambridge, MA, 1964)
Jensen, J. de Lamar, 'Franco-Spanish diplomacy and the Armada', in C. H. Carter, ed., *From the Renaissance to the Counter-Reformation: Essays in honour of Garrett Mattingly* (London, 1965), 205–29
Jensen, J. de Lamar, 'The phantom will of Mary Queen of Scots', *Scotia*, IV (1980), 1–15
Jensen, J. de Lamar, 'The Spanish Armada: the worst-kept secret in Europe', *SCJ*, XIX (1988), 621–41
Jérez-Gómez, J.-D., 'Elizabeth I and Spanish poetic satire: Political context, propaganda, and the social dimension of the Armada', in Olid Guerrero and Fernández, *The image of Elizabeth I*, 251–83
Jervis, R., *Perception and misperception in international politics* (Princeton, NJ, 1976)
Johnson, S., 'Making mathematical practice: gentlemen, practitioners and artisans in Elizabethan England' (Cambridge PhD, 1994)
Jones, C., 'Journal of the Voyage of William of Orange from Holland to Torbay, 1688', *Journal of the Society for Army Historical Research*, LI (1973), 15–18
Jones, C., 'The Protestant wind of 1688: myth and reality', *European Studies Review*, III (1973), 201–22
Jones, E., 'John Lingard and the Simancas archives', *The Historical Journal*, X (1967), 57–76
*Journal of the House of Commons, X: 1688–1693* (London, 1802)
Kagan, R. L., *Lucrecia's dreams: Politics and prophecy in sixteenth-century Spain* (Berkeley, CA, 1990)
Kagan, R. L., 'Politics, prophecy and the Inquisition in late sixteenth-century Spain', in M. E. Perry and A. J. Cruz, eds, *Cultural encounters: The impact of the Inquisition in Spain and the New World* (Berkeley, CA, 1991), 105–24
Kagan, R. L., and A. Dyer, *Inquisitorial inquiries: Brief lives of secret Jews and other heretics* (Baltimore, MD, 2004)
Katz, J., *Kriegslegitimation in der Frühen Neuzeit. Intervention und Sicherheit während des anglo-spanischen Krieges (1585–1604) / The legitimation of war in the early*

*modern period: Intervention and security during the Anglo-Spanish War (1585–1604)* (London, 2021: Veröffentlichungen des Deutschen Historischen Instituts London / Publications of the German Historical Institute London, LXXXVI)

Keegan, J., *The face of battle: A study of Agincourt, Waterloo and the Somme* (London, 1976)

Keeler, M. F., *Sir Francis Drake's West Indian voyage, 1585–6* (London, 1981: Hakluyt Society, 2nd series, CXLVIII)

Kelleher, C., 'La Trinidad Valencera – 1588 Spanish Armada wreck: results of the Underwater Archaeology Unit's work at the site 2004–6', *Journal of Irish Archaeology*, XX (2011), 123–39

Kelly, F., *Captain Francisco de Cuéllar: The Armada, Ireland, and the wars of the Spanish monarchy, 1578–1606* (Dublin, 2020)

Kelly, F., 'The impact of the 1588 Armada campaign and its consequences in Ireland', in *La Armada Española de 1588*, 405–24

Kelly, J., *Gunpowder: Alchemy, bombards, and pyrotechnics* (Cambridge, MA, 2004)

Kelsey, H., *Sir Francis Drake, the Queen's Pirate* (New Haven, CT, and London, 1998)

Kelsey, H., *Sir John Hawkins: The queen's slave trader* (New Haven, CT, and London, 2002)

Kelsey, H., *Philip of Spain, king of England: The forgotten sovereign* (London, 2011)

Kemp, P., ed., *The Papers of Admiral Sir John Fisher*, I (London, 1960)

Kempe, A. J., *The Loseley Manuscripts. Manuscripts and other rare documents, illustrative of some of the more minute particulars of English history, biography, and manners* (London, 1836)

Kennett, W., *Charity and Restitution: A Spital Sermon preached at the Church of St. Bridget, on Easter-Monday, March the 30th, 1719. Before the Right Honourable Sir John Ward, Lord-Mayor, the Court of Aldermen, the Sheriffs, and the Presidents of Hospitals in the City of London. With an Application to the vain Attempts of a Spanish Invasion, in the Year 1588* (London, 1719)

Kenny, R. W., *Elizabeth's admiral: The political career of Charles Howard, earl of Nottingham, 1536–1624* (Baltimore, MD, 1970)

Kermele, N., 'Théorie et pratique de l'histoire du monde dans la *Historia Pontifical y Católica* de Gonzalo de Illescas', *e-Spania* [online], 30 June 2018

Kervyn de Lettenhove, J. M. B. C., *Relations politiques des Pays-Bas et de l'Angleterre, sous le règne de Philippe II*, 11 vols (Brussels, 1882–1900)

Khevenhüller-Metsch, G., and G. Probst-Ohstorff, *Hans Khevenhüller: kaiserliche Botschafter bei Philipp II. Geheimes Tagebuch, 1548–1605* (Graz, 1971); *see also* Veronelli

Kilfeather, T. P., *Ireland: Graveyard of the Spanish Armada* (Tralee, 1967)

Kingsley, C., *Westward Ho!* (London, 1855)

Kinney, A., *Elizabethan backgrounds: Historical documents of the age of Elizabeth I* (Hamden, CT, 1975)

von Klarwill, V., *Fugger-Zeitungen. Ungedruckte Briefe an der Haus Fugger aus den Jahren, 1568–1605* (Vienna, 1923)

Knappen, M. M., ed., *Two Elizabethan Puritan diaries, by Richard Rogers and Samuel Ward* (Chicago, IL, 1933: Studies in Church History, II)

Knighton, C. S., *Calendar of State Papers: Domestic Series of the Reign of Mary I, 1553–1558* (London, 1998)
Knighton, C. S., 'Overgunning the *Mary Rose*: the king was warned', *Journal of the Ordnance Society*, XXIV (2017, for 2012), 5–13
Knighton, C. S., and D. Fontana, 'More documents on the last campaign of the Mary Rose', in B. Vale, ed., *The Naval Miscellany*, VIII (London, 2017), 49–84
Knighton, C. S., and D. Loades, *The navy of Edward VI and Mary I* (Farnham, 2011: Navy Records Society, CLVII)
Knighton, C. S., and D. M. Loades, eds, *The Anthony Roll of Henry VIII's Navy* (Cambridge, 2000)
Kostić, V., 'Ragusa and the Spanish Armada', *Balcanica: Annuaire de l'Institut des Études Balkaniques*, III (1972), 195–235, partially reprinted in R. Filipović and M. Partridge, eds, *Ragusas's relations with England: A symposium* (Zagreb, 1977), 47–61
Kouri, E. I., *Elizabethan England and Europe: Forty unprinted letters from Elizabeth I to Protestant powers* (London, 1982: BIHR Special Supplement, XII)
Kretzschmar, J., *Die Invasionsprojekte der katholischen Mächte gegen England zur Zeits Elisabeths* (Leipzig, 1892)
Kristensen, R. K., and S. E. Jørgensen, 'The mystery of the salvage of *Vasa*'s guns', *The International Journal of Diving History*, XIII (2021), 54–70
*La Armada Española de 1588 y la Contra Armada inglesa de 1589. El conflicto naval entre España e Inglaterra 1590–1607 / The Spanish Armada of 1588 and English Counter-Armada of 1589: Naval conflict between Spain and England 1590–1607*, https://cpage.mpr.gob.es/producto/la-armada-espanola-de-1588-y-la-contra-armada-inglesa-de-1589/
*La Gran Armada. Simposio Hispano-Británico* (Madrid, 1989)
Labanoff, A., *Lettres, instructions et mémoires de Marie Stuart, reine d'Écosse*, 7 vols (London and Paris, 1844)
Laing, D., 'Notice of a scheme, with the warrant of King James VII, and the lords of Privy Council, for a patent to be granted to certain merchants in London, for weighing up and recovering ships in the Scottish seas, 26th May 1686', *Archaeologia Scotica, or transactions of the Society of Antiquaries of Scotland*, IV, part 3 (1857), 428–39
Lang, A., 'The mystery of the Tobermory galleon revealed', *Blackwood's Magazine*, CXCI (March 1912), 422–36
Lapèyre, H., *Une famille des marchands: les Ruiz* (Paris, 1955)
Larkin, J. S., and P. L. Hughes, *Stuart royal proclamations. I: Royal proclamations of King James I, 1603–1625* (Oxford, 1973)
Laspéras, J.-M., 'Los libros de Bernardino de Mendoza (1540 [41] –1604)', *Bulletin Hispanique*, XCIX (1997), 25–39
Latham, R. C., and W. Matthews, eds, *The Diary of Samuel Pepys*, 11 vols (London, 1970–83)
Lathbury, T., *The Spanish Armada, A.D. 1588: or, the attempt of Philip II and Pope Sixtus V to re-establish popery in England* (London, 1840)

Laughton, J. K., 'The Invincible Armada: a tercentenary retrospect', *Notices of the Proceedings at the meetings of the members of the Royal Institution of Great Britain*, XII (1887–9), 307–26

Laughton, J. K., *Memoirs relating to the Lord Torrington* (London, 1889: Camden Society, New Series, XLVI)

Laughton, J. K., *State Papers relating to the defeat of the Spanish Armada, Anno 1588*, 2 vols (London, 1894: Navy Records Society, I–II)

Lazcano González, R., 'Agustinos en la Armada española contra Inglaterra (1588): objetivos, actuaciones y participantes', *Analecta Augustiniana*, LXXXI (2018), 213–24

Lefèvre, J., *Correspondance de Philippe II sur les affaires des Pays-Bas*, III (Brussels, 1956)

Leigh, W., *Queene Elizabeth, paralel'd in her princely vertues with Dauid, Iosua and Hezekia . . . in three sermons* (London, 1611)

Leimon, M., and G. Parker, 'Treason and plot in Elizabethan England: the fame of Sir Edward Stafford reconsidered', *EHR*, CVI (1996), 1,134–58 (reprinted with corrections in Parker, *Success is never final*, 67–95)

Lesaffer, R., *The Twelve Years Truce (1609): Peace, truce, war, and law in the Low Countries at the turn of the 17th century* (Leiden, 2014)

Levillain, C.-E., 'London besieged? The city's vulnerability during the Glorious Revolution', in J. McElligott, ed., *Fear, exclusion and revolution: Roger Morrice and Britain in the 1680s* (Aldershot, 2006), 91–107

Lewis, M., 'The guns of the *Jesus of Lubeck*', *MM*, XXII (1936), 324–45

Lewis, M., 'Fresh light on San Juan de Ulúa', *MM*, XXIII (1937), 296–315

Lewis, M., 'Armada guns: a comparative study of English and Spanish armaments', *MM*, XXVIII (1942), 41–72 (the first of several articles, republished as M. Lewis, *Armada Guns* [London, 1961])

Lewis, M., *The Spanish Armada* (London, 1960)

Lewis, M., *Armada guns* (London, 1961)

Lhermite, J., *Le Passetemps*, ed. C. Ruelens, E. Ouverleaux and J. Petit, 2 vols (Antwerp, 1890–6; facsimile reprint, Geneva, 1971)

Lindsay, A., *A rutter of the Scottish seas* (abridged and edited by I. H. Adams, G. Fortune and A. B. Taylor, Greenwich, 1980)

Lingard, J., *A history of England from the invasion by the Romans to the accession of James I*, V (London, 1823)

Lippincott, J. B., *The Ordnance Manual for use of the officers of the United States Army* (Philadelphia, PA, 1862)

Little, J., *The tercentenary of England's great victory over Spain and the Armada, 1588–1888* (Toronto, 1888)

Loades, D., *The Tudor navy: An administrative, political and military history* (London, 1992)

Loades, D., *Mary Tudor: A life*, revised edn. (Oxford, 1995)

Lodge, E., *Illustrations of British history, biography and manners*, 3 vols (London, 1791)

Loomie, A. J., 'The Armadas and the Catholics of England', *Catholic Historical Review*, LIX (1973), 385–403

Lope Toledo, J. M., 'Logroño en el desastre de la Armada Invencible', *Berceo*, XVII (1962), 231–43

López Mata, T., *La ciudad y el castillo de Burgos* (Burgos, 1949)

Lúcar, C., *Tartaglia's Colloquies and Lúcar's Appendix, the former translated, the latter added by Cyprián Lúcar* (London, 1588)

Lundh, O. G., and I. E. Sars, eds, *Norske rigs-registranter, III: 1588–1602* (Christiania, 1865)

Lyell, J. P. R., 'A commentary on certain aspect of the Spanish Armada drawn from contemporary sources' (B.Litt. thesis, Oxford University, 1932)

Lynch, M., ed., *Mary Stewart: Queen in three kingdoms* (Oxford, 1988)

Macaulay, T. B., *Lays of ancient Rome, with Ivry and the Armada* (London, 1857)

McBride, G. K., 'Elizabethan foreign policy in microcosm: the Portuguese pretender, 1580–1589', *Albion*, V (1973), 193–210

MacCaffrey, W. T., *The shaping of the Elizabethan regime: Elizabethan politics, 1558–72* (Princeton, NJ, 1968)

MacCaffrey, W. T., *Queen Elizabeth and the making of policy, 1572–88* (Princeton, NJ, 1981)

McCarthy, B., 'The surrender of an Armada vessel near Tralee: an exploration of the State Papers', *Journal of the Kerry Archaeological and Historical Society*, XXIII (1990), 91–108

McConnel, J. R. R., 'The 1688 landing of William of Orange at Torbay: numerical dates and temporal understanding in Early Modern England', *Journal of Modern History*, LXXXIV (2012), 539–71

McCue, R. J., 'The ambassadorial career of Sir Edward Stafford, Elizabethan ambassador to France, 1583–1590' (PhD thesis, Brigham Young University, 1970)

McDermott, J., *Martin Frobisher: Elizabethan privateer* (New Haven, CT, and London, 2001)

McDermott, J., *England and the Spanish Armada: The necessary quarrel* (New Haven, CT, and London, 2005)

McElvogue, D., 'The hull', in Marsden, *Mary Rose: Your Noblest Shippe*, 81–105

McGrath, P., 'The Bloody Questions reconsidered', *Recusant History*, XX (1991), 305–19

McGurk, J. J. N., 'Armada preparations in Kent and arrangements made after the defeat (1587–1589)', *Archaeologia Cantiana*, LXXXV (1970), 71–93

McLeay, A., *The Tobermory treasure: The true story of a fabulous Armada galleon* (London, 1986)

McNeill, C., 'Report on the Rawlinson collection of manuscripts preserved in the Bodleian Library, Oxford', *Analecta hibernica*, I (1930), 12–178

Maclean, J., ed., *The life and times of Sir Peter Carew* (London, 1857)

Maginn, C., 'After the Armada: Thanksgiving in Ireland, 1589', *Historical Research*, XCIII (2020), 23–37

Mainwaring, H., 'The seaman's dictionary or, an exposition of all the parts and things belonging to a ship', in G. E. Manwaring and W. G. Perrin, eds, *The life and works of Sir Henry Mainwaring*, II (London, 1922: Navy Records Society, LVI), 83–260

Malcolm, C., 'Solving a sunken mystery: the investigation and identification of a sixteenth-century shipwreck' (PhD thesis, University of Huddersfield, 2017)

Malfatti, C. V., *The accession, coronation and marriage of Mary Tudor as related in four manuscripts of the Escorial* (Barcelona, 1956)

Malfatti, C. V., *Cuatro documentos italianos en materia de la expedición de la Armada Invencible* (Barcelona, 1972)

Mallet, E., ed., *Négociations de Monsieur le Comte d'Avaux en Hollande, depuis 1679 jusqu'en 1688*, 6 vols (Paris, 1752–3)

Manuel de Melo, F., *Epanáphoras de varia historia portuguesa* (1660: ed. E. Prestage, Coimbra, 1931)

Marcus, L., J. Mueller and M. B. Rose, eds, *Elizabeth I: Collected works* (Chicago, IL, and London, 2000)

Mariana, J. de, *Obras del Padre Juan de Mariana*, 2 vols (Madrid 1854–64: Biblioteca de Autores Españoles)

Markham, C. R., ed., *Narratives of the voyages of Pedro Sarmiento de Gamboa to the Straits of Magellan* (London, 1895: Hakluyt Society, XCI)

Marsden, P., ed., *Mary Rose: Your Noblest Shippe. Anatomy of a Tudor warship* (Portsmouth, 2009: The Archaeology of the *Mary Rose*, II)

Martin, C., '*El Gran Grifón*: an Armada wreck off Fair Isle', *International Journal of Nautical Archaeology*, I (1972), 59–71

Martin, C., 'The Spanish Armada expedition 1968–70', in D. J. Blackman, ed., *Marine Archaeology* (London, 1973), 439–59

Martin, C., *Full fathom five: Wrecks of the Spanish Armada* (London, 1975)

Martin, C., 'Spanish Armada tonnages', *MM*, LXIII (1977), 365–7

Martin, C., '*La Trinidad Valencera*: an Armada invasion transport lost off Donegal', *International Journal of Nautical Archaeology*, VIII/1 (1979), 13–38

Martin, C., 'Spanish Armada pottery', *International Journal of Nautical Archaeology*, VIII/4 (1979), 279–302

Martin, C., 'The equipment and fighting potential of the Spanish Armada' (PhD thesis, University of St Andrews, 1983)

Martin, C., '*La Santa María de la Rosa*, un vaisseau de l'Armada naufragé dans le détroit des Iles Blasket, comté de Kerry', in L. Flanagan and R. Sténuit, eds, *Trésors de l'Armada* (Brussels, 1986), 18–23

Martin, C., 'A 16th-century siege train: the battery ordnance of the 1588 Spanish Armada', *International Journal of Nautical Archaeology*, XVII/1 (1988), 57–73

Martin, C., 'The ships of the Spanish Armada', in Gallagher and Cruickshank, *God's obvious design*, 41–68

Martin, C., 'The wreck of the Dutch East-Indiaman Adelaar off Barra in 1728', in R. Mason and N. Macdougall, eds, *People and power in Scotland* (Edinburgh, 1992), 145–69

Martin, C., 'Incendiary weapons from the Spanish Armada wreck *La Trinidad Valencera*, 1588', *International Journal of Nautical Archaeology*, XXIII/3 (1994), 207–17

Martin, C., 'Departicularising the particular: approaches to the investigation of well-documented post-medieval shipwrecks', *World Archaeology*, XXII (2001), 383–99

Martin, C., 'Stowed or mounted: the Spanish Armada of 1588 and the strategic logistics of guns at sea', in C. Beltrame and R. G. Ridella, eds, *The sea ordnance of Venice and Europe between the 15th and 17th centuries* (Oxford, 2011), 85–97

Martin, C., 'Weapons and fighting potential of the 1588 Spanish Armada: the military component', in *La Armada Española de 1588*, 223–45.

Martin, M., *A description of the Western Islands of Scotland* (London, 1703)

Martin, P., *Spanish Armada prisoners* (Exeter, 1988)

Martínez, E., *Cartas de Felipe II al General Pedro de Valdés* (Gijón, 1980: Monumenta historica asturiensia, IX)

Mateo Ripoll, N., and J. J. Oña Fernández, 'Aproximación comparativa al tratamiento museográfico sobre la experiencia de la Gran Armada', unpublished paper at the conference *La Armada Española de 1588*, Cartagena, 2019

Mattingly, G., 'William Allen and Catholic propaganda in England', *Travaux d'humanisme et renaissance*, XXVIII (1957), 325–39

Mattingly, G., *The defeat of the Spanish Armada* (London, 1959)

Maura Gamazo, G., duke of Maura, *El designio de Felipe II y el episodio de la Armada Invencible* (Madrid, 1957)

Mears, N., 'Walls speak: wall paintings of the Spanish Armada in Elizabethan and Jacobean England' (unpublished conference paper)

Mears, N., A. Raffe, S. Taylor and P. Williamson with L. Bates, eds, *National prayers: Special worship since the Reformation: Special prayers, fasts and thanksgivings in the British Isles, 1533–1688* (Woodbridge, 2013: Church of England Record Society, XX)

Melville, J., *The diary of Mr. James Melville, 1556–1601*, ed. R. Pitcairn (Edinburgh, 1829: Bannatyne Club)

Mendoza, B. de, *Theorique and practice of warre* ([Middelburg], 1597)

Meyer, A. O., *England and the Catholic Church under Queen Elizabeth* (London, 1916)

Mihajlović, I., and R. Gianni Ridelli, 'Notes on Ragusan ships and men in Spanish service', in *La Armada Española de 1588*, 249–66

Moir, D. G., *The early maps of Scotland to 1850*, 3rd edn. (Edinburgh, 1973)

Molyneux, T., *Conjunct expeditions: or expeditions that have been carried on jointly by fleet and army* (London, 1759)

Monteith, R., *The Description of the Isles of Orknay and Zetland. With Mapps of them, done from the accurat Observation of the most Learned who lived in these isles* (1633, ed. R. Sibbald, Edinburgh, 1711)

*Monumenta historica societatis Iesu, LX: Ribadeneira*, II (Madrid, 1923); *see also* Ribadeneira

Morel-Fatio, A., *Études sur l'Espagne, 4ᵉ série* (Paris, 1925)

Moretti, T., *Trattato del'Artiglieria* (Brescia, 1672)

Morris, J., ed., *The letter-books of Sir Amias Poulet, keeper of Mary Queen of Scots* (London, 1874)

Moryson, F., *An Itinerary Containing His Ten Yeeres Travell: Through the Twelve Dominions of Germany, Bohmerland, Sweitzerland, Netherland, Denmarke, Poland, Italy, Turky, France, England, Scotland & Ireland*, 4 vols (1617; Glasgow, 1907)

Mosconi, N., *La nunziatura di Spagna di Cesare Speciano, 1586–1588*, 2nd edn. (Brescia, 1961)
Mote, H., *The Primrose of London, with her valiant adventure on the Spanish coast, beeing of the burthen of 150. Tunne. Declaring the maner how 97. Spanyards came aboord* (London, 1585)
Motley, J. L., *A History of the United Netherlands*, 4 vols (London, 1861–9)
Mousset, A., *Dépêches diplomatiques de M. de Longlée, résident de France en Espagne, 1582–1590* (Paris, 1912)
Muller, A., 'Transmitting and translating the excommunication of Elizabeth I', *Studies in Church History*, LIII (2017), 210–22
Muller, A., *The excommunication of Elizabeth I: Faith, politics, and resistance in post-Reformation England, 1570–1603* (Leiden, 2020)
Munby, A. N. L., *Phillipps studies*, 5 vols (Cambridge, 1951–60)
Mundy, P., *The travels of Peter Mundy in Europe and Asia, 1608–1667*, ed. R. C. Temple and L. M. Anstey, 5 vols (London, 1907–36: Hakluyt Society, 2nd series, XVII, XXXV, XLV–XLVI, LV, LXXVIII)
Murdin, W., ed., *A collection of state papers relating to affairs in the reign of Queen Elizabeth from the year 1571 to 1596 … left by William Cecill Lord Burghley* (London, 1759)
Muro, G., *La vida de la princesa de Eboli* (Madrid, 1877)
Naish, G. P. B., 'Documents illustrating the history of the Spanish Armada', in C. Lloyd, ed., *The Naval Miscellany, IV* (London, 1952: Navy Records Society, XCII); reprinted in Waters, *The Elizabethan navy* (from which we quote)
Nash, T., *Pierce penilesse his supplication to the Diuell* (London, 1592)
Nicholas, N. H., *Life of William Davison, Secretary of State and Privy Counsellor to Queen Elizabeth* (London, 1823)
Nichols, J., *The progresses and public processions of Queen Elizabeth: A new edition of early modern sources*, eds. E. Goldring, F. Eales, E. Clarke and J. E. Archer, 5 vols (Oxford, 2014)
Nichols, J. G., *The diary of Henry Machyn, citizen and merchant-taylor of London, 1550–1563* (London, 1848: Camden Society, XLII)
Nicolay d'Arfeville, Nicholas de, *La navigation du Roy d'Ecosse Jacques Cinquiesme du Nom, autour de son Royaume, & Isles Hebrides & Orchades, soubz la conduicte d'Alexandre Lyndsay excellent Pilote Escossois* (Paris, 1583)
Nicolson, H., *Diaries and letters*, ed. N. Nicolson, 3 vols (London, 1966–8)
Noble, T. C., *The names of those persons who subscribed towards the defence of this country at the time of the Spanish Armada, 1588, and the amounts each contributed* (London, 1886)
Nolan, J. S., 'The muster of 1588', *Albion*, XXIII (1991), 387–407
Nolan, J. S., *Sir John Norreys and the Elizabethan military world* (Exeter, 1997)
Norton, R., *The Gunner, shewing the whole practise of artillerie: with all the appurtenances thereunto belonging* (London, 1628)
*Nueva Colección de documentos inéditos para la historia de España y de sus Indias*, 5 vols (Madrid, 1892–5)

Nuttall, Z., *New light on Drake: A collection of documents relating to his voyage of circumnavigation, 1577–1580* (Cambridge, 1914: Hakluyt Society, 2nd series, XXXIV)

Ó Danachair, C., 'Armada losses on the Irish coast', *Irish Sword*, II (1956), 321–31

O'Donnell y Duque de Estrada, H., *La fuerza de desembarco de la Gran Armada contra Inglaterra (1588)* (Madrid, 1989)

O'Donnell y Duque de Estrada, H., 'The Army of Flanders and the invasion of England, 1586–8', in Rodríguez-Salgado and Adams, *England, Spain and the Gran Armada*, 216–35

O'Donnell y Duque de Estrada, H., 'The requirements of the duke of Parma for the conquest of England', in Gallagher and Cruickshank, *God's Obvious Design*, 85–99

O'Neil, B. H. St. J., 'The fortifications of Weybourne Hope in 1588', *Norfolk Archaeology*, XXVII (1940), 250–62

O'Neill, J., *The Nine Years War, 1593–1603: O'Neill, Mountjoy and the military revolution* (Dublin, 2017)

O'Rahilly, A., *The massacre at Smerwick (1580)* (Cork, 1938: Cork Historical and Archaeological Papers I)

O'Sullivan Beare, P., *Historiae Catholicae Iberniae Compendium* (1621; ed. M. Kelly, Dublin, 1850)

Ødegaard, T., *Den spanske armada og Norge* [*The Spanish Armada and Norway*] (Fredrikstad, 1997)

Ødegaard, T., *Alonso de Olmos' etterlatte dokumenter. Om det spanske armadaskipet 'Santiago' som forliste i Sunnhordland i året 1588* [*The surviving documents of Alonso de Olmos. About the Spanish armada ship* Santiago *which was wrecked in Sunnhordland in the year 1588*] (Fredrikstad, 2001)

Ogle, O., and W. H. Bliss, *Calendar of the Clarendon State Papers preserved in the Bodleian Library*, I (Oxford, 1882)

Olid Guerrero, E., and E. Fernández, eds, *The image of Elizabeth I in early modern Spain* (Lincoln, NE, 2019)

Oliveira, F. de, *A arte da guerra do mar* (Lisbon, 1552)

Oosterhoff, F. G., *Leicester and the Netherlands, 1586–7* (Utrecht, 1988)

Oppenheim, M., *A history of the administration of the Royal Navy and of merchant shipping in relation to the navy from MDIX to MDCLX* (London, 1896)

Oppenheim, M., ed., *The naval tracts of Sir William Monson*, 5 vols (London, 1902–14: Navy Records Society, XXII, XXIII, XLIII, XLV and XLVII)

Orr, A., '"Communis Hostis Omnium": The Smerwick Massacre (1580) and the Law of Nations', *Journal of British Studies*, LVIII (2019), 473–93

Orrite Pinedo, R., 'La voz de alarma. La fuga del *Primrose*', in *La Armada Española de 1588*, 107–13

Paine, R. D., *The book of buried treasure, being a true history of the gold, jewels, and plate of pirates, galleons etc., which are sought for to this day* (New York and London, 1911)

Paranque, E., *Elizabeth I of England through Valois eyes: Power, representation and diplomacy in the reign of the queen, 1558–1588* (London, 2019)

Parente, G. et al., *Los sucesos de Flandes de 1588 en relación con la empresa de Inglaterra* (Madrid, 1988)
Parker, G., *Guide to the archives of the Spanish Institutions in or concerned with the Netherlands, 1556–1706* (Brussels, 1970; reprinted 1987)
Parker, G., *The Army of Flanders and the Spanish Road, 1567–1659: The logistics of Spanish victory and defeat in the Low Countries' wars* (Cambridge, 1972; revised edn., 2004)
Parker, G., *Spain and the Netherlands, 1559–1659: Ten studies* (London, 1979)
Parker, G., *The Dutch Revolt*, 2nd edn. (Harmondsworth, 1984)
Parker, G., 'The *Dreadnought* revolution of Tudor England', *MM*, LXXXII (1996), 269–300
Parker, G., *The grand strategy of Philip II* (New Haven, CT, and London, 1998).
Parker, G., *Success is never final: Empire, war and faith in early modern Europe* (New York, 2002)
Parker, G., 'The place of Tudor England in the Messianic vision of Philip II of Spain', *Transactions of the Royal Historical Society*, 6th series, XII (2002), 167–221
Parker, G., 'Queen Elizabeth's Instructions to Admiral Howard, 20 December 1587', *MM*, XCIV (2008), 202–8
Parker, G., 'August 9, 1588: The Spanish Armada (almost) surrenders', in B. Hollingsworth and T. K. Rabb, eds, *I wish I'd been there, Book Two* (New York, 2008), 108–25
Parker, G., *Felipe II. La biografía definitiva* (Barcelona, 2010)
Parker, G., *Imprudent king: A new biography of Philip II* (London and New Haven, CT, 2014)
Parker, G., 'History and climate: the crisis of the 1590s reconsidered', in C. Leggewie and F. Mauelshagen, eds, *Climate change and cultural transition in Europe* (Leiden, 2018), 119–55
Parker, G., *Emperor: A new life of Charles V* (London and New Haven, CT, 2019)
Parker, G., 'The Altamira Collection and the history of the Dutch Revolt', *Cuadernos de Historia Moderna*, XLV (2020), 367–86
Parker, G., 'Lope de Vega really did embark on the Spanish Armada', *Anuario Lope de Vega. Texto, literatura, cultura*, XXVIII (2022), 466–87 c
Parker, G., with the assistance of Andrew Mitchell and Lawrence Bell, 'Anatomy of defeat: the testimony of Juan Martínez de Recalde and Don Alonso Martínez de Leyva on the failure of the Spanish Armada in 1588', *MM*, XC (2004), 314–47
Parshall, J., and A. Tully, *Shattered sword: The untold story of the battle of Midway* (Lincoln, NE, 2005)
Pears, E. A., 'The Spanish Armada and the Ottoman Porte', *EHR*, VII (1893), 439–66
Percyvall, R., *Bibliotheca Hispanica, containing a grammar with a dictionarie in Spanish, English and Latine* (London, 1591)
Pérez Bustamente, C., 'El cronista Antonio de Herrara y la historia de Alejandro Farnesio', *Boletín de la Real Academia de la Historia*, CIII (1933), 737–90
Pérez de Montalbán, J., *El Segundo Seneca de España y príncipe don Carlos, parte segunda* (Madrid, 1632)
Pérez Mínguez, F., *Reivindicación del siglo XVI* (Madrid, 1928)

Philip II, king of Spain, *Premática en que se da la orden que se ha de tener en el traer de los lutos en estos reynos* (Madrid, 1588)

Phillips, C. R., *Six galleons for the king of Spain: Imperial defence in the early seventeenth century* (Baltimore, MD, 1986)

Phillips, C. R., 'The caravel and the galleon', in R. Gardiner, ed., *Cogs, caravels and galleons: The sailing ship, 1000–1650* (London, 1994), 91–114

Phillips, C. R., ed., *The struggle for the South Atlantic: The Armada of the Strait, 1581–1584* (London, 2016: Hakluyt Society, 3rd series XXXI)

Pi Corrales, M., *España y las potencias nórdicas. 'La otra invencible' 1574* (Madrid, 1983)

Pierson, P. O., *Commander of the Armada: The seventh duke of Medina Sidonia* (New Haven, CT, and London, 1989)

Pigafetta, F., *Discorso sopra l'ordinanza del'armata catolica* (Roma, 1588)

Pimentel, Diego, *see* Breeder verclaringhe

Pinto, S. M. G., 'A sixteenth-century draft plan of Lisbon's western suburb', *Imago Mundi: The International Journal for the History of Cartography*, LXX (2018), 27–51

Piot, C., *Chroniques de Brabant et Flandre* (Brussels, 1879)

Pires de Lima, D., 'Um documento português sobre a "Jornada de Inglaterra", procedido de algumas considerações', *Arqueologia e história*, II (Lisbon, 1946), 55–143

Pizarro Llorente, H., *Un gran patrón en la corte de Felipe II. Don Gaspar de Quiroga* (Madrid, 2004)

Pollitt, R., 'Bureaucracy and the Armada: the administrator's battle', *MM*, LX (1974), 119–32

Pollitt, R., 'Contingency planning and the defeat of the Spanish Armada', in D. M. Masterson, ed., *Naval history: The sixth symposium of the US Naval Academy* (Wilmington, DE, 1987), 70–81

Porras Arboledas, P. A., 'La aportación de Castro Urdiales a la Armada Invencible (1586–1618)', *Cuadernos de Historia del Derecho*, XXI (2014), 53–111

Poullet, E., and C. Piot, eds, *Correspondance du Cardinal de Granvelle, 1565–1586*, 12 vols (Brussels, 1877–96)

Powley, E. B., *The English navy in the revolution of 1688* (Cambridge, 1928)

[Price, L.,] *A new Spanish tragedy. Or, more strange newes from the narrow seas discovering two most dreadfull sea fights between the Spaniard and the Hollander* (London, 1639)

Quinn, D. B., 'Spanish Armada prisoners' escape from Ireland', *MM*, LXX (1984), 117–18

Raleigh, W., *The Historie of the World in five books* (London, 1614); in W. Oldys and T. Birch, eds, *The works of Sir Walter Ralegh*, 8 vols (Oxford, 1829)

Raleigh, W., *Judicious and select essayes and observations* (London, 1650)

Ramsay, G. D., *The Queen's merchants and the revolt of the Netherlands* (London, 1986)

Rasor, E., *The Spanish Armada of 1588: Historiography and annotated bibliography* (Westport, CT, 1993)

Rawlinson, H. G., 'The embassy of William Harborne to Constantinople, 1583–8', *Transactions of the Royal Historical Society*, 4th series, V (1922), 1–27

Read, C., *Mr Secretary Walsingham and the policy of Queen Elizabeth*, 3 vols (Oxford, 1925)

Read, C., 'Queen Elizabeth's seizure of the duke of Alva's pay-ships', *Journal of Modern History*, V (1933), 443–64

Read, C., *Lord Burghley and Queen Elizabeth* (New York, 1960)

Read, C., and F. Waddington, eds, *Mémoires inédits de Dumont de Bostaquet, gentilhomme normand, sur les temps qui ont précédé et suivi la révocation de l'édit de Nantes, sur le refuge et les expéditions de Guillaume III en Angleterre et en Irlande* (Paris, 1864)

Redding, B. W. D., 'English naval expansion under the French threat, 1555–1564', *International Journal of Maritime History*, XXVIII (2016), 640–53

Reimer, T., 'Before Britannia ruled the waves. Die Konstruktion einer maritimen Nation' (PhD thesis, Ludwig-Maximilians-Universitat, Munich, 2006)

Renold, P., ed., *Letters of William Allen and Richard Barret, 1572–1598* (London, 1967: Publications of the Catholic Record Society, LVIII)

*Report of the Inspectors of Irish fisheries on the Sea and Inland Fisheries of Ireland for 1891* (Dublin, 1892)

Riaño Lozano, F., *Los medios navales de Alejandro Farnesio, 1587–8* (Madrid, 1989)

Ribadeneira, P. de, *Exhortación para los soldados y capitanes que van a la jornada de Inglaterra en nombre de su Capitán General* (1588; reprinted in *Historias de la Contrarreforma: Biblioteca de Autores Cristianos*, ed. E. Rey, Madrid, 1945), I, 333–49

Ribadeneira, P. de, *Tratado de la tribulación, repartido en dos libros. En el primero se trata de las tribulaciones particulares; y en el segundo de las generales que Dios nos embía y del remedio de ellas* (Madrid, 1589)

Ribadeneira, P. de; *see also* Weinrich

Ridella, R. G., 'Dorino II Gioardi, a 16th-century Genoese gunfounder,' *Journal of the Ordnance Society*, XVI (2004), 27–41

Rizzacasa, G., *Predittioni, o siano Discorsi del Rizzacasa. Sopra gli anni 1586.87.88.89.90* (Carmagnola, 1586)

Rizzacasa, G., *La fisionomia* (Carmagnola, 1588)

Roberts, K., *Pavane* (London, 1968)

Robres, P., and J. R. Ortolá, *La monja de Lisboa. Epistolario inédito entre Fray Luis de Granada y el Patriarca Ribera* (Castellón de la Plana, 1947: *Obras de Fray Luis de Granada*, XIV)

Rodger, N. A. M., *The Armada in the Public Records* (London, 1988)

Rodger, N. A. M., 'The development of broadside gunnery, 1450–1650', *MM*, LXXXII (1996), 301–24

Rodger, N. A. M., *The safeguard of the sea: A naval history of Britain, I: 660–1649* (London, 1997)

Rodger, N. A. M., *The command of the ocean: A naval history of Britain, II: 1649–1815* (London, 2004)

Rodríguez, P. and J., eds, *Don Francés de Álava y Beamonte. Correspondencia inédita de Felipe II con su embajador en París (1564–1570)* (San Sebastián, 1991)

Rodríguez-Salgado, M. J., *The changing face of empire: Charles V, Philip II and Habsburg authority* (Cambridge, 1988)

Rodríguez-Salgado, M. J., ed., *Armada 1588–1988* (London, 1988)

Rodríguez-Salgado, M. J., 'The Spanish story of the 1588 Armada reassessed', *Historical Journal*, XXXIII (1990), 461–78

Rodríguez-Salgado, M. J., 'The Anglo-Spanish war: the final episode in the "Wars of the Roses"?', in Rodríguez-Salgado and Adams, *England, Spain and the Gran Armada*, 1–44

Rodríguez-Salgado, M. J., 'Pilots' navigation and strategy in the Gran Armada', in Rodríguez-Salgado and Adams, *England, Spain and the Gran Armada*, 134–72

Rodríguez-Salgado, M. J., 'Kinship, collaboration and conflict: the complex relations between Alessandro Farnese and Philip II', in R. Valladares, F. Barrios and J. A. Sánchez Belén, eds, *En la corte del rey de España. Liber Amicorum en homenaje a Carlos Gómez-Centurión Jiménez (1958–2011)* (Madrid, 2016), 59–105

Rodríguez-Salgado, M. J., and S. Adams, eds, *England, Spain and the Gran Armada, 1585–1604* (Edinburgh, 1991)

Rogers, E., '1688 and 1888: Victorian society and the bicentenary of the Glorious Revolution', *Journal of British Studies*, L (2011), 892–916

Roiz Soares, P., *Memorias*, ed. M. Lopes de Almeida (Coimbra, 1953)

Romani, R., *Le corti farnesiane di Parma e Piacenza, 1545–1622*, I (Rome, 1978)

Roosens, B., 'Het Arsenal van Mechelen en de wapenhandel 1551–1567', *Bijdragen tot de geschiedenis*, LX (1977), 175–247

Rosales, L., *El sentimiento del desengaño en la poesía barroca* (Madrid, 1966)

Rowe, J., *A demonstration of the diving engine; its invention and various uses* (facsimile and transcription by M. Fardell and N. Phillips, The Historical Diving Society, 2000)

Sacheverell, W., *An account of the Isle of Man, its inhabitants, language, soil, remarkable curiosities, the succession of kings and bishops, down to the eighteenth century*, ed. J. G. Cumming (Douglas, Isle of Man, 1859)

Salazar, J. de, *Política española* (Logroño, 1619; Madrid, 1945)

Salgado, A., *Os navios de Portugal na Grande Armada. O poder naval português (1574–1592)* (Lisbon, 2004)

Saltillo, marquis of, 'El duque de Medina Sidonia y la jornada a Inglaterra en 1588', *Boletín de la Biblioteca de Menéndez Pelayo*, XVI (1934), 167–77

Samson, A., 'Changing places: the marriage and royal entry of Philip, Prince of Austria, and Mary Tudor, July–August 1554', *SCJ*, XXXVI (2005), 761–84

Samson, A., 'Cervantes upending Ribadeneira: Elizabeth I and the Reformation in early modern Spain', in Olid Guerrero, *The image*, 287–312

Samson, A., *Mary and Philip: The marriage of Tudor England and Habsburg Spain* (Manchester, 2020)

San Gerónimo, J. de, *Memorias*, in *Co.Do.In*, VII, 5–442

Sánchez, M. G., 'Anti-Spanish sentiment in English literary and political writing, 1553–1603' (PhD thesis, University of Leeds, 2004)

Santamarta Lozano, L. M., 'Don Guerau de Spes en la Corte Isabelina. La documentación diplomática y el conflicto anglo-español (1568–1571)' (PhD thesis, University of Oviedo, 2001)

Santullano, J., ed., *Obras completas de Teresa de Jesús* (Madrid, 1930)

Sardi, P., *L'artiglieria di Pietro Sardi, Romano, diuisa in tre libri* (Venice, 1621)
Scheltema, J., *De uitrusting en ondergang van de onoverwinnelijke vloot van Philips II in 1588* (Haarlem, 1825)
Schokkenbroek, J. C. A., '"Wherefore serveth Justinus with his shipping of Zeeland?" The Dutch and the Spanish Armada', in Gallagher and Cruickshank, *God's Obvious Design*, 101–11
Schokkenbroek, J. C. A., 'The growth of a nation: the Netherlands after the Spanish Armada campaign of 1588', in *Después de la Gran Armada: la historia desconocida* (Madrid: IX Jornadas de historia marítima, 1993), 85–93
Schokkenbroek, J. C. A., 'The role of the Dutch fleet in the conflict of 1588', *see* Schokkenbroek, '"Wherefore serveth Justinus"'
Schön, E., *Siege of Münster* (woodcut, 1534)
Scott, J. R., 'Pay-list of the Kentish forces raised to resist the Spanish Armada', *Archaeologia Cantiana*, XI (1877), 388–91
Scott, T., *The second part of Vox Populi* ('Goricom', 1624)
Scott, W., ed., *The Somers Collection of Tracts*, I (London, 1809)
Sepúlveda, Fray Juan de, 'Historia de varios sucesos y de las cosas notables que han acaecido en España', in *Documentos para la historia del monasterio de San Lorenzo El Real de El Escorial*, IV (Madrid, 1924)
Serrano, L., *Correspondencia diplomática entre España y la Santa Sede durante el pontificado de San Pio V*, 4 vols (Madrid, 1914)
Sharp, C., ed., *Memorials of the rebellion of 1569* (London, 1840)
Sharpe, K. M., *The personal rule of Charles I* (New Haven, CT, and London, 1992)
Shaw, W. A., *Calendar of Treasury Books, IX: 1689–92* (London, 1931)
Shaw, W. A., ed., *Report on the manuscripts of Lord De L'Isle and Dudley preserved at Penshurst Place* (HMC Report No. 77), III (London, 1936)
Sigüenza, J. de, *La fundación del Monasterio de El Escorial* (1605; Madrid, 1988)
Simmons, J. J., 'Wrought-iron ordnance: revealing discoveries from the New World', *International Journal of Nautical Archaeology*, XVII (1988), 25–34
Sinclair, G., *Ars nova et magna gravitatis et levitatis* (Rotterdam, 1669)
Sinclair, G., *The Hydrostaticks; or, the weight, force, and pressure of fluid bodies: made evident by physical and sensible experiments* (Edinburgh, 1672)
Sinclair, G., *The principles of astronomy and navigation* (Edinburgh, 1688)
Skelton, R. A., and J. N. Summerson, *A description of maps and architectural drawings in the collection made by William Cecil, first Baron Burghley, now at Hatfield House* (Oxford, 1971)
Skilliter, S. A., 'The Hispano-Ottoman armistice of 1581', in C. E. Bosworth, ed., *Iran and Islam* (Edinburgh, 1971), 491–515
Sladen, D. B. W., *The Spanish Armada: A ballad of 1588* (London, 1888)
Smith, G., 'Serpentine gunpowder and the guns that used it', *Journal of the Ordnance Society*, XXVI (2019), 27–39
Smith, S. R., 'Unlocking *Cabala, mysteries of state and government*; the politics of publishing' (PhD thesis, Birkbeck College, University of London, 2018)

Smythe, J., *[Certen] instruct[ions, obseruati]ons and orders militarie, requisit for all chieftaines, captaines [and?] higher and lower men of charge, [and officers] to vnderstand, [knowe and obserue]* (London, 1594)

Soen, V., 'Reconquista and reconciliation in the Dutch Revolt: the campaign of Governor-General Alexander Farnese (1578–1592)', *Journal of Early Modern History*, XVI (2012), 1–22

Spotswood Green, W. M., 'La Rata Encoronada', *Macmillan's Magazine*, LXXXIX (1903–4), 265–75

Spotswood Green, W. M., 'The wrecks of the Spanish Armada on the coast of Ireland', *Geographical Journal*, XXVII (1906), 429–51

Spotswood Green, W. M., 'Armada ships on the Kerry coast', *Proceedings of the Royal Irish Academy*, XXVII (1909), 263–9

Sténuit, R., *Treasures of the Armada* (Newton Abbot, 1972)

Stow, J., *The chronicles of England from Brute vnto this present yeare of Christ 1580* (London, 1580)

Stow, J., *The survey of London*, 4th edn. (London, 1633)

Stoye, J. W., 'An early letter from John Chamberlain', *EHR*, LXII (1947), 522–3

Strada, F., *De bello Belgico, decas segunda* (written 1602; Rome, 1648)

Strype, J., *The life and acts of John Whitgift, D.D., the third and last Lord Archbishop of Canterbury in the reign of Queen Elizabeth*, 3 vols, new edn. (Oxford, 1822)

Strype, J., *Annals of the Reformation and Establishment of Religion, and other various occurrences in the Church of England during Queen Elizabeth's happy reign*, 4 vols, new edn. (Oxford, 1824)

Tamalio, R., 'I Gonzaga e le guerre di Fiandre', in Bertini, *Militari italiani*, 137–51

Tanturri, A., 'La incursión de Francis Drake a Cádiz en 1587: comparación de algunas fuentes documentales inéditas italianas', *Investigaciones históricas. Época moderna y contemporánea*, XXXII (2012), 69–88

Tassis, J. B. de, *Commentarii de tumultibus belgicis sui temporis*, in C. P. Hoynck van Papendrecht, ed., *Analecta Belgica*, 3 vols in 6 pts. (The Hague, 1743), II, pt. 2, 119–600

Taviner, M., 'Robert Beale and the Elizabethan polity' (PhD thesis, St Andrews University, 2000)

Taylor, E. G. R., 'Sir William Monson consults the stars', *MM*, XIX (1933), 22–6

Taylor, E. G. R., ed., *The troublesome voyage of Captain Edward Fenton, 1582–83* (Cambridge, 1959: Hakluyt Society, 2nd series, CXIII)

Taylor, E. G. R., ed., *A Regiment for the Sea, and Other Writings on Navigation, by William Bourne of Gravesend, a Gunner, c. 1535–1582* (London, 1962: Hakluyt Society, 2nd series CXXI)

Taylor, S., ed., *The entring book of Roger Morrice*, IV (Woodbridge, 2007)

Tellechea Idígoras, J. I., *Otra cara de la Invencible: la participación vasca* (San Sebastián, 1988)

Tellechea Idígoras, J. I., *'La Invencible' vista desde la Nunciatura de Madrid* (Salamanca, 1989)

Tetlock, P. E., and A. Belkin, eds, *Counterfactual thought experiments in world politics* (Princeton, NJ, 1996)

Tetlock, P. E., R. N. Lebow and G. Parker, eds, *Unmaking the West: 'What-If?' scenarios that rewrite world history* (Ann Arbor, IL, 2006)

Teulet, A., *Relations politiques de la France et de l'Espagne avec l'Écosse au XVIe siècle*, 5 vols (Paris, 1862)

Thatcher, H. M., *The Downing Street years* (London, 1993)

*The State Letters of Henry earl of Clarendon, lord lieutenant of Ireland during the reign of King James the Second, and his lordship's diary for the years 1687, 1688, 1689 and 1690 . . . with an appendix from Archbishop Sancroft's manuscripts in the Bodleian Library*, 2 vols (Oxford, 1763)

*The true reporte of the prosperous successe which God gaue vnto our English souldiours against the forraine bands of our Romaine enemies, lately ariued (but soone inough to theyr cost) in Ireland, in the yeare 1580* (London, 1581; Dutch translation, *Victorie in Irlandt, van den Coninghinne van Engel-landt, teghen de Spaignarden ende Romanisten* [London, 1581])

Thomas, W., 'The treaty of London, the Twelve Years Truce and religious toleration in Spain and the Netherlands (1598–1621)', in Lesaffer, *The Twelve Years Truce*, 277–97

Thompson, G. S., ed., *The Twysden Lieutenancy Papers* (Maidstone, 1926: Kent Records Society, X)

Thompson, I. A. A., 'Armada guns', *MM*, LXI (1975), 355–71

Thompson, I. A. A., 'Spanish Armada gun policy and procurement', in Gallagher and Cruickshank, *God's Obvious Design*, 69–84

Thompson, I. A. A., *War and society in Habsburg Spain: Selected essays* (London, 1992)

Tilton, W. F., *Die Katastrophe der spanischen Armada, 31 Juli–8. August 1888* (Freiburg-im-Breisgau, 1894)

Tilton, W. F., 'The defeat of the Spanish Armada', *The Atlantic Monthly*, LXXVI (1895), 773–87

Tilton, W. F., 'Lord Burghley and the Spanish invasion', *AHR*, II (1896), 93–8

Tu, Hsuan-Ying, 'The pursuit of God's glory: Francis Walsingham's espionage in Elizabethan politics, 1568–1588' (PhD thesis, York University, 2012)

Ugolini, G., 'Le comunicazioni postali spagnole nell'Italia del XVI secolo', *Ricerche storiche*, XXIII (1993), 283–373

Unwin, R., *The defeat of John Hawkins* (Harmondsworth, 1960)

Usherwood, S. and E., *The Counter-Armada, 1596. The 'Journall' of the* Mary Rose (London, 1983)

van der Essen, L., *Alexandre Farnèse, prince de Parme, gouverneur-général des Pays-Bas (1545–92)*, 5 vols (Brussels, 1933–7)

van der Essen, L., 'Rapport de Don Juan de Idiáquez, adressé à Philippe II, au sujet de l'administration d'Alexandre Farnèse pendant les dernières années du gouvernement de celui-ci [1592]', *BCRH*, C (1936), 167–80

van der Essen, L., 'De auteur en de beteekenis van de *Liber relationum eorum quae gesta fuere in Belgio et alibi per serenissimum D. Ducem Alexandrum Farnesium*', *Mededelingen van de koninklijke Vlaamse Academie. Letteren*, V.1 (Antwerp, 1943) van der Woude, A., 'De crisis in de Opstand na de val van Antwerpen', *Bijdragen voor de Geschiedenis der Nederlanden*, XIV (1959–60), 38–57 and 81–104

van Mander, C., *Het schilder-boeck* (Haarlem, 1604)

van Mander, C., *The lives of the illustrious Netherlandish and German painters*, ed. H. Miedema, 6 vols (Doornspijk, 1994–9)

van Meteren, E., *Historia Belgica nostri* (Cologne, 1598; Hakluyt, *The principal navigations*, II, 369–401, provided an English translation of the passage on the Armada)

van Meteren, E., *Belgische ofte Nederlantsche historie, van onsen tijden* (Delft, 1599: Dutch version of the Latin text, with some important differences)

van Overeem, J. B., 'Justinus van Nassau en de Armada (1588)', *Marineblad*, LIII (1938), 821–31

Vaux, W. S. W., ed., *The world encompassed by Sir Francis Drake* (London, 1854: Hakluyt Society, XVI)

Vázquez, A., 'Los sucesos de Flandes y Francia del tiempo de Alejandro Farnesio', *Co.Do.In.*, LXXII–LXXIV (Madrid, 1879–80)

Vega Carpio, L. de, *La Dragontea* (Valencia, 1598)

Vermeir, R., 'The ransoming of prisoners taken from the Armada, 1589–90', *Notes and Queries*, LXII (2015), 59–64

Veronelli, S., ed., *Diario de Hans Khevenhüller, embajador imperial en la corte de Felipe II* (Madrid, 2001)

Villari, R., and G. Parker, *La política de Felipe II. Dos estudios* (Valladolid, 1996)

Voci, A. M., 'L'impresa d'Inghilterra nei dispacci del nunzio a Madrid, Nicolò Ormanetto (1572–1577)', *Annuario dell'Istituto storico italiano per l'età moderna e contemporanea*, XXXV–XXXVI (1983–4), 337–425

Voorbeijtel Cannenburg, W., 'An unknown "pilot" by Hessel Gerritsz, dating from 1612', *Imago mundi*, I (1935), 49–51

Wagenaer, L. J., *Pars prima. Speculum nauticum super navigatione Maris Occidentalis* (Leiden, 1586)

Wagenaer, L. J., *The Mariner's Mirrour wherin may playnly be seen the courses, heights, distances, depths, soundings, flouds and ebs, risings of lands, rocks, sands and shoalds with the marks for th'entrings of the harbouroughs, havens and ports of the greatest part of Europe* (London, 1588)

Walsh, M. K., 'The anonymous Spaniard of the flight of the earls (Pedro Blanco)', *The Irish Sword*, III (1957–8), 88–90

Walsh, M. K., *'Destruction by Peace': Hugh O'Neill after Kinsale* (Monaghan, 1986)

Walsham, A. M., 'Impolitic pictures: providence, history and the iconography of Protestant nationhood in early Stuart England', in R. N. Swanson, ed., *The Church retrospective* (Cambridge, 1997: Studies in Church History, XXXIII), 307–28

Walsham, A. M., '"Frantick Hacket": prophecy, sorcery, insanity and the Elizabethan Puritan movement', *Historical Journal*, XLI (1998), 27–66

Ward, S., *To God, in memorye of his double deliveraunce from ye invincible navie and ye unmatcheable powder treason/Deo trin-vniBritanniae bis ultori, in memoriam classis invincibilis subversae submersae* (Amsterdam, 1621)

Ward, S., *The life of faith*, 2nd edn. (London, 1622)
Waters, D. W., *The Elizabethan navy and the Armada of Spain* (Greenwich, 1975: National Maritime Museum Monographs, XVII); *see also* Naish
Watson, R., *The History of the Reign of Philip the Second, King of Spain*, 2 vols (London, 1777)
Watts, B., 'Friction in future war', in A. R. Millett and W. A. Murray, eds, *Brassey's Mershon American Defense Annual, 1996–7* (Washington, DC, 1996), 58–94
Weinrich, S. J., *Pedro de Ribadeneyra's Ecclesiastical History of the Schism in the Kingdom of England: A Spanish Jesuit's history of the English Reformation* (Leiden, 2017)
Wernham, R. B., 'Queen Elizabeth and the Portugal expedition of 1589', *EHR*, LXVI (1951), 1–26 and 194–218
Wernham, R. B., *Before the Armada: The growth of English foreign policy, 1485–1588* (London, 1966)
Wernham, R. B., *The making of Elizabethan foreign policy, 1558–1603* (Berkeley, CA, 1980)
Wernham, R. B., *After the Armada: Elizabethan England and the struggle for western Europe, 1588–95* (Oxford, 1984)
Wernham, R. B., *The expedition of Sir John Norris and Sir Francis Drake to Spain and Portugal, 1589* (London, 1988: Navy Records Society, CXXVII)
Wernham, R. B., *The return of the Armadas: The last years of the Elizabethan war against Spain, 1595–1603* (Oxford, 1993)
Whitehead, B. T., *Of brags and boasts: Propaganda in the year of the Armada* (Stroud, 1994)
Whittle, J., *An exact diary of the late expedition of his illustrious highness the prince of Orange (now King of Great Britain)* (London, 1689)
Wickham Legg, L. G., ed., 'A relation of a short survey of the Western Counties, made by a lieutenant of the military company in Norwich in 1635' (London, 1936: The Camden Miscellany, XVI)
Wiener, C. Z., 'The beleaguered isle: a study of Elizabethan and early Jacobean anti-Catholicism', *Past and Present*, LI (1971), 27–62
Wijffels, A., 'The Anglo-Spanish peace treaty of 1604', in Lesaffer, *The Twelve Years Truce*, 69–86
Wilford, T., *A military discourse whether it be better for England to give an invader present battle or to temporize and defer the same*, ed. N. Booth (London, 1734)
Williams, Sir Roger; *see* Evans
Williamson, J. A., *Hawkins of Plymouth: A new history of Sir John Hawkins and of other members of his family prominent in Tudor England* (London, 1949)
Wilson, C., *Queen Elizabeth and the revolt of the Netherlands* (London, 1970)
Winfield, R., *British warships in the age of sail, 1603–1714: Design, construction, careers and fates* (Barnsley, 2009)
Wolseley, G. J., *The soldiers' pocket-book for field service* (London, 1882)
Wright, E. R., 'Epic and archive: Lope de Vega, Francis Drake and the Council of Indies', *Calíope*, III/2 (1997), 37–56
Wright, E. R., 'From Drake to Draque: a Spanish hero with an English accent', in Cruz, *Material and symbolic circulation*, 29–38

Wright, T., *Queen Elizabeth and her times: A series of original letters*, 2 vols (London, 1838)
Wright, W. H. K., *Britain's Salamis: or, The Glorious Fight of 1588. An historical lecture delivered at various places in the West of England... The official souvenir of the Armada Tercentenary Commemoration* (Plymouth, 1888)
Wright, W. H. K., *Catalogue of the Exhibition of Armada and Elizabethan relics, held in the grand saloon of the Theatre Royal, London. Opened October 24th, 1888* (London, 1888)
Wynne, R., 'A brief relation of what was observed by the prince's servants in their journey into Spain in the year 1623', in J. O. Halliwell, ed., *The autobiography and correspondence of Sir Simonds d'Ewes*, 2 vols (London, 1845), II, 415–58
Younger, N., 'If the Armada had landed: a reappraisal of England's defences in 1588', *History*, XCIII (2008), 328–54
Zarco Cuevas, J., G. de Andrés et al., eds, *Documentos para la historia del monasterio de San Lorenzo El Real de El Escorial*, 8 vols (Madrid, 1917–62)

*Acknowledgements*

A*RMADA* SAW ITS GENESIS, gestation and birth in the thirteen years from 1973 to 1986 during which the authors were colleagues at the University of St Andrews. We are deeply grateful to that institution for encouraging our early work, and for the generosity of its Research and Travel Fund in sponsoring so many of our rewarding quests. Other grants have helped us to conduct further research in archives and libraries, and to investigate Armada wrecks off the coasts of Scotland and Ireland. We are indebted to the British Academy, the Carnegie Trust, the Leverhulme Trust, the MacRobert Trusts and the Russell Trust, all of which have given generous support over the years.

Geoffrey Parker also thanks the College of Arts and Sciences and the Mershon Center for International Security Studies of The Ohio State University for supporting his research; the Instituto de Historia y Cultura Naval of the Spanish Ministry of Defence for an invitation to present the early fruit of his research to their 'Armada Research Group' in 1982; and Rear-Admiral José Ignacio González-Aller Hierro for allowing him to work in the Director's suite in the Museo Naval, Madrid, on the documents later published in the magnificent *La batalla del Mar Océano, 1568–1604* (*BMO*), and for his friendship.

We are very grateful to the following for research and technical assistance: Nico Broens, Lucy Byatt, Louis Haas, Jill Hawthorne, Jamie Reid and Bill van de Veen on the first edition, published in 1988; Alison Anderson and Robert Rush on the second edition, published in 1999; and Maurizio Arfaioli, Edward Martin and Felipe Vidales del Castillo on this edition.

We thank the archivists and librarians around the Western world who satisfied our endless quest for documents, especially Mitchell Codding, Patrick Lenaghan and John O'Neill at the Hispanic Society of America in New York City; David and

Marsha Karpeles at the Karpeles Manuscript Library in Santa Barbara, California; and the entire Cuerpo Archivístico in the Archivo General de Simancas, Spain. We also thank the museum curators who welcomed us to their collections: Megan Barford, Richard Ormond and Pieter van der Merwe of the National Maritime Museum, Greenwich; Sjoerd de Meer of the Maritiem Museum Rotterdam; Tom Henderson, Andrew Williamson, Ian Tait and the staff of the Shetland Museum and Archives, Lerwick; Laurence Flanagan and colleagues at the Ulster Museum, Belfast; and Bernadette Walsh and Roisin Doherty at the Tower Museum, Derry/Londonderry.

The archaeological work which has yielded so much new information about the Armada would not have been possible without the far-sighted encouragement of the Ulster Museum, Belfast, and the Shetland Museum, Lerwick. This has resulted in financial support, conservation services and – most important of all – the safe curation of the recovered items as intact collections which have been, and remain, rich resources for study. We warmly thank these institutions and the staff with whom we have had the pleasure of working for their unstinting and enthusiastic help.

Yet another debt is owed to the phalanx of friends and colleagues who have supported us along the way. We can only name the leading few, but we remember and acknowledge our indebtedness to the remaining many. Sydney Wignall must top the list for demonstrating, in 1968, that the discovery of Armada shipwrecks could contribute through archaeological method to a fuller understanding of the campaign. He also put Colin Martin through the stern apprenticeship of diving in Blasket Sound, the exposed seaway off south-west Ireland where the wreck of *Santa María de la Rosa* was found. We salute him, and all the other divers with whom we have been associated – especially the members of the City of Derry Sub-Aqua Club, led by Dave Atherton, Eamonn Molloy and Paddy O'Doherty, whose unselfish forethought has safeguarded for posterity the relics from *Trinidad Valencera*. We have also received valuable assistance from the Moville Sub-Aqua Group. Special acknowledgement is due to the professional diving archaeologists who have helped with the work on the wrecks: Nicholas Dixon, Andrew Fielding, Jeremy Green, Tony Long, Keith Muckelroy and Celie O'Rahilly, as well as Fionnbarr Moore, Connie Kelleher and Karl Brady of the Underwater Archaeology Unit of the Irish National Monuments Service for their support and friendship.

The exciting discoveries off Streedagh Strand since 1985 have been protected by the Irish state for further investigation at some future date. Steve Birch, a member of the initial Streedagh Archaeological Team, generously provided us with unpublished information from these three important wrecks. More recently, we are grateful to members of the Grange and Armada Development Association and Spanish Armada Ireland, and in particular Eddie O'Gorman, for organizing conferences in Grange and Sligo, and inaugurating such splendid and imaginative annual remembrance ceremonies at Streedagh Strand; and Micheál O'Domhnaill for his media input and expertise. At each of the sites of our Armada shipwreck excavations we were made very welcome, and given much practical help (from boats and compressors to milk fresh from the cow), information, hospitality and encouragement, all of which we remember with gratitude.

We are also indebted to Alan Ereira of the BBC for arranging comparative tests of Spanish and English gun-mountings, replicated at full scale for his award-winning 1988 documentary trilogy *Armada*, and to the Portsmouth Field-Gun Team of the Royal Navy for putting them through their paces with such skill and gusto.

We also thank all those who have shared their knowledge of written sources since we started work on this project in 1982. Rayne Allinson in Australia; Roland Baetens, Robert Sténuit and René Vermeir in Belgium; John de Courcy Ireland, Francis Kelly, Brendan McCarthy, Hiram Morgan and Jane Ohlmeyer in the Irish Republic; Jaap Bruijn, Tristan Mostert and Joost Schokkenbroek in the Netherlands; Carlo Beltrame, Marco Morin and Giovanni Muto in Italy; Helen Daae Frøyseth, Knut Geelmuyden and Torbjørn Ødegaard in Norway; José Alcalá-Zamora, Bethany Aram, Fernando Bouza Álvarez, José Luis Casado Soto, Jesús García Calero, José Luis Gonzalo Sánchez-Molero, Santiago Martínez Hernández, Hugo O'Donnell y Duque de Estrada and José Ignacio Tellechea Idígoras in Spain; Simon Adams, John Adamson, Richard Boulind, Trevor Dadson, Natalie Mears, Nicholas Rodger, María José Rodríguez-Salgado, Brian Scott and I. A. A. Thompson in the United Kingdom; and David Cressy, Tom Glasgow Jr, John F. Guilmartin Jr, Harry Kelsey, Paul Lockhart, Peter Pierson, Mary Robertson and Jennifer Sims in the United States.

We are also extremely grateful to Cameron Balbirnie, Samantha Breslin, Robin Dashwood, Alan Ereira, Paul Johnstone and Ray Sutcliffe of the BBC for inviting us to collaborate in their documentaries; to Lucy Buchan, Rachael Lonsdale, Richard Mason, Felicity Maunder, Meg Pettit, Frazer Martin, Heather McCallum and Stuart Weir, our wonderful editorial team at Yale University Press for their enthusiasm and expertise; and to Robert Baldock, who over a long lunch at Bertorelli's restaurant forty years ago suggested that we should write a book about the Spanish Armada.

Our final and greatest debt is to Paula Martin, who has lived with the Armada underwater, in the archives, and at the word processor since the 1970s. As a nautical archaeologist she took part in the excavations of *Gran Grifón* and *Trinidad Valencera*, and conducted her own research into *Spanish Armada Prisoners in England*, published in 1988. She acted as a sounding-board, co-researcher, picture researcher, constructive critic and editorial adviser for the first two editions of this book (1988 and 1999). For this volume, which is effectively a new book, she has moderated and integrated the drafts of two demanding and strong-minded authors separated by the Atlantic Ocean. She has made many helpful comments on the text; provided us with a meticulous typescript; and as this book's picture researcher she has coordinated a new portfolio of images. She has proved a pillar of strength in the unexpectedly complex process of producing this book: supervising the electronic exchange of chapters between the technologically backward authors, proofreading the results with a keen and constructively critical eye, and compiling a new index. Words cannot describe the magnitude of her contribution, and of our debt to her. Quite simply, this book could not have happened without her.

COLIN MARTIN, St Andrews, Scotland
GEOFFREY PARKER, Columbus, Ohio
*April 2025*

## Illustrations

1. The route the Armada took around Britain and Ireland. National Maritime Museum, Greenwich, London, *PBD* 8529(2).
2. Simancas Castle, Spain. Colin Martin.
3. Archaeologist recording a gun on the site of the wreck of *Gran Grifón* off Fair Isle. Colin Martin.
4. Left: Philip II of Spain, by an unknown artist, *c.* 1580, oil on canvas. National Portrait Gallery, NPG 3347; Right: Elizabeth I of England, 'The Ermine Portrait', attributed to William Segar or George Gower, *c.* 1585, oil on panel. Hatfield House. Bridgeman Images.
5. The Theatre of Operations, 1588.
6. Lisbon in 1662. Museu de Lisboa, Palácio Pimenta: 'Cortejo Real no Terreiro do Paço, 23 de Abril de 1662', MC.PIN.0262.
7. Spanish infantry marching. Part of a frieze made of tiles commissioned in the 1580s, formerly in the convent of San Antón in Talavera, now in the city's cathedral. Photo by Felipe Vidales.
8. Map of the provinces of Spain.
9. Items of gold jewellery recovered from the wreck of *Girona*. Colin Martin.
10. Other luxury items found on Armada wrecks. Colin Martin.
11. The insignia of Spanish knightly orders. Colin Martin.
12. Portrait of Don Alonso de Leyva, by El Greco, *c.* 1580. Montreal Museum of Fine Arts, Inv. 1945.885.
13. Re-used piece of carved decoration from a merchant ship. Clare Museum, Ennis, County Clare, Ireland. Paula Martin.
14. *San Martín*, in a fresco painted in the Hall of Battles at the Escorial, by

Niccolò Granello. Patrimonio Nacional de España, Madrid.
15. The battle of Lepanto, 1571. Bibliothèque nationale, Paris, C6669.
16. A galleass, English school, sixteenth century. National Maritime Museum, Greenwich, London, *BHC* 0262.
17. A page from the pamphlet *La felicíssima Armada*, also known as 'The Lisbon Muster', 1588. British Library, books, 192.f.17(i).
18. The Escorial Palace. Colin Martin.
19. Hub of empire: Philip II's study in the Escorial Palace. Patrimonio Nacional de España, Madrid.
20. Religious finds from the *Girona* wreck-site. Colin Martin.
21. Map of south-east England and the Netherlands, 1588.
22. Alexander Farnese, duke of Parma, by Otto van Veen, *c.* 1585. Musée Royale des Beaux-Arts, Brussels, 1327. Bridgeman Images.
23. The hellburners of Antwerp. National Maritime Museum, Greenwich, London, *PAF* 4419.
24. Map showing the areas of Spain and Italy where Philip recruited troops in 1587–8 intended for Flanders and Lisbon (based on O'Donnell, *La fuerza de desembarco*, 41), and also the 'Spanish Road'.
25. Spanish troops on barges. Biblioteca Nacional de España, Ms. Res. 210/272.
26. *Mary Rose*, from the Anthony Anthony Roll, 1546. Pepys Library, Magdalene College, Cambridge, Ms 2991.
27. Elizabeth's leading admirals: Lord Admiral Charles Howard, 2nd Baron Howard of Effingham, by Daniel Mytens, *c.* 1620. National Maritime Museum, Greenwich, London, *BHC* 2786; Sir Martin Frobisher, by Cornelis Ketel, 1577. Bodleian Liibrary, Oxford, *LP* 50; Sir John Hawkins in 1581, artist unknown. National Maritime Museum, Greenwich, London, *BHC* 2755; Sir Francis Drake in 1591, by Marcus Gheeraerts. National Maritime Museum, Greenwich, London, *BHC* 2662.
28. *Graunde Masterys* from the Anthony Anthony Roll, 1546. British Library, Add MS 22047. Bridgeman Images.
29. The firepower of the Elizabethan navy. Hunt *Ellesmere Ms.* 6206B/15v–16, 1574; British Library, Add MS 69,892/5, 24 May 1574.
30. Manning the Elizabethan navy. Hunt *Ellesmere Ms.* 6206B/15v–16, 1574; British Library, Add MS 69,892/5, 24 May 1574.
31. A shipwright and his apprentice at work, from *Fragments of Ancient Shipwrightry* by Matthew Baker, *c.* 1586. Pepys Library, Magdalene College, Cambridge, Ms PL 2820.
32. The profile of a race-built galleon, from *Fragments of Ancient Shipwrightry*

by Matthew Baker, *c.* 1586. Pepys Library, Magdalene College, Cambridge, Ms PL 2820.
33. Hawkins's improvements to English warships. Colin Martin.
34. English naval spending, 1581–8. Geoffrey Parker.
35. The English and Spanish fleets engaged, English school, 16th century, known as the 'Greenwich Cartoon'. National Maritime Museum, Greenwich *BHC* 0262.
36. Replica seal of Francis and Mary Stuart. Geoffrey Parker.
37. A silver coin of Philip and Mary. British Museum.
38. An anonymous sixteenth-century plan of the island of San Juan de Ulúa. Public domain.
39. Smerwick harbour in November 1580. A watercolour map created by or for Sir William Winter. TNA, *MPF* 1/75.
40. The Battle of Alcántara, 25 August 1580. Biblioteca Nacional, Lisbon, Colleção iconografia, D. 319 A.
41. Portrait of the marquis of Santa Cruz, by Juan Pantoja de la Cruz. Fundación Álvaro de Bazán, Madrid.
42. A *consulta*: a minister's recommendation on the right and Philip's reply scrawled in the wide left margin. HSA *Altamira* 1/I/6, folios 189–95, Mateo Vázquez to Philip and rescripts, Lisbon, 6 and 7 September 1582.
43. The amphibious landing at Terceira in 1583, by Niccolò Granello and Fabrizio Castello. Patrimonio Nacional de España, Madrid.
44. 'The World is Not Enough', gold medal. Museo Numismático Português, Lisbon, Inv. 2918.
45. Pewter bowl found on the wreck of *Trinidad Valencera*. Colin Martin.
46. Elizabeth I's triumvirate of advisers: Robert Dudley, 1st earl of Leicester, unknown English workshop, *c.* 1575; William Cecil, 1st Baron Burghley, Lord High Treasurer, unknown artist, after 1587; Sir Francis Walsingham, attributed to John de Critz elder, *c.* 1589. All National Portrait Gallery, 247; 362; 1807.
47. Title page of *The Primrose of London*. British Library, system 0. 002566260.
48. Portrait of Philip II, by Alonso Sánchez Coello, 1587. Galleria Palatina, Pitti Palace, Florence.
49. Some of Philip II's relics at the Escorial. Patrimonio Nacional de España, Madrid.
50. Frontispiece of Luis Cabrera de Córdoba, *History of Philip II, king of Spain*, engraved by Pierre Perret. Biblioteca Nacional de España.
51. Campaign map for the conquest of England sent to Philip by Bernardino de Escalante, 1586. Biblioteca Nacional de España, Ms 5785/168.

52. The execution of Mary Queen of Scots, February 1587. Scottish National Portrait Gallery, PG 1217.
53. A map of the Cadiz raid of 1587, drawn by William Borough. TNA, *MPF* 1/318. Smith Archive / Alamy Stock Photo.
54. The 'Drake Jewel', 1587. Victoria and Albert Museum. World History Archive / Alamy Stock Photo.
55. Portrait of Don Alonso Pérez de Guzmán el Bueno, 7th duke of Medina Sidonia, artist unknown. Fundación Casa Medina Sidonia, Sanlúcar de Barrameda.
56. Philip claims he would like to lead the Armada in a message to Mateo Vázquez. HSA *Altamira* 1/I/46, Vázquez to Philip, 8 March 1588, and rescript.
57. Two examples of the pre-printed forms introduced by Medina Sidonia. AGS *CMC* 2a/772, unfoliated.
58. Musical instruments found on *Trinidad Valencera*. Colin Martin.
59. Medical services on the Armada. Colin Martin.
60. The skull of a rat, from the wreck of *Trinidad Valencera*. Colin Martin.
61. The Narrow Seas from Dieppe to Nieuwpoort. Lucas Wagenaer, *Speculum nauticum super navigatione maris occidentalis* (Leiden, 1586), Vol. I, image 31, Biblioteca Nacional de España.
62. Portuguese chart of the English Channel. National Maritime Museum, Greenwich, London, G218:6/21, 'Mar antre Dobra e Cales'.
63. Map of the Armada's route, 30 May–21 June 1588. Based on *BMO*, IV/1, p. ciii.
64. Two examples of religious medallions, probably distributed at Corunna. Colin Martin.
65. The defences of Plymouth, spring 1587, by Sir Richard Grenville. TNA, *MPF* 1/6.
66. *The Seventh Day of the Battle of the Armada*, by Hendrik Cornelisz Vroom, *c.* 1600. Tiroler Landesmuseum Ferdinandeum, Innsbruck, Gem 1668. Artefact / Alamy Stock Photo.
67. Medina Sidonia's battle plan for the Armada, with (below) a diagrammatic version and translation. Archivo di Stato, Florence, *MdP* 5037/615.
68. A silver bosun's whistle from *Girona*. Colin Martin.
69. A diagrammatic representation of *San Martín*. Based on *BMO*, IV/2, pp. 500–2. Colin Martin.
70. Detail from *The Seventh Day of the Battle of the Armada*, by Hendrik Cornelisz Vroom, *c.* 1600. Tiroler Landesmuseum Ferdinandeum, Innsbruck, Gem 1668. Artefact / Alamy Stock Photo.

# ILLUSTRATIONS

71. Incendiary weapons from *Trinidad Valencera*. Colin Martin.
72. A replica fire-trunk (*bomba*) in action. Colin Martin.
73. Fire-fighting equipment. Colin Martin.
74. The English order of battle, July 1588. Adapted from BL Sloane Ms. 2177/15b copy.
75. Detail from watercolour map created by or for Sir William Winter. TNA, MPF 1/75.
76. Detail of a truck carriage on an English galleon, from *Fragments of Ancient Shipwrightry* by Matthew Baker. Pepys Library, Magdalene College, Cambridge, Ms PL 2820.
77. Venetian and Spanish sea-carriages. Colin Martin; AGS *MPyD* XVIII-48.
78. Portuguese drawing of a truck carriage, 1582–96. Bodleian Library, Oxford, Ms Douce b.2, ff.81-2.
79. Map of the beacon system in Kent in 1585, by William Lambarde. British Library, Add MS 62935.
80. The English fleet leaves Plymouth Sound on the night of 30/31 July. Detail from a hand-coloured engraving by Augustine Ryther of a chart by Robert Adams, made in 1590. National Maritime Museum, Greenwich, London, *PBD* 8529(4).
81. The Armada's advance to Calais.
82. *San Salvador* abandoned and on fire, 31 July. Detail from a hand-coloured engraving by Augustine Ryther of a chart by Robert Adams, made in 1590. National Maritime Museum, Greenwich, London, *PBD* 8528(7).
83. *Nuestra Señora del Rosario* disabled, abandoned, and surrounded by debris, 1 August 1588. Detail from a hand-coloured engraving by Augustine Ryther of a chart by Robert Adams, made in 1590. National Maritime Museum, Greenwich, London, *PBD* 8529(6).
84. A *billete* sent by Juan Martínez de Recalde on Monday 1 August 1588 to the duke of Medina Sidonia. AHN *OM* 3511 expediente 41/6.
85. The battle off Portland Bill, 2 August. Detail from a hand-coloured engraving by Augustine Ryther of a chart by Robert Adams, made in 1590. National Maritime Museum, Greenwich, London, *PBD* 8529(8).
86. The two fleets continue up the Channel. Detail from a hand-coloured engraving by Augustine Ryther of a chart by Robert Adams, made in 1590. National Maritime Museum, Greenwich, London, *PBD* 8529(8).
87. The situation on 6 August. Detail from a hand-coloured engraving by Augustine Ryther of a chart by Robert Adams, made in 1590. National Maritime Museum, Greenwich, London, *PBD* 8529(10).

88. A map of the Dutch-held enclave around Ostend, by Robert Adams, 1590. Hatfield House, *CPM* II/46.
89. Eight fireships attack the Armada off Calais. Museum of the Royal Navy, Portsmouth, Astor Armada Drawings 9.
90. The galleass *San Lorenzo* aground off Calais. Museum of the Royal Navy, Portsmouth, Astor Armada Drawings 10 (detail).
91. At dawn on 8 August, Medina Sidonia found himself exposed. Museum of the Royal Navy, Portsmouth, Astor Armada Drawings 10.
92. A medal celebrating the dispersal of the Armada, 1588. National Maritime Museum, Greenwich, London, *MEC* 0013.
93. The two fleets in the North Sea, off Northumberland. Detail from a hand-coloured engraving by Augustine Ryther of a chart by Robert Adams, made in 1590. National Maritime Museum, Greenwich, London, *PBD* 8529(2).
94. Frontispiece of the English edition of *The Mariner's Mirror*, published in 1588. National Maritime Museum, Greenwich, London, A1730-1.
95. Navigation aboard Armada ships. Colin Martin.
96. The wreck-site of *Trinidad Valencera* in Kinnagoe Bay, County Donegal. Colin Martin.
97. An archaeologist with a Spanish helmet and pewter plate in a copper bucket. Colin Martin.
98. The south-east corner of Fair Isle, Shetland. Colin Martin.
99. Stroms Hellier, where the wreck of *Gran Grifón* lies, in the gully to the left of the central spine of rock. Colin Martin.
100. The title page of *Certaine Advertisments Out of Ireland*, 1588.
101. A string of wrecks along the west coast of Ireland from Counties Sligo to Kerry. Detail from a hand-coloured engraving by Augustine Ryther of a chart by Robert Adams, made in 1590. National Maritime Museum, Greenwich, London, *PBD* 8529(2).
102. Map of shipwreck locations around Ireland.
103. Blasket Sound and Islands, looking south-west. Colin Martin.
104. Route followed by Recalde and Aramburu into Blasket Sound; location of the wreck *of Santa María de la Rosa* and associated anchors. Colin Martin.
105. The standing stone overlooking Blasket Sound. Colin Martin.
106. Pewter plate inscribed 'Matute'. Colin Martin.
107. The last will and testament of Don Antonio de Ulloa y Sandoval from Córdoba. AGS *Estado* 166/63.
108. Detail of a contemporary map depicting the three Streedagh wrecks. TNA, *MPF* 1/91.

109. Streedagh Strand in a gale. Colin Martin.
110. Lacada Point, Co. Antrim, where the galleass *Girona* was wrecked. Colin Martin.
111. The sheltered natural harbour at Tobermory on the Isle of Mull, Scotland. Colin Martin.
112. Two Armada ships wrecked on the coast of Norway. Detail from a hand-coloured engraving by Augustine Ryther of a chart by Robert Adams, made in 1590. National Maritime Museum, Greenwich, London, *PBD* 8529(2).
113. Three designs for a *media culebrina* by Don Juan de Acuña Vela, July 1587. AGS *MPyD* V-17.
114. Shot and powder supplied to and returned by four Portuguese galleons. *BMO*, IV/4, 246-53, 'Relación de la gente de mar y guerra' by Pedro Coco Calderón, 23 October/1 November 1588.
115. Shot sizes and quantities remaining on the wreck of *Gran Grifón*. Colin Martin.
116. The broken muzzle end of a gun from *Gran Grifón*. Colin Martin.
117. A gun from *Juliana* that has suffered a blow-out. Colin Martin.
118. Measuring shot. Colin Martin.
119. Working a replica gun on a replica Spanish sea-carriage in 1988. Colin Martin.
120. Working a replica gun on a replica English truck-carriage in 1988. Colin Martin.
121. Percentage of shot and powder used by the navy royal, 1595–6. Geoffrey Parker.
122. Unknown artist, *The Spanish Armada off the Coast of England*, c. 1600–05 © National Museums Northern Ireland, Ulster Museum Collection.
123. Portrait of Don Balthasar de Zúñiga, *c*. 1615. Castle of Nelahozeves, Czech Republic. Album / Alamy Stock Photo.
124. Portrait of Pedro de Ribadeneira, holding an image of Ignatius Loyola. Rijksmuseum, RP-P-OB-6845.
125. A post-Armada Spanish galleon. TNA, *SP* 9/205/10.
126. Old and new ways of hanging a galleass's rudder. Based on AGS *MPyD*, XIV–89, February 1589. Colin Martin.
127. Drawing defining the sizes of roundshot, by Juan de Acuña Vela. AGS *MPyD*, V–20.
128. All that remains of the standard of *San Mateo*. Museum de Lakenhal, Leiden.

129. Queen Elizabeth reviews her troops at Tilbury. St Faith's church, Gaywood, Norfolk.
130. Queen Elizabeth being carried through the streets, c. 1600. Sherborne Castle, Dorset.
131. The first use of the term 'Invincible Armada'. *Essempio d'una lettera mandata d'Inghilterra a Don Bernardino di Mendozza* [Leiden – recte London – 1588]. British Library.
132. Title page of Percyvall's *Bibliotheca Hispanica* (1591). British Library, 002819850.
133. Don Diego Pimentel's self-portrait. Regionaal Archief, Alkmaar, Catalogusnummer PR 1001474, tracing of the original.
134. The route of the victorious Dutch Armada in 1688.
135. Upnor Castle, on the Medway. Historic England, 26886_039.
136. Edmund Yorke's sketch of Weybourne Hope, Norfolk, in 1588. Hatfield House, *CPM* II/46, Marquess of Salisbury.
137. The tomb of Martin Bond, 1643. St Helen's Church, Bishopsgate, London.
138. Elizabeth: The Armada Portrait. Woburn Abbey, Duke of Bedford.
139. Allegory of the Spanish Armada. Church of St Peter and St Paul, Bratoft, Lincolnshire.
140. Samuel Ward's 'The double deliverance' (Amsterdam, 1621). British Museum, Prints and Drawings, 1847,0723.11.
141. Thomas Deloney's *A new Ballad of the strange and most cruel Whips*, 1588. British Library, books, C.18.e.2, f.63.
142. *The Armada in sight. Plymouth Hoe*, by John Seymour Lucas, 1880. Art Gallery of New South Wales. The Print Collector / Alamy Stock Photo.
143. An Armada tercentenary medal, struck by J. Carter, Birmingham, 1888. National Maritime Museum, Greenwich, London, *MEC* 2088.
144. Commemoration off Streedagh Strand. Spanish Armada Ireland.
145. Commemoration on Streedagh Strand. Colin Martin.
146. A diving bell from George Sinclair's *The Hydrostatics* (1672). Reproduced courtesy of the University of St Andrews Special Collections.
147. Jacob Rowe's 'Diving Engine'. National Maritime Museum, Greenwich, London, ENG/5; MS1980/092.
148. Jacob Rowe's drawings of lifting and the use explosives. National Maritime Museum, Greenwich, London, ENG/5; MS1980/092.
149. Publicity photo of Margaret Naylor, 1924. *Glasgow Herald*.
150. Some of the gold items found on *Girona*. Ulster Museum.

151. Diagram showing swim-line technique used in the search for the wreck of *Santa María de la Rosa*. Colin Martin.
152. An archaeologist with an air-lift removing shingle to reveal a buried bronze gun. Colin Martin.
153. Preparing to lift a heavy gun-carriage wheel from *Trinidad Valencera*. Colin Martin.
154. Everyday objects from *Trinidad Valencera*. Colin Martin.
155. *Elizabeth I and the Spanish Armada*. The Worshipful Society of Apothecaries, London.

## Tables

1.1 The squadrons making up the Spanish fleet, as they left Corunna. Data extracted from *BMO*.
2.1 Parma's invasion army. Tamalio, 'I Gonzaga', 149–50, Ercole Gonzaga to the duke of Mantua, *c.* 7 July 1588.
9.1 Spanish and English weekly rations. *CSPSp*, IV, 269–70.
11.1 Locations of arquebusiers, musketeers and retainers on *San Martín*. Based on *BMO* IV/2, 500–2.
15.1 Relative survival rates of the Spanish fleet's squadrons. *BMO*, V, Anexo 5, and see their table of ship survival in Anexo 6.
16.1 Roundshot fired by selected Armada ships. AGS *CMC* 1a/1736, 2a/460, 772, 905 and 942; KML *MSP CC* 8/32 and 8/37.

# *Index*

Ship names are in italics.
Page references to illustrations are in italics.
'Appx' refers to material online (https://www.yalebooks.co.uk/page/detail/armada/?k=9780300259865).

*Achates 124*, 273, 602 n.25, Appx 3
Acuña, Don Pedro de, commander of galleys, Cadiz 189
Acuña Vela, Don Juan de, Captain-General of Artillery 29, 207, 215, 230–1, 381–2, 393, 595 n.2
  attempt to standardize munitions 432–3, *433*
Adams, Robert, cartographer *3*, 13, 271, *283*, 286–7, *291*, *287*, *304*, *309*, *326*, 485–6, 498, 509, Appx 5 n.2
*Advice* 272, Appx 3
African slave trade *71*, 107–8, 121, 457, 509
Africans serving on Armada 19, 27, 331, 567 n.6
*Aid* 74, *124*, 273, 602 n.25, Appx 3
Álava, Don Francés de, Spanish ambassador in Paris 115–16
Alba, Fernando Álvarez de Toledo, 3rd duke of 15, 50–2, 54, 58, 110–20, 122–3, 126–7, 130, 150, 158–9, 194, 206, 334, Appx 5, chs 4, 18
Alberghetti, Zuanne, gunfounder Appx 4.1B
Albert, cardinal archduke, viceroy of Portugal 16, 18–19, 411, 428
  after the Armada 456–8, 620 n.1
Alcántara bridge, near Lisbon, battle of *128*, 129
Alcázarquivir, battle of, Morocco 126, 492
Alemanni, Vincenzo, Tuscan ambassador in Madrid 258–9, 385, 412, 423, 429, 601 n.7, 624 n.51
Allen, William, cardinal 64–5, 183, 227–9, 468, 473, Appx 5 ch.9
Alva, Andrés de 241, 244
Americas, annual treasure-fleet from 18, 20, 23, 27, 36, 110–11, 121, 150, 157, 191–3, 196, 199, 209, 239, 444
ammunition *see* artillery, projectiles
Amsterdam, Netherlands *49*, 310

Andalucia 25, 36, 147, 209, 257, 383, 385, 429
  preparations for Armada 26, 168, 172, 175, 187, 190–1, 196
  squadron of, commanded by Don Pedro de Valdés 23, 35, 39, 191, 198, 221, 246, 261, 276, 286, 288, 364, 389, 454, Appx 1–2
  troops from 20–1, *21*, 60, 126
Anjou, François de Valois, duke of 54–5, 58, 85, 137–8, 143, 163, 184, 217
Anna of Austria, 4th wife of Philip II 26, 114, 201
Anstruther, Fife, Scotland 338, 368
Anthony, Anthony 69, *69*, 71–2, *72*
Antolínez, Patricio and his infantry company 20, 337, 369, 567 n.8
Antonio, Dom, prior of Crato, claimant to the throne of Portugal 15, 129–30, 132–3, 137–8, 143–4, 147, 149, 163, 178, 196, 366, 445–6
Antwerp, Brabant, Low Countries 46, *49*, 53–4, 55, 57, 58, 65, 110, 144, 148, 161, 216, 218, 227, 256, 308, 356, 496
  'hellburners' of (1585) 55–7, *56*, 312, 377
  sack of (1576) 51, 57, 93, 478
*Anunciada* (Levant) 187, 298, 341–2, *344*, Appx 1–2
  burned, Shannon, Ireland 342, 366
Aramburu, Marcos de *10–11*, 258, 343–6, *347*, 348–50, 352, 372, 426, 432, 457–8, 495, 526, 529
Aranda, Don Martín de, Judge Advocate 322, 356–7, 419
Arcani, Arcano dei, gunfounder, Cesena, Italy Appx 4.2
Arceo, Hierónimo de, secretary to Medina Sidonia 322, 424
archaeology *see* underwater archaeology
archives 3–7, 19, 93, 171, 181, 258, 503–5, 509, Appx 5

recent discoveries 544
Argyll, dukes of 521, 523–5
Argyll, earls of 515–18
*Ark Royal*, English flagship 2, 85, 272, 296, 311, 315, 383, 484, 542, *547*, Appx 3
Armada, 1–2, Appx 1–2
  abandons anchors off Calais 313, 315, 325, 366, 419, 514
  assembly of 16–21, 23–8, 34–6, *35*, *37*, 38, 166–9, 173–5, 187–8, 196–8, 207–8, 214–15, 219–20, 230–2
  battle damage 262, 285, *288*, 296, 299, 317, 319, 323, 332, 335, 346, 350, 360, 362, 365–6
  battle drills 262–4, *263*, *264*, 269
  battle order 258, *259*, 260–1, 270, 280–2, *283*, 284, 286, 294–5, 297, 313, 322
  chaplaincy services 45, *45*, 167, 223
  commanded by military officers 25–8, 495–6
  Council of War 28, 237, 245, 269, 282, 295, 387
  crew 24–5, 382–3
  damage control 266–8, *268*, 313
  draught animals 16, 61, 365, Appx 4.4
  formation discipline 166, 284
  incendiary weapons 230, 265–7, *266*, *267*
  inexperienced officers 384
  into North Sea and homeward 1, *3*, 321–4, *326*, 327–8, 416
  instructions for return to Spain 319
  leaves Corunna 245
  leaves Lisbon 47
  'Lisbon Muster' 38, *38*, 223
  medical services 167, 214, 223, *223*, 243, 331, 417
  moves up Channel 246, 281–300, *283*, *284*, *286*, *287*, *291*, *297*
  multiple languages, weights and measures 384, 395–6, Appx 4

music 220–1, *222*
navigational aids 122, 224–6, *228, 229*, 295, 304, 319, 327–8, *329, 330*, 343–4, 375, 412, 528, Appx 5 ch.9
news of, in Spain 311–20
overcrowding 224, 337
pilots 34, 47, 192, 225–6, 240–1, 245, 278, 299–302, 306, 318, 320, 322, 327–8, 331, 341, 345, 350–2, 366, 371, 375–6, 384–5, 416, 464
printed forms 221
rations 222
religious observance 44–5, *45*, 65, 183, 223, 243, *244*
   blessing of standard 18–19
   return to Spain 416–19
squadron commanders 25–8, Appx 1
squadrons 39, Appx 1–2; *see also* Andalucia; Castile; galleasses; galleys; Guipúzcoa; Levant; *pataches & zabras*; Portugal; *urcas*; Vizcaya
strategy 5, 16, 165–6, 169–70, 173–5, 194, 210, 239–40, 295, 374
supernumeraries *see aventureros; entretenidos*
supplies 187, 207, 215, 223, 231, 234, 236, 245, 324, 326, 328
surviving ships return to Spain 371–2, 416–19, 425–6, Appx 1
tactics 5, 29, 94, 132, 174, 192–3, 206, 255, 258, 261–2, 269–70, 292–4, 299, 314, 391–2
troops on board 16–21, *17*, 23, 342
'troubleshooters' 261, 284, 286, 291–2, 314, 317, 402
weakened by weight of own artillery 335, 360, 426
weaponry *see* artillery
wrecks *see* chs 14, 15, 21
Armada commemorated
   bicentenary (1788) 499
   captured flags displayed 487, 514
   medals *321*, 435, 497, 501, *502*, 599

   paintings 96–7, 250–1, 406–7, *438*, 484–6, 484–7, *492, 546–7*
   quatercentenary (1988) 506–7, 510
   *Rosario* exhibited at Deptford 487, 514
   sermons 489, 498
   shipwreck locations 509–11, *510, 511*
   songs and ballads 486–8, *488*
   statues 500, 503
   tapestries 485–6, 489, 498–9, 508
   tercentenary (1888) in England 459, 490–1, 500–2, *502*, 504
   tercentenary (1888) in Spain 502–3
Armada myths 492, 508
   films 506, 508
   game of bowls, Plymouth Hoe 92, 491–2, *492*
   torture instruments in Tower 490–1
   whips 489–91, *490*
Army of Flanders 51–4, 57–61, 60, 67, 116, 122, 160–2, 164, 169, 171, 173, 182, 184–5, 194–5, 203, 227, 300, 306, 308, 310, 341, 421, 449, 454, 457, 459, 471, 477, 480, 494, 496–7, 539
artillery Appx 4
   comparative nomenclature Appx 4.1–2
   problems of standardization 392, 395–6, 432–3, *433*, Appx 4
   projectiles
      stocks (English) 1–2, 258, 279–80, 295, 325, 397, 400, 404
      stocks (Spanish) 4, 38, 230, 258, 280, 298–9, 385–91, 401, 514, 518–19, 523, 530–1, 533
artillery, English 269, 378, Appx 4.2
   basilico/basilisk 513, Appx 4.1
   bastard cannon Appx 4.1
   breech-loading Appx 4.1
   cannon 69, 75, Appx 4.1
   cannon pedro/perier 513, Appx 4.1
   cannon royal 69, Appx 4.1
   culverin 47, 69, 280, 317, 398–9, *398*, 403, 513, 602 n.25, Appx 4.1

artillery, English (*cont.*)
  demi-cannon 69, 75, 280, 317, 403, 469, Appx 4.1
  demi-culverin 69, 317, 378, 403, 469, 513, Appx 4.1–2
  effectiveness 75, 277, 284, 295–6, 317–19, 350, 378, 389–90, 396–7, 403, 493, 496, Appx 4.2
  falcon 469, Appx 4.1
  falconet 469, Appx 4.1
  minion 519, Appx 4.1
  more and better trained gunners 91–2, 262, 385–7, 397, 399, 420
  more big guns on ships 75–9, 189, 206, 219, 262, 271, 282, 294–5, 376, 396–7, 399, 431
  munitions 71, 86, 279, 294, 325, 396, 401, 542
  reloading faster 396–9, *398*
  robinet Appx 4.1
  saker 469, 602 n.25, Appx 4.1–2
  serpentine Appx 4.1
  siege-guns, lack of 445–6
  speed of firing and reloading 316–17, 387, 389, 393, 397, 493, Appx 4.3
  tactics 108–10, 127, 262, 296
  truck carriage 273–4, *273–4*, 276–7, 376, 397–9, *398*, 401
artillery, Spanish 1, 4, 34, 36–8, 122, 130, 166, 215, 220, 237–8, 260, 285, 292–3, 378, 380, Appx 4
  breech-loaders Appx 4.1C–F
  *cañón* 380–1, Appx 4.1
  *cañoncete* Appx 4.1
  *cañón de batir* 167, 207, 220, 380, 419, 519, 533, Appx 4.1, 4.4
  *cañón grueso* 381, 390, Appx 4.1
  *cañón pedrero* 380, 513, Appx 4.1
  cast iron Appx 4.1E
  *culebrina* 167, 189, 275, 280, 381, 402, 513, Appx 4.1
  effectiveness 189, 269, 378, 379, 403
  *esmeril* 391, Appx 4.1
  *esmeril doble* Appx 4.1
  *falcon* 519, Appx 4.1
  *falcon pedrero* Appx 4.1
  *falconete* Appx 4.1
  foreign trophies 220, Appx 4.1B
  gunner's rule 395–6, *396*
  incendiary weapons 265–7, *266*, *267*
  land carriages 207, 275
  *lombarda* Appx 4.1
  manufacturing faults 220, 393–6, *394*, 514
  *media culebrina* 276, 381, *382*, 390–1, 402, 513, 519, 533, Appx 4.1
  *medio cañón* 381, 389, 393, Appx 4.1
  *medio cañón pedrero* Appx 4.1
  *medio falconete* Appx 4.1
  *medio sacre* 393, 533, Appx 4.1
  munitions 4–5, 16, 34, 36, 38, 63, 166, 175, 182, 186, 189–91, 197, 214–15, 224, 230, 237, 257, 269, 275–6, 294, 328, 340, 342, 353, 365, 387–8, 390, 415, 423–4, 432, 461, 477, 498, 512–15, 522, 531, Appx 4.6
  *pasamuro* Appx 4.1–2
  *pedrero* 381, Appx 4.1
  *quarto cañón* Appx 4.1
  recovered from wrecks 512–15, 518–19, 521, 532–3, *532*, 536, 544, Appx 4
  related equipment Appx 4.3
  reloading 268, 392–3
  royal guns Appx 4.1A
  *sacre* 391, 393, Appx 4.1
  sea carriages 274–6, *275*
  shortage of gunners 386
  shot gauge 395–6, *396*
  siege-train 16, 126, 167–8, 173, 207, 331, 365, 380, 419, 459, 461, 463, 468–9, 477, 480, Appx 4.1, 4.4; *see also cañón de batir*
  smaller numbers of big guns on ships 380
  swivel-guns *37*, 167, Appx 4.1F

*tercio cañón* Appx 4.1
truck carriage 276, *276*
*verso* 391, Appx 4.1
working guns at sea 268, 383–4, Appx 4.3
wrought iron 391, Appx 4.1D
*Ascension* of London 272, Appx 3
Ascoli, Don Antonio Luis de Leyva, prince of 18, 31–2, 263, 313, 322, 350–1, 456, 566 n.3, 569 n.32–4, 608 n.22, 617 n.26, 622 n.28, Appx 5 ch.13
  after the Armada 456
Asheby, William, English ambassador in Scotland 363–4, 369
Austria, Anna of *see* Anna
Austria, Don John of 33, 116
Avancini, Giovanni 360, 362, 385
*aventureros* (gentlemen volunteers) 18, 22, 33, 38
Ávila, Don Cristóbal de 322, 341, 609 n.3
Ávila, Teresa de 148
Azores archipelago
  Spanish conquest of (1581–3) 15, 26–8, 32, *35*, 126, 129–37, *134*, *136*, 174, 374, 411
  subsequent naval operations involving, 20, 24–5, 30, 36, 160, 191–2, 198, 202, 317, 432, 455, 515, 542

Babington, Anthony, English conspirator 176–8, 185
Baker, Matthew, shipwright 76–7, *77*, 79, *80*, 273–4, *274*, 444
Baltic, ships and seamen from 25, 35, 166, 187, 277, 327, 375
Banks of Flanders, sandbanks off Flemish coast *49*, 199, 281, 304, 311, 320–1, 463
*Barca de Amburg* (*urca*) 331, 335, Appx 1–2
*Barca de Danzig* (*urca*) 341–2, 385, 419, Appx 1–2

*Bark Burr* 272, Appx 3
*Bark St Leger* 272, Appx 3
*Bark Talbot* 272, 284, Appx 3
*Bark Young* 272, Appx 3
*Bartholomew* 272, Appx 3
Bazán, Don Alonso de, brother of Santa Cruz 431–2, 612 n.10, Appx 4.2
Bazán, Don Álvaro de *see* Santa Cruz
Bazán, Don Diego de, son of Santa Cruz 352
Beachy Head, Sussex, England 240, 301, *463*, 465, 540, 599 n.13
Beale, Robert, clerk to Privy Council 177–8, Appx 5 ch.7
Bergen, Norway 365
Bergen-op-Zoom, Netherlands *49*, siege of 449
Bertendona, Martín de, commander of Levant squadron 26, 28, 212–13, 258–60, *259*, 277, 292, 314, 322, 355, 372, 375, 385, 419, 432, 447, 455, 495, 515, 571 n.58, Appx 5 ch.8
Bingham, Sir Richard, governor of Connacht 125, 339–40, 354–5, *357*, 366, 370, 512–13
Blacksod Bay, Mayo, Ireland *344*, 360, 512, 526
Blanco, Francisco *see* Ortega
Blanco, Pedro, soldier and bodyguard to Tyrone 448
Blasket Islands and Sound, Kerry, Ireland 6, *10–11*, 343, *344*, 345–9, *346*–7, 351–2, *351*, 492, 510, 519, 526, 529
boats *see* ship and boat types
Bobadilla, Don Francisco de, senior military officer on Armada 17, 28, 32, 47, 53, 161, 215, 232, 241, 258, *259*, 260, 270, 301, 322–3, 383–4, 387, 416, 419–22, 425, 427, 447, 493, 544, 597 n.16, 609 n.3, 629 n.51, 54, Appx 5 chs 8, 10
  after the Armada 456, 458

Boleyn, Anne, queen of England and mother of Elizabeth 87, 102, 104
Boleyn, Mary, sister of Anne 184
Bond, Martin, London merchant 483–4, *484*
Borough, William, naval commander and chart-maker 82, 188–90, *188*, Appx 3
Bothwell, Francis Hepburn, 4th earl of 111
Bothwell, Francis Hepburn, 5th earl of 368
Boulogne, Pas-de-Calais, France *49*, 181–2, 216, 278, *284*, 299, *463*
Bourbon, Cardinal Charles de 137
Bourbourg, Nord, France (Flanders in 1588), peace talks *49*, 66, 217, 228, 242–3, 305, 310, 479, Appx 5 ch.9
Bourne, William, English mathematician and gunnery expert 274, 277, 385, 387
Brabant, Netherlands 48, 53–5, 57–8, 64, 164, 308, 469
*Brave* of London 272, Appx 3
Brentwood, Essex, England, troops sent to *49*, 68
Brill, Netherlands *49*, 148
Brittany, France 138, 225, 246, 327, 412, 432, 450–1, 455, 482, 498
Brochero, Don Diego, naval commander 495
Bruce, John, keeper of State Papers 499, 505, Appx 5 (vi)
Bruges, Flanders *49*, 55, 65–6, *309*, 422–3, 428
Brussels, Low Countries *49*, *49*, 51, 65, 115, 121, 158, 302, 453, 458, 507, 541
Buongiovanni, Muzio, papal collector in Portugal, 46–7, 571 n.58
Burghley, William Cecil, Elizabeth's Secretary of State and (after 1572) Lord Treasurer 18, 38, *38*, 54, 81, 83, 87–9, 102, 111, 115, 119, 138–9, *139*, 141–4, 150, 161, 177–8, 180, 184, 203–4, 228, 310, 339, 357, *357*, 439, 442–4, *442*, 457, 477, 491, 566 n.3, 589 n.7
Burgos, Castile, Spain 20, *21*, 417, 427
Burke, Richard 512
Burt Castle, Donegal, Ireland 334, *344*

Cabrera de Córdoba, Luis, courtier and historian 156, *156*, 494
Cadiz, Andalucia, Spain *10–11*, 20, *21*, 25–6, 30, 32, 46, *60*, 84, 91, 126–7, 186–8, 191–2, 368, 374, 434
  1587 raid by Drake 188–90, *188*, 196–7, 209, 226, 242, 375, 385, 400, Appx 5 ch.7
  1596 raid by Howard 403, 433, 450–1, 454, 457, 482
  1625 Anglo-Dutch raid 495, 542–3
Calahorrano, Diego, friar, Medina Sidonia's confessor 45, 214
Calais, Pas-de-Calais, France *10–11*, 37, *49*, 101, 104, 122, 216, 226, 230, 279–80, *284*, 299–304, *304*, 307–8, 310–11, *312*, 315, *315*, 325, 350, 366–7, 377, *377*, 381, 383–5, 389, 400–2, 420–1, 423–5, 432, 456, 463–4, *463*, 469–70, 474, 476, 496, 514, 540
Calebeg (McSween's Bay), Donegal, Ireland *344*, 361
*camaradas* 21, 205
cannon balls *see* projectiles
Cantabria, Spain *21*, 60, 168, 385, 417, 430, 445
Cardona, Don Juan de 426–7, 430–1
Carew, Sir Francis, 486
Carew, Sir Gawen, naval officer under Henry VIII, 83
Carew, Sir George, drowned on *Mary Rose* 83, 87
Carew, Sir George, Master of the Ordnance in Ireland 513

*Caridad inglesa* (*pataches & zabras*) 187, Appx 1–2
Carleill, Christopher, soldier 148, Appx 5 ch.15
Carnero, Antonio, chief accountant of the Army of Flanders and historian 497, 636 n.28
*Casa de Paz grande*, hospital ship 223, 419, Appx 1–2
Cascais, Portugal 126, 174, 374, 445–7
Castello del Oro *see* Smerwick
Castile, Spain 25, 33, 39, 107, 161, 258, 328, 417, 458
  Cortes (Council) of 153, 170, 234, 446–7, 451
  squadron of, commanded by Diego Flores de Valdés 27, 29, 33, 36, 39, 219, 241, 246, 257, 261, 276–7, 316, 319, 322, 353, 364, 382–3, 385, Appx 1–2
  troops from 20, 59
*Castillo Negro* (*urca*) 331, Appx 1–2
Castro, Don Rodrigo de, archbishop of Seville 164–5, 171
Castro Urdiales, Cantabria, Spain 568 n.42, Appx 1
Catherine of Aragon, queen of England 102–3
Catholics, English 61, 111–12, 119, 141–2, 161, 176, 183, 244, 270, 437, 468, 500
Cavendish, Thomas, circumnavigator 128, 439
Cecil, William *see* Burghley
*Centurion* of London 272, Appx 3
Cerda, Melchor de la, Jesuit 493
*Certaine Advertisements out of Ireland* 338, *339*, 611 n.26
Cervantes, Miguel de, novelist and poet 434, 452, 454, 456
Cesi, count Niccolò 422, 424
Céspedes, Alonso de, commander of field artillery Appx 4.4

Céspedes del Castillo, Guillermo, historian 450
*Chance* 272, Appx 3
Channel, English 5, 16, 43, 46, 48, 58, 62, 71, 91–2, 113, 121, 161, 165, 169, 171–5, 182, 187, 195, 197, 199–200, 202–3, 212, 220, 225–6, 229, *229*, 231, 236, 238–9, 244, 255–6, 261, 271, 280–1, *286*, 290, *297*, 298–300, 303, 305–6, 310–11, 322–3, 325, 345, 360, 364, 377, 383–4, 386–7, 390, 400, 415, 421–3, 428, 447, 462–3, 465, 473, 498, 505–7
Chapman, Richard, shipwright 444
*Charity see Caridad inglesa*
*Charles*, pinnace 272, Appx 3
Charles I, king of England, Scotland and Ireland, 489, 494–5, 539–40, 634 n.6, 639 n.13
Charles II, king of England, Scotland and Ireland, 543
Charles V, emperor, father of Philip II 48–9, 102–3, 152–3, 198, Appx 4.4
  attempt to standardize artillery Appx 4.1
Chatham, Kent, England 71, *470*, 542; *see also* England, dockyards
'Chatham Chest' 440
Chaves, Alonso de, naval writer 258, 260
Cheyney, Edward P., historian 460–1, 481
*Ciervo Volante* (*urcas*) 344, 354–5, Appx 1–2
City of Derry Sub-Aqua Club 533
Clancy, Boetius, sheriff of Clare 341, 612 n.32
Coco Calderón, Pedro, joint chief accountant of the Armada *221*, 317–18, 328, 388, 426–8, 457–8, Appx 5 ch.10
Cohen, Eliot, historian and strategic analyst 373–5, 378, 401, 539

Cole, Mary Hill, historian 88
Collado, Luis Appx 4.1, 4.4, 4.6
Collinson, Patrick, historian 138
Coloma, Don Carlos, soldier and historian 496–7, 636 n.27
Colonna, Oda, soldier and nephew of Cardinal Colonna 184–5, 378
Colquhoun, James, diver 516
Concepción, Antonio de la, friar 46
*Concepción de Castro*, patache 340, *344*, 612 n.31, Appx 1–2
*Concepción de Lastero*, patache 328, Appx 1–2
*Concepción Menor* (Vizcaya) *344*, 354, 388–9, Appx 1–2
Conti, Nicolo di, gunfounder Appx 4.1B
Corbett, Julian S., historian 505, 526, 602 n.22
Córdoba, Don Diego de, chamberlain to Philip II 31, 341, 612 n.32
Córdoba, Don Felipe de 420, 612 n.32
Córdoba, Don Luis de 19, 355
Cornwall, England 66, 231, 278
  1595 Spanish raid, 450
Corunna, Galicia, Spain *10–11*, *21*, 33, 90, 92, 174, 185, 223, 231, 235–47, *235*, 269–70, 294, 301, 303, 307, 331, 335, 352–3, 360, 364–5, 367, 372, 383–4, 386, 388–9, 411, 416–17, 421, 445–7, 458, 477, 515, 539–40
  surviving ships return to 419
Counter-Armada, English (1589) 443–7, 509, 515, Appx 5 ch.18
counter-factual arguments, limitations 479–81, Appx 5 ch.19
Crabb, Lionel 'Buster', diver 524
Creswell, Joseph, Jesuit 43
Croft, James, Privy Councillor 104, 161, 217, 482
Cuéllar, Francisco de, infantry captain 32, 127–8, 322, 324, 356–9, 369–70, 448, 458
  Trail 511

Culmore Castle, Donegal, Ireland 333–4
Cumberland, George Clifford earl of *441*, Appx 3

Dale, Dr Valentine, delegate to Bourbourg peace talks *37*, 64, 228–30, 468, 482, Appx 5 ch.9
Darnley, Lord Henry, king of Scotland 111, 119, 141, 478, 635 n.9
Dartmouth, Devon, England 27, 272, *463*, 464
  Armada survivors ransomed and repatriated from (1590) 35, 335, 354, 360, 367, 370, 544, 611 n.23
Dartmouth, George Legge, Lord, naval commander (1688), 465–6
*David Chico* (urca) 231, Appx 1–2
Davies, David, naval historian 465
Davison, William, joint secretary of state, 177–8, 180, 589 n.3
*Delight* 272, Appx 3
Deloney, Thomas, balladeer 487, 489–90, *490*
Denny, Sir Edward, infantry captain 125, 340–1
Deptford, Kent, England 85, 140, 483, 487, 514
Devon, England 19, 121, 247, 278–9, 366, 415, 462–3, 466, 514
*Diamond* 272, Appx 3
Dieppe, Normandy, France 412
Dingle, Kerry, Ireland *344*, 348
*Disdain*, Lord Admiral's pinnace 272, 283, *283*, Appx 3
diseases on Armada 24, 223, 337, 434, 442, 459
  dysentery 416
  malaria 345
  post-traumatic stress disorder 416
  typhus 24, 208, 416
diseases on English fleet 190, 404, 439–40

divers
  inspect *San Mateo* and repair *San Martín* 317–18
  in salvage from Armada wrecks ch.21
  *see also* underwater archaeology
*Doncella* (*urca*) 318, 371, Appx 1–2
Doona Castle, Mayo, Ireland 360
Doonagore Castle, Clare, Ireland 341
Dorset, England, 462–3, 472, 474
Dovara, Luigi, Tuscan diplomat 162–4, 587 n.33
Dover, Kent, England *49*, 110, 169, 168, 172, 174, 186, 204, 217, 226, 240, 278–9, *284*, 298, 300, 377, 402, 463, *463*, 466, 469, 476, 513
Dover, Strait of *see* Narrow Seas
Downs, The, anchorage between Kent coast and Goodwin Sands *49*, 205, 226, *229*, 242, 279, *284*, 296, *304*, *463*, 465–6, 468, 476, 540, battle of 542–3
Drake, Sir Francis 2, 24, 43 *71*, 71, 82–5, 89–92, 108, 121, 130, 143–4, 147, 163–5, 203–5, 219, 243, 247, 260, 271–2, 278, 282–4, *283*, 293, 296, 314, 319, 378, 400–3, 414, 423, 425, 435–6, 439–40, 444–6, 448–50, 482, 491–3, *492*, 501–2, 506, 508–9, 543, Appx 3
  Azores 190–1, 375, 446
  Cadiz raid (1587) 186–92, *188*, 196–7, 209, 226, 242, 375, 385, 400, 403
  capture of *Rosario* 286–90, *287*, 401–2, 439, 453
  Caribbean (1585) 82, 84, 91, 164, 168, 170, 366, 375, 400, 403
  Caribbean (1596) 375, *403*, 450, 482
  circumnavigation 71, 85, 148
  Counter-Armada 443–6, 509, 515
  Galicia raid (1585) 149, 163–4
  'haul and draw' philosophy 82–4, 401
  jewel 70, *190*, 190
  knighted 85, 140
  Pacific voyage 127, 140
  Panama raid 121
  San Juan de Ulúa (1567) 108–10
Drake, Richard 453
*Dreadnought* 77–9, 121, 272, Appx 3
Drogheda, Louth, Ireland 334, *344*
Dudley, John *see* Lisle
Dudley, Robert *see* Leicester
Dunkirk, Nord, France 48, *49*, 61–4, 84, 122, 174, 195, 200, 218, *229*, 242, 282, 295, 299, 301, 303, 305–6, 308–11, 315, 367, 369, 377, 415, 420–4, 429, 438, 456, 473, 539–40
Dunluce Castle, Antrim, Ireland *344*, 501, 513
Dunquin, Kerry, Ireland 349, 351, 510
*Duquesa Santa Ana* (*urca*, Andalucia) 297–8, *344*, 360, Appx 1–2
Dutch blockading fleet 50, 199, 218, 304–10, 423, 444
Dutch Republic 5, *49*, 133, 137, 143–4, 147, 168, 217, 226, 444, 452, 461, 479, 481, 491
Dutch Revolt 48–58, 120, 138, 141, 217, 480, 539

Écija, Andalucia, Spain 21
Edinburgh, Scotland, *10–11*, 501
  Armada survivors in 334, 363–4, 368
Edward VI, king of England 87, 103
*Edward Bonaventure* 127, 272, Appx 3
Ehrman, John, naval historian 543
Elizabeth I, queen of England and Ireland 9, 16, 55, 58, 73, 85, 87–90, 102–8, 110–11, 140–1, 150, 158, 184, 190, 203, 214, 227–8, 291, 368, 377, 405, *406–7*, 409, 437, 440–1, 446, 449–50, 452–3, 495, *502*
  'Armada portrait' 484–5, *485*, 508
  defensive measures and weaknesses 68, 74–5, 121, 141, 185, 194–5, 199, 202, 227, 278, 378, 443, 468, 470–3, 476–8, 504

Elizabeth I (*cont.*)
  development of navy 5, 68, 72–6, 79–82, 84–6, 88, 91, 138, 172, 271–4, 373, 376, 379–80, 504
  excommunicated by Pius V 112
  financial problems 444, 452, 476–7
  foreign policy 5, 65–6, 74, 101–7, 110–14, 121–3, 125, 129–30, 137–40, 142, 150, 163–4, 169, 180–2, 185–6, 190, 216–17, 374, 452, 471, 477, 479
  imprisonment and execution of Mary Queen of Scots 111, 114–16, 118–20, 176–80, *179*
  instructions to navy 186, 202–5, 277–8, 289, 373–4, 444
  peace negotiations 64, 66 204, 217, 228, 243, 479
  privateering 66, 85, 121, 130, 393
  Privy Council 5, 67, 72–3, 89, 92–3, 138, 140–3, 147, 177–8, 180, 204, 230, 247, 278–9, 290, 340, 366–7, 400, 437, 440, 458, 468–9, 472–4, 478, 488, 491, 513–14
  progresses 116, 441, *441*
  reaction to failure of Armada 368, 370, 438, 441–2
  relations with Philip II 104–23, 129–30, 145, 160–2, 173, 175, 193–5
  religion 104–5, 112
  safe-conduct to Dunkirk for survivors 369
  Tilbury visit and speech 436–8, *438*, 449, 468, 478, 484, 486, 489, 508, Appx 5 ch.18
*Elizabeth Bonaventure* 272, 439, Appx 3
Elizabeth de Valois, wife of Philip II, brother of Francis II, 112
*Elizabeth Drake* 272, Appx 3
*Elizabeth Jonas* 73–4, 81, 84–5, 272, Appx 3
Ellis, Sir Henry, British Museum Librarian 503

Empel, miracle of (1585) 47
England
  beacons 278–9, *279*, *407*, 466, 476, 484, *492*, 498
  Catholic exiles 61, 65, 160–1, 183, 270, 458, 468, 491
  celebrations after failure of Armada 435–43
  defences 5, 16, 67–8, 73–4, 84, 86, 88, 121, 142–3, 160, 185, 199, 218, 247, *248*, 440, 468, 474–6, *475*, 504
  dockyards 73–4, 77, 542
    Chatham 71, 85, 379, 440, 444, 469, 542
    Deptford 85
    survey of damage after Armada 378–80
    Woolwich 74
  extent of coast to be defended 473
  House of Commons 86, 467
  Lord Admiral *see* Howard
  merchant ships 121, 185
  Navy Board 68, 73, 75–6, 85, 185, 444
  Ordnance Office 5, 69, 279, 403
  past invasions of 68, 85, 165–6, 467
  Treasurer of the Navy 1, 5, 73, 79, 85–6, 379
Enríquez, Don Diego, son of Don Martín 261, 314
Enríquez, Don Diego Téllez 314, 356, 358
Enríquez, Don Martín, viceroy of Mexico 109–10, 261, 376
'Enterprise of England' *see* Philip II
*entretenidos* (staff officers, reserve officers) 18, 21, 22, 27, 32, 38, 221
Ereira, Alan, BBC documentary trilogy 397–9, 507
Escalante, Bernardino de 171–2, *172*, 457, 588 n.44
Escalante Mendoza, Juan de 209
Escorial, the (San Lorenzo el Real de El Escorial, Madrid, Spain) *10–11*,

39, 40, *40*, *41*, 44, 135, 152, 155, *155*, *156*, 171, 191, 200, 232–3, 235, 239, 255–7, 411–12, 416, 493, 570 n.41
  Hall of Battles *35*, 132, *134*, 135
Espinosa, Diego Felipe de, physician, Salamanca 459
Essex, England 93, 449, 466, 579 n.29
Essex, invasion expected in (1588) 68, 118, 204, 278, 291, 378, 462–3, 469, 471, 473–4, 476, 478, 483, 633 n.32
Essex, invasion expected in (1688) 462–3
Essex, Robert Devereux, earl of 87, 90, 433, 440, 606 n.35
Exeter, Devon, England *463*, 464
Exmouth, Devon, England 462, 464, 466
Extremadura, Spain, troops from 20–1

failure in war 373–5, 378, 401, 539
Fair Isle, Shetland, Scotland 6, 335, *336*, 337, 509, 521, 532
  wreck of *Gran Grifón* 6, 327–9, *328*, 390, 402, 531–3, *532*
*Falcon Blanco Mediano* (urcas) *344*, 354–5, Appx 1–2
Falmouth, Cornwall, England 242, 281, 462
Farnese, Alessandro, cardinal 421, 424
Farnese, Alexander *see* Parma, duke of
Farnese, Ranuccio, son of Alexander, duke of Parma 494
Faro, Portugal, captured and burned (1595) 450
Fenton, Edward 82, 91, 127, 273, 375, 399–400, 483, Appx 3
Fenton, Sir Geoffrey, secretary to Irish Privy Council 512–13
Feria, Don Gómez Suárez de Figueroa, count and later duke of, Spanish ambassador in England 105–6, 115, 634 n.2

Fernández Duro, Cesáreo, naval historian 503–5, 544
Ferrol, Galicia, Spain 385, 433, 515, 544
Finisterre, Cape, Spain 186, 231, 234–5, *235*, 241, 269, 301, 303, 306, 326, 416
fireships 55, 249, 266, 279, 284, 304, 311–13, *312*, 315, 324–5, 374, 376–7, 400, *406*–7, 421, 425, 456, 465, 481, 484, 540–1
Fitzwilliam, Sir William, lord deputy of Ireland 340, 354, 358–9, 370–1, 448, 512–13
Flanagan, Laurence 528, 534, 640 n.31
Flanders, Netherlands 36, *49*, 53, 55, 57–8, 64–6, 161, 164, 172, 175, 194–6, 199, 203–4, 217, 225–7, 234, 255, 288, 294, 299, 303, 305–6, 310, 318–20, 348, 419, 422–3, 425, 454, 469, 494, 496
  Armada survivors in 369, 448
  coast of 48, 122, 169–70, 225–6, 301, 308, 318, 320
  *see also* Army of Flanders; Banks of Flanders; Netherlands, provinces
fleet, Dutch (1588), 48, 121, 175, 217–18, 302–4, 305, 306, 308–10, 318, 369–70, 423, 444, 445, 447, 450, 607 n.17, 636 n.25, Appx 5 (v)
fleet, Dutch (after 1588) 461–6, *463*, 470, 496, 539–42
fleet, English (1588) *see* navy royal
fleet, English (after 1588) 463–6, 539–44
fleet, Spanish (1588) *see* Armada
fleet, Spanish (after 1588) 431–3, 539–42
Fleming, Captain Thomas 92, 247, Appx 3
*Florencia* (Portugal/Levant) 36, 261, 380, Appx 1–2
*Florencia*, misidentification of *San Juan de Sicilia* 517

Flores de Valdés, Diego, commander of Castilian squadron 27–30, 32, 46, 108, 121, 127–8, 209, 241, 245, 247–8, 257–8, 261–2, 270, 287–8, 290, 293, 313–14, 322–4, 327–8, 371–2, 383, 392, 419, 544
   after the Armada 427, 454
   blamed for failure of Armada 426–8
Florida, North America 27, 108, 121, 125
Flushing, Zeeland *49*, 58, 84, 148, 174, 212, 226, 256, 310, 318–19, 496–7, 514
Fogaza, Antonio, spy in London 271, 273
Forman, Simon, astrologer 92
Forth, Firth of, Scotland 181, 325, 327, 338, 374, 435
Foss, Kenneth Mackenzie, Colonel 523–4, 639 n.25
Fotheringhay Castle, Northamptonshire, England 176, 178
France
   Catholic League 137–8, 181–2, 216, 457, 477
   Huguenot privateers 110
   Protestants (Huguenots) 108, 115, 118, 137, 182, 216, 457, 514
   reaction to death of Mary Queen of Scots 179
   *see also* Florida
*Frances* of London 272, Appx 3
Francis I, king of France 220, Appx 4.1B–C
Frederick II, king of Denmark 65, 66, 179, 477
Frobisher, Sir Martin 70, 71, 82, 90, 271, 289, 291–2, 296, 298–9, 400, 403, 440, 482, 501–2, *502*, 605 n.23, Appx 3, Appx 5 (vi)
Froude, James Anthony, historian 504–5
Fuentes, Don Pedro Enríquez de Acevedo, count of 206–7, 214, 456–7, 458, 594 n.33

Galicia 2, 231, 234, 372, 386, 415, 432, 515, 544
   raided by Drake (1585) 149, 163–4, 161, 433
   raided by Drake (1589) 445
   soldiers from 20
galleasses, squadron of 28, 39, 198, 236, 258, *259*, 260, 286–7, *291*, 294, 296–8, 304, 314, 364, 380, 390, 444, Appx 1–2
*Galleon Dudley* 272, Appx 3
*Galleon Leicester* 77, 127, 272, Appx 3
galleys, squadron of 39, 220, 230–1, 234–5, *235*, 241, 246, 258, *259*, 261, 279, 327, 374, 381, 385, 459, Appx 1–2
Galway, Ireland 339, 354, 436
   Galway town *344*, 354, 366, 448, 512–13
García de Palacio, Diego, judge and author 24, 276
Garnet, Henry, Jesuit 441
Gascoigne, George 57, 478
Ghent, Flanders *49*, 55, 64–5, 308
Ghislieri, Paolo 380
Giambelli, Federico, engineer 55–6, *56*, 312, 474
Gil, Juan, ensign/lieutenant 281–2, 303
Gillray, James, satirist 499
Gioardi, Dorino II, gunfounder, Genoa Appx 4.1B–C
*Girona*, Neapolitan galleass 22, 360–1, 432, 508, 513, Appx 1–2
   gold jewellery from 22, 30, *30*, *528*
   wreck, Lacada Pt, Antrim, N Ireland 6, 22, 244, 263, *344*, 360–1, *361*, 508, 510, 513, 527–8, *528*, Appx 4.1F
*Golden Hind*, Drake's flagship on circumnavigation 85
*Golden Hind*, pinnace 92, 247, 272, Appx 3
*Golden Lion* 85, 272, Appx 3
*Golden Noble* 272, Appx 3

*Golden Ryall* 272, Appx 3
Gómez de Medina, Juan, commander, squadron of *urcas* 26, 28–9, 127, 209, 238, 258, 295, 322, 335, 337–8, 368–9, 372, 402, 521
Góngora, Bernardo de, friar 243, 287
González-Aller Hierro, José Ignacio, Admiral 8, 247, 507
Gooch, John, historian 373–5, 378, 401, 539
Goodwin Sands, large sandbank off E coast of Kent 49, 226, *463*
Gorgas, Sir Arthur 387
Gorges, Nicholas 85
Gorrochategui Santos, Luis 509
Gourdan, Giraud de Mauléon, lord of, governor of Calais 311, 315
Gower, George, artist 9, 484–5, *485*
*Gran Grifón* (*urcas*) 20, 35, 187, 236, *259*, 295–7, 312, 317, 319, 324, 368, 390–4, 402, 509, Appx 1–2
   wreck, Fair Isle, Scotland 6, *6*, 331, 335–8, *336*, 368–9, 381, *394*, 521, 531–3, *532*, Appx 4
*Gran Grin* (*Vizcaya*) 261, Appx 1–2
   wreck, off Clare Island *344*, 354, 512
Granada, Fray Luis de 18, 231, 428, Appx 5 ch.1
Grand Fleet *see* fleet, Spanish
Grand Strategy *see* Philip II, Enterprise of England
Granvelle, Antoine Perrenot, cardinal and chief minister of Philip II 22, 135, 137, 144–5, 154, 164, 175, 362
Grattan, John, naval officer 524–5, 529
*Graunde Masterys* (Grand Mistress) 71–2, *72*
Gravelines, Nord, France *49*, battle off 310, 316, 319, 339, 341, 353, 356, 362, 366, 371, 391, 396, 399, 401–3, 425, 436, 458, 484
Gregory XIII, pope (1572–85) ix, 161–2, 587 n.27

Gregory, James, Scottish academic 517
Grenville, Sir Richard 247–8, *247*
Grey, Arthur, baron, lord deputy of Ireland 123, 127
Guevara, Francisco de, 145, 262
Guipúzcoa *21*, 60, 175, 419
   ships and seamen from 166, 207
   squadron of, commanded by Miguel de Oquendo 23, 27, 35, 39, 236, 241, 261, 285, 314, 341, 349, 364, 389, 513, Appx 1–2
Guise, Henry of Lorraine, duke of 137, 181–2, 216, 449
gun-founding 72, 214, 393, Appx 4.1, 4.4
gunpowder 2, 4, 21, 38, 63, 92, 123, 132, 168, 215, 217, 230–1, 247, 258, 265, 267, 269, 279–80, 285–6, 295, 298–9, 352, 363–5, 371, 383, 385–8, 390, 396–7, 399, 400–1, 403, 417, 469, 472, 514, 521, Appx 4.5
Gunpowder Plot (1605) 438, 487–8, *488*
Gush, James, diver 522
Guy, John, historian 102, 142
Guzmán de Silva, Don Diego, Spanish ambassador in England 88, 106–7

Hainaut, Netherlands 48, 64
Hakluyt, Richard, diplomat and writer 91
Hall of Battles *see* Escorial
Halut, Remigy de, gunfounder, Mechelen 419, 533, Appx 4
Hamburg, Germany *10–11*, 187, 308, 365
Harborne, William, secret agent in Istanbul 147–8, 181
Harris, Augustus, London theatre-owner 501
*Hart* of Dartmouth 272, Appx 3
Harwich, Essex, England 118, 142, 203, 463

Hawkins, Sir John, Treasurer of the Navy (1577–95) 1–2, *70*, 71, 79–82, 85, 89–90, 92, 107–10, *109*, 113, 115, 117–19, 143, 145, 148, 177, 186, 204, 219, 273, 284, 290, 296–7, 299, 314, 375–6, 379–80, 392, 399, 403, 440, 444, 450, 482, 501–2, *502*, 509, 543, 579 n.24, 580 n.32, Appx 3, 4.2, 5 ch.3
Henry III, king of France 129, 137–8, 144, 179, 181, 216, 449, 457
Henry VII, king of England 165
Henry VIII, king of England, 102, 104
  artillery on ships 69, 72, 273
  coastal defences 68, 468
  navy 68–74, *69, 72*, 82–5, 108
Henry of Navarre, later King Henry IV of France 137, 182, 444, 457
*Hercules* of London 272, Appx 3
Herrera y Tordesillas, Antonio de, historian 494
*Hind* of Exeter 272, Appx 3
Hobbes, Thomas, political philosopher 483
Holland, Netherlands 6, 48, 50–1, 54–5, 58, 122, 144–6, 162–3, 168, 171, 183, 192, 217, 305, 308, 310, 369, 385, 455, 471, 479, 540–1
*Hope* 272, 376, Appx 3
*Hope* of Plymouth 272, Appx 3
*Hopewell* of London 272, Appx 3
Horozco y Covarrubias, Juan de 428
Howard, Lord Charles of Effingham, Lord Admiral 2, 5, 26, 68, *70*, 71, 73, 81–5, 87–92, 94, 114, 144, 148, 161, 178, 181, 184, 186, 203–5, 227, 239, 243, 247, 271, 277, 278–80, 282–4, 287, 290–3, 295–6, 298, 300, 304, 310–15, 325, 339, 375, 377–8, 387, 396–7, 400–2, 435, 437, 439–40, *441*, 444, 450, 452–3, 482–3, 502, 508, 579 n.22, 586 n.22, 589 n.3, 634 n.2

  archives of Appx 5 (vi)
  Armada tapestries commissioned by 485–6, 489, 498–9, 508
  campaign journal 5, 298
  Council of War advises 82, 296, 311, 325, 401
  Elizabeth's Instructions to 88–90, 203
Howard, Lord Thomas, nephew of Lord Admiral 85, Appx 3
Huerta, Juan de, Armada Paymaster-General 311
Huguenots *see* France, Protestants
Hume, Martin A. S., historian, 505–6, 526
Hunsdon, Henry Carey, baron 177, 441, *441*

Idiáquez, Don Juan de, principal secretary of state to Philip II 26, 53, 168, 192, 195–6, 210–11, 224–5, 233–5, 237–8, 240, 242, 270, 377, 412–14, 416–17, 420, 423, 429, 457
Idiáquez, Martín de, minister of state to Philip II 281
Illagh Castle, Donegal, Ireland 334
Illescas, Gonzalo de, polemical author 107, 214, 578 n.12
India, Portuguese 182, 191–2, 449, 481
Infantado, Iñigo López de Mendoza, 5th duke of 233
Inquisition *see* Spain
'Invincible Armada', first use of term 442–3, *442*
Iran, shah of 147, 163, 201
Ireland
  Catholic exiles 38, 53, 61, 65, 113, 123, 160
  commemoration of loss of life in shipwrecks 509–11, *510*, *511*
  English troops in 333–4, 339, 349–50, 351, 358–9, 366, 370

hostility to English 114, 129, 340, 349, 359, 371, 448, 468, 479
massacre of survivors 334, 340–1, 353–5, 358, 366, 370, 512
plans for diversionary attack on 113, 165–6, 168, 171, 173, 194–7, 199
plans to invade 114, 117, 147, 413
Privy Council 512
reaction to failure of Armada 448
Spanish soldiers in 125, 353, 355, 367, 448
treatment of survivors by Irish 23, 332–3, 354, 358–9
wrecks on coast 2, *3*, 6, 23, 125, 327–8, 339–40, *342*, 343, *344*, 350–1, 354–6, *357*, 364, 370, 419, 512–13, 526, 536–7, 544; *see also entries for individual shipwrecks*
*see also* Smerwick

Iriarte brothers, from Zumaya 24, 419
Isabella Clara Eugenia, daughter of Philip II 115, 232, 411, 456, 620 n.1
*Isabella* (Vizcaya), *patache* 352, Appx 1–2
Isla, Nicolás de, *maestre de campo* 18, 258, 277, 419

Jackson, Clare, historian 461
James I, king of England and Ireland and James VI of Scotland 107, 111, 147, 179, 181, 363, 368, 438, 452, 482, 487
James II, duke of York and later king of England, Ireland and Scotland 461–7, 497, 518–19, 543
James V, king of Scotland 103, 327
*Jesus of Lübeck* 74, 108–10, 432, Appx 4.2
Joinville, treaty of (1584) 137, 181, Appx 5 ch.5
Juan, Marolín de, chief pilot 241, 263, 322, 608 n.22
*Judith* 108, 110

*Juliana* (Levant) 34, 187, *344*, Appx 1–2
wreck of, Streedagh, Sligo, Ireland 6, 355, *357*, 358, 360, 393, *394*, 448, 511, 519, 536–7, Appx 4.1B–C, 4.4

Kahane, Nicholas 512
Kelly, John, major, Burt Castle 334
Kent, 103, 166, 172, 467, 470, 478–9, 481
beacon system 278, *279*
landing-zone for Armada 16, 48, 68, 169, 173, 196, 199, 256–7, 305, 307, 459, 476
weak defences 378, 400, 468–9, 472–4
Kent, Henry Grey, 6th earl of *179*
Khevenhüller, count, Imperial ambassador in Spain 149–50, 170, 201, 208, 237, 387, 418, 423, 477, 480, Appx 5 (vii)
Kingsley, Charles, historian and novelist 499–500
Kinnagoe Bay, Donegal, Ireland 6, 332, *332*, 533
Kinsale, Cork, Ireland 173, *344*, 452
knighthood, English 83, 84, 140, 299, 637 n.53
knighthood, Spanish 16, 18, 29–31, *30*, 108, 132, 152–3, *153*, 361, 420, 454–6, 568 n.29, 569 n.31–2
Knollys, Francis, privy councillor 148, 177

La Hogue, France 246
La Torre, Gerónimo de, friar 322, 324, 331
Lambarde, William, antiquary 278, *279*
landing-craft 133–4, *134*, 166
Lang, Andrew, identified 'Tobermory galleon' 523
*Lark* 272, Appx 3
Laughton, John Knox, naval historian 459, 505, 526

*Lavia* (Levant) 219, 275, 322, 326, 375, Appx 1–2
  wreck of, Streedagh, Sligo, Ireland 6, *344*, 355–6, *357*, 360, *510*, *511*, 536
Le Havre, Normandy, France 246, 353, 385, 419, *432*, 614 n.16
Leicester, Robert Dudley, earl of 55, 57, 68, 87–9, 104, 138, *139*, 140–1, 147–8, 161, 164, 177–8, 184, 216–17, 468, 473–6, 482, 576 n.33, 584 n.35, 589 n.1
  in Netherlands 216–17
  at Tilbury 436–7, 474, 489, 491, Appx 5 (vi), chs 7, 17
Leiden, Holland, Netherlands *49*, 226, 435, *436*, 514, 634 n.8
Leigh, William, preacher 487
Leighton, Sir Thomas, soldier 475–6
Leith, Scotland 338, 369
León, Lucrecia de, plaza prophet 43–4, 570 n.50
Lepanto, battle of (1571) 20, 36, *37*, 52, 120, 132, 158, 220, 378, 380, Appx 5 ch.11
Levant squadron, commanded by Martín de Bertendona 26, 34, 39, 198, 207, 212, 238, 261, 285, 326, 331, 341, 355, 362, 364, 389, 392, Appx 1–2, Appx 4.4
Leveson, Sir Richard 85, Appx 3
Lewis, Michael, naval historian 271
Leyva, Don Alonso Martínez de 17, 22, 27–8, 30, 32, *33*, 46, 53, 161, 198, 205–6, 214, 223, 245, 247, 256–7, 260–1, 270, 277, 282–3, 285, 291, 294, 314, 320, 322–4, 326, 331, 360–2, 371, 419, 425–6, 434, 456, 508, 513, 544, 569 n.36, 594 n.30, 622 n.25, 624 n.40, 42, Appx 5 chs 14–15
Lingard, John, Catholic historian 503

Linschoten, Jan Huyghen van, Dutch world traveller 393
*Lion* 73, 85, 188–90, 272, Appx 3
Lippomano, Hieronimo, Venetian ambassador in Madrid 41, 157, 180, 201, 445
Lisbon *14*, 18–20, *21*, 28, 40, 45–7, *60*, 123, 129–30, 158, 257, 355, 374, 376, 428, 446, 450, 467
  archbishop of 18
  naval base 15–16, 20, 23–8, 31–4, 36, 63, 85, 126, 131–2, 164, 166–8, 170–5, 183, 185, 187–92, 196–200, 202, 204–10, 212, 214–16, 219–20, 225–7, 231, *235*, 238, 243–4, 244–6, 255, 301, 306, 327, 331, 345, 351, 365, 381, 383, 385, 388, 390, 393, 411, 416, 419, 434, 455–6, 459, 508, 533, 535, Appx 4
  Ribeira Palace *14*, 15–16
  'Lisbon Muster' 38–9, *38*, 223, 570 n.41, Appx 4.1D
Lisle, John Dudley, viscount, father of Robert 87
Lizard, Cornwall, England 248, 281, *284*, 377
Loeffler, Gregorio, gunfounder, Augsburg 419, 519, Appx 4.4
London 16, 23, *49*, 67, 88, 92, 103–7, 114, 116, 125, 138, 141, 146, 158, 160, 167, 169–73, 178, 184–6, 190, 203, 205, 226, 230, 244, 271, 278–9, 288, 292, 305, 311, 338, 340, 353, 363, 378, 402, 434, 436–7, 439–40, 450, 452–3, 458–9, 461–3, 466–7, 469, 473, 476–80, 482–3, 486–7, 499–501, 504, 507–8, 513–14, 519–20, 524, 541, 543
  river of (Thames) 16, 103, 199, 437, 473–4
  Tower of 87, 110, 118, 120, 141, 172, *172*, 180, 279, 458, 474, 490, 501, Appx 4.2

weak defences 470–2
William III of Orange enters (1688) 466
Longin, Carlos, 367
López del Árbol, Balthasar, sergeant-major of Spanish infantry 149, 334, 497
Louis XIV, king of France 461
Low Countries *see* Netherlands
Loyola, Ignatius, founder of Jesuit Order 155, *430*
Lucar, Cyprian, gunner Appx 4.1
Lucas, John Seymour, artist 492, *492*
Luzón, Don Alonso de, *maestre de campo* 17, 20, 31, 214, 223, 314, 331–5, 361, 377, 383, 419, 569 n.31, 617 n.22, 629 n.47
after the Armada 454

McClancy, Tadhg óg, Rossclogher, Irish chieftain 359, 448
MacDonnell, Sorley Boy, Irish chieftain 513
McGurk, J.J., historian 472
Maclean, Sir Lachlan of Duart, Mull, Scotland 362–3, 369
Maclean clan, Mull 518
McLennan, Murdoch 373
Madrid, Spain *21*, 31, 33, 39–41, 43–4, 106, 115, 120–2, 135, 144, 149, 152, 157, 164, 170, 175, 180–1, 186, 190, 192, 201, 205, 209, 212, 216, 220, 231–2, 237, 241, 258, 302, 385, 387, 412, 414–15, 417, 421, 423, 427–9, 445–6, 454, 457–8, 474, 489, 494–5, 502–3, 507, 515, 526, 544
Magellan, Fernando, explorer 324, 326
Magellan, Strait of 29, 127–8, 140, 343, 392, Appx 5 ch.4
Mainwaring, Sir Henry, naval writer 275
Man, Dr John, English ambassador in Madrid 106–7, 111

Manona, Giovanni 350–1
Manrique, Don Antonio, *maestre de campo* 59
Manrique, Don Jorge, Inspector-General 237–8, 311, 322, 422, 606 n.8
*Margaret and John* 272, 288, Appx 3
Margate, Kent, England 16, 169, 173, 199–200, 300, 306, 375, 467, 477, 479–81
defences 469
Margate Cape (North Foreland) *49*, 199–200, 206, 240, 255–6, 281, 299
*María Juan* (Vizcaya) 261, 314, *316*, 319, 362, 364, Appx 1–2
Mariana, Juan de, Jesuit historian 493–4
*Marlyon* 124, 273, Appx 3
*Mary Rose* (1509–45) 69, *69*, 71, 79, 80, 83, 87, 273, *273*, *398*, 525, Appx 4.1D, 4.2
*Mary Rose* (1557–1618) 73, 81, 272, Appx 3
Mary Stuart, queen of Scotland 101–7, *101*, 111–19, 130, 137–8, 141–2, 147, 161–2, 165, 172, 176–9, *179*, 181, 184–5, 327, 441–2, 469, 487, 500–1
Mary Tudor, queen of England 73, 87, 103–4, 141, 176, 487
married to Philip II of Spain 26, 72–3, 101, *103*, 104–5, 478, Appx 4.4
Mattingly, Garrett, historian 506, 571 n.58
Matute, Francisco Ruiz 20, 351, *351*, 531
Mauld, James, diver 518
Maxwell, John 8th Lord 181
*Mayflower* of London 272, Appx 3
Medici, Catherine de, queen dowager of France 137
Medici, Giovanni de' 422, 428–9
Medina, Pedro de, humanist 28

Medina Sidonia, Don Alonso Pérez de Guzmán el Bueno, 7th duke of, commander of Armada 4, 15–17, 19–20, 23, 25, 27–32, 34, 36, 38, 40, 44, 47, 126, 129, 168, 175, 187, 189, 191, 196, 198, 208–11, *208*, 213–15, 218–21, 224–5, 231, 234–47, 256–8, 260–3, 265, 269–71, 276–7, 281–2, 287–8, 290–300, 313–14, 316, 318, 320, 322, 324–5, 371, 375–7, 380–1, 383, 401, 412–13, 420–2, 424–6, 435, 456, 470, 481–2, 493, 521, 578 n.12, 598 n.5, 607 n.12, 623 n.31, 32, Appx 5 ch.9
  after the Armada 416–17, 419, 422
  blamed for failure of Armada 425–6
  campaign *diario* 5, 299, 328, 446
  communication with Parma 218, 234, 240, 246–7, 255, 279, 281, 296, 299–307, 328, 387, 415, 421
  correspondence with Philip II 210–12, 234–6, 239–40, 257–8, 260, 269–70, 281, 306–7, 412–13, 416
  correspondence with Recalde 288, *288*, 324
  Council of War 28, 237, 245, 269, 282, 295, 387
  fighting instructions 262–3, *263*, *264*, 264–8
  Instructions to fleet 231, 243
  Instructions from Philip II 255–6, 262, 413
  order of battle 258, *259*, 260–2, 282, *286*
  preparations for Armada 209–10, 214–15, 219–26, *221*, *223*, 230–2
  religious devotion 46, 297
  return to Spain 325, 327–8, 341, 345, 352–3, 371, 404
  slow to care for survivors 416–17
Medrano, Diego de, commander of the galleys 28

Medway river, Kent, England 118, 469–70
Melville, James, minister, Anstruther, Fife, Scotland 338
Mendoza, Don Bernardino de, Spanish ambassador in London, then Paris, 99, 129–30, 142, 149, 177, 185–6, 412, 415, 421, 443, 449, 457–8, 581 n.1–2, 586 n.23, 589 n.1
Menéndez de Avilés, Pedro, admiral and colonizer of Florida 108, 121–2, 125, 271, 495
*Merchant Royal* 272, Appx 3
Mexía, Don Agustín, *maestre de campo* 15, 18, 53, 383, 419, 426
  after the Armada 456, 495
Mexico, 108–9, *109*, 118, 261, 276, 457–8, 502; see also New Spain
Millar, Archibald, diver 518–19, 524, 531
*Minion* 108–10
*Minion* of Bristol 272, Appx 3
*Minion* of London 272, Appx 3
*Minion* of Plymouth 272, Appx 3
Moncada, Don Hugo de, commander of the galleasses 28, 291–4, 315, 322, 380, 419, 605 n.23
Monson, Sir William, seaman 92, 274, 473, 577 n.44
Montalbán, Juan Pérez de, playwright 493
Montenegro, Francisco de, soldier 417
*Moon* 272, Appx 3
Morán, Perucho, galleass commander 380
Moresin, Francesco, staff officer and courier *235*, 303, 306–7, 572 n.17, 607 n.12–13
Mountgomerie, John, naval writer 253, 280, 444, 627 n.19
Mount's Bay, Cornwall, England 231, 246

Moura, Don Cristóbal de, minister of Philip II, 211, 232, 234, 237, 240, 451, 457
Mull, Isle of, Scotland 6, 362, *363*, 364, 492, 515–19
Mundy, Peter, world traveller 540, 542
munitions *see* artillery
Muros, Galicia, Spain, surviving ships return to 372, 419, 515
museums and collections
　Clare Museum, Ennis, Ireland *34*
　Inveraray Castle, Argyll, Scotland 518, Appx 4.1B
　Mull Museum, Tobermory, Scotland 523
　Museo Nacional de Arqueología Subacuática, Cartagena, Spain 511
　Museo Naval, Madrid 515
　Museum of London 268
　National Museum of Ireland, Dublin 537
　National Museum of the Royal Navy, Portsmouth, England 509
　Royal Museums Greenwich, London 508
　Shetland Museum and Archives 532–3
　Tower Museum, Derry/Londonderry, N Ireland 534
　Ulster Museum, Belfast 351, 507, 528, 531, 533–4
　West Highland Museum, Fort William, Scotland 523

Naples, Spanish viceroyalty 38, *103*, 166, 175, 196, 275, 597 n.25, Appx 5 (iii)
　troops from 17, 20, *21*, 23, 28, 60, *60*, 331–5, 589 n.48
*Napolitana*, galleass 380, 390, 618 n.32, Appx 1–2
Narrow Seas 16, 173, 195, 200, 204, *229*, 230, 295, 300, 305, 340, 375, 428
　fleet 48, 67, 72, 82, 173, 205, 277–8, 304, *304*, 311–12, 314, 325, 401, 440, 540

Nash, Thomas, satirist 300
Nassau, Justinus of, illegitimate son of William 55, 57, 218, 310
Nassau, Maurice of, son of William 58, 321, 435, 542
Nassau, William of *see* William of Nassau
Navarre, Henry of *see* Henry of Navarre
Navy Board *see* England
navy royal (1588) 67–8, 89–90, Appx 3
　abandons pursuit *10–11*, 325
　ability to carry heavy artillery 78, 80, 121
　ability to operate artillery at sea 397, *398*, 399
　after the campaign 82, 378–80, 383, 436, 439–40
　battle formation 272, 296–7, *297*
　common language, weights and measures 277, 397
　cost of maintenance 86
　Council of War 82, 296, 311, 401
　crews 76, 82–4, 91–2, 277
　development of 68–73, 76–81, *77*, *78*, 80
　England's best defence 68, 74
　firepower 75, 291, 317, 402
　follows Armada up Channel 284, *284*, 291–2
　leaves Plymouth 92, 282–3, *283*
　music 293
　navigational aids 278, *329*, *330*
　private vessels 84–5, 272
　race-built ships 72, 76, *78*, 79–80, 82, 121, 271, 273, 277, 382
　rations 222
　strategy 295
　superior sailing qualities 277, 304, 308, 316, 382, 399
　supplies 205, 243, 247, 279–80
　tactics 271, 291–2, 295
Naylor, Margaret, 'lady diver' 523, *523*

Netherlands 16–17, 20, 23, 25–7, 33, 42, 46, 48, *49*, 50–5, 57, 59, 61, 63–6, 102, 105–6, 110–11, 114, 116, 118, 120–1, 130–1, 135, 138, 141–5, 149, 151, 158–9, 161–5, 168–9, 171, 173–4, 180–2, 185–6, 192, 195–7, 200, 216–18, 225, 227, 237, 305, 308, 328, 334, 367, 375, 400, 421, 435, 445, 447, 449, 452, 456, 458, 468, 471, 479–80, 497
  refugees from, in England 121
  religious diversity 49–50
  Spanish embargo of shipping from (1585) 144–5, 182, 584 n.27
  Spanish reconquest of 50, 53–8, 137, 162–4, 217
  States-General of 6, 51, 54–5, 58, 66, 217, 467, 479, 542
  *see also* Army of Flanders; Banks of Flanders; Brabant; Dutch Republic; Dutch Revolt; Flanders; Hainaut; Holland; Parma; Zeeland
Neumann, John von, mathematician 213
New Spain, Spanish viceroyalty 108–9, *109*, 118, 376, 454, 457–8; *see also* Mexico
Nicolay, Nicholas de, pilot and chart-maker 327
Nieuwpoort, Flanders 48, *49*, 61–3, 218, *229*, 308–10, *309*, 318, 422–4, 438
Nombre de Dios, New Spain, captured 450
*Nonpareil* 73, 272, 376, Appx 3
Nonsuch, treaty of (1585) 148, 185
Norfolk, England *438*, 474–6, *475*, 478, 483, 486
Norfolk, Henry Fitzalan-Howard, 15th duke of, 500
Norfolk, Thomas Howard, 4th duke of 116–20, 579 n.25
Normandy, France 225, 255, 412, 469
Norris, Sir John 87–8, 444–6, 474, 476
North Foreland *see* Margate Cape

North Sea 1, 35, 51, 122, 241, 299–300, 303, 320–1, 326, *326*, 328, 420, 436, 449
Northumberland, 10th earl of, Lord Admiral 540–1
Norton, Robert, gunner and author 393
Norway, Armada survivors in 323, 325, 335, 364–5, *365*, 369, 435, 544, 615 n.30
*Nuestra Señora de Begoña* (Castile) 261, Appx 1–2
*Nuestra Señora del Rosario* (Andalucia) 21, 23, 35, 229, 243–4, 246, 270–1, 275, 286–90, *287*, 367, 371, 381–2, 401–2, 414, 425, 427, 439, 453–4, 458, 487, 513–14, Appx 1–2, Appx 4.2; *see also* Valdés, Don Pedro de
'Nun of Lisbon' *see* Visitación, Sor Maria de la

Ødegaard, Torbjørn 544
O'Donnell, Hugh Roe, Irish chieftain 334
Ojeda, Agustín de, commander of *pataches* & *zabras* 27–8, 322, 430
Olivares, count of, Spanish ambassador in Rome 122, 157–8, 161–2, 165, 183–4, 411, 580 n.41, 587 n.33
Olivares, Don Gaspar de Guzmán, count-duke of, son of ambassador 445–6, 495–6, 539, 569 n.32, Appx 5 (ii)
Oliveira, Fernando, naval writer 258, 260
Olmos, Alonso de, captain of Spanish infantry 365
O'Malley, Dowdarra Roe, Irish chieftain 354, 512
Oquendo, Don Antonio de, son of Miguel, admiral 496, 539–40
Oquendo, Miguel de, commander of Guipúzcoan squadron 26–31, 46, 231, 241, 258, 261, 291–2, 314, 319,

322, 372, 381, 383, 390, 417, 419, 495, 514, Appx 4.4
Orange *see* Nassau; William of Orange
Orkney islands, Scotland 2, 6, *10–11*, 327–8, 335, 338, 435
O'Rourke, Sir Brian, Irish chieftain 359, 448
Ortega, Juan (formerly Francisco Blanco), soldier 20
Ostend, Flanders *49*, 148, 309, *309*, 316, 318, 422, 471
O'Sullivan Beare, Philip, Irish Catholic historian 448
Ottoman empire 105, 120, 147, 163, 180
Padilla, Don Martín de, count of Santa Gadea, 191–2, 451
Palmer, Sir Henry 82, Appx 3
*Paloma Blanca* (*urca*) 383, Appx 1–2
Panama, isthmus of 121, 484
Paredes, count of 31, 362, 384
Paris, France 38, 40, 115, 138, 158, 177, 179, 181, 184, 186, 216, 302, 412, 415, 421, 457, 470
Parma, Alexander Farnese, duke of 2, 16, 30, 47–8, 52–66, *52*, 144, 161, 163–5, 169–74, 183–6, 194–5, 197, 199–204, 206, 216–18, 225–32, 239–40, 242, 255–7, 270, 279–81, 295–6, 298–311, 313, 316, 319, 323–5, 353, 369–70, 378, 387, 401–2, 412–16, 428–9, 435–8, 447, 449, 454, 476, 479–81, 496, 514
  archives of Appx 5 (iii)
  blamed for failure of Armada 420–4, 494
  communication with Medina Sidonia 218, 234, 240, 246–7, 255, 279, 281, 296, 299–307, 328, 387, 415, 421
  if he had landed 455–73
  Instructions from Philip II 256–7
  ransoms prisoners 367
  religious devotion 63–4
Parma, Margaret of, mother of Alexander, regent in Netherlands 50
Pasajes, Guipúzcoa, Spain 24, 372, 383, 390, 514, Appx 1
*Passport* 272, Appx 3
*pataches* & *zabras*, squadron of, commanded by Agustin de Ojeda 27, 35, 39, 364, 430, Appx 1–2
Paulet, Sir Amias, custodian of Mary Queen of Scots 178
peace between England and Spain (1603) 452
Pedroso, Bernabé de, Victualler-General 311, 322
Peñafiel, Juan Téllez Guzmán, marquis of (later duke of Osuna) 32, 314, 383
Peniche, Portugal 445
Pennington, Sir John, admiral 540–1
Percyvall, Richard, compiler of Spanish-English dictionary 453, *453*, 457
Pereda, Don Melchor de, staff officer 367
Perrenot, Tomás, nephew of Cardinal Granvelle 22, 362
Peru, Spanish viceroyalty of 127
Philip II, king of Spain 1, 5, 9, 15–19, 25–9, 31–2, 36, 38–43, *40*, *41*, 50–2, 54–5, 57–8, 60, 64–6, 85, 87–8, 90, 104–8, 112–23, 135, 134, 137–8, 140, 142–4, 146–8, 150–3 *153*, 155–65, *155*, *156*, 167–8, 170–5, 177, 179, 181–6, 190, 192–203, 205–13, *213*, 216–19, 225–7, 229, 232–7, 240–2, 255–8, 260, 269, 271, 288, 303, 306–7, 310, 337–9, 365, 368, 374, 395, 423, 425–8, 431, 439, 445–52, 454–7, 461–2, 465, 467, 476–8, 480–2, 489, 491, 503, 506, 539
  after the Armada 411–20, 446–8
  archives of Appx 5 (ii)
  armchair strategist 174

Philip II (*cont.*)
   authorizes 12 galleons of new design 430, 541
   bankruptcy (1575) 51, (1596) 451
   blamed for failure of Armada 428–9, 493–4
   children 151–2, 232, 411
   Council of War 39, 198, 206, 241, 418, 420, 426, 495
   desire to restore Catholicism in England 1, 65, 106, 113–16, 164, 183–4, 195, 199
   dress 152–3
   empire *10–11*, 18, 39, *41*, 48, 126, 135, 151–2, 157–60, 196, 205, 434, 484
   'Enterprise of England' 4, 7, 16, 18, 33, 44, 48, 59, 61, 68, 99, 115–16, 151, 160–3, 165–75, *172*, 182, 184, 192, 194, 196, 198–9, 201, 207, 211, 212–13, 227, 236, 255, 258, 291, 305–6, 373, 377, 415, 421–4, 457, 462, 477, 479–81, 494, 496–7
   'Grand Design' *see* 'Enterprise of England'
   ill-health 197–8, 205, 211, 239, 418
   improves English navy 72–3
   inbred 481
   Instructions to Medina Sidonia 255–6, 262, 413
   Instructions to Parma 64, 200, 202, 256–7
   Instructions to Santa Cruz 200, 202
   intelligence service 158
   married to Mary Tudor 26, 72–3, 101, *103*, 104–5, 478, Appx 4.4
   Masterplan *see* 'Enterprise of England'
   offer to marry Elizabeth 105
   plans to invade Ireland 114, 117, 147, 194–6, 413, 451
   postal service 158
   religious devotion 154–7, *155*, 418
   style of government 151–4, 157–60, 198
   support for bereaved and survivors 420
   would like to lead Armada 213
Philip III, king of Spain 411, 448, 452, 457, 481, 482, *488*, 586 n.21, 635 n.21
*Philip and Mary see Nonpareil*
Phillips, Carla Rahn, historian 127
Piatti, Giovanni Battista, engineer and courier 170, 174, 197, 422
Piedrola, Miguel de, plaza prophet 43–4, 428, 625 n.49
Pimentel, Don Diego, maestre de campo 18, 20, 28, 149, 190, 305, 314, 318, 383–4, 419, 454–6, *455*, 495, 600 n.22
Pine John, engraver 498
pirates 109, 219, 383
Pitt, Henry, gunfounder, London Appx 4.2
Pius V, pope (1566–72) 111–13
Plymouth, Devon, England 5, 66–7, 71, 90–2, 107, 110, 118, 140, 148, 185–6, 190, 202, 204–5, 227, 242–3, 247–8, 2, 260, 271–2, 278, 281–3, *283*, *284*, 285, 301, 303, 305, 366, 377, 425, 433, 439, *463*, 491–2, *492*, 500–2, 504, 509
Portland Bill, Dorset, England *284*, 291–2, *291*, 303, *463*, 464
Portsmouth 69, 86, 92, 279, *284*, 291, 295, *398*, 399–400, *463*, 466, 478, 509
Portugal 15–17, 19–20, 25, 32, 39, 107, 126, 144–5, 175, 177, 185–6, 192, 195, 233, 237, 258, 328, 376, 415, 428, 433–4, 445–6, 450, 456–7
   Anglo-Dutch invasion (1589) 375, 443–6, 451
   soldiers and sailors from 19–20, 341, 345, 366
   Spanish conquest of 15–16, 25, 32, 40, 126, 129–37, 159–60, 174, 207, 374, 449, 467, 481

squadron of, commanded by the duke of Medina Sidonia, 23, 25, 32, 36, 39, 166, 231, 246, 261, 277, 284, 297, 314, 317, 324, 326, 345, 364, 376, 380, 382–4, 388, 390, 392, 435, 445, 458, 508, 514, Appx 1–2
*Primrose* 145–6, *146*, 148, 262, Appx 5 ch.5
*Prince Royal* 542
privateers
　Dutch 130
　English 66, 77, 85, 121, 130, 393, 499
　French Huguenot 110, 115, 121
prophets of doom in England 93
prophets of doom in Spain 43–4, 428

Quendale *see* Sinclair
Queralt, Don Luis, *maestre de campo* 59, 61
Querquerman, Burgat, owner and master of *Gran Grifón* 337
Quiroga, Gaspar de, Inquisitor-General 121–3, 368

Raggazoni, Giacomo, owner of *Regazona* 515
Ragusa (Dubrovnik), merchant ships from 34, 166, 187, 354, 536, Appx 1, Appx 5 (iii) ch.21; *see also San Juan de Sicilia*
Raleigh, Sir Walter, soldier, explorer and historian 68, 79–80, 125, 396–7, 440, 468, 513, 543
*Rata (Santa María) Encoronada* (Levant) 32, 187, 261, 285, 292, 297, 314–15, 319, *344*, 360, 382, 385, 392, Appx 1–2
　burned, Blacksod Bay, Mayo, Ireland 512
Recalde, Juan Martínez de, commander of Vizcayan squadron 4, 26–8, 33, 36, 51, 122–3, 125, 168, 175, 191–2, 214–15, 223, 225–6, 237–43, 245–7, 257–8, 261, 277, 281–5, 288, *288*, 290–4, 298–300, 313–14, 320, 322–7, 331, 345–50, *347*, 352, 374–5, 381–4, 419, 433, 447, 455, 495, 526
　blames Medina Sidonia for failure of Armada 425–6
　campaign journal 4–5, 293, 318, 345–6, 348, 390
　in Blasket Sound 343–51, *347*
　religious devotion 46
　surveys coast of SW Ireland 123
*Red Lion* of London 272, Appx 3
*Regazona* (Levant) 219, 292, 314, 372, 385, 419, 455, 515, 544, Appx 1–2, Appx 4.4
Requena, Alonso, prisoner escaped from flag galley 459
Requesens, Don Luis de, governor-general of the Netherlands 51, 58, 122, 130, 159
*Revenge*, flagship of Sir Francis Drake 2, 77, *124*, 272–3, 293–4, 296, 380, 401–3, 432, 444, 515, Appx 3, 4.2
Ribadeneira, Pedro de, Jesuit 44, 46, 209, 226–7, 429, *430*, 443, 452, 570 n.51, 597 n.25
Ribadeo, Galicia 35
　surviving ship returns 419
Ridolfi, Roberto, Florentine banker in London and conspirator 579 n.29
Ridolfi Plot 114–21, 137–8, 141, 160, 164, 176, 194, 634 n.2, Appx 5 ch.4
Rinaldi, Paolo, Parma's chamberlain and chronicler 57, 63–4, 623 n.31, Appx 5 (iv)
Rizzacasa, Giorgio, mathematician and astrologer 43, 448–9
Roanoke, North Carolina 144, 168
Rodger, Nicholas, historian 68, 81–2, 89, 542–3, 602 n.22
*Roebuck* 513–14, Appx 3
Rogers, Richard, parson, Essex 476, 478, 483

Romney, Kent, England 240, 599 n.13
*Rosario see Nuestra Señora del Rosario*
Ross, John Leslie, bishop of 119–20
Rossclogher Castle, Leitrim, Ireland 359
Rostock, Germany, Baltic port 6, 35, 337
Rowe, Jacob, diver 520–2, *520, 522*, 524, 532
*Royal Defence* 272, Appx 3
Ruiz, Simón, banker 175
Ryther, Augustine, engraver 3, 272, *283, 286, 287, 291, 297, 304, 326, 342, 365*, 485, 508–9

Sagres, Algarve, Portugal 189, 375
*St Andrew see San Andrés*
St Andrews University, Scotland 4, 516, 517, 523, 533–4
St James *see* Santiago
Salazar, Eugenio de, judge 220–1
*San Andrés* (*urcas*) 187, Appx 1–2
*San Andrés*, one of Twelve Apostles 433
San Antón island, Corunna, Spain 243, 515
*San Bernardo* (Portugal) 381 Appx 1–2
*San Cristóbal* (Castile) 36, 246, 382, Appx 1–2
*San Cristóbal* (Portugal) 381, 388, Appx 1–2
*San Esteban* (Guipúzcoa) 341, *344*, 513, Appx 1–2
*San Esteban* (Vizcaya) 345–6, Appx 1–2
*San Felipe* (Portugal) 36, 85, 231, 261, 314, *316*, 317–18, 514, Appx 1–2
*San Francisco* (Andalucia) 388–9, Appx 1–2, Appx 4.4
*San Francisco* (Castile) *221*, Appx 1–2
*San Francisco* (Portugal/Levant) *see Florencia*
*San Juan* (Portugal), vice-flagship of fleet 10–11, 33, 231, 261, 284–5, 288, 290, 296, 345, 349, 372, 380, 383, 397, 445, 458, 508, 515, Appx 1–2

*San Juan Bautista de la Esperanza* (Levant) 389, Appx 1–2
*San Juan Bautista* (Castile) 261, 343, 348, 352, 372, Appx 1–2
*San Juan Fernandome* (Castile) *344*, 352, 383, 510, 526, Appx 1–2
*San Juan Menor* (Castile) 261, 314, Appx 1–2
*San Juan de Sicilia* (Levant) 34, 187, 220, 261, 298, 314, 319, 326, 362–4, 383, 395, 515, Appx 1–2
wreck of, Tobermory, Mull, Scotland 6, 515–26, Appx 4.1B–C, 4.4
San Juan de Ulúa, Mexico 108–10, *109*, 115, 261, 273, 376, 399, Appx 4.2
prisoners from 118, 580 n.32
*San Lorenzo*, galleass flagship *37*, *259*, 275, 292, 312–13, 315–16, *315*, 382, 385, 390, 402, 414, *432*, 514, 600 n.29, 605 n.23, Appx 1–2
*San Luís* (Portugal) 261, 297–8, 381, 388, Appx 1–2
*San Marcos* (Portugal) 32, 261, 314, 383, 544–5, Appx 1–2
*San Martín* (Portugal), Armada flagship 23, *35*, 36, 224, 236, 261, 263, *264*, 264, 268–9, 281, 285, 291, 293, 295–6, 299, 305–6, 313–14, 316–17, 322–3, 331, 352, 371, 376, 380, 383, 380, 388, 392, 397, 402, 416, Appx 1–2
*San Mateo* (Portugal) 36, 132, 261, 314, *316*, 317–18, 374, 384, 392, 433, 435, *436*, 455, 514, Appx 1–2
*San Mateo*, one of Twelve Apostles 433
*San Nicolás Prodaneli 344*, 354, Appx 1–2
*San Pedro* 109–10
*San Pedro* (Castile) 32, 319, 322, Appx 1–2
*San Pedro Mayor* (*urcas*) 19, 187, 223, 286, 365–7, 384, Appx 1–2
wrecked Hop Cove, Devon, England 365–7, 514

*San Salvador* (Guipúzcoa) 23, 261, 285–6, *286*, 290, 367, 381–4, 414, 419, 514, Appx 1–2, Appx 4.2, 4.4
*San Salvador* (*urcas*) 261, 317, Appx 1–2
San Sebastián, Guipúzcoa 24, 26, 30, 35, 351, 372, 417
  surviving ships return to 419
Sánchez, Ciprián, chart-maker 226, Appx 5 ch.9
Sánchez Coello, Alonso, artist 153
Sanlúcar de Barrameda, Andalucia, Spain 4, 20, 25, 196, 198, *208*, 214, 257, 260, 322, 425, 454–5
*Santa Ana* (Guipúzcoa) 23, 27, 253, 292, 314, 319, 381, 383, 417, 514, Appx 1–2, Appx 4.4
*Santa Ana* (Vizcaya) 23, 236, 246, 261, 277, 353, Appx 1–2
*Santa Ana* (*urcas*) 274–5, Appx 1–2
*Santa Bárbara* (Guipúzcoa) 389, Appx 1–2
*Santa Bárbara* (*urcas*) 322, 341, *344*, Appx 1–2
*Santa Catalina* (Andalucia) 389, Appx 1–2
*Santa Clara* 109–10
Santa Cruz, Don Álvaro de Bazán, marquis of 15–17, 20, 24–8, 32–3, 35–6, 43, 126, 130–4, *131*, 160–7, 160–1, 165–8, 171, 173–5, 183, 189, 191–2, 198–202, 205–8, 210, 212, 215, 219, 224, 255, 303, 374, 381, 400, 419, 451, 456, 502–3
*Santa María de la Rosa* (Guipúzcoa) 20, 24, 35, 236, 239, *244*, 261, 319, 384, Appx 1–2, Appx 4.6
  wreck, Blasket Sound, Kerry, Ireland 6, *347*, 349–51, *351*, 510, 519, 524, 526, 529–31, *530*, 533
*Santa María de Visón* (Levant) Appx 1–2
  wreck, Streedagh, Sligo, Ireland 6, 347, 349, *349*, 352, 511, 536

Santander, Spain 36, 116, 118, 174, 371–2, 494–5
  surviving ships return 384, 386, 388, 392, 397, 416, 419, 425–6
*Santiago* (Portugal) 246, 324, 381–2, 388, Appx 1–2
*Santiago* (*urcas*) 23, 187, wrecked off Bergen, Norway 365, 544, Appx 1–2
Santiago, patron saint of Spain 43, *136*
Santillán, Don Rodrigo de, judge 426–8
Santo Domingo, Caribbean 135, sacked by Drake 168
São Miguel, Azores, 15, 35–6, *35*, 129, 132, 166, 190, 374
*São Phelipe*, captured by Drake 190
Savoy, Charles Emanuel, duke of 152, 162, 421
Scheldt *see* Antwerp
Scilly, Isles of, Cornwall, England 142, 231, 236, 238, *284*, 234, 331, 335, 353
Scotland 2, 5–6, 50, 54, 71, 73–4, 89, 99, 101–6, 111–12, 117–18, 147, 172, 177, 179, 181, 203–5, 218, 227, 325, 327, 338, 343, 359–65, 367–9, 375, 413, 415, 438, 452, 461–2, 478, 487, 492, 498, 500, 509, 515–16, 518, 539
Scott, Sir Thomas, soldier 476
Scott, Thomas, pamphleteer 491
sea crossings, health effects on men and animals 464, 469–70, 477
Sebastian, king of Portugal, 126, 492
Sepúlveda, Jerónimo de, friar 493
Seville, Andalucia, Spain 21, *21*, 23, 29, 157, 187–8, 206, 209, 414, 456–7, *535*, 580 n.32, 630 n.51
Seymour, Lord Henry 82–5, 205, 277–9, 304, 310, 314, 401, 440, 482, 502
Sharpe, Kevin, historian 541
Sharpe, Lionel 489, 491
Sheffield, Douglas, sister of Admiral Howard and wife of Sir Edward Stafford, 184, Appx 5 ch.7

Sheffield, Edmund, 3rd baron 85, *441*, Appx 3
Shetland islands, Scotland 2, 6, *10–11*, 331, 335–7, 416, 532–3
ship and boat types
  caravel, with Armada 35, 39, 47
  cromster 444
  felucca, with Armada 34, 39, 47, 226–7, 230–1, 282, 290, 313, 322, 456
  galleass 6, 36, *37*, *38*, 46, 133, *134*, 166, 171, 175, 196, 275, 312, 315–16, 353, 360–1, 374, 380, 385, 402–3, 431, 432, 444, 484, 514
    rudder problems 246, 315, 352–3, 382, 431, *432*
  galley 15, 20, 25, 28, 36, *37*, 47, 108, 122, 126, 133–4, *134*, 148, 157–8, 166–8, 171, 188–92, 199, 201, 207, 219–20, 260, 304, 308, 374, 403, 482
  Indies Guard vessels 188, 191, 196, 219, 257, 276–7, 454, 495, 535
  *patache* 35, 168, 171, 238, 246, 258, 281, 285–7, 290, 294, 301, 303, 306, 313, 320, 341–2, 371
  pinnace 84–5, 144–5, 148, 185–6, 247, 271, 278, 322, 415
  *see also* Glossary
shipbuilding
  English 76–8
  Spanish 35, 541
shipworm (*Teredo navalis*) 80, 81
Shovell, Sir Cloudesley, admiral 543–4
Shrewsbury, George Talbot, earl of *179*, *441*, 442
Sicily, Spanish viceroyalty 175, 589 n.48
  merchant ships from 166, 187, 197, 331
  troops from 18, 20, 190, 351, 623 n.30
Sidney, Sir Philip 148

siege-guns *see* artillery
Sigüenza, José de, friar, keeper of relics at Escorial and historian 493–4, Appx 5 ch.6
Silva, Don Juan de, councillor to Philip II 154, 159–60, 450
Silva, Don Vasco de, prisoner in England 453
Simancas Castle, Valladolid, Spain, archives in 4, *4*, 181, 386, 388, 503, 505–6, 533, 588 n.37, 637 n.46, Appx 5 (ii)
Sinclair, George 516–17, *517*
Sinclair, Malcolm of Quendale, Shetland 337–8
Sixtus V, pope (1585–90) 64–5, 153, 162, 164, 183–4
Sluis, Flanders, 216–18, 308–10
Smerwick, Kerry, Ireland, Hispano-Papal landing at (1580) 26, 123–6, *124*, 129, 160, 165, 273, 339, 341, *344*, *347*, 348, 370, 375, 399
Smollett, John, of Dumbarton 363
Smythe, Sir John, English ambassador to Spain 122–3, 474
Solent 26, 28, 85, 103, 256, 273, *284*, 295–6, 298, 375, 402; *see also* Wight, Isle of
Soranguren, Juan de, sailor 364
South Atlantic, fleet to *see* Magellan, Strait of
Southampton, Hampshire, England, 26–8, 168, 172, 174, 197, 242
Southwell, Sir Robert 85, Appx 3
*Sovereign of the Seas* 542
Spain 2, 5, 7, 16, *21*, 23, 28–9, 33, 43–4, 107–8, 151
  amphibious operations 15, 25, 34, 113, 126, 130, *134*, 160, 163, 165–6, 168, 173–4, 302, 374
  Council of the Indies 175, 182
  Council of State 39, 120, 454, 456, 495

Council of War 28, 39, 198, 206, 241, 418, 420, 426, 495
depression after failure of Armada 434, 492–5
Inquisition 28–9, 31, 39, 50, 121, 145, 153, 156, 171, 368, 428, 452, 457, 491, 499
Spanish America 163, 168, 185, 197
treasure-fleets from 18, 20, 23, 110, 121, 150, 157, 192, 196, 198
*see also* Mexico; New Spain; Peru
'Spanish Fury' in Antwerp (1576) 51, 57, 478
'Spanish Road', military corridor from Lombardy to the Netherlands *10–11*, 52, 57, 59–60, 158, 161, 170, 218, 456
*Spark* of Plymouth 272, Appx 3
Speciano, Cesare, papal nuncio in Spain 414–15, 418, 429, 592 n.16, 622 n.29, Appx 5 (vii)
Spes, Don Guerau de, Spanish ambassador in England 107, 110–11, 114–15, 118, 119, 129, 149, Appx 5 ch.4
Spierincx, François, tapestry weaver 485–6
Spotswood Green, William, antiquarian and Fisheries Inspector 526
Stafford, Sir Edward, English ambassador in Paris 184–6, Appx 5 ch.7
Stanley, Sir William 431, 471, 625 n.55
Start Point, Devon, England 278, *284*
Sténuit, Robert, diver 527–8
Strada, Famiano, historian, 56, Appx 5 ch.4
Strait of Magellan *see* Magellan
Streedagh Strand, Sligo, Ireland, 3 wrecks 6, 275, *344*, 356–9, *357*, 393, 448, 510–13, *510–11*, 519, 536–7

Strozzi, Filippo, naval commander for Dom António 130, 132
Stuart *see* Mary Stuart
Stukeley, Thomas, Irish adventurer 114–15, 160
Stukeley, William, son of Thomas, aboard *Rosario*, then *San Martín* 271, 278, 283, 285, 287–90, 293, 314, 321, Appx 5 ch.10
*Swallow* 272, Appx 3
*Swiftsure* *124*, 272–3, 602 n.25, Appx 3

Tagus, river *see* Lisbon
Tasovčić, Stefan Olisti 342, Appx 1–2
Teixeira, Luis, chart-maker 225, Appx 5 ch.9
Terceira, Azores 15, 17, 27–9, 31, 46, 126, 132–6, *134*, 160–1, 166, 174, 215, 238, 374, 380, 467, Appx 4.2
commemorative bowl *136*
Thames, river *see* London
Thanksgiving service and day (1588), England 440–1, 489
*Thomas* of Plymouth 272, Appx 3
Thomas, William, master gunner 396–7
Thompson, I.A.A., historian 536
Throckmorton, Francis, Catholic conspirator 141–2
Throckmorton, Sir Nicholas, ambassador to France 74
*Tiger* of London 272–3, 369, Appx 3
*Tiger* of Plymouth 272, Appx 3
Tilbury, Essex, army camp *49*, 57, 68, 89, 436–8, *438*, 443, 468, 474–5, 478, 483–4, *484*, 486, *488*, 489, 491, 508, Appx 5 ch.18
Elizabeth's speech at 436–8, *438*, 468, 478, 484, 486, 489, 508, Appx 5 ch.18
Tilton, William F., historian 505
Tobermory, Mull, Scotland 6, 362–3, *363*, 383, 492, 504, 515–25, 530–1
*Toby* of London 272, Appx 3

Toledo, Don Francisco de, *maestre de campo* 18, 20, 314, 317–18, 383, 419
tonnage measurements Appx 5 ch.16
Torbay, Devon, England *463*, 464, 466
Traunte, Captain James 349–50
Treleben, Hans Albrecht van, diver 518
*Trinidad* (Castile) 344–5, Appx 1–2
*Trinidad (de) Escala* (Levant) 320, 383–4, 389, 393, 617 n.24, Appx 1–2
*Trinidad Valencera* (Levant) 20, 34, 187, 220, 224, 236, *244*, 261, 314, 326, 361, 383, *398*, 454, 497, Appx 1–2
  wreck, Kinnagoe Bay, Donegal, Ireland 6, 22–3, *22*, *136*, 220–1, *222–3*, 225, 266–8, 275, *275*, *330*, 331–2, *332–3*, 335, 353, 361, 395, *396*, 533–6, *534–5*, Appx 4
*Triumph* 74, 81, 272, 292, 294, 298, Appx 3
Tromp, Maarten Harpertszoon, Dutch admiral 540–1
'troubleshooters 261, 284, 286, 291–2, 314, 317, 402
Tuscany, Ferdinand, grand duke of 53, 153, 164–5, 182, 258, 422
Tutbury Castle, Staffordshire, England 112
'Twelve Apostles', new design Spanish galleons 430–3, *431*, 541
Tyrone, Hugh O'Neill, earl of 448, 452

Ubaldini, Petruccio, Italian historian in England 376–7, 485, Appx 5 ch.20
Ugolini, Giovanni, historian 158
Ulloa y Sandoval, Don Antonio de 354–5, *355*
underwater archaeology 6–7, 511, 527–37, 544
underwater salvage 513–26
*Unity* 272, Appx 3
Upnor Castle, Kent, England 469–70, *470*

*urca* 6, 20, 23, 47, 166, 187–8, 206, 223–4, 231, 274–5, 297, 318, 322, 327, 331, 337, 341–2, 354, 360, 365, 371, 375, 377, 383, 387, 392, 521, 532, 544
  squadron of 26, 35, 39, 198, 230, 238, 261, 295, 335, Appx 1–2
Utrecht, Netherlands 49, 479

Valdés, Diego Flores de *see* Flores de Valdés, Diego
Valdés, Don Pedro de, commander of Andalusian squadron 27–31, 51, 108, 122, 125–7, 132, 238, 246, 258, 260–1, 270, 274–5, 277, 286–90, *287*, 294, 322, 374, 378, 401–2, 419, 425, 487, 491, 495, 513, 544, Appx 5 ch.18
  after the Armada 453–4
Valladolid *21*, 425–6, 458, 493
  English College of St Alban 458–9, 482
van Meteren, Emanuel, Dutch historian 401
Vanegas, Alonso, gunnery officer 268, 285, 293–4, 296, 313, 317, 319–20, 323, 331, 385, 390, 397, 402, Appx 5 ch.10
*Vanguard* 369, 403, Appx 3
*Vasa*, Swedish warship 518, 525
Vázquez, Alonso, soldier and chronicler 623 n.30, Appx 5 (iv)
Vázquez, Mateo, private secretary to Philip II 25, 42, *133*, 135, 170, 211–13, 232–3, 411, 413–14, 418, 447, 450, 457
Vega, Lope de, Spanish poet and playwright 33, 349, 458, 508
Venice 10–11, 34, 120, 158, 166, 187, 331, 536
Vera, Gerónimo de, Jesuit 458
*Victory* 1, 74, 272, Appx 3
Villafranca, Martín de 24, 351

Visitación, Sor María de la, the 'Nun of Lisbon' 18, 46, 428, Appx 5 ch.1
Vitoria, Juan de, friar and historian 493, Appx 5 (ii)
Vizcaya 175, 189, 328, 345
  merchant ships from 166
  squadron of 23, 26, 35, 39, 187, 189–90, 236, 246, 261, 277, 286, 314, 319, 352–4, 364, 374, 381, 389, 455, 459, Appx 1–2
  troops from 20
Vroom, Hendrik Corneliszoon, Dutch artist *250–1, 265*, 484–6, 634 n.5

Wagenaer, Lucas, Dutch cartographer 226, 229, *229*, 278, 327, *329*, Appx 5 ch.9
Wales, plans for diversionary attack 171
Walsingham, Sir Francis, secretary of state 1–2, 55, 87, 91, 138–41, *139*, 143–4, 146–8, 176–8, 180, 184–6, 294, 319, 363, 400, 437, 443, 446, 449, 471, 482, Appx 5 (vi) ch.7
Ward, Samuel, preacher and pamphleteer 487–8, *488*
Waterford, Ireland 166, 171, 341, *344*, 413
Westmoreland, Charles Neville, earl of 65
Weybourne Hope, Norfolk, England, defences 474–5, *475*
Weymouth, Dorset, England *284*, 290
White, Henry 284, Appx 3
*White Bear* 85, 272, 311, Appx 3
Whitelocke, James, judge 483
Whitgift, John, Archbishop of Canterbury 93, 147–8
Wight, Isle of 86, 103, 142, 195, 197, 212, 242, 256, 278, 281, *284*, 295–6, 298, 301, 303, 305–6, 347, 401–2, 447, 462–3, 465, 514; *see also* Solent
Wignall, Sydney, diver 529, 531, 675

William of Nassau, prince of Orange 50, 51, 53–5, 58, 111, 133–4, 136–8, 140, 142, 143, 216, 217, 566 n.3
William III, prince of Orange and later king of England, Scotland and Ireland, invasion of England (1688) 461–7, 469, 479, 497–8, 499
Williams, Sir Roger 57, 471
Windsor Castle, Berkshire, England 141
Winslade, Tristram, English Catholic exile aboard *Rosario* 244, 270, 289, 458
Winter, Sir William, Master of Ordnance of the Navy 26, 61–2, 75, 81–2, 84, 87, 89, 98, 102, 104, 123–4, *124*, 148, 186, 204–5, 272–3, 277, 304, 314, 317, 359, 374–5, 396, 399, 401, 403, 444, 471, 482, *502*, 508, 637 n.53, Appx 3
Wyatt, Sir Thomas, rebel leader 103–4, 160

York, James Stuart, duke of *see* James II
Yorke, Edmund, quartermaster-general and brother of Roland 471, 474–5, *475*
Yorke, Roland, captain 471
Younger, Neil, historian Appx 5 ch.19

*zabra* 27, 35–6, 39, 364, 372, 430, Appx 1–2
Zárate, Don Francisco de 290
Zayas, Alonso de, captain of Spanish infantry 21
Zayas, Gabriel de, secretary of state to Philip II 116, 570 n.43
Zeeland, Netherlands 6, 48, 50–1, 54, 58, 63, 122, 144–5, 162, 168, 192, 217, 305, 308, 310, 369, 423, 435, 479
Zúñiga, Don Antonio de, *maestre de campo* 59

Zúñiga, Don Balthasar de, staff officer on Armada 31, 263, 328, 331, 385, 387, 415–16, *415*, 421, 446, 621 n.14
  after the Armada *415*, 455
Zúñiga, Don Juan de, foreign policy adviser to Philip II 137, 161–3, 171–3, 175, 198, 211, 256, 582 n.10–11, Appx 5 ch.4
*Zúñiga*, galleass 246, 352–3, 380, 385, 416, 432, 610 n.15, 616 n.13, 618 n.32, Appx 1–2